What's New in this Edition

The second edition of the *Microsoft SQL Server 6.5 DBA Survival Guide* has been significantly enhanced to help administrators and developers understand the features of Microsoft SQL Server 6.5. As soon as you install version 6.5, you will notice that it is much more than just a maintenance release. Microsoft has added many new features and enhanced several existing components. This book was designed to help you understand and incorporate these features into your database environment.

The following list is a brief summary of the new chapters we have added to this edition to help keep you up to date with the features found in version 6.5:

- ◆ **Chapter 13, "Distributed Transaction Coordinator."** The DTC is a new and exciting transaction management technology that provides complete transaction management in a distributed environment. This chapter explains how to configure, manage, and maximize the DTC.

- ◆ **Chapter 24, "Using Stored Procedures and Cursors."** Stored procedures are nothing new to SQL Server—they have been around since the early days of the product. However, the first edition of this book did not have a section dedicated to stored procedures. In this edition, we decided to add an extensive and detailed section on stored procedures and merge it with the cursor appendix from the previous version. This chapter answers a lot of the questions about how to use stored procedures and cursors to solve common DBA problems.

- ◆ **Chapter 28, "New SQL Server Utilities."** The Web Assistant and MS-Query are two new utilities included with version 6.5. This chapter discusses how these products work; we have thrown in a few tips to make the use of these products even easier.

The following list is a brief summary of the chapters we have significantly revised or improved:

- ◆ **Chapter 5, "Planning an Installation or Upgrade," and Chapter 6, "Installing or Upgrading SQL Server."** These chapters have been improved to make the installation of SQL Server even easier. We have also added several tips to help you through those *troublesome* installations.

- ◆ **Chapter 12, "Replication."** This chapter provides several new examples and explains how to replicate to an ODBC subscriber. The chapter also includes a section on how to incorporate stored procedures with the replication process to provide special data formatting.

- ◆ **Chapter 14, "Backups," and Chapter 15, "Recovery."** These chapters have been enhanced to correspond to the significantly improved backup engine found in SQL Server 6.5. We have also added explanations of how to work with single table backups and point-in-time recovery.

- ◆ **Chapter 18, "Monitoring SQL Server," Chapter 22, "Understanding the Query Optimizer," and Chapter 23, "Multi-User Considerations."** All three chapters have been considerably modified to cover SQL Trace, new optimization techniques and query plans, and dynamic locking. Each of these chapters have several new examples and tips.

- ◆ **Chapter 27, "SQL OLE Integration."** With version 6.5, the SQL-DMO object model has been extensively improved to allow even more automation. We discuss how to use SQL-DMO to automate those tasks and show you how the product we have developed for the CD-ROM that accompanies this book—the DBA Assistant—can simplify SQL Server administration. SQL Server administrators should take a look at the graphical BCP component found in the DBA Assistant—no more command-line BCP syntax!

We have also identified which features are new with version 6.5 and which features have been enhanced from versions 6.0 and 4.21. If the feature has changed between versions, we explain the changes and also show any compatibility issues. Whenever you see a sentence that includes the version number *6.x*, we refer to a feature available in *both* versions 6.5 and 6.0.

Happy reading!

Orryn & Mark

MICROSOFT® SQL SERVER® 6.5 DBA
SURVIVAL GUIDE
SECOND EDITION

Orryn Sledge

Mark Spenik

SAMS
PUBLISHING

201 West 103rd Street
Indianapolis, Indiana 46290

Orryn's Dedication

This book is dedicated to my soon-to-be born child. I can't wait to meet ya!

Mark's Dedication

To my grandmother, Mary Spenik — Happy 90th Birthday!

COPYRIGHT © 1996 BY SAMS PUBLISHING

PUBLISHER AND PRESIDENT	Richard K. Swadley
ACQUISITIONS MANAGER	Greg Wiegand
DEVELOPMENT MANAGER	Dean Miller
MANAGING EDITOR	Cindy Morrow
MARKETING MANAGER	John Pierce

ACQUISITIONS EDITOR
Rosemarie Graham

DEVELOPMENT EDITOR
Todd Bumbalough

SOFTWARE DEVELOPMENT SPECIALIST
Cari Skaggs

PRODUCTION EDITOR
Alice Martina Smith

TECHNICAL REVIEWERS
Jeff Perkins
Karen Jaskolka
Michael Gilbert

RESOURCE COORDINATOR
Deborah Frisby

TECHNICAL EDIT COORDINATOR
Lynette Quinn

FORMATTER
Frank Sinclair

EDITORIAL ASSISTANT
Sharon Cox

COVER DESIGNER
Tim Amrhein

BOOK DESIGNER
Alyssa Yesh

PRODUCTION TEAM SUPERVISOR
Brad Chinn

ART/ILLUSTRATION
Stephen Adams
Daniel Harris
Clint Lahnen
Ryan Oldfather
Casey Price
Laura Robbins
Jeff Yesh

PAGE LAYOUT
Mary Ann Abramson,
Carol Bowers, Judy Everly,
Louisa Klucznik, Steph Mineart,
Ian Smith, Andrew Stone,
Mark Walche

PROOFREADING
Christine Berman, Georgiana
Briggs, Bruce Clingaman, Mike
Henry, Donna Martin, Ginger
Morgan, SA Springer

INDEXER
Chris Cleveland

Overview

Contents

PART III   PLANNING AND INSTALLING/UPGRADING SQL SERVER

5   Planning an Installation or Upgrade   59

PART VI   MAINTAINING THE SHOP

25   Developing a SQL Server Maintenence Plan   591

26   Automating Database Administration Tasks   605

27   SQL OLE Integration   637

Acknowledgments

We would like to thank the following people for helping us put this book together: Andrew Coupe of Microsoft for providing us with his support, knowledge, and timeliness. Without Andrew's help, this project would not have been possible. And to Paul Galaspie, for putting in a lot of time and effort in developing the Database Estimator—thanks, Paul! The staff at Sams did such a great job—especially our production editor, Alice Martina Smith. Special thanks to Rosemarie Graham and Todd Bumbalough for keeping the project going at a quick pace with a changing product.

ORRYN'S ACKNOWLEDGMENTS

Once again, I would like to thank my wife, Victoria, for her encouragement and motivation. To my parents, Larry and Lucile Sledge, thanks for starting me in the right direction during those adolescent years. To everyone at The Future Now, Mohammed Kateeb at Microsoft, and everyone else who has provided feedback on the book (especially the online folks at the MSSQL forum on CompuServe)—thanks for the great suggestions! And to Mark Spenik—thanks for the keeping the ideas going!

MARK'S ACKNOWLEDGMENTS

I want to thank my wife, Lisa, for her enduring love and support. Lisa is my number one fan and was the driving force behind the scenes for this second edition. Without her and her sacrifices, this endeavor would not have been possible! To my big family John, Denise, David, Kim, Adam, Chris, Gary, Debbie, Lisa, David, and all my nieces and nephews, thanks for the support! The Meyer (Sam, Marge, and Jonathan) and the Rimes (Denise and Pat) families for all their encouragement. To my father, John, and my late mother, Anna Jane—thanks for the great childhood and for giving me the tools to succeed. Everyone at Keiter, Stephens Computer Services, Inc. for their support and feedback. And lastly, Orryn and Victoria Sledge for being such a great coauthor and supporting cast!

About the Authors

Orryn Sledge is a client/server consultant in the metropolitan Pittsburgh, PA, area. He specializes in developing high-performance, mission-critical systems using Microsoft SQL Server, Sybase SQL Server, PowerBuilder, Visual Basic, and Access. He has been actively involved with SQL Server consulting since 1992. In addition to SQL Server consulting, he has trained several Fortune 500 companies on SQL Server administration and development. In early 1995, he was one of the first developers in the nation to complete the Microsoft Certified Solution Developer (MCSD) program. He is also certified by Microsoft in SQL Server Administration, SQL Server Database Implementation, Windows NT Server and Workstation, Access, Windows System Architecture I, and Windows System Architecture II. In addition to his Microsoft certifications, he is a Certified PowerBuilder Developer (CPD). Orryn can be reached on CompuServe at 102254,2430 or on the Internet at 102254.2430@compuserve.com.

Mark Spenik is the manager of Client/Server Technologies at Keiter, Stephens Computer Services, Inc. Mark, who is a graduate of George Mason University in Fairfax, VA, entered the computer industry in 1985. He has designed and coded large scale C/S applications and has consulted with numerous firms in C/S development, implementation, and migration. He has a broad programming background including assembly language, C, C++, and Visual Basic. Mark has hands-on experience with database implementation and administration including Oracle RDBMS, Sybase SQL Server, and Microsoft SQL Server. His specialty is Microsoft SQL Server, which he has used extensively since the early OS/2 days. Currently, Mark is involved with clients in Richmond, VA, who are using Windows NT, SQL Server, and Visual Basic. Mark is a Microsoft Certified Solution Developer and charter member, and is frequently invited to speak at Microsoft Developer Days. He is also certified in Microsoft SQL Server administration, SQL Server database implementation, and Windows NT. Mark can be reached on CompuServe at 102045,1203 or on the Internet at mspenik@kscsinc.com.

Introduction

In the late 1980s and early 1990s, the Sybase RDBMS (Relational Database Management System) was one of the most popular and innovative RDBMS systems. RDBMS systems could be found in UNIX and NetWare environments. But the entry fee to purchase an RDBMS system was out of the reach of many small businesses and workgroups.

To this end, Sybase and Microsoft entered into a joint venture. Microsoft would license and sell the Sybase RDBMS system, SQL Server, under the Microsoft name on the OS/2 platform. Microsoft SQL Server for OS/2 became a good, affordable workgroup RDBMS system. The product, however, was limited by OS/2 in its scalability and performance.

The relationship between Microsoft and Sybase became strained and ended around the time Microsoft announced that they had rewritten SQL Server for the Windows NT platform. The Windows NT platform is Microsoft's operating system of the future, slated to take on the UNIX and NetWare operating systems. Because of its great pricing and performance, Microsoft SQL Server for Windows NT quickly became one of the most popular Windows NT applications.

The split between Sybase and Microsoft becomes quite apparent when you look at the two SQL Server products. Microsoft SQL Server is tightly integrated into the NT operating system and the database administration tasks are packaged into several graphical front-end tools. Administering Microsoft SQL Server for Windows NT is not the same as administering a Sybase SQL Server, which lacks the graphical administrating and scheduling tools.

It was about this time that we first started hearing cries from customers and various online services for a book that specifically covered Microsoft SQL Server. Microsoft began previewing to customers and SPs the next generation of SQL Server for Windows NT that was to compete in the VLDB (Very Large Database) arena against Sybase and Oracle.

The next generation of SQL Server had a brand-new graphical interface, code-named *starfighter*, and was designed to allow database administration in an enterprise environment. When we saw the sweeping changes being added to SQL Server, we began to realize that it was time for a book that concentrated on Microsoft SQL Server. At the same time, Sams Publishing was introducing a brand-new series of books called the *DBA Survival Guides* that concentrated on real-world experience in managing RDBMS systems. When we saw the format for the *DBA Survival Guide* series, Orryn and I realized that this was the type of book everyone had been asking for!

To make a long story short, Orryn and I and the folks at Sams Publishing put out the very first SQL Server 6.0 book on the market, the *Microsoft SQL Server DBA Survival Guide*. The book has been very well received by the Microsoft SQL Server community. Orryn and I have appreciated all the e-mail and feedback we have received from readers of that first edition. When we learned that Microsoft was preparing the new release, SQL Server Version 6.5, we were excited to learn that Sams wanted us to do a second edition of the book for the new release. This second edition incorporates all the popular features of the first edition plus additional tips and tricks and descriptions of all the new and exciting features of the by-far-best-release-to-date of Microsoft SQL Server—version 6.5.

THE GOALS OF THIS BOOK

Managing a Microsoft SQL Server is quite different from managing several other RDBMS packages because of the graphical nature and ease of use of the overall SQL Server system. The trick to becoming a good Microsoft DBA is to become familiar with the graphical front-end, to understand what happens behind the scenes (that is, what happens when you push a particular button), and to have a good understanding of the product and your job. The goals of this book are as follows:

- ◆ To provide the knowledge and know-how to administrator a SQL Server database
- ◆ To appeal to all levels of DBAs: beginner, intermediate, and experienced
- ◆ To appeal to all levels of developers: beginner, intermediate, and experienced
- ◆ Offer any tips, tricks, and suggestions buried deep within the documentation
- ◆ Offer real-world insight and experience and to pass on any tips, tricks, or suggestions learned the hard way
- ◆ Provide checklists and examples for SQL Server DBA tasks
- ◆ Provide conventions and naming standards
- ◆ Provide insight into the tasks that make up a DBA's job description

THE ORGANIZATION OF THE BOOK

The book is organized into several parts that compromise the various jobs and tasks the DBA performs. Part I, "Introduction," is an overall introductory section that includes the following chapters. For DBAs new to the world of client/server computing, Chapter 1 provides an overview of general client/server concepts. It explains what *client/server* really means (all vendors seem to attach the term *client/server* to their products, even when it really does not meet the definition of client/server). This chapter also explains the benefits of client/server computing compared to other types of computing (such as mainframe and PC/file server). Not sure what a DBA is or what the responsibilities of a DBA are? Chapter 2 is for you.

Part II, "The World of Microsoft's SQL Server," is a high-level overview. Chapter 3 discusses enhancements made to SQL Server 6.x. Chapter 4 details how SQL Server integrates with Windows NT and also explains the benefits of SQL Server being tightly integrated with Windows NT—and how this integration helps differentiate the product from its competitors.

Part III, "Planning and Installing/Upgrading SQL Server," does just what its title suggests. Chapter 5 covers the planning steps required before you attempt a SQL Server upgrade or installation. Do you have all your bases covered in the event an upgrade fails? This chapter covers this topic and many more. Chapter 6 discusses installation and upgrade.

Part IV, "Database Operation," is the largest section of the book and includes chapters about many of the functions you will perform as a DBA.

Chapter 7 provides a high-level explanation of the types of tasks that can be performed through the Enterprise Manager. Chapter 8 discusses how to manage devices. Chapter 9 explains how to create, manage, and delete a database. The chapter includes a discussion about making logs an integral part of a database. If you are a DBA new to SQL Server, you will not want to skip the topic titled "The Two Most Common Database Errors." Without exception, every DBA encounters the errors discussed in this section. Knowing how to deal with these errors ahead of time will simplify a DBA's life. Chapter 10 discusses user management.

Every organization should be concerned with data security; Chapter 11 discusses in detail how to implement data security through SQL Server. Several strategies are offered to help simplify security administration while maintaining an effective security model.

Not sure what Microsoft SQL Server's replication is all about? Having trouble installing the distribution database? Not sure why a replicated database should be read-only? Find these answers and more in Chapter 12.

Wondering what distributed transactions are all about and how to administer them with SQL Server 6.5? See Chapter 13.

Curious how to use your backups? When and how often to back up? These are standard questions all new DBAs face. What happens if a database fails after a backup? Can you provide up-to-the-minute recovery? See Chapters 14 and 15.

Can't get BCP to work? You're not alone—almost every DBA hits a snag or two when trying to work with BCP. Chapter 16 discusses in detail how BCP works and provides numerous tips and examples on how to make BCP work. Also included in this chapter are several alternatives to BCP. Having problems? You won't want to miss Chapter 17, which discusses checkups and problem detection.

What would a database book be without a section on performance and tuning? Part V, "Performance and Tuning," fills that role. Having performance problems with SQL Server? Look at Chapter 18. SQL Server provides numerous tools to help diagnose and isolate bottlenecks. The secret is knowing how to effectively use these tools. For example, the Performance Monitor allows you to monitor over 40 different SQL Server counters and several hundred different operating system counters. Which counters do you look at? Chapter 18 guides you in the right direction if you are wondering which Performance Monitor counters you should analyze. The chapter also discusses how to monitor user activity, a feature that has been extensively enhanced in version 6.5.

Need to configure SQL Server? Which knobs do you turn? Check out Chapter 19. Chapter 20 provides information on database design issues. Do indexes have you all tangled up? If so, don't miss Chapter 21.

Chapter 22 explains in easy-to-understand vernacular the inner workings of SQL Server's cost-based optimizer. When transactions are slow to process or you are experiencing blocking or deadlocks, you will want to refer to the tips and tricks in this chapter. Knowing how to read a showplan is a key element to diagnosing query performance problems. The hard part about reading a showplan is knowing what to look for because lots of cryptic information is generated. This chapter explains what to look for in the output generated by a showplan, what the output really means, and how to improve performance based on showplan information.

I think every DBA has seen an application that runs fine when a single user is logged in to the system, but when multiple users log on, the system bogs down. With multi-user applications, issues such as blocking and deadlocks must be addressed. Chapter 23 offers solutions that can reduce the headaches associated with a multi-user system. Be sure to take a look at the section titled, "Ten Tips to Help Minimize Locking and Prevent Deadlocks."

Do you want to learn more about stored procedures and cursors? Look at Chapter 24. This chapter provides a detailed discussion on these two topics and includes several examples the DBA can use to automate common tasks.

The chapters in Part VI, "Maintaining the Shop," consist of ways to automate and help you plan and schedule various DBA tasks.

Chapter 25 explains why maintenance should be periodically performed on SQL Server and the Windows NT operating system. In addition to explaining why you should perform maintenance, the chapter provides step-by-step instructions on how to maintain the system.

After reading Chapter 25, you will want to automate several of the maintenance tasks discussed in the chapter. Chapter 26 explains how to automate common DBA tasks through the use of two core components of SQL Server: Task Scheduler and Alert Manager. Graphical automation and advanced features such as e-mail and pager notification are two examples of how these components can help simplify a DBA's life.

You already know that OLE is included with SQL Server, but what can you do with it? Chapter 27 walks through the construction of an application that helps simplify database administration task using Visual Basic. Chapter 28 describes some utilities that are new to SQL Server 6.5—don't miss out on what's new!

Part VII, "Appendixes," is dedicated to some useful quick-references that can provide additional information. Every DBA should understand how to use DBCC commands; inadequate DBCC knowledge can prolong data corruption and complicate data restoration. Be sure to look at the appendix on DBCC commands. It details each command, provides a comparison of the commands, and recommends which commands should be frequently run as part of a maintenance schedule.

Conventions Used in this Book

The following conventions are used in this book:

The `computer font` is used for commands, parameters, statements, and text you see on-screen.

A **`boldfaced computer font`** indicates text you type.

Italics indicate new terms or items of emphasis.

Note

Notes provide additional information pertinent to the current subject matter.

Tip

Tips offer useful hints and information.

Caution

Caution boxes present warnings and describe the consequences of particular actions.

Stranger than Fiction!

Some say that truth is stranger than fiction. These boxes offer fun facts to know and tell that *are* stranger than fiction!

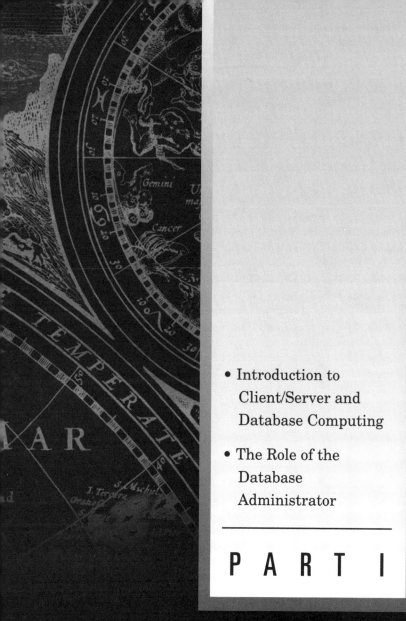

- Introduction to
  Client/Server and
  Database Computing

- The Role of the
  Database
  Administrator

PART I

Introduction

CHAPTER 1

by Orryn Sledge

Introduction to Client/Server Database Computing

Client/server (C/S) database computing is a relatively new technology that only recently has been adapted as a system architecture for the deployment of applications. C/S database computing is the wave of the 90s and it is anticipated that C/S database computing will continue to gain popularity. To understand the reasons behind the success of C/S database computing, it helps to understand the other common types of database computing: mainframe and PC/file server.

MAINFRAME DATABASE COMPUTING

Before the late 80s and early 90s, *mainframe computing* was about the only computer choice for organizations that required heavy-duty processing and support for a large number of users. Mainframes have been in existence for over 20 years. Their longevity has lead to their reliability. The ability of mainframes to support a large number of concurrent users while maintaining a fast database retrieval time contributed to corporate acceptance of mainframes.

Mainframe computing, also called *host-based computing*, refers to all processing carried out on the mainframe computer. The mainframe computer is responsible for running the Relational Database Management System (RDBMS), managing the application that is accessing the RDBMS, and handling communications between the mainframe computer and dumb terminals. A *dumb terminal* is about as intelligent as its name implies: it is limited to displaying text and accepting data from the user. The application does not run on the dumb terminal; instead, it runs on the mainframe and is echoed back to the user through the terminal (see Figure 1.1).

Figure 1.1.
Mainframe database
computing.

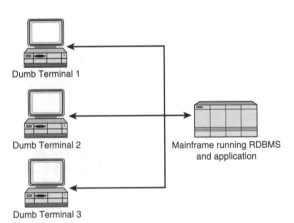

The main drawback of mainframe computing is that it is very expensive. Operating a mainframe computer can run into the millions of dollars. Mainframes are expensive to operate because they require specialized operational facilities, demand extensive support, and do not use common computer components. Additionally, the idea of paying thousands of dollars to rent software that runs on the mainframe is almost inconceivable for PC users who have never used mainframe technology.

Rather than using common components, mainframes typically use hardware and software proprietary to the mainframe manufacturer. This proprietary approach can lock a customer into a limited selection of components from one vendor.

PC/FILE SERVER DATABASE COMPUTING

PC/file server-based computing became popular in the corporate environment during the mid to late 80s when business users began to turn to the PC as an alternative to the mainframe. Users liked the ease with which they could develop their own applications through the use of fourth-generation languages (4GL) such as dBASE III+. These 4GL languages provided easy-to-use report writers and user-friendly programming languages.

PC/file server computing is when the PC runs both the application and the RDBMS. Users are typically connected to the file server through a LAN. The PC is responsible for RDBMS processing; the file server provides a centralized storage area for accessing shared data (see Figure 1.2).

Figure 1.2.
PC/file server database computing.

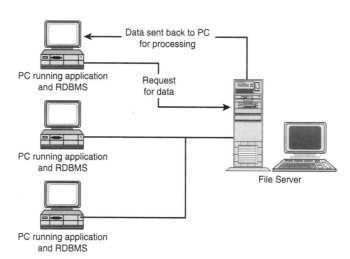

The drawback of PC-based computing is that all RDBMS processing is done on the local PC. When a query is made to the file server, the file server does not process the query. Instead, it returns the data required to process the query. For example, when a user makes a request to view all customers in the state of Virginia, the file server might return all the records in the customer table to the local PC. In turn, the local PC has to extract the customers that live in the state of Virginia. Because the

RDBMS runs on the local PC and not on the server, the file server does not have the intelligence to process queries. This can result in decreased performance and increased network bottlenecks.

PC/FILE SERVER HEADACHES

As a consultant, I am often called into projects that are running behind schedule and require additional resources. About two years ago, a mortgage banking corporation called me in to convert a mainframe application to the PC environment. The majority of the company's income was generated from the application I was converting. Not only was I converting their money maker, the system was required to be up and running within six weeks. The project manager decided that I should build the system using a popular PC/file server database product.

The application design specified a maximum of three concurrent users. Based on the type of queries that were to be performed, I felt comfortable in stating that the performance would be acceptable for the users. After rushing to meet my deadline, the system was implemented. Everything went smoothly until this company's business skyrocketed and more loans than anticipated had to be processed. Before I knew it, the number of users had increased to fifteen.

With fifteen users on the system, the network came to a standstill. The reason the application brought the network to standstill is simple: in a PC/file server architecture, all database processing occurs on the local PC. Therefore, when the users issued complicated queries to the server, the network jammed with data being sent back to the local workstations. Often, the queries being issued from the applications required thousands of rows to be returned to the local PCs.

In the PC/file server environment, this is the equivalent of calling a car dealership and asking how many blue pickup trucks they have in stock. To get the answer, the dealer drives every car to your house and you count the number of blue pickup trucks. Obviously, this is not very efficient. In the C/S database computing environment, a different approach is taken. Someone at the dealership counts the number of blue pickup trucks and passes the information back to the caller.

Eventually, the mortgage banking system was rewritten using a C/S computing database. Performance was improved, network bottlenecks were decreased, and users were happy.

THE ADVENT OF CLIENT/SERVER DATABASE COMPUTING

C/S database computing evolved as an answer to the drawbacks of the mainframe and PC/file server computing environments. By combining the processing power of the mainframe and the flexibility and price of the PC, C/S database computing combines the best of both worlds (see Figure 1.3).

Figure 1.3.
Client / server database
computing.

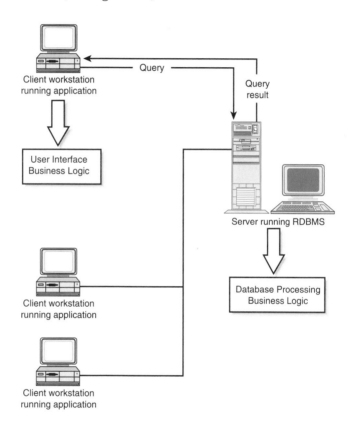

C/S database computing can be defined as the logical partitioning of the user interface, database management, and business logic between the client computer and the server computer. The network links each of these processes.

The *client computer*, also called a *workstation*, controls the user interface. The client is where text and images are displayed to the user and where the user inputs data. The user interface may be text based or graphical based.

The server computer controls database management. The server is where data is stored, manipulated, and retrieved. In the C/S database environment, all database processing occurs on the server.

Business logic can be located on the server, on the client, or mixed between the two. This type of logic governs the processing of the application.

In the typical corporate environment, the server computer is connected to multiple client computers. The server computer is a high-powered computer dedicated to running the RDBMS. The client workstations are usually PC based. The client computer and database server communicate through a common network protocol that allows them to share information.

WHY CLIENT/SERVER DATABASE COMPUTING IS THE ANSWER

Many corporations have turned to client/server database computing as their computing answer. Following are some of the underlying reasons for its popularity:

◆ **Affordability**: C/S database computing can be less expensive than main-frame computing. The underlying reason is simple: C/S database computing is based on an open architecture, which allows for more vendors to produce competing products, driving the cost down. This is unlike mainframe-based systems, which typically use proprietary components available only through a single vendor. Also, C/S workstations and servers are often PC based. PC prices have fallen dramatically over the years, which has led to reduced C/S computing costs.

◆ **Speed**: The separation of processing between the client and the server reduces network bottlenecks, which allows a C/S database system to deliver mainframe performance while exceeding PC/file server performance.

◆ **Adaptability**: The C/S database computing architecture is more open than the proprietary mainframe architecture. Therefore, it is possible to build an application by selecting an RDBMS from one vendor, hardware from another vendor, and development software from yet another vendor. Customers can select components that best fit their needs.

◆ **Simplified data access**: C/S database computing makes data available to the masses. Mainframe computing was notorious for tracking huge amounts of data that could be accessed only by developers. With C/S database computing, data access is not limited to those who understand procedural programming languages (which are difficult to learn and require specialized data access knowledge). Instead, data access is provided by common software products that hide the complexities of data access. Word processing, spreadsheet, and reporting software are just a few of the common packages that provide simplified access to C/S data.

FAT CLIENT OR FAT SERVER: WHERE TO PLACE BUSINESS LOGIC

Now you understand that with C/S database computing, the user interface runs on the client computer and the RDBMS runs on the server computer. A third component in the C/S database computing environment is the placement of business logic. As mentioned previously, *business logic* is the rule that governs the processing of the application. Business logic can be placed on the server, on the client, or mixed between the two.

A *fat server* locates business logic within the RDBMS on the server (see Figure 1.4). The client issues remote procedure calls to the server to execute the process. The advantage of the fat server is centralized control and decreased network traffic. Fat servers are best suited for structured and consistent business logic, such as online transaction processing (OLTP). Modern RDBMS products support fat servers through stored procedures, column rules, triggers, and other methods.

Figure 1.4.
A fat server.

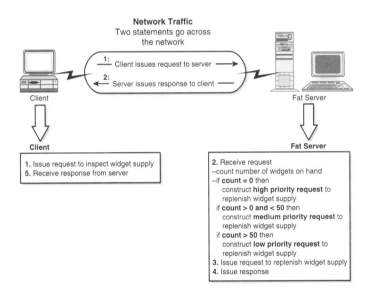

A *fat client* embeds business logic in the application at the client level (see Figure 1.5). Although a fat client is more flexible than a fat server, it increases network traffic. The fat client approach is used when business logic is loosely structured or when it is too complicated to implement at the RDBMS level. Additionally, fat client development tools, such as 4GL languages, typically offer more robust programming features than do RDBMS programming tools. Decision support and ad-hoc systems are often fat client based.

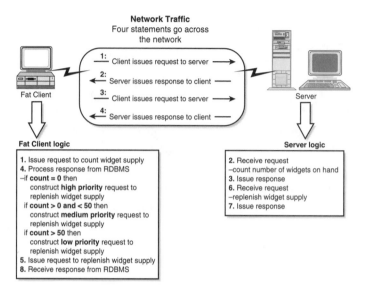

Figure 1.5.
A fat client.

A *mixed environment* partitions business logic between the server and the client (see Figure 1.6). For practical reasons, an application may have to implement this approach. This balancing act is a common approach with C/S database computing.

Figure 1.6.
A mixed environment.

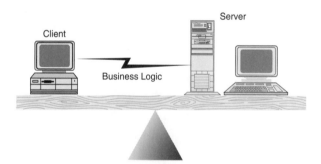

RDBMS: THE STANDARD DATABASE FOR CLIENT/SERVER COMPUTING

RDBMS (Relational Database Management System) has become the standard for C/S database computing. Database software vendors and corporate IS departments have rapidly adapted the RDBMS architecture. It is based on the relational model that originated in papers published by Dr. E.F. Codd in 1969. In an RDBMS, data is organized in a row/column manner and is stored in a table. Records are called *rows* and fields are called *columns* (see Figure 1.7).

Figure 1.7.
Row and column layout
in a relational model.

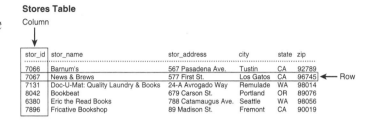

Stores Table

Column

stor_id	stor_name	stor_address	city	state	zip
7066	Barnum's	567 Pasadena Ave.	Tustin	CA	92789
7067	News & Brews	577 First St.	Los Gatos	CA	96745	← Row
7131	Doc-U-Mat: Quality Laundry & Books	24-A Avrogado Way	Remulade	WA	98014
8042	Bookbeat	679 Carson St.	Portland	OR	89076
6380	Eric the Read Books	788 Catamaugus Ave.	Seattle	WA	98056
7896	Fricative Bookshop	89 Madison St.	Fremont	CA	90019

Data is structured using relationships among data items. A *relationship* is a link between tables (see Figure 1.8); relationships allow flexibility of the presentation and manipulation of data.

Figure 1.8.
Relationships among
data items in a rela-
tional model.

Stores Table

stor_id	stor_name	stor_address	city	state	zip
7066	Barnum's	567 Pasadena Ave.	Tustin	CA	92789
7067	News & Brews	577 First St.	Los Gatos	CA	96745
7131	Doc-U-Mat: Quality Laundry & Books	24-A Avrogado Way	Remulade	WA	98014
8042	Bookbeat	679 Carson St.	Portland	OR	89076
6380	Eric the Read Books	788 Catamaugus Ave.	Seattle	WA	98056
7896	Fricative Bookshop	89 Madison St.	Fremont	CA	90019

Sales Table

stor_id	ord_num	date	qty	payterms	title_id
7066	QA7442.3	Sep 13 1985 12:00AM	75	On invoice	PS2091
7067	D4482	Sep 14 1985 12:00AM	10	Net 60	PS2091
7131	N914008	Sep 14 1985 12:00AM	20	Net 30	PS2091
7131	N914014	Sep 14 1985 12:00AM	25	Net 30	MC3021
8042	423LL922	Sep 14 1985 12:00AM	15	On invoice	MC3021
8042	423LL930	Sep 14 1985 12:00AM	10	On invoice	BU1032
6380	722a	Sep 13 1985 12:00AM	3	Net 60	PS2091
6380	6871	Sep 14 1985 12:00AM	5	Net 60	BU1032
8042	P723	Mar 11 1988 12:00AM	25	Net 30	BU1111
7896	X999	Feb 21 1988 12:00AM	35	On invoice	BU2075
7896	QQ2299	Oct 28 1987 12:00AM	15	Net 60	BU7832
7896	TQ456	Dec 12 1987 12:00AM	10	Net 60	MC2222
8042	QA879.1	May 22 1987 12:00AM	30	Net 30	PC1035
7066	A2976	May 24 1987 12:00AM	50	Net 30	PC8888
7131	P3087a	May 29 1987 12:00AM	20	Net 60	PS1372
7131	P3087a	May 29 1987 12:00AM	25	Net 60	PS2106
7131	P3087a	May 29 1987 12:00AM	15	Net 60	PS3333
7131	P3087a	May 29 1987 12:00AM	25	Net 60	PS7777
7067	P2121	Jun 15 1987 12:00AM	40	Net 30	TC3218
7067	P2121	Jun 15 1987 12:00AM	20	Net 30	TC4203
7067	P2121	Jun 15 1987 12:00AM	20	Net 30	TC7777

Discounts Table

stor_id	discount
7131	6.7
8042	5.0

WHY RDBMS IS THE STANDARD IN CLIENT/SERVER DATABASE COMPUTING

The RDBMS has become the standard in client/server database computing for the following reasons:

◆ **Data integrity**: The primary goal of the relational model is *data integrity*. Data integrity prevents incorrect or invalid data from being stored. In an RDBMS, data integrity can be implemented at the server level rather than the application level. This approach offers the advantage of centralized control. When data integrity is changed at the RDBMS level, it is automatically represented at the application level, ensuring consistency and alleviating the need to modify application logic. For example, a data integrity constraint states that the `ship_to_state` for a customer's order must be a valid two-digit state code. Whenever `ship_to_state` data is entered or updated, it is checked against a list of valid state codes. If an invalid state code is entered, the RDBMS prevents the data from being saved.

◆ **Structured Query Language** (SQL, pronounced *sequel*): The SQL language was developed by IBM during the mid-1970s. The SQL language provides a common method for accessing and manipulating data in a relational database. This common language has been adapted by RDBMS vendors as an industry standard. The standardization of SQL allows someone to move to a new RDBMS without having to learn a new data access language.

◆ **Flexibility**: Modifications can be made to the structure of the database without having to recompile or shut down and restart the database. New tables can be created on the fly and existing tables can be modified without affecting the operation of the RDBMS.

◆ **Efficient data storage**: Through a process called *normalization* (see Chapter 20, "Database Design Issues," for more information), redundant data is reduced. Normalization is a primary concept of the relational model.

◆ **Security**: Data security can be implemented at the RDBMS level rather than the application level. As with data integrity, this approach offers the advantage of centralized control at the database level as opposed to the application level.

WHO ARE THE POPULAR RDBMS VENDORS?

The number of RDBMS vendors has increased over the years as C/S has grown in popularity. Although each vendor's database product stems from the relational model, vendors take different approaches to implementing it. These differences—combined with price, performance, operating systems supported, and a host of other items—make choosing the right RDBMS difficult. Following is a brief summary of popular RDBMS vendors:

Vendor: Microsoft
Product: SQL Server
The SQL Server product was originally developed by Sybase in the mid-1980s. Microsoft partnered with Sybase and, in 1988, released SQL Server for OS/2. In 1993, Microsoft shipped the NT version of SQL Server. In 1994, Microsoft and Sybase ended their partnership. Microsoft's SQL Server has grown to be a huge success in the RDBMS market. Microsoft has been successful in combining performance, support for multiple platforms, and ease of use. When SQL Server shipped in 1993, it set a new price/performance TPC benchmark. Since then, it has continued to be a leader in the price/performance benchmark. Support for multiple platforms is accomplished through Microsoft's NT operating system, which runs on the Intel, RISC, and other chip sets. Ease-of-use is accomplished through SQL Server's graphical management tools.

Vendor: Computer Associates
Product: INGRES
The INGRES database software was one of the original RDBMS products to be offered. INGRES supports the OS/2, UNIX, and VAX/VMS platforms. Computer Associates was the first company to provide cost-based optimization, which has become an industry standard. Distributed processing support is available as an INGRES add-on product.

Vendor: IBM
Product: DB2
DB2 is IBM's mainframe relational database that offers impressive processing power. DB2's support for massive databases and a large number of current users gained it corporate acceptance during the 1980s. IBM is the original developer of the relational model and SQL.

Vendor: Centura Technologies
Product: SQL Base
Centura introduced SQL Base for the PC/DOS platform in 1986. Since then, Centura has added support for the NT, OS/2, Novell NLM, and UNIX platforms. Price, fully scrollable cursors, and declarative referential integrity help differentiate SQL Base from its competitors.

Vendor: INFORMIX Software
Product: INFORMIX OnLine
INFORMIX Software was the first vendor to release a UNIX RDBMS. Although available on other operating systems, INFORMIX for UNIX is the

company's most popular offering. INFORMIX offers high-performance transaction processing, advanced security, and distributed processing capabilities.

Vendor: Oracle
Product: Oracle
Oracle is one of the largest and most popular vendors in the RDBMS industry. They have the honor of being the first company to offer an RDBMS for commercial use. Oracle's portability to practically every major hardware and operating system platform is impressive. This means that Oracle code written on a VAX/VMS platform can easily be ported to run on a Macintosh platform. Currently, Oracle supports over 80 different hardware platforms.

Vendor: Sybase
Product: System 11
Sybase originally released SQL Server in the mid-1980s. Its latest product is known as System 11. Sybase's System 11 is designed to run on UNIX, Novell NLM, NT, and VMS platforms. Sybase has proven its innovativeness by being one of the first companies to offer features such as triggers and symmetrical multiprocessing support. UNIX is Sybase's predominate platform. Reliability, performance, and scalability have enabled Sybase to become one of the most respected RDBMS vendors in the industry.

Vendor: XDB Systems
Product: XDB-Server
XDB-Server's strength lies in its 100 percent DB2 compatibility. Developers can downsize to XDB-Server from IBM's DB2 or can upsize from XDB-Server to DB2. In addition to full DB2 support, the product also offers SQL/DS and ANSI level 2 compatibility. XDB-Server is available for DOS, OS/2, and Novell.

THE EVOLUTION OF THE CORPORATE SYSTEM: ENTERPRISE NETWORK

An *enterprise network* links multiple information servers so that they can be accessed and managed from a centralized source (see Figure 1.9). In the 1980s and early 1990s, distributed computing grew in popularity. Distributed computing physically moved computer systems closer to the source of the information. In doing so, distributed systems are more widely dispersed, geographically, than are their stay-at-home mainframe counterparts.

Figure 1.9.
An enterprise network.

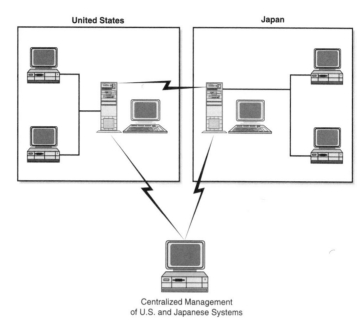

Centralized Management
of U.S. and Japanese Systems

With distributed computing comes decentralized control; with decentralized control comes increased difficulty in managing and accessing data among distributed systems. To solve this problem, tools such as SQL Server's Enterprise Manager have been developed to manage the enterprise network.

SUMMARY

In this chapter, you learned about the following:

- ◆ C/S database computing evolved as an answer to the drawbacks of the mainframe and PC/file server environments.
- ◆ C/S database computing partitions the user interface, database management, and business logic between the client computer and the server computer. The network links each of these processes.
- ◆ The client computer controls the user interface. The server computer controls database management. Business logic can be located on the server, on the client, or mixed between the two.
- ◆ Advantages of C/S database computing include affordability, speed, adaptability, and simplified data access.
- ◆ A fat server locates business logic within the RDBMS on the server; a fat client embeds business logic in the application at the client level.

◆ An RDBMS is the standard database in the C/S environment. RDBMS data is organized in a row/column manner and is stored in a table. Records are called rows and fields are called columns. Data is structured using relationships among data items.

◆ Advantages of an RDBMS include data integrity, SQL, flexibility, efficient data storage, and security.

◆ Multiple vendors offer powerful and robust RDBMS products.

◆ An enterprise network links multiple information servers that can be accessed and managed from a centralized source.

The next chapter discusses the role of the database administrator in RDBMS computing.

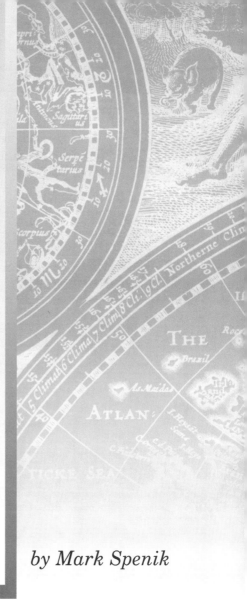

CHAPTER 2

by Mark Spenik

The Role of the Database Administrator

In Chapter 1, you read about the new world of client/server computing and the different RDBMS systems. What about the people that manage and maintain these systems? This chapter looks at a small client/server network with 2 servers (a file/print server and a database server) and 15 client workstations that access the servers.

In this chapter, you learn about the different jobs and responsibilities required to maintain a client/server network. Begin by examining the type of tasks required to maintain the client/server network shown in Figure 2.1.

Figure 2.1.
A small client / server
network.

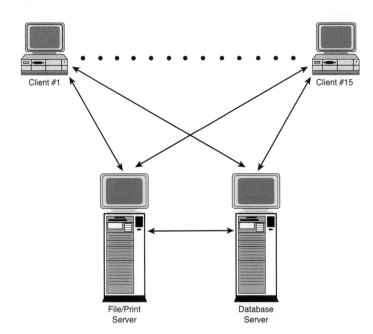

HARDWARE

Figure 2.1 shows a total of 15 client machines and 2 servers. Someone must be responsible for maintaining the physical machines to ensure that they are continually running. This person is responsible for routine maintenance and upgrades such as adding more disk space and memory.

NETWORK

The 15 client machines communicate with the 2 servers over the *network*. The network consists of the hardware and software that ties all the machines together and includes the cabling, routers, repeaters, and network protocols (TCP/IP, named-pipes, SPX/IPX, and so on). Again, someone must take responsibility to make sure that the network stays up and running. If the network goes down, none of the machines can talk to each other.

OPERATING SYSTEMS

All machines—clients and servers—use some sort of *operating system*. Because this is a book about NT SQL Server, you can safely assume that the servers shown in Figure 2.1 are running Microsoft Windows NT and that the clients are running Microsoft Windows or Microsoft Windows NT Workstation. Each client and server machine must be properly configured and set up.

FILE/PRINT SERVER

The *file/print server* needs general maintenance, backups, and upgrades to protect against the loss of data. Someone must be responsible for adding user accounts and installing new applications and maintaining the stability of the file/print server. After all, if the file and print server go down, users cannot perform their jobs.

DATABASE SERVER

The *database server* requirements are similar to those of the file/print server. The difference is that the administration occurs with the RDBMS package. The database server must be set up and tuned correctly to produce the best performance. Above all, the data in the databases must be protected; if data is lost, the data must be restored. Someone also has to manage the users' access and security on the database server.

WHO DOES WHAT?

You may be asking yourself, "For such a small client/server network, there seem to be a lot of different jobs and responsibilities to keep the whole network up and running." Imagine a client/server network 10 to 100 times the size of the relatively small network used in this example! So, who is responsible for which task? The answer to who does what can become quite complex because the size of an organization and the size of the client/server network dictates who is responsible for each task. In some organizations, a single individual may wear many different hats. In other organizations, an individual may be more specialized. The following sections examine some of the general job titles and the responsibilities that accompany each position.

PC AND TECH SUPPORT

The PC and tech support group is responsible for maintaining and setting up the hardware on the different client machines and sometimes on the server machines. If a new software package is installed or more disk space or memory must be added, the PC and tech support group is called in.

NETWORK ADMINISTRATOR

The network administrator is responsible for maintaining the network. A network administrator makes sure that all the hardware components are working correctly and that the networking software is set up correctly. In many cases, the network administrator is also responsible for maintaining the network operating system.

SYSTEM ADMINISTRATOR

The system administrator is responsible for maintaining the many different servers in the organization. The responsibilities include backup and recovery, maintaining user access and security, scheduling task and batch runs, and upgrading and maintaining the operating system.

DATABASE ADMINISTRATOR

Someone once told me that the database administrator (DBA for short) is simply responsible for the data. Well, there is a lot more to being a DBA than just being responsible for the data; that is what you will concentrate on for the rest of the chapter!

Note

In many cases, you may notice that a fine line separates job responsibilities (where one job starts and ends), such as the possible overlap of the network administrator and the system administrator. Depending on their size, most organizations divide the work realistically (that is, no one person has too many responsibilities). One of the most important things to remember is that it takes a team effort to keep a client/server network healthy. Cooperation among the different individuals is a must.

WHAT IS A DATABASE ADMINISTRATOR?

In a very general sense, a *database administrator* is the individual responsible for maintaining the RDBMS system (in this book, the Microsoft SQL Server). The DBA has many different responsibilities, but the overall goal of the DBA is to keep the server up at all times and to provide users with access to the required information when they need it. The DBA makes sure that the database is protected and that any chance of possible data loss is minimized.

WHO ARE THE DBAS?

Who are the DBAs and how do you become one? A DBA can be someone who, from the start, has concentrated in the area of database design and administration. A DBA can be a programmer who, by default or by volunteering, took over the responsibility of maintaining a SQL Server during project development and enjoyed the job so much that he or she switched. A DBA can be a system administrator who was given the added responsibility of maintaining a SQL Server. To start your journey to becoming a Microsoft SQL Server DBA, you need the following:

◆ A good understanding of Microsoft Windows NT

◆ Knowledge of Structured Query Language (SQL)

◆ Sound database design

◆ Knowledge about Microsoft SQL Server

Tip

If you are part of a technical team looking for a Microsoft SQL Server DBA, do yourself a favor and volunteer. It is a great job and good DBAs are in demand.

DBA RESPONSIBILITIES

The following sections examine some of the responsibility of the database administrator and how they translate to various Microsoft SQL Server tasks.

INSTALLING AND UPGRADING A SQL SERVER

The DBA is responsible for installing SQL Server or upgrading an existing SQL Server. In the case of upgrading SQL Server, the DBA is responsible for making sure that, if the upgrade is not successful, the SQL Server can be rolled back to an earlier release until the upgrade issues can be resolved.

MONITORING THE DATABASE SERVER'S HEALTH AND TUNING ACCORDINGLY

Monitoring the health of the database server means making sure that the following is done:

◆ The server is running with optimal performance.

◆ The server is properly configured with the correct amount of memory and the proper configuration parameters.

◆ The error log or event log is monitored for database errors.

◆ Databases have routine maintenance performed on them and the overall system has periodic maintenance performed by the system administrator.

USING STORAGE PROPERLY

Maintaining the proper use of storage means making sure that databases and transaction logs are created correctly, monitoring space requirements, and adding new storage space when required.

PERFORMING BACKUP AND RECOVERY DUTIES

Backup and recovery are the DBA's most critical tasks; they include the following aspects:

◆ Establishing standards and schedules for database backups

◆ Developing recovery procedures for each database

◆ Making sure that the backup schedules meet the recovery requirements

MANAGING DATABASE USERS AND SECURITY

The DBA is responsible for setting up user's database server login IDs and determining the proper security level for each user. Within each database, the DBA is responsible for assigning permissions to the various database objects such as tables, views, and stored procedures.

WORKING WITH DEVELOPERS

It is important for the DBA to work closely with development teams to assist in overall database design, such as creating normalized databases, helping developers tune queries, assign proper indexes, and aiding them in creating triggers and stored procedures.

Tip

> I have too often seen DBAs who were content to sit back and watch developers make bad design and SQL Server decisions. I have also seen situations in which the DBA wanted to be involved in design decisions but management prevented it because it was not the DBA's "job." Don't be underutilized. If you are in this situation, show your management this tip! Take an active role in new project development. The entire team will benefit from your insight and knowledge!

Establishing and Enforcing Standards

The DBA should establish naming conventions and standards for the SQL Server and databases and make sure that everyone sticks to them.

Transferring Data

The DBA is responsible for importing and exporting data to and from the SQL Server. In the current trend to downsize and combine client/server systems with mainframe systems, importing data from the mainframe to the SQL Server is a common occurrence.

Replicating Data

SQL Server version 6.x has added a new requirement and responsibility for the DBA: setting up and maintaining data replication throughout the workplace. Replication is a tremendous feature that will play a big part in many organizations.

Scheduling Events

The database administrator is responsible for setting up and scheduling various events using Windows NT and SQL Server to aid in performing many tasks such as backups and replication.

Providing 24-Hour Access

Although you may say to yourself, "No way!," the database server must stay up and the databases must always be protected and online. Be prepared to perform some maintenance features and upgrades after hours. If the database server should go down, be ready to get the server up and running. After all, that's your job.

LEARNING CONSTANTLY

To be a good DBA, you must continue to study and practice your mission-critical procedures, such as testing your backups by recovering to a test database. In this business, things change very fast so you must continue learning about SQL Server, available client/servers, and database design tools. It is a never-ending process.

TRICKS OF THE TRADE

Now that you understand the different responsibilities of a DBA, how can you learn the tricks of the trade? You are off to a good start by reading this book. The following sections examine some other ways to learn the tricks of the trade.

CLASSES AND TRAINING

Taking a Microsoft-certified SQL Server training class is very good way to get started. Find a class that gives you hands-on classroom training. The class can introduce you to many of the concepts and procedures required to maintain SQL Server. To find out about authorized Microsoft SQL Server training centers near you, call 1-800-SOL-PROV and ask for information on Microsoft Solution Provider Authorized Technical Education Centers. On CompuServe, GO MECFORUM.

Tip

If you go to class, make sure that when you return, you start practicing immediately what you learned in class. Most classes are three to five days; to retain the information, you must start practicing and using it immediately.

ON THE JOB

The real school of how to be a DBA is on the job; for many DBAs, that is where they learned. On-the-job training can be difficult when you are the only one learning a system with which no one else is familiar. You may have the luxury of having a seasoned DBA teach you the ropes. Ultimately, we all learn on the job.

Tip

Practice, practice, practice. Constantly practice different procedures and tasks, such as backing up and recovering data or importing data on a nonproduction server. When the day comes to perform the task, you will be well prepared.

MICROSOFT TECHNET, MICROSOFT DEVELOPERS NETWORK, AND ONLINE SERVICES

Take advantage of the vast knowledge base of articles Microsoft makes available on the TechNet and Microsoft Developers Network (MSDN) CDs. Many times, you can solve a problem simply by searching the two CDs for the problem and possible resolution. Use online services that provide a Microsoft SQL Server forum. On the forum, you can post problems and get help from other DBAs or you can scan through the various messages posted and learn how to solve problems you have not yet encountered. The CompuServe SQL Server forum is GO MSSQL. Microsoft's Web page for SQL Server is http://www.Microsoft.com/SQL. You can learn more about Microsoft TechNet by calling 1-800-344-212, navigating the Internet to technet@microsoft.com, or using CompuServe's forum, GO TECHNET. To learn more about the Microsoft Developers Network (MSDN), call 1-800-759-5474 or use CompuServe's forum (GO MSDN).

MAGAZINES AND BOOKS

Subscribe to various database magazines that keep you abreast of topics such as the latest database design and development tools, relational database concepts, and SQL Server. Also search the book store for books on database design and SQL Server (like this book). Pinnacle Publishing publishes a magazine called the *Microsoft SQL Server Professional*; they can be reached at CompuServe 76064,51, on the Internet at 1119390@mcimail.com, or by fax at 1-206-251-5057. Another magazine that provides very good articles on SQL Server and Windows NT is *Windows NT Magazine*; reach the publishers at 1-800-621-1544 or on the Internet at winntmag@duke.com.

CERTIFICATION

Microsoft offers product certification for SQL Server database administration and SQL Server database implementation. It is strongly encouraged that you take the test to become certified. Certification does not replace experience and training but it will help point out possible weakness in your understanding of SQL Server and give you credibility (because you understand the concepts and procedures to maintain SQL Server). To find out more about Microsoft certification, look on CompuServe at GO MECFORUM or on the Internet at http://www.Microsoft.com. You also can call 1-800-636-7544 and ask for the Certification Roadmap.

Tip

We are often asked, "What do I need to do to pass certification? Will this book help?" Of course this book will help! Here are some words of advice about the certification test: Before taking the test, review the test outline for SQL Server (which is part of the Certification Roadmap). The certification test asks questions on only the topics listed in the test outline. Make sure that you are familiar with each of the topics.

Although managing a Microsoft SQL Server is a graphical experience, the test will more than likely ask you about the command to create a database (instead of how to create a database using the Enterprise Manager), so make sure that you are familiar with the commands required to perform various administration tasks.

Last but not least, take the practice test that comes with the Certification Roadmap. The practice test gives you a general idea of the types of questions asked on the test. Do not take the real test until you do well on the practice test.

HOW THE DBA INTERACTS WITH OTHER TEAM MEMBERS

Now that you have decided to become a DBA, how will you interact with other team members such as the system administrator, network administrator, developers, and users? Many times, these relationships are hard to determine because each organization has people filling one or many different roles. Based on earlier job descriptions, however, the following sections quickly examine the types of interaction to expect.

SYSTEM ADMINISTRATOR AND NETWORK ADMINISTRATOR

A DBA's interaction with the network administrator is mostly concerned with the type of network protocols that can be used and the network address or port number that can be used for the server. If users are complaining about query times and SQL Server is executing the queries very fast, you and the network administrator should examine possible networking problems.

The interaction of the system administrator and the DBA is much tighter than the interaction of the network administrator and the DBA. The system administrator is responsible for tuning the Windows NT server on which your SQL Server runs. The system administrator is responsible for adding the hard drives and storage space required for you to create database devices. If you choose to use integrated user security with SQL Server, you must work with the system administrator to set up the correct NT user accounts and groups. The different types of backup and recovery procedures for the NT Server and the SQL Server should be worked out by both parties because, in some cases, the system administrator may have to restore a system drive that contains a database.

DEVELOPERS

The interaction of DBAs with developers is where I have seen the greatest differences in organizations' definitions of a DBA. In some organizations, the DBA works very closely with the developers; in other organizations, the DBAs work very little with the developers and are stuck maintaining the developers' systems and designs without any input. It is my firm belief that the DBA should work very closely with the developers; after all, the DBA is the one maintaining the database side of the application; in many cases, the DBA has the most experience in relational database design and tuning. The DBA should design, aid, or review any and all database designs for the organization. The DBA should also provide assistance in helping the developers select proper indexes, optimize queries and stored procedures, as well as being a source of information to the developers.

USERS

In most organizations, the DBA's interaction with the users of the system is limited to user account maintenance, security, and database recovery requirements.

SUMMARY

The role of the database administrator is very important in an organization. The job can be challenging and exciting. If you are a DBA or want to be a DBA, remember that it is important to constantly study SQL Server and database tools. Become certified and practice your backup and recovery procedures. Following is a quick list of the many duties and responsibilities of a DBA:

- ◆ Installing and upgrading SQL Server
- ◆ Monitoring the database server's health and tuning it accordingly
- ◆ Using storage properly
- ◆ Backing up and recovering data
- ◆ Managing database users and security

◆ Establishing and enforcing standards
◆ Performing data transfer
◆ Setting up and maintaining data replication
◆ Setting up server scheduling
◆ Providing 24-hour access
◆ Working with development teams
◆ *Learning!*

PART II

The World of Microsoft's SQL Server

- What's New in Version 6.5

- Features Common to Versions 6.5 and 6.0

- Summary

CHAPTER 3

by Orryn Sledge

The Evolution of SQL Server

In 1988, Microsoft released its first version of SQL Server. It was designed for the OS/2 platform and was jointly developed by Microsoft and Sybase. During the early 1990s, Microsoft began to develop a new version of SQL Server for the NT platform. While it was under development, Microsoft decided that SQL Server should be tightly coupled with the NT operating system. In 1992, Microsoft assumed core responsibility for the future of SQL Server for NT. In 1993, Windows NT 3.1 and SQL Server 4.2 for NT were released. Microsoft's philosophy of combining a high-performance database with an easy-to-use interface proved to be very successful. Microsoft quickly became the second most popular vendor of high-end relational database software. In 1994, Microsoft and Sybase formally ended their partnership. In 1995, Microsoft released version 6.0 of SQL Server. This release was a major rewrite of SQL Server's core technology. Version 6.0 substantially improved performance, provided built-in replication, and delivered centralized administration. In 1996, Microsoft released version 6.5 of SQL Server. This version brought significant enhancements to the existing technology and provided several new features.

WHAT'S NEW IN VERSION 6.5

SQL Server version 6.5 is more than a maintenance release. It includes numerous features that further extend SQL Server. Following are several of the key features found in version 6.5:

◆ Distributed Transaction Coordinator (DTC)

◆ Replication to ODBC subscribers

◆ Internet integration

◆ Improved performance

◆ Data warehousing extensions

◆ Simplified administration

DISTRIBUTED TRANSACTION COORDINATOR (DTC)

The Distributed Transaction Coordinator (DTC) controls transactions that span multiple SQL Server systems. This feature allows applications to update multiple databases in a distributed environment while providing transaction management. Through DTC, a data modification is guaranteed to run to completion or the modification is rolled back in its entirety. For example, if a modification updates data in two servers and the second server crashes during the update, the entire transaction is rolled back from both servers.

REPLICATION TO ODBC SUBSCRIBERS

Version 6.5 has extended replication to database products other than SQL Server. Through Open Database Connectivity (ODBC), SQL Server can replicate changes to products such as Oracle, Sybase, IBM DB2, Access, and other database products. This feature offers administrators and developers a simplified and reliable method for distributing data.

INTERNET INTEGRATION

SQL Server provides direct Internet support through the SQL Web Assistant and Microsoft's Internet Information Server (IIS). The SQL Web Assistant is included with version 6.5; it generates HTML scripts for SQL Server data. This product allows you to create Web pages that contain SQL Server data. SQL Server version 6.5 also provides direct support for Microsoft's IIS product, which means that complete Internet solutions can be delivered through the combination of SQL Server, NT, and IIS.

IMPROVED PERFORMANCE

SQL Server version 6.5 delivers improved performance over previous versions through enhancements such as reduced checkpoint serialization, faster sorting and indexing, and improved integration with the NT operating system. Version 6.5 also offers several new counters to help tune SQL Server for maximum performance.

DATA WAREHOUSING EXTENSIONS

SQL Server version 6.5 provides several data warehousing extensions and improved support for Very Large Databases (VLDB). These extensions include several new commands for online analytical processing (OLAP). Two of these new commands, CUBE and ROLLUP, allow a developer to create a single query that returns a recordset based on multiple dimensions and that contains aggregate information. Version 6.5 also provides improved VLDB support through single table backups/restorations and point-in-time recovery.

SIMPLIFIED ADMINISTRATION

SQL Server version 6.5 continues to simplify database administration through improvements to the Enterprise Manager and through wizards. In version 6.5, the Enterprise Manager offers a customizable toolbar and menu system, an improved Transfer Manager, and other interface enhancements. Version 6.5 also includes a Database Maintenance wizard that automates common DBA tasks such as backups, database consistency checks (DBCC), and index maintenance (such as UPDATE STATISTICS).

FEATURES COMMON TO VERSIONS 6.5 AND 6.0

Many of the features found in version 6.5 were originally released in version 6.0. Version 6.0 was a significant upgrade from the previous version of SQL Server (version 4.2x). Many of these changes were made in response to the complaint that version 4.2x was better suited to handle the needs of a department rather than an enterprise. Version 6.x meets the demanding requirements of an enterprise and also includes several other features that help differentiate it from its peers.

ENTERPRISE MANAGER

The Enterprise Manager combines the functionality of version 4.2x's Object Manager and SQL Administrator into a single easy-to-use interface. From the Enterprise Manager, you can administer multiple servers, configure data replication, and develop databases.

Tip

In addition to managing SQL Server 6.x, you can manage SQL Server 4.2x from the Enterprise Manager. To do this, you must first run—from your 4.2x version of SQL Server—the `SQLOLE42.SQL` script that ships with version 6.x.

DATA REPLICATION

Before SQL Server version 6.x, if you wanted replication, you had to buy a replication product or build your own replication services. Neither alternative was very appealing. Data replication products are expensive to purchase and building your own replication service can be complex and time consuming. Fortunately, SQL Server 6.x provides a robust replication component that can meet the needs of an enterprise. The uses for replication are endless. Data warehousing, distributed processing, and end-user reporting are just a few examples of how SQL Server's data replication component can be used.

SQL EXECUTIVE

SQL Executive helps automate many of the routine tasks a DBA must perform. Event scheduling, alert notification, replication management, and task management are some of the functions that SQL Executive provides.

Note

SQL Executive replaces version 4.2x's SQL Monitor.

OLE AUTOMATION

Distributed Management Objects (SQL-DMO) allow developers to tap into the power of SQL Server through the ease of OLE automation. Developers can use Visual Basic, Excel, and other products that support the VBA programming language to build custom administration scripts. These objects simplify the process of creating management scripts by allowing programs to interface with SQL Server through objects, methods, and properties.

PARALLEL DATA SCANNING AND READ-AHEAD MANAGER

Through parallel data scanning and read-ahead algorithms, version 6.x has significantly improved SQL Server performance. Certain types of queries, such as table scans, execute 400 percent faster over version 4.2x.

MULTITHREADED KERNEL

SQL Server version 6.x features a redesigned kernel that results in improved transaction performance and scalability. Previous versions of SQL Server were unable to effectively scale beyond two or three processors. Version 6.x is better suited to take advantage of multiple processors.

OPTIMIZER IMPROVEMENTS

Version 6.x's optimizer has been significantly improved. The likelihood of a proper query execution plan has increased through better index usage and improved subquery support.

Also new with version 6.x are optimizer *hints*. Now you can explicitly force the optimizer to choose an index. Before version 6.x, developers sometimes had to use nonstandard techniques to force the optimizer to choose an appropriate index.

HIGH-PERFORMANCE BACKUP AND RESTORATION

Version 6.x uses parallel optimization techniques to minimize backup and restoration times. These techniques allow Very Large Databases to be backed up and restored in a reasonable amount of time.

VERY LARGE DATABASE (VLDB) SUPPORT

Earlier versions of SQL Server had a practical size limitation of 50 to 60 gigabytes. Version 6.x can effectively support databases in excess of 100 gigabytes. SQL Server uses parallel optimization techniques to maximize performance. This enables SQL Server to post significant performance gains over previous versions.

DATATYPES

The following three datatypes have been added to version 6.x:

◆ Decimal

◆ Numeric

◆ Double-precision

Additionally, an *identity* property has been added. It is a value that is automatically incremented when a new record is inserted into a table. You can have only one identity column per table.

Note

Version 6.x is ANSI SQL 92-compliant.

DATA INTEGRITY

Several new data constraints have been added to version 6.x. These constraints relieve the developer from having to code declarative referential integrity (DRI). Constraints are defined with the CREATE TABLE and ALTER TABLE statements. See Table 3.1. for a comparison of data constraints.

TABLE 3.1. COMPARISON OF DATA CONSTRAINTS.

Version 6.x	Earlier Versions
CHECK	CREATE trigger or rule
DEFAULT	CREATE default
FOREIGN KEY	CREATE trigger, sp_foreignkey
PRIMARY KEY	CREATE UNIQUE index, sp_primarykey
REFERENCE	CREATE trigger
UNIQUE	CREATE UNIQUE index

Note

In SQL Server 4.2x, the system procedures sp_primarykey and sp_foreignkey were strictly for documenting primary keys and foreign keys. They *do not* enforce data integrity and have been removed from version 6.x.

CHECK CONSTRAINT

The CHECK constraint limits the range of data values a column can contain. The CHECK constraint can be created at the table or column level.

DEFAULT CONSTRAINT

A DEFAULT constraint automatically enters a default value into the column when a value is not specified. The DEFAULT constraint can be created at the table or column level.

FOREIGN KEY CONSTRAINT

The FOREIGN KEY constraint enforces foreign key relationships. It is used with the REFERENCE and PRIMARY KEY constraints.

PRIMARY KEY CONSTRAINT

The PRIMARY KEY constraint uniquely identifies a primary key and enforces referential integrity. The column it references must contain unique data values and cannot be NULL. It is used with the REFERENCE and FOREIGN KEY constraints.

REFERENCE CONSTRAINT

The REFERENCE constraint is used to enforce referential integrity in conjunction with the PRIMARY KEY and FOREIGN KEY constraints.

UNIQUE CONSTRAINT

The UNIQUE constraint prevents duplicate data values. This constraint is similar to the PRIMARY KEY constraint, except that it allows NULLs.

Note

Before version 6.x, referential integrity (RI) could be enforced only through the use of triggers. This meant that you had to build extensive code to enforce RI. With version 6.x, you can use the REFERENCE, PRIMARY KEY, and FOREIGN KEY constraints to enforce RI. However, you must still use triggers to perform cascading updates and deletes.

CURSORS

ANSI-SQL cursors and engine-based cursors are part of version 6.x. In previous versions of SQL Server, cursors could be created only by using DB-LIB or ODBC API calls. SQL Server's cursors are fully scrollable and permit data modifications. ANSI cursors (which are row oriented) are preferred to engine-based cursors (which are set oriented).

SUMMARY

SQL Server 6.x offers significant improvements and enhancements over earlier versions. These changes are discussed throughout this book.

_____

by Orryn Sledge

CHAPTER 4

SQL Server:
The Big Picture

SQL Server is a high-performance relational database system that is tightly integrated with the Windows NT operating system. This arrangement allows SQL Server to take advantage of the features provided by the Windows NT operating system. SQL Server is an excellent choice for meeting the challenging needs of today's complex client/server systems.

ARCHITECTURE

SQL Server's integration with the Windows NT operating system provides the following important features:

◆ Symmetric multiprocessing (SMP)
◆ Portability
◆ Network independence
◆ Reliability

SYMMETRIC MULTIPROCESSING (SMP)

SMP allows SQL Server to increase performance through the use of additional processors. SQL Server uses a single process and multiple threads in conjunction with NT's scheduler so that Windows NT can balance work loads across multiple processors. All this occurs without user interaction; it also relieves administrators from the complexities of managing multiple processors.

PORTABILITY

SQL Server can run on different hardware platforms because Windows NT is a portable operating system. Currently, Windows NT supports the Intel platform, Digital's Alpha architecture, various RISC machines, PowerPC, and other hardware platforms.

NETWORK INDEPENDENCE

The Windows NT operating system supports several different types of network protocols. This level of support extends to the client-side connectivity of SQL Server. This allows you to choose the network protocol that best fits your present and future needs. TCP/IP, IPX/SPX, named-pipes, and Banyan Vines are currently supported.

RELIABILITY

Windows NT provides crash protection, memory management, preemptive scheduling, and remote management. These types of features enable you to keep SQL Server up and running 24 hours a day, 7 days a week.

NT Integration

SQL Server is designed to take advantage of the NT operating system. This means that several common NT components provide additional functionality to SQL Server.

Control Panel

SQL Server (MSSQLServer), SQL Executive (SQLExecutive), and Distributed Transaction Coordinator (DTC) are defined as services in the NT control panel (see Figure 4.1). You use the control panel to start, stop, and monitor the status of SQL Server, SQL Executive, and Distributed Transaction Coordinator.

Figure 4.1.
Integration with the
Windows NT control
panel.

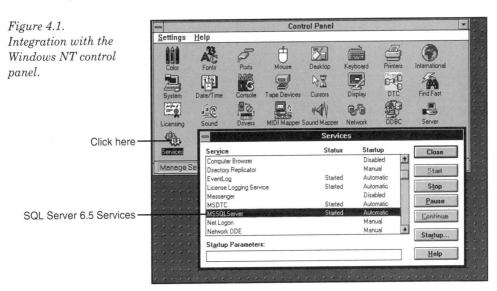

Note

Version 4.2x of SQL Server uses different service names: *SQLServer* and *SQLMonitor*. In version 6.x, SQLServer became MSSQLServer and SQLMonitor was replaced by SQLExecutive.

Event Viewer

The *Event Viewer* allows administrators to view and track information pertaining to SQL Server (see Figure 4.2). SQL Server logs the following types of messages to the Event Viewer: information, errors, and warnings.

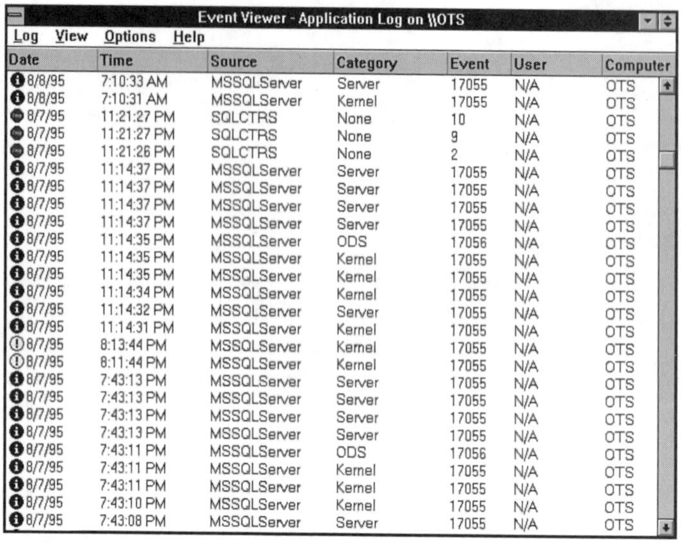

Date	Time	Source	Category	Event	User	Computer
8/8/95	7:10:33 AM	MSSQLServer	Server	17055	N/A	OTS
8/8/95	7:10:31 AM	MSSQLServer	Kernel	17055	N/A	OTS
8/7/95	11:21:27 PM	SQLCTRS	None	10	N/A	OTS
8/7/95	11:21:27 PM	SQLCTRS	None	9	N/A	OTS
8/7/95	11:21:26 PM	SQLCTRS	None	2	N/A	OTS
8/7/95	11:14:37 PM	MSSQLServer	Server	17055	N/A	OTS
8/7/95	11:14:37 PM	MSSQLServer	Server	17055	N/A	OTS
8/7/95	11:14:37 PM	MSSQLServer	Server	17055	N/A	OTS
8/7/95	11:14:37 PM	MSSQLServer	Server	17055	N/A	OTS
8/7/95	11:14:35 PM	MSSQLServer	ODS	17056	N/A	OTS
8/7/95	11:14:35 PM	MSSQLServer	Kernel	17055	N/A	OTS
8/7/95	11:14:35 PM	MSSQLServer	Kernel	17055	N/A	OTS
8/7/95	11:14:34 PM	MSSQLServer	Kernel	17055	N/A	OTS
8/7/95	11:14:32 PM	MSSQLServer	Server	17055	N/A	OTS
8/7/95	11:14:31 PM	MSSQLServer	Kernel	17055	N/A	OTS
8/7/95	8:13:44 PM	MSSQLServer	Kernel	17055	N/A	OTS
8/7/95	8:11:44 PM	MSSQLServer	Kernel	17055	N/A	OTS
8/7/95	7:43:13 PM	MSSQLServer	Server	17055	N/A	OTS
8/7/95	7:43:13 PM	MSSQLServer	Server	17055	N/A	OTS
8/7/95	7:43:13 PM	MSSQLServer	Server	17055	N/A	OTS
8/7/95	7:43:13 PM	MSSQLServer	Server	17055	N/A	OTS
8/7/95	7:43:11 PM	MSSQLServer	ODS	17056	N/A	OTS
8/7/95	7:43:11 PM	MSSQLServer	Kernel	17055	N/A	OTS
8/7/95	7:43:11 PM	MSSQLServer	Kernel	17055	N/A	OTS
8/7/95	7:43:10 PM	MSSQLServer	Kernel	17055	N/A	OTS
8/7/95	7:43:08 PM	MSSQLServer	Server	17055	N/A	OTS

Figure 4.2.
The Event Viewer.

Tip

In the Event Viewer, you can control the size of the event log. To control its size, select the Log Settings option from the Log menu. This action opens the Event Log Settings dialog box. From this dialog box, you can specify a maximum log size and the overwrite behavior.

From within SQL Server, you can write your own messages to the event log. Use the extended stored procedure `xp_logevent`, as in the following example:

```
xp_logevent error_number, message, [severity]
```

THE REGISTRY

Windows NT configuration information is stored in a database called the *Registry*. To view and edit the Registry, run `REGEDT32.EXE` (see Figure 4.3). Normally, the Registry is automatically maintained by your software. You should change information in the Registry only when absolutely necessary. Otherwise, you may inadvertently introduce errors into your software and operating system.

Following is the registry key to SQL Server 6.x:

```
HKEY_LOCAL_MACHINE
 \SOFTWARE
 \Microsoft
 \MSSQLServer
```

Figure 4.3.
The Registry.

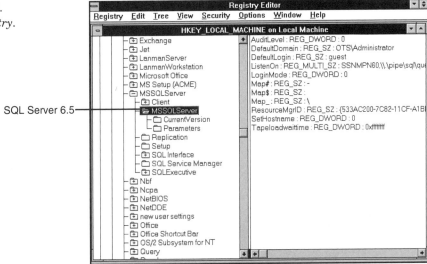

NOTE

If you want to view registry information about SQL Server 6.x, be sure to look at the MSSQLServer section and *not* the SQLServer section. SQLServer is version 4.x.

NT USER ACCOUNTS

Through *integrated security*, SQL Server can use Windows NT user accounts and passwords (see Figure 4.4). This means that a single user account can be used to control access to NT and SQL Server. This significantly reduces account maintenance, eliminates duplication, and simplifies login procedures.

For more information on user accounts, see Chapter 10, "Managing Users."

Figure 4.4.
NT user accounts.

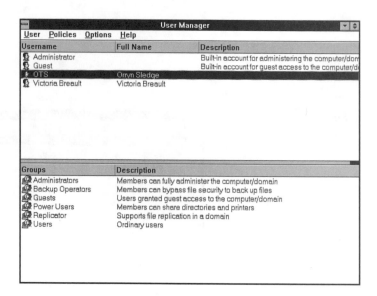

PERFORMANCE MONITOR

The *Performance Monitor* provides graphical statistics about the performance of SQL Server and Windows NT (see Figure 4.5). For more information about using the Performance Monitor, see Chapter 18, "Monitoring SQL Server." You also can define alerts in the Performance Monitor. *Alerts* enable you to track and monitor the frequency of an event (see Figure 4.6).

Figure 4.5.
Performance Monitor.

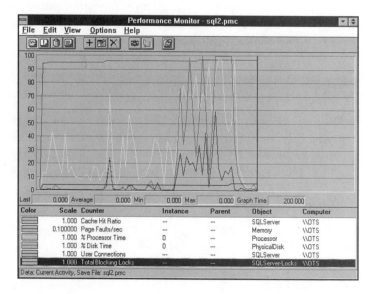

Figure 4.6.
Alerts in the Perfor-
mance Monitor.

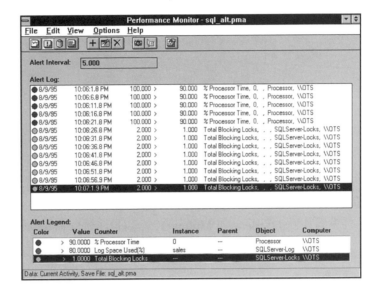

VISUAL ADMINISTRATION TOOLS

A primary goal of SQL Server for NT was to provide administrators with easy-to-use graphical administration tools. The ease with which someone can administer SQL Server for NT is a testimony to the success of Microsoft's development efforts. This is quite a different philosophy from SQL Server's competitors: the majority of their products are not intuitive and are command-line based.

The following tools allow you to easily set up, administer, and interact with SQL Server.

SQL SERVER SETUP

Through SQL Setup, you can perform the following functions (see Figure 4.7):

◆ Set up SQL Server

◆ Configure an existing SQL Server installation

◆ Rebuild the `master` database

◆ Remove SQL Server

Figure 4.7.
SQL Server Setup.

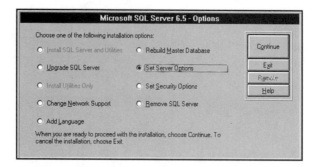

 ## SQL SERVICE MANAGER

From the SQL Service Manager, you can start, stop, and pause SQL Server, SQL Executive, and Distributed Transaction Coordinator (see Figure 4.8).

Figure 4.8.
The SQL Service
Manager.

Tip

What is the purpose of the yellow stop light in the SQL Service Manager? This a commonly asked question. The reason it exists is to pause the server. By pausing the server, you can prevent users from logging in to SQL Server while still keeping it up and running. This feature is useful when you want to halt users from making new connections but allow existing connections to continue processing; it also allows users a chance to log off normally before bringing down the database.

Note

SQL Server can also be started as a service through the control panel or from the command line by using the command NET START MSSQLSERVER.

ISQL/w

ISQL/w is the Windows-based version of ISQL (see Figure 4.9). Generally, it is used by developers and end-users who need to execute SQL statements. It does not provide graphical administration (use the Enterprise Manager for graphical administration).

Figure 4.9.
ISQL/w.

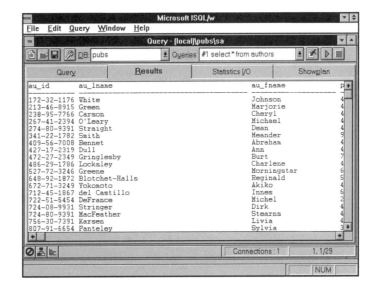

Using ISQL/w, you can perform the following functions:

◆ Execute SQL statements

◆ Analyze query plans

◆ Display query statistics

SQL SECURITY MANAGER

The SQL Security Manager allows you to graphically manage how Windows NT users interact with SQL Server (see Figure 4.10).

Note

You must be running integrated or mixed security to take advantage of SQL Security Manager. There is no benefit from the Security Manager if you are using standard security.

Figure 4.10.
The SQL Security
Manager.

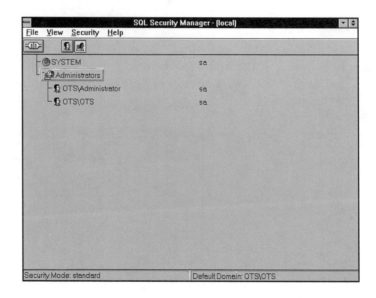

From the Security Manager, you can perform the following functions:

◆ Manage security

◆ Grant and revoke privileges to Windows NT groups

◆ Search account information

SQL ENTERPRISE MANAGER

As an administrator, you will probably spend the majority of your time interacting with SQL Server through the Enterprise Manager. This is where you can administer multiple database servers through a single interface (see Figure 4.11).

Using the Enterprise Manager, you can perform the following functions:

◆ Start or shut down SQL Server, SQL Executive, SQL Mail, and Distributed Transaction Coordinator

◆ Manage backups

◆ Manage databases

◆ Manage devices

◆ Manage logins and permissions

◆ Manage replication

◆ Manage tables, views, stored procedures, triggers, indexes, rules, defaults, and user-defined datatypes

◆ Schedule tasks

◆ Generate SQL scripts

Figure 4.11.
SQL Enterprise
Manager.

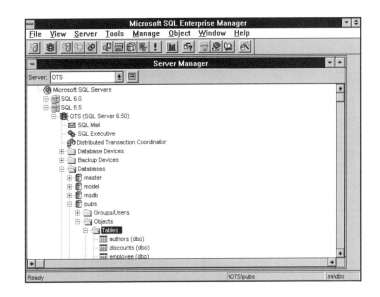

SQL CLIENT CONFIGURATION UTILITY

From the SQL Client Configuration utility, you can perform the following functions (see Figure 4.12):

◆ Determine DB-Library version information

◆ Configure client-side connections

Figure 4.12.
The SQL Client
Configuration utility.

SQL TRACE

SQL Trace is new with SQL Server 6.5; it is a graphical tool that displays Transact-SQL activity for a selected server (see Figure 4.13). SQL Trace can be used by an administrator or developer to probe user activity and to generate audit trails. The output from SQL Trace can be saved as a script or as an activity log. See Chapter 28, "New SQL Server Utilities," for more information on SQL Trace.

Figure 4.13.
SQL Trace.

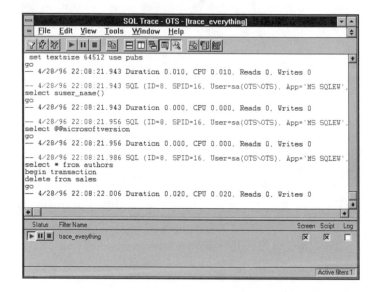

MS QUERY

MS Query is new with SQL Server 6.5; it is Microsoft's graphical query tool (see Figure 4.14). Common operations such as viewing data, modifying data, and viewing table definitions can be performed through MS Query. In addition to being shipped with SQL Server, this tool can be found in Microsoft Office.

Figure 4.14.
MS Query.

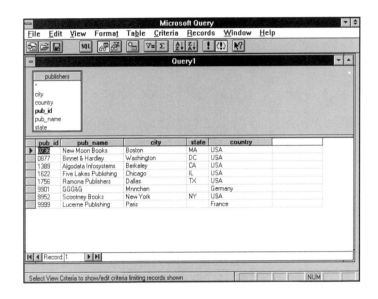

NON-VISUAL ADMINISTRATION TOOLS AND COMMAND-LINE TOOLS

A DBA will probably spend the majority of his or her time using the visual administration tools included with SQL Server. However, there are two non-visual administration tools that a DBA may also use: BCP and ISQL.

BCP

BCP stands for *Bulk Copy Program*. It is a command-line utility that enables you to import and export data to and from SQL Server. The advantage of BCP is that it is fast. Users new to SQL Server are often amazed at how fast it operates. The drawback of BCP is that it can be difficult to use.

By default, BCP.EXE is installed in the mssql\binn directory. For more information on BCP, see Chapter 16, "Importing and Exporting Data."

Following is the syntax for BCP:

```
bcp [[database_name.]owner.]table_name {in | out} datafile
[/m maxerrors] [/f formatfile] [/e errfile]
[/F firstrow] [/L lastrow] [/b batchsize]
[/n] [/c] [/E]
[/t field_term] [/r row_term]
[/i inputfile] [/o outputfile]
/U login_id [/P password] [/S servername] [/v] [/a packet_size]
```

4

SQL SERVER: THE BIG PICTURE

Note

BCP switches are case sensitive.

ISQL

ISQL is a command-line utility used for executing queries and administering SQL Server. With the advent of graphical administration tools for SQL Server, the importance of ISQL has diminished. Most people prefer to perform day-to-day administration tasks from the Enterprise Manager instead of ISQL.

Its minimal overhead, however, makes ISQL useful for processing noninteractive routines such as nightly batch jobs.

By default, ISQL.EXE is installed in the mssql\binn directory.

Following is the syntax for ISQL:

```
isql [-U login id] [-e echo input]
  [-p print statistics] [-n remove numbering]
  [-c cmdend] [-h headers] [-w columnwidth] [-s colseparator]
  [-m errorlevel] [-t query timeout] [-l login timeout]
  [-L list servers] [-a packetsize]
  [-H hostname] [-P password]
  [-q "cmdline query"] [-Q "cmdline query" and exit]
  [-S server] [-d use database name]
  [-r msgs to stderr] [-E trusted connection]
  [-i inputfile] [-o outputfile]
  [-O use Old ISQL behavior disables the following]
         <EOF> batch processing
         Auto console width scaling
         Wide messages
         default errorlevel is -1 vs 1
  [-? show syntax summary]
```

Note

ISQL switches are case sensitive.

Common SQL Server Objects

SQL Server uses the term *object* to describe a database component. Common database objects include tables, rules, defaults, user-defined datatypes, views, triggers, and stored procedures.

Note

Do not be misled by the term *object*. SQL Server is ***not*** an object-oriented database.

TABLES

A *table* is used to store data. It is organized in a row/column manner (see Figure 4.15). You can retrieve, modify, and remove data from a table by using the SQL language.

Figure 4.15.
An example of a table.

stor_id	stor_name	stor_address	city	state	zip	last_update
7066	Barnum's	567 Pasadena Ave.	Tustin	CA	92789	8/1/1995 4:25 PM
7067	News & Brews	577 First St.	Los Gatos	CA	96745	8/15/1995 3:00 PM
7131	Doc-U-Mat	24-A Avrogado Way	Remulade	WA	98014	3/11/1995 1:00 PM
8042	Bookbeat	679 Carson St.	Portland	CA	89076	4/25/1995 3:00 PM

RULES

A *rule* is used to enforce a data constraint (see Figure 4.16). Rules are column specific and cannot perform table lookups. Generally, rules are used to enforce simple business constraints.

Figure 4.16.
An example of a rule.

stor_id	stor_name	stor_address	city	state	zip	last_update
7066	Barnum's	567 Pasadena Ave.	Tustin	CA	92789	8/1/1995 4:25 PM
7067	News & Brews	577 First St.	Los Gatos	CA	96745	8/15/1995 3:00 PM
7131	Doc-U-Mat	24-A Avrogado Way	Remulade	WA	98014	3/11/1995 1:00 PM
8042	Bookbeat	679 Carson St.	Portland	CA	89076	4/25/1995 3:00 PM

Business Rule: All store ids must be between 1 and 9999.

SQL Server Translation: CREATE RULE stor_id_rule AS
@stor_id > = 1 AND @stor_id < = 9999

sp_bindrule stor_id_rule, 'stores. stor_id'

Note

In SQL Server 6.x, an alternative to creating a rule is using the CHECK constraint. Another alternative to creating a rule is using a trigger.

DEFAULTS

Defaults are used to populate a column with a default value when a value is not supplied (see Figure 4.17).

Figure 4.17.
An example of defaults.

stor_id	stor_name	stor_address	city	state	zip	last_update
7066	Barnum's	567 Pasadena Ave.	Tustin	CA	92789	8/1/1995 4:25 PM
7067	News & Brews	577 First St.	Los Gatos	CA	96745	8/15/1995 3:00 PM
7131	Doc-U-Mat	24-A Avrogado Way	Remulade	WA	98014	3/11/1995 1:00 PM
8042	Bookbeat	679 Carson St.	Portland	CA	89076	4/25/1995 3:00 PM

stor_name
Barnum's
News & Brews
Doc-U-Mat
Bookbeat
Johnston

Business Rule: Store id is an integer and can not be null.

SQL Server Translation: sp_addtype stor_id_data type, 'integer,' 'null'

CREATE TABLE stores (stor_id stor_id_datatype,
stor_name char (35),

Note

In SQL Server 6.x, an alternative to creating a default is to use the DEFAULT constraint.

USER-DEFINED DATATYPES

With a *user-defined datatype*, you can create a custom reusable datatype based on an existing SQL Server datatype (see Figure 4.18). By using user-defined datatypes, you can ensure datatype consistency.

Figure 4.18.
An example of a user-defined datatype.

stor_id	stor_name	stor_address	city	state	zip	last_update
7066	Barnum's	567 Pasadena Ave.	Tustin	CA	92789	8/1/1995 4:25 PM
7067	News & Brews	577 First St.	Los Gatos	CA	96745	8/15/1995 3:00 PM
7131	Doc-U-Mat	24-A Avrogado Way	Remulade	WA	98014	3/11/1995 1:00 PM
8042	Bookbeat	679 Carson St.	Portland	CA	89076	4/25/1995 3:00 PM
8100	Johnston	**unknown**	Fairfax	VA	23294	8/1/1995 1:00 PM

stor_name
Barnum's
News & Brews
Doc-U-Mat
Bookbeat
Johnston

Business Rule: If store address is not known when adding a new record, enter "unknown."

SQL Server Translation: CREATE DEFAULT stor_address_default AS
'unknown'

sp_bindefault stor_address_default, 'stores. stor_address'

VIEWS

A *view* is a virtual table that looks and feels like a real table. Views limit the amount of data a user can see and modify. Views may be used to control user access to data and to simplify data presentation (see Figure 4.19).

TRIGGERS

A *trigger* is a user-defined collection of Transact SQL commands that are automatically executed when an INSERT, DELETE, or UPDATE is executed against a table (see Figure 4.20). Triggers are flexible and powerful, which makes them useful for enforcing business rules, referential integrity, and data integrity. Triggers can be column, row, or table specific.

Figure 4.19.
An example of a view.

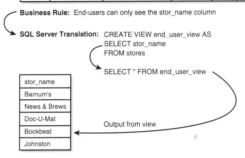

Figure 4.20.
An example of a trigger.

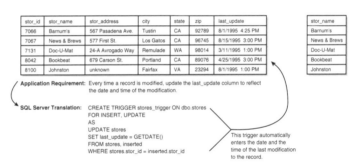

Note

Before version 6.x, SQL Server triggers had to be used to enforce referential integrity. New with version 6.x is the capability to create declarative referential integrity by using the FOREIGN KEY, PRIMARY KEY, and REFERENCE statements. Triggers must still be used to cascade table changes.

STORED PROCEDURES

A *stored procedure* is a compiled SQL program (see Figure 4.21). Within a stored procedure, you can embed conditional logic (if/else logic), declare variables, pass parameters, and perform other programming tasks.

Figure 4.21.
An example of a stored
procedure.

stor_id	stor_name	stor_address	city	state	zip	last_update
7066	Barnum's	567 Pasadena Ave.	Tustin	CA	92789	8/1/1995 4:25 PM
7067	News & Brews	577 First St.	Los Gatos	CA	96745	8/15/1995 3:00 PM
7131	Doc-U-Mat	24-A Avrogado Way	Remulade	WA	98014	3/11/1995 1:00 PM
8042	Bookbeat	679 Carson St.	Portland	CA	89076	4/25/1995 3:00 PM
8100	Johnston	unknown	Fairfax	VA	23294	8/1/1995 1:00 PM

Application Requirement: Store name can be retrieved by passing a parameter to a stored procedure.

SQL Server Translation: CREATE PROCEDURE retrieve_store_name @stor_id integer AS
SELECT stor_name
FROM stores

execute retrieve_store_name 8100

Output from
stored procedure

stor_name
Johnston

SUMMARY

SQL Server delivers performance and ease of use by tightly integrating SQL Server
and Windows NT. The next chapter discusses how to prepare for the installation of
SQL Server.

- Planning an Installation or Upgrade

- Installing or Upgrading SQL Server

PART III

Planning and Installing/ Upgrading SQL Server

CHAPTER 5   *by Mark Spenik*

Planning an Installation or Upgrade

In this chapter, you develop plans and strategies to help you correctly install or upgrade SQL Server. Why bother with a planning stage? Why not just skip right to the installation or upgrade? SQL Server installation is a simple process but by planning ahead, you can make the correct decisions before the installation that affect the performance and operation of SQL Server. In the case of an upgrade, you can never make too many plans to limit server downtime and protect your database against problems encountered during the upgrade. Start by examining installation strategies and plans.

DEVELOPING AN INSTALLATION STRATEGY AND PLAN

Developing an installation plan starts with the assessment of the requirements of your business or users, includes the selection and purchase of the hardware, and finishes with making decisions for specific SQL Server options. You begin the process by collecting user and system requirements. Then you examine possible hardware configurations and SQL Server options. You then create a checklist to use during system installation. Finally, you install SQL Server.

STEP 1: DETERMINE SYSTEM AND USER REQUIREMENTS

How do you determine the hardware system requirements and user requirements for SQL Server? How else: You ask questions and do some homework. Start with the user requirements or business requirements. Based on the requirements of the users or business, you can determine the size and type of hardware system you need to meet the requirements. Start with the following questions:

◆ What is the purpose or goal of the system?

◆ What are the database requirements?

◆ What are the user or business requirements?

◆ How much money will it cost?

Note

One decision you won't have to make is which operating system to use. Microsoft SQL Server 6.x is supported only on Windows NT Server and Windows NT Workstation. If you have decided to use Microsoft SQL Server, the operating system war is already over!

The following sections expand on each of the preceding questions to help you determine the type of system you need.

What Is the Purpose or Goal of the System?

The first questions you might ask yourself are, "What is the system for?" and "Is the system for a single department with 10 users or for a very large database with several hundred users?" In most cases, a system supporting more users requires more memory, disk space, and processing power. Is the system a dedicated SQL Server system or does it perform other activities like file and printing services? Is the system replacing another system as a result of downsizing or right-sizing? If it is replacing an existing system, you already have a lot information available to you (such as the current load on the system and the current system's shortcomings). Is the system a production system or a development/test system? You will want more fault tolerance and more storage capability on a production server than you typically need on a development server.

What Are the Database Requirements?

What are the database requirements for the system? Will the SQL Server primarily be used for decision support systems or transaction systems? How heavy is the expected transaction load? If the system is transaction driven, try to determine the number of expected transactions per day and how the transactions are processed. For example, is the server idle for eight hours and does it then process all the transactions during a few hours, or does it process the transactions evenly throughout the day? What is the expected size of the database? Are you moving databases from another system to SQL Server because of downsizing or right-sizing? If so, you should be able to obtain information such as the current database size, expected database size, and the transaction load of the system from the current system.

Tip

If you have the means, dedicate a machine for SQL Server. Then you can tune the hardware to give the best SQL Server performance.

What Are the User or Business Requirements?

It is always important to understand the requirements and expectations of the individuals who use SQL Server. What type of query response time do the users expect? How many users will be logged on to SQL Server at one time? What are the backup and storage requirements of the users or business?

HOW MUCH MONEY WILL IT COST?

Maybe this question should be listed first! In the real world, the difference between the system you need and the system you get is the amount of money you have available to spend on the system. (Enough said!)

STEP 2: SELECT THE RIGHT PLATFORM

After you obtain the answers and information to the questions described in "Step 1: Determine System and User Requirements," in the first part of this chapter, you are ready to select the hardware platform for your SQL Server. For this discussion, the hardware platform is divided into four areas:

◆ Hardware (including the processor or processors and peripherals)

◆ Memory

◆ Disk drives

◆ File system

The following sections examine each area and the type of decisions you need to make for each area.

HARDWARE

When determining which type of hardware platform to use, the first and last place to check is the Windows NT Hardware Compatibility List to make sure that the brand and model of the machine you are considering is on the list. If the brand and model you are interested in is not on the compatibility list, download the latest list from an electronic bulletin board. If the machine is still not listed, check with the manufacturer or Microsoft.

Tip

Save yourself a lot of problems and potential headaches: Use only the machines approved for Microsoft Windows NT. Although you may get other machines to work, I have seen the difficulty involved and the potential to *not* get the machine up and running when using non-approved platforms and configurations.

At the time this book goes to press, Windows NT is supported on the following microprocessors:

◆ Digital Alpha AXP

◆ Intel 32-bit x86 (486, Pentium, and so on)

- ◆ MIPS
- ◆ Power PC

Note

Remember to check the compatibility list; support for new systems is an ongoing process.

So, how do you determine the correct hardware platform for your business or organization? Start with cost and examine hardware platforms within your budget. There is no point wasting your time researching hardware platforms you can't afford.

The next step is to use the information you gathered earlier—such as the expected number of transactions during a given time period—and talk to the hardware manufacturers or integrators to see whether the platform you are considering can meet those goals and requirements. Check for SQL Server benchmarks on the particular platform and ask to speak to other clients currently using the platform. Consider other factors such as manufacture reliability, service, and maintenance. These three factors are extremely important if the machine runs into a hardware problem and you are faced with downtime. Consider expandability; for example, will you require multiple processors in the future? If so, can the current platform be expanded to accept more processors?

Do I Need SMP (Symmetric Multiple Processors)?

Right out of the box, Windows NT 3.51 supports up to four processors; SQL Server can take advantage of these processors without any special add-ons or configuration changes. In theory, a perfect scaleable SMP machine would scale 100 percent, meaning that if your SQL Server performed 20 transactions per second and you added a second processor, you would increase the number of transactions to 40 per second. The scalability of systems varies widely and can range from nearly 100 percent to below 60 percent. Check with the manufacturer.

What does it mean to you and SQL Server? If you are performing heavy transaction database processing, you can expect your transaction performance to increase with the scalability of the system. If you perform 10 transactions per second and add a second processor on a system that provides 80 percent scalability, you can expect roughly 18 transactions per second. SMP works very well for transaction-based systems.

What if you do primarily decision support (such as database queries)? Adding a second processor may not be the best way to improve your system performance. In decision support systems, the queries are I/O bound and not processor bound, so adding additional processors does not provide the same substantial performance gain you get with transaction-based systems.

MEMORY

A common theme in this book is *give SQL Server enough memory*. Not because SQL Server is an inefficient memory hog, but because SQL Server uses memory very intelligently. Extra memory can provide you with some very cost-effective performance enhancements. The minimum memory requirement for an Intel-based Windows NT Server with SQL Server is 16M (RISC machines like the Alpha AXP and the MIPS require slightly more memory). If you want to use replication, the minimum requirement jumps to 32M of memory with at least 16M assigned to SQL Server.

Tip

Although a Windows NT server with 16M of memory is the minimum requirement, I recommend starting with 32M, allocating 16M for Windows NT and 16M for SQL Server. You can tune up from there.

The setup program allocates up to but does not exceed 8M of memory to SQL Server. Once SQL Server is up and running, you can increase the amount of memory allocated to SQL Server. How does SQL Server get memory? When SQL Server starts, requests are made to the operating system to obtain the configured amount of memory. Memory is allocated for the SQL Server executable code, static memory, data structures, and miscellaneous overhead. SQL Server divides the remaining memory into the procedure cache and data cache (as discussed in Chapter 19, "Which Knobs Do I Turn?").

Tip

When SQL Server starts, it requests the amount of memory in the configuration parameter. The operating system then allocates as much physical memory as possible to SQL Server; if needed, it uses virtual memory to meet the memory configuration requirement. Avoid setting the memory configuration option higher than the amount of physical memory available to SQL Server (subtract the memory required for Windows NT from your machine's total memory; the remainder can be allocated to SQL Server). Using virtual memory can slow performance. Never set the memory parameter too high; if SQL Server cannot get the required amount of memory from physical and virtual memory, the server does not start.

In later chapters, you learn to tune your server for the correct amount of memory. At installation time, however, how much memory should you use? Microsoft has published the following suggestions as rough estimates for SQL Server and Windows NT memory configurations. These figures are from SQL Server's online documentation:

Machine Memory (Megabytes)	Approximate SQL Server Memory Allocation (Megabytes)
16	4
24	8
32	16
48	28
64	40
128	100
256	216
512	464

Configuration & Tuning of Microsoft SQL Server for Windows NT on Compaq Servers (February 1994, Database Engineering, Compaq Computer Corporation) suggests the following formula to use as a rough estimate for memory allocation:

```
SQL Server Memory = 5MB for Kernel and Data Structures
          + (2% Total Data and Index Space) + (50 KB * Number of Users)
```

Regardless of the amount of memory you start with, once SQL Server is up and running, you can monitor SQL Server to more accurately determine your memory requirements.

DISK DRIVES

One of the most important system decisions you can make is the type of disk drives and disk controllers you select. Selecting the proper disk system has a big impact on the overall performance of the SQL Server system and the type of data fault tolerance used to protect the databases.

Caution

Take special care in selecting your disk system. Disk I/O is the typical bottleneck found in database systems.

Before you get into the specifics, you want to select fast disk drives and smart controller cards to take advantage of Windows NT multitasking and asynchronous read-ahead features. When buying disk drives for a database server, consider using more, smaller physical drives rather than one large physical drive. Doing so allows you to spread your databases and transaction logs over several different physical devices. If you are considering buying one 2G hard drive, for example, reconsider and purchase two 1G hard drives or four 500M hard drives.

Tip

The asynchronous read-ahead technology in SQL Server 6.x is beneficial only with multiple disk configurations and smart disk controllers that have asynchronous capabilities.

Just as important as the speed of your hard disk system is the fault tolerance offered in modern disk drive systems. You want the best protection for your databases with optimum performance. One option available to you is the use of RAID (Redundant Array of Inexpensive Disks) disk drive configurations. RAID disk configurations use several disk drives to build a single logical striped drive. Logically, a striped drive is a single drive; physically, the logical drive spans many different disk drives. *Striping the drives* allows files and devices to span multiple physical devices. By spreading the data over several physical drives, RAID configurations offer excellent performance. Another benefit of RAID configurations is fault tolerance and recovery. A RAID 5 configuration can lose a single disk drive and recover all the data on the lost drive. When a new drive is added, the RAID configuration rebuilds the lost drive on the new drive. A RAID 5 system offers good protection and performance for your databases. RAID configurations can be hardware-based solutions or Windows NT software-based solutions. Hardware-based RAID solutions are typically faster than software-based RAID solutions.

FILE SYSTEM

Should you use NTFS (New Technology File System) or FAT (File Allocation Table)? From a performance standpoint, it does not really matter (the performance difference between the two file systems is negligible). In general, NTFS performs faster in read operations and FAT performs faster in write operations. If you use the NTFS file system, you can take advantage of Windows NT security. If you are required to have a dual boot computer, you should use a FAT partition.

Tip

I typically recommend NTFS, which can take advantage of NT security and auditing features.

THE RIGHT PLATFORM

What is the right platform for SQL Server? The best system you can afford that will do the SQL Server processing you require! A good configuration for a SQL Server system is shown in Figure 5.1: a computer configured with one or many processors and starting with 32M of memory. Use a RAID 5 stripe set disk configuration for the databases and the operating system and place SQL Server on a nonstriped drive. How could this system be enhanced? Add additional stripe sets or more memory. Additional stripe sets can give you additional logical drives so that you can place a table on one logical drive and its index on another. For the memory requirements, monitor your SQL Server and determine the correct amount of memory for your Server. After all, SQL Server can run with as little as 4M of memory and as much as 2G of memory.

Figure 5.1.
A typical SQL Server hardware configuration.

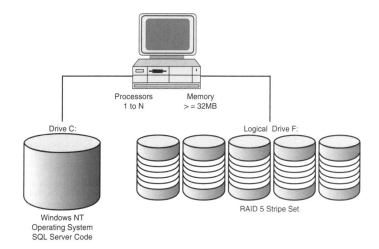

STEP 3: ANSWER REQUIRED QUESTIONS AND UNDERSTAND WHY THEY ARE IMPORTANT

When you begin a new SQL Server installation, you are asked several questions such as your name, company name, and the type of license agreements for the SQL Server. You should be able to answer these questions with no problem—but you are also asked to answer other questions that affect SQL Server performance, maintenance, and behavior. Examine the following installation topics in more detail to help you make the correct choices for your SQL Server:

- ◆ master device
- ◆ Character set
- ◆ Sort order
- ◆ Network
- ◆ SQL Server executive account

THE master DEVICE

During installation, you are asked to give the drive, path, and filename of the master device. The master device is the most important database device and is described in more detail in Chapter 8, "Managing Devices." The master device contains the master database, which houses all the SQL Server information required to manage and maintain the server's databases, users, and devices (basically, all the information required to maintain and run SQL Server). The master device also contains the model and tempdb databases, as well as the optional pubs database. The default name for the master device is master.dat and the default path is the drive and root directory selected for the SQL Server installation in the directory \DATA. The default/minimum size for the master device is 25M.

Note

The default size for SQL Server version 4.21 is 15M.

The minimum installation size for the master device in version 6.x is 25M. You should use a size of 35M to 40M to give you room for expansion. A larger master device size gives you more room to create SQL Server objects and enables you to expand the temporary database (tempdb) beyond the default of 2M (if tempdb is not placed in RAM).

CHARACTER SET

The *character set* is the set of valid characters in your SQL Server database. A character set consists of 256 uppercase and lowercase numbers, symbols, and letters; the first 128 characters in a character set are the same for all the different character sets.

Note

If you plan to use SQL Server replication, you must select the same character set for all the SQL Servers participating in replication.

Following are some common character sets you can choose from at installation time:

Code page 850 (Multilingual)	Code page 850 includes all the characters for North American, South American, and European countries.
	Code page 850 is the default character set for SQL Server 4.21 installations.
ISO 8859-1 (Latin 1 or ANSI)	This character set is compatible with the ANSI characters used by Microsoft Windows NT and Microsoft Windows.
	ISO 8859-1 is the default sort order for SQL Server version 6.x.
Code Page 437 (US English)	The common character set used in the United States. Code Page 437 also contains many graphical characters that are typically not stored in databases.

Other available character sets are as follows:

- Code Page 932   Japanese
- Code Page 936   Chinese (simplified)
- Code Page 949   Korean
- Code Page 950   Chinese (traditional)
- Code Page 1250   Central European
- Code Page 1251   Cyrillic
- Code Page 1253   Greek
- Code Page 1254   Turkish
- Code Page 1255   Hebrew
- Code Page 1256   Arabic
- Code Page 1257   Baltic

Caution

Deciding on the correct character set is important because the character set cannot be changed easily. Changing the character set requires rebuilding and reloading all your databases.

SORT ORDER

The sort order you select for your SQL Server determines how the data is presented in response to SQL queries that use the GROUP BY, ORDER BY, and DISTINCT clauses. The sort order also determines how certain queries are resolved, such as those involving WHERE clauses. For example, if you choose a sort order that is case sensitive and you have a table called MyTable, the query to select all the rows from MyTable must have the following format:

```
Select * from MyTable
```

If the sort order selected is case insensitive, the preceding query could be written in following manners:

```
Select * from MyTable
Select * from mytable
Select * from MYTABLE
```

SQL Server offers many different sort orders, each with its own set of rules. The following sections briefly examine some of the possible sort order choices. Not all sort orders are available for every character set.

DICTIONARY ORDER, CASE INSENSITIVE

Dictionary order means that the characters, when sorted, appear in the order you find them in a dictionary. Dictionary order, case insensitive, uses the following rules to compare characters:

◆ Uppercase and lowercase characters are treated as equivalents.

◆ Characters with diacritical marks are treated as different characters.

Note

Dictionary order, case insensitive, is the default sort order for SQL Server 6.x.

BINARY SORT ORDER

The *binary sort order* uses numeric values to collate the data. Each charter is compared to its numeric representation of 0 to 255. Data does not always come back in dictionary order; for example, UUU returns before aaa in ascending order.

DICTIONARY ORDER, CASE SENSITIVE

Dictionary order, case sensitive, uses the following rules:

◆ Uppercase and lowercase characters are not treated the same.

◆ Characters with diacritical marks are treated as different characters.

Tip

If you have two servers available and you want to change the sort order or character set, use the Transfer Manager built into the Enterprise Manager to rebuild the database and transfer the data.

The sort order affects the speed and performance of SQL Server. Binary sort order is the fastest of the sort orders; the other sort orders are 20 to 35 percent slower than the binary sort order. The default sort order (dictionary order, case insensitive) is about 20 percent slower than the binary sort order.

Caution

Selecting the correct sort order is important because changing the sort order—just as changing the character set—requires rebuilding your databases and reloading the data.

Tip

If you have several SQL Servers in your organization, you should use the same character set and sort order for each of the servers, especially if you want to share databases using the DUMP and LOAD commands. You can't load a database that was dumped with a different character set and sort order.

NETWORK

Because SQL Server supports many different network options simultaneously, clients running TCP/IP can connect to SQL Server along with clients using IPX/SPX—all at the same time. SQL Server installs different network libraries during installation to handle network communication with other servers and client workstations. SQL Server always installs the named-pipes protocol. You have the option during installation (and after) to install one or more network libraries. Keep in mind that the type of network support you select determines the security mode you can use for SQL Server. Before you examine the network libraries available to you, look at the three different security modes (for detailed information, see Chapter 10, "Managing Users"):

◆ **Standard.** An individual logging on to SQL Server supplies a user name and a password that is validated by SQL Server against a system table. Standard security works over all network configurations.

♦ **Integrated.** Integrated security takes advantage of Windows NT user security and account mechanisms. Integrated security can be implemented over the named-pipes protocol or multi-protocol network protocols.

♦ **Mixed.** Users using trusted connections (named-pipes or multi-protocol) can log in using integrated security; users from trusted or nontrusted connections can log in using standard security.

The following sections describe the network options available for SQL Server 6.x.

NAMED-PIPES PROTOCOL

The named-pipes protocol is the default protocol installed with SQL Server. Named-pipes allows for interprocess communication locally or over networks and is used in NT networks using the NetBUI protocol.

MULTI-PROTOCOL

Multi-protocol is new for SQL Server version 6.x. The multi-protocol uses Windows NT Remote Procedure Call (RPC) mechanisms for communication and requires no setup parameters. Multi-protocol currently supports IPX/SPX and TCP/IP, enabling users of those protocols to take advantage of SQL Server integrated security features.

Note

Before SQL Server version 6.0, integrated security was supported only by named-pipes protocol.

NWLINK IPX/SPX PROTOCOL

IPX/SPX is the familiar network protocol used for Novell networks; it is the default network protocol for Windows NT 3.5x servers. If you select NWLink IPX/SPX during installation, you are prompted for the Novell Bindery service name to register SQL Server.

TCP/IP PROTOCOL

TCP/IP is a popular communications protocol used in many UNIX networks. If you select TCP/IP, you are asked to provide a TCP/IP port number for SQL Server to use for client connections. The default port number and the official Internet Assigned Number Authority socket number for Microsoft SQL Server is 1433.

BANYAN VINES

Banyan Vines is another popular PC-based network system. Support for Banyan Vines is included only on Intel-based SQL Server systems. If you install Banyan Vines, you are prompted for a valid street talk name that must first be created using the Vines program MSERVICE.

APPLETALK ADSP PROTOCOL

AppleTalk ADSP allows Apple Macintosh clients to connect to SQL Server using AppleTalk. If you select AppleTalk, you are prompted for the AppleTalk service object name.

DECNET PROTOCOL

Decnet is a popular network protocol found on many Digital networks running VMS and Pathworks. If you select Decnet, you are prompted for a Decnet object ID.

Note

For performance, the named-pipes protocol is the fastest of the network protocols. Running TCP/IP and IPX/SPX is faster than using the multi-protocol but limits your security mode options.

SQL EXECUTIVE USER ACCOUNT

The SQL Executive was first introduced in SQL Server 6.0. The SQL Executive is the service responsible for managing SQL Server tasks such as replication, events, alerts, and task scheduling. During system installation and upgrade, you are required to assign an NT system user account for the SQL Executive. You can use the local system account (in which case, you do not have to create a new NT user account) but you will not be able to perform tasks with other servers like replication or task scheduling. It is recommended that you set up a Windows NT domain user account for the SQL Server Executive. Then you can access files on other servers, such as a Novell NetWare server or Microsoft LAN Manager and perform server-to-server replication and scheduling.

Note

Version 6.5

SQL Server 6.5 has added a new Windows NT user account, installed during installation/upgrade, called SQLExecutiveCmdExec which defaults to a member of the NT local users group. The new user account allows nonsystem administrators (nonSA) to run the CmdExec task in the security context of the SQLExecutiveCmdExec user.

STEP 4: INSTALL SQL SERVER

The next step is to read the next chapter and begin the installation process. Use the following worksheet to help you prepare for the installation; use the worksheet later as a reference:

```
                    SQL Server Installation WorkSheet
Installation Date:
Installed By:
Name:
Company:
Product ID:
# of Client Licenses:
SQL Server Installation Path:
Master Device Path:
Master Device Size:
Character Set:
Sort Order:
Network Support
_X_ Named Pipes         ___ TCP/IP          ___ DecNet
___ NWLink IPX/SPX      ___ Banyan Vines    ___ Apple Talk ADSP
Auto Start SQL Server at Boot Time?
Yes    No
Auto Start SQL Executive at Boot Time?
Yes    No
SQL Executive Log On Account
Start the SQL Server Installation
```

DEVELOPING AN UPGRADE STRATEGY AND PLAN

The plan and strategy for an upgrade is different from the plan and strategy for a new installation. In an upgrade, you have already decided on a platform and are currently running SQL Server. You may have many large production databases and hundreds of users who depend on the databases, or you may have small development databases with a few users. In many ways, upgrading an existing SQL Server is more critical than installing a new SQL Server. The existing SQL Server contains data being used and depended on by your organization.

Now you know why it is important to develop a plan that enables you to upgrade to the new release; if the upgrade is not successful, your plan should allow you to return the system to its pre-upgrade state.

MARK AND ORRYN'S FIRST RULE OF UPGRADING

Never under estimate the difficulty of an upgrade. Remember Mark and Orryn's first rule of upgrading: *expect something to go wrong*; when it does, make sure that you can get the system back and running to its previous state. Creating an upgrade plan is essential. I was once involved with what was to be a simple upgrade for a banking organization that gave me a six-hour window to get their high-powered multi-processor SQL Server upgraded from SQL Server 4.21 to SQL Server 4.21a. No problem, right? After all, the upgrade was not even a major revision number—just a revision letter. Nothing could go wrong...*NOT!* Five hours later, when the SQL Server was still not working correctly and tech support was trying to resolve the problem, we opted to restore the system to the pre-upgrade state. Once the SQL Server was restored, it did not work either! It appears that the problem had to do with the SQL Server registry entries. This was not a problem because our upgrade plan called for backing up the system registry. Once the registry was restored, the SQL Server was up and running with no problems, and the upgrade was pushed off to another day, awaiting information from tech support.

The moral of this story is never underestimate the potential problems that may be encountered during an upgrade, and be overly cautious. It's better to have too many files backed up and ready to restore than not enough.

Once you perform a SQL Server 6.5 upgrade on a 6.0 or 4.2*x* database, there is no turning back. The upgrade process to version 6.5 makes modifications to the databases such as new system tables and datatypes that are not supported in SQL Server versions 6.0 or 4.2*x*.

Note

Upgrades from SQL Server 1.x are not supported with SQL Server 6.x. OS/2 SQL Server version 4.2x systems can be upgraded, but you must first upgrade the operating system to Windows NT 3.51.

When upgrading an existing SQL Server to SQL Server 6.5, you have two options available:

◆ Upgrade the existing SQL Server
◆ Install a new SQL Server and migrate the databases to the new server

Version 6.5 UPGRADE THE EXISTING SQL SERVER

You upgrade SQL Server to the next release by running the setup program and selecting the Upgrade SQL Server option. The upgrade option installs the new SQL Server software and upgrades the databases with new system tables and datatypes.

Before running a SQL Server upgrade, you must make sure that you have adequate disk space on the drive where SQL Server is located. Upgrading from SQL Server 6.0 to SQL Server 6.5 requires an additional 20M of free disk space and 2M of free space in the master database. Upgrading SQL Server 4.2x to version 6.5 requires the following:

◆ 65M of free disk space.

◆ The master database must have at least 9M of free space. If the master database does not have at least 9M free, the setup program alters the master database and increases the size of the database.

The installation program automatically increases the size of the master database. You must make sure that the SQL Server Open Databases configuration parameter is equal to or greater than the number of databases on your server (including master, pubs, model, and tempdb). If the parameter is less than the total number of databases on your system, use the SQL Enterprise Manager or the system stored procedure sp_configure to increase the value. SQL Server 6.5 added several new keywords and is now fully ANSI-92 compliant. If you are upgrading from SQL Server 6.0 or 4.2x to SQL Server 6.5, run the utility program CHKUPG65 before upgrading to SQL Server 6.5. CHKUPG65 checks to make sure that the database status is fine, that all required comments are in the SQL Server system table syscomments, and that there are no keyword conflicts in your databases. In SQL Server 6.0, the CHKUPG65 utility was called CHKUPG. If you are upgrading from SQL Server 6.0 and have not used any of the published reserved words, you will not have any problems with keyword conflicts.

Tip

Fix them now or fix them later! Although keyword conflicts found in your databases do not prevent the successful upgrade of SQL Server from 4.2x to 6.5, you will have to make the corrections on SQL Server and your applications that reference the keywords before or after the upgrade.

The syntax for the CHKUPG65 utility is as follows:

```
CHKUPG65 /Usa /Ppassword /Sservername /ofilename
```

In this syntax, password is the password for the sa user, servername is the SQL Server being upgraded, and filename is the output file to print the CKKUPG65 report. The filename parameter must be fully qualified with drive, path, and filename. The following is a sample output from the CHKUPG65 utility:

```
==================================================================
Database:  master
     Status: 8
         (No problem)
     Missing objects in Syscomments
         None
     Keyword conflicts
         Column name: MSscheduled_backups.DAY [SQL-92 keyword]
==================================================================
Database: pubs
     Status: 0
         (No problem)
     Missing objects in Syscomments
         None
     Keyword conflicts
         Column name: sales.DATE [SQL-92 keyword]
```

If you have problems with syscomments entries, drop and re-create the objects. Databases with the read only option set to TRUE must be changed so that the read only option is set to FALSE.

Tip

A full list of the new keywords and future keywords can be found in the SQL Server documentation. The following keywords have given me trouble during several 4.2x upgrades: CURRENT_TIME, CURRENT_USER, KEY, CURRENT_DATE, and USER.

Tip

This caution does not apply to users upgrading from SQL Server 6.0 to SQL Server 6.5. If you are moving from SQL Server 4.2x to SQL Server 6.5, be prepared after the upgrade to rewrite and recompile some stored procedures. SQL Server 6.5 is not SQL ANSI-92 compliant. You may get this error message after upgrading when you try to execute a stored procedure: You must drop and re-create the stored procedure <stored procedure name>. What's the problem? Transact SQL treatment of some subqueries and SQL statements such as GROUP BY were not ANSI-92 compliant. When you upgrade and try to execute these stored procedures that break ANSI-92 SQL rules, you get the preceding error message. For example, the following pubs database query works and can be compiled as a stored procedure with SQL Server version 4.2x:

```
Select au_id, au_lname
From Authors
Group By (au_id)
```

With SQL Server 6.5, however, you get an error. To correct the SQL statement for use with SQL Server 6.5, change the query as follows:

```
Select au_id, au_lname
from authors
Group By (au_id), (au_lname)
```

The CHKUPG65 utility does not report ANSI-92 SQL violations in stored procedures.

THE UPGRADE PLAN

Before you begin to upgrade an existing SQL Server installation, it is important to create an upgrade plan. The following sections provide you with an example of an upgrade plan to upgrade an existing SQL Server installation to SQL Server 6.5:

1. **Determine whether you have the required disk space.**

   Make sure that you have the required amount of disk space to upgrade your existing SQL Server. If you are upgrading a SQL Server 6.0 installation, you need approximately 20M; if you are upgrading a SQL Server 4.2x installation, you need approximately 65M.

2. **Run the CHKUPG65 utility.**

   When upgrading from 4.2x or 6.0, run the CHKUPG65 utility and review the output report. Correct any errors such as keyword conflicts reported by the utility. Repeat step 2 until errors are no longer reported.

3. **Estimate downtime and schedule the upgrade with users.**

   Estimate the amount of time you expect the upgrade to take. Remember that the larger the database, the longer the upgrade will take. Don't forget to give yourself time to perform any necessary backups before the upgrade begins, time to test the upgraded server, and time to handle any possible problems—including going back to the original installation, if necessary. Once you have determined the amount of time required to perform the upgrade, schedule a date to perform the upgrade with your users. If you have a Microsoft Technical Support contract, notify tech support of your upgrade plans and check for any last minute instructions or known problems.

On the day of the upgrade, follow these steps:

1. **Perform database maintenance.**

   Before backing up the databases, perform the following DBCC commands on each database: CHECKDB, NEWALLOC, and CHECKCATALOG.

2. **Check the SQL Server Open Databases configuration parameter.**

   Make sure that the SQL Server Open Databases configuration parameter is equal to or greater than the number of databases on your server (including master, pubs, model, and tempdb). If the parameter is less than the total number of databases on your system, use the Enterprise Manager or the system stored procedure sp_configure to increase the value.

3. **Back up all databases.**

   Perform SQL Server backups on the databases, including the master database. If possible, shut down SQL Server and use the Windows NT backup facilities to back up the SQL Server directories, including all the SQL Server devices for possible restoration.

4. **Back up the NT registry.**

   Back up the NT system registry again, in case you need to restore the system to the original SQL Server installation.

5. **Turn off read-only on databases.**

   For any databases that have the read only option set to TRUE, use sp_dboption to set the read only option to FALSE. The CHKUPG65 utility reports any databases in read-only mode.

6. **Make sure that no SQL Server applications are executing.**

   Before upgrading the SQL Server, ensure that no one is using SQL Server.

7. **Upgrade the server.**

   Run the setup program and select the Upgrade SQL Server option.

THE FALL BACK PLAN

A SQL Server upgrade is a straightforward process, but because you are usually dealing with valuable data and systems that can be down only for a limited amount of time, upgrades should be treated with extreme caution and care. Just as important as a good upgrade plan is a good fall back plan in case the upgrade does not go as smoothly as you hoped. Here are some suggestions on how to protect yourself. Above all, make sure that you have the backups (tapes, and so on) to return your SQL Server to its earlier state if necessary.

Caution

Always make sure that you have a valid backup of the Windows NT system registry before starting any upgrade.

SUGGESTION 1: COMPLETE SYSTEM BACKUP RECOVERY PLAN

If possible, shut down the SQL Server before the upgrade and perform a backup of the SQL Server directories and all the data devices. You must shut down SQL Server to back up files that SQL Server is using, such as devices. If the upgrade fails for some reason, you can restore the SQL Server directories, devices, and the NT registry, returning your system to its earlier setup.

SUGGESTION 2: COMPLETE DATABASE BACKUPS—REINSTALL PREVIOUS VERSION

Perform SQL Server database backups on the databases, including the master. Make sure that you have all the valid SQL Server configuration information such as the server name, character set, sort order, network configuration, and device and database layouts. If you cannot get the SQL Server 6.5 upgrade to work correctly, having the database dumps and the required SQL Server information enables you to reinstall your previous SQL Server system and reload your databases if necessary.

SUGGESTION 3: COMPLETE SYSTEM BACKUP AND DATABASE BACKUPS

Perform suggestions 1 and 2. You can never be too careful!

The bottom line is that the information and data completely recover your system if the upgrade fails. Play it safe. Have a backup plan to use if the backup plan fails!

THE UPGRADE CHECKLIST

Use the checklist on the next page to help prepare for a SQL Server upgrade. Check off each item on the list as it is completed. Perform each step in order from top to bottom.

INSTALL A NEW SERVER AND MIGRATE THE DATABASES

The option to install a new server does not qualify as an *upgrade* to an existing system, but it is mentioned here for two special cases. The first case is that SQL Server 6.5 can be installed alongside SQL Server 4.2x SQL Server on the same machine.

CHECKLIST

- ☐ Free disk space (6.0 > 20M; 4.2x > 65M)
- ☐ The Open Databases configuration parameter is equal to or greater than the number of databases on your server (including `master`, `pubs`, `model`, and `tempdb`).
- ☐ Run the CHKUPG65 utility
- ☐ `syscomments` errors corrected
- ☐ Read-only databases set to `FALSE`
- ☐ Keyword conflicts resolved

Estimated Down Time:_____hours

- ☐ Alert users
- ☐ Fall back recovery plan in place
- ☐ Fall back recovery plan in place in case fall back plan fails
- ☐ SQL Server DBCC maintenance commands of *all* databases
- ☐ SQL Server backup of *all* databases
- ☐ SQL Server backup of `master` database
- ☐ Back Up Windows NT system registry
- ☐ Operating system backup of SQL Server directories and files (including devices)
- ☐ Make sure that no users are on the system
- ☐ Make sure that no applications are using SQL Server
- ☐ Start the SQL Server upgrade

Caution

You cannot install SQL Server 6.5 alongside SQL Server 6.0 on the same machine. Because the two products share the same registry entries, installing SQL Server 6.5 on a machine with SQL Server 6.0 results in an upgrade.

SQL Server 6.x uses a different directory structure and registry entries than does SQL Server 4.2x. You can run the two SQL Servers simultaneously and migrate the databases from SQL Server 4.2x to the new SQL Server 6.5 installation. This enables you to test each database with SQL Server 6.5 and migrate all the databases without worrying about unexpected problems because the 4.2x installation is still operating and functional. This option is not for everyone because it requires enough disk space and memory to support both SQL Servers *and* your existing databases.

The second case is mentioned for the situation in which an existing SQL Server's machine is being upgraded to a new machine. In this scenario, you can install SQL Server on the new machine and migrate the existing databases from the old machine.

If you decide to use either method, you should perform all the normal upgrade steps and follow the installation procedure for a new SQL Server. Use the Enterprise Manager interface (Transfer Manager in SQL Server 6.0 and 4.2x) to transfer the databases and data or the DUMP and LOAD commands.

Tip

When installing version 6.5 alongside a SQL Server 4.2x installation, remember to change the named-pipes name used for the SQL Server 6.x installation; otherwise, the SQL Server 6.x will not run correctly. The named-pipes used by SQL Server 6.x and SQL Server 4.2 are the same: \\.\pipe\sql\query. To change the named-pipes name for SQL Server 6.x, use the setup program and select the Change Network option. Make sure that the Named-Pipe checkbox is selected and click OK. A dialog box displaying the default named-pipe appears. Change the name of the named-pipe and click the Continue button. Although you can also use the registry editor, regedt32, this method is not recommended.

SUMMARY

This chapter has helped you prepare for a SQL Server upgrade or installation. In the next chapter, you walk through the installation and upgrade process.

- Installing SQL Server

- Upgrading SQL Server

- Starting and Stopping SQL Server

- Removing SQL Server

- Installing Client Tools

- Configuring Clients

- Troubleshooting Installation and Upgrade

- Summary

CHAPTER 6 *by Mark Spenik*

Installing or Upgrading SQL Server

In this chapter, you walk through the actual installation and upgrade of SQL Server as well as the installation of software for the client PCs. Take a look at what the SQL Server installation program actually loads on your computer. Following are the directories created from the SQL Server root directory (MSSQL) during installation:

◆ BACKUP: Default backup directory

◆ BIN: Windows-based and DOS-based DB-Library TSRs and DLLs

◆ BINN: SQL Server NT server, Dynamic Link Library files (DLLs) and client executable files as well as online help files

◆ CHARSETS: Character sets and sort order files

◆ DATA: SQL Server devices and DTC log file

◆ INSTALL: Installation scripts and output files

◆ LOG: Error log files

◆ REPLDATA: Distribution databases' working directory

◆ SNMP: The MSSQL.MIB file for SNMP

◆ SQLOLE: SQLOLE DMO Visual Basic samples

◆ SYMBOLS: SQL Server debug files

The following services are installed:

◆ MSDTC (SQL Server Distributed Transaction Coordinator)

◆ MSSQLServer (SQL Server)

◆ SQLExecutive (SQL Executive)

The following utilities are installed:

◆ SQL Setup: Enables you to configure some SQL Server startup parameters and network support, and remove SQL Server after installation

◆ SQL Service Manager: Used to start and stop SQL Server

◆ ISQL/W: Utility to issue SQL queries

◆ SQL Security Manager: Used to set up integrated security

◆ SQL Performance Monitor: Used to tune SQL Server performance

◆ SQL Enterprise Manager: Primary tool used to manage SQL Server and SQL Server objects

◆ SQL Client Configuration utility: Used to set up SQL Server connection information and check versions of the DB-Library installed

◆ SQL Trace: Utility to monitor and record database activity

◆ MS Query: Query application that provides many features for querying data (such as creating queries using drag and drop)

◆ MS DTC: Microsoft Distributed Transaction Coordinator

◆ SNMP Support: Simple Network Management Protocol Management Information Base (SNMP MIB) and SNMP agent

◆ SQL Server Web Assistant: Creates HTML files as the result of a query

◆ BCP: Bulk Copy utility to import and export flat files with SQL Server

INSTALLING SQL SERVER

Before installing SQL Server, make sure that you have read through the documentation regarding installation that ships with SQL Server 6.5. Also make sure that your system meets the minimum requirements. To help you with your installation, use the worksheet at the end of this chapter.

Tip

One of the problems that occurs quite often on new SQL Server installations is trying to install SQL Server with a user account that does not have the correct NT permissions to create new directories and files. If you get the error message `Can't create directory`, make sure that you are using an account with the correct privileges. Try creating the directory with **File Manager**. If you have the correct privileges, you will be able do so; otherwise, use an account that has the correct permissions.

STEP 1: RUNNING SETUP

Installing SQL Server requires running the setup program, located on the SQL Server 6.5 CD-ROM. The CD-ROM contains several directories, including different directories for each of the currently supported microprocessors:

◆ \I386 for Intel machines

◆ \ALPHA for Digital Alpha AXP machines

◆ \PPC for PowerPC machines

◆ \MIPS for MIPS processors

Select the correct directory for the processor you are using and run the setup program. The window displayed in Figure 6.1 appears.

Figure 6.1.
The SQL Server
setup window.

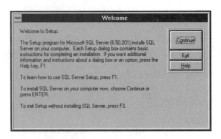

STEP 2: NAME AND ORGANIZATION

Click the Continue button. The Name and Organization dialog box appears (see Figure 6.2).

Figure 6.2.
The Name and Organi-
zation dialog box.

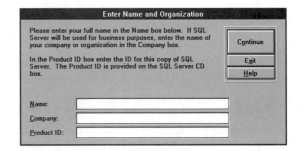

Fill in your name, organization, and the product ID and click the Continue button. Another dialog box appears, prompting you to verify that the information you just entered is correct. If the name, organization, and product ID are correct, click the Continue button. The SQL Server 6.5 Options dialog box appears (see Figure 6.3).

STEP 3: LICENSING MODE

Make sure that the Install SQL Server and Utilities option button is selected in the SQL Server 6.5 Options dialog box. Click the Continue button. The Choose Licensing Mode dialog box appears (see Figure 6.4). Select the correct licensing mode for the SQL Server you have purchased and click the Continue button. When the licensing verification dialog box appears, read the agreement, check the verification checkbox, and click the OK button.

Figure 6.3.
The SQL Server 6.5
Options dialog box.

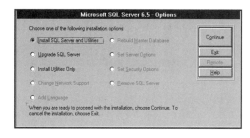

Figure 6.4.
The SQL Server
Licensing Mode
dialog box.

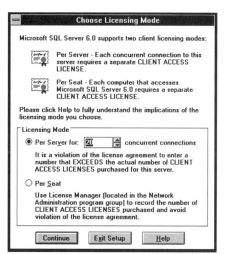

STEP 4: INSTALLATION PATH

After you have read the licensing agreement, the SQL Server Installation Path dialog box appears (see Figure 6.5). Select the correct drive and directory for the SQL Server installation and click the Continue button.

Figure 6.5.
The SQL Server
Installation Path
dialog box.

STEP 5: MASTER DEVICE

The Master Device Creation dialog box appears (see Figure 6.6). Select the correct drive, directory, filename, and size for the master device and click the Continue button.

Figure 6.6.
The Master Device
Creation dialog box.

Tip

The minimum default size is 25M. I recommend making the master device at least 35M to allow for expansion and a larger temporary database. I also recommend using the default filename, master.dat, because it has become a standard and makes for easy reference when looking at documents or talking to tech support. By default, the master device is located in the \DATA directory off the SQL Server home directory.

STEP 6: BOOKS ONLINE

The SQL Server Books Online dialog box appears (see Figure 6.7). Select one of the following radio buttons:

◆ Install on Hard Disk

◆ Install to Run from CD

◆ Do Not Install

Click the Continue button.

Figure 6.7.
The SQL Server Books
Online dialog box.

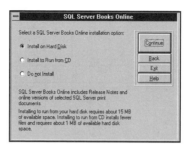

Tip

I recommend installing Books Online. Although the space requirements are about 15M, it is space well spent. The documentation is
very good and has search and find features that help you quickly track
down specific topics and problems.

STEP 7: INSTALLATION OPTIONS

The Installation Options dialog box appears (see Figure 6.8). Use this dialog box to
change the default character set or sort order, or to add additional network support.
You can also enable SQL Server and the SQL Executive to automatically restart
when Windows NT is rebooted by checking the Auto Start checkboxes for SQL
Server and the SQL Executive.

Figure 6.8.
The Installation
Options dialog box.

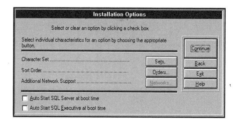

To change the character set, click the Sets button. The Select Character Set dialog
box appears (see Figure 6.9). Select a character set from the list and click the OK
button.

To change the sort order, click the Orders button in the Installation Options dialog
box. The Select Sort Order dialog box appears (see Figure 6.10). Select the new sort
order and click the OK button.

Figure 6.9.
The Select Character
Set dialog box.

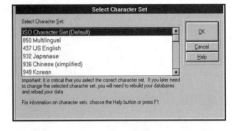

Figure 6.10.
The Select Sort Order
dialog box.

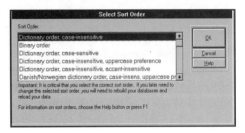

To add additional network support, click the Networks button in the Installation Options dialog box. To start SQL Server and the SQL Executive as NT services when the NT server is booted, select the proper checkbox options (refer back to Figure 6.8). After you have made your selections, click the Continue button.

Tip

If you are setting up the NT server to be a dedicated SQL Server system, select the Auto Start SQL Server at Boot Time and the Auto Start SQL Executive at Boot Time checkboxes. If the NT server goes down momentarily because of a power outage, SQL Server starts automatically when the NT server reboots (if SQL Server and SQL Executive are NT services).

STEP 8: SET UP SQL EXECUTIVE USER ACCOUNT

The next step is to assign an NT user account to the SQL Executive service using the SQL Executive Log On Account dialog box (see Figure 6.11). If you created a special account for the Executive Service, enter the account name, password, and password confirmation. To use the local system account instead, check the appropriate option button. When you have made your choice, click the Continue button.

Figure 6.11.
The SQL Executive Log
On Account dialog box.

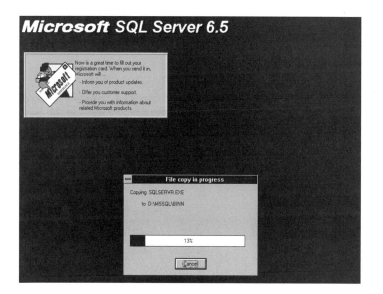

STEP 9: WAIT AND WATCH

Step 9 is the "wait-and-watch" step or the "go-do-something-else" step. The setup program begins to create the SQL Server directories and load the appropriate files (see Figure 6.12).

Figure 6.12.
SQL Server setup
copying files.

Once the file copy is complete, SQL Server begins to create the `master` device (see Figure 6.13).

Figure 6.13.
SQL Server setup
creating the `master`
device.

The other devices and databases are created and the registry is updated; when the setup program is complete, the SQL Server Completed dialog box appears (see Figure 6.14). To use SQL Server, you must now reboot the server.

Congratulations—SQL Server installation is complete!

Figure 6.14.
The SQL Server
Completion dialog box.

UPGRADING SQL SERVER

The upgrade procedure is very similar to the installation procedure, except that a few questions are skipped because the server is already running. Before starting the upgrade, make sure that you have performed all the items on the upgrade checklist described in Chapter 5, "Planning an Installation or Upgrade." As a reminder, make sure that you do the following:

◆ Perform database backups

◆ Back up SQL Server files, devices, and directories

◆ Back up the NT registry

◆ Make sure that the SQL Server configuration parameter open databases is equal to or greater than the current number of databases on the SQL Server you are upgrading

◆ Run CHKUPG65.EXE

SQL SERVER 6.0 TO SQL SERVER 6.5

Before upgrading from SQL Server 6.0 to SQL Server 6.5, here is a quick checklist of the compatibility issues between the two systems:

◆ You cannot run SQL Server 6.0 and SQL Server 6.5 side by side on the same machine.

◆ SQL Server 6.5 can read SQL Server 6.0 databases.

◆ SQL Server 6.0 with service pack 3.0 (available from Microsoft) can read a SQL Server 6.5 database.

STEP 1: RUN SETUP

Upgrading SQL Server requires running the setup program located on the SQL Server 6.5 CD-ROM. The CD-ROM contains several directories, including directories for each of the currently supported microprocessors:

- ◆ \I386 for Intel machines
- ◆ \ALPHA for Digital Alpha AXP machines
- ◆ \PPC for PowerPC machines
- ◆ \MIPS for MIPS processors

Select the correct directory for the processor you are using and run the setup program. When the SQL Server Welcome dialog box appears, click the Continue button. The SQL Server Already Installed dialog box appears (see Figure 6.15). Click Continue. The SQL Server 6.5 Options dialog box appears.

Figure 6.15.
The SQL Server
Already Installed
dialog box.

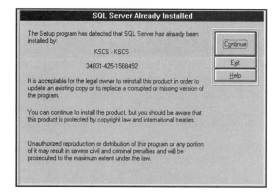

STEP 2: CHECK UPGRADE OPTION

Make sure that the Upgrade SQL Server option button is selected in the SQL Server 6.5 Options dialog box and click the Continue button (see Figure 6.16).

Figure 6.16.
The SQL Server 6.5
Options dialog box.

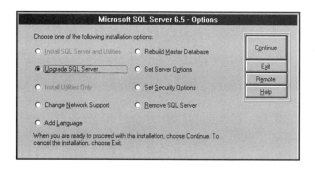

STEP 3: NAME, ORGANIZATION, AND LICENSING MODE

The Name and Organization dialog box appears with the current name and organization filled in from the previous SQL Server (refer back to Figure 6.2). Fill in the product ID and click the Continue button. Another dialog box appears, prompting you to verify that the information you just entered is correct. If the name, organization, and product ID are correct, click the Continue button. The Choose Licensing Mode dialog box appears (refer back to Figure 6.4). Select the correct licensing mode for the SQL Server you have purchased and click the Continue button. When the licensing verification dialog box appears, read the agreement, check the verification checkbox, and click the OK button.

STEP 4: CONTINUE OR EXIT UPGRADE

The SQL Server Upgrade dialog box appears (see Figure 6.17). To stop the upgrade, click the Exit button. To continue the upgrade, click the Resume button.

Figure 6.17.
The Upgrade SQL
Server dialog box.

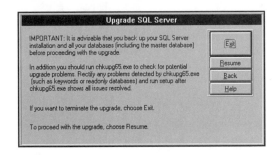

STEP 5: INSTALLATION PATH

The SQL Server Installation Path dialog box appears (refer back to Figure 6.5). The current directory and drive for the existing SQL Server is the default. To change the directory and drive, select the correct drive and path for the SQL Server installation and click the Continue button.

STEP 6: UPGRADE MASTER DEVICE

The SQL Server Upgrade Master Device Path dialog box appears (see Figure 6.18). The drive and path must point to the master device being upgraded to SQL Server 6.5. If the drive and directory displayed are invalid, select the correct drive, directory, and filename and click the Continue button.

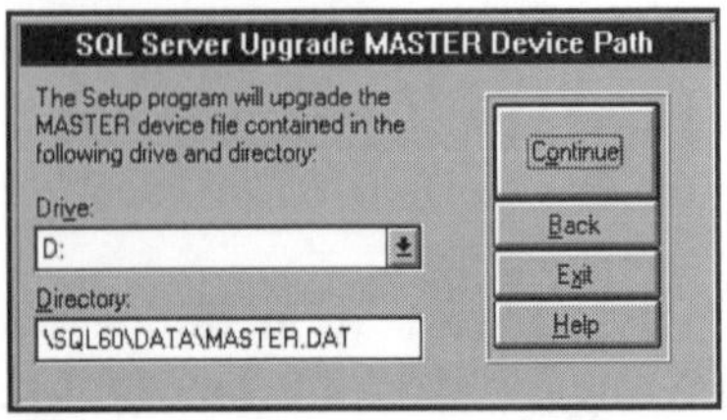

Figure 6.18.
The SQL Server
Upgrade Master Device
Path dialog box.

STEP 7: BOOKS ONLINE

The SQL Server Books Online dialog box appears (refer back to Figure 6.7). Select one of the following radio buttons:

◆ Install on Hard Disk

◆ Install to Run from CD

◆ Do Not Install

Click the Continue button.

STEP 8: EXECUTIVE SERVICE USER ACCOUNT

The SA (SQL Server system administrator) Password dialog box appears (see Figure 6.19). Enter the sa password and confirmation password and click the Continue button. The SQL Executive Log On Account dialog box appears (refer back to Figure 6.11). If you created a special account for the Executive Service, enter the account name, password, and password confirmation. If you want to use the local system account instead, check the appropriate option button. When you have made your choice, click the Continue button.

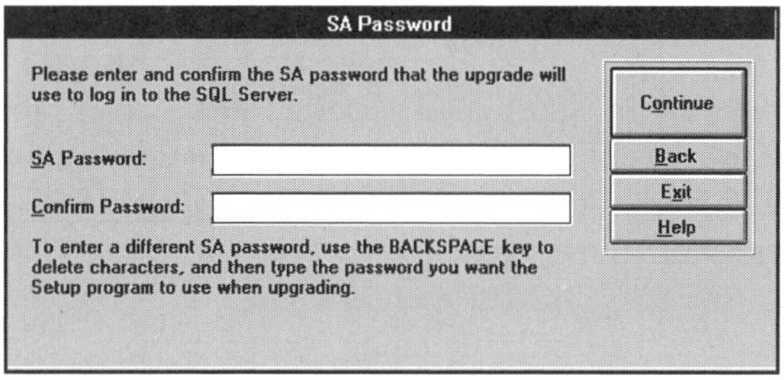

Figure 6.19.
The SA Password
dialog box.

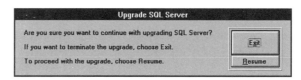

STEP 9: WAIT AND WATCH

You are prompted by the Upgrade SQL Server dialog box (see Figure 6.20). To continue the SQL Server upgrade, click the Resume button. To halt the upgrade, click the Exit button. If you click the Resume button, you enter a waiting period while the SQL Server 4.2x or 6.0 installation is upgraded to SQL Server 6.5. When the upgrade is complete, the Microsoft SQL Server 6.5 Completed dialog box appears. To run SQL Server 6.5, you must now reboot the server.

Figure 6.20.
The Upgrade SQL
Server dialog box.

STARTING AND STOPPING SQL SERVER

If you checked the Auto Boot options for SQL Server and the SQL Executive, the two services start automatically when the NT server reboots. The easiest way to start, stop, pause, or check the status of SQL Server and SQL Executive is to use the SQL Service Manager (see Figure 6.21).

Figure 6.21.
The SQL Service
Manager.

The SQL Server Manager is located in the Microsoft SQL Server 6.5 program group, which was created during the installation or upgrade. To start the SQL Server Manager, double-click the icon. If SQL Server is running, the traffic light is green. If the service is stopped, the traffic light is red. To start the server, double-click the light next to the Start/Continue label.

To stop SQL Server, double-click the light next to the Stop label. To pause SQL Server, double-click the light next to the Pause label. Pausing SQL Server does not halt queries in process; it prevents new users from logging in to SQL Server. When SQL Server is paused, users currently logged in to SQL Server can continue to work as normal.

Controlling the SQL Executive is the same as controlling SQL Server, except that you cannot pause the SQL Executive. To perform stop, start, and status checks on SQL Executive, use the drop-down Services list box and select SQLExecutive instead of MSSQLServer.

You can also start SQL Server and SQL Executive from the Windows NT Services dialog box located in the Windows NT control panel. If you want to set up SQL Server and SQL Executive to start when the NT server is rebooted, use the Services dialog box in the control panel or the SQL setup program to set the Auto Boot options (refer back to Figure 6.8).

Note

The service name for Microsoft SQL Server has changed. In previous versions, the name used for the service was *SQLServer*. With SQL Server 6.5, the name is *MSSQLServer*.

REMOVING SQL SERVER

If you want to remove a SQL Server installation, do not delete the SQL Server directories. Run the setup program and select the Remove SQL Server option from the SQL Server Options dialog box (see Figure 6.22).

Figure 6.22.
The SQL Server
Options dialog box.

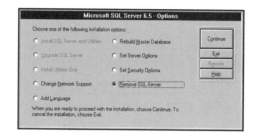

Click the Continue button; the Remove SQL Server dialog box appears. Select the Remove Files option to clear the SQL Server entries from the system registry and remove all the SQL Server files installed; otherwise, only the registry is cleared. If you select Remove Files, you must manually delete a few files used by the setup program when the SQL Server removal is complete. Remove the leftover files by removing the SQL Server home directory, which also is left over after a file removal.

INSTALLING CLIENT TOOLS

SQL Server provides several different tools that allow computers acting as clients to connect to SQL Server. The following are the current 32-bit operating systems supported by the SQL Server client tools:

◆ Microsoft Windows NT Server version 3.51

◆ Microsoft Windows NT Workstation version 3.51

◆ Microsoft Windows 95

If you are using one of these 32-bit operating systems, you can install the following tools:

◆ **ISQL/W:** Utility to issue SQL queries

◆ **SQL Security Manager:** Used to set up integrated security

◆ **SQL Enterprise Manager:** Primary tool used to manage SQL Server and SQL Server objects

◆ **SQL Client Configuration utility:** Utility to set up SQL Server connection information and check versions of the DB-Library installed

◆ **SQL Trace:** Utility to monitor and record database activity

◆ **MS Query:** Query application that provides many features for querying data (such as creating queries using drag and drop)

◆ **MS DTC:** Microsoft Distributed Transaction Coordinator client support

◆ **SQL Server Web Assistant:** Creates HTML files as the result of a query

◆ **ODBC drivers:** Installs other ODBC drivers for replication use

◆ **BCP:** BulkCopy utility to import and export flat files with SQL Server

The following 16-bit operating systems are supported:

◆ Windows 3.1 and Windows 3.11 (Workgroups)

◆ MS-DOS

The following tools are available for Windows 3.1 and Windows 3.11:

◆ **ISQL/W:** Utility to issue SQL queries

◆ **SQL Client Configuration utility:** Utility to set up SQL Server connection information and check versions of the DB-Library installed

◆ **BCP:** BulkCopy utility to import and export flat files with SQL Server

The following tools are available for MS-DOS:

◆ **ISQL:** Utility to issue SQL queries

◆ **BCP:** BulkCopy utility to import and export flat files with SQL Server

Note: The BCP utility is an MS-DOS-based utility for all client utility versions.

Note

You can use the SQL Administrator and SQL Object Manager client tools installed with SQL Server 4.2x on 32-bit and 16-bit clients. For 32-bit clients, I recommend using the new 32-bit tools, such as the SQL Server Enterprise Manager, rather than the SQL Server 4.2x tools. But the 4.2x SQL Object Manager does provide graphical BCP capabilities.

To use SQL Administrator and SQL Object Manager, you must install the following scripts on the version 6.5 SQL Server, located on the SQL Server root directory \INSTALL:

◆ ADMIN60.SQL for the SQL Server Administrator

◆ OBJECT60.SQL for the Object Manager

Before you can administer a SQL Server 6.0 installation with a SQL Server 6.5 Enterprise Manager, you must install the following script on the version 6.0 SQL Server:

◆ SQLOLE65.SQL for the SQL Server 6.5 Enterprise Manager to attach to a SQL Server 6.0 installation

The following sections walk through a SQL Server client utilities installation from Windows 95.

STEP 1: RUN SETUP

Installing SQL Server utilities on 32-bit operating systems requires running the setup program located on the SQL Server 6.5 CD-ROM. The CD-ROM contains several directories, including directories for each of the currently supported micro-processors:

◆ \I386 for Intel machines

◆ \ALPHA for Digital Alpha AXP machines

◆ \PPC for PowerPC machines

◆ \MIPS for MIPS processors

Note

For 16-bit operating systems (Windows 3.1 and Windows 3.11), run setup from the correct processor directory under the directory \CLIENTS\WIN16. For MS-DOS, use the directory \CLIENTS\MSDOS.

Select the correct directory for the processor you are using and run the setup program. The SQL Server Welcome dialog box appears (see Figure 6.23). To install the client utilities, click the Continue button.

Figure 6.23.
The SQL Server
Welcome dialog box.

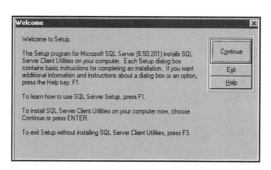

STEP 2: INSTALL CLIENT UTILITIES

The next dialog box that appears is Install/Remove Client Utilities (see Figure 6.24). To continue the installation, select the Install Client Utilities option and click the Continue button.

Figure 6.24.
The Install/Remove
Client Utilities
dialog box.

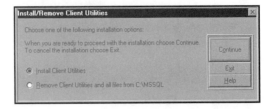

Note

To remove client utilities, select the Remove Client Utilities and Files option and then click the Continue button.

STEP 3: SELECT UTILITIES

The Install Client Utilities dialog box appears (see Figure 6.25). Use the Drive combo box to select the correct drive; enter a directory in the Directory text box (the default directory is \MSSQL). All the utilities checkboxes are selected in the Utilities To Be Installed area. If you do not want a utility installed, deselect the appropriate checkbox. When you have made all your utility selections, click the Continue button.

Figure 6.25.
The Install Client
Utilities dialog box.

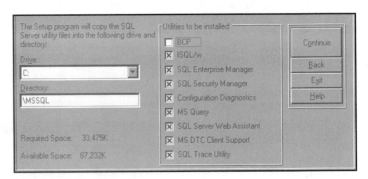

The utilities begin to load on your computer. When the utilities are loaded, a completion dialog box appears and the client utility installation is complete. Reboot the computer and you are ready to test the utilities. Figure 6.26 shows the Windows 95 program group created by the utilities setup program. The SQL Server utilities installation is complete.

Figure 6.26.
The Windows 95 SQL
Server 6.5 Utilities
program group.

CONFIGURING CLIENTS

Now that you have the client utilities installed, you are ready to connect to SQL Server. SQL Server clients establish connections with SQL Server over named-pipes using dynamic server names. SQL Server clients can connect over named-pipes or any of the Microsoft-supplied protocols, including TCP/IP sockets and IPX/SPX.

Typically, you can connect to SQL Server from a client utility without any special configuration. When using ISQL/W or the Enterprise Manager, click the List Servers button to get a list of the active SQL Servers.

To connect to a SQL Server that is using a different network protocol or listening on an alternate named-pipe, you can set up an entry for the SQL Server using the Advanced page of the Client Configuration Utility dialog box (see Figure 6.27).

Tip

If you are trying to connect to SQL Server on a local machine, leave the server name blank.

Figure 6.27.
The Advanced page of
the SQL Server Client
Configuration Utility
dialog box.

6

INSTALLING OR UPGRADING SQL SERVER

To add a new client configuration, select a server or enter the server name in the Server combo box. Select the network used to communicate with the server in the DLL Name list box. The DLL name refers to the network library that provides the communication between SQL Server and the client. Selecting the network assigns the correct DLL to the server entry. The network DLLs for each operating system are listed in Table 6.1.

TABLE 6.1. SQL SERVER NET LIBRARIES.

Network Protocol	Windows NT DLL	Windows 3.1 and 3.11 DLL	MS-DOS TSR
Named-Pipes	DBNMPNTW	DBNMP3	DBNMPIPE.EXE
NWLink IPX/SPX	DBMSSPXN	DBMSSPX3	DBMSSPX.EXE
Banyan Vines	DBMSVINN	DBMSVIN3	DBMSVINE.EXE
TCP/IP Sockets	DBMSSOCN	DBMSSOC3	None
Multi-Protocol	DBMSRPCN	DBMSRPC3	None

Add the proper connection string information in the Connection String text box. For example, if the network is TCP/IP and the address of the server is 200.12.20.123 and the SQL Server port is 1433, add the following in the Connection String box:

200.12.20.123,1433

Click the Add/Modify button in the Client Configuration Utility dialog box. The server name is now available for the SQL Server client utilities.

WHAT ABOUT ODBC?

If you are trying to connect to SQL Server using the Open Database Connectivity standard (ODBC), remember that the Client Configuration Utility does not set up ODBC data sources for applications such as Microsoft Access or Powerbuilder. You must run the ODBC setup program that ships with the application or the operating system. See Chapter 12, "Replication," for examples of configuring ODBC sources.

TROUBLESHOOTING INSTALLATION AND UPGRADE

As stated earlier, the installation and upgrade process for SQL Server is fairly straightforward; however, even in the most straightforward operations, problems can and do occur. Hopefully, you will be provided with error messages that pinpoint your problem. In some cases, you will have to do some debugging and observation to determine what has gone wrong. In the worst case, you may find yourself on the telephone with tech support trying to determine the problem.

Some of the common errors encountered during an installation or upgrade are improper Windows NT permissions or insufficient disk space. If you receive an error message telling you that you can't create a directory or file, you probably have a permissions problem. Switch to an account with the correct permissions. If the installation fails, check your disk space to make sure that you have enough free space to install SQL Server.

Typical problems encountered during an upgrade—other than problems with disk space and permissions—are trying to upgrade a suspect (corrupted) database or a database with a read-only flag set. Use the CHKUPG utility and make sure that you resolve any suspect database problems and reset the read-only database options to FALSE before upgrading.

What can you do if you have completed an installation or upgrade and your SQL Server does not work? You have to start debugging and try to determine the problem. The best place to start is the SQL Server error log.

ERROR LOG AND WINDOWS NT APPLICATION LOG

The error log, located on the SQL Server root directory in the directory \LOG, is a text file used to log audit and error information for SQL Server.

The Windows NT application log is a Windows NT system log used by applications and Windows NT to log audit and error information. The Windows NT application log contains the same information as the SQL Server error log, except that only SQL Server writes to the error log but any Windows NT application can write to the application log. You can configure SQL Server to write to both logs (the default) or to either log.

Tip

When I try to read consecutive error or audit messages, I find that the SQL Server error log is easier to view than the Windows NT application log; however, one benefit of the Windows NT application log is that error messages are highlighted with a stop-sign icon and are easy to find.

Following is an example of a SQL Server error log entry during system startup:

```
96/04/29 07:39:12.97 kernel   Microsoft SQL Server  6.50 - 6.50.201 (Intel X86)
     Apr  3 1996 02:55:53
     Copyright (c) 1988-1996 Microsoft Corporation

96/04/29 07:39:13.06 kernel   Copyright (C) 1988-1994 Microsoft Corporation.
96/04/29 07:39:13.07 kernel   All rights reserved.
96/04/29 07:39:13.07 kernel   Logging SQL Server messages in file
'C:\MSSQL\LOG\ERRORLOG'
96/04/29 07:39:13.14 kernel   initconfig: number of user connections limited to 15
96/04/29 07:39:13.15 kernel   SQL Server is starting at priority class 'normal'
with dataserver serialization turned on (1 CPU detected).
96/04/29 07:39:13.31 kernel   Attempting to initialize Distributed Transaction
Coordinator
96/04/29 07:39:13.71 server   Failed to obtain TransactionDispenserInterface:
XACT_E_TMNOTAVAILABLE
96/04/29 07:39:13.79 kernel   initializing virtual device 0,
C:\MSSQL\DATA\MASTER.DAT
96/04/29 07:39:13.82 kernel   Opening Master Database ...
96/04/29 07:39:14.02 spid1    Loading SQL Server's  default sort order and charac-
ter set
96/04/29 07:39:14.13 spid1    Recovering Database 'master'
96/04/29 07:39:14.19 spid1    Recovery dbid 1 ckpt (7953,34) oldest tran=(7953,0)
96/04/29 07:39:14.39 spid1    Activating disk 'MSDBData'
96/04/29 07:39:14.40 kernel   initializing virtual device 127,
C:\MSSQL\DATA\MSDB.DAT
96/04/29 07:39:14.40 spid1    Activating disk 'MSDBLog'
96/04/29 07:39:14.41 kernel   initializing virtual device 126,
C:\MSSQL\DATA\MSDBLOG.DAT
96/04/29 07:39:14.42 spid1    Activating disk 'mypubs'
96/04/29 07:39:14.43 kernel   initializing virtual device 2,
C:\MSSQL\DATA\mypubs.DAT
96/04/29 07:39:14.43 spid1    Activating disk 'repdata'
96/04/29 07:39:14.44 kernel   initializing virtual device 3,
C:\MSSQL\DATA\repdata.DAT
96/04/29 07:39:14.45 spid1    Activating disk 'replog'
96/04/29 07:39:14.46 kernel   initializing virtual device 4,
C:\MSSQL\DATA\replog.DAT
96/04/29 07:39:14.47 spid1    Activating disk 'sales_data2'
96/04/29 07:39:14.48 kernel   initializing virtual device 7,
C:\MSSQL\DATA\sales_data2.DAT
96/04/29 07:39:14.48 spid1    Activating disk 'Sales_Datat'
96/04/29 07:39:14.49 kernel   initializing virtual device 5,
C:\MSSQL\DATA\Sales_Datat.DAT
96/04/29 07:39:14.50 spid1    Activating disk 'sales_log'
96/04/29 07:39:14.51 kernel   initializing virtual device 6,
C:\MSSQL\DATA\sales_log.DAT
96/04/29 07:39:14.51 spid1    Activating disk 'test_data'
96/04/29 07:39:14.52 kernel   initializing virtual device 1,
C:\MSSQL\DATA\test_data.DAT
96/04/29 07:39:14.56 spid1    server name is 'KSCSNT'
96/04/29 07:39:14.63 spid1    Recovering database 'model'
96/04/29 07:39:14.68 spid1    Recovery dbid 3 ckpt (338,0) oldest tran=(339,0)
96/04/29 07:39:14.94 spid1    Clearing temp db
96/04/29 07:39:16.73 kernel   Read Ahead Manager started.
96/04/29 07:39:16.80 kernel   Using 'SQLEVN60.DLL' version '6.00.000'.
96/04/29 07:39:16.99 kernel   Using 'OPENDS60.DLL' version '6.00.01.02'.
```

```
96/04/29 07:39:17.03 kernel   Using 'NTWDBLIB.DLL' version '6.50.201'.
96/04/29 07:39:17.08 ods      Using 'SSNMPN60.DLL' version '6.5.0.0' to listen on
'\\.\pipe\sql\query'.
96/04/29 07:39:19.01 spid10   Recovering database 'pubs'
96/04/29 07:39:19.03 spid10   Recovery dbid 4 ckpt (865,2) oldest tran=(865,0)
96/04/29 07:39:19.05 spid11   Recovering database 'msdb'
96/04/29 07:39:19.06 spid12   Recovering database 'products'
96/04/29 07:39:19.10 spid11   Recovery dbid 5 ckpt (3594,11) oldest tran=(3594,0)
96/04/29 07:39:19.21 spid12   Recovery dbid 6 ckpt (338,10) oldest tran=(338,0)
96/04/29 07:39:19.68 spid12   6 transactions rolled forward in dbid 6.
96/04/29 07:39:19.80 spid11   Recovering database 'MyPubs'
96/04/29 07:39:19.85 spid11   Recovery dbid 7 ckpt (801,15) oldest tran=(801,0)
96/04/29 07:39:19.88 spid10   Recovering database 'distribution'
96/04/29 07:39:20.03 spid10   Recovery dbid 8 ckpt (5505,1) oldest tran=(5505,0)
96/04/29 07:39:20.18 spid12   Recovering database 'Sales'
96/04/29 07:39:20.22 spid12   Recovery dbid 9 ckpt (1029,9) oldest tran=(1029,8)
96/04/29 07:39:20.29 spid12   1 transactions rolled forward in dbid 9.
96/04/29 07:39:20.40 spid10   10 transactions rolled forward in dbid 8.
96/04/29 07:39:20.62 spid1    Recovery complete.
96/04/29 07:39:20.65 spid1    SQL Server's default sort order is:
96/04/29 07:39:20.65 spid1            'nocase' (ID = 52)
96/04/29 07:39:20.65 spid1    on top of default character set:
96/04/29 07:39:20.66 spid1            'iso_1' (ID = 1)
96/04/29 07:39:20.84 spid1    Launched startup procedure 'sp_sqlregister'
96/04/30 10:34:09.84 kernel   SQL Server terminating due to 'stop' request from
Service Control Manager
```

You can view the error log using any text file editor, such as Windows Notepad or SQL Server Enterprise Manager. You can view the Windows NT application log using the Windows NT Event Viewer (see Figure 6.28).

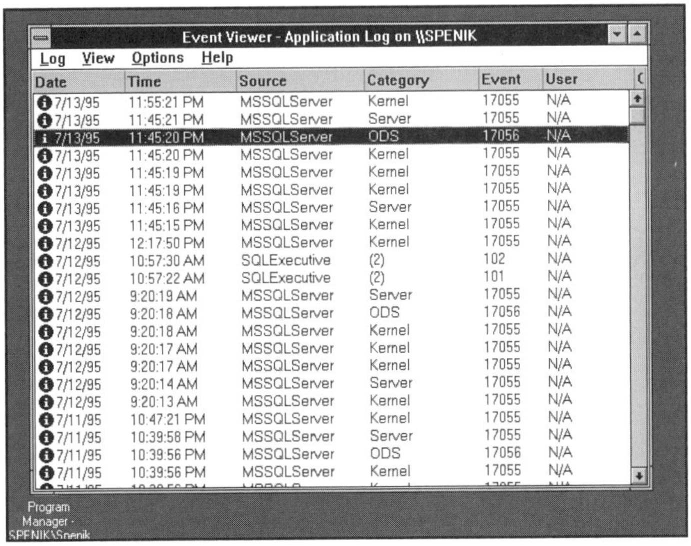

Figure 6.28.
The Windows NT
application log.

Scan through the error log or application log and look for possible error messages. Every time you stop and restart SQL Server, a new error log is started. SQL Server archives the error logs by saving the previous six error log files, named as follows (where *x* is 1 through 6, and the current error log is ERRORLOG):

ERRORLOG.*X*

Another possible place to find error messages is the \INSTALL directory on the SQL Server root directory. Each installation script file writes to an output file with an OUT extension. To find the last script that was executed, enter the following on a DOS command line from the \INSTALL directory:

dir *.out /od

The last file displayed is the last script to execute. Check the OUT file for possible errors.

START SQL SERVER FROM THE COMMAND LINE

If you are having trouble starting SQL Server from the Windows NT Service Manager or the SQL Server Service Manager after an installation or upgrade, try starting SQL Server from the command line. Starting SQL Server from the command line is a great way to debug because the messages usually logged to the error log or Windows NT application log are displayed directly in the DOS command window. To start SQL Server from the command line, enter the following:

sqlservr *<command line options>*

Not all the command-line options are discussed here, but read on to find out about a few of the important options you can use to help get your SQL Server debugged and up and running.

-d

The -d option specifies the path and filename of the master device.

-c

The -c option starts SQL Server independent of the Windows NT Service Control Manager.

Tip

> The -c option is supposed to quicken SQL Server startup time by bypassing the Windows NT Service Control Manager. If you are having problems starting SQL Server, include the -c option to help further isolate the problem. I was working with one upgraded SQL Server installation in which the NT Service Control Manager kept shutting down SQL Server every time it started. By specifying the -c option, we were able to get the server up and running and correct the problem. The only drawback is that you cannot stop the SQL Server with any of the conventional methods (such as the SQL Server Service Manager). SQL Server can be halted by logging off of Windows NT or pressing Ctrl+C in the DOS command window running SQL Server. When you press Ctrl+C, you are prompted with a message asking if you want to shut down the server. Select Y to shut down the server.

-m

The -m option enables you to start SQL Server in single-user mode, which means that only one user can log into SQL Server. Use the -m option when restoring databases or trying to fix suspect or corrupted databases.

-f

You decide to push the limits of your system's capabilities and you place tempdb in RAM, not really understanding where the RAM is coming from for the temporary database. You restart SQL Server and you get an error trying to open the tempdb database because you don't have enough physical or virtual memory on your machine to create tempdb in RAM and run SQL Server. Does this problem sound familiar? How do you correct this problem? Use the -f startup option.

The -f option enables you to start SQL Server in a minimal configuration. Use the -f option only when SQL Server does not start because of a configuration parameter problem, such as placing a 40M tempdb in RAM when only 20M of RAM is available.

Following is an example of how to start SQL Server from the command line using some of the preceding options:

```
sqlservr -c -dc:\sql\data\master.dat -f
```

SQL Server Installation Checklist

Check off the following items as you complete or verify them:

Hardware and PC Setup

☐　Computer is Alpha AXP, MIPS, PowerPC, or Intel (32-bit x86) and is on the Windows NT Hardware Compatibility list

☐　Memory: 16M for nondistribution server, 32M for distribution server

☐　Operating System: Windows NT 3.51 or greater

☐　Free Disk Space >= 96M on the hard drive to which SQL Server is to be installed

File System:　☐　FAT

☐　NTFS

NT Server Name

SQL Server Options (Check or fill in)

User Name:_____Company Name:_____Product ID:_____

SQL Server Root Directory:_____

Master Device Location and Filename: _____

Master Device Size (Min: 25M): _____

Selected Character Set

☐　ISO 8859-1 (Default)　　☐　Code Page 850 (Multilingual)

☐　Code Page 437 (US English)　☐　Other _____

Selected Sort Order:_____

Network Protocols:

☐　Named-Pipes (Default)　　☐　Multi-Protocol

☐　NWLink IPX/SPX　　　　☐　TCP/IP Sockets

☐　Banyan Vines　　　　　☐　AppleTalk ADSP

☐　DECnet

Books Online Installed: ☐　Yes ☐　No (Requires an additional 1M to 15M)

Auto-Start Options:

☐   SQL Server

☐   SQL Executive

Licensing Mode:_____

Windows NT User Accounts:

MS SQL Server User Account: _____ (Required for SQL Server network access for features such as ODBC replication or Web page generation)

SQL Executive User Account: _____

Summary

You now have completed the chapters on installing and upgrading SQL Server. The remaining chapters in this book teach you how to perform database administration tasks such as database backups, SQL Server tuning and configuration, and many other activities.

PART IV

Database Operation

CHAPTER 7

by Orryn Sledge

Managing the Enterprise

The SQL Server 6.x Enterprise Manager greatly simplifies database management. The Enterprise Manager combines the features found in version 4.2x's Object Manager and SQL Administrator. Now, from a single interface, a DBA can concurrently administer multiple servers without the burden of having to use multiple administration products.

STARTING THE ENTERPRISE MANAGER

To start the Enterprise Manager, double-click the SQL Enterprise Manager icon in the Microsoft SQL Server 6.5 (Common) group (see Figure 7.1).

Figure 7.1.
The SQL Enterprise
Manager icon.

Note

Because of its 32-bit architecture, Enterprise Manager can be run only from Windows NT or Windows 95. It *cannot* be run from Windows 3.1.

NAVIGATING THE ENTERPRISE MANAGER

Because of its graphical interface, the Enterprise Manager minimizes the number of commands required to administer a server. Following are common methods of navigation in the Enterprise Manager:

◆ Menu items

◆ Double-click

◆ Right mouse click

◆ Drag and drop

REGISTERING A SERVER

The first time you start the Enterprise Manager, you are prompted to register a server. When you *register a server*, you provide the Enterprise Manager with a logical name and user login with which to connect to the SQL Server database engine.

Follow these steps to register a server (see Figure 7.2):

1. From the Register Server dialog box, enter the name of the server you want to register.

2. Select the type of login to use: trusted or standard. *Trusted security* offers the advantage of having to maintain only a Windows NT login account and password. With *standard security*, you must maintain a network account as well as a SQL Server account and password.

    If using standard security, enter the login ID and password.

Note

> To use trusted security, SQL Server must be installed with Windows NT integrated security or mixed security.

3. Select a server group or create a new server group.

4. Click the Register button to register the server with the Enterprise Manager.

Figure 7.2.
Registering a server.

Note

You can use the Enterprise Manager to administer a 4.2x version of SQL Server. Run the script SQLOLE42.SQL. This script can be found in the install subdirectory of SQL Server (for example, c:\mssql\install\sqlole42.sql).

STARTING, PAUSING, AND STOPPING SQL SERVER

To start, pause, or stop SQL Server, select a server and click the Start/Pause/Stop Server toolbar button. This action takes you to the SQL Server Manager dialog box (see Figure 7.3). From this dialog box, you can start, pause, or stop SQL Server.

Figure 7.3.
The SQL Server
Manager dialog box.

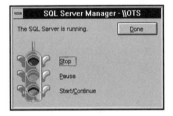

CONNECTING TO A SERVER

Once you have opened the Enterprise Manager and started SQL Server, click the plus (+) sign next to the server icon to connect to a server. If a connection is successfully made, the connected symbol appears next to the server status icon (see Figure 7.4).

Note

If you are unable to establish a connection to SQL Server from the Enterprise Manager, make sure that the MSSQLServer service is currently running.

Figure 7.4.
A successful server
connection.

The connected
server status icon

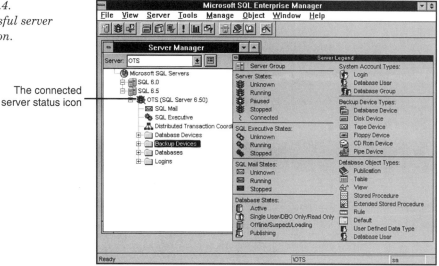

DISCONNECTING FROM A SERVER

To disconnect from a server, select the server and right-click. From the shortcut menu, select Disconnect.

Note

You are automatically disconnected from SQL Server when you close the Enterprise Manager.

STARTING, STOPPING, AND CONFIGURING SQL MAIL, SQL EXECUTIVE, AND DISTRIBUTED TRANSACTION COORDINATOR

To start, stop, or configure SQL Mail, SQL Executive, or the Distributed Transaction Coordinator (DTC), right-click the desired service and select the appropriate option (see Figure 7.5). This action opens the corresponding dialog box (see Figures 7.6, 7.7, and 7.8).

Figure 7.5.
Services associated
with the server.

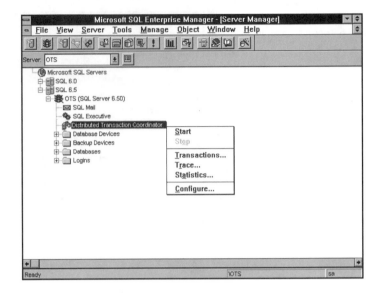

Figure 7.6.
The SQL Mail Configu-
ration dialog box.

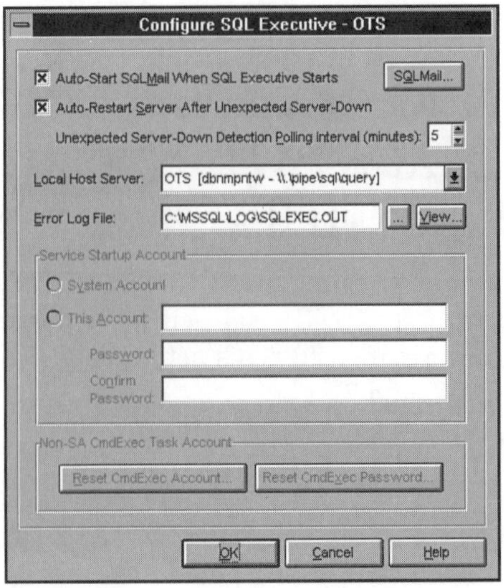

Figure 7.7.
The Configure SQL
Executive dialog box.

Figure 7.8.
The DTC Configuration
dialog box.

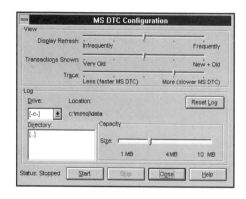

COMMON TASKS

The following sections provide brief descriptions of how to perform common administration tasks from the Enterprise Manager. Many of these tasks are explained in greater detail in other sections of this book.

EXECUTE AND ANALYZE QUERIES

To execute and analyze queries, select a server from the Enterprise Manager and click the SQL Query Tool toolbar button. This action takes you to the Query dialog box (see Figure 7.9). From this dialog box, you can issue Transact SQL statements, view results, and analyze query performance and optimization plans.

Figure 7.9.
The Query dialog box.

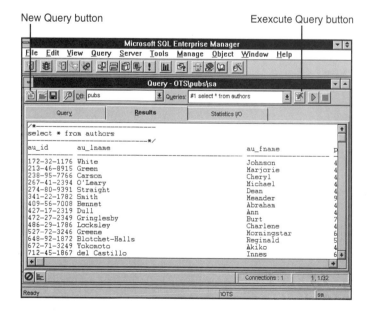

Tip

From the Query dialog box, you can concurrently run multiple SQL statements against the server. Click the New Query toolbar button in the Query dialog box. This action opens a new connection to SQL Server, which can be used to issue a new query while maintaining previous connections. This feature enables you to switch connections while queries are being processed. Because the processing takes place on the server and not on the client, your machine is free to continue with other tasks. Queries that are being processed have a globe icon next to the query number (see Figure 7.10).

The spinning globe indicates that a query is being processed

*Figure 7.10.
An example
of multiple-
query
processing.*

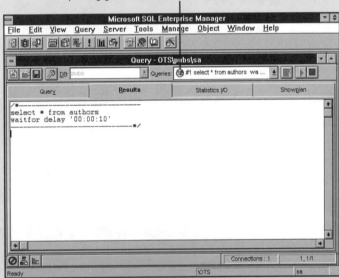

Also from the Query dialog box, you can run an individual Transact SQL statement by highlighting just the text and clicking the Execute Query toolbar button (see Figure 7.11).

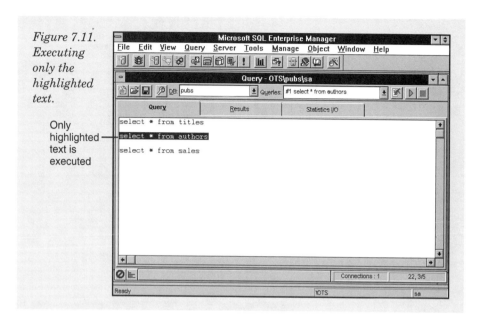

Figure 7.11. Executing only the highlighted text.

Only highlighted text is executed

MANAGE SERVER CONFIGURATIONS

Follow these steps to configure a server:

1. Select a server to configure from the Enterprise Manager.

2. Click the Configure SQL Server toolbar button in the Enterprise Manager. The Server Configuration/Options dialog box appears (see Figure 7.12). From this dialog box, you can configure server level options and security and view SQL Server build information.

MANAGE DEVICES

Follow these steps to create, manage, and delete devices:

1. Select the server from the Enterprise Manager for which you want to manage a device.

2. Open the Database Devices folder by clicking the plus (+) sign next to the Database Devices folder. To manage an individual device, right-click the appropriate device. To manage multiple devices, right-click the Databases Devices folder. The shortcut menu appears.

3. From the shortcut menu, select Edit. The Manage Database Devices dialog box appears (see Figure 7.13).

Figure 7.12.
The Server Config-
uration / Options
dialog box.

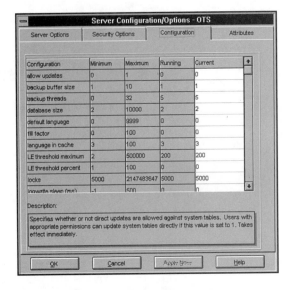

Figure 7.13.
The Manage Database
Devices dialog box.

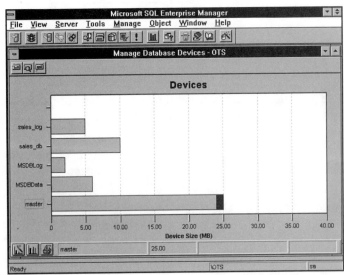

4. Double-click a device in the Manage Database Devices dialog box to open the Edit Database Devices dialog box (see Figure 7.14). Use this dialog box to edit an existing device.

Figure 7.14.
The Edit Database
Device dialog box.

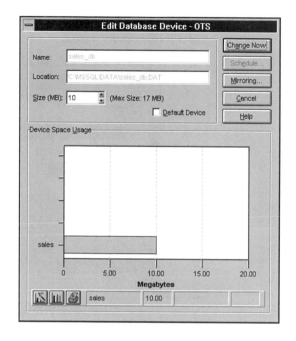

Refer to Chapter 8, "Managing Devices," for more information on managing devices.

MANAGE DATABASES

Follow these steps to create, manage, and delete a database:

1. From the Enterprise Manager, select the server for which you want to manage a database.

2. Open the Databases folder by clicking the plus (+) sign. From this folder, you can create a new database, edit an existing database, or delete a database. Right-click the appropriate object to activate the corresponding database menu.

3. To manage multiple databases, right-click the Databases folder. From the shortcut menu, select Edit. This action displays the Manage Databases dialog box (see Figure 7.15). Double-click a database in the Manage Databases dialog box to open the Edit Database dialog box (see Figure 7.16). Use this dialog box to edit an existing database.

Refer to Chapter 9, "Managing Databases," for more information on managing databases.

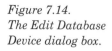

Figure 7.15.
The Manage Databases
dialog box.

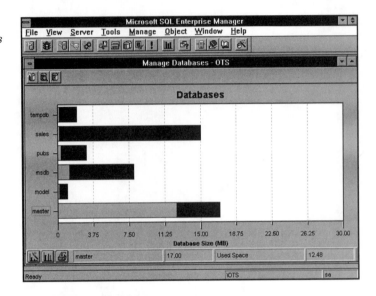

Figure 7.16.
The Edit Database
dialog box.

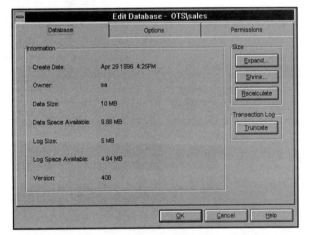

MANAGE DATABASE OBJECTS

Follow these steps to create, manage, and drop database objects such as tables, indexes, triggers, views, stored procedures, rules, defaults, and user-defined datatypes:

1. From the Enterprise Manager, select the server for which you want to manage a database object.

2. Open the Database folder by clicking the plus (+) sign. Open the database that contains the objects you want to work with by clicking the plus (+) sign next to the corresponding database.

3. Open the Objects folder by clicking the plus (+) sign. From this folder, you can manage tables, views, stored procedures, rules, defaults, and user-defined datatypes (see Figure 7.17). For example, to manage a table, click the plus sign next to the Tables folder. From the Tables folder, double-click a table. This action opens the Manage Tables dialog box; use this dialog box to alter an existing table or create a new table (see Figure 7.18).

Figure 7.17.
Managing database objects.

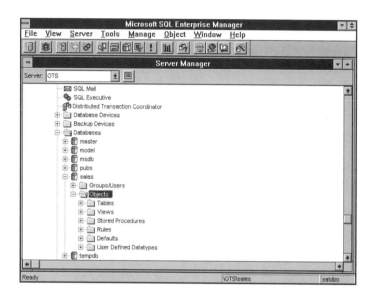

Figure 7.18.
Managing tables.

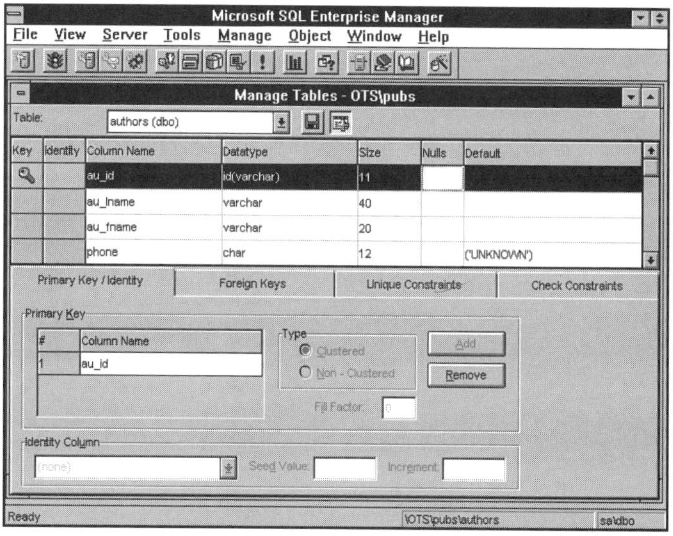

You can also manage object permissions by right-clicking the appropriate object and selecting the Permission option from the shortcut menu. This action displays the Object Permissions dialog box (see Figure 7.19).

Figure 7.19.
The Object Permissions
dialog box.

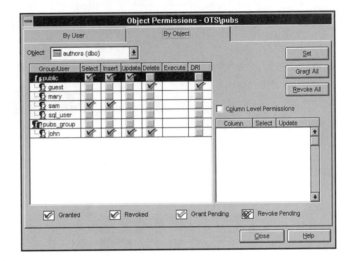

MANAGE LOGINS

Follow these steps to manage logins:

1. From the Enterprise Manager, select the server for which you want to manage logins.

2. Click the Manage Logins toolbar button in the Enterprise Manager window. The Manage Logins dialog box appears. From this dialog box, you can add, edit, and drop server logins (see Figure 7.20). You can also control a user's database access and default database from the Database Access section of the dialog box.

Refer to Chapter 10, "Managing Users," for more information on controlling logins.

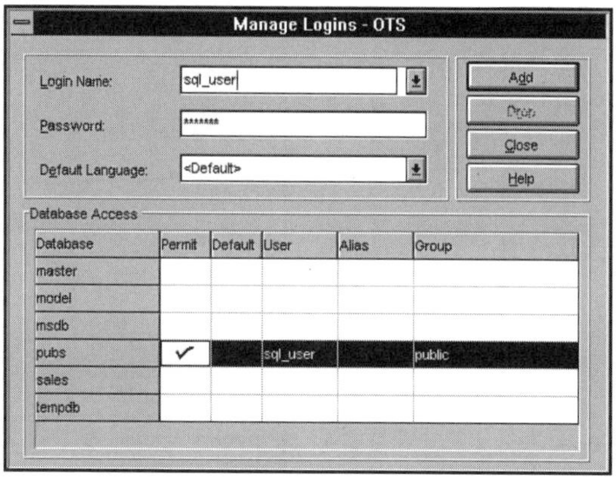

Figure 7.20.
The Manage Logins
dialog box.

GENERATE SQL SCRIPTS

From the Enterprise Manager, you can generate SQL scripts that contain the data definition language used to create an object in a database. This enables you to reverse-engineer existing objects.

Tip

An easy way to add or delete a column from a table is to generate the corresponding SQL scripts, modify the script, and then re-create the object from the modified script.

SQL scripts are also useful for performing keyword searches. Suppose that you want to determine how many tables have the column au_id varchar(11). An easy way to determine this is to generate the data definition language for all the tables in the database and then search with a text editor for au_id.

Follow these steps to generate SQL scripts:

1. From the Enterprise Manager, select the server and database from which you want to generate a SQL script.

2. From the Object menu, select Generate SQL Scripts. This action displays the Generate SQL Scripts dialog box. From this dialog box, you can generate the appropriate SQL syntax (see Figure 7.21).

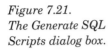

Figure 7.21.
The Generate SQL
Scripts dialog box.

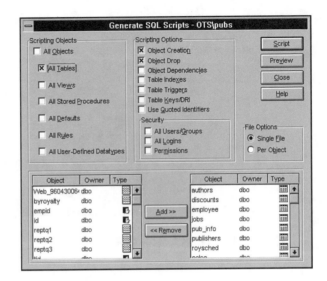

MANAGE BACKUPS AND RECOVERY

SQL Server provides a robust backup and restoration component that enables you to tailor your backup strategy to maximize data recovery. Follow these steps to manage backups:

1. From the Enterprise Manager, select the server and database you want to back up or restore.

2. From the Tools menu, select Database Backup/Restore. This action displays the Database Backup/Restore dialog box. From this dialog box, you can back up and restore databases (see Figure 7.22).

Refer to Chapter 14, "Backups," and Chapter 15, "Recovery," for more information on backups and restoration.

Tip

Use the Enterprise Manager's Task Scheduler to schedule backups on a recurring basis.

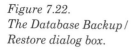

Figure 7.22.
The Database Backup/
Restore dialog box.

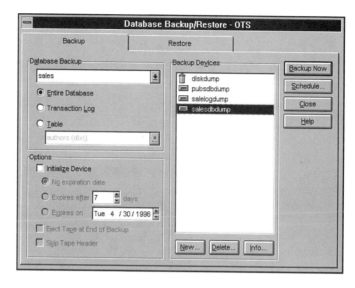

SCHEDULE TASKS

The Task Scheduler can automatically execute a task at a preset time interval. Database dumps, transaction log dumps, and DBCC commands are just a few of the types of administrative tasks that can be automated with Task Scheduler. To manage scheduled tasks, follow these steps:

1. Click the Manage Scheduled Tasks toolbar button. This action displays the Manage Scheduled Tasks dialog box (see Figure 7.23).
2. From this dialog box, you can add, edit, or delete a task. You can also view currently running tasks.

Figure 7.23.
The Manage Scheduled
Tasks dialog box.

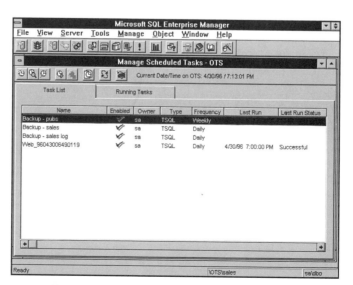

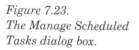

7

MANAGING THE ENTERPRISE

MANAGE ALERTS

The Enterprise Manager provides a built-in Alert Manager that enables you to define various types of alerts. The Alert Manager can automatically notify an operator through e-mail or a pager, providing a more proactive approach to database administration. To manage alerts, follow these steps:

1. Click the Manage Alerts and Operators toolbar button. This action displays the Manage Alerts and Operators dialog box (see Figure 7.24).

Figure 7.24.
The Manage Alerts and
Operators dialog box.

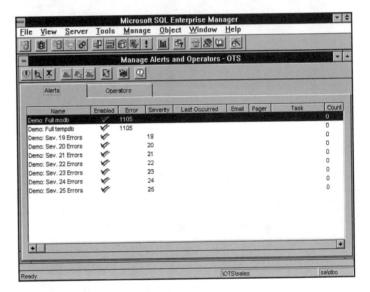

2. From the Manage Alerts and Operators dialog box, you can add, edit, and delete alerts. You can also define operators for e-mail and pager notification.

Refer to Chapter 26, "Automating Database Administration Tasks," for more information on alerts.

MANAGE REPLICATION

SQL Server provides a graphical replication model that uses a publish and subscribe metaphor to simplify replication initialization and management.

Replication management has three components: Replication Topology, Replication—Manage Publications, and Replication—Manage Subscriptions.

To manage each of these components, click the corresponding toolbar button (see the following chart). Refer to Chapter 12, "Replication," for more information on replication.

Toolbar Button	Associated Component
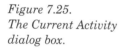	Replication Topology
	Replication—Manage Publications
	Replication—Manage Subscriptions

Monitor User Activity

With SQL Server 6.x, you can easily monitor user activity to help you pinpoint query problems and isolate bottlenecks. From the User Activity dialog box, you can kill a process and send an e-mail message to a user.

To monitor user activity, click the Current Activity toolbar button. This action opens the Current Activity dialog box (see Figure 7.25). From this dialog box, you can view and terminate different processes.

Refer to Chapter 23, "Multi-User Considerations," for more information on monitoring user activity.

Figure 7.25.
The Current Activity
dialog box.

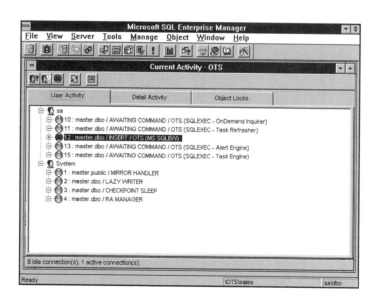

SUMMARY

As you can see, the graphical interface provided by the Enterprise Manager simplifies the tasks required to manage SQL Server. However, to manage a production environment, a DBA must know more than how to right-click an object. A DBA must be knowledgeable about the various components of SQL Server and how they interact. With that in mind, the next chapter discusses one of the most fundamental components of SQL Server: devices.

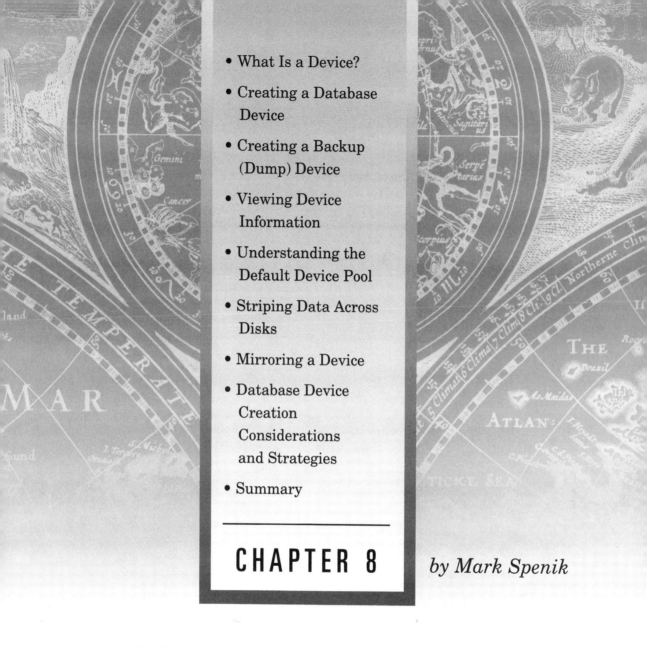

CHAPTER 8

by Mark Spenik

Managing Devices

This chapter discusses SQL Server devices. You learn the difference between a data device and a dump device and how to create, delete, use, and maintain SQL Server devices.

WHAT IS A DEVICE?

A very general definition of a Microsoft SQL Server device is a storage area from which SQL Server can read and write. Devices are used for database storage, transaction log storage, database backups, and database recovery. Figure 8.1 shows several examples of SQL Server devices.

Figure 8.1.
Examples of SQL
Server devices.

8 mm tape

Floppy disk

Hard disk file

UNDERSTANDING DIFFERENT TYPES OF DEVICES

Not only can a device be represented by different physical objects such as a floppy disk or hard drive, but devices come in two types: database devices and dump (backup) devices.

DATABASE DEVICES

A *database device* is a disk file used to store databases and transaction logs. Creating a database device requires preallocating storage space for later use. A database device can be larger or smaller than the database or transaction log you allocate to the device because databases and transaction logs can span multiple devices. When SQL Server is first installed, three database devices are created in the \MSSQL\DATA directory: MASTER.DAT, MSDB.DAT, and MSDBLOG.DAT.

The master Device

MASTER.DAT is the master database device and is the most important SQL Server device. The master device stores the master, model, tempdb, and pubs databases, described in detail in Chapter 9, "Managing Databases." It is important to understand that the master database, stored on the master device, contains all the SQL Server information required to manage and maintain the server's databases, users, and devices (basically all the information required to maintain and run SQL Server). If the master device becomes corrupted, all databases are unusable until the master device can be restored.

Caution

Never use the master device for any database allocation except for the default databases installed on the master device during SQL Server setup. Even though SQL Server allows you to allocate space on the master device for other databases, don't do it! The master device should be used only for its intended purpose: to store the master, model, and tempdb databases! Following this advice can save you many headaches if you have to recover the master device.

The minimum master device size required to install SQL Server 6.x is 25M.

The Scheduler Database and Log

MSDB.DAT is the database device created at installation time to store the msdb database used by the SQL Executive for scheduling information. The device MSDBLOG is used to store the transaction log for the msdb database. The default device size used during setup is 2M for MSDB.DAT and 2M for MSBDLOG.DAT.

Note

MSDB.DAT and MSDBLOG.DAT were added in version 6.0 and do not exist in previous 4.2x versions. Also, the SQL Server documentation incorrectly states that the size of MSDBLOG.DAT is 1M; installation allocates 2M to MSDBLOG.DAT.

DUMP DEVICES

Dump devices are used to back up and restore databases and transaction logs.

Version
6.5

Note

The SQL Server 6.5 SQL Enterprise Manager now refers to dump devices as *backup devices* (previous versions of SQL Server always referred to them as dump devices). I welcome the change because a dump device is a backup device—but then again, the command to perform a backup is DUMP...make a mental note that the terms *dump device* and *backup device* are equivalent.

When a dump (backup) device is allocated, unlike a database device, no storage space is preallocated. Dump devices can be tapes, floppy disks, disk files, or named pipes.

Note

Named-pipe dump devices are new for version 6.x. A named-pipe dump device is not created like other dump devices; it is a parameter used in the DUMP and LOAD commands. For more information, see Chapter 13, "Distributed Transaction Coordinator," and Chapter 14, "Backups."

Three dump devices are created during SQL Server installation: DISKDUMP, DISKETTEDUMPA, and DISKETTEDUMPB. DISKETTEDUMPA and DISKETTEDUMPB are dump devices for floppy drives A and B for the machine on which SQL Server is running. The floppy drive backup devices are added strictly for backward compatibility and require you to use a special command-line utility called console.

Note

I received a few e-mail messages after the first edition of this book was published, asking where the backup devices DISKETTEDUMPA and DISKETTEDUMPB were because they do not show up on the SQL Enterprise Manager. You can verify that they really do exist by issuing the command sp_helpdevice from the SQL Query tool. As stated earlier, the two devices were included only for backward compatibility. The Microsoft documentation suggests that if you want to back up a database to floppy, you should back it up to another device (such as a hard drive) and then copy it to the floppy.

The DISKDUMP device is a special backup device referred to as the *NULL dump device* because the backup device represents no physical media, only thin air.

Tip

DISKDUMP (the NULL dump device) can be very helpful during database application development. Use DISKDUMP to clear out databases and transaction logs when developers are filling the databases and logs with test data that does not need to be backed up.

CREATING A DATABASE DEVICE

Now that you understand the different types of devices, you can create a database device.

Note

If you are using SQL Server version 6.0 and not version 6.5, the following steps for creating a device are essentially the same except that the Manage Database Devices dialog box differs slightly between versions and that scheduling device creation is not available in version 6.0.

From the SQL Server Manager, perform the following steps:

1. Select the server on which you want to create the device.
2. Click the Manage Database Devices button on the SQL Manager toolbar. The screen shown in Figure 8.2 appears.

Figure 8.2.
The Manage Database
Devices dialog box.

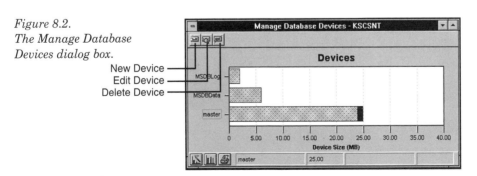

8

3. Click the New Device button; the New Database Device dialog box appears (see Figure 8.3).

The following list describes the different parameters in the New Database Device dialog box:

◆ **Name**: The name field specifies the logical name that will be given to the device. The logical name is used to manage the device in SQL Server. The maximum size of the name field is 30 characters.

Tip

Choose meaningful names for devices. Include the database you plan to store on the device in the device name. For example, if the device will be used for a transaction log, include log in the name. Doing so can help you remember what the device is for. Consider the device names given to the default devices: MSDBData for the msdb database and MSDBLOG for the msdb database transaction log.

◆ **Location**: The drive and path to create the device. The Location combo box is used to select the disk drive on which the device is to be created. *Note:* A database device can be created only on a local disk drive; it cannot be created on an attached network drive.

The Location text box contains the directory in which the device will be created. The default path is \MSSQL\DATA. Clicking the button at the end of the Location text box displays the Database Device Location dialog box (see Figure 8.4), which you can use to select the directory in which the new device will reside.

Figure 8.3.
Creating device
test_data in the New
Database Device
dialog box.

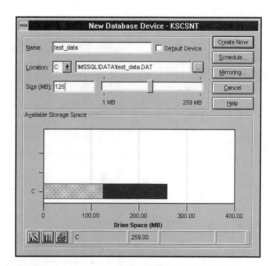

Figure 8.4.
The Database Device
Location dialog box.

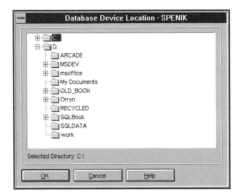

- ◆ **Size**: Enter the device size in megabytes or use the slider bar to increase or decrease the device size. The minimum device size is 1M; there is no practical maximum size.

- ◆ **Default Device**: Check this box to add the device to the pool of default devices.

4. Add the necessary parameters to create the device. Figure 8.3 shows the New Database Device dialog box with the required parameters filled in to create a SQL Server device called `test_data`.

5. To add the new device, click Create Now to create the device immediately; click the Schedule button to schedule the device creation for a later time.

Figure 8.3 specifies a 125M device named `test_data` to be created in the default directory `\MSSQL\Data` on drive C. So what happens when the device `test_data` is created with the SQL Server Manager? The SQL Server Manager performs a command called `DISK INIT`. The `DISK INIT` command creates a 125M initialized file, `test_dat.DAT`, located in `C:\MSSQL\DATA`, and adds a new entry in the system table, `sysdevices`, located in the `master` database.

Note

Device creation in SQL Server version 6.x happens much faster than in earlier 4.2x versions. Version 6.x does not zero-out each page of the device—it takes advantage of the fact that a DOS FAT file or NTFS file is already initialized with zeroes. Because previous 4.2x versions of SQL Server zeroed out each page, creating a large device with those older versions took longer.

The DISK INIT command can also be issued from an ISQL prompt; the command has the following format:

```
DISK INIT
NAME = logical_name,
PHYSNAME = physical_name,
VDEVNO = virtual_device_number,
SIZE = number_of_2K_blocks
[, VSTART = virtual_address]
```

NAME is the logical name of the device; it is the same as the name field shown in Figure 8.3.

PHYSNAME is the physical location and filename of the database device (that is, the path and filename).

VDEVNO is a number between 1 and 255, assigned to the new device. The number 0 is reserved for the master device. VDEVNO uniquely identifies a device; once the number is used for a device, it cannot be used again until the device is dropped.

SIZE is the size of the device to create. When using the DISK INIT command from ISQL/w, the size is in 2K pages (2048) bytes; the SQL Server Enterprise Manager uses megabytes. 1M is equal to 512 2K pages.

VSTART is an optional parameter that represents the starting offset (in 2K blocks) in the device file. The value is 0 and should be modified only if you are instructed to do so.

CREATING A BACKUP (DUMP) DEVICE

To create a backup device, select the server to which you want to add the backup device from the SQL Server Manager and then perform the following steps:

1. Select the Backup Devices folder and right-click the folder. A shortcut menu appears.

2. Select New Backup Device from the shortcut menu to display the New Backup Device dialog box (see Figure 8.5).

Figure 8.5.
The New Backup
Device dialog box.

The following list describes the different parameters in the New Backup Device dialog box:

◆ **Name**: The SQL Server logical name for the backup device. The rules and limitations for a backup device name are the same as those for database devices.

◆ **Location**: This parameter applies only if the backup device being created is a hard disk file. The location is the path and filename of the hard disk. *Tip:* The location for a backup device can be on a network drive.

◆ **Type**: Select either Disk Backup Device or Tape Backup Device. If you select Tape Backup Device, you can also select or clear the Skip Headers checkbox. Skip Headers determines whether SQL Server will search for ANSI labels that may be on a tape before a backup is performed.

Note

No file size is required for a disk type backup device. If you use disk backup devices, make sure that you have enough storage to dump the object. For example, if you have 20M free on a hard drive for a disk backup device called MYDBDUMP and you want to back up a full 150M transaction log, you cannot use MYDBDUMP because you do not have enough space.

3. Enter the required information, described in the preceding step, and click the Create button to create the backup device.

Adding a backup device with SQL Server Manager is the same as executing the stored procedure sp_addumpdevice, which has the following parameters:

```
sp_addumpdevice Type, 'Logical_Name',
'Physical_Name'
[,@devstatus = {noskip | skip}]
```

The Type parameter specifies the type of device and can be 'disk', 'diskette', or 'tape'. Logical Name is the logical name of the dump device. Physical Name is the physical path and name of the dump device.

Set @devstatus to skip or noskip. These parameters determine whether SQL Server will try to read ANSI labels before performing a backup.

When a dump device is added, SQL Server makes an entry in the sysdevices table (the same table used for database devices).

Note

In older versions of SQL Server (versions before 4.21), `sp_addumpdevice` included the parameters `cntrltype` and `media_capacity`. Because these parameters were never used in NT versions of SQL Server, they are not included in version 6.x.

Caution

Always back up the `master` database after adding any devices. If the `master` database should become corrupted or damaged, you will have a valid backup of the database with the newly created devices.

Figure 8.6 shows the system table `sysdevices` after the devices `test_data` and `test_dump` have been added.

Figure 8.6.
The system table,
sysdevices.

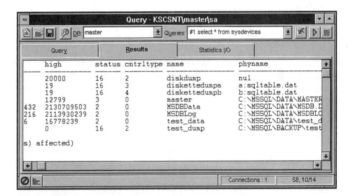

SYBASE BEWARE!

Microsoft has taken care of the most common problem (besides syntax problems) that I have encountered during device creation: running out of configured devices. SQL Server 4.2x had a configuration parameter called `devices`, which is the maximum number of devices that can be configured. In SQL Server 4.2x, the initial setting for `devices` was 10, which means that you can have up to 10 devices, device numbers (VDEVNO) 1 through 9. But what about device number 10? Device numbers are zero-based (remember that the device number 0 is reserved for the master device). When the device limit was exceeded, you could not add any more devices until you reconfigured the SQL Server using the stored procedure, sp_configure. The zero-based numbering and the error message(s) were very confusing to beginning administrators, who often called to say that SQL Server would not let them add another device.

With version 6.x, this is no longer a problem. In version 6.x, the configuration parameter devices no longer exists. You now have access to all possible devices, 1 through 255.

VIEWING DEVICE INFORMATION

You can view device information in several ways. To see the current devices installed on a server, use the Server Manager window to select a server and then click the Database Devices folder. Backup devices can be viewed in the same manner by clicking the Backup Devices folder.

Figure 8.7 shows a view of database devices and backup devices using the SQL Enterprise Manager. To see more detailed information, click the Manage Database Devices button on the Enterprise Manager toolbar.

Figure 8.7.
The SQL Enterprise Manager, showing database and backup devices.

Manage Database Devices

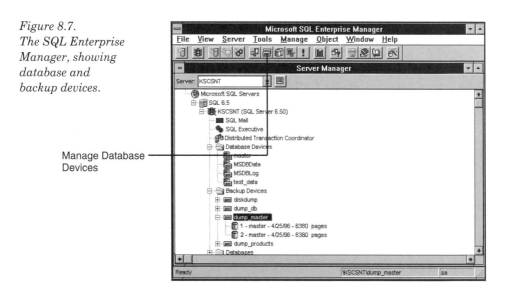

Figure 8.8 shows the detailed database window. Each bar graph represents a database device. The graph shows the amount of space used on each device and the space available.

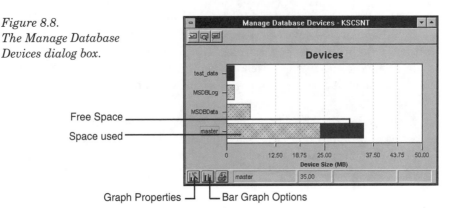

Figure 8.8.
The Manage Database
Devices dialog box.

Tip

In SQL Server 6.5, the graphical display of the devices can be changed using the Graph Properties button and the Bar Graph Options button. The Graph Properties button allows you to change the graph labels, color, legend display, and types of graphs. You can use the Bar Graph Options button to make the graph vertical or horizontal and selectable or stretched.

The stored procedure, `sp_helpdevice`, can be used to display device information from the ISQL command line and has the following syntax:

```
sp_helpdevice [device_name]
```

The *device name* parameter is the logical name of the device for which you want information. If the parameter is omitted, all the devices in the sysdevices table are listed.

REMOVING A DEVICE

Now that you can add and view devices you have created, how do you get rid of them? Removing a database or a backup device is called *dropping* a device in SQL Server terms. When a device is dropped, the row containing the dropped device is removed from the system table, sysdevices. The logical name and device number (VDEVNO) can then be reused. Before you can reuse the physical name of the device, however, you must first delete the file. When a database device is dropped, the actual physical file created for the device is not removed. To remove the file and regain the space, you must delete the file using the NT File Manager or the DOS DEL command to delete the file. Once the file is deleted, you can reuse the physical name.

Caution

For versions of SQL Server before version 6.x, you must shut down SQL Server after a device is dropped before the physical file can be removed.

Database and dump devices can be dropped with the stored procedure sp_dropdevice. The syntax for sp_dropdevice is as follows:

```
sp_dropdevice device name
```

The *device name* parameter is the logical name of the device you want to drop.

To drop a database device using the SQL Enterprise Manager, access the Manage Database Devices dialog box. Select the device by clicking it (make sure that the graph mode is selectable) and then click the Delete Device button (refer back to Figure 8.2). Before the device is dropped, a confirmation box appears to prevent accidental deletions.

Caution

When a device is dropped, any databases or transaction logs using that device are also dropped. SQL Server displays a warning message that lists any database(s) and transaction log(s) currently using the device. If you decide to continue the operation, first the databases or transaction logs on the device are dropped and then the device itself is dropped.

To delete a backup device using the SQL Enterprise Manager, select the server on which the device resides. Select the Backup Devices folder and choose the backup device to delete. Right-click the backup device to display a shortcut menu. Choose Delete from the shortcut menu. The Delete Backup Device dialog box appears (see Figure 8.9). To delete the backup device, click the Delete button. A confirmation dialog box appears to prevent accidental deletions.

8

MANAGING DEVICES

Figure 8.9.
The Delete Backup
Device dialog box.

EXPANDING A DATABASE DEVICE

Once a database device is created, the size of the device cannot be decreased, but it can be increased. To increase the database device size with the SQL Enterprise Manager, open the Database Device folder and double-click the database device. From the Manage Database Devices dialog box, double-click the database device to expand the bar graph. The Edit Database Device dialog box appears (see Figure 8.10).

Figure 8.10.
The Edit Database
Device dialog box.

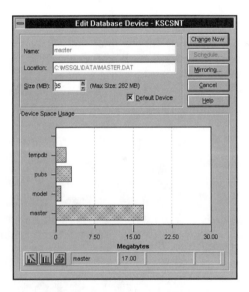

To increase the size of the device, change the Size parameter to the new device size; click Change Now to immediately alter the size of the database device. Click Schedule to change the database device size at a latter time.

Note

The drive or drives on which the device resides must have available free space greater than or equal to the amount by which you want to increase the device.

The corresponding command to increase disk space is the DISK RESIZE command, which has the following syntax:

```
DISK RESIZE
NAME = 'logical device name',
SIZE = device final size
```

NAME is the logical device name of the device to expand. SIZE is the size of the database device after the device is expanded. The size is specified in 2K pages. Remember that 512 equals 1M.

UNDERSTANDING THE DEFAULT DEVICE POOL

SQL Server maintains a pool of database devices that are used if a database is created without specifying a device. Devices in the pool are referred to as *default devices*. The default device pool can consist of one or many database devices. SQL Server allocates the default space one device at a time, going in alphabetical order. When a default device runs out of space, SQL Server uses the next default device available. You can designate a database device as a default device *during device creation* with the SQL Enterprise Manager: check the Default Device checkbox in the Create Database Device dialog box. You can designate a database device as a default device *after the device has been created*: check the Default Device checkbox in the Edit Database Device dialog box. The database device can be removed from the default database pool by deselecting the Default Device checkbox in either dialog box.

Caution

At installation, the SQL Server master device is placed in the default disk pool. Remove the master device from the pool immediately so that a database or transaction log is not accidentally placed on the master device.

The stored procedure used to add and remove devices from the default device pool is sp_diskdefault. Following is the syntax for sp_diskdefault:

```
sp_diskdefault device name, defaulton ¦ defaultoff
```

The device name parameter is the logical device name for the device; defaulton and defaultoff are the flags used to add or remove the device from the default device pool. The defaulton flag adds the device; defaultoff removes the device.

STRIPING DATA ACROSS DISKS

SQL Server disk configurations were briefly covered in an earlier chapter; this section expands on some of the points mentioned earlier and shows how they relate to SQL Server devices and performance. In SQL Server (or any other database server), one of the most likely bottlenecks is the disk I/O from clients reading and writing from different tables or different databases simultaneously.

Suppose that you have a PC configured as a server; it has a fast processor and a large amount of memory, but you bought a single 2 gigabyte hard drive with a single disk controller to store all your database information. Because you have only one disk drive, any devices you create physically reside on the single hard drive. What happens when users start inserting and retrieving data simultaneously? SQL Server has more than enough memory and the processor is fast enough to handle the requests, but what about the single disk drive and disk controller? A bottleneck will quickly form as I/O requests queue up to the single disk. An old SQL Server trick, dating back to the days of Sybase, has been to use a smart disk controller card or disk array; rather than a single 2 gigabyte hard drive, use four 512M hard drives. Devices can then be created on different physical hard drives, enabling you to spread databases and transaction logs across different physical devices. Although this arrangement is a better solution than a single hard drive, it still has some deficiencies. Databases and transaction logs can be placed on different physical devices, improving transaction processing. Databases can be spread over multiple SQL Server devices (thus different physical devices), but the hot data everyone is after may be on a single drive causing disk I/O bottlenecks similar to those on a single large drive. Smart SQL Server DBAs take advantage of segments (described in Chapter 9, "Managing Databases"). The NT operating system and new advanced hardware systems have created better solutions: hardware or software *disk striping*.

Figure 8.11 is a conceptual diagram of disk striping for a drive labeled J. Drive J looks like a single physical drive to the SQL Server DBA who is creating devices. Logically, a striped drive is a single drive, but physically, the logical drive spans many different disk drives. A striped disk is made up of a special file system called a *striped set*. All the disks in the disk array that make up the logical drive are part of the striped set. Data on each of the drives is divided into equal blocks and is spread over all the drives. By spreading the file system over several disk drives, disk I/O performance is improved because the disk I/O is spread over multiple drives. The balancing of the I/O is transparent to the DBA, who no longer has to worry about spreading out file I/O. Disk striping is also referred to as *RAID 0* (Redundant Array of Inexpensive Disks). RAID level 0 is the fastest RAID configuration. The level of fault tolerance is measured in levels 0 through 5, with 0 providing no fault tolerance. If a single disk fails in a RAID 0 system, none of the data in the stripe set can be accessed. Windows NT provides software level disk striping. Disk striping can also be handled by special hardware disk arrays.

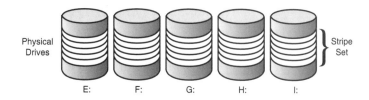

Figure 8.11.
Disk striping.

Note

Hardware-based disk striping (RAID configurations) outperform Windows NT software disk striping. NT's implementation is done through software and requires system processor resources. The disadvantage of hardware striping solutions is cost. RAID systems can be quite expensive, depending on the level of fault tolerance you select.

A RAID 0 system has no fault tolerance; the entire file system can be rendered useless if a single drive fails. RAID 1 is also known as *disk mirroring*. In a RAID 1 configuration, data written to a primary disk is also written to a mirrored disk. RAID 2 uses disk striping along with error correction. RAID 3 and RAID 4 also use disk striping and error correction and vary in their degrees of effectiveness and disk space requirements. A RAID 5 system has the maximum fault tolerance: a single disk can fail and the system continues to function. A backup drive can be placed in the disk array so that the lost device can be re-created on the new drive by the RAID system. RAID 5 technology can be implemented using Windows NT disk striping with parity or as a hardware-based solution.

Mirroring a Device

SQL Server provides a method of redundancy to protect against a device failure called *device mirroring*. When a SQL Server device is mirrored, a duplicate copy of the device is maintained. If either device becomes corrupted, the uncorrupted device takes over SQL Server operations to provide uninterrupted processing.

Figure 8.12 shows a mirrored device. NT SQL Server mirrors a drive using *serial writes*: Information is written to the primary device first. When the I/O operation is complete, the information is then written to the secondary device.

Note

Non-Windows NT SQL Servers can perform nonserial writes to mirror devices; that is, they can write to both devices simultaneously or they can perform serial writes. Mirroring with Windows NT SQL Server always results in serial writes.

Figure 8.12.
A mirrored device.

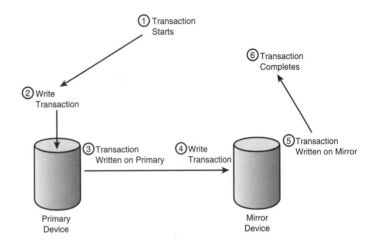

If an error occurs when writing to either of the mirrored devices, the bad device becomes unmirrored and the uncorrupted device takes over as the primary device, protecting your server from downtime caused by a lost device.

Note

Remember that *devices* are mirrored—the databases are not mirrored. If you want to mirror a database, you must mirror all the devices that make up the database.

To mirror a device using the SQL Enterprise Manager, select the server and device you want to mirror and perform the following steps:

1. Access the Edit Database Device dialog box (refer back to Figure 8.10).

2. Choose the Mirroring button. The Mirror Database Device dialog box appears (see Figure 8.13).

Figure 8.13.
The Mirror Database
Device dialog box.

3. Use the default device name in the Mirror Device Filename text box or modify it to change the location or filename of the mirrored device.

4. Click the Mirror Now button. The device will be mirrored.

Tip

Mirroring a device requires SQL Server to create the mirror device, which uses the same name as the device being mirrored but with a MIR file extension. Once the mirror device is created, used pages from the primary device are copied to the new mirror device. Large databases can take a while to mirror.

The SQL Server command to mirror a device is the DISK MIRROR command, which has the following syntax:

```
DISK MIRROR
NAME='logical device name',
MIRROR = 'mirror device physical name',
[,WRITES=SERIAL | NOSERIAL]
```

NAME is the SQL Server logical device name of the device to be mirrored. MIRROR is the location and filename of the mirrored device. WRITES SERIAL and NOSERIAL are not required; they are provided for SQL Server compatibility on non-Windows NT platforms.

Tip

If the master device is mirrored and fails, the mirror device takes over and operation continues uninterrupted. If the SQL Server is later halted and restarted, the server fails because of a bad master device. To prevent this failure at startup, use the SQL Server Setup utility to add the following startup parameter to the server:

```
-rphysical mirror device path and name
```

The -r startup option tells SQL Server at startup to use the mirrored device when the primary device fails.

When a device is mirrored, the sysdevices table is modified. The physical name of the mirrored device is placed in the mirrorname column and the status column is modified to indicate that mirroring has been turned on.

UNMIRRORING AND REMIRRORING DEVICES

Unmirroring a device prevents SQL Server from performing writes to the mirrored device. Unmirroring is performed automatically by SQL Server when an I/O error occurs on the primary or mirrored device.

Tip

Devices can be mirrored and unmirrored without shutting down SQL Server.

A DBA can also unmirror a device using the SQL Enterprise Manager. To unmirror a drive, select the server and the device you want to unmirror and perform the following steps:

1. Display the Edit Database Device dialog box.

2. Click the Mirroring button. The Unmirror Device dialog box appears (see Figure 8.14).

Figure 8.14.
The Unmirror Device
dialog box.

3. Select one of the checkbox options and click Unmirror.

   The checkbox options enable you to perform the following unmirroring options:

   ◆ **Switch to Mirror Device—Retain Original Device**: Makes the mirrored device the primary device but keeps the original device. Use this option if you want to temporarily turn off mirroring plan to remirror later.

   ◆ **Switch to Mirror Device—Replace Original Device**: Replaces the primary device with the mirrored device.

   ◆ **Turn Off Mirroring—Retain Mirror Device**: Pauses SQL Server mirroring. Use this option if you plan to remirror to the same device later.

   ◆ **Turn Off Mirroring—Remove Mirror Device:** Stops mirroring on the selected device, clears the status bits, and sets the `mirrorname` column in `sysdevices` to `NULL`.

Note

Removing a mirrored device does not remove the operating system file. Use the Windows NT File Manager or the DOS DEL command to remove the physical mirrored file.

The SQL command to unmirror a disk is the DISK UNMIRROR command, which has the following syntax:

```
DISK UNMIRROR
NAME = 'logical name'
[, SIDE = PRIMARY ¦ SECONDARY]
[, MODE = RETAIN ¦ REMOVE]
```

NAME is the SQL Server logical device name to unmirror. SIDE specifies the device to disable (the primary or the secondary device). The default value of MODE is to retain the mirror device entry in the sysdevices table. The REMOVE flag clears mirror information in the sysdevices table.

If mirroring has been paused or halted because of device failure, mirroring can be turned on by remirroring the device. To remirror a device with SQL Enterprise Manager, select the server and the device to remirror and perform the following steps.

Note

You can only remirror a database if you chose the Retain Mirror Device option when you unmirrored the device.

1. Display the Edit Database Device dialog box.
2. Click the Mirroring button to display the Re-Mirror Database Device dialog box (see Figure 8.15).

Figure 8.15.
The Re-Mirror Data-
base Device dialog box.

3. Click the Re-Mirror Now button. The device is remirrored.

The command to remirror a device is DISK REMIRROR, which has the following syntax:

```
DISK REMIRROR
NAME = 'logical name'
```

NAME is the logical name of the SQL Server device to remirror.

DEVICE MIRRORING STRATEGIES

To mirror or not to mirror: that is the question. In the old days, mirroring a device was the best protective measure available for ensuring nonstop SQL Server operation. Today, other options such as RAID 5 hardware configurations and NT software-based striping exist; in most cases, these newer options may be a better recovery strategy for your system. Because better options do exist, Microsoft has recently suggested that, instead of using SQL Server mirroring, you can take advantage of Windows NT mirroring. Although SQL Server mirroring is still supported in SQL Server 6.5, future versions of SQL Server may not support SQL Server mirroring (although Windows NT mirroring will be supported). However, if you decide to use SQL Server mirroring, you must develop a strategy that is cost effective for your organization and provides acceptable downtime in case of a recovery. Following are some suggested mirroring strategies:

◆ Always mirror the master device.

◆ Mirror transaction logs of production databases.

◆ To prevent downtime with a database, all devices that make up the database must be mirrored (if you do not mirror one of the devices that makes up the database, you have the potential to be down).

Device mirroring provides a level of protection against data corruption. The price you pay for device mirroring is that you use more disk space and add overhead by requiring the server to perform more disk I/O.

DATABASE DEVICE CREATION CONSIDERATIONS AND STRATEGIES

When creating SQL Server database devices, consider the following:

◆ What purpose will the device serve?

◆ How large should the device be?

◆ On which drive will the device be located?

◆ How do you name the device?

◆ How will the device be recovered if an error occurs?

Many decisions made about a database device depend on the hardware configuration and the database that resides on the device. The following sections examine each of these considerations and present possible strategies to implement.

WHAT PURPOSE WILL THE DEVICE SERVE?

Before creating a database device, determine the purpose that the device will serve. Will the device be used for transaction logs, database storage, or both?

I like to create a separate device for each transaction log. Doing so allows more efficient disk allocation because databases have different sizes and backup requirements. If you decide to mirror some production transaction logs but not all of them, you can select only the transaction log devices that need to be mirrored. I do not like to create a single device for all transaction logs. SQL Server maintains an I/O queue for each device. Placing all the database transaction logs on a single device also places all requests on a single device I/O queue. By placing each transaction log on its own device, you limit the overall requests to the device I/O queue.

Another advantage of a single device per transaction log is device failure. If a single database device with a transaction log fails, you lose access to only one database. If a device with several transaction logs fails, you lose access to many databases.

Databases can be placed on several devices or can span multiple devices. One of the deciding factors should be the physical disk layout. If the disk drives are striped or have a RAID configuration or a single disk drive, you do not have to concern yourself with balancing the database across different physical devices. Although I do not do so with transaction logs, I *do* share database devices for small databases (those less than 200M in size).

It is good practice not to mix database and transaction logs on the same device.

HOW LARGE SHOULD THE DEVICE BE?

Transaction log and database sizing is detailed in Chapter 9, "Managing Databases"; however, this section examines the size issue as it relates to devices.

Recommended transaction log sizes are 10 to 25 percent of the size of the database. These percentages are just a starting point. Take into consideration the frequency of transaction log dumps and the number of transactions. A transaction-intensive database that has the log dumped every 15 minutes requires a smaller transaction size than the same database being dumped daily.

For database devices, I tend not to create devices larger than 1 gigabyte. If the device fails, it is much faster to recover smaller devices than larger devices. The drawback is that several smaller devices are harder to manage than a single large device. It is a good idea to come up with a standard size for database devices. For a large database, create database devices anywhere from 512M to 1G; 256M is a good average for smaller databases.

ON WHICH DRIVE WILL THE DEVICE BE LOCATED?

The correct drive to select for a device typically depends on available space and whether disk striping or a RAID configuration is being used.

HOW DO I NAME THE DEVICE?

Establish consistent naming conventions for devices and logs. Include the word LOG for transaction log devices and the word DATA or DB for database devices. For dump devices, include the word DUMP. If the device belongs to a single database, use the name of the database. For example, a transaction log and database device for the pubs database would be PUBSLOG, PUBSDB, or PUBSDATA.

HOW WILL THE DEVICE BE RECOVERED IF AN ERROR OCCURS?

Take precautions to protect against data loss by using device mirroring, NT disk mirroring, or RAID configurations. When you create a device, it is important to make sure that you have a hardware or software plan that allows you to recover the device if it is lost—in a acceptable amount of time—especially the master device.

BETWEEN THE LINES

Following are some of the important points in this chapter that you should remember when managing SQL Server devices:

◆ Devices can be used to store databases and transaction logs or for backup and restore purposes.

◆ The master device is the most important device. Protect it at all costs!

◆ The minimum master device size in SQL Server version 6.x is 25M.

◆ Use the DISKDUMP (NULL) device to clear out transaction logs or databases in a development environment when saving the data is not critical.

◆ Use naming conventions for devices.

◆ The devices configuration parameter no longer exists in SQL Server version 6.x.

◆ Always delete the physical file after a device is dropped. You do not have to shut down the server in version 6.x (previous versions require you to shut down the server before you can release the file).

◆ Devices can be expanded but cannot be shrunk.

◆ Mirroring a device does not use up a VDEVNO or add a new entry to sysdevices. It only updates a current entry.

◆ RAID software and hardware solutions may provide better device protection than SQL Server mirroring.

◆ Back up the master database after any device changes are made.

SUMMARY

You should now have a good understanding of SQL Server devices and how to create them, modify them, and remove them. It is also very important to realize the need to protect the devices (in case of device failure) and the different options available to you, such as mirroring or RAID configurations. In the next chapter, you learn how to assign databases to the devices you have created and examine in more detail the placement of databases and transaction logs on devices.

8

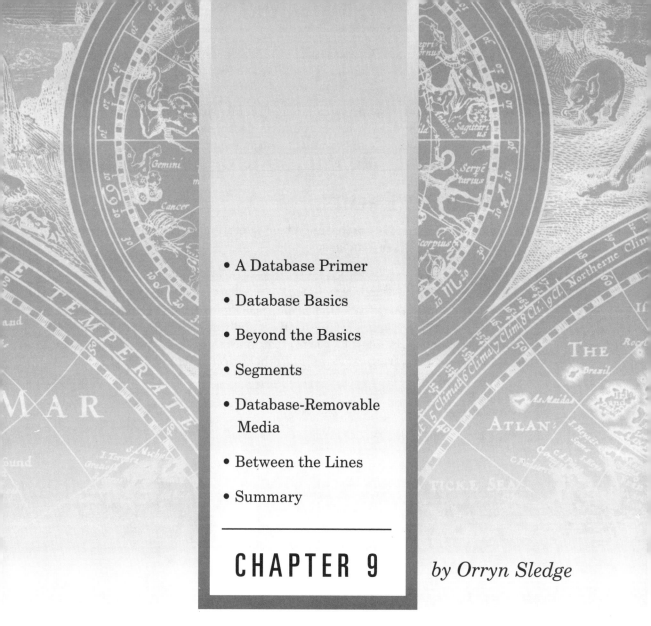

CHAPTER 9

by Orryn Sledge

Managing Databases

It is important to understand how to manage a database in SQL Server. Every object and its corresponding data revolves around the database. If a database isn't properly managed, you may experience system downtime, countless headaches, and loss of data.

A DATABASE PRIMER

The following sections discuss the fundamental terminology and concepts necessary to manage a SQL Server database.

WHAT IS A DATABASE?

A *database* is an organized collection of data (see Figure 9.1). This collection of data is logically structured and systematically maintained. SQL Server extends the concept of a database by allowing you to create and store other types of objects, such as stored procedures, triggers, views, and other objects that interact with the data.

Figure 9.1.
A database.

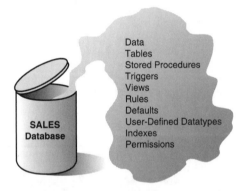

Data
Tables
Stored Procedures
Triggers
Views
Rules
Defaults
User-Defined Datatypes
Indexes
Permissions

SALES
Database

WHAT IS THE TRANSACTION LOG?

The *transaction log* is the history of data modifications to a database (see Figure 9.2). Whenever you create a database, SQL Server automatically creates a corresponding database transaction log. SQL Server uses the transaction log to ensure transaction completeness and to incrementally restore data changes (see Chapter 14, "Backups," for more information on restoring the transaction log).

Figure 9.2.
A transaction.

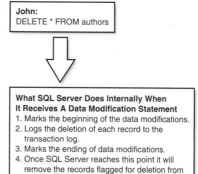

The capability to guarantee transaction completeness helps separate SQL Server from less well-equipped RDBMS software. To SQL Server, virtually every data modification must have a starting point and an ending point. If the ending point isn't reached, SQL Server automatically reverses any changes that were made. Suppose that the power goes out to the server midway through a process that is deleting all the rows from a table. When SQL Server restarts, it automatically restores all the rows that had been deleted, thus returning the table to its original state before the delete process was run. Through the use of the transaction log, SQL Server can guarantee that all the work was done or that none of the work was done.

SQL Server automatically uses a *write-ahead* type of transaction log. This means that changes to the database are first written to the transaction log and then they are written to the database. Examples of database changes written to the transaction log include data modified through the UPDATE, INSERT, and DELETE commands; any type of object creation; and any security changes.

SQL Server automatically marks the starting point and ending point whenever you execute a command that performs data modifications. For greater control, you can define the starting point and ending point for a group of data modifications. This is often done when more than one set of data modifications occurs within a unit of work.

For example, if a user transfers $1,000 from checking to savings, you can use a user-defined transaction to ensure that the checking account was debited and the savings account was credited. If the transaction did not complete, the checking and saving accounts return to their original states (their states before the transaction began).

To specify the beginning of a user-defined transaction, use the following statement:

`BEGIN TRANsaction [transaction_name]`

To specify the end of a user-defined transaction, use the following statement:

`COMMIT TRANsaction [transaction_name]`

To roll back any changes made within a user-defined transaction, use the following statement:

`ROLLBACK TRANsaction [transaction_name ¦ savepoint_name]`

The transaction log is a table within the database, named `syslogs`. The `syslogs` table has two columns: `xactid` (binary) and `op` (tinyint). The data contained in the `xactid` column is useless to look at because it is in binary format. Only SQL Server can understand the contents of the transaction log.

Note

No, you cannot disable the transaction log. This question is commonly asked when the log is not part of someone's backup strategy. Consequently, many people would rather not periodically dump the transaction log. Unfortunately, you can't avoid having transactions written to the log. But you *can* have the transaction log truncated automatically in SQL Server; set the database option Truncate Log On Checkpoint to TRUE (see "Setting Database Options," later in this chapter, for more information about Truncate Log On Checkpoint).

HOW DATABASES AND DEVICES INTERACT

Every database in SQL Server must use at least one device. Whenever you create a database, you are dedicating a predefined amount of device space to the database. Depending on your needs, you can create your entire database on one device or multiple devices (see Figure 9.3).

Figure 9.3.
The way in which
databases and devices
interact.

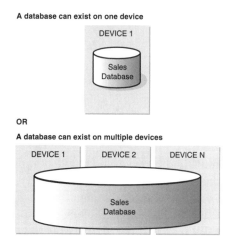

ESTIMATING THE SIZE OF A DATABASE

When you create a database, you must specify how much space to allocate to it. Other than "guesstimating," the second easiest way to estimate database size is to use the Estimator application included on the CD that accompanies this book (see Figure 9.4). The Estimator automatically calculates database storage requirements for a new table or an existing table.

Figure 9.4.
The Estimator
application.

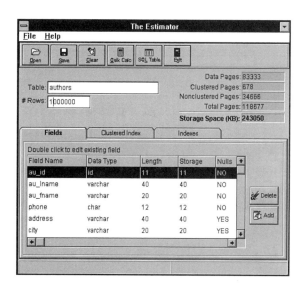

Tip

Use the Estimator application on the CD that accompanies this book to estimate the size of a database. The application works great when calculating the size of a new or existing database.

ESTIMATING THE SIZE OF THE TRANSACTION LOG

When estimating the size of the transaction log, a good starting point is to take the database size and multiply it by a factor of 10 to 25 percent. Whether you should use 10 percent or 25 percent (or some other factor) depends on the frequency between transaction log dumps and the average size of your transactions. With SQL Server, you can easily increase the size of your transaction log but you *cannot* easily decrease it.

DATABASE PRE-FLIGHT CHECKLIST

Before you create a database, review the following checklist:

CHECKLIST

☐ Does the database device already exist? If not, you must create the device before continuing.

☐ Did you decide whether you should use one device or multiple devices for the database?

☐ Did you decide whether the transaction log will be on the same device as the database or on a separate device?

☐ Did you estimate the size of the database?

☐ Did you estimate the size of the transaction log?

DATABASE POST-FLIGHT CHECKLIST

After you create a database, review the following checklist:

CHECKLIST

☐ Do you need to set any database options?

☐ Did you dump the `master` database?

☐ Did you document the configuration of the database (use the output from `sp_helpdb` to document the database)?

DATABASE BASICS

The following sections provide step-by-step instructions for managing a database.

CREATING A DATABASE

Before you can create tables and start to manage your data, you must create a database. Follow these steps to create a new database:

1. From the Enterprise Manager, access the Server Manager dialog box and select a server.

2. From the toolbar, click the Manage Databases toolbar button. The Manage Databases dialog box appears (see Figure 9.5).

Figure 9.5.
The Manage Databases dialog box.

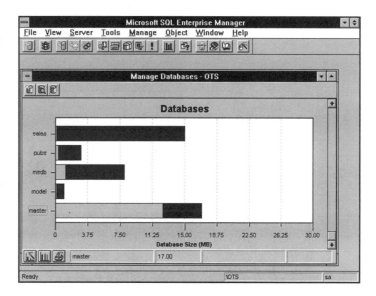

3. Click the New Database toolbar button at the top left corner of the Manage Databases dialog box. The New Database dialog box appears (see Figure 9.6).

4. Enter a name for the database.

Figure 9.6.
The New Database
dialog box.

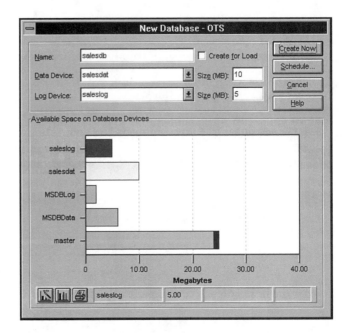

Note

Database names can be up to 30 characters long and must conform to valid SQL Server naming conventions (no spaces, table names must begin with a character, and so on).

Be consistent when naming a database. Use all uppercase or lowercase characters. Database names are case sensitive. Don't forget that you may often need to type the database name in a SQL statement—this may make you think twice about using all 30 characters! Try to make the name meaningful and relatively short.

5. Select a data device. This is the device on which the database will reside.

Caution

Do not put the database on the master device! Doing so will cause a major headache if you ever have to recover the master device.

6. Enter the size of the database (in megabytes). The size automatically defaults to the amount of available space on the selected device. Although you can override the default size, remember that it cannot be larger than the amount of available space on the selected device. If the device does not

have enough free space for the database, you must increase the size of the device before proceeding (refer to Chapter 8, "Managing Devices," for more information on increasing the size of a device).

Note

The minimum size of a database is 1M. In versions of SQL Server before version 6.x, the minimum size was 2M. The maximum size of a database is 1 terrabyte.

Tip

Don't worry if you allocate too little or too much space to your database. You can go back and change the size of the database after it is created.

7. Select a log device. Although it usually isn't recommended, you may set this option to None if you want to place the log on the same device as the database.

Caution

Always select a separate log device when creating production databases. Doing so improves performance and allows the log to be backed up. If you do not place the log on a separate device, you will be unable to dump the transaction log.

8. If you selected a log device in step 7, enter the size of the log (in megabytes). The size automatically defaults to the amount of available space on the selected device. Although you may override the default size, remember that it cannot be larger than the amount of available space on the selected device. If the device does not have enough free space for the log, you must increase the size of the device before proceeding.

Caution

Under normal circumstances, *do not* select the Create For Load option when creating a database. This option is used only when restoring a database from a backup (see Chapter 15, "Recovery," for more information on restoring a database).

9. Choose Create Now to create the database.

Tip

Always back up the `master` database after you create a new database. Doing so makes it easier to recover your database should the `master` database become damaged.

Note

The `sa` is the only user who can create a database, unless the statement permission is granted to another user (see Chapter 11, "Managing SQL Server Security," for more information about managing statement permissions).

You can use the following Transact SQL command to create a database:

```
CREATE DATABASE database_name
[ON {DEFAULT ¦ database_device} [= size]
[, database_device [= size]]...]
[LOG ON database_device [= size]
[, database_device [= size]]...]
[FOR LOAD]
```

VIEWING INFORMATION ABOUT A DATABASE

After you create a database, you can view information such as data size, data space available, log size, and log size available. Follow these steps to view information about a specific database:

1. From the Enterprise Manager, access the Server Manager window, open the Databases folder, and double-click a database. The Edit Database dialog box appears (see Figure 9.7).

2. From the Edit Database dialog box, you can view information about a database, set database options, and set statement permissions (see Chapter 11, "Managing SQL Server Security," for more information about statement permissions).

You can use the following Transact SQL command to view information about a database:

```
sp_helpdb [dbname]
```

9

Figure 9.7.
Viewing information
about a database.

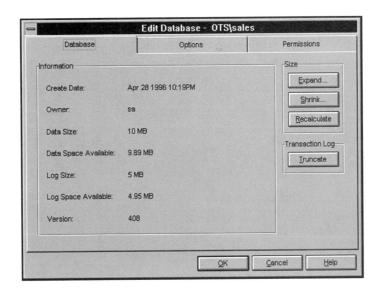

SETTING DATABASE OPTIONS

Each database in SQL Server has its own database options. Follow these steps to set database options:

1. From the Enterprise Manager, access the Server Manager dialog box, open the Databases folder, and double-click a database. The Edit Database dialog box appears.

2. Select the Options tab in the Edit Database dialog box (see Figure 9.8).

Figure 9.8.
Setting database
options on the
Options tab.

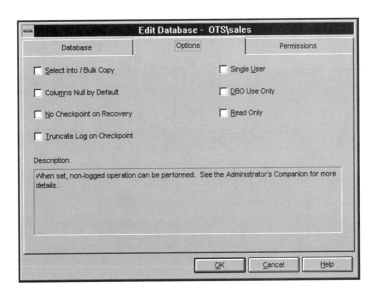

3. Check the options you want selected.

   The following sections describe each of the database options available on this tab.

4. Click OK to save your changes.

Tip

When you change database options, the changes take effect immediately. You do not have to restart the server for the option to take effect.

SELECT INTO/BULK COPY

Default setting: FALSE

The underlying consideration for how to set the Select Into/Bulk Copy option depends on how you handle the backup of the transaction log. Use the following information to help determine how you should set this option.

Set this option to FALSE if you depend on the transaction log for recovery (see Chapter 15, "Recovery," for more information on database recovery). This setting is typically used for production databases. When this option is set to FALSE, you cannot perform the following operations: Select Into, fast mode BCP, or Writetext.

Set this option to TRUE if you do not depend on the transaction log for recovery. This setting is typical for development databases and non-mission critical databases. By setting this option to TRUE, you can perform the following operations:

◆ **Select Into a destination table:** The Into portion of the SQL statement creates a copy of the source's table structure and populates the newly created table with data returned from the SQL statement.

Note

If Select Into/Bulk Copy = FALSE, you get the following error message when you use the SELECT [column_list] INTO [destination_table] statement:

Msg 268, Level 16, State 2
You can't run SELECT INTO in this database. Please check with the Database Owner.

◆ **Fast mode BCP:** BCP may run significantly faster when this option is set to TRUE because the fast mode of BCP bypasses the transaction log. (Fast BCP works only on a table that does not have an index; see Chapter 16, "Importing and Exporting Data," for more information about using BCP.)

Tip

> Those shops that use the transaction log for database recovery can temporarily set this option to TRUE, run a nonlogged operation (such as Select .. Into or fast-mode BCP), reset the option to FALSE, and dump the database. You must dump the database before you resume dumping the log. If you do not dump the database after performing a nonlogged operation, the next time you try to dump the transaction log, you receive an error message.

◆ **Writetext statement:** You can use this statement to perform nonlogged updating of text or image fields.

DBO USE ONLY

Default setting: FALSE

When the DBO Use Only option is set to TRUE, only the database owner (DBO) can access the database. Use this option if you want to keep everyone but the database owner and sa out of the database.

NO CHECKPOINT ON RECOVERY

Default setting: FALSE

The No Checkpoint on Recovery option controls the issuance of a checkpoint record to the log after the database has been recovered. In SQL Server terminology, the word *recovered* means that the database was successfully loaded during the startup of SQL Server. Typically, you leave this option set to FALSE unless you are dumping the log to a standby server. If you are dumping the log to a standby server, set this option to TRUE on the standby server's database. Doing so allows you to dump the log from the primary server and apply the log to the standby server.

READ ONLY

Default setting: FALSE

When the Read Only option is set to TRUE, the contents of the database can be viewed but not modified.

SINGLE USER

Default setting: FALSE

When the Single User option is set to TRUE, only one user at a time (including the sa) can be in the database.

COLUMNS NULL BY DEFAULT

Default setting: FALSE

The Columns Null by Default option determines whether a column is defined as NULL or NOT NULL when it is created. This option is implemented for ANSI compatibility.

The following examples explain the impact of setting this option.

Example A:

```
Columns Null By Default = FALSE
CREATE TABLE sales (sales_id int)
```

Result: The column sales_id is defined as NOT NULL.

Example B:

```
Columns Null By Default = TRUE
CREATE TABLE sales (sales_id int)
```

Result: The column sales_id is defined as NULL.

Note

Explicitly specifying a column as NULL or NOT NULL with the CREATE TABLE command overrides the Columns Null By Default option.

TRUNCATE LOG ON CHECKPOINT

Default setting: FALSE

When the Truncate Log on Checkpoint option is set to TRUE, the transaction log is automatically truncated when a CHECKPOINT is issued by the system. (A CHECKPOINT is issued by the system about once every minute.)

Set this option to FALSE if you use the transaction log as part of your backup recovery process.

Note

If you try to dump the transaction log when the database option Truncate Log on Checkpoint = TRUE, you will receive an error.

Set this option to TRUE if you are not concerned about using the transaction log as part of your backup recovery process. This option is useful for development databases or non-mission critical databases. When you set this option to TRUE, you significantly lessen the chance of the transaction log running out of space.

OTHER DATABASE OPTIONS

Three additional database options are not accessible through the Edit Database dialog box. You can use sp_dboption command to change any database option.

Note

> The offline, published, and subscribed database options are new to SQL Server 6.x.

You can use the following Transact SQL command to set database options:

```
sp_dboption [dbname, optname, {TRUE | FALSE}]
```

Offline

Default setting: FALSE

When the offline option is set to TRUE, the database is taken offline from the system. It is not recovered during system startup and remains inaccessible until it is placed online.

Set this option to FALSE unless you are working with a removable media database.

Published

Default setting: FALSE

When the published option is set to TRUE, it permits the database to be published for replication. It does not perform the replication, it only allows it to be replicated.

When this option is set to FALSE, it prevents the database from being published. Set this option to FALSE unless you want this to be a published database.

Subscribed

Default setting: FALSE

When the subscribed option is set to TRUE, it permits the database to be subscribed for replication. It does not perform the subscription, it only allows it to be subscribed to.

When this option is set to FALSE, it prevents the database from being subscribed. Set this option to FALSE unless you want this to be a subscribed database.

EXPANDING THE DATABASE

You can easily expand the size of the database after it has been created. SQL Server offers two approaches to increasing the size of a database. Before proceeding, you should review which approach best suits your needs.

APPROACH 1: USE THE CURRENTLY ASSIGNED DEVICE

One way you can allocate more space to the database is to use more space on the device currently in use by the database (see Figure 9.9). The existing device must have sufficient space to accommodate the increase in database size (refer to Chapter 8, "Managing Devices," for more information on managing devices).

Tip

To determine which device or devices are in use by a database, use `sp_help`:

`sp_helpdb [dbname]`

Figure 9.9.
Approach 1: Expanding the database.

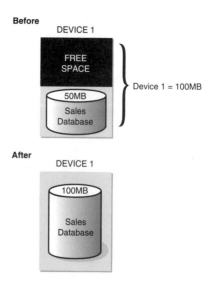

APPROACH 2: USE ANOTHER DEVICE

The second way you can expand the database is to assign another device to the database (see Figure 9.10). Doing so allows the database to grow in size by spanning multiple devices. The device must exist already, and it must have sufficient space to accommodate the increase in database size.

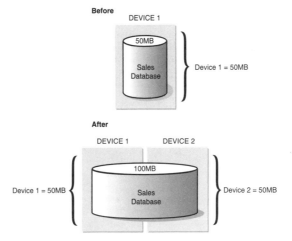

Figure 9.10.
Approach 2: Expanding
the database.

Follow these steps to use another device to increase the size of a database:

1. From the Enterprise Manager, access the Server Manager dialog box and select a server.

2. Click the Manage Databases button on the toolbar; the Manage Databases dialog box appears. Double-click a database to display the Edit Database dialog box.

3. From the Edit Database dialog box, select the Database tab. Click the Expand button. The Expand Database dialog box appears (see Figure 9.11).

4. Select a data device.

5. In the Size text box, enter the amount of additional space you want allocated to the database.

Caution

Do *not* use the `master` device to gain additional database space. Doing so can cause a major headache if you ever have to recover the `master` device.

6. Click Expand Now to save your changes.

Note

You can increase the size of a database up to a maximum of 32 times. After 32 times, you must drop and re-create the database.

Tip

Always back up the `master` database after you increase the size of a database. Doing so makes it easier to recover your database should the `master` database become damaged.

Figure 9.11.
The Expand Database
dialog box.

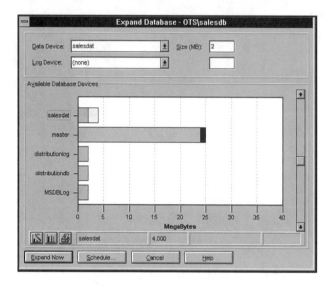

You can use the following Transact SQL command to expand a database:

```
ALTER DATABASE database_name
[ON {DEFAULT | database_device} [= size]
[, database_device [= size]]...]
[FOR LOAD]
```

EXPANDING THE DATABASE LOG

You can easily expand the size of the database log after it has been created. The concept behind expanding the database log is the same as for expanding the database: space can be added to the device currently in use by the log, or another device can be assigned to the log (see "Expanding the Database," earlier in this chapter, for more information).

Follow these steps to increase the size of the database log:

1. From the Enterprise Manager, access the Server Manager dialog box and select a server.

9

2. From the toolbar, click the Manage Databases button; the Manage Databases dialog box appears. Double-click a database to display the Edit Database dialog box.

3. From the Edit Database dialog box, select the Database tab. Click the Expand button. The Expand Database dialog box appears.

4. Select a log device.

5. In the Size text box, enter the amount of additional space you want allocated to the database log (see Figure 9.12).

Caution

Do not use the master device to gain additional database log space. Doing so can cause a major headache if you ever have to recover the master device.

6. Click Expand Now to save your changes.

Tip

Always back up the master database after you increase the size of a database. Doing so makes it easier to recover your database should the master database become damaged.

Figure 9.12.
Expanding the data-
base log.

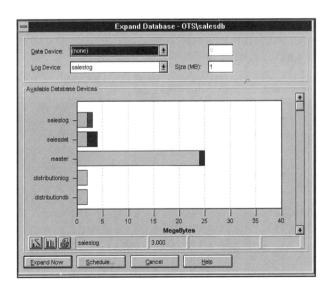

You can use the following Transact SQL command to expand the database log:

```
ALTER DATABASE database_name
[ON {DEFAULT ¦ database_device} [= size]
[, database_device [= size]]...]
[FOR LOAD]
```

SHRINKING A DATABASE

Follow these steps to decrease the size of a database:

1. From the Enterprise Manager, access the Server Manager dialog box and select a server.

2. From the toolbar, click the Manage Databases button; the Manage Databases dialog box appears. Double-click a database to display the Edit Database dialog box.

3. From the Edit Database dialog box, select the Database tab. Click the Shrink button. The Shrink Database dialog box appears (see Figure 9.13).

4. Enter the new database size in megabytes and click OK.

Figure 9.13.
Shrinking a database.

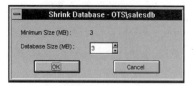

You cannot make the database smaller than the amount of space currently occupied by data and objects. (Refer to "Determining Database Size and Available Space," earlier in this chapter, for more information on database size.) Also, you can only decrease the size of the database; you cannot decrease the size of the database's log.

Tip

Always back up the master database after you create a new database. Doing so makes it easier to recover your database should the master database become damaged.

Use the following Transact SQL command to shrink a database:

```
dbcc shrinkdb (database_name [,new_size [[,'MASTEROVERRIDE']]])
```

Note

The capability to shrink a database is new to SQL Server 6.x.

RENAMING A DATABASE

You can rename any database after it has been created. Only the sa can rename a database. Follow these steps to rename a database:

1. Set the database you are going to rename to single-user mode. (Refer to "Setting Database Options," earlier in this chapter, for more information about single-user mode.)

2. From the Enterprise Manager, access the Query dialog box and select the Query tab.

3. Enter the following syntax:

   ```
   sp_renamedb oldname, newname
   ```

4. Run the query.

5. Reset the database to multi-user mode.

Caution

When renaming a database, watch out for SQL statements that explicitly refer to the database name; for example, SELECT * FROM pubs..authors. If you rename the pubs database to pub_db, you must remember to change the statement to SELECT * FROM pubs_db..authors. Some common areas in which you should look for database references are views, stored procedures, triggers, BCP scripts, and embedded SQL commands in applications.

DROPPING A DATABASE

When you drop, or delete, a database, you physically remove the database from the device(s) on which it resides and you destroy all objects contained within the database. Any device space allocated to the database is reclaimed. Only the sa and database owner can drop a database. Follow these steps to drop a database:

1. From the Enterprise Manager, access the Server Manager dialog box, select a server, and open the Databases folder. Right-click the database you want to drop and select Delete from the shortcut menu (see Figure 9.14).

Figure 9.14.
Dropping a database.

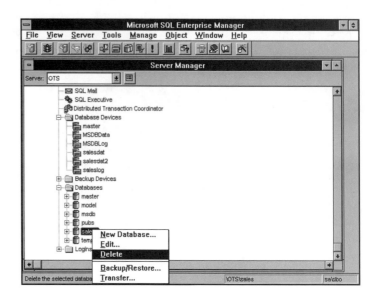

2. At the prompt, click Yes to delete the database.

You can use one of the following Transact SQL commands to shrink a database:

```
DROP DATABASE database_name [, database_name...]
```

```
sp_dbremove database[,dropdev]
```

Tip

Always back up the master database after you drop a database. Doing so makes it easier to recover your database should the master database become damaged.

New to SQL Server 6.x is the capability to drop a damaged database with the DROP DATABASE command. In SQL Server versions before 6.x, you could use only the DBCC DBREPAIR (database_name, DROPDB) command. You can also use sp_dbremove to drop a database (sp_dbremove is new to version 6.x).

THE TWO MOST COMMON DATABASE ERRORS

Without a doubt, you will encounter the following errors when you work with SQL Server:

- **The database log ran out of space**. Following is a typical error message:

```
Msg 1105, Level 17, State 2
Can't allocate space for object 'Syslogs' in database '[dbname]' because the
'logsegment' segment is full. If you ran out of space in Syslogs, dump the
transaction log. Otherwise, use ALTER DATABASE or sp_extendsegment to
increase the size of the segment.
```

- **The database ran out of space**. Following is a typical error message:

```
Msg 1105, Level 17, State 1
Can't allocate space for object '[object name]' in database '[database name]'
because the 'default' segment is full. If you ran out of space in Syslogs,
dump the transaction log. Otherwise, use ALTER DATABASE or sp_extendsegment
to increase the size of the segment.
```

DBAs new to SQL Server are frequently confused about why they get these error messages. The confusion occurs because you must preallocate space to the database and database log. If you do not allocate sufficient space, you get these error messages. Remember that the amount of remaining database space and log space has nothing to do with the amount of space left on your hard drive. Remaining database and log space is based on the amount of unused space allocated to the database or log.

The following sections explain in greater detail what each error means and how best to correct the error.

THE DATABASE LOG RAN OUT OF SPACE

Whenever you fill up the transaction log, you receive the following error message:

```
Msg 1105, Level 17, State 2
Can't allocate space for object 'Syslogs' in database '[dbname]' because the
'logsegment' segment is full. If you ran out of space in Syslogs, dump the
transaction log. Otherwise, use ALTER DATABASE or sp_extendsegment to increase
the size of the segment.
```

To resolve the error, you must dump the log or increase the size of the log before continuing. (See "Expanding the Database Log," earlier in this chapter, for more information on increasing the size of the database log.)

To help avoid this error, do one of the following:

- **Increase the size of the log until the problem goes away.** Although this is the simplest solution, it may not be the most effective solution. If you do not properly manage your transactions, you can fill up the transaction log regardless of how much space has been allocated to it.

- **Increase the frequency of the log dump.** Doing so may reduce the frequency of the error or prevent it from occurring.

- **Set the database option Truncate Log On Checkpoint to TRUE.** Only use this option if you are not backing up the transaction log—this option *is not* recommended for production databases!

◆ **Use a nonlogged command to perform the equivalent SQL command.** Nonlogged operations are not written to the transaction log; therefore, you invalidate the effectiveness of backing up your transaction log after you perform a nonlogged operation. For mission-critical data, you should dump your database after you perform a nonlogged command.

You can substitute the following nonlogged commands for SQL commands:

SQL Command	Nonlogged Command Equivalent	Notes
DELETE FROM [tablename]	TRUNCATE TABLE [tablename]	Use TRUNCATE TABLE [tablename] to remove all rows from the table. Also, because the TRUNCATE command is a nonlogged operation, it runs much faster than the DELETE command.
INSERT INTO [tablename] SELECT * FROM [tablename]	BCP	Rather than using an INSERT statement, try using BCP. Use BCP to export the data out of a table and into another table.

THE DATABASE RAN OUT OF SPACE

Whenever you deplete the available database space, you get this error message:

```
Msg 1105, Level 17, State 1
Can't allocate space for object '[object name]' in database '[database name]'
because the 'default' segment is full. If you ran out of space in Syslogs, dump the
transaction log. Otherwise, use ALTER DATABASE or sp_extendsegment to increase the
size of the segment.
```

To resolve this error, you must increase the size of the database or reduce the amount of space used by existing objects. (Refer to "Expanding the Database," earlier in this chapter, for more information on increasing the size of the database.)

Follow these suggestions to help avoid this error in the future:

◆ **Ward off the problem before it happens.** You should frequently review your production databases for space allocation problems. (Refer to "Determining Database Size and Available Space," earlier in this chapter, for more information about space allocation.)

◆ **Always leave yourself more space in the database than you expect to use.** I recommend that you should leave at least 25 percent more space than you think is necessary. Doing so can give you room to work when you need to copy data and tables.

BEYOND THE BASICS

The following sections list helpful tips and tricks that can help improve the management of databases. These tips can help simplify database maintenance and improve database recoverability.

TIP 1: PLACE THE TRANSACTION LOG ON A SEPARATE DEVICE

For most databases, you will want to place the transaction log on a separate device. By segregating the transaction log and database onto separate devices, you gain the following benefits:

◆ **You can dump the transaction log to a backup device.** Only when the transaction log is on a separate device can you back up the transaction log to a backup device. This is the best way to recover your data from a database failure.

◆ **You improve database performance.** By placing the transaction log on a separate device, the contention for page space is reduced, thus improving performance.

◆ **You reduce the likelihood of a damaged database and damaged transaction log.** By splitting the database and transaction log, you use two devices instead of one device. This helps diffuse the risk of a damaged device.

◆ **You can control the amount of space allocated to the database transaction log.** When the database and transaction log are on the same device, it can be difficult to control the size of the log. This may result in the log eating up space that you thought would be allocated to your data.

TIP 2: DOCUMENT THE DATABASE

Always document the configuration of the database after it has been modified. This is in addition to dumping the `master` database. The easiest way to document the configuration of a database is to use the `sp_helpdb` command. I recommend saving the output from the command to a text file (preferably somewhere other than the server's hard drive).

TIP 3: TAKE ADVANTAGE OF THE `model` DATABASE

Use the `model` database to simplify object creation. The `model` database allows you to define a template for the creation of new databases. When you create a new database, SQL Server copies the contents of the model database into the newly created database. This makes a handy mechanism for copying frequently used database options and objects into a new database. Anything you want automatically copied into a new database should be placed in the model.

Note

The model database is automatically created when you install SQL Server. It cannot be deleted.

Changes to the model database will not impact existing databases. The model database is used only when creating new databases.

Following are common types of objects and settings that can be stored in the model database:

◆ Frequently used user-defined datatypes, rules, and defaults.

◆ Database options. Any database option you set in the model database is copied into a new database. For example, if you always set the Select Into / Bulk Copy option to TRUE, go ahead and set it in the model database.

◆ Any tables, views, or stored procedures that you always add to a new database can be placed in the model database.

◆ Database size. If you expand the model database (the default size is 1M), that becomes the minimum size for any new databases.

Caution

Be careful when you increase the size of the model database. It will become the minimum size for all new databases. Whenever SQL Server creates a new database, it copies the contents of the model database into the new database. Therefore, the new database cannot be smaller in size than the model database.

SEGMENTS

Segments allows you to gain performance by placing frequently accessed tables and indexes on their own devices (see Figure 9.15). Using segments is an old trick that DBAs employ to improve read/write access to frequently used tables. For segments to be effective, they must have their own physical disk controller.

Figure 9.15.
Segments.

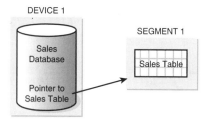

Tip

Before going to the trouble of using segments, you should explore Windows NT-based alternatives. Very few SQL Servers for NT installations use segments because they can be tedious to implement, difficult to maintain, and can complicate database recovery.

Windows NT offers easier-to-use alternatives, such as Windows NT stripe sets—RAID 0 (striping) and RAID 5 (striping with parity)—and hardware disk arrays. Refer to Chapter 8, "Managing Devices," for more information on striped sets and hardware disk arrays. Windows NT striping performs as well as segments and is much easier to implement and maintain.

CREATING A SEGMENT

Use the `sp_addsegment` command to create a segment:

```
sp_addsegment segname, logical_name
```

In this statement, *segname* is the name you are going to assign to the segment; *logical_name* is the name of the device you are going to use for the segment. (The device must already exist. See Chapter 8 for more information on creating devices.)

To create a segment named `seg_sales` and using `device1`, use the following command:

```
sp_addsegment seg_sales, device1
```

Note

Each database in SQL Server can have up to 32 segments.

CREATING A TABLE ON A SEGMENT

Use the CREATE TABLE command with the ON *segment_name* option to create a table on a segment:

```
CREATE TABLE [database.[owner].]table_name
({col_name column_properties [constraint [constraint [... constraint]]]
¦ [[,] constraint]}
[[,] {next_col_name ¦ next_constraint}...]
)
[ON segment_name]
```

To create the sales table on the seg_sales segment, use the following command:

```
CREATE TABLE sales
(sales_id integer,
sales_amount money)
ON seg_sales
```

CREATING AN INDEX ON A SEGMENT

Use the CREATE INDEX command with the ON *segment_name* option to create an index on a segment:

```
CREATE [UNIQUE] [CLUSTERED ¦ NONCLUSTERED] INDEX index_name
ON [[database.]owner.]table_name (column_name [, column_name]...)
[WITH
[FILLFACTOR = x]
[[,] IGNORE_DUP_KEY]
[[,] {SORTED_DATA ¦ SORTED_DATA_REORG}]
[[,] {IGNORE_DUP_ROW ¦ ALLOW_DUP_ROW}]]
[ON segment_name]
```

For example, to create a clustered index on the seg_sales segment for the sales table, use the following command:

```
CREATE CLUSTERED INDEX sales_id_idx
ON sales(sales_id)
ON seg_sales
```

INCREASING THE SIZE OF A SEGMENT

Use the sp_extendsegment command to increase the size of a segment:

```
sp_extendsegment segname, logical_name
```

For example, to extend the seg_sales segment to device2, use the following command:

```
sp_extendsegment seg_sales, device2
```

Viewing Information about a Segment

Use sp_helpsegment to list information about a particular segment or all the segments in a database:

sp_helpsegment [*segname*]

For example, to view information about the seg_sales segment, use the following command:

sp_helpsegment seg_sales

Use sp_helpdb to view which segments are in use for a particular database:

sp_helpdb [*dbname*]

To view segment information within the sales database, use the following command:

sp_helpdb sales

Dropping a Segment

Use the sp_dropsegment command to drop a segment:

sp_dropsegment *segname*

Note

You cannot use the sp_dropsegment command if an object resides on the segment you are trying to drop. You must drop the object before dropping the segment.

For example, to drop the seg_sales segment, use the following command:

sp_dropsegment seg_sales

Database-Removable Media

New to SQL Server 6.x is the capability to create database-removable media. This enables you to distribute databases on media such as CD-ROM, floppy drives, WORM drives, or optical drives. You can also create new databases from removable media.

Note

The database-removable feature provides new possibilities for archiving and distributing databases.

CREATING A REMOVABLE DATABASE MEDIA

Use the `sp_create_removable` command to create a removable database:

```
sp_create_removable dbname, syslogical, 'sysphysical', syssize,
loglogical, 'logphysical', logsize, datalogical1, 'dataphysical1', datasize1
[... , datalogical16, 'dataphysical16', datasize16]
```

For example, to create a 4M sales database for distribution on removable media, with a 2M device for the system catalog, and a 2M device for the transaction log, use the following command:

```
sp_create_removable sales, salessys, 'c:\mssql\data\salessys.dat',2,
saleslog,'c:\mssql\data\saleslog.dat',2,
salesdat,'c:\mssql\data\salesdat.dat',4
```

> ## STRANGER THAN FICTION!
>
> The `sp_create_removable` example in the SQL Server documentation is incorrect.
>
> **Incorrect Example**:
> ```
> sp_create_removable inventory, invsys, 'c:\mssql\data\invsys.dat, 2',
> invlog,'c:\mssql\data\invlog.dat',4
> invdata,'c:\mssql\data\invdata.dat',10,
> ```
> **Correct Example**:
> ```
> sp_create_removable inventory, invsys, 'c:\mssql\data\invsys.dat',2,
> invlog,'c:\mssql\data\invlog.dat',4,
> invdata,'c:\mssql\data\invdata.dat',10
> ```

CERTIFYING A DATABASE FOR REMOVABLE DISTRIBUTION

When you are ready to distribute the database, use the `sp_certify_removable` command. This command takes the database offline, thus making it available for distribution:

```
sp_certify_removable dbname[, AUTO]
```

The optional AUTO parameter automatically drops all database users and transfers ownership of the database to the sa.

To certify the sales database for distribution, use the following command:

```
sp_certify_removable sales, AUTO
```

9

Tip

Be sure to save the information returned from the `sp_certify_removable` procedure. Whenever you distribute a removable database, you should include the output from the `sp_certify_removable` command. This information will be needed by anyone who plans to install the database.

In SQL Server version 6.5, `sp_certify_removable` automatically generates a text file containing the information returned from the procedure. The information is saved in a file named `CertifyR_[dbname].txt` in the `LOG` subdirectory in the SQL Server installation directory structure. In version 6.0, the output from `sp_certify_removable` must be manually saved to a text file.

Version 6.5

The following is sample output from the `sp_certify_removable` command:

```
DBCC execution completed. If DBCC printed error messages, see your System
Administrator.
DBCC execution completed. If DBCC printed error messages, see your System
Administrator.
DBCC execution completed. If DBCC printed error messages, see your System
Administrator.
File: 'c:\mssql\data\saleslog.dat' closed.
Device dropped.
The following devices are ready for removal. Please note this info. for use when
installing on a remote system:

Device name   Device type    Sequence  Device frag.    Physical file name
                                       used by database
------------------------------------------------------------------------------
salessys      System + Log   1         2 MB            c:\mssql\data\salessys.dat
salesdat      Data           2         4 MB            c:\mssql\data\salesdat.dat

Database is now offline
Closing device 'salesdat' and marking it 'deferred'.
Device option set.
Closing device 'salessys' and marking it 'deferred'.
Device option set.
```

INSTALLING AND ACTIVATING A REMOVABLE MEDIA DATABASE

When you are ready to install a removable media database, use the `sp_dbinstall` command. This command copies the system tables and transaction log from the removable media to the hard drive and optionally copies the data device to the hard drive:

```
sp_dbinstall database,logical_dev_name,'physical_dev_name',size,
'devtype'[,'location']
```

To install the system catalog tables and transaction log from the removable media, use the following syntax:

```
sp_dbinstall sales,salessys,'e:\salessys.dat',2,
'SYSTEM','c:\mssql\data\salessys.dat'
```

To install the data tables from the removable media, use the following syntax:

```
sp_dbinstall sales,salesdat,'e:\salesdat.dat',4,
'DATA','c:\mssql\data\salesdat.dat'
```

Note

The sp_dbinstall command is run for each database device. For this example, the sales database used two devices: a system plus log device and a data device. To install the entire database to the server's hard drive, run the sp_dbinstall option twice—once with the devtype parameter set to SYSTEM and once with the devtype parameter set to DATA.

After the database has been successfully installed, you must place it online. To place a database online, use sp_dboption with the offline parameter:

```
sp_dboption dbname, offline, {TRUE ¦ FALSE}
```

For example, to bring the sales database online, use the following syntax:

```
sp_dboption sales, offline, FALSE
```

Note

Combining the offline and FALSE parameters brings a database online. To take the database offline, use the offline and TRUE parameters.

DELETING A DATABASE INSTALLED FROM REMOVABLE MEDIA

Use the sp_dbremove command to delete a database installed from removable media:

```
sp_dbremove database[,dropdev]
```

Note

The optional parameter dropdev drops any devices used by the removable database media. It does not delete the actual device from the hard drive.

Following is an example of the `sp_dbremove` command:

```
sp_dbremove sales, dropdev
```

BETWEEN THE LINES

Following are some important notes to remember when managing databases:

- ◆ Use the Enterprise Manager or Transact SQL commands to manage databases. For ease of use, the Enterprise Manager is generally preferred over Transact SQL commands.
- ◆ Every database in SQL Server has a transaction log.
- ◆ SQL Server uses the transaction log to ensure transaction completeness and to incrementally restore data changes.
- ◆ Virtually all changes to the database are first written to the transaction log and then are written to the database.
- ◆ Every database in SQL Server must use at least one device.
- ◆ The `sa` is the only user who can create a database unless the statement permission is granted to another user.
- ◆ Watch out for the Select Into/Bulk Copy and Truncate Log On Checkpoint database options. When these options are set to `TRUE`, they may impact your backup strategy.
- ◆ Use the `sp_help` command to document important database information.
- ◆ You can expand or shrink the size of a database.
- ◆ You can only expand the size of the transaction log—you cannot shrink the size of the transaction log.
- ◆ Always place the transaction log on a separate device.
- ◆ Use the `model` database to simplify object creation.
- ◆ Use NT stripe sets or hardware disk arrays before going to the trouble of using segments.
- ◆ New to SQL Server 6.x is the capability to create database-removable media.

SUMMARY

Basic database management techniques combined with supplemental tips provide you with the skill set to intelligently manage a database. Remember that intelligent database management is the key to keeping your database up and running. In the next chapter, you learn how to manage users.

CHAPTER 10

by Mark Spenik

Managing Users

In this chapter, you examine how to manage user login IDs and database users. A *login ID* is the name that allows an individual to access SQL Server. For example, sa is the system administrator user login ID. A database user name allows an individual access to a specific database on SQL Server.

Note

The difference between a *user login ID* and a *database user name* can become confusing. Remember that adding a login allows an individual to log in to the server; it does not allow the individual access to databases except for the login ID's default database. A database user name does not allow an individual access to SQL Server, but is assigned to the login ID to provide access to a specific database. The login ID and the database user name can be the same, and in many cases are.

UNDERSTANDING THE LOGIN ID

A *login ID* (name) allows a user to log in to SQL Server. When SQL Server is first installed, the server adds the SQL Server login IDs described in the following sections.

Note

Throughout this chapter, you see references to *login ID* and *login name*. The two are one and the same. Many of the system's stored procedures like sp_adduser and sp_dropuser ask for a login ID, while the Enterprise Manager Manage Login dialog box asks for a login name.

SA

The sa login ID is the login ID of the SQL Server system administrator. The sa user has permission to do anything and everything on the server, from creating users and devices to backing up and restoring databases.

Caution

Protect the sa login ID. The sa account should be used only by the database administrator! Do not allow developers and users access to SQL Server with the sa login ID.

PROBE

The probe login ID is used only in standard mode for some SQL Server administrative applications, such as the Performance Monitor, to connect to SQL Server. In integrated security mode, the sa login ID is used.

If your server has been set up to support replication, one or both of the following login IDs will be installed.

REPL_PUBLISHER

The repl_publisher login ID is set up if the server has been configured to handle subscription replication services.

REPL_SUBSCRIBER

The repl_subscriber login ID is created if the server is set up as a publication server for replication.

Caution

Do not use the probe, repl_publisher, or repl_subscriber login IDs for user logins to SQL Server. These login IDs are reserved for SQL Server services.

UNDERSTANDING TYPES OF SECURITY MODES

The type of security mode selected determines how SQL Server login IDs are created and maintained. SQL Server supports three different security modes:

- ◆ Standard
- ◆ Integrated
- ◆ Mixed

The security mode is selected during SQL Server installation but can be modified at any time. One factor that limits the security mode you can select is the type of network protocol you will be using (refer to Chapter 5, "Planning an Installation or Upgrade," for more details). The following sections look at the different security modes and how they relate to user management.

STANDARD SECURITY

Standard security is the standard SQL Server login facility inherited from Sybase 4.x systems and implemented in the Microsoft OS/2 versions of SQL Server. An individual logging on to SQL Server must supply a user name and a password that is validated by SQL Server against a system table. Standard security works over all network configurations.

INTEGRATED SECURITY

Integrated security takes advantage of Windows NT user security and account mechanisms. SQL Server user management integrates directly with the NT operating system. Users with a valid Windows NT account can log on to SQL Server without supplying a user name and password once the user account has been granted access to SQL Server. Integrated security can be implemented over the following network protocols: named-pipes protocol or multi-protocol.

Tip

In versions of NT SQL Server before version 6.0, only the named-pipes protocol supported integrated security.

MIXED SECURITY

Mixed security is the best of both worlds; it is a combination of the integrated and security modes. Users using trusted connections (named-pipes or multi-protocol) can log in using integrated security; users from trusted or nontrusted connections can log in using standard security.

Study Figure 10.1 to get a better idea of the different types of security modes and the options available.

Figure 10.1.
Security modes.

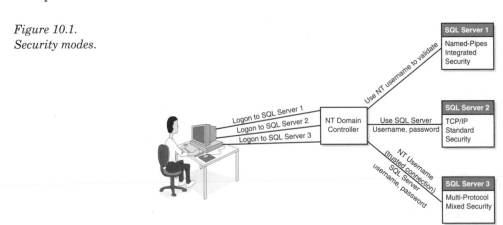

UNDERSTANDING LOGINS THAT USE STANDARD SECURITY

The standard security access mode dates back to the days of Sybase and the Microsoft pre-NT SQL Server. In standard security mode, a login ID is added to SQL Server for a user. The user must then use the login ID name and password to log in to the server. The login ID does not tie into the NT user name and password scheme. Standard logins are used for standard and mixed security modes.

Tip

Understanding how the standard security mode works makes using integrated security logins easier to understand.

To add a user login for standard security, follow these steps using the SQL Server Enterprise Manager:

1. Select the server to which you want to add the login.

2. Click the Manage Logins button on the Enterprise Manager toolbar to display the Manage Logins dialog box (see Figure 10.2).

Figure 10.2.
The Manage Logins dialog box.

3. Add the necessary parameters to create the new login. Figure 10.2 shows the Manage Logins dialog box with the required parameters to create a SQL Server login ID called Sam_Meyer.

4. To add the new login ID, click the Add button. A dialog box prompts you to verify the login ID password. Enter the password for verification and click the OK button.

The following list describes the different parameters in the Manage Logins dialog box:

◆ **Login Name**: The login name is the login ID used to log in to the server. The login name must conform to the SQL Server identifiers standards. Briefly stated, the name can be from 1 to 30 characters in length and the first character must be a letter or number. No embedded spaces are allowed in the name.

◆ **Password**: The password is the string required to log in to the SQL Server. NULL password is the default.

Caution

SQL Server version 6.x encrypts the password. Previous versions of SQL Server did not encrypt the password, so on previous versions of SQL Server, the sa user can read user passwords by performing a select * from syslogins.

◆ **Default Language**: The language used when the user logs in to the server. The default is the default language set up on the server. Only languages installed on the server appear as options.

◆ **Database Access**: The database access grid allows you to assign a login ID to multiple databases quickly.

Note

Always assign a login ID to a default database; otherwise, users will be in the master database when they log in.

WHAT HAPPENS WHEN A LOGIN ID IS ADDED?

When a new login ID is added to SQL Server, an entry is placed in the syslogins table. Figure 10.3 shows a query displaying several columns from syslogins. The column suid stands for the *Server User ID*. The suid is a unique number used throughout SQL Server to identify a login ID. When assigning a suid, SQL Server uses the lowest suid available (filling any possible hole left when a login ID is removed); if no numbers are available, the suid number is incremented by one and assigned as the new suid for the login ID.

Tip

The suid, not the login name, is used internally by SQL Server to uniquely identify a login name.

Figure 10.3.
SQL Query, displaying
several columns of the
system table syslogins.

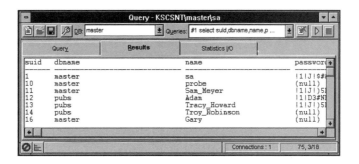

The command to add a login ID is the system stored procedure sp_addlogin, which has the following syntax:

```
sp_addlogin login_id [, password [, default database [, default
language[,login_suid]]]]
```

Note

The parameter login_suid is a new parameter added for SQL Server 6.5. Use login_suid to remap a new user login ID with a database user name that has become orphaned. An orphaned user name in a database occurs when an entry in the sysusers table of the database contains an entry with a suid that does not have a matching suid in the syslogins table. This can occur when you load a new database from a backup from another server or from an older backup that includes users you have since removed from syslogins. This feature is not the same as using an alias (discussed later in this chapter).

Version
6.5

USING GROUPS

Groups are used in SQL Server to simplify assigning security and permissions to databases objects, such as tables and stored procedures, by logically grouping users together. A group name can be any name you like, as long as the name follows the rules for SQL Server identifiers. You can create groups to represent your business groups. For example, a software development company may have groups for developers, testers, and analysts. SQL Server installs a single default group called public on every database when the database is created.

Tip

Groups are created for a database, not for the entire server. If you end up adding the same groups to every database, you can create the groups in the model database. When a new database is created, the new groups are included in the new database.

CREATING A GROUP

To create a group, perform the following steps using the SQL Server Enterprise Manager:

1. Select the server and database on which you want to create the group.
2. From the Manage menu on the Enterprise Manager menu bar, select the Groups option to display the Manage Groups dialog box (see Figure 10.4).

Figure 10.4.
The Manage Groups
dialog box.

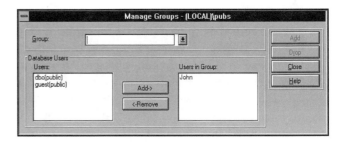

3. Type the group name in the Group combo box.
4. Use the Add-> button to add users to the group.
5. Click the Add button to add the new group.

Caution

A user can belong to only one user-defined group at a time and to the system group public. A user always belongs to the group public and cannot be removed from the public group. The only-one-group limitation is a design limitation because groups are stored in a column of the user row in the sysusers table. *Beware:* If you use the SQL Server Enterprise Manager to add a user to a group who belongs to another group, the user is removed from the first group and placed in the new group. SQL Server Enterprise Manager does not warn you that the user has been removed from the first group.

When a group is added to a database, a new entry for the group is made in the system table called `sysusers`, covered in more detail later in this chapter. The system stored procedure to add a group is called `sp_addgroup`, which has the following syntax:

```
sp_addgroup groupname
```

The system stored procedure to change a users group is `sp_changegroup`, which has the following syntax:

```
sp_chagegroup groupname, username
```

MANAGING LOGINS USING INTEGRATED SECURITY

Integrated security allows SQL Server to share the same user name and password used for Windows NT and allows the user to bypass the SQL Server login process. Some of the benefits of integrated security are that the user does not have to remember a separate password and user name; when the password changes in NT, the user does not have to change the password in SQL Server.

How does integrated security work? When a user logs in to Windows NT and accesses SQL Server, which has been set up with integrated or mixed security over a trusted connection, the standard SQL Server login process is bypassed. SQL Server obtains the user and password information from the user's NT network security attributes, which are established when the user logs on to Windows NT. Using integrated security allows you to take advantage of Windows NT features such as password aging and login auditing.

Tip

> You can set up more than one sa user account with integrated security. All members of the Windows NT Admin group have sa privileges on SQL Server in integrated security mode.

Integrated security requires more NT hands-on experience or working closely with the NT system administrator when setting up user accounts and groups. Setting up integrated security requires a few more steps than setting up standard security, but integrated security offers many benefits. Follow these steps to set up integrated security:

1. Make sure that SQL Server is running a network protocol that supports trusted connections. In version 6.x, named-pipes and multi-protocol can be used. In versions 4.21 and 4.21a, only named-pipes is supported. If you are not running these protocols, you cannot use integrated security.

2. Make sure that the server is properly configured (see the following section, "Configuring the Server for Integrated and Mixed Security").

3. Once all the security options are set up on SQL Server, the next step is to create the Windows NT user accounts and Windows NT groups. NT users and groups are created using the NT User Manager.

Note

Windows NT groups are not the same as SQL Server groups, although the SQL Security Manger will create a SQL Server group for you from a Windows NT group.

4. To add the Windows NT users and groups to SQL Server, use the SQL Security Manager (refer to "Adding Groups (Users) with the SQL Security Manager," later in this chapter).

Integrated or mixed security setup is complete. The following sections cover steps 2 and 4 in more detail.

CONFIGURING THE SERVER FOR INTEGRATED AND MIXED SECURITY

Setting up the server for integrated or mixed security mode requires configuring the server. Take a look at the Security Options tab of the Server Configuration/Options dialog box (see Figure 10.5).

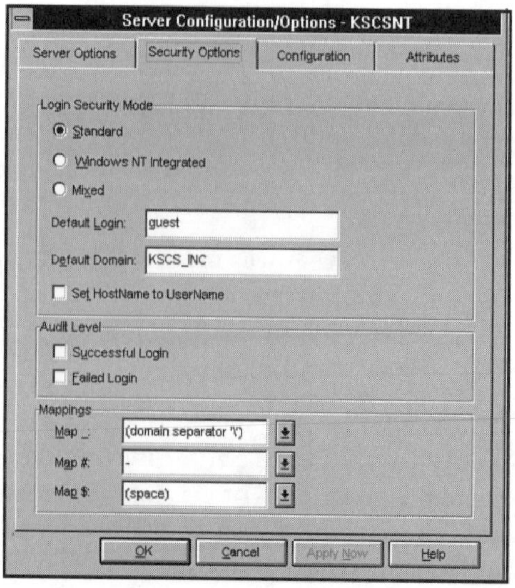

Figure 10.5.
The Security Options
tab in the Server
Configuration/Options
dialog box.

- **Login Security Mode**: To use integrated security, you must select the Windows NT Integrated or the Mixed radio button in the Login Security Mode panel.

  Only the sa can change the security mode of the server.

- **Default Login**: The default login name is the NT user name used as a default login ID for NT users logging in to SQL Server without a valid SQL Server login ID that matches their NT login name.

  NT users must be in the same group as the DEFAULT user in order to use the default login; otherwise, access is denied when they attempt to connect to the SQL Server.

- **Default Domain**: Set this option to the NT domain you are a member of or to the server name of the computer if you are not a member of an NT domain.

- **Set HostName to UserName**: Checking this option means that the user's network name will appear when you issue the stored procedure sp_who.

- **Audit Level—Successful Login and Failed Login**: Check either option (or both) to monitor successful and unsuccessful user logins. The audit messages are logged in the SQL Server error log and the Windows NT event log.

- **Mappings**: The mapping characters replace valid NT account characters, such as the domain separator \, that are illegal identifier characters in SQL Server, with valid SQL Server characters.

10

MANAGING USERS

Tip

If you are going to use integrated security, simplify your life and come up with a naming convention that uses valid SQL Server characters. Doing so can prevent possible account conversion problems.

The Apply Now button is new in version 6.x. Selecting Apply Now changes the security mode without requiring you to restart the server, which is required in older versions.

ADDING GROUPS (USERS) WITH THE SQL SECURITY MANAGER

The SQL Security Manager is a separate application and not part of the Enterprise Manager. The SQL Security Manager is located in the Microsoft SQL Server 6.0 or 6.5 program group.

Note

Only the sa or a member of the sa group can log on to SQL Server using the SQL Security Manager.

Using the SQL Security Manager is similar to using the Enterprise Manager (see Figure 10.6). You can view the Windows NT users and groups that currently have access to SQL Server by using the View option from the SQL Security Manager menu. Two types of privileges are available from the view option: sa and User. All Windows NT administrators have sa privileges with SQL Server. All other users added through the SQL Security Manager belong to the User privilege group.

Figure 10.6.
The SQL Security
Manager.

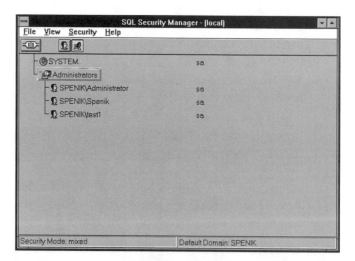

When using the SQL Security Manager, you cannot select individual Windows NT users to add—instead, Windows NT groups are added. Adding the group adds all the users in the group to SQL Server. To add a group with user permissions, perform the following from the SQL Security Manager:

1. Select View from the menu.
2. Select the User Privilege option.
3. Select the Security menu item and then select Grant New to display the Grant User Privilege dialog box (see Figure 10.7).
4. Select the group to add to SQL Server from the Grant Privilege panel in the Grant User Privilege dialog box. Use the Show checkboxes to display Local or Default NT groups.

Figure 10.7.
The Grant User
Privilege dialog box.

5. Select the Add Login IDs for Group Members checkbox. If the box is checked, a SQL Server login ID is created for each user in the group. If the box is not checked, the default user setup during security configuration is used.

6. Select the Add Users to Database checkbox to select a default database for each user.

7. Click the Grant button to transfer the selected Windows NT group to SQL Server. A dialog box appears, showing the status of the accounts transferred, such as the login IDs, database users, groups, and errors that occurred during the transfer.

Tip

Most errors are caused by invalid characters in the user name or group.

What happened? If the Add Login ID for Group Members checkbox was selected, the SQL Security Manager uses the Windows NT group and user account information to create SQL Server login IDs for each user in the selected NT group. The selected NT group and user names are added to the selected SQL Server default database. Removing the users from SQL Server is just as easy. Use the SQL Security Manager and, rather than selecting the Grant New option under the Security menu, select Revoke. The Revoke command removes all the users login IDs and the group from SQL Server. The system commands used to add and revoke users for integrated security are the extended stored procedures `xp_grantlogin` and `xp_revokelogin`. For more details on these commands and extended stored procedures, see Appendix B.

INTEGRATED SECURITY CHECKLIST

Following is a simple checklist to use to help set up integrated security:

CHECKLIST
☐ Running trusted connection protocol (named-pipes or multi-protocol).
☐ Configure SQL Server with integrated or mixed security. Add default user and map characters if necessary.
☐ Create Windows NT local or domain group for SQL Server using the NT User Manager.
☐ Add local Windows NT users and assign them to the new SQL Server group.
☐ Use the SQL Security Manager to create groups and login IDs on SQL Server.

CREATING DATABASE USERS

Once you have created a login ID for a user, you grant the login ID access to various databases by creating a database user for the login ID. A database user must be added and associated to the login ID in every database the login ID has access to, the exception being databases that have the user guest and that make use of aliases.

Note

When you create a login name, you automatically add the user to a database by selecting a default database for the user.

ADDING A USER TO A DATABASE

When you add a user to a database, you associate the login ID with the database user name and enable the login ID to access the database. There are several ways you can add a user to a database. You can add a login ID to one or more databases when you create the login ID by using the grid in the Manage Logins dialog box. To add the user to a database, check the database in the grid. When the login ID is added, the login ID and user name are added to each of the databases selected. To add a user to a database using the Manage User dialog box, perform the following steps using SQL Server Enterprise Manager:

1. Select the server and database for the new user.
2. Open the Manage menu from the Enterprise Manager menu bar.
3. Select Users to display the Manage Users dialog box (see Figure 10.8).

Figure 10.8.
The Manage Users
dialog box.

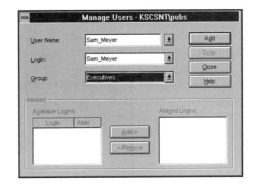

4. Add the necessary parameters to create the new user. Figure 10.8 shows the Manage User dialog box with the required parameters to create a SQL Server `pubs` database user named `Sam_Meyer`, with the login ID `Sam_Meyer`, who is a member of the group `Executives`.

5. To add the new user to the database, click the Add button. A dialog box prompts you to verify the login ID password. Enter the password for verification and click the OK button.

The following list describes the parameters in the Manage Users dialog box:

◆ **User Name**: The name of the user while he or she is in the database. The user name can be the same as the login name for the selected login ID or it can be different. The size and format of the user name must conform to the same rules as the login name. To add a new user, open the drop-down list box and select `<new user>`.

◆ **Login**: This drop-down list box contains the possible login IDs to associate with the database user.

◆ **Group**: The group to which the user will belong (the default is `public`).

The system stored procedure to add a new user to a database is `sp_adduser`, which has the following syntax:

```
sp_adduser login_id [, username [, groupname]]
```

When a new user is added to a database using the SQL Enterprise Manager or `sp_adduser`, an entry for the user is made in the `sysusers` table of the database to which the user was added. Figure 10.9 shows the results of the a `select * from sysusers` query. The column `uid` stands for *User Identifier* and shows the unique numbers within the database that represent the users. In Figure 10.9, notice that the `uid` of the group `Executives` is 16384, which is the starting `uid` for groups. A group's `uid` is greater than or equal to 16384, except for the `public` group, which always has a `uid` of 0. The column `gid` stands for *Group Identifier* and represents the group to which the user belongs. In Figure 10.9, notice that name `Sam_Meyer` has a `gid` of 16384, which corresponds to the `uid` 16384 of the group `Executives`. Figure 10.10 shows the relationship between the `suid` in `syslogins` and `sysusers`.

Figure 10.9.
A SQL query of the
sysusers table.

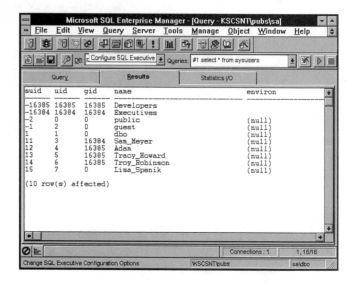

Figure 10.10.
The relationship
between syslogins *and*
sysusers.

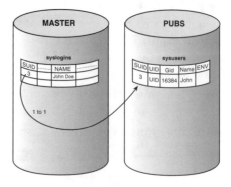

REMOVING A USER FROM A DATABASE

To remove a user from a database, use the Manage Users dialog box (refer back to Figure 10.8). Select the user to remove and click the Drop button. You are prompted by a confirmation dialog box. Click the OK button to drop the user from the database. The row in the `sysusers` table for the user is deleted.

The corresponding system stored procedure to drop a user from a database is `sp_dropuser`, which has the following syntax:

```
sp_dropuser User_Name
```

Understanding the guest User

A special user name, guest, can be added to a database to allow anyone with a valid SQL Server login to access the database. The guest user name is a member of the group public. Once a guest user has been added to a database, any individual with a valid SQL Server login—regardless of security mode—can access the database as the guest user. A guest user works as follows:

1. SQL Server checks to see whether the login ID has a valid user name or alias assigned. If so, it grants the user access to the database as the user name or aliases. If not, go to step 2.

2. SQL Server checks to see whether a guest user name exists. If so, the login ID is granted access to the database as guest. If the guest account does not exist, SQL Server denies access to the database.

Note

The guest user always has a uid of 2.

A guest user is added to the master database and the pubs database when the system is installed. SQL Server version 6.x prevents you from accidentally dropping the guest user from the master database. If you removed guest from the master database, only the sa user could log in to SQL Server! When users log in to SQL Server, they have access to the master database as the guest user. (Don't worry, the guest user has very few permissions in the master database.)

Using Aliases

What is an alias? An *alias* enables you to assign more than one login ID to a specific user name in a database. For example, suppose that you are running a bank and you have a database called BIG_BUCKS. You have a user name in the BIG_BUCKS database called banker. You also have three other SQL Server login IDs: banker1, banker2, and banker3, which perform the same function as the user banker. Instead of adding each login ID to the database, you alias the three users to the database user banker (see Figure 10.11).

In the database BIG_BUCKS, shown in Figure 10.11, a single entry is placed in the sysusers table for the user banker. When the three other users are aliased to the user banker, an entry is made in the database system table sysalternates for each login ID aliased. When one of the alias users tries to access the database, the table sysusers is scanned for the suid of the user. When the suid is not found, the sysalternates table is checked. If suid is found, the column altsuid in sysalternates is used as the suid to search the sysusers table for the correct uid.

Figure 10.11.
An example of an alias.

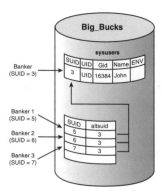

Aliases are typically used to assign more than one login ID as the DBO (database owner).

Note

The DBO can be assigned only to a single login ID. Using an alias is the only way to allow multiple logins to be DBOs.

Tip

If you use the DUMP and LOAD commands to move databases to a new server, the sysusers table travels with the database. The suids in the new server may not correctly match the suids in the database to the proper users. You can use aliases to remap object permissions in the moved database.

SQL Server 6.5 provides an alternative method to using aliases when you use the DUMP and LOAD commands to move a database: a system stored procedure called sp_change_users_login. The topics of mismatched login IDs and database user names, as well as sp_change_users_login, are discussed in "Suggested User Account Management Strategies," later in this chapter.

Version
6.5

ADDING AN ALIAS

Aliases can be assigned in several ways. To add an alias from the Manage Logins dialog box, follow these steps:

1. In the Database Access grid of the Manage Logins dialog box, select the database to which you want to add the login ID alias. For example, in Figure 10.12, the pubs database is selected.

2. Access the pull-down list in the Alias column and select the user name you want to alias. In Figure 10.12, the login ID Sam_Meyer is selected. You can alias Sam_Meyer to any of the users shown in the drop-down combo box (***Note:*** Do not alias to guest because anyone using a database without a user ID is automatically aliased to guest).

Figure 10.12.
Adding an alias using
the Database Access
grid in the Manage
Logins dialog box.

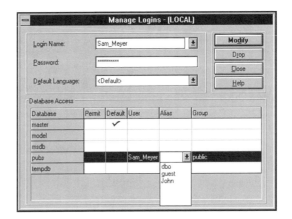

3. Click the Modify button if you are working with existing login IDs; click the Add button if you are adding a login ID.

To add an alias using the Manage Users dialog box, follow these steps:

1. Select the server, database, and user you want to alias to other users.

2. Copy the login IDs to alias using the Add-> button. In Figure 10.13, the user Lisa_Spenik has been selected in the pubs database. The logins Anne and Gary have been selected to be aliases of Lisa_Spenik.

Figure 10.13.
Adding an alias using
the Manage Users
dialog box.

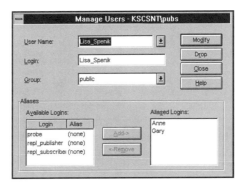

3. Click the Modify button if you are working with existing users; click the Add button if you are adding a user.

The system stored procedure to add aliases is `sp_addalias`, which has the following syntax:

```
sp_addalias login_id, user_name_in_database
```

Caution

Be careful when dropping from a database a user being used as an alias for other login IDs. When the user name is dropped from the database, the alias users lose access to the database.

VIEWING LOGIN ID, DATABASE USER, AND GROUP INFORMATION

Login ID, database user, and group information can be viewed in several ways. To see the current login IDs on a server, use the Enterprise Manager and select the server; then click the Logins folder. The user logins for the server are displayed as shown in Figure 10.14.

Figure 10.14.
The SQL Enterprise
Manager Logins folder.

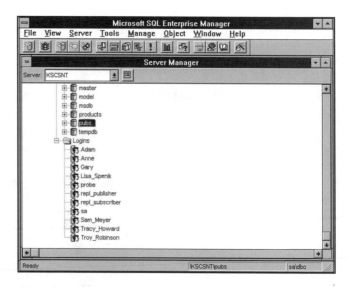

To see the current groups and users in a database, select the database and click the Groups/Users folder; a list of the database's groups is displayed. Click a group to see the users in that group. Figure 10.15 shows a drill down of groups and users.

Tip

To see detailed user information, double-click the folder to display the Manage Users dialog box (refer back to Figure 10.8).

Figure 10.15.
The SQL Enterprise
Manager Groups/Users
folder.

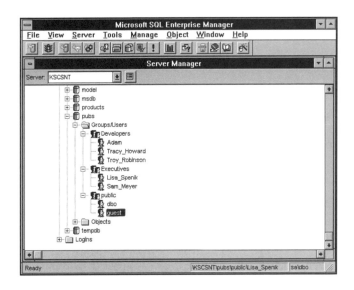

To see more detailed information for login IDs, use the Manage Logins dialog box (refer back to Figure 10.2). SQL Server 6.5 includes a new stored procedure called sp_helplogins, which has the following syntax:

```
sp_helplogins [Login_Name_Pattern]
```

The sp_helplogins procedure displays information about the current logins such as remote logins and database users and aliases. Output from the sp_helplogins stored procedure is shown in Figure 10.16.

For more detailed group information, use the Manage Groups dialog box (refer back to Figure 10.4). For information about database users or aliases, use the Manage Users dialog box (refer back to Figure 10.8).

The stored procedure sp_helpuser displays user information for a specific user or for all users in a database; the procedure has the following syntax:

```
sp_helpuser [user_name]
```

Figure 10.16.
Sample output from the
stored procedure
`sp_helplogins`.

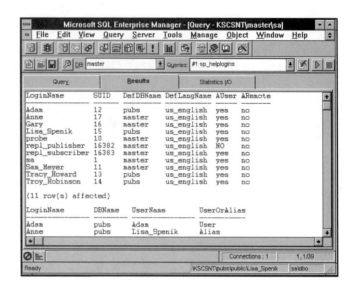

MODIFYING AND REMOVING LOGIN IDs

Once you have created a login ID, you can easily perform the following tasks:

◆ Change the password

◆ Add the login ID to a new database

◆ Remove the login ID from a database

◆ Alias the login ID to add a user in a database

Performing maintenance tasks requires using the Manage Logins dialog box (see Figure 10.17). The following sections explain how to change a password and drop a login ID.

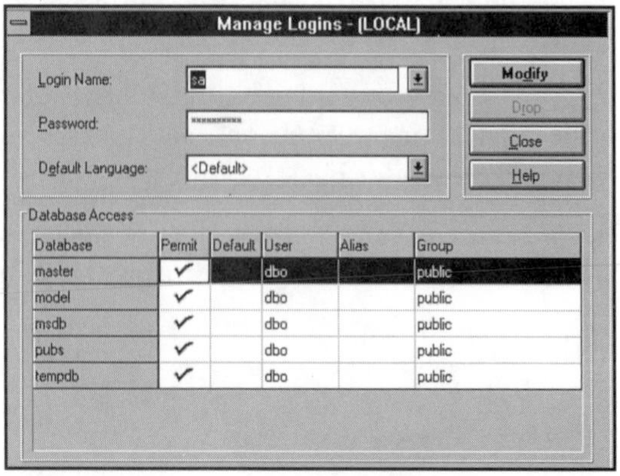

Figure 10.17.
The Manage Logins
dialog box.

CHANGE THE PASSWORD

To change the password for a login ID, select the login ID you want to change from the Login Name drop-down list box in the Manage Logins dialog box. Enter the new password in the Password text box and click the Modify button. You are prompted by the Confirm Password dialog box (see Figure 10.18).

Figure 10.18.
The Confirm Password
dialog box.

10

Enter the new password and click the OK button. The password has been changed.

Note

Users can change their own passwords, but only the sa can change another user's password.

The system stored procedure to change the password is sp_password, which has the following syntax:

```
sp_password old_password, new_password [, login_id]
```

Caution

I cannot begin to tell you how many "secure environments" I have walked into and then logged on to their secure SQL Server as the sa, using the NULL password. As stated in Chapter 6, "Installing or Upgrading SQL Server," always give the sa account a password. The environment is not secure when anyone who has ever used Microsoft SQL Server or Sybase SQL Server knows your sa password. If you are using integrated security, you do not have to give sa a password; however, if you are using standard or mixed security, *please do*! One last thing—don't forget the sa password. If you do, and you are using standard security mode, you must reinstall SQL Server.

REMOVING A LOGIN ID

To remove a login ID, select the login ID you want to change from the Login Name drop-down list box in the Manage Logins dialog box and click the Drop button. When you are prompted by the confirmation dialog box, click the OK button. The login ID is dropped.

Tip

Before you can drop a login ID with the Enterprise Manager, you must first drop and re-create any user-owned objects in the databases using another login ID. When a login ID is dropped using the Enterprise Manager, the login ID is removed from any databases to which it was explicitly granted access.

The system stored procedure to drop a login is `sp_droplogin`, which has the following syntax:

```
sp_droplogin Logon_name
```

Caution

This caution applies to users of SQL Server 4.2x. I am happy to say that the caution does not apply to SQL Server 6.x. With SQL Server 4.x, the stored procedure `sp_droplogin` *does not* check to see whether the login ID has been removed from all databases or whether it owns any objects. With SQL Server 6.x, `sp_droplogin` *does* check to see whether the login ID has been removed from all databases or whether it owns objects. However, I still recommend that you use the Enterprise Manager to drop user login IDs.

With SQL Server 4.x, *never* use `sp_droplogin`. Always use the SQL Administrator to drop user logins, for two reasons:

1. `sp_droplogin` does not check to see whether you have removed the user from all the databases. Because `sp_droplogin` does not check, you can drop a login ID from the system and leave a `sysusers` entry in another database. When the `suid` is reused later, the new user can automatically access any database left over from the previous login ID that used the same `suid`.

2. `sp_droplogin` does not check to see whether the login ID being dropped owns any database objects. Because `sp_droplogin` does not check for database objects, it is possible to leave database objects (such as tables and stored procedures) that have no owner. Even worse, these objects will be owned by the next login ID added.

SUGGESTED USER ACCOUNT MANAGEMENT STRATEGIES

Now that you know all about user management, what about some of the important maintenance and implementation issues: When should you use integrated security or standard security? What about user naming conventions? When should you use aliases? The following sections answers these question and present some suggested strategies to follow for user account management.

WHEN TO USE WHICH SECURITY MODE

If your organization is part of an NT domain or your users log in to a single NT server, consider using integrated security if you are running the proper network protocols. Your users will appreciate a single login name and password, and you can take advantage of login auditing. The downside is that anyone who is a Windows NT system administrator can get SQL Server administrator privileges. Remember that if you are *not* using the network protocols multi-protocol or named-pipes, you must use standard security.

LOGIN NAME CONVENTIONS

Come up with a standard convention for your login names, whether it is the user's first and last name, such as John_Doe, or an abbreviation, such as JohnD. Just be consistent.

DATABASE USER NAMES

It is nice that SQL Server allows you to have a different user name than the login ID in a database. However, I find that the database is easier to manage by keeping the two names the same.

HOW TO GROUP

Groups are very important to object security. Create groups that make sense. Grouping users by business function is a very good approach.

WHEN TO USE ALIASES

There are two cases in which I recommend using aliases:

- ◆ When you have a development database and you want all the objects created by the DBO, alias the login IDs to the DBO in the database.

◆ If you plan to share a database with another SQL Server by using the DUMP and LOAD commands. The login IDs (suid) for the two SQL Servers may not be the same or may have missing entries. When the system database table sysusers contains suids not found in the system table syslogins, the suids in sysusers are said to be *orphan users* because they do not have a corresponding entry in the syslogins table (that it, it is a referential integrity problem). Orphan users can occur when you transfer a database using DUMP and LOAD from one server to another or when you restore from an older database that contains suids that no longer exist on the current system.

Other issues that can arise when moving databases from one server to another are security and proper suid mappings. Because the sysusers table travels with the database when you use DUMP and LOAD, the DBA for the second server can have a difficult task of properly mapping his or her users' suids to those in the moved database. Suppose that, in the first server, the DBO has a suid of 10. However, on the second server, suid 10 maps to a business user who barely knows how to run a query. A big security problem: the business user has full database access! If you plan to share a database by using the DUMP and LOAD commands, set up user accounts on the first database as if they were groups (login IDs of developer and tester, for example) and then use aliases. For example, alias all users who are developers to the developer login ID. When you move the database, the second DBA can drop the improper aliases (the sysalternates table also travels) and then correctly alias the logins.

Version
6.5

SQL SERVER 6.5 ALTERNATIVE TO ALIASES FOR ORPHANED USERS

SQL Server 6.5 comes with a new stored procedure that can be used to correct the missing relationships between the syslogins and sysusers tables. The sp_change_users_login stored procedure can be used to list orphaned database users; it can also be used to reestablish the links between the syslogins and sysusers tables. sp_change_users_login corrects the link problem by adding new login IDs to the syslogins table or by updating the sysusers table with existing suids. The syntax for the command is as follows:

```
sp_change_users_login {'Auto_Fix' ¦ 'Report' ¦ 'Update_One'}
[,User_Name_Or_Pattern [, Login_Name]]
```

Use the 'Report' option to list the orphaned users in a database. To assign an orphaned user to an existing login ID, use the 'Update_One' option. To reestablish the links between the two tables, use the

'Auto_Fix' option. Be warned that when you use 'Auto_Fix', you must check the outcome with the 'Report' option. 'Auto_Fix' may make incorrect assumptions when reestablishing the link between sysusers and syslogins. The output from the execution of the following example is show in Figure 10.19.

```
sp_change_users_login 'Auto_Fix', 'Lisa%'
```

Figure 10.19.
Sample output
from the
sp_change_users_login
stored procedure.

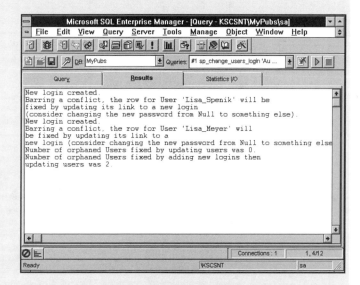

Caution: Although sp_change_users_login can correct missing links between the sysusers and syslogins tables, if cannot correct security problems of improperly mapped suids. Suppose that you decided to move a database from Server1 to Server2. On Server1, the DBO has a suid of 11. On Server2, suid 11 is assigned to a general user with limited database access. When you move the database from Server1 to Server2, the general user on Server2 becomes the DBO. sp_change_users_login does not report this type of problem because the suid of the database has a matching suid in the syslogins table.

BETWEEN THE LINES

Following are some important tips and tricks to keep in mind for user management:

◆ A login ID gives a user access to SQL Server.

◆ A database user name gives a SQL Server login access to the database.

◆ SQL Server for NT supports three security modes: standard, integrated, and mixed. The security mode influences the way user logins are added and maintained.

◆ SQL Server version 6.x encrypts passwords stored in `syslogins`.

◆ Create groups that match your business and place users in the groups accordingly. You can use groups to set up security in the database.

◆ A user always belongs to the system group `public` and can also belong to a single user-defined group.

◆ If you use integrated security mode, choose Windows NT user account names that make use of valid SQL Server characters to simplify adding users to SQL Server.

◆ Always assign a default database to a login ID so that the `master` database is not the default.

◆ If you plan to share a database with another server by using the `DUMP` and `LOAD` commands, add the minimum number of login IDs to the database and then use aliases.

◆ Always use the Enterprise Manager to drop login accounts.

◆ Always give the `sa` user a password. Otherwise, someone who knows the default Sybase and SQL Server `sa` password may illegally access your system someday.

◆ Do *not* forget the password for `sa`. If you do this in standard security mode, you will have to reinstall SQL Server.

SUMMARY

You should now have a good understanding of user management in SQL Server and how and when to use the different security modes. In the next chapter, you learn about database object permissions and how to assign them to users and groups.

- Levels of Security

- Security Hierarchy

- Permissions

- Beyond Security
  Basics: Suggested
  Strategies

- Between the Lines

- Summary

CHAPTER 11 *by Orryn Sledge*

Managing SQL Server Security

SQL Server provides built-in security and data protection. Its security features are trustworthy and relatively easy to administer. By taking advantage of SQL Server's security features, you can create a secure database that prevents unauthorized access and allows data modification to occur in a controlled and orderly manner.

LEVELS OF SECURITY

The term *security* is a broad term that carries different meanings depending on how it is applied. It can be applied to the following levels (see Figure 11.1):

◆ **Operating System**: To connect to the server, a user typically must go through some type of operating system login routine that validates system access.

◆ **SQL Server**: To connect to SQL Server, the user must have a valid SQL server user login (refer to Chapter 10, "Managing Users," for more information about user logins).

◆ **Database**: To access a database within SQL Server, the user must have been granted permission to the database (refer to Chapter 10 for more information about permitting access to a database).

◆ **Object** (table, view, or stored procedure): To access an object within a database, the user must be granted permission to the object.

When dealing with security, you spend the majority of your time working at the database and object level. Therefore, the remainder of this chapter concentrates on database and object security.

Figure 11.1.
The four levels of
security.

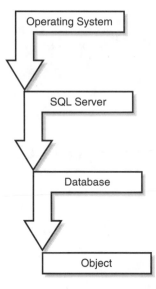

SECURITY HIERARCHY

SQL Server's security mechanism is hierarchically based. Within the hierarchy exists four types of users: the system administrator, database owners, database object owners, and other users of the database (see Figure 11.2).

Figure 11.2.
Security hierarchy.

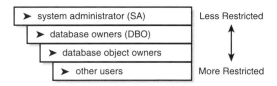

SYSTEM ADMINISTRATOR

The system administrator (login ID sa) is "the almighty one" who has unrestricted access to SQL Server. Any SQL Server statement or command can be executed by the sa. The sa can also grant permissions to other users.

DATABASE OWNERS (DBO)

The database owner (DBO) is the user who created the database or has had ownership assigned to him or her. The DBO has complete access to all objects within his or her database and has the ability to assign object permissions to other users.

Tip

> To determine the owner of a database, use sp_helpdb [*database name*] or double-click the database name in the Enterprise Manager (refer to Chapter 9, "Managing Databases," for more information on managing databases).

DATABASE OBJECT OWNERS

The person who creates the database object is considered the owner of the object and is called the *database object owner*. SQL Server assumes that if you have the necessary permission to create the object, you are automatically given all permissions to that object (SELECT, UPDATE, INSERT, DELETE, REFERENCE, and EXECUTE). With the exception of the database object owner and the sa, no one else can access an object until the appropriate permission is granted.

Tip

Use sp_help [*object name*] to determine the owner of an object within a database.

There is no SQL Server command to transfer ownership of an object within a database. To get around this limitation, the sa or *existing* database object owner must drop the object and the *new* database object owner must re-create the object.

To simplify object access, the DBO should create all objects within the database. This automatically makes the DBO the database object owner.

OTHER USERS

Other users must be granted object permissions (SELECT, UPDATE, INSERT, DELETE, REFERENCE, and EXECUTE) to operate within the database. The system administrator can also grant statement permissions to other users so that they can create and drop objects within the database.

PERMISSIONS

A *permission* allows someone to do something within a database. There are two types of permissions: *object* and *statement*. As a DBA, you will probably spend more time with object permissions. Object permissions control who can access and manipulate data in tables and views and who can run stored procedures. Statement permissions control who can drop and create objects within a database.

SQL Server uses the commands GRANT and REVOKE to manage permissions.

◆ GRANT: When you GRANT a permission to an object, you allow someone to perform an action against the object (for example, SELECT, UPDATE, INSERT, DELETE, EXECUTE). When you GRANT permission to a statement, you allow someone to run the statement (for example, CREATE TABLE).

◆ REVOKE: When you REVOKE a permission from an object, you prevent someone from performing an action against the object (for example, SELECT, UPDATE, INSERT, DELETE, EXECUTE). When you REVOKE permission from a statement, you take away a user's capability to run the statement (for example, CREATE TABLE).

OBJECT PERMISSIONS

Object permissions control access to objects within SQL Server. You can grant and revoke permissions to tables, table columns, views, and stored procedures through the Enterprise Manager or through system procedures. When a user wants to perform an action against an object, he or she must have the appropriate permission. For example, when a user wants to SELECT * FROM table1, he or she must have SELECT permission for the table. Table 11.1 summarizes the different types of object permissions.

TABLE 11.1. SUMMARY OF OBJECT PERMISSIONS.

Object Type	Possible Actions
table	SELECT, UPDATE, DELETE, INSERT, REFERENCE
column	SELECT, UPDATE
view	SELECT, UPDATE, INSERT, DELETE
stored procedure	EXECUTE

GRANTING OBJECT PERMISSIONS

Perform the following steps to grant object permissions:

1. From the Enterprise Manager, access the Server Manager dialog box, select a server, open the Databases folder, select a database, and select the Objects folder.

2. From the Object menu, select Permissions.

3. Select the By Object tab or the By User tab. The By Object tab allows you to select an object and manage each user's permissions to the object. The By User tab allows you to select a user or group and manage the user's or group's permissions to several objects.

4. If you selected the **By Object tab**:

   From the Object list, select an object (table, view, or stored procedure) to work with. After you select the appropriate object, a list of groups and users is displayed along with the corresponding permissions to the object (see Figure 11.3).

   If you selected the **By User tab**:

   From the User/Group list, select a user or group to work with. After you select the user or group, a list of objects and their corresponding permissions is displayed (see Figure 11.4).

Figure 11.3.
Granting object
permissions using the
Object Permissions
dialog box.

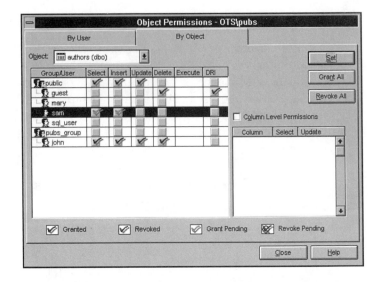

Figure 11.4.
Granting object
permissions by user.

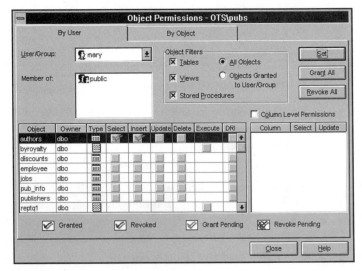

5. If you selected the **By Object tab**:

   To grant all permissions to all users and groups, click the Grant All button.

   If you selected the **By User tab**:

   To grant all permissions to all objects, click the Grant All button.

6. For **either the By Object tab or By User tab**:

   To grant individual permissions to a group or user, select the appropriate row and click the appropriate checkbox.

7. For **either the By Object tab or the By User tab**:

   To grant column-level permissions to a table or view, select Column Level Permissions and click the appropriate checkbox.

8. Click the Set button to commit any changes that have been made.

REVOKING OBJECT PERMISSIONS

Perform the following steps to revoke object permissions:

1. From the Enterprise Manager, access the Server Manager dialog box, select a server, open the Databases folder, select a database, and select the Objects folder.

2. From the Object menu, select Permissions.

3. Select the By Object tab or the By User tab. The By Object tab enables you to select an object and manage each user's permissions to the object. The By User tab enables you to select a user or group and manage the user's or group's permissions to several objects.

4. If you selected the **By Object tab**:

   From the Object list, select an object (table, view, or stored procedure) to work with. After you select the appropriate object, a list of groups and users is displayed along with the corresponding permissions to the object (see Figure 11.5).

Figure 11.5.
*Revoking object
permissions by object.*

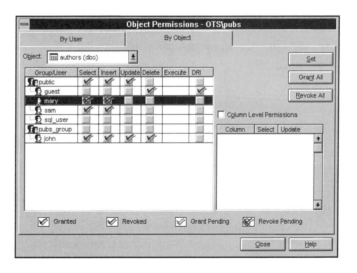

If you selected the **By User tab**:

From the User/Group list, select a user or group to work with. After you select the user or group, a list of objects and their corresponding permissions is displayed (see Figure 11.6).

Figure 11.6.
Revoking object
permissions by user.

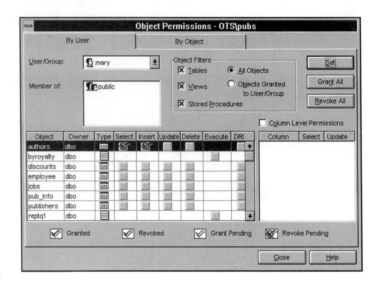

5. If you selected the **By Object tab**:

   To revoke all permissions to all users and groups, click the Revoke All button.

   If you selected the **By User tab**:

   To revoke all permissions to all objects, click the Revoke All button.

6. For **either the By Object tab or the By User tab**:

   To revoke individual permissions to an object, select the appropriate row and click the appropriate checkbox.

7. For **either the By Object tab or the By User tab**:

   To revoke column-level permissions to a table or view, select Column Level Permissions and click the appropriate checkbox.

8. Click the Set button to commit any changes that have been made.

TIPS FOR MANAGING OBJECT PERMISSIONS

Use the following tips to help manage object permissions:

◆ When an object (table, view, or stored procedure) is first created, only the creator of the object or the sa can access and manipulate the object. Object permissions must be assigned to users so that they can access the object.

◆ Object and statement permissions take effect immediately. Unlike other systems, a user does not have to log out and log back in to SQL Server for the change to take effect.

◆ Permissions are object specific, not database specific; therefore, each object (table, view, or stored procedure) must be assigned the appropriate permission.

◆ By default, the sa automatically has all permissions for all objects; therefore, you do not need to assign permissions to the sa.

◆ With the Enterprise Manager, you can limit the type of object to be displayed for an individual user or group by making the appropriate choice in
the Objects Filters area of the dialog box. For example, to look at only table
permissions assigned to the public group, select the Tables option in Object
Filters and deselect the other options (see Figure 11.7). To look at only
stored procedure permissions, select the Stored Procedures option in Object
Filters and deselect the other options (see Figure 11.8).

Figure 11.7.
*Viewing permissions
through object filters
(table filter).*

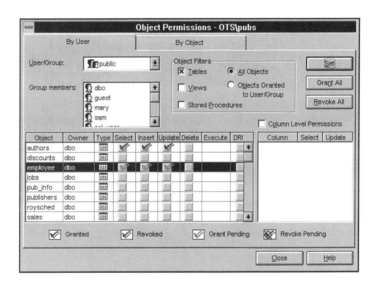

Figure 11.8.
*Viewing permissions
through object filters
(stored-procedure
filter).*

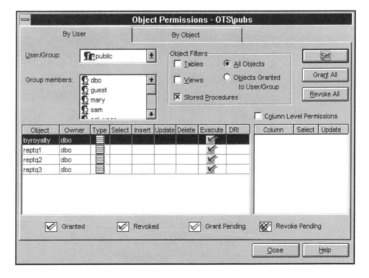

◆ If you are logged in as sa or the database owner, you can use SETUSER to impersonate another user within the system. This is an easy way to test changes without having to log out and log back in. Also, you do not have to know the password of the user you are trying to impersonate. Look at the following syntax:

```
SETUSER ['username' [WITH NORESET]]
```

If the WITH NORESET parameter *was not* specified, you can issue the SETUSER statement without any parameters to revert back to the profile of the logged-in user. If the WITH NORESET parameter *was* specified, you can reopen the database (USE database_name) to revert back to the profile of the logged-in user.

If you forget who you are impersonating, you can use the user_name() function to determine the active user profile, as in the following syntax:

```
SELECT user_name()
```

◆ Be sure to save an object's permissions before you drop and re-create a table, view, or stored procedure. All permissions to the object are removed when it is dropped and SQL Server does not prompt you to save permissions to the object. An easy way to save the permissions to an object is to select the object from the Enterprise Manager and then, from the Object menu, select Generate SQL Scripts. From the Generate SQL Scripts dialog box, select the Permissions checkbox and generate the script. After you re-create the object, you can apply the script to restore permissions.

PERMISSION DIFFERENCES BETWEEN VERSIONS 6.0 AND 6.5

When assigning and revoking permission in version 6.0, it was important to keep in mind the order in which the assignment occured. The order in which permissions were assigned determined a user's access to an object. If the order of permission assignment was not properly followed, it would often lead to undesirable results. Consider the following:

1. Grant the SELECT permission to the authors table for Joe.

2. Revoke the SELECT permission to the authors table from the public group (by default, Joe is a member of the public group).

In version 6.0, when Joe tried to issue a SELECT against the authors table, he was denied access because the SELECT permission was revoked from the public group *after* the SELECT permissions were granted to Joe. In version 6.5, Joe can still access the authors table because the SELECT permission granted in step 1 still allows Joe access to the object.

CORRESPONDING TRANSACT SQL COMMANDS TO MANAGE OBJECT PERMISSIONS

The following command syntax can also be used to manage object permissions.

TO ADD OBJECT PERMISSIONS (VERSION 6.5):

```
GRANT {ALL [column_list]¦ permission_list [column_list]}
ON {table_name [(column_list)] ¦ view_name [(column_list)] ¦
stored_procedure_name} TO {PUBLIC ¦ name_list } [WITH GRANT OPTION]
```

TO ADD OBJECT PERMISSIONS (VERSION 6.0):

```
GRANT {ALL ¦ permission_list}
ON {table_name [(column_list)] ¦ view_name [(column_list)] ¦
stored_procedure_name ¦ extended_stored_procedure_name}
TO {PUBLIC ¦ name_list}
```

Note

11

In SQL Server version 6.5, the GRANT statement has been enhanced to conform to ANSI-SQL standards. The GRANT statement now provides ANSI column-level grants (previous versions provided a non-ANSI standard syntax); through WITH GRANT OPTION, permissions can be granted to other users.

For example, the following GRANT statement uses the ANSI column-level syntax to grant mary the permission to SELECT the au_id column in the authors table:

```
GRANT SELECT (au_id) ON authors to mary
```

Using non-ANSI SQL (versions 6.x, 4.2x), the following example grants mary the permission to SELECT the au_id column in the authors table (this example has the same effect as the preceding example, it just uses a different syntax):

```
GRANT SELECT ON authors(au_id) to mary
```

With version 6.5, you can now grant a permission to a user and through WITH GRANT OPTION, that user can in turn grant the permission to another user.

For example, the following statement grants the SELECT permission for the authors table to mary:

```
GRANT SELECT ON authors to mary WITH GRANT OPTION
```

User mary can, in turn, grant the SELECT permission to user sam:

GRANT SELECT ON authors to sam

User sam is now granted the SELECT permission for the authors table.

The GRANT enhancements in version 6.5 are available only when using the GRANT statement; they are not available when graphically managing security from the Enterprise Manager.

Version
6.5

To REMOVE OBJECT PERMISSIONS (VERSION 6.5):

```
REVOKE [GRANT OPTION FOR] {ALL ¦ permission_list } [(column_list)]
ON { table_name [(column_list)] ¦ view_name [(column_list)] ¦
stored_procedure_name} FROM {PUBLIC ¦ name_list ¦ role_name} [CASCADE]
```

To REMOVE OBJECT PERMISSIONS (VERSION 6.0):

```
REVOKE {ALL ¦ permission_list}
ON {table_name [(column_list)] ¦ view_name [(column_list)] ¦
stored_procedure_name ¦ extended_stored_procedure_name}
FROM {PUBLIC ¦ name_list}
```

Version
6.5

Note

In SQL Server version 6.5, the REVOKE statement has been enhanced to conform to ANSI-SQL standards. The REVOKE statement now provides the GRANT OPTION FOR and CASCADE syntax. When revoking a permission that was granted through the WITH GRANT OPTION, you must use the CASCADE option in conjunction with the REVOKE statement.

These version 6.5 REVOKE enhancements are available only when using the REVOKE statement; they are not available when graphically managing security from the Enterprise Manager.

To VIEW PERMISSIONS BY OBJECT OR BY USER:

```
sp_helprotect objectname [, username]
```

STATEMENT PERMISSIONS

Statement permissions control who can drop and create objects within a database. Only the sa or database owner can administer statement permissions. I advise prudence in granting access to statement permissions such as CREATE DATABASE, DUMP

DATABASE, and DUMP TRANSACTION. Usually, it is better to let the sa or database owner manage these statements. Following is a list of statement permissions that can be granted or revoked:

◆ CREATE DATABASE: Creates a database. This permission can be granted only by the sa and only to users in the master database.

◆ CREATE DEFAULT: Creates a default value for a table column.

◆ CREATE PROCEDURE: Creates a stored procedure.

◆ CREATE RULE: Creates a table column rule.

◆ CREATE TABLE: Creates a table.

◆ CREATE VIEW: Creates a view.

◆ DUMP DATABASE: Dumps the database (backup database) to a dump device.

◆ DUMP TRANSACTION: Dumps the transaction log to a dump device.

GRANTING STATEMENT PERMISSIONS

Perform the following steps to grant statement permissions:

1. From the Enterprise Manager, access the Server Manager dialog box, select a server, and double-click a database.

2. Select the Permissions tab. Existing permissions are indicated with checkmarks (see Figure 11.9).

3. Select the appropriate user and statement permission until a green check appears in the checkbox.

4. Click OK to commit any changes that have been made.

Figure 11.9.
Granting statement
permissions.

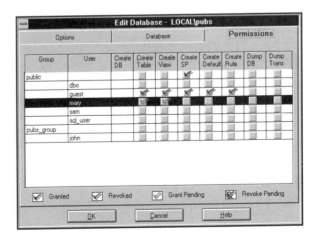

Note

The CREATE DB permission can be granted only by the sa and only to
users in the master database.

REVOKING STATEMENT PERMISSIONS

Perform the following steps to revoke statement permissions:

1. From the Enterprise Manager, access the Server Manager dialog box, select
   a server, and double-click a database.
2. Select the Permissions tab. Existing permissions are indicated with
   checkmarks (see Figure 11.10).

Figure 11.10.
Revoking statement
permissions.

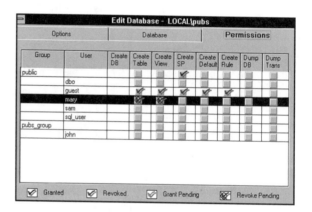

3. Select the appropriate user and statement permission until a red circle and
   slash appears in the checkbox.
4. Click OK to commit any changes that have been made.

CORRESPONDING TRANSACT SQL COMMANDS TO MANAGE STATEMENT PERMISSIONS

The following command syntax can also be used to manage statement permissions.

TO ADD STATEMENT PERMISSIONS:

```
GRANT {ALL ¦ statement_list}
TO {PUBLIC ¦ name_list}
```

TO REMOVE STATEMENT PERMISSIONS:

```
REVOKE {ALL ¦ statement_list}
FROM {PUBLIC ¦ name_list}
```

To view statement permissions by user or group:

```
sp_helprotect username
```

Beyond Security Basics: Suggested Strategies

In addition to object and statement permissions, you can combine different components within SQL Server to facilitate administration and provide improved security. Following is a list of suggested security strategies:

◆ Group-based security management

◆ Views for data security

◆ Stored procedures for data security

◆ Triggers for audit trails

Group-Based Security Management

In the corporate environment, users often work in groups. People in these groups require similar permissions to the database. Whenever multiple users require similar permissions, you should use group-based security. With group-based security, you reduce the number of GRANT and REVOKE statements that must be maintained (refer to Chapter 10, "Managing Users," for more information on the creation and management of groups).

Before diving headfirst into group-based security management, you should keep in mind the following points:

◆ A user can belong to only one user-defined group per database plus the public group (a user automatically becomes part of the public group when he or she is permitted access to the database). From a maintenance standpoint, this limitation may result in a less-than-optimal security strategy. You may want to assign a user to a user-defined group that gives him or her the majority of his or her permissions and then grant the user additional individual permissions.

◆ When everyone in a database needs the same permission to the same object, use the public group. When you grant or revoke a permission to the public group, everyone feels the effect. This is often an easy way to streamline security administration.

◆ When a user is assigned to a group other than the public group, it appears that the user is no longer a member of the public group. Don't worry—the user is still a member of the public group! Any permissions assigned to the public group impact all users within the database.

VIEWS FOR DATA SECURITY

Views help control data security for the following reasons:

◆ A view can limit the amount of data a user can see and modify. To the user, a view looks and acts like a real table, even though he or she may be working with a subset of the data. Behind the scenes, a view is a virtual table that defines the presentation and manipulation of the actual table(s).

◆ A user only needs permissions to the view, not to the table(s) that make up the view.

USING VIEWS FOR COLUMN-LEVEL SECURITY

Often, you use a view when a user needs access to a table but, for security reasons, you want to restrict access to certain columns (such as salary data) within the table. By using a view, you can easily restrict access to sensitive data.

Syntax:

```
CREATE VIEW [owner.]view_name
[(column_name [, column_name]...)]
[WITH ENCRYPTION]
AS select_statement [WITH CHECK OPTION]
```

The following listing shows the schema for the employee table:

```
employee_ssn char (9)
name char (35)
address char (35)
city char (35)
state char (35)
zip char (35)
salary money
last_updated_by char (50)
last_update_datetime datetime
```

For example, to prohibit access to the employee_ssn, salary, last_updated_by, and last_update_datetime columns in the employee table, use the following syntax:

```
CREATE VIEW  employee_view AS
SELECT name, address, city, state, zip
FROM employee
```

When the user issues SELECT * FROM employee_view, he or she gets back only the following columns:

```
name
address
city
state
zip
```

To users, the view looks like a real table except that they never see the employee_ssn, salary, last_updated_by, and last_update_datetime columns. If they can't see it, they can't modify it.

USING VIEWS FOR ROW-LEVEL AND COLUMN-LEVEL SECURITY

A simple way to implement row-level security is to add a WHERE clause to the CREATE VIEW statement. For example, use the following syntax to create a view that limits column and row access:

```
CREATE VIEW  employee_view_by_state AS
SELECT name, address, city, state, zip
FROM employee
WHERE state = 'VA' OR state = 'MA'
```

When users issue this statement, they see only the employees with a state code of VA or MA:

```
SELECT * FROM employee_view_by_state
```

Tip

To further ensure data security and to prevent typing errors, you can add the WITH CHECK OPTION to the CREATE VIEW statement. The WITH CHECK OPTION is new to SQL Server 6.x.

The WITH CHECK OPTION prevents users from inserting rows or updating columns that do not conform to the WHERE clause, as in the following example:

```
CREATE VIEW  employee_view_by_state AS
SELECT name, address, city, state, zip
FROM employee
WHERE state = 'VA' OR state = 'MA'
WITH CHECK OPTION
```

With this view, users can only add rows with a VA or MA state code; they can only update a state code to MA or VA. If users try to change the state code to something other than VA or MA, they receive the following message:

```
Msg 550, Level 16, State 2
The attempted insert or update failed because the target view either
specifies WITH CHECK OPTION or spans a view which specifies WITH CHECK
OPTION and one or more rows resulting from the operation did not qualify
under the CHECK OPTION constraint.
Command has been aborted.
```

HOW VIEWS AND PERMISSIONS WORK TOGETHER

When you grant object permissions to a view, you do not have to grant permissions to the underlying tables in the view. Therefore, users can SELECT employee data from the employee view, even though they do not have SELECT permission for the employee table. This feature can simplify administration when the view consists of multiple tables.

Tip

You may be wondering, "Why not use column-level permissions to prevent access to the `employee_ssn`, `salary`, `last_updated_by`, and `last_update_datetime` columns?" Good question! Both views and column-level permissions can prevent users from accessing restricted columns.

The reason for using a view rather than column-level security is that the view allows a user to issue the `SELECT *` statement without receiving error messages while still providing column-level security. Consider the following examples:

Example A:

John's `SELECT` permission has been revoked from the `employee_ssn` column in the `employee` table. When John issues `SELECT * FROM employee`, he receives the following error message:

```
Msg 230, Level 14, State 1
SELECT permission denied on column employee_ssn of object employee, data-
base xxx, owner dbo
```

To avoid the error message, John must explicitly name each column in the `SELECT` statement.

Example B:

A view has been developed for John to use. The view does not include the `employee_ssn` column. John can issue a `SELECT *` statement against the view and he will see only the columns specified in the view. He does not receive any error messages.

STORED PROCEDURES FOR DATA SECURITY

The advantage of using stored procedures to access and modify data is that users only need `EXECUTE` permission to run a stored procedure; they do not need access to the tables and views that make up the stored procedure. This alleviates the headache of assigning permissions to all underlying tables and views referenced within a stored procedure. The following syntax is an example of a stored procedure that returns all rows in the `employee` table:

```
CREATE PROCEDURE usp_employee AS
SELECT * FROM employee
```

To run the procedure, the user needs only `EXECUTE` permission for `usp_employee`. The user does *not* need the `SELECT` permission for the `employee` table.

GOING TO EXTREMES (BUT IT MAY BE WORTH IT!)

You can really clamp down on end-user data modifications by implementing stored procedures to handle *all* data modifications. To implement this strategy, you must design your applications to use only stored procedures and not embedded SQL to handle data modifications. Next, you must revoke all UPDATE, DELETE, and INSERT (and maybe even SELECT) privileges to *all* tables and views in the database. End users are now denied access whenever they try to modify data. For this approach to be successful, it requires extensive use of stored procedures, careful planning, and tight coordination between the application developers and the DBA.

TRIGGERS FOR AUDIT TRAILS

Triggers are comprised of Transact SQL statements that automatically execute when a table is modified through INSERT, UPDATE, or DELETE statements. Because a trigger is automatically executed, it can be a useful facility for auditing data changes. Additionally, you do not have to grant a user the privilege to execute a trigger.

An often-used type of trigger is one that tracks who made the last change to a table and when the change occurred. To track this information, use the following syntax:

```
CREATE TRIGGER tiu_employee ON dbo.employee
FOR INSERT,UPDATE
AS
UPDATE employee
SET employee.last_updated_by = USER_NAME(),
employee.last_update_datetime = GETDATE()
FROM inserted,employee
WHERE inserted.employee_ssn = employee.employee_ssn
```

Whenever an INSERT or UPDATE statement is run against the employee table in this example, the column last_updated_by is set to the name of the user who made the change and the column last_update_datetime is set to the time the change was made.

Caution

BCP bypasses triggers! Therefore, any audit trail that is maintained through a trigger must be manually updated after using BCP.

11

MANAGING SQL SERVER SECURITY

BETWEEN THE LINES

Following are some important notes to remember when managing security:

◆ Use the Enterprise Manager or Transact SQL commands to grant and revoke permissions. For ease of use, the Enterprise Manager is generally preferred over Transact SQL commands.

◆ When an object (table, view, or stored procedure) is first created, only the creator of the object, the sa, or the database owner can access and manipulate the object. Object permissions must be assigned to users so that they can access the object.

◆ Object and statement permissions take effect immediately. Unlike other systems, a user does not have to log out and log back in to SQL Server for the change to take effect.

◆ Permissions are object specific, not database specific. Therefore, each object (table, view, or stored procedure) must be assigned the appropriate permission.

◆ By default, the sa automatically has all permissions to all objects. You do not have to assign permissions to the sa.

◆ Use SETUSER to impersonate another user within the system. This is an easy way to test permission changes without having to log out and log in again.

◆ Use groups to implement security, but don't forget that a user can belong to only one user-defined group (the user also belongs to the public group).

◆ Use the public group to assign object permissions to a table, view, or stored procedure to which everyone needs access.

◆ Use views to control column and row access.

◆ Use stored procedures to control data modifications.

◆ Use triggers for audit trails.

SUMMARY

You now should have a good understanding of object and database security. By having a solid understanding of SQL Server's security architecture, you can lock down your data and ward off unauthorized data changes. In the next chapter, you discover how to implement data replication.

CHAPTER 12

by Mark Spenik

Replication

One of the exciting new features that first shipped with SQL Server version 6.0 and that has been enhanced in version 6.5 is *data replication*.

Note

I throw in the fact that the data replication feature ships with the standard product because several other RDBMS vendors treat replication as a separate product for which you must pay extra.

In a nutshell, *replication* is the capability to reliably duplicate data from a source database to one or more destination databases. Using Microsoft SQL Server replication, you can automatically distribute read-only transaction-based data from one SQL Server to many different SQL Servers through ODBC (Open Database Connectivity). SQL Server 6.5 extends replication by allowing you to replicate non-SQL Server ODBC sources such as an Oracle RDBMS or a Microsoft Access database. When would you want to use SQL Server replication? Here are some examples:

◆ To distribute the workload across servers (such as moving ad-hoc query and reporting capability from a source server).

◆ To move specific subsets of data (such as a company department or one month's worth of data) from a main central server.

◆ When you have a central database that is updated and the updates must be moved out to other databases (such as a department store changing prices for an item).

◆ Environments in which several servers are importing similar flat-file information. Use a central database to import the flat file and replicate the information to the other sites.

SQL Server replication uses a loose consistency distributed data model. *Loose consistency* means that the data synchronization between the source and destination server does not occur simultaneously. Before going into more detail, look at another distributed data model: tight consistency. A *tight consistency* distributed data model can be accomplished with SQL Server using two-phase commits. In a tight consistency model, all transactions are committed or rolled back on all the servers so that the data is in synch 100 percent of the time. In a loose consistency model, transactions are committed or rolled back on a source server. The transactions on the source server are then replicated asynchronously to subscribing servers. The big difference between the tight consistency model and the loose consistency model is that, on the loose consistency model, there is some lag time between when changes are made to the source server and when they are replicated to the destination servers (that is, the databases are temporarily out of synch).

SQL Server replication is not designed to be used in a hot backup server situation (that is, for another machine to be used when the primary machine goes down). The loose consistency model used by SQL Server replication does not keep the two servers "in synch" at all times.

REPLICATION OVERVIEW

SQL Server can perform replication by using the existing transaction log. If a table is marked for replication, the changes made to the table are automatically replicated to other servers. It sounds simple, but in reality, the replication process is a little complicated. Before getting into the details of replication, it is important to understand some of the terminology used when discussing SQL Server replication. In Figure 12.1, SQL Server A is replicating data from the pubs database to several other servers. Using Figure 12.1, review the terminology used in SQL Server replication defined in the following sections.

Figure 12.1.
Overview of replication.

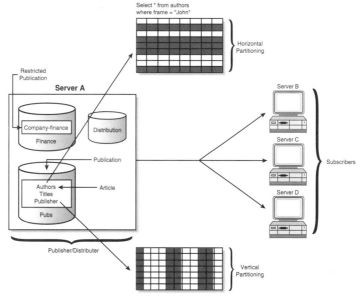

PUBLISH AND SUBSCRIBE

SQL Server replication uses a *publish and subscribe* metaphor. Servers publish publications to which other servers can subscribe. A SQL Server that makes data available to other servers for subscribing purposes is called a *publisher*. For example, Server A in Figure 12.1 is a publisher. A SQL Server that subscribes to a publication published by another SQL Server is said to be a *subscriber* (an example of a subscription server is Server B in Figure 12.1). A SQL Server that contains the distribution database is said to be a *distributor* (the distribution server is Server A in Figure 12.1).

PUBLICATION AND ARTICLES

A publisher publishes a collection of one or more articles called a *publication*. The publication shown in Figure 12.1 contains the authors, titles, and publishers article. An *article* is the basic unit of replication and can be a table or a subset of a table.

Note

Articles are always associated with a publication and cannot be published by themselves.

Publications can contain one or more of the following:

◆ Tables
◆ Vertically partitioned tables
◆ Horizontally partitioned tables
◆ Horizontally and vertically partitioned tables

A *vertical partitioned table* is an article that uses a filter to select only certain columns of a table. A *horizontal partitioned table* is an article that uses a filter to select only specific rows in the table.

The following cannot be published:

◆ The `model`, `tempdb`, and `msdb` databases
◆ The system tables in the `master` database
◆ The SQL Server `identity` columns and `timestamp` columns
◆ Tables without a primary key (a subscriber table that is populated with a snapshot replication process does not require a primary key)

Version
6.5

In SQL Server 6.5, data replication for text and image datatypes are supported with fewer restrictions then in SQL Server 6.0. See the Microsoft documentation for the exact restrictions on image and text datatypes.

SQL Server replication provides a level of security. For example, publications can be selectively marked `restricted` or `unrestricted` to different subscribing servers. In Figure 12.1, Server B has been restricted from viewing the `company_finance` publication, which is marked *restricted*.

Note

Subscribing servers can see only the publications to which they have access.

SERVER ROLES

SQL Server can play one or more of the following roles during the replication process:

- **Publisher.** A publisher server is responsible for maintaining its source databases, making the data available for replication, and sending the data to the distribution database to be replicated to subscribing servers.
- **Subscriber.** A subscriber server is a server that receives and maintains published data.
- **Distributor.** The distribution server maintains the distribution database, which is responsible for the store and forward capabilities of SQL Server replication. The job of the distribution server is to replicate data from the distribution database to the appropriate subscribing servers.

Non-SQL Server systems such as Oracle and Microsoft Access can only be subscribers.

REPLICATION MODELS

SQL Server can participate in one or more replication roles. For example, in many cases, a publication server also serves as a distribution server and can also subscribe to other publications from other publishers (in which case, the same server that was acting as a publisher and distributor is also acting as a subscriber). When setting up replication, there are several publisher and subscriber models you can use. Figure 12.1 is an example of a single publisher server providing information to multiple subscribers. Figure 12.2 shows a single publisher server using a distribution server to replicate data to subscribers.

Figure 12.2.
Replication model: a single publisher using a distribution server.

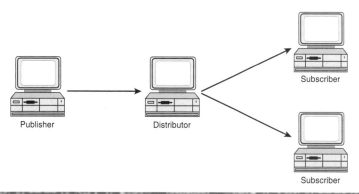

Publisher   Distributor   Subscriber

Subscriber

12

REPLICATION

The replication model in Figure 12.3 shows multiple publishers and multiple subscribers.

Figure 12.3.
Replication model:
multiple publishers
and multiple
subscribers.

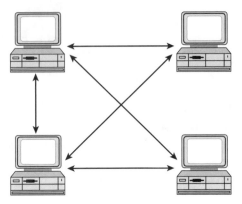

Another replication model, similar to the one shown in Figure 12.3, is multiple publishers to a single subscriber. The important point to understand is that there are many ways to set up SQL Server replication. Study the various replication models and plan before implementing.

Tip

Microsoft SQL Server documentation covers the different replication models in much more detail. Make sure that you review the replication chapters before implementing replication.

WALKING THROUGH THE REPLICATION PROCESS

Now that you have a general understanding of replication terminology, walk through the SQL Server replication process using Figure 12.4.

To begin the overview of SQL Server replication, assume that Server A has published the entire pubs database in a publication titled MyPubs for replication. Server A is also the distribution server. Before you begin your walk through, you need to learn about some of the components that make up SQL Server replication:

◆ **Log reader process.** The *log reader* process searches the transaction log of published databases for transaction log entries marked for replication. The log reader process moves the marked transactions to the distribution database.

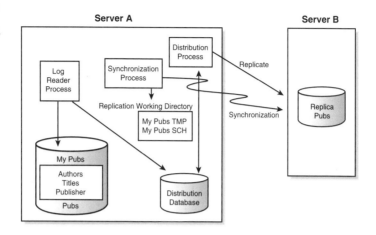

Figure 12.4.
An overview of the SQL
Server replication
process.

◆ **Distribution database.** The *distribution database* stores all the transactions to be replicated to subscribing servers and acts as a store-and-forward database for replicated transactions. Transactions stay in the distribution database until all subscribers have successfully received the transaction.

◆ **Synchronization process.** The synchronization process ensures that the published database and the subscribing database are in synch with one another before data replication begins.

◆ **Distribution process.** The distribution process distributes the transactions stored in the distribution database to the subscribing servers.

Note

The log reader process, synchronization process, and distribution process are all part of the SQL Executive service.

Now you are ready to walk through two of the main replication processes: synchronization and replicating data. Referring to Figure 12.4, Server B subscribes to the MyPubs publication. Before data replication can begin between the two databases, the synchronization process must complete successfully.

SERVER A AND SERVER B PERFORM SYNCHRONIZATION

When Server B subscribes to Server A's pubs database publication, the subscriber, Server B, has the choice of accepting several different synchronization modes:

◆ Automatic
◆ Manual

◆ No Synchronization

◆ Snapshot Only

SYNCHRONIZATION MODES

The default synchronization mode is automatic, which means that SQL Server performs the synchronization process automatically at a scheduled interval. Manual synchronization requires you to synchronize the databases and notify SQL Server when the synchronization process has completed.

Tip

> Use manual synchronization when dealing with very large tables or a slow communications line. The files required for synchronization can be copied to a tape or other media and applied to the destination server or servers.

The no synchronization option assumes that the articles in the source are already in synch with articles in the destination. SQL Server does nothing to verify that the databases are synchronized—that task is up to you. The last option, snapshot only, is also referred to as a *table refresh*. If snapshot synchronization is selected, SQL Server ignores any changes to the published articles and instead performs the synchronization process at defined intervals (that is, it refreshes the destination tables).

AUTOMATIC SYNCHRONIZATION

For this example, assume that Server B selects automatic synchronization during the subscription process. The distribution server creates two files, referred to as a *synchronization set*, in the replication working directory (the default is \REPLDATA off the SQL Server home directory). The synchronization set consist of a BCP data file with the actual data of the subscribed articles and the article's table schema file.

Tip

> Schema files created for replication have a SCH extension; the data files have a TMP file extension.

Once the synchronization set is created, a synchronization job is added to the distribution database. The distribution process reads the distribution database and applies the synchronization file set to the subscribing server, (in this example,

Server B). First the schema file is applied to create the table schema. The table information is then copied to the subscribing server using BCP. The distribution server is notified that synchronization has completed, and Server A can begin to replicate the publication MyPubs to Server B.

Note

Once all other subscriptions have acknowledged successful synchronization, the TMP files are removed from the replication working directory.

Any transactions that occurred to the published articles after the subscribing server first subscribed but before the synchronization process occurred are then replicated to the subscriber.

Caution

Be careful when trying to perform synchronization with tables that exist on the publishing and the subscribing server, such as the pubs database. The distribution process attempts to drop a table on the subscribing server if it exists during the synchronization process. If the table being dropped has declarative referential integrity defined and is referenced, for example, by a foreign key constraint from another table, the table cannot be dropped and the synchronization process will fail. If this occurs, use manual synchronization (or no synchronization mode), or do not drop the table during synchronization. With SQL Server 6.5, constraints can be turned off during the replication process by using the NOT FOR REPLICATION option with the ALTER and CREATE table statements.

Version
6.5

ARTICLES ON SERVER A ARE MODIFIED AND REPLICATED

The two servers, shown in Figure 12.4, are synchronized. Modifications are made to articles (tables) on Server A. Because the tables are published, the transactions are marked in the pubs database transaction log for replication. The log reader process, searching transaction logs for marked transactions, creates SQL statements for any marked transactions found and sends the SQL statements to the distribution database.

12

REPLICATION

Note

> Transactions marked for replication in a published database's transaction log remain in the transaction log until the distribution process copies the marked transactions to the distribution database. That is, transaction log backups do not truncate the transactions in the transaction log marked for replication until they have been copied to the distribution database.

The distribution process replicates the transactions found in the distribution database to the subscriber (Server B) using the preconstructed SQL statements or stored procedures, removes the transactions from the distribution database, and updates the Mslast_job_info table on the subscription server.

Note

> Using SQL statements to perform the data modifications rather than sending the actual data greatly reduces the network traffic required to perform replication. The use of SQL statements makes it quite clear why the databases must first be synchronized. Using SQL statements also highlights the point of keeping subscribing databases read-only in practice so that SQL statements applied on the source database have the same effect on the records in the destination database.

PLANNING FOR DATABASE REPLICATION

Unlike many other database operations you perform using SQL Server, replication requires some planning before implementing. The following sections review the requirements before setting up replication.

TRUSTED NETWORK CONNECTIONS ARE REQUIRED

SQL Servers participating in replication are required to use a *trusted connection*, which means that you must have trusted relationships established for NT servers residing in other domains. The SQL Server acting as the distribution server must have a client configuration default protocol setting of named-pipes or multi-protocol.

Note

> SQL Server replication works with any of the security modes (standard, integrated, or mixed). But because replication uses a trusted connection, the distribution server always connects to the subscribing servers in an integrated security mode.

32-BIT ODBC DRIVERS MUST BE INSTALLED

SQL Server replication uses ODBC (Open Database Connectivity) to replicate the data. The 32-bit ODBC drivers must be installed on all SQL Servers involved with replication.

Note

The ODBC drivers are installed automatically during setup. You do not have to configure the ODBC sources.

MEMORY REQUIREMENTS

If the server is a distribution server or a distribution server and publication server, then the NT server requires at least 32M of memory with 16M of memory assigned to SQL Server.

CHARACTER SET

In Microsoft SQL Server 6.5, replication between SQL Servers with different character sets (that is, code pages) is supported. For Microsoft SQL Server 6.0, all version 6.0 SQL Servers participating in replication must have the same character set.

Version
6.5

ADEQUATE TRANSACTION LOG SPACE FOR PUBLISHER DATABASES

Because transactions remain in the transaction log until moved to the distribution database, your publishing databases may require extra space for the added overhead of active replication transactions in the log.

ALL TABLES YOU WANT TO PUBLISH HAVE PRIMARY KEYS

You cannot publish a table that does not have a primary key declared for the table (tables without primary keys do not appear when you select articles for publication). In SQL Server 6.5, if the table uses snapshot replication, you do not need a primary key. You must use the stored procedure sp_addarticle to add an article without a primary key for snapshot replication because only tables with primary keys show up in the Enterprise Manager.

Version
6.5

12

REPLICATION

PREREPLICATION CHECKLIST

Following is a checklist you can use before setting up replication:

PREREPLICATION SETUP CHECKLIST

TRUSTED NETWORK

☐ Default network protocol on distribution server client configuration

    ☐ named-pipes

    ☐ multi-protocol

☐ 32-bit ODBC drivers installed

MEMORY REQUIREMENTS

☐ NT Server 32M (total including SQL Server)

☐ SQL Server 16M

OTHER

☐ Distribution server character set (optional; for record keeping)

☐ Distribution server sort order (optional; for record keeping)

☐ Adequate transaction log space for publisher databases

☐ SQL Executive is using a user domain account, not a local account

☐ All tables you want to publish have primary keys (non-snapshot)

CREATING THE DISTRIBUTION DATABASE

Now it's time to walk through the steps required to set up replication. First, you examine how to set up the distribution database. Follow these steps to create the distribution database, using the Enterprise Manager:

1. Select the server on which you want to install the distribution database.

2. From the Enterprise Manager menu, select Server and then select the Replication Configuration option. A drop-down menu appears (see Figure 12.5).

   Select the Install Publishing option. The Install Replication Publishing dialog box appears (see Figure 12.6).

Figure 12.5.
The Replication
Configuration menu
and option list.

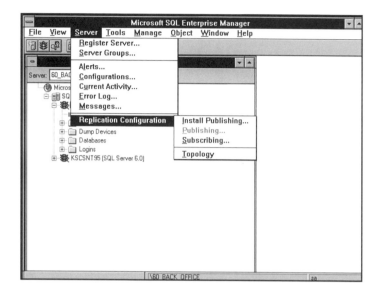

Figure 12.6.
The Install Replication
Publishing dialog box.

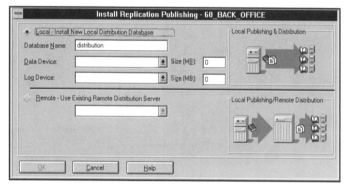

3. To install the distribution database, use the default option, Local - Install New Local Distribution Database. Select an existing device for the data and the transaction log of the distribution database using the combo selection boxes or create a new device by selecting <new> from the Data Device and Log Device combo boxes.

Note

In most cases you encounter, you typically use a distribution server that has already been set up, so select the second option shown in Figure 12.6 (Remote - Use Existing Remote Distribution Server).

12

4. Once you select the proper devices, enter the size for the database and transaction log and click the OK button to create the distribution database.

A message box appears when the process completes, stating the success or failure of the operation. If the operation succeeds, you can begin to add publishing databases and subscribers by selecting the Yes option from the message box.

Note

As you do for every database, put the transaction log for the distribution database on a separate device.

The recommended minimum size for the distribution database is 30M for the data and 15M for the transaction log. To help determine the correct amount of space, determine the number of transactions, average transaction size, and the retention time of the data (that is, typical database size requirements).

TROUBLESHOOTING DISTRIBUTION DATABASE SETUP

While creating the distribution database, you can easily run into a few *gotcha*s. Here is a list of a few of the problems I have encountered while setting up replication distribution databases:

◆ Do not try to create the distribution database while connected to a SQL Server that is on the same machine as the Enterprise Manager using the default server name of (local). You will get midway through the distribution process and encounter error number 21271 (see Figure 12.7 for actual error message). Make sure that you connect to the server using the server name.

Figure 12.7.
The message
box for error
number 21271.

◆ Make sure that you are using trusted connection or you will not be able to replicate.

◆ If you run into problems while creating the distribution database, check the file INSTDIST.OUT in the \INSTALL directory for errors.

♦ If your SQL Server is not configured with at least 16M of memory, you are warned and will be unable to build the distribution database until you allocate at least the minimum amount.

The process of creating a distribution database can be performed manually by following these steps:

1. Create the distribution database and transaction log on separate devices.

2. Run the install script INSTDIST.SQL from the distribution database. The script file adds all the required system tables and stored procedures.

3. Dump the transaction log for the distribution database using the NO_LOG option.

4. Use the system stored procedure sp_serveroption to set the option dist to TRUE for the server.

WHAT HAPPENS WHEN THE DISTRIBUTION DATABASE IS CREATED?

When you create the distribution database, you create a SQL Server database named *distribution*. The distribution database is created with the standard database system tables, as well as the following user tables:

♦ Msjob_commands: Used by the distribution process, the Msjob_commands table contains one command for each transaction.

♦ Msjob_subscriptions: Associates a subscriber with an article.

♦ Msjobs: Contains the transactions used for replication.

♦ Mssubscriber_info: Used by the SQL Executive for passing jobs.

♦ Mssubscriber_jobs: Stores information that associates each subscriber with the commands they need to receive.

♦ Mssubscriber_status: Stores status information about batches of transactions sent to subscribing servers.

CONFIGURING REPLICATION PUBLISHING AND DISTRIBUTION OPTIONS

Once the distribution database has been successfully installed, or you have been given permission to publish to a remote distribution server, you can then configure

12

a server to be a publisher. Using the Enterprise Manager, you can set up which servers can subscribe to published databases, which publisher servers can use the distribution server as a remote distribution server, and which replication schedule used is to replicate the data to each subscribing server.

Note

To set up SQL Server as a publisher, you must have one of the following:

◆ A local distribution database

◆ Access to a remote distribution database

If you have a local distribution database on your server (that is, your server is acting as a distribution server), you can do the following:

◆ Set the distribution working directory

◆ Allow other servers access to your distribution database for publishing

Both distribution servers and publisher servers can control which servers allow access to published articles and which databases on your local server can publish articles.

CONFIGURING PUBLISHING

To set up publications options, following these steps:

1. Select the server from the Enterprise Manager.

2. From the Enterprise Manager menu, select Server and then select Replication Configuration. From the menu that appears, select Publishing. The Replication Publishing dialog box appears (see Figure 12.8).

3. To enable a database for publication, select the Enable checkbox next to the appropriate database.

4. To enable a server to subscribe, select the server's Enable checkbox.

5. To save the changes, click the OK button. To ignore changes made, click the Cancel button.

SETTING DISTRIBUTION OPTIONS

You can administer various distribution options for each subscriber by clicking the Distribution Options button in the Replication Publishing dialog box (refer to Figure 12.8). When you click this button, the Distribution Options dialog box appears (see Figure 12.9).

Figure 12.8.
The Replication
Publishing dialog box.

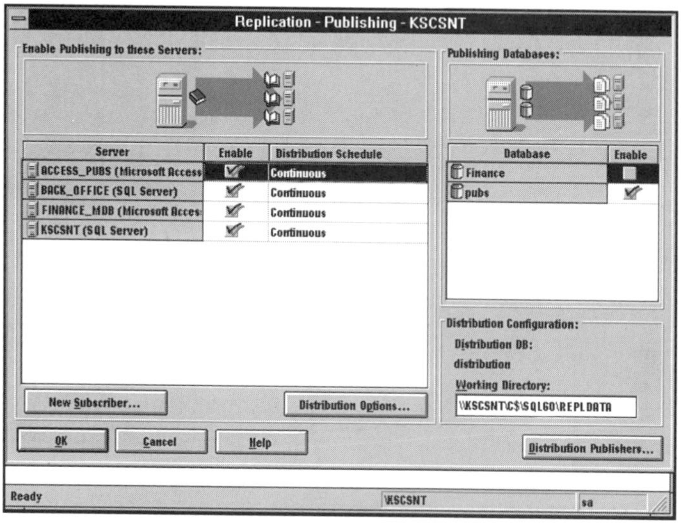

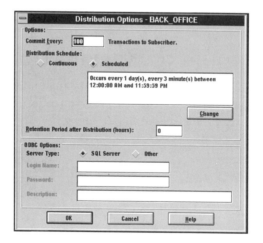

Figure 12.9.
The Distribution
Options dialog box.

The Distribution Options dialog box enables you to set replication scheduling to subscribing servers and ODBC options such as login name and password for non-SQL Server subscribing servers. Non-SQL Server ODBC subscribers are detailed later in this chapter; for now, examine the scheduling options. If you select the Continuous schedule, transactions are replicated continuously to the subscribing servers. If you do not want continuous replication, you can specify a schedule for how often transactions are replicated to the subscribing service.

To allow a remote publisher server to use this SQL Server as a remote distribution server, select the Distribution Publishers button in the Replication Publishing dialog box. The Replication Distribution dialog box appears (see Figure 12.10).

Figure 12.10.
The Replication
Distribution dialog box.

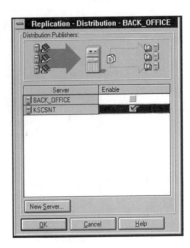

To allow a remote publishing server to use the local server as a distribution server, select the Enable checkbox next to the appropriate remote server and click the OK button.

CONFIGURING REPLICATION SUBSCRIBING

To allow local databases to subscribe to publications or to allow publishing servers to replicate data to the local server, you must enable permissions for the publication servers and the local databases using the Enterprise Manager.

Note

Setting up subscribers enables you to determine which databases can receive published articles and which remote publisher servers you can receive publications from.

To set up subscription options, follow these steps:

1. Select the server from the Enterprise Manager.

2. From the Enterprise Manager menu, select Server and then select the Replication Configuration option. From the menu that appears, select Subscribing. The Replication Subscribing dialog box appears (see Figure 12.11).

3. To enable a server to subscribe, select the Enable checkbox next to the server or database. When you are done, click the OK button.

Figure 12.11.
The Replication
Subscribing dialog box.

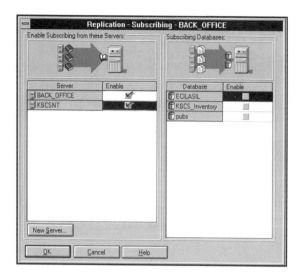

VIEWING REPLICATION TOPOLOGY

Once you have set up your replication, you can view the overall replication topology. Using the Enterprise Manager, follow these steps:

1. Select the server from the Enterprise Manager.

2. From the Enterprise Manager menu, select Server and then select the Replication Configuration option. From the drop-down list box, select Topology. The Replication Topology dialog box appears (see Figure 12.12).

Figure 12.12.
The Replication
Topology dialog box.

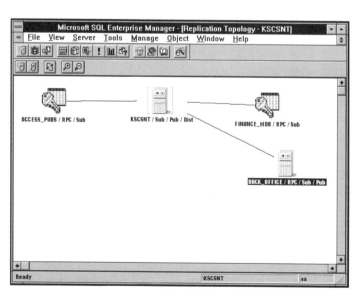

Tip

The Replication Topology dialog box gives you a graphical view of how replication is set up between servers. If a server is a distribution server, the server has the abbreviation DIST next to its picture. Publishing servers have the abbreviation Pub and subscribing servers have the abbreviation Sub. Notice that non-SQL Server ODBC servers are also graphically displayed. You can add a subscriber by selecting a SQL Server from the Enterprise Manager and dropping the server into the topology window.

MANAGING PUBLICATIONS

After you set up your SQL Server as a publisher, you can create publications to which other SQL Servers can subscribe. Changes made to your published databases are then replicated to subscribing databases. Remember that a publication consists of one or many articles (tables). To create a publication using the Enterprise Manager, follow these steps:

1. Select the server you want to use to manage publications from the Enterprise Manager.

2. From the Enterprise Manager menu, select Manage and then select Replication. From the menu that appears, select Publications. The Manage Publications dialog box appears (see Figure 12.13).

   Published databases are displayed in the Publications list box. The databases have the typical Enterprise Manager drill-down features. Drilling down through a database displays the publications in the database. Drilling down through a publication shows the articles in the publication. If you drill down through the article(s), you can see the current subscribers.

Figure 12.13.
The Manage Publications dialog box.

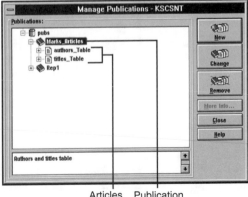

Articles   Publication

3. To create a new publication, click the database to which you want to add the publication and then click the New button. The Edit Publications dialog box appears (see Figure 12.14).

   The Edit Publications dialog box enables you to create a new publication and assign articles to the publication.

Figure 12.14.
The Edit Publications
dialog box.

Selected table —
Available tools —

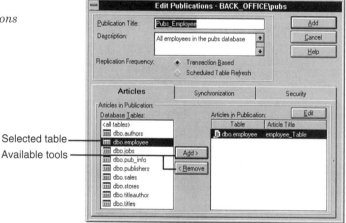

4. To create a publication, enter the name of the publication in the Publication Title text box. In the Description text box, enter the description for the publication.

5. To add tables to the publication, select a table from the Database Tables list in the Edit Publications dialog box and click the Add button. The table is added to the Articles in Publication list.

6. To remove an article from the publication, select the article and click the Remove button.

12

the transaction log are marked and copied to the distribution database and later applied to the destination databases. The Scheduled Table Refresh option is applied at scheduled intervals and is sometimes referred to as a *snapshot*. When a table refresh is performed, the destination table is dropped and re-created. The data in the source table is copied into the destination (or snapshot) table.

7. To add a new publication, click the Add button.

SYNCHRONIZATION OPTIONS

To set synchronization options for a publication, use the Synchronization page in the Edit Publications dialog box (see Figure 12.15). You can control the type of BCP formats used (Native or Character format) and you can schedule the frequency of automatic synchronization by clicking the Change button.

Figure 12.15.
The Synchronization
page in the Edit
Publications
dialog box.

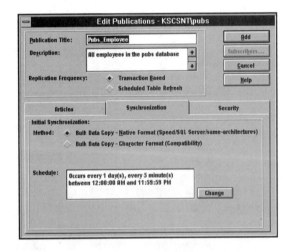

SECURITY OPTIONS

The Security page in the Edit Publications dialog box enables you to restrict which servers can view the publication (see Figure 12.16). The default is unrestricted.

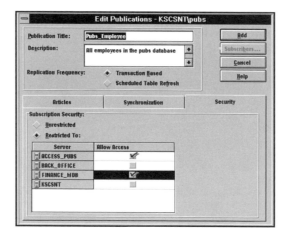

Figure 12.16.
The Security page in
the Edit Publications
dialog box.

MANAGING ARTICLES

To edit an article, to apply a filter, or to add scripts, select the article and click the Edit button in the Edit Publications dialog box (refer back to Figure 12.14). The Manage Article dialog box appears (see Figure 12.17).

Figure 12.17.
The Manage Article
dialog box.

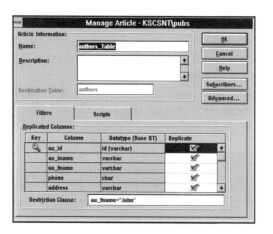

Using the Manage Article dialog box, you can perform vertical partitioning by deselecting columns for the table listed in the Replicated Columns area or you can perform horizontal partitioning by applying a filter in the Restriction Clause text box. For example, in Figure 12.17, a restriction has been added to the pubs database authors_table column, au_fname, to select only records where au_fname is equal to John. If you want to further tune the article by adding stored procedures or editing a script, select the Scripts tab. The Manage Article dialog box with the Scripts page active is shown in Figure 12.18.

Figure 12.18.
The Scripts page in
the Manage Article
dialog box.

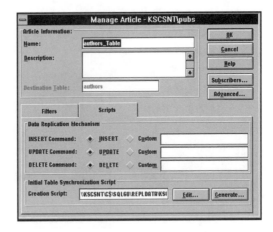

The Scripts page enables you to specify the type of replication mechanism used by SQL Server during replication.

The radio buttons marked Insert Command, Update Command, and Delete Command represent the default replication mechanism used by SQL Server when constructing SQL statements for each of the commands. Select the Custom checkbox if you want to make one of the following choices:

◆ Enter NONE in the Custom text box to prevent the type of transaction from being replicated. For example, if you select Custom from the Update Command row and enter NONE in the Custom text box, any transactions that are UPDATE commands are not replicated.

◆ Enter a stored procedure to perform the proper SQL command UPDATE, INSERT, or DELETE. You must enter the stored procedure in the format `Call stored_procedure_name`.

USING STORED PROCEDURES WITH REPLICATION

Why use stored procedures during replication? Let's start with the obvious: Use stored procedures to improve the performance of the replication process. Stored procedures improve performance by using precompiled SQL statements during replication. Stored procedures also reduce network traffic because you pass only the stored procedure name and parameters instead of the entire SQL statement. You can also use stored procedures to perform custom processing on the subscribing server such as reformatting the data to simplify end-user queries. The customer stored procedures may be as simple as translating an integer status field to a character field that reports "SUCCESS" or "ERROR".

Here's an example of using custom replication stored procedures to reduce the number of joins (that is, denormalizing a table for a data warehouse). Suppose that you are replicating to a database that is to be used by several end users. The primary table the end users are concerned with, My_Customer, consists of several ID columns that reference description values in other tables. You want to prevent the end users from having to join the My_Customer table to any other tables to retrieve the descriptions associated with the ID columns (that is, you want to flatten the table). Here are the steps required to perform this operation using replication:

1. Create an article on the publishing server for the table My_Customer.

2. Using the Scripts page in the Manage Article dialog box (refer back to Figure 12.18), select the Custom boxes and add stored procedure names for the data modification statements you plan to support (for example, INSERT, UPDATE, and DELETE).

3. Subscribe the end-user database server to the article set up on the publishing server for the My_Customer table. Select No Data Synchronization for the type of replication synchronization.

4. On the subscribing server, create the My_Customer table with a different table schema than the one found on the publishing server (that is, replace the ID columns' datatypes with the datatypes for the description columns).

5. Create stored procedures for all the data modifications you plan to support (for example, INSERT, UPDATE, and DELETE) on the subscribing server. For example, the INSERT stored procedure uses the ID columns of the My_Customer table passed in during replication to retrieve the description columns from the other tables in the database and inserts them (along with the other associated information for a row) into the subscriber's My_Customer table.

6. Once everything is in place, you must sync the data between the two tables. The easiest and safest way to sync the data is to copy all the data from the publisher server's My_Customer table to a holding table on the subscribing server (use the stored procedures DUMP and LOAD, or use BCP). Create a cursor that reads each

row in the holding table and executes the replication INSERT stored procedure to place the information in the correct format in the subscriber's My_Customer table.

Once the two tables are synched and the data is the same, you are ready to go. When data is changed on the publisher, the changes are replicated to the subscribing server. The stored procedure is executed on the subscribing server, retrieving the correct columns and inserting them in the subscribing server's copy of the My_Customer table. You have created a more user-friendly table on the subscribing server by using custom stored procedures.

One more thing: If you use stored procedures for replication, all subscribing servers must have the stored procedures in the subscribing database. The stored procedures do not have to exist on the publishing server.

If you are editing an existing article, the Creation Script text box in the Manage Article dialog box contains the path and filename of the synchronization schema file. To generate the schema file, click the Generate button.

Tip

To set the schema options such as table index options, truncating the table, dropping or not dropping the table during synchronization, or including the primary key, click the Generate button in the Manage Article dialog box to display a schema option dialog box.

The Advanced button in the Manage Article dialog box allows you to add a stored procedure to filter the replication results. You may want to use this feature to further limit the results of an article that has already been partitioned horizontally or vertically. The stored procedure must follow this format:

```
If SQL Statement Return 1 Else Return 0
```

The Use Column Names in SQL Statements checkbox adds column headers to replication INSERT statements for the selected article. Check this option when the column order of the subscribing table does not match the column order of the publishing table.

When you have completed any modifications or changes to the article, click the OK button to save your changes; click the Cancel button to ignore your changes. Review the other tab options available in the Edit Publications dialog box.

MANAGING SUBSCRIPTIONS

SQL Server supports two types of subscription methods: a *pull subscription* and a *push subscription*. A pull subscription is when you are managing the subscribing server and you select one or more publications to subscribe to. A push subscription occurs when you are managing a publication server and you set up subscribers from the publication server (that is, you push the article out to other servers).

Note

Push subscriptions cannot be performed at the publication level. Only articles can be pushed.

PULL SUBSCRIPTIONS

A *pull subscription* is when you are the subscribing server and you subscribe to one or more publications. To manage a pull subscription, follow these steps:

1. Select the server from the Enterprise Manager.

2. From the Enterprise Manager menu, select Manage and then select Replication. From the menu that appears, select Subscriptions. The Manage Subscriptions dialog box appears (see Figure 12.19).

Figure 12.19.
The Manage Subscriptions dialog box.

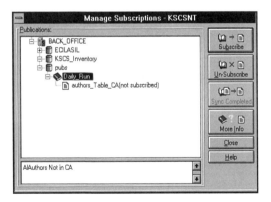

3. To subscribe to a publication or an article, select a publication or an article from the Publications list. To subscribe to the selected publication or article, click the Subscribe button. The Subscription Options dialog box appears (see Figure 12.20).

Figure 12.20.
The Subscription
Options dialog box.

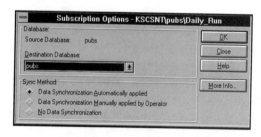

4. Select the destination database for the replicated publication from the Destination Database combo box. Select the synchronization method and then click the OK button. The subscription has been added. The process is completed when the data synchronization occurs between the source and destination databases.

Tip

The Sync Completed button in the Manage Subscriptions dialog box informs SQL Server that the synchronization process has been completed (use only for manual synchronization). In most cases, you probably want to use automatic synchronization methods and allow SQL Server to handle the required synchronization steps. There are exceptions, however. If the database you are replicating is extremely large or the servers you are replicating to are linked with a slow data line, use the manual replication mechanism instead. If you are creating a duplicate database on another server using a current backup of the database or if you are positive that the two databases participating in replication are identical, you may want to use the no synchronization option.

PUSH SUBSCRIPTIONS

In a *push subscription*, you set up subscribers from the publication server (that is, you push the article out to other servers). To manage a push subscription, follow these steps:

1. Select the server from the Enterprise Manager.

2. From the Enterprise Manager menu, select Manage and then select Replication. From the menu that appears, select Publications. The Manage Publication dialog box appears (refer back to Figure 12.13). Select the publication you want to push and click the Change button. The Edit Publications dialog box appears (refer back to Figure 12.14). You can push an entire publication or a specific article. In this example, you push a single article (for an example of pushing an entire publication, refer to the following section, "SQL Server Replication to ODBC Subscribers"). To push an article to a subscribing server, select an article and click the Edit button. The Manage Article dialog box appears (refer back to Figure 12.17). Click the Subscribers button and the Publication Subscribers dialog box appears (see Figure 12.21).

Figure 12.21.
The Publication
Subscribers dialog box.

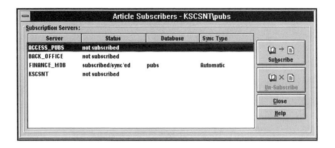

3. Select a server to push the article to and click the Subscribe button. The Subscription Options dialog box appears (see Figure 12.22).

Figure 12.22.
The Subscription
Options dialog box.

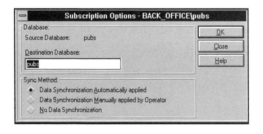

4. Type the name of the destination database and select the synchronization method. Click OK to push the subscription to the selected server and database.

Version 6.5 SQL SERVER REPLICATION TO ODBC SUBSCRIBERS

SQL Server 6.5 can replicate to non-SQL Server ODBC subscribers such as Microsoft Access, IBM DB2, Sybase, and Oracle databases. As stated earlier in this chapter, non-SQL Server ODBC sources can only be subscribers, they cannot be publishers.

Note

Because non-SQL Server subscribers use ODBC, I'm sure that the list of possible ODBC subscribers will increase. For an updated list of supported ODBC subscribers, refer to your Microsoft documentation or check the SQL Server forums on the Internet or CompuServe. From this point on in this chapter, when we discuss *ODBC subscribers*, we mean *non-SQL Server ODBC sources*.

ODBC subscribers must be set up by the publishing server using the push subscription method. Each ODBC subscriber participating in SQL Server replication has its own individual requirements and restrictions. For example, when creating the ODBC DSN with Oracle, you must include a username; with Microsoft Access DSN, you must enter a username and a password. Check out the Microsoft SQL Server documentation for the various restrictions that apply between Microsoft SQL Server and the selected ODBC subscriber.

Here are a few known restrictions that apply to all ODBC subscribers:

◆ ODBC DSN must follow SQL Server naming conventions

◆ Batch statements are not supported

Also review the datatype conversions between Microsoft SQL Server and the ODBC subscriber. The following sections describe how to set up an ODBC subscriber using Microsoft Access 7.0.

STEP 1: CREATE AN ODBC DATA SOURCE NAME

The first step in setting up replication to an ODBC subscriber is to create a system ODBC Data Source Name (DSN) for the subscribing server. To create a system ODBC DSN, follow these steps:

1. Double-click the ODBC icon located in the control panel to start the ODBC Administrator (see Figure 12.23).

Figure 12.23.
The ODBC Administra-
tor dialog box.

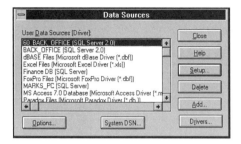

2. Click the System DSN button. The System Data Sources dialog box appears
   (see Figure 12.24).

Tip

The System ODBC DSN must be set up on the SQL Server that is
participating as the distribution server (that is, the ODBC DSN
cannot be set up on a client machine or subscriber server).

Figure 12.24.
The System Data
Sources dialog box.

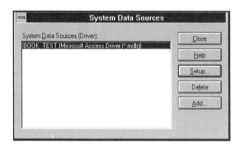

3. To add a new system DSN, click the Add button. A list of installed ODBC
   drivers appears. Select the correct ODBC driver for your subscribing server
   (for this example, select Microsoft Access). Once you select the correct
   ODBC driver, click OK. The ODBC Microsoft Access 7.0 Setup dialog box
   appears (see Figure 12.25).

12

Figure 12.25.
The ODBC Microsoft
Access 7.0 Setup
dialog box.

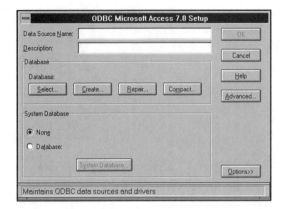

Note

The look of the ODBC Setup dialog box varies for different data sources. For this example, Microsoft Access is used. Compare the Microsoft Access Setup dialog box in Figure 12.25 to the ODBC Setup screen for SQL Server (shown in Figure 12.26).

Figure 12.26.
The ODBC SQL
Server Setup
dialog box.

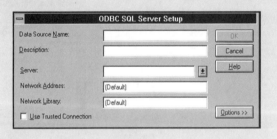

4. Enter the Data Source Name for the Microsoft Access database. The Data Source Name is how the ODBC subscriber will be referenced by SQL Server. Select the Access database to push the replicated data to and click the Advanced button. Add a user name and password for the Access

database (this is one of the requirements for setting up an Access ODBC subscriber). Once you have entered the correct information, click the OK button to add the ODBC subscriber.

Tip

The Access database can be located on a network drive.

STEP 2: REGISTER THE ODBC SOURCE AS A SUBSCRIBING SERVER

The next step is to add the ODBC DSN to SQL Server's list of subscribing servers. To add an ODBC DSN to the list of subscribing servers, follow these steps:

1. Select the server from the Enterprise Manager.

2. From the Enterprise Manager menu, select Server and then select Replication Configuration. From the menu that appears, select Publishing. The Replication Publishing dialog box appears (see Figure 12.27).

Figure 12.27.
The Replication
Publishing dialog box.

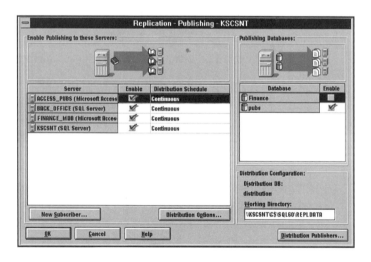

3. Click the New Subscriber button. The New Subscriber dialog box appears. Click the ODBC Subscriber button. The New ODBC Subscriber dialog box appears (see Figure 12.28).

Figure 12.28.
The New ODBC
Subscriber dialog box.

4. Use the combo box to select the correct ODBC DSN. Enter the login ID and password if required. The login ID and password are optional because they may be stored when the system DSN is created. In the case of Microsoft Access, leave the login and password fields blank because this information is stored with the ODBC system DSN. To register the ODBC subscriber, click the OK button. This action adds the DSN to the SQL Server system table sysservers.

STEP 3: PUSH THE PUBLICATION OR ARTICLE TO THE ODBC SUBSCRIBER

Once the ODBC DSN has been registered as a subscribing server, follow these steps to push a publication or article to the ODBC subscriber:

1. Select the server from the Enterprise Manager.

2. From the Enterprise Manager menu, select Manage and then select Replication. From the drop-down list box, select Publications. The Manage Publication dialog box appears (refer back to Figure 12.13). Click the Change button; the Edit Publications dialog box appears (refer back to Figure 12.14). You can push an entire publication or a specific article. In "Push Subscriptions," earlier in this chapter, a specific article was used as an example; this example pushes a publication. Select the publication you want to push and click the Subscribers button; the Publication Subscribers dialog box appears (see Figure 12.29).

Figure 12.29.
The Publication
Subscribers dialog box.

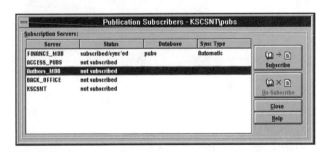

3. Select the subscribing server to push the publication to and click the Subscribe button. The Subscription Options dialog box appears (refer back to Figure 12.20). Select the type of synchronization mode and click the OK button. The push subscription is complete.

Tip

When performing replication to an Access database, make sure that the type of synchronization method selected is Bulk Data Copy - Character Format. You can also check the status of replication to ODBC sources just as you can check the status of replication to another SQL Server: by using the Task Scheduling dialog box.

WRAPPING UP

To wrap up this chapter on replication, the following sections review a last few pointers, tips, and reminders when dealing with SQL Server replication.

SUBSCRIBING (REPLICATED) DATABASES ARE READ-ONLY

Databases that are subscribed from a publisher server should not be modified on the subscribing server and should be used for read-only purposes. SQL Server does not prevent you from modifying the data, but if you do modify data in the replicated databases, the database will become out of synch with the published database. Also, any changes you make in the replicated database can easily be overwritten by changes made in the published database. Suppose that you modify an amount field in row 1 of a table called bank_account on the subscribing server's replicated database. You set the value of the field to $1,000.00. A few minutes later, someone on the publishing database modifies the same record but they set the value to -$1000.00. A few minutes later, the changed record is replicated to your database, overwriting your changes—unknown to you! The values in your database are no longer valid (another reason to use SQL Server replication for read-only databases). SQL Server replication does *not* have a mechanism that allows you to replicate records to various databases and make changes on any of the databases (subscriber or publisher). Then replicate all the changes back to subscribing servers, notifying users of record conflicts (records modified by more than one server). Do not be discouraged—the read-only database replication scheme is very powerful and useful in many real-world scenarios.

DATABASE READ-ONLY OPTION

Replication cannot occur on a subscribing database if the read-only database option is set to TRUE.

TABLE CONSTRAINTS

Version 6.5

SQL Server 6.5 allows you to disable constraints during replication.

REPLICATION IS TRANSACTION DRIVEN

Remember that SQL Server replication is transaction driven. Keep this in mind as you publish and subscribe various articles and monitor the number of transactions that are replicated. Pay close attention to update transactions. If SQL Server performs a deferred update on a table, the update consists of a delete followed by an insert. Updating 10,000 records can translate to 10,000 deletes and 10,000 inserts for a total of 20,000 transactions. If you intend to perform many updates, you may want to examine the rules SQL Server uses to perform direct updates, better known as *updates in place*. Rather than performing a DELETE and an INSERT, SQL Server updates the record in place.

DEADLOCKS

Because of exclusive table-lock conditions, deadlocks can sometimes occur between the distribution process and the log reader. If you experience deadlocks between the two processes, try reducing the commit batch size using the Enterprise Manager; alternatively, reduce the frequency of the distribution process.

ODBC SUBSCRIBERS

When setting up the system DSN for an ODBC subscriber, you must add the DSN on the Windows NT server with the distribution server. Remember, non-SQL Server ODBC sources can only be subscribers.

BETWEEN THE LINES

Following are some of the important things to remember for SQL Server replication:

◆ SQL Server replication is transaction based and follows a loose consistency data distribution model.

◆ Replication uses a publish and subscriber metaphor.

◆ Subscribing databases should be treated as read-only.

- NT servers participating in replication require a trusted connection.
- SQL Server uses ODBC for replication.
- A server can play multiple roles and be a subscriber, publisher, or distributor.
- To set up replication to a non-SQL Server ODBC source, add the ODBC DSN using the ODBC administrator on the distribution server.
- Non-SQL Server ODBC sources can only be subscribers.
- You can tune or schedule the frequency of replicating publications.
- Use stored procedures instead of SQL statements for replication to enhance performance.

SUMMARY

Replication is a new and exciting technology that will play an important part in many real-world solutions. As a Microsoft SQL Server DBA, you must fully understand how to correctly set up and administer database replication and how to correctly use replication to benefit your company or organization.

12

REPLICATION

Version
6.5

*by Mark Spenik
and
Orryn Sledge*

CHAPTER 13

Distributed Transaction
Coordinator

SQL Server 6.5 includes a distributed transaction coordinator, the Microsoft Distributed Transaction Coordinator (DTC). DTC provides an easy-to-use distributed transaction capability for the Windows NT and Windows 95 environments. The DTC uses OLE transaction objects to provide complete transaction management in a distributed environment. This technology allows applications to modify data in multiple SQL Server databases through a single transaction object. By using the distributed transactions through the MS DTC, you can guarantee that each data modification will complete in its entirety; in the event of an aborted transaction, the modified data will retain its original state (before the transaction was initiated).

Note

The DTC was introduced in SQL Server 6.5. Previous versions of SQL Server must be upgraded to version 6.5 to take advantage of the DTC service.

The MS DTC is integrated into the SQL Server Enterprise Manager. You can easily start, stop, trace, view statistics, and configure the MS DTC all from the Enterprise Manager. Before you look at the Microsoft DTC, you should understand the different components involved in distributed transactions. The following sections explain the key components involved in a distributed transaction and the role played by SQL Server and the Distributed Transaction Coordinator.

TRANSACTION MANAGER

The Transaction Manager is responsible for the coordination and management of a transaction. The MS DTC serves as the Transaction Manager. The MS DTC creates transaction objects on behalf of the calling application. Resource Managers participating in the transaction enlist with the Transaction Manager. The Transaction Manager is then responsible for initiating and coordinating the two-phase commit protocol for the participants. The Transaction Manager is also responsible for keeping a log of transaction events. For the MS DTC, this log is the sequential file MSDTC.LOG. The log is used in case Transaction Manager should fail, so that the Transaction Manager can reconstruct the transaction by reading the log.

RESOURCE MANAGER

The Resource Manager is responsible for performing the request of the transaction. In the case of a SQL Server acting as a Resource Manager, this request could be an

INSERT, UPDATE, or DELETE statement. Resource Managers are responsible for keeping enough information so that they can commit or roll back the transaction. Currently, the DTC supports only the SQL Server 6.5 Resource Manager.

TWO-PHASE COMMIT

The MS DTC uses a two-phase commit algorithm to guarantee that a distributed data modification will run in its entirety or that the modified data will return to its original state (the state it was in before the transaction was initiated). The two-phase commit algorithm is based on the following logic.

When a commit statement is issued, the Transaction Manager (in the case of SQL Server, the MS DTC) asks the resources involved in the transaction if they are ready to commit the transaction. This step is known as *preparing to commit*. If every resource is ready to commit the transaction, the Transaction Manager broadcasts a message to commit the transaction. Each resource sends back a message stating that the transaction is committed. If each resource successfully commits the transaction, the Transaction Manager marks the transaction as successfully committed. If a resource fails to commit a transaction, the Transaction Manager continues to hold the transaction in a pending state. This state must be resolved before the transaction is considered complete; otherwise the transaction is rolled back.

WALKING THROUGH A DISTRIBUTED TRANSACTION PROCESS

Refer to Figure 13.1 as you walk through a simple example of a distributed transaction. The transaction begins with the application, which issues a BEGIN DISTRIBUTED TRANSACTION command, causing the Transaction Manager (MS DTC) to create a transaction object for the transaction. When the application begins to perform a SQL statement as part of the transaction (for example, an INSERT statement), the Resource Manager (in this case, SQL Server) calls the Transaction Manager to enlist in the transaction. Keeping track of enlisted Transaction Managers is part of the responsibility of the Transaction Manager.

During the life of the transaction, the Transaction Manager (MS DTC) records in the MSDTC.LOG file events such as transaction starts, enlistments, and commits or aborts. By keeping the log file up to date, the Transaction Manager ensures that it can reconstruct a transaction in case the Transaction Manager should go down. When the application commits or aborts the transaction, the Transaction Manager begins the two-phase commit with all the enlisted Resource Managers. (The example in Figure 13.1 involves only a single computer with a single Transaction Manager and Resource Manager.)

Figure 13.1.
Walking through a
distributed trans-
action process.

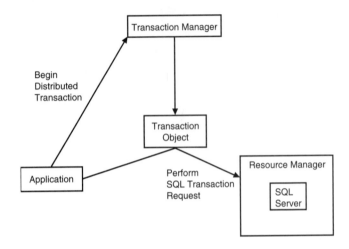

The real power behind the DTC is that you can use it in a distributed environment for transactions that span multiple computers and Transaction Managers. In a distributed environment, each system has a local Transaction Manager. The Transaction Manager for each system works with the other Transaction Managers in the distributed environment to manage transactions that span multiple systems. The Transaction Manager that initiates a distributed transaction is referred to as the *global commit coordinator* (or the *root Transaction Manager*). When a transaction crosses to other systems, the Transaction Managers from each system establish relationships. The system making the request is said to have an *outgoing relationship* with the Transaction Managers on the other systems. Transaction Managers receiving the request establish an *incoming relationship* with the root Transaction Manager. The relationships between the different Transaction Managers are called a *commit tree*. The general idea is that, when a distributed transaction is committed or aborted, the request flows outward. Any Transaction Manager in the commit tree can abort the transaction before it agrees to prepare to commit or abort the transaction.

DEVELOPING AN APPLICATION WITH DISTRIBUTED TRANSACTIONS

By using Transact SQL, stored procedures, or C/C++ functions, you can develop an application that incorporates distributed transactions. The following sections explain each method.

USING STORED PROCEDURES

By using SQL Server's stored procedures, you can implement distributed transaction logic. To implement distributed transaction logic, use the following syntax: `begin distributed tran`, `commit tran`, `rollback tran`. You can also use stored procedures to make remote procedure calls (RPC) to stored procedures located on servers. These RPC calls allow you to modify data located on another server.

USING C/C++ FUNCTIONS

You can also implement distributed transaction logic by using C or C++ functions with DB-Library or ODBC. If you use C or C++ functions, you can directly initiate a DTC transaction within an application through an OLE transaction-compliant Resource Manager.

INSTALLING THE DTC SERVER COMPONENT

Preparing to use the DTC service on the server where SQL Server resides is relatively straightforward. By default, the DTC service is automatically installed when you install SQL Server 6.5. When you install SQL Server, the MSDTC service is automatically added to the NT operating system.

When you use remote procedure calls (RPC) to modify data on another server, the remote server must be added to the list of available remote servers. Follow these steps to add a remote server:

1. From the Enterprise Manager, select the server that will act as the DTC coordinator. Select the Remote Server option from the Server menu. The Manage Remote Servers dialog box opens.

2. In the Manage Remote Servers dialog box, enter the remote server's name. Select the RPC option and enter Remote Login information (see Figure 13.2). Click the Add button to save the information.

Figure 13.2.
The Manage Remote
Servers dialog box.

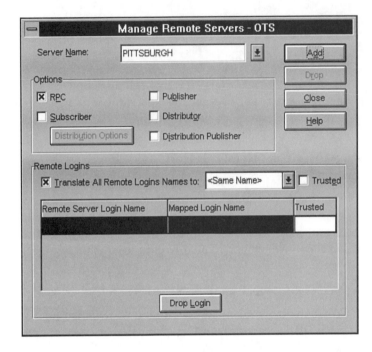

INSTALLING THE DTC CLIENT COMPONENT

If you want a client to initiate a DTC transaction, the MS DTC client utility must be installed on a client machine.

Note

The DTC client utility is required only when a client initiates a DTC transaction. It is not required when a client calls a stored procedure in SQL Server and the stored procedure initiates the DTC transaction. Therefore, if you code the `begin distributed tran`, `commit tran`, and `rollback tran` logic using stored procedures, you do not have to install the DTC client utility.

The DTC client must be installed on a 32-bit client. It does not work with Windows for Workgroups or Windows 3.1.

Before you can install the Microsoft DTC client component, you must first install the Microsoft Remote Registry Service. To determine whether the Microsoft Remote Registry Service is installed on your computer, double-click the Network icon in the control panel. If you do not see Microsoft Remote Registry listed as an installed component (see Figure 13.3), you must install it by performing the following steps:

1. Double-click the Network icon in the control panel. The Network dialog box appears.

2. Click the Add button in the Network dialog box. The Select Network Component Type dialog box opens.

3. Select Service and click the Add button. The Select Network Service dialog box opens.

4. Click the Have Disk button. The Install From Disk dialog box opens.

5. Enter the location of the REGSRV.INF file. This file can be found in the \i386\remotereg directory on the SQL Server v6.5 CD-ROM. Click the OK button to install the service. You return to the Select Network Service dialog box. At this point, you are ready to install the Microsoft Remote Registry Service. Click the OK button to continue the installation.

6. The Microsoft Remote Registry Service begins to install. Depending on your Windows 95 configuration, you may be prompted for additional files that reside on the Windows 95 installation CD or disks. When the installation is complete, you will see Microsoft Remote Registry listed as an installed component (see Figure 13.3).

Figure 13.3.
The Microsoft Remote
Registry service.

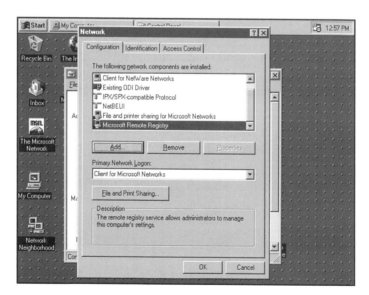

7. In addition to installing the Microsoft Remote Registry service, you must also enable user-level access control. To enable user-level access control, select the Access Control tab in the Network dialog box. On this page, click the User-Level Access Control option and enter the source for user information (see Figure 13.4).

Figure 13.4.
Enabling user-level
access control.

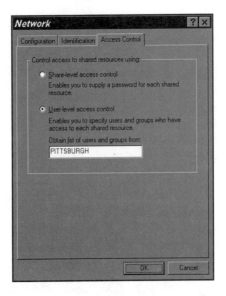

After you successfully complete the installation of the Microsoft Remote Registry Service, you must run the DTCCFG.CPL control panel extension to configure the default commit coordinator. Follow these steps to configure the DTCCFG.CPL control panel extension:

1. Find the installed location of DTCCFG.CPL and double-click the file. The MS DTC Client Configuration dialog box opens (see Figure 13.5).

2. From the MS DTC Client Configuration dialog box, enter a default MS DTC server and a network protocol. Click the OK button to save the information.

Figure 13.5.
Configuring the MS
DTC client.

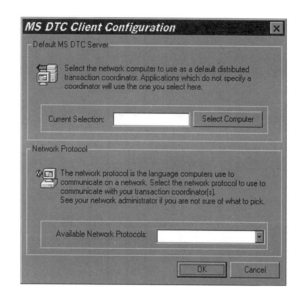

STARTING THE DTC

Follow these steps to start the DTC from the Enterprise Manager:

1. To manually start the DTC from the Enterprise Manager, select the server that will be running the DTC service and right-click the Distributed Transaction Coordinator icon. From the shortcut menu that appears, select the Start option (see Figure 13.6).

Figure 13.6.
Starting the Distrib-
uted Transaction
Coordinator from the
Enterprise Manager.

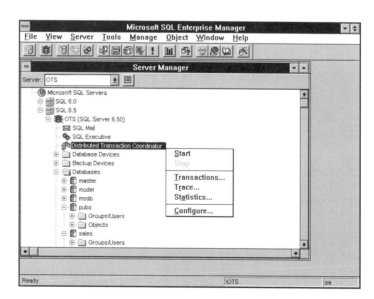

2. Once the Distributed Transaction Coordinator has started, the DTC icon appears with a green dot. This indicates that the DTC is currently running.

Note

You can also start the DTC from the Services icon in the control panel or by typing `net start msdtc`.

Tip

If you plan to use the DTC on a regular basis, you should configure it to start automatically whenever the NT Server starts. To automatically start the DTC service, double-click the Services icon in the Windows NT control panel. The Services dialog box opens. In the Services dialog box, double-click the MSDTC service. A dialog box containing information about the MSDTC service opens. From this dialog box, select Automatic as the Startup Type (see Figure 13.7). Click the OK button to save the changes.

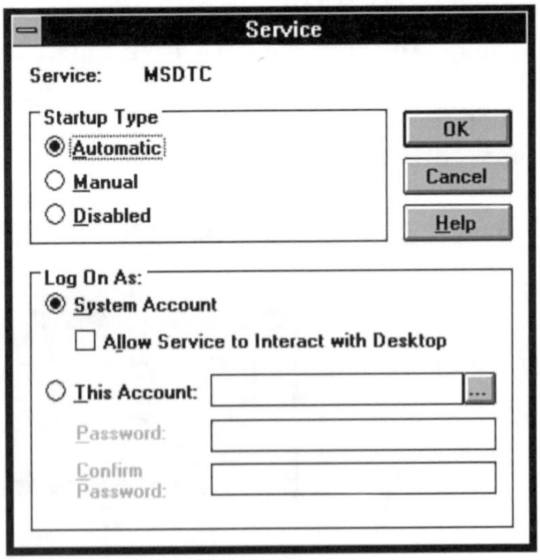

Figure 13.7.
Configuring the DTC service to start automatically.

TESTING THE DTC

Follow these steps to verify that the DTC is properly configured:

1. From the Enterprise Manager, right-click the Distributed Transaction Coordinator icon. From the shortcut menu that appears, choose the Statistics option. The MS DTC Statistics dialog box opens. Keep this dialog box open for the remainder of the test.

2. From the Enterprise Manager, open a Query dialog box by clicking the SQL Query Tool button.

3. In the Query dialog box, type `begin distributed tran` and click the Execute Query button to execute the query. Keep this dialog box open for the remainder of the test.

4. Return to the MS DTC Statistics dialog box. If the DTC is properly configured, you should see one active transaction in the Current/Active counter section of the dialog box (see Figure 13.8).

5. Return to the Query dialog box. Type `rollback tran` and click the Execute Query button to execute the query.

6. Return to the MS DTC Statistics dialog box. If the DTC is properly configured, you should see no active transactions in the Current/Active counter section of the dialog box.

Figure 13.8.
The MS DTC Statistics dialog box, showing one active transaction.

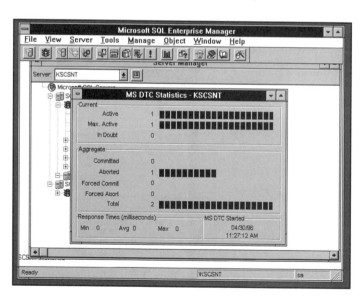

ADMINISTERING THE DTC

Although DTC sounds complex, Microsoft supplies several graphical tools built into the Enterprise Manager to simplify the administration of DTC. The following Enterprise Manager tools are used to manage DTC:

- ◆ **MS DTC Configuration dialog box.** Allows you to set advanced MS DTC options.
- ◆ **MS DTC Trace window.** Allows you to monitor trace messages issued by the MS DTC.
- ◆ **MS DTC Transaction window.** Provides a graphical view of transaction states and enables you to manually resolve a transaction.
- ◆ **MS DTC Statistics window.** Provides a graphical view of transaction statistical information.

MS DTC CONFIGURATION DIALOG BOX

You can use the MS DTC Configuration dialog box to set advanced parameters. For example, you can set MS DTC display parameters or reset the MS DTC log and timers.

To view the MS DTC Configuration dialog box, perform the following steps:

1. From the Enterprise Manager, select the server you want to administer.
2. Select the Distributed Transaction Coordinator icon (see Figure 13.9).

Figure 13.9.
The Enterprise Manager, with the Distributed Transaction Coordinator selected.

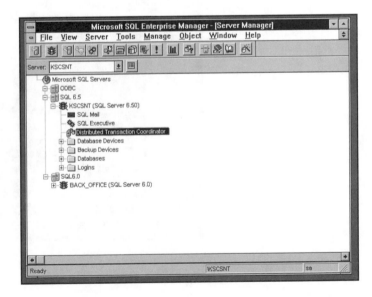

3. Right-click the Distributed Transaction Coordinator to display the Distributed Transaction Manager shortcut menu (see Figure 13.10).

Figure 13.10.
The Distributed Transaction Coordinator shortcut menu.

4. Select the Configure option. The MS DTC Configuration dialog box appears (see Figure 13.11). Using the MS DTC Configuration dialog box, you can set various MS DTC options. Once you set the necessary options, click the Close button to save the changes and return to the Enterprise Manager. You can also stop or start the MS DTC by clicking the Start or Stop button.

Figure 13.11.
The MS DTC Configuration dialog box.

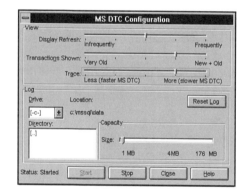

The following sections examine the MS DTC Configuration dialog box in more detail.

VIEW FRAME

The View frame shown in Figure 13.11 is used to control how often the MS DTC updates information. To adjust any values in the View frame, move the slider bars.

The **Display Refresh slider bar** determines how often the statistical, transaction list, and trace information is sent to the various graphical interfaces. The more frequently the information is updated, the more accurate the information. However, frequent updating increases the administrative overhead required. The Display Refresh slider bar starts at Infrequently and goes to Frequently. Following are the display update intervals for each value:

◆ Every 20 seconds (Infrequently)
◆ Every 10 seconds

- ◆ Every 5 seconds (Default value)
- ◆ Every 3 seconds
- ◆ Every 1 second (Frequently)

The **Transactions Shown slider bar** determines how long a transaction must be active before it appears on the graphical interfaces. The Transactions Shown slider bar goes (from left to right) from `Very Old` to `New + Old`; the associated values are as follows:

- ◆ Transaction 5 minutes old (Very Old)
- ◆ Transactions 1 minute old
- ◆ Transactions 30 seconds old
- ◆ Transactions 10 seconds old
- ◆ Transactions 1 second old (New + Old)

The **Trace slider bar** controls the amount of trace information sent to the graphical interface. The Trace slider bar goes from `Less (faster MS DTC)` to `More (slower MS DTC)`. The more trace statements you send back to the graphical interface, the slower MS DTC performs. The values for the Trace slider bar are as follows:

- ◆ Send no traces (Less; faster MS DTC)
- ◆ Send only error traces
- ◆ Send error and warning traces
- ◆ Send error, warning, and informational traces (default)
- ◆ Send all traces (More; slower MS DTC)

Tip

You can change the parameters in the View frame dynamically while the MS DTC is running.

LOG FRAME

The Log frame allows you to adjust the size of the MS DTC log. The MS DTC log file is called `MSDTC.LOG`.

Caution

Do not modify the size of the MS DTC log while MS DTC has unresolved transactions.

To modify the size of the MS DTC log, follow these steps:

1. Make sure that the MS DTC has no unresolved transactions by viewing the MS DTC Transaction window (discussed later in this chapter). If no unresolved transactions exist, click the Stop button to stop the MS DTC.

2. Once the MS DTC has stopped (that is, when the Status indicator at the bottom of the MS DTC Configuration dialog box shown in Figure 13.11 reads Stopped), you can change the size of the log by using the slider bar. You can also change the location of the file by using the Drive and Directory boxes.

3. Once you have modified the MS DTC log (either the size or the location or both), click the Reset Log button.

4. Click the Start button to restart the MS DTC.

MS DTC TRACE WINDOW

The MS DTC Trace window allows you to view the trace messages issued by MS DTC. Use this information to track or debug problems or potential problems. The type of information displayed in the Trace window depends on the message trace level set with the MS DTC Configuration dialog box. You can view errors, warnings, or informational messages. To view the MS DTC Trace window, follow these steps:

1. From the Enterprise Manager, select the server you want to trace.

2. Select the Distributed Transaction Coordinator icon.

3. Right-click the Distributed Transaction Coordinator icon to display the shortcut menu.

4. Select the Trace option. The MS DTC Trace window shown in Figure 13.12 appears.

Figure 13.12.
The MS DTC Trace window.

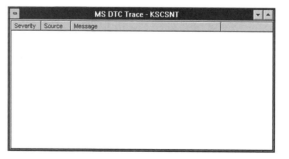

MS DTC Transaction Window

The MS DTC Transaction window allows you to quickly view current transactions and resolve the transaction manually if required. The following sections explain how to accomplish both these tasks.

Viewing Current Transactions

The MS DTC Transaction window allows you to quickly view current transactions that may require a DBA's intervention or attention. Because a single MS DTC can have many concurrent transactions, the MS DTC Transaction window displays only those transactions that have remained in the same state for an extended period of time or whose status is in doubt. You can configure the time interval for which transactions must remain in the same state before they appear in the MS DTC Transaction window by using the MS DTC Configuration dialog box discussed earlier in this chapter. To view the MS DTC Transaction window, follow these steps:

1. From the Enterprise Manager, select the server for which you want to view current transactions.

2. Select the Distributed Transaction Coordinator icon.

3. Right-click the Distributed Transaction Coordinator icon to display the shortcut menu.

4. Select the Transactions menu option. The MS DTC Transaction window appears (see Figure 13.13).

Figure 13.13.
The MS DTC Transac-
tion window (Large
Icons).

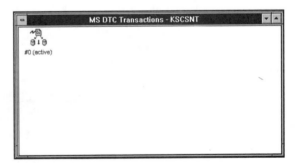

You can change the view of the Transaction window by right-clicking anywhere in the MS DTC Transaction window and selecting View from the shortcut menu. Figure 13.13 shows the Large Icon view. You can also display transactions in Small Icon view, List view, or Detail List view. The transactions displayed in the MS DTC window will be in one of the following states:

◆ **Active.** The transaction has been started and work has been done on it by the Resource Manager.

- ◆ **Aborting.** The transaction is aborting.
- ◆ **Aborted.** Subordinate Transaction Coordinators and Resource Managers have been notified or are currently unavailable.
- ◆ **Preparing.** The application has issued a commit request.
- ◆ **Prepared.** All enlisted Resource Managers and MS DTC have agreed to prepare.
- ◆ **In-doubt.** The transaction is prepared and initiated by a different server; the MS DTC coordinating the transaction is unavailable.
- ◆ **Forced Commit.** An in-doubt transaction has been manually committed.
- ◆ **Forced Abort.** An in-doubt transaction has been manually aborted.
- ◆ **Notifying Committed.** The transaction has prepared and MS DTC is notifying all enlisted Resource Managers that the transaction has committed.
- ◆ **Only Fail Remain to Notify.** All connected Resource Managers and subordinates have been notified of the transaction commit; the only ones left to notify are not connected.
- ◆ **Committed.** The transaction has been successfully committed.

Manually Resolving Transactions

From time to time, you may be required to resolve a distributed transaction manually because of a break in the commit tree (for example, one caused by a break in the communications link). Transactions that remain in the in-doubt state can prove to be a problem because transactions that remain in the in-doubt state may cause the Resource Manager to hold all the locks on the various resources, making them unavailable to others.

To determine the proper action to take when manually resolving an in-doubt transaction, use the MS DTC Transaction window to locate the transaction's immediate parent. Examine the parent using the MS DTC Transaction window to determine the fate of the transaction. If the transaction does not appear in the MS DTC Transaction window, the transaction has been aborted. If the transaction shows up with the Only Failed To Notify state, the transaction has been committed and you can manually commit the transaction. If the status reads In-Doubt, you must look at the next parent node in the chain. Continue to search the nodes until you can determine whether the transaction has been aborted or committed. Once you know the status of the transaction, commit or abort the transaction on the child node and forget the transaction with the Failed To Notify status on the parent node.

To manually resolve a transaction, follow these steps:

1. From the MS DTC Transaction window, select the transaction you have to resolve.

2. Right-click the transaction; the shortcut menu shown in Figure 13.14 opens.

Figure 13.14.
The MS DTC Transac-
tion window shortcut
menu.

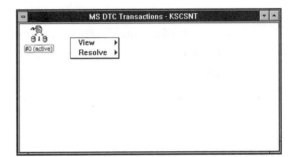

3. Select the Resolve option. The menu shown in Figure 13.15 appears.

Figure 13.15.
The MS DTC Transac-
tion window Manual
Transaction Resolution
menu.

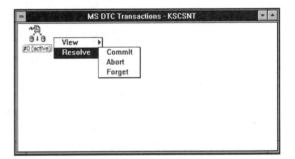

4. Select the proper command from the menu.

MS DTC STATISTICS WINDOW

The MS DTC Statistics window provides cumulative and current information about the transaction in which a server has participated. The DBA can use this information to monitor the performance of MS DTC and make adjustments if required. If possible, you should leave the MS DTC up and running at all times to get the most out of the cumulative statistics. The cumulative statistics displayed in the MS DTC Statistics window are reset to zero when the MS DTC is stopped and restarted. To view the MS DTC Statistics window, follow these steps:

1. From the Enterprise Manager, select the server for which you want to view statistics.

2. Select the Distributed Transaction Coordinator icon.

3. Right-click the Distributed Transaction Coordinator icon to display the shortcut menu.

4. Select the Statistics option. The MS DTC Statistics window appears (see Figure 13.16).

Figure 13.16.
The MS DTC Statistics window.

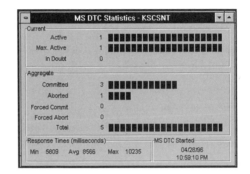

The MS DTC Statistics window has several frames, each of which is described following.

The **Current frame** displays the following information:

◆ **Active.** The current number of transactions yet to complete in the two-phase commit protocol.

◆ **Max Active.** The peak number of transactions reached at any time while the MS DTC is running.

◆ **In-Doubt.** The current number of transactions that are unable to commit because of communication problems between the commit coordinator and the local SQL Server.

The **Aggregate frame** displays the following information:

◆ **Committed.** The cumulative total of committed transactions (excluding those committed manually).

◆ **Aborted.** The cumulative total of aborted transactions (excluding those aborted manually).

◆ **Forced Commit.** The cumulative total of manually committed transactions.

◆ **Forced Abort.** The cumulative total of manually aborted transactions.

◆ **Total.** The cumulative total of all transactions.

The **Response Time frame** displays the average, minimum, and maximum response times in milliseconds. The *response time* is the time between when the transaction was started and when it was committed by the commit coordinator.

The **MS DTC Started frame** displays the date and time on which the current MS DTC was started.

BETWEEN THE LINES

Here is a list of the important points to review when using the Microsoft Distributed Transaction Coordinator:

- ◆ The Transaction Manager is responsible for the coordination and management of a transaction.
- ◆ The Resource Manager is responsible for performing the request of the transaction.
- ◆ As this book went to press, only SQL Server 6.5 can serve as a Resource Manager.
- ◆ The DTC uses a two-phase commit algorithm to guarantee that a distributed data modification will run in its entirety or that the modified data will return to its original state (that is, the state it was in before the transaction was initiated).
- ◆ The Enterprise Manager provides several tools you can use to monitor and tune the MS DTC.

SUMMARY

With the Microsoft Distributed Transaction Coordinator, the process of distributed transactions and two-phase commits has been greatly simplified. Read through this chapter—as well as the Microsoft documentation—and experiment with setting up and administering a Distributed Transaction Coordinator.

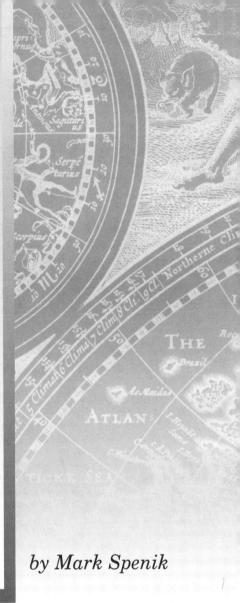

CHAPTER 14

by Mark Spenik

Backups

Backups are copies of SQL Server databases or transaction logs used to recover a database if the database becomes corrupted or is lost in a catastrophic event. The task of backing up and protecting the data is probably the number one job responsibility of the DBA. I have been to many organizations where the sole job responsibility of the DBAs is backup and database maintenance. Being able to recover a database when several disk drives crash or a table or database becomes corrupted is when good DBAs earn their keep. Remember that your ability to recover depends on current backups of your databases. SQL Server 6.5 has made many improvements and enhancements to the backup and recovery process. For example, you can now back up and restore an individual table. One improvement that will greatly simplify your life is that SQL Server 6.5 maintains a history of database backups in the msdb database; this history allows you to back up a database without knowing on which devices the backup is stored.

In this chapter, you learn about the different methods available to you to back up SQL Server databases, tables, and transaction logs. Even more important, you learn how to create a backup and recovery strategy.

Note

Database, table, and transaction log backups are commonly referred to as *dumps* (that is, a database dump, a table dump, or a Transaction log dump). The name *dump* comes from the SQL Server Transact SQL command used to back up databases and transaction logs: the DUMP command. Having worked with SQL Server for many years, I use the terms *dump* and *backup* interchangeably—as you will in the real world. As mentioned in Chapter 8, "Managing Devices," before SQL Server 6.5, a backup device was referred to as a *dump device*; don't be confused if you see a reference to a dump device—it's just another (older) name for a backup device.

BETTER SAFE THAN SORRY!

I learned the value of having a good set of database backups the hard way. Several years ago, while working on a Sybase 4.2 UNIX system, I was hired as a contractor to help out an organization with several large Sybase databases. They had recently lost several key MIS employees and were short handed.

I was working with a gentleman whom I'll refer to as Don, "The Man," one of the few really good jack-of-all trades (UNIX system administrator, Sybase DBA, and client/server developer) individuals I have met. I had been at the organization for only two days; Don and I were busy trying to get a clean set of backups for the database and the UNIX system. The nightly UNIX backup had failed for the last two days and the database backups were going slow because several databases were flagged with errors during DBCC (database consistency check).

We were working with Sybase tech support to correct the database problems. Don was preparing one of the larger databases for a backup when I heard him exclaim "Oh no! I can't believe I did that, I can't believe what I just did. We are doomed!"

It turned out that Don had entered a SQL statement incorrectly that had started one large transaction that was deleting all the rows of a table with about four million rows! I said, "No problem. We'll just recover from a database backup." It was then that Don informed me that the only database backup was 30 days old and outdated! What to do?

Because Don had blocked the delete within a single transaction, we killed the server before it could complete the operation and commit the transaction. The server took a while to come back up as several thousand transactions were rolled back. We then verified the table row count from some numbers taken earlier that day to verify that no data had been lost (information was always added to the table, but never updated).

At this point, Don and I realized that we needed backups—*now*. We stayed late that night verifying previous backup tapes that we found could not be read because of media problems. We continued to work early into the morning and created a whole new set of UNIX system backups and database backups.

The moral of the story is "backups are serious business!" Too often I have heard someone say, "The nightly backup did not run; not sure why, but I'll run it again tonight." Big mistake. Remember that you don't know the hour, day, or minute when the disk drive will give up, the building will be hit by a natural disaster, or someone like Don will issue a SQL command that will ruin the production database! If you don't have a good backup, you will find yourself trying to explain to your boss how you lost a day's worth of data because the nightly backup did not work and you did nothing about it that morning.

14

BACKUPS

WHAT IS A DATABASE BACKUP (DUMP)?

Think of a database backup as a full backup of a database. When you perform a database backup, SQL Server copies all user-defined objects, system tables, and data to the backup device, including the transaction log. Remember from Chapter 8, "Managing Devices," that backup devices can be files, floppy drives, or tape drives. SQL Server 6.x supports backup devices on a Novell file server and can perform striped backups to multiple devices.

Tip

You can dump (back up) a database or transaction log while the database is in use. When a database DUMP command is issued, SQL Server writes all completed transactions to disk and then begins to copy the database. Any incomplete transactions or transactions that occur after the database dump process is started are *not* backed up. To back up changes that occurred while the backup process was running, you must dump the transaction log after the backup completes. Backing up a database slows SQL Server down, so consider performing backups during nonpeak hours. *Note:* When backing up a table, an exclusive lock is placed on the table, prohibiting user access to the table until the table backup is complete.

WHAT IS A TRANSACTION LOG BACKUP (DUMP)?

If you think of a database dump as a full backup, think of a transaction log dump as an incremental database backup (as stated in Chapter 9, "Managing Databases," a transaction log contains all the various transactions that have occurred on a database before the last transaction log dump).

Note

If you create your database and transaction log on the same device, you cannot perform an incremental (transaction log) backup.

A transaction log backup performs one or both of the following operations, depending on the dump options selected:

- ◆ Copies the inactive part of the transaction log to the backup device
- ◆ Truncates (clears and frees up space in) the inactive part of the transaction log

The inactive part of the transaction log is all the completed transactions up to and not on the same page as the earliest outstanding transaction or the earliest transaction that has not been moved to the distribution database and is marked for replication.

Note

Performing a full database backup does not clear out the inactive part of the transaction log. If you only perform database backups, eventually your transaction log will fill up and you will be unable to perform any transactions in the database (no INSERT, UPDATE, or DELETE actions) until you dump the transaction log. You have to perform transaction log dumps, even if you rely on full database backups, to clear out the inactive part of the transaction log.

WHAT IS A TABLE BACKUP (DUMP)?

Version
6.5

A table backup is a copy (snapshot) of a single table within the database. Table backups are a new feature in SQL Server 6.5. Backing up an individual table allows you to perform selective backups that use fewer system resources and save time because you are backing up only a table and not the entire database. You can also use a table backup to move an individual table to another database—for example, if you want to manually synchronize a table between a publisher and subscriber for data replication or in any particular case for which your only previous option was BCP (BulkCopy). You cannot back up a table with columns that have text or image datatypes.

Caution

Although being able to back up an individual table is a powerful enhancement, be careful how you use this feature. You can get into a lot of trouble loading a table that has many different relationships (for example, one that has FOREIGN KEY constraints) with other tables. Loading a copy of a table into such an environment can cause data inconsistencies between the tables. Data in the table you are loading may have changed since the last backup, cascading changes to other tables. Other tables that participate in relationships with the table may have changed since the last table backup (for example, there may be referential integrity problems). Microsoft's documentation recommends restoring from a table backup only in disaster recovery situations. As such, I would rely on transaction log dumps to pick up any

14

BACKUPS

changes that occur in the database and database dumps to recover a database. I recommend using table dumps only in cases where a snapshot of the table makes sense (for example, tables that have no FOREIGN KEYS or relationships), such as when you move a single table to another server.

PERFORMING DATABASE, TRANSACTION LOG, AND TABLE BACKUPS

Examine the steps required to perform a database backup or transaction log backup using the SQL Server Enterprise Manager.

Tip

Before running a database backup, it is good practice to run database maintenance commands. The commands recommended by Microsoft documentation and backed up by real-world experience are the following DBCC commands: CHECKDB, NEWALLOC (or CHECKALLOC), and CHECKCATALOG. It is important to keep up with database maintenance even though it adds time to the backup process. A database backed up with errors will have the same errors on a restored database and, in some severe cases, may prevent a successful restoration of the database. Also consider performing DBCC commands after the backup occurs to validate that the database is still in good order (because changes to the database can occur during backups).

From the Enterprise Manager, select Tools and then select Database Backup/ Restore. The Database Backup/Restore dialog box appears (see Figure 14.1).

Note

When SQL Server performs a database or transaction log backup, SQL Server reads one extent at a time (an extent is eight 2K data pages), skipping unallocated extents, and writes the extent to the database device.

The following sections quickly review the options in the Database Backup/Restore dialog box.

Figure 14.1.
The Database Backup /
Restore dialog box.

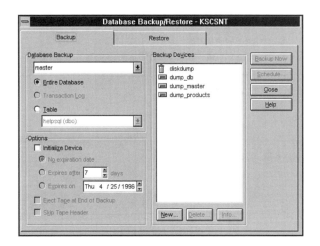

Backup and Restore Tabs

The Database Backup/Restore dialog box has two tabs: the Backup tab and the Restore tab. In this chapter, you concentrate on the functionality provided with the Backup tab. The functionality of the Restore tab is covered in Chapter 15, "Recovery."

Backup Devices Frame

The Backup Devices frame contains a list and icon representations of the backup devices on the server. The functions performed by the three buttons located at the bottom of the Backup Devices frame are as follows:

◆ **New button.** The New button allows you to add a new backup device to the server.

◆ **Delete button.** The Delete button removes the currently selected backup device from the server. Adding and deleting backup devices is covered extensively in Chapter 8, "Managing Devices."

◆ **Info button.** The Info button displays information about the backup device through the Backup Device Information dialog box (see Figure 14.2). You can also display the Backup Device Information dialog box by double-clicking the backup device in the Backup Devices frame.

The Backup Device Information dialog box displays important information about the backups on the backup device, such as the size of the backup device, the database(s) and transaction log(s) currently on the backup device, and the date/time the database or transaction log was dumped to the device.

The information displayed in the Backup Device Information dialog box is the header information for the backup devices. The Transact SQL command to display the header information for a backup devices is LOAD HEADERONLY and has the following format:

```
LOAD HEADERONLY
From dump device
```

Figure 14.2.
The Backup Device
Information dialog box.

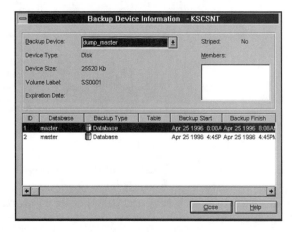

> ## *Note*
>
> **Version**
> **6.5**
>
> Some of the improved features added to SQL Server 6.x are the enhancements for backing up to a disk file instead of to a tape. Many of the features that existed for tape backups in previous versions (such as displaying header information or multiple dumps to a single tape) have now been implemented with disk file dump devices. In version 6.5, the procedures to back up to tape and disk file dump devices are almost identical except for one or two option flags specific to tape drives.

THE STEPS TO PERFORM A BACKUP

To back up a database, transaction log, or table, follow these steps:

1. From the Database Backup/Restore dialog box, select a backup device from the Backup Device frame by clicking the device.

2. Using the Database Backup combo box, select the database for which you want to perform the database, table, or transaction log backup.

3. Select the Entire Database radio button to perform a database backup; select the Transaction Log radio button to perform a transaction log backup; select the Table radio button to perform a table backup. If you select the Table radio button, you must also select the table you want to back up from the drop-down list box under the Table radio button.

4. To write over an existing backup on the selected device, select the Initialize Device checkbox. *Note:* You must select Initialize Device when attempting to back up to a newly created backup device (that is, one that has never been used). The Skip Tape Header and Eject Tape at End of Backup checkboxes are specific to tape drive devices. If the Skip Tape Header box is selected, SQL Server skips reading the ANSI label on the tape. If the Eject Tape at End of Backup checkbox is selected, SQL Server rewinds and unloads the tape at the end of the backup.

Note

The capability to append database and transaction log dumps to a disk file dump device is a welcome feature first added to SQL Server 6.0. SQL Server 4.2x did not have this capability and many DBAs were forced to write script files that would execute after a dump was executed and then move the disk dump file to another directory or rename the file so that the next backup would not overwrite the previous backup. I have seen some very good disk dump file management schemes using directories and file-naming conventions. Being able to append to an existing dump device should eliminate many script files and the problem of overwriting previous backups. However, be careful about how much information is appended to a single backup device. The danger in using a single large dump device for an extended period of time with many different databases and transaction log dumps is that you run the risk of losing all your backups with a single media failure.

5. If you select the Initialize Device checkbox, set one of the following three checkboxes to determine at what time an existing dump device tape or file can be overwritten with new information:

   ◆ **No expiration date:** The file or tape can be overwritten immediately.

   ◆ **Expires after:** Sets the number of days before the tape or file can be overwritten.

   ◆ **Expires on:** Sets the date on which the tape or file can be overwritten.

Tip

> Use the Expires On or the Expires After options to protect your
> database and transaction log dumps from being accidentally over-
> written.

6. To start the database, table, or transaction log backup, click the Backup
   Now button in the Database Backup/Restore dialog box. The Backup
   Volume Labels dialog box appears (see Figure 14.3).

Figure 14.3.
The Backup Volume
Labels dialog box.

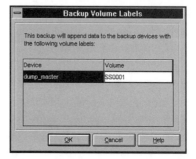

7. Each backup device involved in the backup is displayed along with the
   volume label of the backup device. Volume labels can be changed only if the
   Initialize Device checkbox has been selected. To change the volume label on
   the backup device, enter the name of the volume in the Volume column.
   Volume labels can be up to six ASCII characters; the default volume name
   is SS0001.

8. To continue the backup, click the OK button in the Backup Volume Labels
   dialog box. The database, table, or transaction log backup begins writing to
   the selected devices. The Backup Progress dialog box is displayed (see
   Figure 14.4).

   The Backup Progress dialog box uses a progress indicator to display the
   progression of the backup. To cancel a backup in progress, click the Cancel
   button. When the backup is complete, the Backup Progress Completion
   dialog box is displayed (see Figure 14.5). ***Note:*** If you enable the Select into/
   BulkCopy option for a database and a nonlogged operation such as a bulk
   copy has occurred, you cannot perform a transaction log dump on the
   database.

Figure 14.4.
The Backup Progress
dialog box.

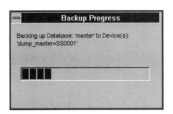

Figure 14.5.
The Backup Progress
Completion dialog box.

Note

To dump a database or transaction log to the floppy disk dump devices `diskettedumpa` or `diskettedumpb`, you must run the Console utility program from a DOS shell. Alternatively, you can dump the database or transaction log to a disk file backup device and then copy the dump file to the floppy disk.

The Transact SQL command used to back up the database and transaction log is the DUMP command, which has the following format for a database:

```
DUMP DATABASE {dbname ¦ @dbname_var}
TO dump_device [, dump_device2 [..., dump_device32]]
[WITH [[,] {UNLOAD ¦ NOUNLOAD}]
[[,] {INIT ¦ NOINIT}]
[[,] {SKIP ¦ NOSKIP}]
[[,] {{EXPIREDATE = {date ¦ @date_var}}
¦ {RETAINDAYS = {days ¦ @days_var}}]
[[,] STATS [ = percentage]]]
```

To dump a transaction log, use the following format:

```
DUMP TRANSACTION {dbname ¦ @dbname_var}
[TO dump_device [, dump_device2 [..., dump_device32]]]
[WITH {TRUNCATE_ONLY ¦ NO_LOG ¦ NO_TRUNCATE}
[[,[{UNLOAD ¦ NOUNLOAD}]
[[,] {INIT ¦ NOINIT}]
[[,] {SKIP ¦ NOSKIP}]
[[,] {{EXPIREDATE = {date ¦ @date_var}}
¦ {RETAINDAYS = {days ¦ @days_var}}]]
```

SQL Server also recognizes the following shortcut syntax (rather than DUMP TRANSACTION) to dump the transaction log:

```
DUMP TRAN
```

To dump a table, use the following format:

```
DUMP TABLE [[[dbname.]owner]Table_Name
TO dump_device [, dump_device2 [..., dump_device32]]
[WITH [[,] {UNLOAD | NOUNLOAD}]
[[,] {INIT | NOINIT}]
[[,] {SKIP | NOSKIP}]
[[,] {{EXPIREDATE = {date | @date_var}}
| {RETAINDAYS = {days | @days_var}}]
[[,] STATS [ = percentage]]]
```

For all three DUMP DATABASE, DUMP TRANSACTION, and DUMP TABLE commands, dump_device has the following format:

```
{dump_device_name | @dump_device_namevar}
| {DISK | TAPE | FLOPPY | PIPE} =
{'temp_dump_device' | @temp_dump_device_var}}
[VOLUME = {volid | @volid_var}]
```

The optional parameters INIT and NOINIT, available with tape devices on SQL Server 4.2x, are now available for other backup devices on SQL Server 6.x. Use the INIT option to overwrite the information stored on the dump device. Use NOINIT to append the information. Remember that the capability to overwrite a device also depends on the expiration and retention dates set for the backup device.

TEMPORARY BACKUP DEVICES

SQL Server 6.x enables you to create and use temporary backup devices when backing up databases or transaction logs. A *temporary backup device* is a backup device that is created at the time of the DUMP command and that has not been added to the system table sysdevices with the system stored procedure sp_addumpdevice. To back up a database to a temporary backup device, you must specify the type of media the backup device is on (use the options DISK, FLOPPY, TAPE, or PIPE) and then specify the complete path and filename. In the case of PIPE, you must specify the name of the named-pipe used in the client application. You can also use variables to create a temporary backup device. Look at some examples using temporary devices.

Example: Dump the master database to a temporary disk backup device called tdump_master.dat, located in the directory C:\MSSQL\BACKUP.

Using the path and filename:

```
DUMP DATABASE master
to DISK='C:\MSSQL\BACKUP\tdump_master.dat'
```

Using a variable:

```
Declare @temp_dump varchar[255]
Select @temp_dump = 'C:\MSSQL\BACKUP\tdump_master.dat'
DUMP DATABASE master
to DISK = @temp_dump
```

UNDERSTANDING DUMP TRANSACTION OPTIONS

The different options available for a transaction log and when to use the different options can be confusing to new DBAs. Examine each of the options individually and determine the correct time to use them.

TRUNCATE_ONLY

The TRUNCATE_ONLY option removes the inactive part of the transaction log (truncates) without backing up (copying) the log to a dump device. You do not have to specify a dump device when using TRUNCATE_ONLY because the log is not copied to a dump device. For example, the syntax to dump the master database transaction log with the TRUNCATE_ONLY option is as follows:

```
DUMP TRANSACTION master
WITH TRUNCATE_ONLY
```

Use the TRUNCATE_ONLY option in the following cases:

◆ If you do not use the transaction log for recovery purposes and rely on full database backups, use TRUNCATE_ONLY immediately after a full database backup has been performed to clear out the inactive part of the transaction log.

◆ To truncate the transaction log when the database and the transaction log share the same device (the master database, for example).

Caution

Always perform a full database backup before using the TRUNCATE_ONLY option. If you use the TRUNCATE_ONLY option without a full database backup, you will not be able to recover the completed transactions in the inactive part of the transaction log at the time the DUMP TRAN with TRUNCATE_ONLY command was issued.

14

NO_LOG

When a DUMP TRANSACTION command is issued with the NO_LOG option, SQL Server truncates the inactive part of the transaction log without logging the DUMP TRANSACTION command.

Caution

After using the NO_LOG option, always perform a full database backup; otherwise, the changes that had been in the transaction log at the time the log was truncated with the NO_LOG option will not be recoverable.

Use the NO_LOG option only when the transaction log has become so full that you cannot dump the transaction log normally to free up space. This occurs when SQL Server is attempting to log the DUMP TRANSACTION command with no room left in the transaction log. Like the TRUNCATE_ONLY option, the NO_LOG option does not require a database device because the log is not copied to a device.

Tip

Microsoft SQL Server has added a feature, available with the first NT release, called a *threshold dump* (or *threshold alert*). The threshold dump monitors the space in the transaction log and prevents the log from filling up by performing a transaction dump when the log reaches a user-defined threshold. See Chapter 26, "Automating Database Administration Tasks," to learn how to set up a transaction log threshold. Once you have set up SQL Server to automatically dump transaction logs, you should not have to use the NO_LOG option. If you do need to use the NO_LOG option, you can execute the command by clicking the Truncate button on the database's Edit Database dialog box.

NO_TRUNCATE

Use the NO_TRUNCATE option when the database you are trying to access is corrupted and you are about to rebuild the database. To use NO_TRUNCATE, the following must be true:

◆ The transaction log must reside on a separate device from the database.

◆ The master database is not corrupted.

The NO_TRUNCATE option writes all the transaction log entries from the time of the last transaction dump up to the point of the database corruption. You can then load the transaction log dump as the last dump in the recovery process for up-to-the-minute data recovery.

Tip

Become familiar with the NO_TRUNCATE option. I have met many DBAs who were unfamiliar with the option or were not sure when to use it.

PERFORMING STRIPED BACKUPS

SQL Server 6.x adds the capability to perform a database, table, or transaction log backup to multiple backup devices called *parallel striped backups*. A parallel striped backup lessens the amount of time required to back up a database, table, or transaction log by creating a single thread for each backup device. The backup device threads read an allocated extent in a round-robin fashion and then write the extents to the thread's assigned backup device, taking advantage of asynchronous I/O capabilities. An example of a parallel striped backup is shown in Figure 14.6.

Figure 14.6.
An example of a
parallel striped backup.

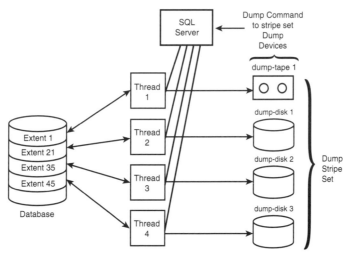

The database, table, or transaction log can be dumped to multiple devices of the same or different media (tape, disk, and so on) called the *striped set*. If a database or transaction log is dumped to multiple devices, it must also be read from multiple devices during restoration. SQL Server can perform parallel backups from 2 to 32 database backup devices. To perform a parallel striped backup to multiple devices using the DUMP DATABASE command, list the backup devices separated by commas. For example, to back up the master database to three backup disk devices called dump1, dump2, and dump3, the syntax is as follows:

```
DUMP DATABASE master
to dump1, dump2, dump3
```

To use the SQL Server Enterprise Manager to perform a parallel striped backup, access the Database Backup/Restore dialog box (refer back to Figure 14.1). Select the database, table, or transaction log you want to back up and set the appropriate backup options. To create a striped dump set, follow these steps:

1. Select a backup device displayed in the Backup Device frame.

2. Press and hold the Ctrl key and use the mouse to select backup devices that are to be part of the dump striped set. When you are done selecting backup devices, release the Ctrl key and click the Backup Now button. The Backup Volume Labels dialog box appears (see Figure 14.7), showing each backup device that is a part of the striped set. Click the OK button to perform the striped backup.

Figure 14.7.
The Backup Volume
Labels dialog box with
a backup striped set.

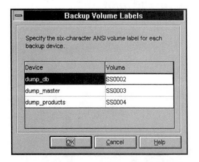

Use the striped parallel backup feature when you have very large databases or are in a production environment that tolerates little or no downtime.

Caution

When you use a striped dump set and then have to restore the transaction log, table, or database, you must read the entire striped set. SQL Server 6.5 simplifies this requirement if you restore from a backup using backup history information that tracks all the devices used to create the backup. If any of the striped devices fail, you cannot recover the data.

Remember that striping is not done to protect the data; it is done to speed up the system.

SCHEDULING BACKUPS

Microsoft SQL Server 6.x excels with scheduling capabilities (the scheduling capabilities and improvements are covered in Chapter 26, "Automating Database Administration Tasks"). Setting up SQL Server to automatically perform database and transaction log backups is a snap. To use SQL Server scheduling, you must run the SQL Server Executive service installed during SQL Server installation.

Note

SQL Server 6.x backup scheduling capabilities have improved substantially over those in SQL Server 4.21. SQL Server 4.21 scheduling involved running the SQL Monitor. I heard many complaints and problems about scheduled backups and the SQL Monitor under SQL Server 4.21. For example, if a backup took an extended period of time and the SQL Monitor properties in the system registry for the backup time were not set high enough to allow the backup to complete, SQL Monitor would halt the backup. I also ran into a few people who used the NT scheduler and AT command instead of SQL Monitor to schedule backups. SQL Server 6.x scheduling has improved substantially; I recommend using the new features along with the SQL Server Executive service.

Backups are scheduled from the Database Backup/Restore dialog box (refer back to Figure 14.1). To schedule a database, table, or transaction log for backup, select the appropriate options and the backup device(s), and then click the Schedule button. The Backup Volume Labels dialog box appears (refer back to Figure 14.3). Use the default volume label or assign a volume label to the selected backup device(s) and click the OK button. The Schedule Backup dialog box appears (see Figure 14.8).

Figure 14.8.
The Schedule Backup
dialog box.

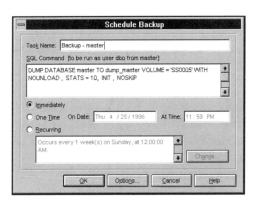

14

BACKUPS

To schedule the backup, follow these steps:

1. Enter a name for the scheduled task in the Task Name text box in the Schedule Backup dialog box or accept the default name Backup - *databasename*.

Tip

> Use a descriptive name for the scheduled task. Using a descriptive name makes it easier to identify the task later in the NT event log or in the SQL Server scheduled task history log.

2. The Transact SQL command scheduled to be executed when the scheduled task runs is displayed in the SQL Command list box. You can edit the SQL command by typing over the existing text or by typing new text.

Tip

> If you were wondering how to use the Enterprise Manager to perform a DUMP TRANSACTION with NO_LOG, TRUNCATE_ONLY, or NO_TRUNCATE, you won't find any checkbox options like the ones in SQL Server 4.21 SQL Administrator! Instead, you must select the device and database for the transaction log dump, click the Schedule button, and then edit the command in the SQL Command list box, adding the transaction log dump options.
>
> If you do not back up the transaction log for recovery purposes and rely on full database dumps, you may want to add a DUMP TRANSACTION with TRUNCATE_ONLY command before or after the DUMP DATABASE command in the SQL Command list box. That way, the inactive part of the transaction log will be cleared out when the database is dumped and is scheduled as a single task instead of scheduling two separate tasks (one to dump the database and one to truncate the transaction log). If data modifications occur during backups, back up the transaction log to a backup device for full database restoration instead of using the TRUNCATE_ONLY option.

3. Select when you want the scheduled backup to occur. For the backup to occur immediately as a background task, select the Immediately radio button. For the task to occur one time only, select the One Time radio button and then set the date and time you want the backup to occur. To set up a recurring backup, select the Recurring radio button. To schedule the recurring backup, click the Change button; the Task Schedule dialog box appears (see Figure 14.9).

Using the Task Schedule dialog box, you can easily schedule the backup to occur daily, weekly, or monthly on a given day or time. (The Task Schedule dialog box is covered in detail in Chapter 26, "Automating Database Administration Tasks.")

Figure 14.9.
The Task Schedule
dialog box.

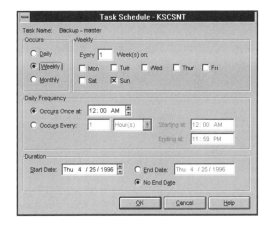

4. After you choose when you want the backup to occur, click OK to schedule the backup.

Note

The Options button on the Schedule Backup dialog box allows you to set up e-mail notification on the success or failure of the scheduled backup, the number of retries, and whether the event is to be written to the event log. The Options button is covered in detail in Chapter 26.

The success or failure of the scheduled task can be viewed from the task scheduling window using the Enterprise Manager (select the Server menu and then select Scheduled Tasks). Scheduled backups and user-initiated backups are now written to the NT event log.

DUMPING A SQL SERVER 6.5 DATABASE INTO A SQL SERVER 6.0 FORMAT

Version
6.5

You can create a database backup from SQL Server 6.5 that can be loaded into SQL Server 6.0. To create a 6.0 backup, the following must be true before generating the backup:

◆ The database you want to back up must be set to read-only or the server must be started in stand-alone mode. It is very important that no activity

(UPDATE, INSERT, or DELETE) occurs while the database backup is being performed, otherwise SQL Server 6.0 will be unable to use the backup.

◆ The database must not contain any SQL Server 6.5 specific features.

◆ Before performing the backup, use DBCC to set the trace flag 3002, which causes SQL Server 6.5 to dump databases in SQL Server 6.0 format. ***Do not forget to turn the trace flag off after you are done.***

Once you have met the necessary requirements, perform the normal backup procedures.

Note

You can load SQL Server 6.5 databases in SQL Server 6.0 if you use service pack 3.0.

UNDERSTANDING DATABASE OPTIONS AND THE TRANSACTION LOG

The following database options affect your ability to perform transaction log dumps on a database:

◆ **The trunc. log on chkpt. option.** If the trunc. log on chkpt. option is set on a database, SQL Server performs the equivalent of a DUMP TRANSACTION with TRUNCAT_ONLY command when SQL Server's checkpoint handler or a user performs a checkpoint on the database. How often a checkpoint is performed on a database by the checkpoint handler depends on the SQL Server configuration parameter recovery interval. If the trunc. log on chkpt. option is set, you get an error message if you attempt to perform a transaction log dump. If the trunc. log on chkpt. option is set, you must rely on full database dumps for backups. Use the trunc. log on chkpt. option in a development environment when you are not concerned about the potential loss of data.

◆ **The select into/bulkcopy option.** The select into/bulkcopy option enables you to perform operations, such as select into or bulk copy, using BCP. Operations such as select into and fast BCP are nonlogged operations (that is, the changes to the database are not logged in the transaction log). If a nonlogged operation is performed on a database, you cannot perform a transaction log dump on the database. To use the DUMP TRANSACTION command, you must use the DUMP DATABASE command to back up the database with the nonlogged operations. Once you have successfully performed a full database dump, you can then use the DUMP TRANSACTION command until a nonlogged operation is performed in the database.

USING DATABASE DUMPS AND TRANSACTION LOG DUMPS TO RECOVER A DATABASE

Before you learn how to create a backup database schedule, it is important to understand how to use database dumps and transaction log dumps to restore a database with up-to-the minute information. To help you understand how to use database and transaction dumps in the real world, walk through the following example (see Figure 14.10).

Figure 14.10.
An example of database and transaction log dumps.

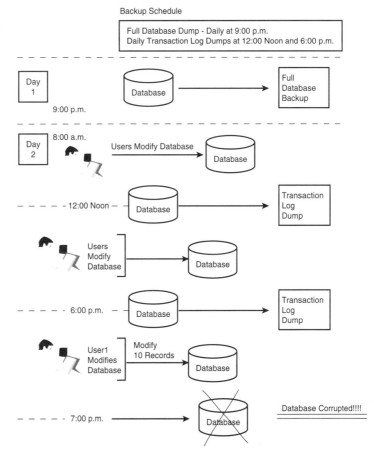

Backup Schedule

Full Database Dump - Daily at 9:00 p.m.
Daily Transaction Log Dumps at 12:00 Noon and 6:00 p.m.

Day 1 — 9:00 p.m. — Database → Full Database Backup

Day 2 — 8:00 a.m. — Users Modify Database → Database

12:00 Noon — Database → Transaction Log Dump

Users Modify Database → Database

6:00 p.m. — Database → Transaction Log Dump

User1 Modifies Database — Modify 10 Records → Database

7:00 p.m. — Database — Database Corrupted!!!!

Using the example in Figure 14.10, the backup schedule for a database is as follows:

◆ Full database backup performed daily at 9:00 P.M.

◆ Transaction log backups performed daily at 12:00 (noon) and 6:00 P.M.

The backup schedule was set up this way because the majority of the people working on the database go to lunch at noon and go home for the evening before 6:00 P.M.. The two incremental backups and the daily full database backup meet the user's recovery needs. Follow through the drawing starting with Day 1.

DAY 1: FULL DATABASE BACKUP OCCURS

Day 1 is the starting point for this example. All you are concerned about is that at 9:00 P.M. on Day 1, SQL Server successfully performs a full database backup.

DAY 2: DATABASE MODIFIED, DATABASE CORRUPTED

Between 8:00 A.M. and 11:59 A.M., the database users log on to the database and make minor modifications and changes to the data stored in the database.

Between 12:00 noon and 12:59 P.M., many of the database users are at lunch, although some continue to work. The SQL Executive kicks off the scheduled transaction log dump. The transaction log of the database is dumped to a dump device, saving all the changes made to the data since the last full backup at 9:00 P.M. the previous evening.

Between 1:00 P.M. and 5:59 P.M., the database users continue to make minor modifications to the data in the database. By 6:00 P.M., the majority of the users have logged off the database and are on their way home.

Between 6:00 P.M. and 6:59 P.M., the SQL Executive starts the evening transaction log dump, saving all the committed transactions made to the database before the previous transaction log dump at noon. Shortly after the transaction log backup completes, User 1 modifies ten records on the database.

At 7:00 P.M., the database becomes corrupted and users are no longer able to access the database. The DBA is called in to remedy the problem. Now what?

USING THE DUMPS TO RECOVER THE DATABASE

In Chapter 15, "Recovery," the commands and requirements to recover a corrupted database are discussed in detail. In this chapter, an example of a high-level walk-through of restoring the database using the available backups is covered. As you understand from this example, the database has become corrupted. So where do you start the recovery process?

The first thing to do is to dump the transaction log with the NO_TRUNCATE option and then drop the corrupted database and re-create it. Once the database has been re-created, you are ready to restore the data.

Next, you must load a full database backup to the newly created database. So you load the database dump performed on Day 1 at 9:00 P.M. The new database now exists in the exact same state as the corrupted database on Day 1 at 9:00 P.M. But how do you get back the work that was done on Day 2? You guessed it: you use the incremental database dumps (that is, the transaction log dumps).

Transaction log dumps are sequenced and must be loaded in the correct order. You load the first transaction log dump that was made at 12:00 noon on Day 2. Loading a transaction log (also referred to as *applying the transaction log*) causes the transactions in the transaction log to re-execute. When the transaction log has completed, the database is now in the exact state the database was in as of 12:00 noon on Day 2.

To regain the 12:00 noon until 6:00 P.M. transactions, you load the second transaction log dump performed at 6:00 P.M. on Day 2. Once the second transaction log successfully loads, the database is in the same state as the original database at 6:00 P.M. on Day 2. But what about the ten records modified by User 1 after the transaction log dump completed but before the database was corrupted? If the database and transaction log were on the same device or you forgot to run the DUMP TRANSACTION with NO_TRUNCATE command, those modified records are lost because you do not have a transaction log dump or a full database dump with the modifications in them. User 1 would have to manually go back and update the records. But because you had the database and transaction log on separate devices and you executed the DUMP TRANSACTION with NO_TRUNCATE command, you load the transaction log dump produced by the NO_TRUNCATE dump command, and the database is back in the same state (including the ten modified records) as the original database just before it became corrupted. You now know how transaction logs and database dumps are used to recover a database—but when should you dump your databases and transaction logs?

UNDERSTANDING WHEN TO DUMP A DATABASE AND TRANSACTION LOG

You know *how* to schedule and dump transaction logs and databases but *when* should you dump them? To answer this question, you are going to create two separate categories: Category 1 consists of actions performed in a database that warrant an immediate database dump. Category 2 consists of the dumps required to meet your recovery needs.

CATEGORY 1: ACTIONS THAT WARRANT DUMPING A DATABASE

In general, you are aware that you should perform database backups on a timely schedule. Backups should also be performed after certain actions occur in a database to ensure full and easy recovery.

USER DATABASES

After you perform certain actions on a user database, you should dump the database as soon as possible to guarantee the recovery of your changes. For example, perform a database backup in the following cases:

◆ After the database is created.

◆ After performing nonlogged operations such as fast BCP, SELECT INTO, or DUMP TRANSACTION with NO_LOG or TRUNCATE_ONLY.

◆ After you make substantial database modifications (new triggers, stored procedures, tables, and so on).

◆ After you create a large index (doing so can speed up the recovery process because SQL Server does not have to rebuild the index during recovery).

THE master DATABASE

Of course, the master database has its own set of rules for when it should be backed up. Remember that keeping a healthy master database is a high priority, so backing up the master database regularly is a must. The master database should be backed up when changes are made to system tables. A list of the commands that modify the system tables can be found in the SQL Server documentation. Here is a short list of some of those commands:

◆ ALTER DATABASE

◆ DISK INIT

◆ DISK MIRROR

◆ DISK RESIZE

◆ sp_addlogin

◆ sp_droplogin

Because many of you use the Enterprise Manager to perform your database administrative tasks, you may be unaware of the SQL Server commands and system stored procedures being executed. In Enterprise Manager lingo, back up the master database after you have done the following:

◆ Added/removed devices or databases

◆ Altered the size of a database

◆ Added system login IDs

◆ Modified system configuration parameters

CATEGORY 2: SCHEDULED DATABASE DUMPS

Unfortunately, there is no exact formula to tell you when you should dump your databases. Why? Because each database has its own backup requirements. For example, in the backup and recovery example you stepped through earlier in this chapter, transaction log dumps were performed twice a day. In the example, it was acceptable to lose a half day's work if the example SQL Server suddenly lost all its databases, including the master. Many organizations cannot afford to lose any data and require up-to-the minute recovery.

As another example, maybe you are in a development environment in which a bimonthly database backup is all that is required. Your backup strategy should enable you to recover any of your databases within an acceptable amount of time and for an acceptable data loss limit for each database. Before discussing backup strategies, I want to point out that it is just as important to perform routine database and table maintenance (database maintenance plans are discussed in more detail in Chapter 25, "Developing a SQL Server Maintenance Plan") as it is to properly back up your databases.

In general, you can find more information on setting up appropriate backup schedules in the documentation that ships with SQL Server or the white papers found on Microsoft TechNet. Now review a few questions and suggestions you can use to help you set up a backup plan.

Note

In my opinion, a backup plan and a recovery plan are one in the same. To test and verify your backup plan, you must use the database backups to restore your SQL Server databases; thus, the two go hand-in-hand. Also, don't forget that databases require routine maintenance, including the use of DBCC commands.

SYSTEM DATABASES

Having up-to-date, valid database backups can save you a lot of time, especially if you need to restore a system database (such as the master database). Take special care with the master database; consider mirroring the master device for added

14

BACKUPS

protection. I recommend backing up the following system databases (at the minimum) daily:

- ◆ `master`
- ◆ `msdb`
- ◆ `model`
- ◆ distribution database (for distribution replication servers)

TRANSACTION LOG THRESHOLD ALERTS

All database transaction logs should have threshold events scheduled to prevent the database transaction logs from filling up. (Enough said!)

HOW OFTEN SHOULD I DUMP THE TRANSACTION LOG DATABASE?

If the database and the transaction log both became corrupted, how many transactions can you afford to lose? How many transactions are performed in an hour? A day? You must ask and answer these questions and more to determine how often you should dump the transaction log and database. Try to perform your database and transaction log dumps during nonpeak hours.

Also keep in mind what is required to recover a database using full database dumps and transaction logs. For example, if you perform transaction log dumps (incremental backups) six times a day and a full database backup every five days, what do you have to do to recover the database? Depending on when the database became corrupted, you stand the possibility of having to load a full database backup and 0 to 30 transaction log dumps. Is this acceptable? Get the picture? If you have a database that is not updated very often, performing a biweekly transaction log dump and a weekly database dump may meet your requirements.

HOW DO I MANAGE THE DUMPS?

How are you going to manage the various database and transaction log dumps on tapes or dump files and how long are you going to keep your backups? Believe me, this is a problem in organizations with several databases. Organization is the key here. Come up with a consistent naming convention and filing system for your backups. You will want to keep old backups around for several weeks or months. Organization makes it easy to find dumps that are several weeks or months old.

HOW LONG WILL IT TAKE TO RECOVER THE DATABASE?

If your database becomes corrupted, how long will it take to recover the database? Is the recovery time acceptable? If you find that the recovery time is not acceptable, you may have to consider hot backups. A *hot backup* is a term given to a system that uses specialized hardware to mirror the main database server; the hot backup can be used immediately if the main database server goes down. SQL Server 6.5 now provides a mechanism to support fallback recovery when two computers share the same hard drive. If one computer fails, the other computer takes over. The bottom line is that by using a hot backup or fallback recovery configuration, you decrease the chance that you will experience any downtime.

IN WHAT OTHER WAYS IS THE DATABASE PROTECTED?

It never hurts to have more than one level of data protection for very sensitive data. For example, is the database on a device that is mirrored or does it reside on a RAID 5 drive configuration? Is the SQL Server shut down weekly and the SQL Server directory and database devices backed up to tape by a system administrator? Always know what other recovery options are available to you, just in case your well-constructed backup and recovery plan fails.

TEST AND PRACTICE

Once you have created a backup plan, don't stop there and say, "Well, I've got a plan—I'm done." Make sure that you test your backup plan by actually recovering the databases. And when you are done testing, test your recovery plan again. When the day comes and a database fails, you should feel very comfortable and confident in your ability to recover the database. The bottom line is, test and practice your backup and recovery plans.

BETWEEN THE LINES

For database backups, keep in mind the following:

◆ A SQL Server backup is commonly referred to as a *dump*.

◆ Database dumps are full backups of the data and database objects.

◆ Transaction log dumps are incremental backups that reflect the changes in the database since the previous transaction log dump.

◆ Users can still use the database during backups.

◆ SQL Server 6.5 allows you to perform a backup on an individual table. Users cannot access the table during a table backup because SQL Server places an exclusive lock on the table. Do not rely on table backups to restore a database. Use table backups in cases where a snapshot of the data makes sense or as a last resort in a disaster recovery situation.

◆ Use the header information on backup devices to display important information about the currently stored backups.

14

BACKUPS

Version
6.5

Version
6.5

- ◆ You can append dumps to disk dump devices as to well as to tape dump devices.

- ◆ SQL Server 6.5 keeps a history of database backups in the msdb database.

- ◆ SQL Server 6.x allows you to use temporary dump devices.

- ◆ Review the section in this chapter about the DUMP TRANSACTION log options: TRUNCATE_ONLY, NO_LOG, and NO_TRUNCATE.

- ◆ To decrease the amount of time required for database backups, use the new parallel striped backup features of SQL Server 6.x.

- ◆ Backups can be reliably and easily scheduled from the Enterprise Manager.

- ◆ It is a good practice to perform database maintenance (that is, DBCC commands) on a database before performing a backup. It is also a good idea to perform the same maintenance commands after the backup completes.

- ◆ Create a backup and recovery plan to protect your databases. Make sure that you test and practice the plan.

- ◆ Back up the master database at least once a day.

SUMMARY

Maintaining a good set of database backups is one of the most important responsibilities of a DBA. Use the ideas and suggestions in this chapter to help build your own backup plan. The next chapter examines the other side of the coin: how to use the database and transaction log backups to restore or move a database.

CHAPTER 15

by Mark Spenik

Recovery

In the previous chapter, you learned how to back up a database, table, and transaction log and how to set up a backup schedule to prevent data loss. In this chapter, you learn how to use the database, table, and transaction log backups to restore a corrupted database or move a database or table to another server. This chapter builds on what you learned in the previous chapter and puts your backup and recovery plans to the test. A restore operation is also referred to as a *database load* (after the Transact SQL LOAD statement used to restore a database, table, or transaction log).

This chapter explains the steps to follow when a database becomes corrupted and the DBA restores (recovers) the database. But first, let's look at another type of database recovery performed by SQL Server: *automatic recovery*.

AUTOMATIC RECOVERY

Whenever SQL Server is started, a process called *automatic recovery* occurs. During the automatic recovery process, SQL Server checks each database for uncommitted transactions to roll back or for committed transactions to roll forward.

You may be wondering what it means to *roll a transaction back* or to *roll a transaction forward*. First, you must understand what a transaction is. In simple database terminology, a *transaction* is defined as a unit of work. A transaction can consist of a single SQL statement that modifies one row or 10,000 rows or a transaction can consist of many SQL statements bunched together as a single unit of work.

The following is a single SQL statement:

```
Insert jobs
Values(12, "Write SQL Books", 1,4)
```

The following are multiple SQL statements:

```
Begin TRAN
Insert jobs
Values(12, "Write SQL Books", 1, 4)
if(@@error != 0)
begin
Rollback tran
else
Update employee
set job_id = 12
end
if(@@error = 0)
Commit TRAN
else
Rollback TRAN
```

Note

Data modification statements such as INSERT, DELETE, and UPDATE are treated as transactions. To group several data modifications together to be treated as a single transaction, use one of the following syntaxes:

```
BEGIN TRAN
```
```
BEGIN TRANSACTION
```

To commit the changes (that is, to save them in the database), use one of the following syntaxes:

```
COMMIT TRAN
```
```
COMMIT TRANSACTION
```

To roll back the changes (that is, to *not* save them in the database), use one of the following syntaxes:

```
ROLLBACK TRAN
```
```
ROLLBACK TRANSACTION
```

If a transaction is written to the database, the transaction is said to be *committed*. A transaction is said to be *rolled back* when the transaction is written to the data cache and transaction log and then removed from the log without being written to the database. Using the diagrams in Figure 15.1, walk through a series of transactions and a SQL Server automatic recovery.

Step 1: Start Transactions

Figure 15.1 shows two users issuing two separate transactions to SQL Server called TRAN1 and TRAN2. SQL Server receives the transactions and marks the start of transactions TRAN1 and TRAN2 in the transaction log. TRAN1 modifies page 5 in the cache; TRAN2 modifies page 7 in the cache. No data has been written to the transaction log or the database.

Step 2: Commit Transaction TRAN1

User 1 sends a statement to SQL Server to commit TRAN1. SQL Server writes the committed transaction to the transaction log and marks page 5 in the cache as a *dirty* page. The transaction is still not written to the database.

Figure 15.1.
Transactions and
automatic recovery.

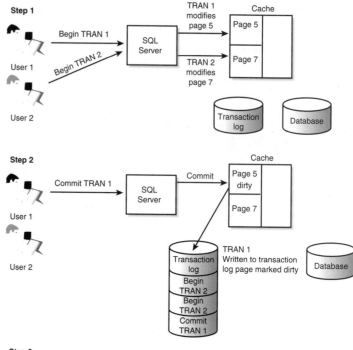

Step 3
SQL Server goes down due to power outage, before checkpoint.

Step 4
Automatic recovery

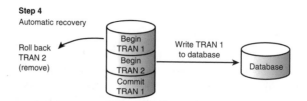

Note

SQL Server uses a write-ahead log scheme. Data is written to the transaction log first before it is written to the database. The term *dirty page* refers to a page in the disk cache that has been modified by a committed transaction; the page has been written to the transaction log but not to the database (pages modified by uncommitted transactions are considered active and not dirty).

STEP 3: POWER OUTAGE—SQL SERVER UNEXPECTEDLY SHUTS DOWN

Before SQL Server issues a checkpoint in the database and User 2 can commit TRAN 2, a power outage occurs, bringing down the NT server and SQL Server.

Note

Dirty pages are written to the database when SQL Server performs an automatic checkpoint or when a user (the database owner or sa) issues a CHECKPOINT command in the database. A checkpoint causes all dirty pages to be written to the database and typically takes a second or two to execute. The frequency of automatic checkpoints depends on the SQL Server configuration parameter recovery interval. The recovery interval parameter determines the maximum number of minutes required to recover a database. The CHECKPOINT process checks every minute to see which databases have matched or exceeded the recovery interval and performs a checkpoint in each of these databases. For more information on the recovery interval, see Chapter 19, "Which Knobs Do I Turn?"

STEP 4: RESTART AND AUTOMATIC RECOVERY

In this step, NT server is restarted and restarts SQL Server. SQL Server begins to go through the automatic recovery process. The master database is first checked, followed by the model database and the temporary database; tempdb is cleared; the scheduling database is recovered, followed by the pubs database and the distribution database for servers configured as a replication distributor. Last, but not least, the user databases are recovered. In the user database, the committed transaction TRAN1 is *rolled forward*, that is, it is written to the database. The uncommitted transaction, TRAN2, is *rolled back*, that is, it is removed from the transaction log without being written to the database. You can view the results of the SQL Server automatic recovery process by viewing the error log shown in Listing 15.1 or by viewing the NT event log.

LISTING 15.1. PARTIAL ERROR LOG LISTING OF THE SQL SERVER AUTOMATIC RECOVERY PROCESS.

```
96/05/07 20:27:40.67 spid10    Recovering database 'pubs'
96/05/07 20:27:40.69 spid11    Recovering database 'msdb'
96/05/07 20:27:40.70 spid12    Recovering database 'test'
```

continues

LISTING 15.1. CONTINUED

```
96/05/07 20:27:40.74 spid11   Recovery dbid 5 ckpt (1283,20) oldest tran=(1283,19)
96/05/07 20:27:40.75 spid11   1 transactions rolled forward in dbid 5.
96/05/07 20:27:40.75 spid10   Recovery dbid 4 ckpt (777,24) oldest tran=(777,23)
96/05/07 20:27:40.76 spid10   1 transactions rolled forward in dbid 4.
96/05/07 20:27:40.77 spid12   Recovery dbid 6 ckpt (1522,27)
96/05/07 20:27:41.62 spid1    Recovery complete.
```

Tip

When the transaction log is truncated, only committed transactions up to the oldest open active transaction are removed. An outstanding transaction can result in the inability of the transaction log to be cleared when truncating. If you suspect you are having this problem, use the DBCC command option OPENTRAN for information on the oldest outstanding transaction. If you have an open transaction preventing you from clearing the transaction log, in SQL Server 6.x you can use the spid (system process ID) displayed in the DBCC output and terminate the offending process using the KILL command. In SQL Server 4.2x, all users were required to log off SQL Server and the server had to be shut down and restarted to close the open transaction.

LOADING A DATABASE OR TABLE BACKUP OR APPLYING A TRANSACTION LOG BACKUP USING THE BACKUP HISTORY ENTRY

Version
6.5

Before covering the steps required to recover a corrupted database, examine how to use the SQL Enterprise Manager to load a database or table backup or apply a transaction log backup using a backup history entry. The term *backup history entry* is used to represent the backup history information maintained by SQL Server 6.5 and stored in the msdb database in the system tables sysbackupdetails, sysbackuphistory, sysrestoredetails, and sysrestorehistory. When a successful backup of a database, table, or transaction log occurs in SQL Server 6.5, the information is stored in the database msdb system tables. Using the backup history entry simplifies the restoration process: you don't have to know which, what, or how many devices the backup is on. The backup history information is a new SQL Server 6.5 feature. The steps to load an existing database using the backup history differ slightly from loading a database using backup devices. I highly recommend using the backup history entry except in the case where backup history does not exist (such as in the case of moving a database to another server).

Note

You can perform the following to load or recover databases; however, to recover a damaged master database, you must run a special utility, described later in this chapter.

From the SQL Enterprise Manager, select Tools and then select Database Backup/Restore. The Database Backup/Restore dialog box appears (see Figure 15.2). Click the Restore tab (see Figure 15.3).

Figure 15.2.
The Database Backup/
Restore dialog box.

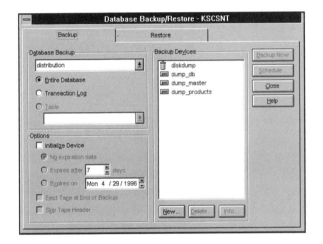

To load a database, table, or transaction log backup, perform the following steps:

1. Using the Database drop-down combo box in the Restore page of the Database Backup/Restore dialog box, select the database to which you want to restore. The backup history for the selected database is displayed in the Backup History frame (see Figure 15.4).

2. To load a database or transaction log backup, select the Database and/or Transaction Logs radio button. To load a table, select the Single Table radio button and then select the table you want to load from the drop-down combo box.

3. Select the proper checkbox for the database, transaction log, or table backup history entry from which you want to restore in the Backup History frame. The Backup History frame displays various information about the backups for the database (for example, the type of backup, the start and end time of the backup, and the size of the backup to name a few of the items). For additional information about the selected backup, click the Info

button; the Backup History Information dialog box appears (see Figure 15.5). The Backup History Information dialog box displays further information for the selected backup such as the device or devices on which the backup is stored. By using a backup history entry to restore from, you no longer have to worry about the device on which the backup resides—in the case of a striped backup set, you no longer have to remember which devices comprise the backup set—because the information is stored in the backup history entry.

Figure 15.3.
The Restore page of the
Database Backup/
Restore dialog box.

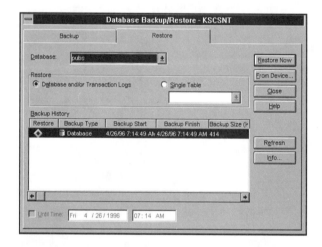

Figure 15.4.
The Restore page of the
Database Backup/
Restore dialog box,
showing the backup
history.

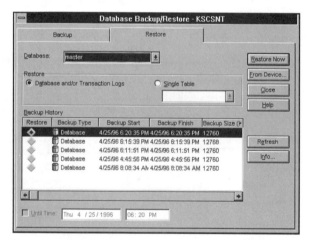

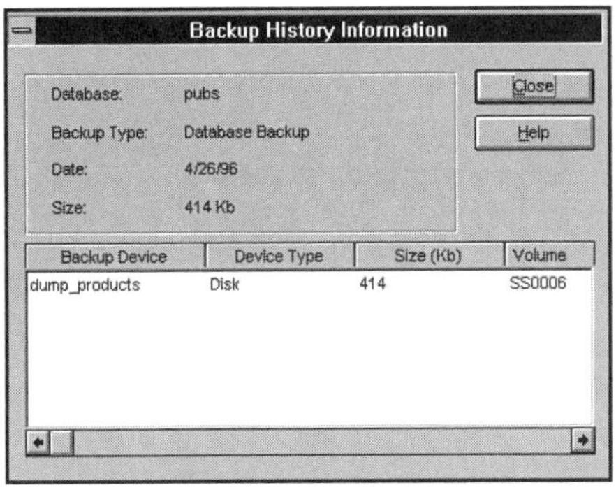

Figure 15.5.
The Backup History
Information dialog box.

4. After you select the proper backup history entry, click the Restore Now button. A Restore Progress dialog box appears (see Figure 15.6), showing the progress of the recovery process. To cancel the recovery process, click the Cancel button. Once the recovery has completed, a successful restore dialog box appears, informing you that the operation has successfully completed.

Figure 15.6.
The Restore Progress
dialog box.

15

RECOVERY

Note

A new feature of SQL Server 6.x speeds up the load and recovery process. This feature loads database or transaction dumps in 64K chunks. Also note that although a table can be loaded from a database backup, the Microsoft documentation discourages doing so because of possible inconsistencies that can result when using a database backup (the entire table is not locked during a database backup—as it is for a table backup).

The Transact SQL command to load a database backup is the LOAD DATABASE command, which has the following syntax:

```
LOAD DATABASE { dump_device_name ¦ @dump_device_namevar}
FROM dump_device [, dump_device2 [..., dump_device32]]
[WITH [[,] {UNLOAD ¦ NOUNLOAD}]
[[,] {SKIP ¦ NOSKIP}]
[[,] {FILE = fileno}]
[[,] STATS [ = percentage]]]
```

For LOAD DATABASE, LOAD TRANSACTION, and LOAD TABLE, dump_device can have the following format:

```
dump_device =
{dump_device_name ¦ @dump_device_namevar} ¦{DISK ¦ TAPE ¦ FLOPPY ¦ PIPE} =
{'temp_dump_device' ¦ @temp_dump_device_var}}
[VOLUME = {volid ¦ @volid_var}]
```

Tip

You can load dumps from temporary dump devices.

The Transact SQL command to load a transaction log is the LOAD TRANSACTION command, which has the following syntax:

```
LOAD TRANSACTION { dump_device_name ¦ @dump_device_namevar}
FROM dump_device [, dump_device2 [..., dump_device32]]
[WITH [[,] {UNLOAD ¦ NOUNLOAD}]
[[,] {SKIP ¦ NOSKIP}]
[[,] {FILE = fileno}]
[[, ] {STOPAT = date_time ¦ @date_time_var}]
```

The Transact SQL command to load a table is the LOAD TABLE command, which has the following format:

```
LOAD Table [[database.]owner.]Table Name
FROM dump_device [, dump_device2 [..., dump_device32]]
[WITH [[,] {UNLOAD ¦ NOUNLOAD}]
[[,] {SKIP ¦ NOSKIP}]
[[,] {FILE = fileno}]
[[, ] {SOURCE = source_name}]
[[, ] {APPEND}]
[[,] STATS [ = percentage]]]
```

RESTRICTIONS AND RULES FOR LOADING A TABLE

There are several rules and restrictions that apply when loading a table from a backup. The rules and restrictions for loading an individual table are as follows:

- ◆ A table load cannot occur on a table that has indexes or columns with the `image` or `text` datatypes or that has been published for replication.

- ◆ You can load an individual table from a database backup.

- ◆ Declarative referential integrity (DRI), rules, triggers, and defaults are not enforced during a table load.

- ◆ You cannot load a table into a system table, only into user-defined tables.

- ◆ The database `select into/bulkcopy` option must be set.

- ◆ The source and target tables can have different names.

- ◆ Once you load a table, you must perform a full database backup before you can use the `DUMP TRANSACTION` statement.

LOADING A DATABASE OR TABLE BACKUP OR APPLYING A TRANSACTION LOG BACKUP USING BACKUP DEVICES

You may encounter a situation in which you do not have any backup history information for a database, table, or transaction log but you want to recover the database, table, or transaction log using backup devices (for example, if you lost the `msdb` or the `master` database). When you select a backup device or file, the header information is read so that you can validate what type of backup and what databases are on the device or file. Another example of a database with no backup history information is a database created for the sole purpose of loading a database backup from another server. In this case, the newly created database has no backup history from which you can restore it. To restore a database, table, or transaction log using backup devices, follow these steps:

1. From the Restore page in the Database Backup/Restore dialog box (refer back to Figure 15.3), click the From Device button; the Restore From Device on Server dialog box appears (see Figure 15.7).

2. From the Destination Database drop-down combo box, select the database to restore to.

3. Select the backup device(s) or files from which you are going to restore the database, transaction log, or table. Press and hold the Ctrl key and select multiple backup devices. If the database or transaction log backup was performed using a parallel striped set, you must select all the devices in the

backup stripe set before you can restore. Select the backup from which you want to load in the Backup Information window.

4. Once you have selected the destination database and backup device(s) and selected the correct backup to load from in the Backup Information window, click the Restore Now button to load the selected backup from the selected device(s).

Figure 15.7.
The Restore From
Device on Server
dialog box.

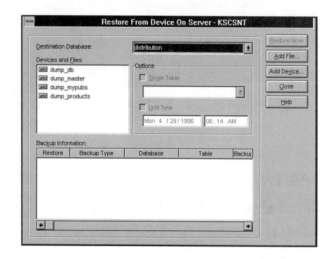

Version 6.5 POINT-IN-TIME RECOVERY

SQL Server 6.5 allows you to perform point-in-time recovery when applying (restoring) a transaction log to a database. Point-in-time recovery allows you to specify a point in time from which the transactions in the transaction log are to be rolled forward. Suppose that a transaction log spans from 11:30 A.M. to 2:30 P.M. In previous versions of SQL Server, you had to load the entire transaction log (that is, all or nothing). All the transactions that occurred from 11:30 A.M. to 2:30 P.M. are applied to the database. In SQL Server 6.5, you do not have to load the entire transaction log. For example, you can choose to load only all the committed transactions from 11:30 A.M. to 12:30 P.M. In a normal restoration process, you will always want to load the entire transaction log; however, in some instances when the database has become corrupted (for example a user error such as an invalid UPDATE or DELETE), you can use point-in-time recovery to bring the database back to the point before the data corruption occurred. To perform point-in-time-recovery, follow these steps:

1. Start at the Restore page in the Database Backup/Restore dialog box (see Figure 15.3). From the Database drop-down combo box, select the database

to which you want to restore the transaction log. The backup history for the selected database is displayed in the Backup History frame.

2. Select the Database and/or Transaction Logs radio button.

3. In the Backup History frame, select the proper checkbox for the history entry of the transaction log backup from which you want to restore.

4. Once you have selected the proper transaction log backup history entry, select the Until Time checkbox. Adjust the date and time. Transactions committed after the date and time setting will be rolled back (see Figure 15.8).

Figure 15.8.
The Restore page in the Database Backup/Restore dialog box, showing point-in-time recovery.

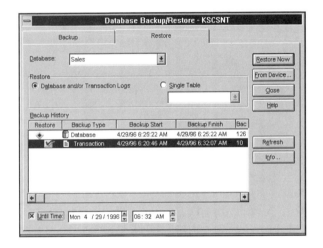

5. Click the Restore Now button. A Restore Progress dialog box appears, showing the progress of the recovery process. Once the recovery has completed, a successful restore dialog box appears, informing you that the operation has successfully completed.

PREPARING FOR A DATABASE LOAD (RESTORE)

Whether you are trying to recover a corrupted database or moving a database to another server, certain conditions must be met to load the backup. First, any existing data in the database is overwritten by the loaded backup. A backup cannot be loaded while the database is in use; the database to which you are loading the backup must be at least as large or larger than the database that created the backup. The SQL Server to which you are loading the backup must have the same sort order and character set as the SQL Server that backed up the database.

Tip

> If you are creating a database to load a database backup, use the SQL Server 6.x FOR LOAD option on the CREATE DATABASE Transact SQL command. The FOR LOAD option saves time when creating the database by not initializing the data pages.

One of the most overlooked aspects of preparing a database for recovery is that the database must not only be the same size or larger than the dump database, but it must have the exact same device allocation order and size.

THE RESTORE DATABASE MYTH

Requiring the exact device size and allocation is one of the deep dark secrets of SQL Server database recovery. I have run into many DBAs who were trying to restore databases and were having problems because the device allocation was not the same. Many assumed that the database only had to be the same size or larger!

What does having the same device allocation and size mean? Consider a few examples. In the first example, you create a database called test1 that is created with 40M for data on data_dev1 and 10M for the transaction log on log_dev1. To load a database backup of the database test1 to another database, you must create a database at least 50M in size (40M of data followed by at least 10M for the transaction log). Now suppose that you performed an alter database command and added 5M for data on data_dev2 and 2M for the log on log_dev2 and 10M of data on data_dev1. Now the test1 database contains many different device fragments (that is, the space allocated to the database by the create and alter statements) as shown in Table 15.1.

TABLE 15.1. DATABASE test1 DEVICE FRAGMENT MAP.

Device Type	Size in Megabytes
Data	40
Log	10
Data	5
Log	2
Data	10
Total Database Size	67

To create a database to load the `test1` database dump, you need a database of at least 67M in size with a 40M data fragment followed by a 10M log fragment, followed by 5M data fragment, followed by a 2M log fragment, followed by at least a 10M data fragment—get the picture? If all of this sounds complex, relax. Microsoft has added two system stored procedures in SQL Server 6.5 (`sp_coalesce_fragments` and `sp_help_revdatabase`) that simplify the process of determining the proper device allocation required to create a database to load a database backup. Before discussing the two new stored procedures, let's review the manual process of determining database device allocation.

Note

To load or recover a database from a backup, the actual device on which the database is located is not important. However, the size and type of device fragmentation allocation is. The actual device(s) on which a database resides is important if the device fails and must be re-created.

To manually determine the device allocation for a database, perform the following device fragment query in the `master` database. (Note that the following query is for the database `test1`. Substitute your database name for *test1*):

```
select segmap 'fragment type', size 'fragment size'
from sysusages
where dbid = (select dbid
from sysdatabases
where name = "test1")
```

Running the query on SQL Server displays the following output:

```
Fragment Type Fragment Size
3            1024
4             512
```

The `Fragment Type` column translates as follows:

◆ `3` = Data device

◆ `4` = Log device

◆ `7` = Log and data are on the same device

◆ Any other values are user-defined segments

The fragment size is displayed in 2K blocks (512 = 1M). If you don't want to compute the size of the device segment, execute the system stored procedure `sp_helpdb`, which has the following syntax:

```
sp_helpdb [database name]
```

15

RECOVERY

Following is the output of the `sp_helpdb` command on the `test1` database:

```
name   db_size  owner  dbid created  status
---------------------------- ------------ ---------------------------- ------- ----------- --
------------------------------------------------------------------------------------------------
------------------------------------------------------------------------------------------------
-------
test1  3.00 MB sa  6   Aug  6 1995 no options set

device_fragments  size   usage
-------------------------------------- ------------ -------------------
test1                                  2.00 MB data only
test1_log                              1.00 MB log only
```

Version 6.5

SQL Server 6.5 has added two system stored procedures to aid you in determining how to correctly create a database with the proper device allocation. The two stored procedures are `sp_coalesce_fragments` and `sp_help_revdatabase`. The stored procedure `sp_coalesce_fragments` deletes and updates rows in the system table `sysusages`. The purpose of `sp_coalesce_fragments` is to reduce the number of rows in `sysusages` for database fragments on the same device and physically contiguous by combining them into a single row in the `sysusages` table. The syntax for `sp_coalesce_fragments` is as follows:

```
sp_coalesce_fragments [DataBase Name Pattern]
```

Run the `sp_coalesce_fragments` stored procedure before executing the stored procedure `sp_help_revdatabase`. `sp_help_revdatabase` analyzes a database and generates a script to re-create the database with the proper device allocation. The format for `sp_help_revdatabase` is as follows:

```
sp_help_revdatabase [DataBase Name Pattern]
```

The optional parameter `Database Name Pattern` specifies a database name pattern and follows the rules used for a LIKE statement. `sp_help_revdatabase` may not be able to generate the correct script to re-create the database in cases where device fragments are not evenly divisible by 512. Check the script for cautionary comments that indicate that the ALTER database size has been rounded up. You can avoid this problem by creating devices in multiples of 512 2K pages. A sample output from the stored procedure `sp_help_revdatabase` is shown in Listing 15.2.

LISTING 15.2. A SAMPLE SCRIPT GENERATED BY THE STORED PROCEDURE `sp_help_revdatabase`.

```
/********1*********2*********3*********4*********5*********6**
Reverse generated at 1996/04/29  08:11:39:130

Server / Database / Default sortorder ID :
KSCSNT / Sales / 52

DBName                          FromLPage  ToLPage   segmap
------------------------------- ---------- --------- ----------
```

```
Sales                          0         1023      3
Sales                       1024        2047      4
Sales                       2048        3071      3


@@version:  Microsoft SQL Server  6.50 - 6.50.201 (Intel X86)
*********1*********2*********3*********4*********5*********6**/
go

USE master
go

--------------- Space and Log allocations -------------


CREATE  Database  Sales
      on  Sales_Datat  =  2  -- 1024  of two Kb pages
go



ALTER   Database  Sales
      on  sales_log  =  2  -- 1024  of two Kb pages
go
EXECute sp_logdevice Sales ,sales_log
go

ALTER   Database  Sales
      on  sales_data2  =  2  -- 1024  of two Kb pages
go

------------------- DB Options -----------------


EXECute sp_dboption  Sales ,'ANSI null default'
                          , false

EXECute sp_dboption  Sales ,'dbo use only'
                          , false

EXECute sp_dboption  Sales ,'no chkpt on recovery'
                          , false

/***
EXECute sp_dboption  Sales ,'offline'
                          , false
***/

/***
EXECute sp_dboption  Sales ,'published'
                          , false
***/

EXECute sp_dboption  Sales ,'read only'
                          , false

EXECute sp_dboption  Sales ,'select into/bulkcopy'
                          , false
```

continues

LISTING 15.2. CONTINUED

```
EXECute sp_dboption  Sales ,'single user'
                           , false

/***
EXECute sp_dboption  Sales ,'subscribed'
                           , false
***/

EXECute sp_dboption  Sales ,'trunc. log on chkpt.'
                           , false

go

------------------- sa  is  dbo -------------------


go
--
```

Tip

Keep a script generated by sp_help_revdatabase for each database. Check the script to make sure that no cautionary comments have been added because of fragments that are not multiples of 512. In the event of a recovery or a simple database move, you will be well prepared because you will have the Transact SQL statements required to properly create the database. Update your database scripts whenever you alter the size of a database or transaction log. It is also a good idea to keep a device fragment and device allocation map for each database generated by the device fragment query shown earlier in this section as a fallback.

RECOVERING A DATABASE

Now that you understand how to use the tools and commands required to load a database, review the following steps to recover a damaged database:

1. If the transaction log for the corrupt database is on a separate device, use the DUMP TRANSACTION command with the NO_TRUNCATE clause to dump the transaction log to a dump device so that the transactions can be recovered (that is, load it as the last transaction log).

2. Perform the device fragment query described earlier in this section to determine the correct fragment map required to re-create the database.

3. Drop the damaged database using the Enterprise Manager or the DROP DATABASE command. If the DROP DATABASE command fails, use DBCC DBREPAIR (*database name*, DROPDB) or the system stored procedure, sp_dbremove.

4. Create the database with the correct device fragments using the CREATE DATABASE command or the SQL Server Enterprise Manager and, if necessary, the ALTER DATABASE command.

5. Reload the database using the Enterprise Manager or the LOAD DATABASE command.

Tip

You can load a database dump from SQL Server 4.2x or SQL Server 6.0 to SQL Server 6.5, but you cannot load a SQL Server 6.5 formatted database to a SQL Server 4.2x database. You can load a SQL Server 6.5 database into a SQL Server 6.0 that is using SQL Server 6.0 service pack 3.0. You can create a backup from SQL Server 6.5 in SQL Server 6.0 format that can be read by SQL Server 6.0 without SQL Server 6.0 service pack 3.0. For more information on producing a backup in SQL Server 6.0 format from SQL Server 6.5, refer to Chapter 14, "Backups."

LOADING TRANSACTION LOGS

After you load the most recent database backup, you can begin to load (apply) the transaction log dumps to the database. When you load a transaction log dump, database modifications made in the transaction log are reexecuted in the database. To maintain database integrity, transaction logs must be loaded in correct order. SQL Server checks the timestamp value of each transaction log and ensures that the transaction sequence is correct. If you try to load a transaction log out of sequence, you get an error and the transaction load halts. To load transaction logs, use the Enterprise Manager or the LOAD TRANSACTION command.

MOVING A DATABASE

If you plan to move a database to another server or another database using a database dump, follow the guidelines outlined in "Preparing for a Database Load," earlier in this chapter. Create the database using the correct segment map and load the database using the steps outlined in "Loading a Database or Table Backup or Applying a Transaction Log Backup Using Backup Devices," earlier in this chapter.

The SQL Server Enterprise Manager provides another tool to move a database: the Transfer Manager. Chapter 16, "Importing and Exporting Data," explains how to use the Transfer Manager to move a database when the character set or sort order of the two database servers is different. You can also use the Transfer Manager to transfer databases between servers on different platforms such as from an Intel platform to an Alpha platform.

Caution

If you use the DUMP command and then the LOAD command to move a database from one server to another, remember that the database user IDs travel with the database and the mappings, between the server login IDs, and that database IDs may not be correct on the new server. Use aliases or the system stored procedure sp_change_users_login to correct the problem.

RECOVERING THE `master` DATABASE

You have probably guessed by now that the `master` database is definitely not just another database. To recover the `master` database, you need a separate recovery procedure. You will know when the `master` database is corrupted because you will see output from a DBCC command, you will find an error message in the error log or the NT event log, or SQL Server will not start.

Note

The procedure to restore the `master` database is much improved in SQL Server 6.x than it was in previous versions. You no longer have to use the utility `buildmaster` or run the `installmaster` and `installmodel` scripts. As a matter of fact, these utilities are no longer shipped with SQL Server.

To rebuild the `master` database, use the SQL setup program. Start the SQL setup program and follow these steps:

1. Select the Rebuild Master Database checkbox in the SQL Server Setup dialog box and click the Continue button (see Figure 15.9). The Rebuild Master Database dialog box appears (see Figure 15.10).

Figure 15.9.
The SQL Server Setup
program dialog box.

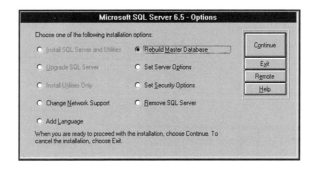

Figure 15.10.
The Rebuild Master
Database dialog box.

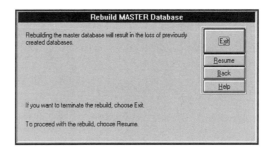

Note

The Rebuild Master Database dialog box warns that you will lose all previously created databases. You recover the previous databases by loading a backup of the master database later in the rebuild process.

2. Click the Resume button. The SQL Server 6.5 Rebuild Options dialog box appears (see Figure 15.11).

Figure 15.11.
The SQL Server 6.5
Rebuild Options
dialog box.

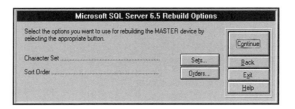

3. To recover the master database and all your other databases, you must select the same sort order and character set that were used by the corrupted master database. Once you have selected the correct character set and sort order, click the Continue button. The SQL Server Installation Path dialog box appears (see Figure 15.12).

15

RECOVERY

Figure 15.12.
The SQL Server
Installation Path
dialog box.

4. Select the correct path of your current SQL Server installation and click the Continue button. The Rebuild Master Device dialog box appears (see Figure 15.13).

Figure 15.13.
The Rebuild Master
Device dialog box.

5. Enter the path and the size of your current master device and click the Continue button. The master device and database are then re-created. When the process finishes, a completion dialog box appears. Click the Exit to Windows NT button.

6. Start SQL Server and log on to the server using the Enterprise Manager. The master database is in the same state as when SQL Server was first installed. You now must use a previous database dump of the master database to restore it. Add to the master database the dump device from which you plan to restore.

7. Shut down SQL Server. To load the master database, either with the Enterprise Manager or from an ISQL command prompt, you must start SQL Server in single-user mode. To start SQL Server in single-user mode, use the SQL setup program and the Set Server Options selection to add the single-user flag /m or enter the following on the command line:

```
startserver /c /dpath and filename of the master device /m
```

8. Once SQL Server is started in single-user mode, use the Enterprise Manager or the LOAD DATABASE command to load a backup of the master database. When using the Enterprise Manager, use the Restore from Backup Devices

File option to load the previous backup files. When you use the Restore from File option, the header information for each file is read so that you can determine the database and the date and time at which the backup was created. When the load operation completes, the completion message box appears (see Figure 15.14).

Restart SQL Server in multi-user mode. The `master` database has now been successfully rebuilt.

Figure 15.14.
The completion mes-
sage box.

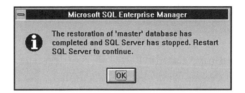

If changes such as new logins or database modifications have been made since the `master` database backup, you must manually apply the changes or use a script file. Some changes, such as new devices added after the loaded backup can be recovered using the `DISK REINIT` command.

To recover database `CREATE` or `ALTER` database statements, use the `DISK REFIT` command. Remember, if you loaded from a current `master` database dump, recovery is complete. *Always* maintain a current backup of the `master` database.

Tip

If you are a new DBA or a DBA in training, find a test system on which you can practice recovering the `master` database. Think about how crucial the `master` database is to the proper operation of your SQL Server. The first time you rebuild the `master` database should not be on a production database while you are under a lot of stress and pressure to get the database back up and running. Practice makes perfect!

I contracted once for a Fortune 100 company that was using a UNIX Sybase system (before the release of Windows NT). The DBA was new and inexperienced and the UNIX system had many system and drive problems during the first month. The DBA had to rebuild the `master` database twice. (Unfortunately, I was not allowed to help because I was contracted to support another group!) The first time resulted in failure, frustration, and then just an "Oh heck, it's not production. Let's reinstall." The second time, the DBA had learned from the previous experience and was able to rebuild the `master` database. Fortunately, Microsoft has now made rebuilding the `master` database a simple and graphical task!

15

RECOVERY

BETWEEN THE LINES

Here are some of the important points to remember about SQL Server recovery:

◆ Automatic recovery is performed on all the databases when SQL Server is started.

◆ Use the Enterprise Manager and backup history information to load transaction log and database backups.

◆ When creating a database that will be loaded with a database backup, use the FOR LOAD option with the CREATE DATABASE command.

◆ Restoring from a striped dump set requires reading from the striped set.

◆ Loading a database dump requires the new database to have the same size and device fragment allocation.

◆ When moving or loading databases, the SQL Server must have the same character set and sort order as the SQL Server that produced the database dump.

◆ Use the SQL setup program to rebuild the master database.

◆ Practice performing database recovery procedures.

SUMMARY

Database backups and recovery are serious business and an important part of a DBA's job responsibility. Set up a database backup plan; from time to time, practice your recovery procedures so that, in an emergency, you are prepared to properly recover the database.

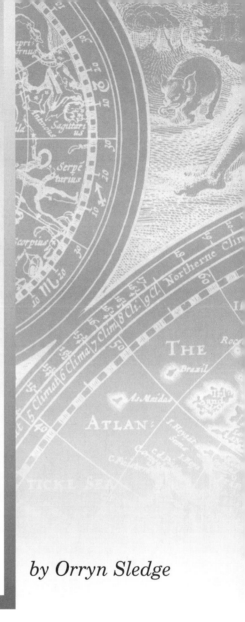

CHAPTER 16

by Orryn Sledge

Importing and Exporting Data

You can use various methods to import and export SQL Server data. Almost all systems require some type of data transfer. BCP is the utility provided by SQL Server to transfer data. This chapter discusses in detail the BCP utility and also covers alternatives to BCP.

BCP

BCP stands for *Bulk Copy Program*. It is the only tool SQL Server provides (with the exception of a few tricks discussed later in this chapter) to import and export data. Data can be either *native mode* (SQL Server specific) or *character mode* (ASCII text). ASCII text data is commonly used to share data between SQL Server and other systems (see Figure 16.1).

Figure 16.1.
Common uses of BCP.

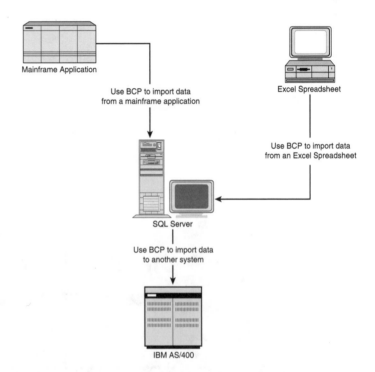

IS IT LOVE OR HATE?

As a DBA, you will probably have a love/hate relationship with BCP. BCP is limited in scope and lacks common file formats, but it does provide excellent performance.

For those new to SQL Server, the following list provides some insight into BCP. These are the reasons why I like BCP:

◆ **Performance**: BCP is one the fastest raw data loaders around. I have seen BCP turn in impressive performance numbers compared to other import/export products.

◆ **Minimal overhead**: Because BCP is command-line based, it requires a nominal amount of memory to run compared to today's memory-intensive GUI applications. This leaves memory for other tasks.

Now for the drawbacks of BCP. These are the reasons why I hate BCP:

◆ **Unforgiving syntax**: BCP's switches are case- and order sensitive. This is because BCP's origins stem back to Sybase and the UNIX world, where commands are case sensitive. I wish that Microsoft would break with tradition and implement a user-friendly version of BCP.

◆ **Minimal file support**: Basically, the choices are ASCII text, native SQL Server format, or nothing at all. Do not try to load an Excel spreadsheet or an Access database directly into SQL Server; it will never work. To load non-SQL Server data, you must export the data as ASCII text and then import the text file into SQL Server. It would be nice if BCP could directly import/export today's popular file formats such as Access, Excel, dBASE, and so on.

◆ **Inadequate error messages**: BCP's error messages are minimal and too generic. I wish that Microsoft would enhance BCP's error messages to be more informative and specific.

As you can see, BCP is far from perfect, but it is the only utility provided by SQL Server to import/export data. Oh well! With this in mind, the remainder of this chapter will provide you with some useful tips and tricks to make your life easier when you use BCP.

BCP SYNTAX

Use the following syntax to perform BCP operations:

```
bcp [[database_name.]owner.]table_name {in ¦ out} datafile
[/m maxerrors] [/f formatfile] [/e errfile]
[/F firstrow] [/L lastrow] [/b batchsize]
```

```
[/n] [/c] [/E]
[/t field_term] [/r row_term]
[/i inputfile] [/o outputfile]
/U login_id [/P password] [/S servername] [/v] [/a packet_size]
```

Note

With BCP, you can use - or / to preface a switch. For example, the following two statements are equivalent:

```
bcp pubs..sales out sales.out /c /Usa /P

bcp pubs..sales out sales.out -c -Usa -P
```

Parameter	Explanation
database_name	Name of the database being accessed. The database name is optional; if the database name is omitted, the user's default database is used (optional).
owner	Owner of the table or view being accessed (optional). **Tip:** Use the .. symbol to specify ownership. The .. syntax is more generic than specifying an owner (for example: pubs..authors instead of pubs.dbo.authors).
table_name	Name of the table or view being accessed (required). **Tip:** Use the # or ## symbol to copy a temporary table.
in ¦ out	Direction of data transfer, where in means import and out means export (required).
datafile	The name of the data file for an import or the name of the file to be created during an export. A path can be included with this statement, such as c:\mssql\binn\authors.txt (required).
/m maxerrors	Maximum number of errors that can occur before the BCP operation is terminated. Each failed insert counts as one error. Default value is 10 (optional).
/f formatfile	The name of the format file used to import or export data. A path can be included with this statement, such as c:\mssql\binn\authors.fmt (optional).
/e errfile	The name of the error file to store BCP error messages and unsuccessfully transferred rows. A path can be included with this statement, such as c:\mssql\binn\authors.err (optional). **Tip:** Error files are useful for pinpointing BCP errors during unattended operations such as nightly data imports.

Parameter	Explanation
/F *firstrow*	The number of the first row to copy (optional).
/L *lastrow*	The number of the last row to copy (optional). ***Tip:*** The /F and /L switches are useful when copying portions of data. For example, to export the first 1,000 records from a table, use the following syntax: /F 1 /L 1000
/b *batchsize*	The number of rows transferred in a batch. The default setting is the number of rows in the data file (optional).
/n	Native data mode. Native data is SQL Server specific. Native data mode does not prompt the user for field information (optional).
/c	Character data mode. Character data (ASCII) can be transferred to and from SQL Server tables and other non-SQL Server products. Character mode does not prompt the user for field information. By default, fields are tab delimited and rows are newline delimited (optional). ***Tip:*** Character data mode is usually easier to work with than native data mode.
/E	New with version 6.x. Used when importing data into a table that contains an identity datatype and you want to populate the column with values from the data file. If this switch is omitted, SQL Server automatically populates the identity column and ignores the field's corresponding data values in the import file (optional). The following example shows how the /E switch impacts data imports:

```
Sample table structure:
id int identity(1,1)
descr char(15)
Sample data file:
5    xxx
6    yyy
7    zzz
BCP syntax WITHOUT the /E switch:
bcp sales..table2 in
table2.txt /c /U sa /P
Results:
id          descr
---------- ----------------------------------
1           xxx
2           yyy
3           zzz
```

Notice the values in the id column. SQL Server populated the id column with an automatically incremented data value. It ignored the values 5,6,7 in the data file.

continues

Parameter	Explanation
	The following is BCP syntax with the /E switch: ``` bcp sales..table2 in table2.txt /c /E /U sa /P Results: id descr ----------- ------------- 5 xxx 6 yyy 7 zzz ``` With the /E switch, the values in the text file were observed and SQL Server did *not* automatically generate a set of data values for the id column. *Tip:* Use the /E switch to preserve data values when you are unloading and reloading data in a table that contains an identity datatype. Otherwise, SQL Server automatically populates the identity column with its own set of values.
/t *field_term*	Field terminator (optional). See Table 16.1 for BCP terminators.
/r *row_term*	Row terminator (optional). See Table 16.1 for BCP terminators.
/i *inputfile*	File to redirect input. This switch is not generally used (optional).
/o *outputfile*	File to redirect BCP output (optional). *Tip:* Use the /o switch to log BCP output during unattended BCP operation. This creates a useful trail of BCP output that can be used to monitor and diagnose BCP performance and execution.
/U *login_id*	SQL Server login ID (required).
/P *password*	SQL Server password. If the *password* is omitted, BCP prompts you for a password (required). *Note:* If you are using integrated security or your SQL Server login does not have a password, BCP still prompts you for a password. To bypass BCP's prompt, use the /P switch without a *password*, as in the following example: ``` BCP pubs..authors in authors.txt /U sa /P ```
/S *servername*	The name of the server that contains the database and table you are working with. The /S *servername* switch is required if you are using BCP from a remote client on a network (optional).

Parameter	Explanation
/v	Displays the version of DB Library in use (optional). ***Note:*** If you are concurrently running SQL Server version 6.x and version 4.2x, be certain that you are using the correct version of BCP. To determine which version of BCP is in use, type **BCP** /v. Version 6.x's copyright date will be greater than or equal to 1995.
/a packet_size	The number of bytes contained in a network packet. The default value for Windows NT Server and Windows NT clients is 4096 ; the default value for MS-DOS clients is 512. Valid sizes are 512 to 65535 bytes (optional). ***Tip:*** Depending own your network architecture, you may be able to improve BCP performance by increasing the packet size. Try setting the packet size between 4096 and 8192 bytes. Use the statistics returned by BCP (the clock time and rows per second) to help tailor this setting.

TABLE 16.1. VALID BCP TERMINATORS.

Terminator Type	Syntax
tab	\t
new line	\n
carriage return	\r
backslash	\\
NULL terminator	\0
user-defined terminator	character (^, %, *, and so on)

PERMISSIONS REQUIRED TO RUN BCP

No permissions are required to run the BCP command-line utility. However, to use BCP to copy data into a table, the user must be granted INSERT permission to the target table. To export data from a table, the user must be granted SELECT permission for the source table.

CHARACTER MODE VERSUS NATIVE MODE

BCP can import/export data in character file format or native file format. *Character mode* is plain old ASCII text. Use the /c switch or a format file to specify character

16

IMPORTING AND EXPORTING DATA

mode. *Native mode* uses special formatting characters internal to SQL Server to represent data. Use native mode only when you are transferring data between SQL Server tables. Use the /n switch to specify native mode. Following is sample output from character mode BCP:

```
bcp pubs..jobs out jobs.txt /c /U sa /P

1       New Hire - Job not specified    10      10
2       Chief Executive Officer         200     250
3       Business Operations Manager     175     225
```

Tip

> Character mode is usually easier to work with than native mode because you can view the contents of a character mode data file with a standard text editor.

INTERACTIVE BCP

Interactive BCP is used to selectively import or export data. Interactive mode is automatically activated when the following switches are *not* included in the BCP statement:

/n (native format)

/c (character format)

/f (format file)

Through the use of interactive prompts, you can tailor BCP to your import and export specifications. Interactive BCP prompts you for four pieces of information:

◆ File storage type

◆ Prefix length

◆ Field length

◆ Field and row terminator

The following are sample interactive BCP prompts:

```
Enter the file storage type of field discounttype [char]:
Enter prefix-length of field discounttype [0]:
Enter length of field discounttype [40]:
Enter field terminator [none]:
```

Tip

When importing data, you can skip a column by entering 0 for prefix length, 0 for length, and no terminator. You cannot skip a column when exporting data.

At the end of an interactive BCP session, you receive the following prompt:

```
Do you want to save this format information in a file? [Y/n]
Host filename [bcp.fmt]:
```

If you answer *yes* at this prompt, your interactive responses are saved to a format file. This enables you to specify at a later time the /f switch (format file) to automatically reuse the information from your interactive BCP session.

FILE STORAGE TYPE

The *file storage type* specifies the datatypes used to read from and write to data files. Table 16.2 lists valid file storage types.

Tip

When working with ASCII files, set all file storage types to char, regardless of the table's datatypes. This is the only way you can load ASCII data into SQL Server using BCP.

TABLE 16.2. FILE STORAGE TYPES.

```
char

varchar

text

binary

varbinary

image

datetime

smalldatetime

decimal
```

continues

Table 16.2. continued

```
numeric

float

real

int

smallint

tinyint

money

smallmoney

bit

timestamp
```

Prefix Length

SQL Server uses the *prefix length* to store compacted data. When working in native mode, accept the default values whenever possible.

Tip

> When working with fixed-width ASCII data, set the prefix length to 0.

Field Length

The *field length* specifies the number of bytes required to store a SQL Server datatype. Use default field lengths whenever possible, otherwise data truncation or overflow errors may occur. Table 16.3 lists default field lengths.

Table 16.3. Default field lengths.

Datatype	Length in Bytes
bit	1
char(n)	n
datetime	26
decimal	28
float	25
int	12
money	24

Datatype	Length in Bytes
numeric	28
real	25
smalldatetime	26
smallint	6
smallmoney	24
tinyint	3
varchar(n)	n

Tip

When importing and exporting ASCII fixed-width data files, you may need to modify the field length to match your import/export specification. For example, to export a char(15) column as a 25-byte piece of data, specify a field length of 25. This pads the data length to 25 bytes.

FIELD TERMINATOR

The *field terminator* prompt controls how field data is delimited (separated). The default delimiter is no terminator. See Table 16.4 for valid field terminators.

Tip

The last field in a table acts as a row terminator. To separate rows with a newline delimiter, specify \n at the field terminator prompt.

Note

At the BCP command line, you can also use the /t (field terminator) and /r (row terminator) switches to specify terminators.

TABLE 16.4. VALID FIELD TERMINATORS.

Terminator Type	Syntax
tab	\t
new line	\n
carriage return	\r

continues

16

IMPORTING AND EXPORTING DATA

TABLE 16.4. CONTINUED

Terminator Type	Syntax
backslash	\\
NULL terminator	\0
user-defined terminator	character (^, %, *, and so on)

FORMAT FILES

A *format file* is a template for BCP to use when you import or export data. With this template, you can define how BCP should transfer your data.

The easiest way to create a format file is to initiate an interactive BCP session. Interactive mode is initiated when you do *not* specify one of the following switches:

◆ /n (native format)

◆ /c (character format)

◆ /f (format file)

At the end of your interactive session, you see the following prompt:

```
Do you want to save this format information in a file? [Y/n] y
Host filename [bcp.fmt]:sample.fmt
```

At this prompt, enter a filename to save the format information. SQL Server then creates a format file, which is really just an ASCII text file (see Figure 16.2). You can make modifications to an existing format file by using a standard text editor.

Tip

Use the FMT extension when saving format files to simplify file identification.

Figure 16.2.
A sample format file.

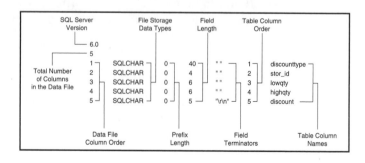

Once you have saved the format file, you can reuse the format file by specifying the /f (format file) switch, as in the following example:

```
bcp sales..discounts in discount.txt /f sample.fmt /U sa /P
```

> ## Note
>
> If a table has a corresponding format file, any column modification to the table must be reflected in the format file. For example, if you drop a column from a table, you must also remove the column from the format file.

SAMPLE BCP SCRIPTS

This section describes how to use BCP to perform typical import and export routines. The examples discussed in this section use the pubs..discounts table.

The following is the structure of the discounts table:

```
discounttype varchar (40)
stor_id varchar
lowqty smallint
highqty smallint
discount decimal(0, 0)
```

The following is discounts table data:

```
discounttype                             stor_id lowqty highqty discount
---------------------------------------- ------- ------ ------- --------
Initial Customer                         (null)  (null) (null)  10.50
Volume Discount                          (null)  100    1000    6.70
Customer Discount                        8042    (null) (null)  5.00
```

SIMPLE IMPORT

This example uses the /c switch to load a data file that contains tab-delimited fields and newline-delimited rows. For this example, the import data is contained in a file named disc.txt. Following are the contents of the sample import file:

```
Preferred Customer 6380 200 800  5.5
Valued Customer    7896 100 1000 8.5
```

The following syntax shows how to import the contents of the disc.txt file into the discounts table:

```
bcp pubs..discounts in disc.txt /c /U sa /P
```

SIMPLE EXPORT

This example uses the /c switch to export data to a file with tab-delimited fields and newline-delimited rows. The following syntax shows how to export the contents of the discounts table to the discount.out file:

```
bcp pubs..discounts out discount.out /c /U sa /P
```

Following is the output:

```
Initial Customer                                    10.50
Volume Discount              100    1000    6.70
Customer Discount           8042                    5.00
```

COMMA-DELIMITED IMPORT

This example imports a data file that contains comma-delimited fields and newline-delimited rows. The /t switch specifies a comma delimiter; the /r\n switch specifies a newline row delimiter. For this example, the import data is contained in a file named disc2.txt. Following are the contents of the sample import file:

```
Preferred Customer,6380,200,800,5.5
Valued Customer,7896,100,1000,8.5
```

The following syntax shows how to import the contents of the disc2.txt file into the discounts table:

```
bcp pubs..discounts in disc2.txt /c /t, /r\n /U sa /P
```

COMMA-DELIMITED EXPORT

This example exports the discounts table to a file with comma-delimited fields and newline row delimiters. The following syntax shows how to export the contents of the discounts table to the disc3.txt file:

```
bcp pubs..discounts out disc3.txt /c /t, /r\n /U sa /P
```

Following is the output:

```
Initial Customer,,,,10.50
Volume Discount,,100,1000,6.70
Customer Discount,8042,,,5.00
```

FIXED-LENGTH IMPORT

This example uses a fixed-length ASCII text file named disc4.txt. Table 16.5 shows the layout of the text file.

TABLE 16.5. THE FILE LAYOUT OF `disc4.txt`.

Column Name	File Length	File Position
discounttype	40	1-39
stor_id	4	40-43
lowqty	6	44-49
highqty	6	50-55
discount	5	56-60

The following is sample data from `disc4.txt`:

```
12345678901234567890123456789012345678901234567890123456789 0
Preferred Customer                  6380200   800   5.5
Valued Customer                     7896100  1000   8.5
```

For fixed-length data transfers, SQL Server needs to know the field positions in the data file. An easy way to do this is to use interactive BCP. To begin interactive BCP, use the following command:

```
bcp sales..discounts in disc4.txt /U sa /P
```

For the first two prompts, you can accept the default values because they match the layout in the data file. For the third, forth, and fifth prompts (see the highlighted text in Figure 16.3), you have to override the default prompts.

Note

When importing fixed-length ASCII data, *always* use char for the file storage type and 0 for the prefix length.

FIXED-LENGTH EXPORT

Suppose that you need to export the discounts table in a fixed-length file format and the format must follow the specification used in the previous example. No problem; you can reuse the format file you created in the previous example (see Figure 16.4).

The following syntax shows how to export the contents of the discounts table to the `disc4.out` file:

```
bcp pubs..discounts out disc4.out /c /f disc4.fmt /U sa /P
```

Figure 16.3.
Interactive BCP
responses.

Figure 16.4.
The `disc4.fmt` *format*
file.

```
6.0
5
1    SQLCHAR    0    40    " "      1    discounttype
2    SQLCHAR    0    4     " "      2    stor_id
3    SQLCHAR    0    6     " "      3    lowqty
4    SQLCHAR    0    6     " "      4    highqty
5    SQLCHAR    0    5     "\r\n"   5    discount
```

SKIPPED FIELDS ON IMPORT

Suppose that you want to skip the columns stor_id, lowqty, and highqty when you load the disc4.txt ASCII file. To do this, you must modify the format file. To skip a column, enter **0** for the table column order (see Figure 16.5).

Figure 16.5.
The format file used to
skip columns.

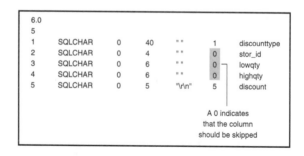

After you modify your format file, you can use the following BCP syntax to load the data:

```
bcp pubs..discounts in disc4.txt /c /f disc4.fmt /U sa /P
```

SKIPPED FIELDS ON EXPORT

BCP does not allow you to skip a column in a table during an export. However, you can trick BCP into skipping a column by creating a view that references only the columns you want to export, thus skipping unwanted columns. Then use BCP to export the data from the view.

The following syntax shows how to export only the discounttype and discount columns from the discounts table:

```
create view discounts_view as
select output = convert(char(40),discounttype) + convert(char(5),discount)
from discounts
```

Next, create a format file that contains one column (see Figure 16.6). Only one column is listed in the format file because the view concatenates the discounttype and discount columns.

Figure 16.6.
The format file used to
export data from a
view.

```
6.0
1
1    SQLCHAR    0    45    "\r\n"    1    output
```

Finally, use BCP to export the data from the view:

```
bcp pubs..discounts_view out discview.txt /f discview.fmt /U sa /P
```

The following is sample output:

```
Initial Customer                      10.50
Volume Discount                        6.70
Customer Discount                      5.00
```

MODES OF OPERATION

When importing data, BCP has two modes of operation: fast mode and slow mode. As you probably guessed, the fast mode runs faster than the slow mode. The performance difference is caused by the logging of transactions. Fast mode bypasses the transaction log; slow mode posts all data inserts to the transaction log.

Note

You need to be concerned with fast and slow mode BCP only when you import data. BCP does not use a fast or slow mode when you export data.

When you run BCP, SQL Server automatically decides which BCP mode to run. There is no BCP switch that allows you to toggle between fast and slow modes.

ACHIEVING FAST MODE BCP

In SQL Server 6.x, two factors determine whether BCP can run in fast mode: the SELECT INTO/BULKCOPY option and indexes. For BCP to run in fast mode, the following two conditions must be true:

◆ The database option SELECT INTO/BULKCOPY must equal TRUE.

◆ Indexes must not exist on the target table.

If either of these conditions is FALSE, BCP runs in slow mode (see Figure 16.7).

Figure 16.7.
How SQL Server
determines which BCP
mode to run.

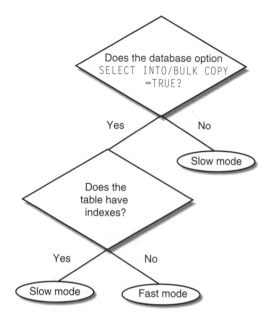

WHY YOU SHOULD BE CONCERNED WITH WHICH BCP MODE IS RUNNING

You may be asking yourself, "Why not always run BCP in fast mode?" The answer is based on the following three factors:

◆ Backup strategy
◆ Window of opportunity
◆ Available database space

BACKUP STRATEGY

To run the fast mode of BCP, you must have the SELECT INTO/BULKCOPY option set to TRUE. By setting this option to TRUE, you may be sacrificing data recovery for BCP performance. When SELECT INTO/BULKCOPY is set to TRUE, you cannot back up the transaction log for a database. Instead, you can only back up the entire database. This means that you will be unable to use the transaction log to provide up-to-the-minute data recovery.

WINDOW OF OPPORTUNITY

Fast mode BCP requires that the target table not contain any indexes. This means that you must consider the downtime involved with dropping the indexes, loading the data, and re-creating the indexes. For a table that requires 24-hour data access, it is not feasible to drop and re-create indexes.

Tip

To significantly reduce the time required to create a clustered index, have your import data presorted on the fields that make up your clustered index. Then use the WITH SORTED_DATA option to create the clustered index, as in the following example:

```
CREATE CLUSTERED INDEX pk_idx ON table1 (id) WITH SORTED_DATA
```

The WITH SORTED_DATA option bypasses the physical data sort step normally used to create a clustered index.

AVAILABLE DATABASE SPACE

A clustered index requires free space equal to approximately 120 percent the size of the table. For example, a 100M table requires approximately 120M of free database space to create the clustered index. If you are tight on disk space, you may not be able to drop and re-create a clustered index for a large table.

16

Table 16.6 helps clarify the differences between the two modes.

Table 16.6. Fast BCP versus slow BCP.

	Fast Mode	*Slow Mode*
PROS	Fast! Operations are not logged. Don't have to worry about filling up the transaction log.	Maximum recoverability.
CONS	Zero recoverability. Must dump the database after using BCP. Cannot dump the transaction log. Indexes must be rebuilt after loading the data	Slow! Every insert is written to the transaction log. Can easily fill up the transaction log during large data imports, thus complicating the import process.

Note

BCP may or may not notify you about which mode it is using. You do not receive a message that slow mode is in use when you import data into a table with an existing index.

BCP and Enforcement of Triggers, Rules, Defaults, Constraints, and Unique Indexes

When using BCP to import data into a SQL Server table, it is important that you understand how triggers, rules, defaults, constraints, and unique indexes are enforced. Many people forget that certain types of objects are bypassed when using BCP to import data. Table 16.7 summarizes which objects are enforced when BCP is used to import data.

Table 16.7. Enforcement of objects.

Object	*Enforced?*
Default	Yes
Unique index/unique constraints	Yes
Primary key and foreign key constraints	Yes
Check constraint	No

Object	Enforced?
Rule	No
Trigger	No

Caution

Do not forget that triggers, check constraints, and rules are not enforced when using BCP. To prevent data integrity problems, load your data into a work table and run it through a validation routine similar to the validation defined in your triggers, constraints, and table rules. Once you are satisfied that the data meets your integrity requirements, transfer the data to your target table.

Note

Before version 6.x, you could enforce primary key and foreign key relationships only through the use of triggers. Because BCP bypasses triggers, additional steps were required to ensure that you did not violate primary key and foreign key integrity. This problem has been resolved in version 6.x through the use of primary key and foreign key constraints, which *are* enforced by BCP.

COMMON BCP TRAPS

Be on the lookout for the following traps. They always seem to be lurking out there.

◆ **Invalid dates**: When importing data, a data file that contains dates represented as 00/00/00 and 000000 will fail. These are invalid SQL Server date formats. This problem often arises when data is transferred from a mainframe system to SQL Server. You must adhere to SQL Server date formats when importing date information into datetime columns.

◆ **Space-filled dates**: When importing spaces into a datetime column, SQL Server defaults the column to 1/1/1900. This is probably not what you want! To avoid this problem, do not pad the column with any data; just follow the column with a delimiter. SQL Server sets the data column to NULL, which is presumably more in line with what you expected.

◆ **Improper delimiter**: Do not use a delimiter that exists in your data or you will have problems. For example, if the first and last name are stored as one field and a user enters Smith, Mike, do not use a comma delimiter. For this example, use a tab or another type of delimiter.

BCP TIPS

Use the following tips to help simplify data imports and exports:

◆ **Use views to export data.** Views allow increased flexibility to filter and physically arrange your data. For example, to export only the date portion of a datetime column, use a view and the CONVERT function.

Sample table:

```
emp_id char(3)
hire_date datetime
```

Sample view:

```
CREATE VIEW date_example_view AS
SELECT emp_id,convert(char(12),hire_date,1)
FROM sample_table
```

Sample BCP statement:

```
bcp sales..date_example_view out sample.out /c /Usa /P
```

> *Note*
>
> Refer to the CONVERT function in Appendix D for other date formats.

◆ **Always issue an UPDATE STATISTICS command after importing data into a table with existing indexes.** An index's statistics will not reflect the data loaded with BCP. This may cause the optimizer to overlook a useful index. To avoid this problem, you must use the UPDATE STATISTICS command.

> *Note*
>
> You do not have to issue an UPDATE STATISTICS command if the table's indexes are dropped before the BCP operation is performed and re-created after the BCP operation. Under this scenario, the statistics will be up to date.

◆ **Echo BCP output and errors to a text file.** To capture BCP's output, use the /o switch. To capture BCP's error messages, use the /e switch.

◆ **Many systems import data on a recurring basis.** Once the data is loaded into the system, various routines are run to summarize the data, generate reports, and so on. Any easy way to automate this process is to create a stored procedure that calls BCP and then runs the subordinate processes. The advantage of creating a single stored procedure to run your import process is that you can schedule it through SQL Server's Task Scheduler. The following syntax is an example of a stored procedure that calls BCP to load data into the system and then executes summary procedures against the data:

```
CREATE PROCEDURE usp_load_example AS
/* flush out work table */
truncate table table1

/* BCP in data */
exec master..xp_cmdshell "bcp sales..table1 in C:\mssql\binn\table1.txt /c
/Usa /P"

/* run summary procedures */
exec usp_summary1
exec usp_summaryN
```

Caution

Do not use xp_cmdshell to call BCP from within a user-defined transaction in a stored procedure. Doing so can lead to endless blocking!

Tip

Do you ever have to export or import data for all the tables in a database? To perform this task, you could manually create BCP scripts, but that can be tedious and time consuming—especially if you must use BCP to copy data from numerous tables in the database. An alternative to manually creating the scripts is to build a SQL statement that automatically generates the BCP syntax. Suppose that you need to export data from all the tables in the pubs database. To generate the BCP syntax, create a query that references the sysobjects table (each database in SQL Server has a sysobjects table and a corresponding record for each object in the database). In the WHERE clause of the query, specify type = 'U' (this clause returns only user tables). The following is a sample query used to generate the BCP syntax (the -c switch is used in this example to export the data in a tab-delimited character format):

```
select 'bcp pubs..' + name + ' out ' + name + '.txt' + ' -c -Usa
-Ppassword -Stfnserver'
          from pubs..sysobjects
          where type ='U'
          order by name
```

Following is the output from the query:

```
bcp pubs..authors out authors.txt -c -Usa -Ppassword -Stfnserver
bcp pubs..discounts out discounts.txt -c -Usa -Ppassword -Stfnserver
bcp pubs..employee out employee.txt -c -Usa -Ppassword -Stfnserver
bcp pubs..jobs out jobs.txt -c -Usa -Ppassword -Stfnserver
bcp pubs..pub_info out pub_info.txt -c -Usa -Ppassword -Stfnserver
```

continues

16

```
bcp pubs..publishers out publishers.txt -c -Usa -Ppassword -Stfnserver
bcp pubs..roysched out roysched.txt -c -Usa -Ppassword -Stfnserver
bcp pubs..sales out sales.txt -c -Usa -Ppassword -Stfnserver
bcp pubs..stores out stores.txt -c -Usa -Ppassword -Stfnserver
bcp pubs..titleauthor out titleauthor.txt -c -Usa -Ppassword -Stfnserver
bcp pubs..titles out titles.txt -c -Usa -Ppassword -Stfnserver
```

Now that you have the proper BCP syntax, you can save the output from the query to a BAT file and automatically run the file from the command line. As you see, the combination of SQL Server syntax with information from the system tables can simplify common DBA chores.

ALTERNATIVES TO BCP

The following sections discuss alternatives to BCP. These alternatives are simple tips and tricks that can simplify data transfers.

SQL SERVER DBA ASSISTANT

The SQL Server DBA Assistant allows you to graphically export data from SQL Server into common file formats. The product was developed using Visual Basic 4.0 and SQL-OLE technology.

Note

The SQL Server DBA Assistant is on the CD that accompanies this book. The product requires a 32-bit operating system (NT or Windows 95).

Follow these steps to use the SQL Server DBA Assistant to export data:

1. Double-click the SQL Server DBA Assistant icon to start the SQL Server DBA Assistant.

2. In the SQL Server DBA Assistant window, select the Bulk Copy tab (see Figure 16.8).

3. On the Bulk Copy tab, select a database, a table, a file type, and any other options. Then click the Export Data button to export the data. When the export has completed, you receive a message specifying the number of rows exported (see Figure 16.9).

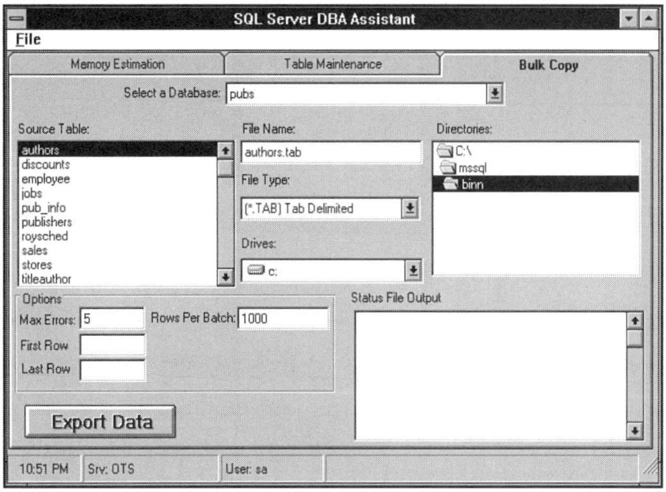

Figure 16.8.
The Bulk Copy tab in
the SQL Server DBA
Assistant window.

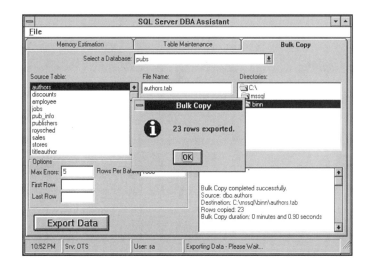

Figure 16.9.
The number of rows
exported.

SELECT INTO AND INSERT COMBINED WITH SELECT

The SELECT INTO statement creates a new table with a structure identical to the structure in the SELECT statement, along with any matching data. For example, the following SQL statement copies the authors table from the pubs database to the sales database:

```
SELECT *
INTO sales..authors
FROM pubs..authors
```

Note

The database option SELECT INTO/BULKCOPY must be set to TRUE if you want to use SELECT INTO to create a new table in a database. However, the SELECT INTO/BULKCOPY setting has no impact on your ability to create a temporary table in SQL Server.

An INSERT statement combined with a SELECT statement appends data into a target table with data from the source table. For example, the following SQL statement copies any rows returned from the SQL statement into the target_table:

```
INSERT INTO target_table
SELECT * FROM source_table
```

Tip

Sometimes you must drop and re-create a table to perform a table modification. Most people use BCP to copy out the data, drop and re-create the table, and then use BCP to copy the data back in. In this scenario, it may be complicated to use BCP to reload your data if you made extensive changes to your table. An alternative to using BCP is to use SELECT INTO to create a working copy of your table. Drop and re-create the table and then use INSERT INTO to reload the data from the work table.

SAVE SQL OUTPUT AS A TEXT FILE

An easy way to save data in a fixed-width format is to issue a SQL SELECT query from the Query window in the Enterprise Manager. The query results are displayed in the Results tab. Click the Save Query/Result button to save the query's output. The output is saved in an ASCII text file in a fixed-width data format with newline separators (see Figure 16.10).

Figure 16.10.
Saving SQL output as
a text file.

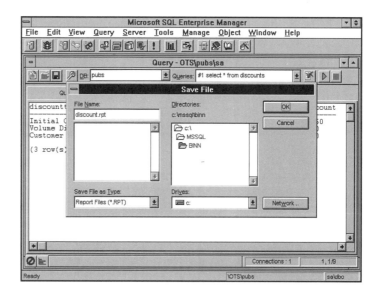

Use Query Options to prevent column names and row counts from
being displayed in the Results tab. From the Query dialog box, click
the Query Options button; the Query Options dialog box appears.
From this dialog box, select the Query Flag tab. Set No Count Display
to TRUE. On the Format Options tab, set Print Headers to FALSE.

SQL SERVER 4.2X'S OBJECT MANAGER

For some inexplicable reason, the graphical version of BCP found in SQL Server
4.2's Object Manager was not included in SQL Server 6.x. This is unfortunate
because the graphical version of BCP in SQL Server 4.2x's Object Manager greatly
simplified BCP usage. However, you can still run Version 4.2x's Object Manager
against SQL Server 6.x to take advantage of graphical BCP. The following steps
explain how to install and use version 4.2x's Object Manager to access the graphical
version of BCP.

Caution

The Object Manager works only with version 6.x tables that use
version 4.2x datatypes. This means that you cannot use BCP to
copy tables that use identity, decimal, or other SQL Server 6.x
enhancements.

1. Load the `object60.sql` script included with version 6.*x* (see Figure 16.11). The file is located in the `\mssql\install\` directory. Ignore any error messages generated by the script.

Figure 16.11.
The `object60.sql` *script.*

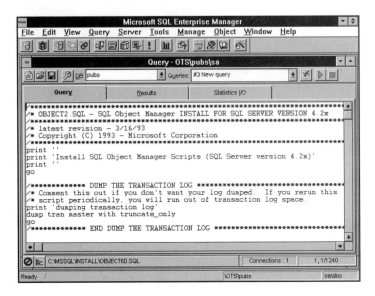

2. Click the SQL Object Manager icon in the SQL Server for Windows NT group (see Figure 16.13). Remember that SQL Object Manager is a 4.2x product that is not included with SQL Server 6.x.

3. In the Connect Server dialog box, enter the server name, login ID, and password for SQL Server 6.x. Click the Connect button to connect to SQL Server 6.x.

Tip

To determine which version of SQL Server you are logged in to, use the `@@version` global variable. For example:

```
SELECT @@version
```

Following is the output:

```
Microsoft SQL Server 6.50 - 6.50.201 (Intel X86)
Apr  3 1996 02:55:53
Copyright (c) 1988-1996 Microsoft Corporation
```

4. Select a database.
5. Click the Transfer button in the Object Manager. The Transfer Data dialog box appears; from this dialog box, you can use BCP to graphically copy data (see Figure 16.12).

Figure 16.12.
Object Manager's
Transfer Data dialog
box.

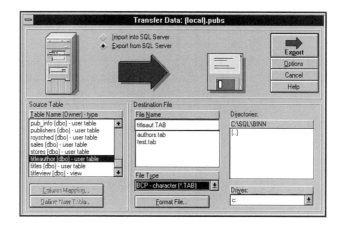

TRANSFER MANAGER

The *Transfer Manager* is a graphical tool used to transfer databases and objects. These objects can be transferred between different databases, different servers, and even different versions of SQL Server. Following are the types of objects that can be transferred:

- ◆ Tables (including data)
- ◆ Views
- ◆ Triggers
- ◆ Rules
- ◆ Defaults
- ◆ User datatypes
- ◆ Stored procedures
- ◆ Logins (including permissions)

Tip

The Transfer Manager is useful for moving a database from a development server to a production server or for moving a table and its data between the two servers.

Note

> The Transfer Manager allows you to transfer objects and data be-tween SQL Server 6.x and SQL Server 4.2x. Be aware that several new reserved words were added in SQL Server 6.x. If a reserved word is present in your 4.2x Transact SQL statement, the transfer to SQL Server 6.x will fail.
>
> The Transfer Manager also enables you to transfer a SQL Server 6.x database to a SQL Server 4.2x server. However, the database can-not contain any SQL Server 6.x language enhancements such as `identity` datatypes, `decimal` datatypes, declarative referential integrity, and so on.

The following steps explain how to use the Transfer Manager:

1. From the Enterprise Manager, access the Server Manager dialog box and select a server. Open the server object and then open the database folder. Right-click the appropriate database. From the shortcut menu, select the Transfer option (see Figure 16.13).

Note

Version
6.5

> In version 6.5, the Transfer Manager is integrated with the Enterprise Manager. In version 6.0, the Transfer Manager was a separate appli-cation in the Microsoft SQL Server 6.0 (Common) group.

Figure 16.13.
The Transfer menu
option.

2. From the Database/Object Transfer dialog box, enter the destination server and destination database. If necessary, set other options in the Database/Object Transfer dialog box.

Tip

The destination server can be the same as your source server. Use this feature to transfer objects between different databases on the same server.

Note

To transfer individual objects, deselect the Transfer All Objects checkbox. This enables the Choose Objects button. From the list that appears when you click this button, you can select individual objects to transfer.

3. Click the Start Transfer button to transfer the objects and data (see Figure 16.14). If errors occur during the transfer process, click the View Logs button to review the error log.

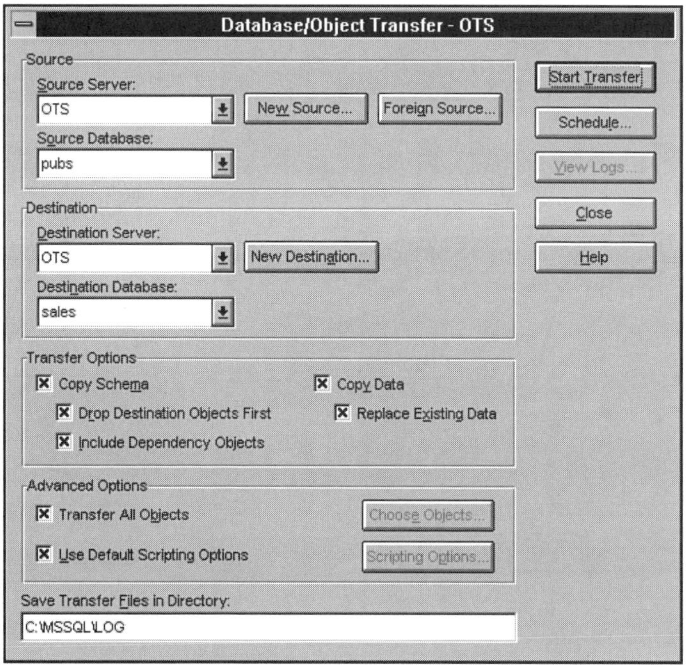

Figure 16.14.
The Transfer Manager window.

BETWEEN THE LINES

Following are important notes to remember when importing and exporting data:

◆ BCP uses two file types to transfer data: character mode and native mode. Character mode is ASCII text; native mode is a SQL Server file type. Character mode is usually easier to work with.

◆ When working with fixed-length ASCII files, always use the `char` datatype and `0` prefix length.

◆ To skip a column in interactive BCP, enter `0` for prefix length, `0` length, and no terminator.

◆ When importing data, BCP has two modes of operation: fast and slow. Fast mode bypasses the transaction log; slow mode posts all data inserts to the transaction log.

◆ To achieve fast mode BCP, set the database option `SELECT INTO/BULKCOPY` to `TRUE` and drop the indexes on the target table.

◆ Your ability to continuously run fast mode BCP depends on the backup and data access requirements in your production environment.

◆ Check constraints, rules, and triggers are not enforced when using BCP.

◆ When importing data into a date column, spaces in a data file convert to `1/1/1900`.

◆ Always use `UPDATE STATISTICS` after using BCP to import data into a table that contains indexes.

SUMMARY

As you can see from reading this chapter, you need to know a lot when it comes to importing and exporting data in SQL Server. The next chapter discusses common SQL Server errors.

CHAPTER 17   *by Mark Spenik*

Troubleshooting SQL Server

So far, each chapter in this book has covered common problems and resolutions. This chapter steps back and focuses on how SQL Server alerts you to possible problems with databases, objects, or the server; how to find more information about the problem; how to fix the problem; and how to get help in determining and fixing your problem. You also learn about several tools that ship with SQL Server to help you track and debug problems, as well as other resources readily available to aid in problem resolution. Start by taking a look at SQL Server error messages.

SQL ERROR MESSAGES

If you run a query and accidentally make a mistake by entering a table that does not exist in the database, what happens? SQL Server returns an error message. Actually, SQL Server reacts to all errors in the same manner, whether those errors are generated by users, databases, objects, or the system. SQL Server returns a formatted error message and/or writes the error message to the error log and/or event log. Here is a quick example that executes a SQL statement to update a nonexistent table in the pubs database. The SQL statement for the example is as follows:

```
UPDATE new_authors
Set author1 = "Spenik",
author2 = "Sledge",
title="Microsoft SQL Server DBA Survival Guide"
```

When the statement is executed, the following error message is returned:

```
Msg 208, Level 16, State 1
Invalid object name 'new_authors'.
```

The preceding error message demonstrates the standard message format for error messages returned by SQL Server.

Tip

> The first thing presented in the error message is the message number, severity level, and the state. To most users, these numbers are just garbage to be ignored, so they skip down to the message and try to resolve the problem. In reality, the error message number is very useful for obtaining more error information. You can use the severity levels to help find errors that need to be handled. When tracking a problem, always write down all the error information, including the message number, severity level, and state. In many cases, these will be of more assistance than the actual message.

Examine the format of a standard SQL Server error message.

ERROR MESSAGE NUMBER

Each error message displayed by SQL Server has an associated error message number that uniquely identifies the type of error.

Tip

You can define your own error messages. User-defined error message numbers must be greater than 50,000 and less than 2,147,483,647. You can use the system stored procedure sp_addmessage (described in detail in Appendix C) to add the error message to the system table, sysmessages. From a trigger or stored procedure, you can use the RAISERROR statement to report a user-defined error message to the client and SQL Server.

ERROR SEVERITY

The error severity levels provide a quick reference for you about the nature of the error. The severity levels range from 0 to 25.

Severity Level	Meaning
0 to 10	Messages with a severity level of 0 to 10 are informational messages.
11 to 16	Severity levels 11 to 16 are generated as a result of user problems and can be fixed by the user. For example, the error message returned in the invalid update query used earlier had a severity level of 16.
17	Severity level 17 indicates that SQL Server has run out of a configurable resource, such as user connections or locks. Severity error 17 can be corrected by the DBA, and in some cases, by the database owner.
18	Severity level 18 messages indicate nonfatal internal software problems.

Note

Severity errors 19 through 25 are fatal errors. When a fatal error occurs, the running process that generated the error is terminated (nonfatal errors continue processing). For error severity levels 20 and greater, the client connection to SQL Server is terminated.

Severity Level	Meaning
19	Severity level 19 indicates that a nonconfigurable resource limit has been exceeded.
20	Severity level 20 indicates a problem with a statement issued by the current process.
21	Severity level 21 indicates that SQL Server has encountered a problem that affects all the processes in a database.
22	Severity level 22 means that a table or index has been damaged. To try to determine the extent of the problem, stop and restart SQL Server. If the problem is only in the cache and not on the disk, the restart will correct the problem. Otherwise, use DBCC to determine the extent of the damage and the required action to take.
23	Severity level 23 indicates a suspect database. To determine the extent of the damage and the proper action to take, use the DBCC commands.
24	Severity level 24 indicates a hardware problem.
25	Severity level 25 indicates some type of system error.

STATE NUMBER

The error state number is an integer value between 1 and 127; it represents information about the invocation state of an error.

ERROR MESSAGE

The error message is a description of the error that occurred. The error messages are stored in the sysmessages system table. Figure 17.1 shows a query result of the sysmessages table. *Note:* The Query Analyzer is the new SQL Server 6.5 name for the SQL Server 6.0 Query window.

Figure 17.1.
Query results of
sysmessage using the
SQL Query tool.

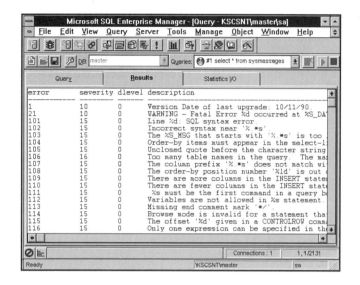

USING THE ERROR MESSAGE NUMBER TO RESOLVE THE ERROR

Earlier in this chapter, you learned that, by using the error message number, you could quickly retrieve detailed information about the error and possible ways to resolve the error. How, you may ask? Books Online!

INFORMATION AT YOUR FINGER TIPS

Isn't technology great! I believe that to really appreciate Microsoft's Books Online, you have to have been a Sybase DBA from the 4.2 UNIX days. When an error would occur that displayed the error number, you jotted down the error number and then tried to locate the error messages and the troubleshooting guide. Of course, the book was never in the same place. And if you had my luck, once you found the book, the error number was never in the book—it always fell within the "reserved" section or something similar. New DBAs who start with SQL Server 6.x will truly be spoiled by Microsoft's Books Online.

Hopefully, when you installed SQL Server, you included the Books Online utility shown in Figure 17.2.

Figure 17.2.
The SQL Server Books
Online.

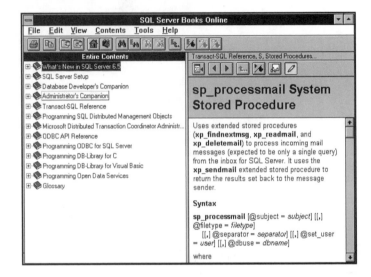

To see how to use Books Online to find more information on the error message number displayed during the invalid query example (error message number 208), follow these steps:

1. Select Tools, Query from the menu in the SQL Server Books Online window. The Query dialog box appears (see Figure 17.3).

Figure 17.3.
The Query dialog box.

Note

In Books Online in SQL Server 6.0, the Query dialog box is found by selecting Tools, Find. In version 6.0, the dialog box is called the Find dialog box instead of the Query dialog box.

2. The Query dialog box allows you to quickly search Books Online for specific information. In the Query combo box, type the error message number: **208**. In the Scope of Search frame, select the Entire Contents radio button. In the Topic Area To Search frame, select the Title Only radio button.

3. To run the search, click the Run Query button. The query runs, searching for **208** in the title of any of the book topics. If one or more items are found, they are displayed in a Query Results dialog box (see Figure 17.4).

Figure 17.4.
The Query Results
dialog box.

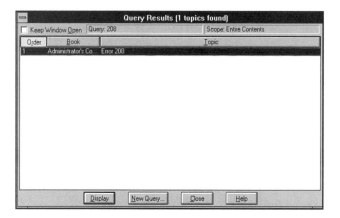

4. To view the document(s) found in the search, double-click the item or select the item and click the Display button. The detailed information for the error message number, including a detailed explanation and the action to take, is displayed. You can even print the document! Just think, no more trying to locate a troubleshooting or error message book! No more flipping through pages searching for error messages; if the error number is not in the book, you know immediately! The detailed information found for error number **208** is displayed in Figure 17.5.

Figure 17.5.
The Books Online
description of error
message 208.

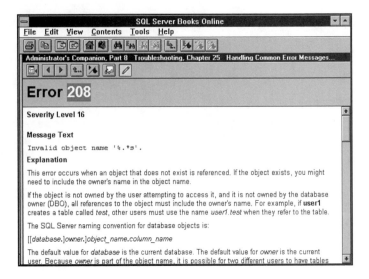

DECIPHERING THE ERROR LOG

The error log is a standard text file that holds SQL Server information and error messages and can provide meaningful information to help you track down problems or to alert you to potential or existing problems. SQL Server maintains the current error log and the six previous error log files. The current error log filename is ERRORLOG; the previous error log files, referred to as *archived error logs*, are named ERRORLOG.1 (most recent) to ERRORLOG.6 (the oldest). The default location of the error log file is in the \LOG directory off the SQL Server home directory. The following is an example of a SQL Server error log:

```
96/03/04 22:23:51.43 spid1     server name is 'SPENIK'
96/03/04 22:23:51.47 spid1     Recovering database 'model'
96/03/04 22:23:51.48 spid1     Recovery dbid 3 ckpt (394,4) oldest tran=(394,0)
96/03/04 22:23:51.56 spid1     Clearing temp db
96/03/04 22:23:52.83 kernel    Read Ahead Manager started.
96/03/04 22:23:52.85 kernel    Using 'SQLEVN60.DLL' version '6.00.000'.
96/03/04 22:23:52.91 kernel    Using 'OPENDS60.DLL' version '6.00.01.02'.
96/03/04 22:23:52.92 kernel    Using 'NTWDBLIB.DLL' version '6.50.163'.
96/03/04 22:23:52.96 ods       Using 'SSNMPN60.DLL' version '6.3.0.0' to listen on
➥'\\.\pipe\sql\query'.
96/03/04 22:23:55.01 spid10    Recovering database 'pubs'
96/03/04 22:23:55.04 spid11    Recovering database 'msdb'
96/03/04 22:23:55.07 spid11    Recovery dbid 5 ckpt (1799,18) oldest tran=(1799,17)
96/03/04 22:23:55.08 spid10    Recovery dbid 4 ckpt (1090,28) oldest tran=(1090,27)
96/03/04 22:23:55.10 spid11    1 transactions rolled forward in dbid 5.
96/03/04 22:23:55.10 spid10    1 transactions rolled forward in dbid 4.
96/03/04 22:23:55.38 spid1     Recovery complete.
96/03/04 22:23:55.40 spid1     SQL Server's default sort order is:
96/03/04 22:23:55.40 spid1             'nocase' (ID = 52)
```

The error log output includes the time and date the message was logged, the source of the message, and the description of the error message. If an error occurs, the log contains the error message number and description.

Tip

> Spend some time looking at and understanding the messages in the error log, especially the proper startup sequence messages. This knowledge can come in handy in times of trouble!

You can view the error log using any text editor, such as Notepad, or you can use the SQL Server Enterprise Manager. To use the Enterprise Manager, select Error Log from the Server menu. The Server Error Log dialog box appears (see Figure 17.6). To view archived error logs, use the combo box shown in Figure 17.6.

Figure 17.6.
The Server Error Log
dialog box.

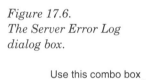

Use this combo box
to select an archive

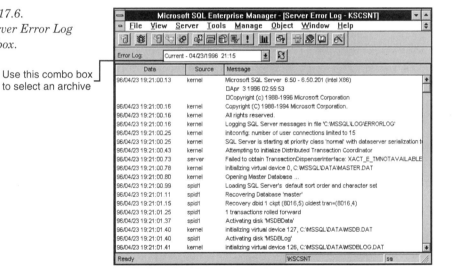

USING THE EVENT VIEWER

SQL Server also logs information and error messages to the Windows NT event log. The event log is used by Windows NT as a repository for the operating system and applications to log informational and error messages. The Event Viewer is located in the Windows NT Administrative Tools group. The advantage of using the Event Viewer over the error log is that errors are easy to spot because NT highlights all error messages with a red stop sign; it highlights information messages with a blue exclamation mark (see Figure 17.7).

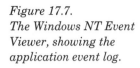

Figure 17.7.
The Windows NT Event
Viewer, showing the
application event log.

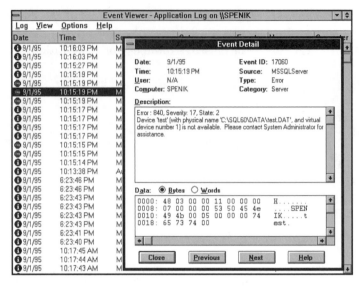

To view the detailed error message description, severity level, and state, double-click the line item. An Event Detail dialog box appears. The Event Viewer also provides a search utility that enables you to search for specific types of events in the event log. For example, you can search for all the error messages in the event log.

KILLING A PROCESS

A SQL Server *user process* is a task or request made to SQL Server by a user. Occasionally, you may be required to halt (stop) a user process before it completes. Perhaps the user has incorrectly formatted a query or launched a massive transaction that will take hours to complete and that has blocked out other users from necessary table information. Whatever the case may be, you can bet that sooner or later someone will ask you to stop his or her process or someone else will complain about not getting any information back. The proper terminology for halting a process is called *killing a process*, which sounds much more severe than just halting or stopping the process. When you kill a process, you completely remove the process from SQL Server.

Tip

The number one reason to kill a process is interference with other users' p rocessing (that is, the rogue process prevents users from getting to the required information by "blocking" them out, as in exclusive table locks, for a lengthy transaction).

SQL Server assigns each task a unique identity number called a spid (system process ID). To view the currently running processes and their spids, issue the system stored procedure sp_who, which has the following format:

```
sp_who [login id ¦ 'spid']
```

In this syntax, *login_id* is the specific user login ID for which you want to report activity and *spid* is a specific process ID for which you want to report activity.

Issuing the sp_who command with no parameters displays a report on all the current processes on SQL Server, as in the following example:

```
spid   status     loginame     hostname    blk    dbname    cmd
------  --------   ---------    ---------   -----  ------    --------------
1      sleeping   sa                       0      master    MIRROR HANDLER
2      sleeping   sa                       0      master    LAZY WRITER
3      sleeping   sa                       0      master    CHECKPOINT SLEEP
4      runnable   sa                       0      master    RA MANAGER
10     sleeping   sa           SPENIK      0      master    AWAITING COMMAND
11     runnable   sa           SPENIK      0      master    SELECT
```

To kill a process, use the KILL command, which has the following syntax:

```
KILL spid
```

In this syntax, *spid* is the system process ID of the process you want to terminate.

You can kill only one spid at a time and the statement cannot be reversed. Once you have issued the command, the process *will* be killed. To kill spid number 11 shown in the previous sample, you issue the following command:

```
kill 11
```

Note

In pre-system 10 versions of Sybase and pre-Windows NT versions of Microsoft SQL Server, the KILL command did not always work. If the spid was a sleeping process, the only way to kill the process was to shut down the server. The inability to kill a process with the KILL statement was a kind of joke among DBAs; the processes were nick-named *zombies*. A zombie process was a serious problem when a process really did need to be shut down and the KILL command was ineffective. Microsoft corrected the problem in SQL Server for Windows NT 4.21.

You also can kill a process using the SQL Server Enterprise Manager by performing the following steps:

1. After you select a server from the Enterprise Manager, select Current Activity from the Server menu. The Current Activity dialog box appears (see Figure 17.8).

   All the current processes running on SQL Server as well as the spids of the processes are displayed in the Current Activity dialog box.

Figure 17.8.
The Current Activity
dialog box.

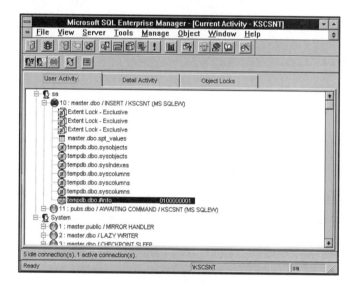

Note

In SQL Server 6.0, the Current Activity dialog box is found under the Tools menu.

2. To kill a process, select the process you want to terminate and then click the Kill Process toolbar button in the Current Activity dialog box. The selected process is terminated.

VIEWING DETAILED PROCESS ACTIVITY

The day will come when your phone is ringing off the hook because suddenly the system is slow or a user has been waiting a very long time for a report to complete. With SQL Server 6.x, you can easily view the current activity of the system using the Current Activity dialog box (refer back to Figure 17.8). Click the Detail Activity tab in the Current Activity dialog box; the Detail Activity page of the Current Activity dialog box appears (see Figure 17.9).

Figure 17.9.
The Detail Activity
page of the Current
Activity dialog box.

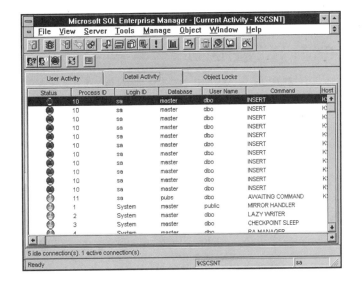

The Detail Activity page allows you to quickly view the current state of executing processes and helps you determine possible problems such as a blocked process (covered in detail in Chapter 23, "Multi-User Considerations").

You can view the last command executed by a process or the resource usage of the process (CPU and disk usage) by double-clicking the process in the Current Activity dialog box (either the User Activity or Detail Activity page). The Process Information dialog box appears (see Figure 17.10). The Process Information dialog box not only shows you the last command executed by the process but also the CPU and disk usage.

Figure 17.10.
The Process Informa-
tion dialog box.

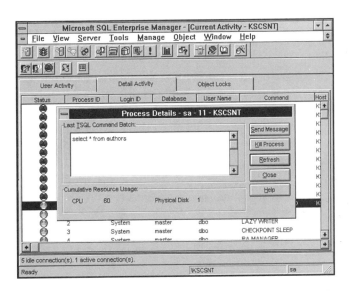

USING DBCC AND TRACE STATEMENTS TO TROUBLESHOOT

DBCC stands for *Database Consistency Checker*. DBCC consists of a series of commands that perform many different functions on databases and database objects. You use DBCC commands to perform database and database object maintenance but you also use the output of DBCC commands to find errors—and in some cases, fix them. Trace flags can be used to provide additional information about SQL Server actions such as process deadlock information (trace flags 1204 and 1205) or the estimated and actual cost of a sort (trace flag 326).

Note

DBCC and trace flag settings are detailed in Appendix E. It is highly recommended that you read and re-read Appendix E. Understanding when and how to use DBCC can save you a lot of headaches.

For starters, when tracking errors or problems, you will want to examine the output of your daily DBCC maintenance commands for standard SQL Server error messages. If you find an error message in a DBCC output, treat the error message like any other SQL Server error message and use Books Online or technical support to resolve the error. When you call technical support or find the error number in Books Online, one or many of the resolution steps may be to execute DBCC command(s) to resolve the problem. Suppose that you are trying to create an index in sorted order on the authors table, column au_lanme, in the pubs database; the CREATE INDEX statement fails with the following error message:

```
Msg 1520, Level 18, State:1
Sort failed because dpages in the Sysindexes row for table 'authors' in database
'pubs' had an incorrect value. Please run DBCC CHECKTABLE on this table to correct
the value, then re-run your command.
```

The description in the error message suggests that you execute the DBCC command with the option CHECKTABLE. If you search Books Online for error 1520, you see a more detailed description of why the error message occurred and the following Action section (taken from Administrator's Companion, Books Online):

```
Action
To correct the page count, use one of the following statements:
dbcc tablealloc(tablename)
dbcc newalloc(databasename)
dbcc checktable(tablename)
After running DBCC, you should be able to create the index.
```

Become familiar with DBCC commands. Use the correct DBCC options (if any) to fix a problem in your database when instructed to do so.

Follow the Clues

Last night, while working late to help a group fix a SQL Server problem, I was reminded of a very important tip when troubleshooting SQL Server problems: ***Follow the clues. Do not speculate first.*** The reason I was reminded of this tip is that, when I arrived on the scene, everyone involved was ready to blame the problem on the new release of SQL Server that they had upgraded to two weeks ago (the upgrade was from release 4.21 to release 6.0—and I performed the upgrade). When I looked over the error log and the general state of the system, I quickly ruled out the upgrade.

The problem they were having was running a new stored procedure that pulled information in from a mainframe flat file and massaged and reformatted the data to be output to another flat file to feed the mainframe. Whenever the stored procedure ran, the transaction log filled up before the process could complete. They had expanded the log several times and still the stored procedure could not run to completion. One important fact to mention is that the procedure had been tested with 500 rows on versions 4.21 and 6.0 but now they were attempting to run 16,000 rows.

One problem I spotted and fixed immediately with DBCC commands was that the transaction log's size was invalid and would not respond correctly to the DUMP TRANSACTION WITH NO_LOG command. Once the transaction log problem was corrected, I set up a threshold to dump the log when it was 80 percent full. Still the procedure would not run. When I examined the stored procedure, I found nothing unusual. A transaction was started and then the 16,000 rows were copied to four tables. This organization had several stored procedures that performed the same operation and nothing looked unusual with the stored procedure. Again the cry of "maybe it's version 6.0—let's try 4.21" was echoed.

Because there was no evidence to suggest that it was a version 6.0 problem, we tried the procedure again. This time we monitored the server from the version 4.21 Object Manager using sp_who, sp_lock, and DBCC SQLPERF(LOGSPACE) to track what was going on. It was not long before we noticed that the spid executing the stored procedure seemed to be stuck on an UPDATE statement. That seemed odd because the only UPDATE occurred outside of the transaction and had already occurred. Again moans about the upgrade or the corrupted transaction log rose across the room. Except for the developer, who quietly stated, "I bet there is an update trigger on the table I'm inserting into." Well, she was right. Not only was there an update trigger but the SQL statement was incorrectly copying 16,000 rows into a table with an update trigger when only 39 rows should have been copied. The problem was quickly solved.

The moral of this story is that troubleshooting can be difficult and often consists of more then one clue (such as an upgrade, a corrupted transaction log, and a new process). Try not to jump to conclusions. Solve each problem, one at a time, and if something does not make sense, keep searching for the real reason the process fails so that you can fix it. It is very easy to go down the wrong road. Oh, by the way: beware of triggers on tables when troubleshooting a developer process. They are easy to forget and, in some cases, may be the unexpected root of the problem!

TABLE FRAGMENTATION

I have heard a lot of noise on various SQL Server forums about table fragmentation. *Table fragmentation* occurs on tables that have a lot of insert/update/delete activity. As the table is modified over a period of time, the fullness of each data page begins to vary (that is, pages are not full). You can defragment the table by dropping and re-creating the clustered index on the table, which packs each page with the fill factor amount of data. Not only does this improve performance when you read the table, it also can increase the amount of available database space. Because rebuilding a clustered index on a very large table can take a fair amount of time, SQL Server 6.x provides the DBCC SHOWCONTIG command that enables you to determine how fragmented a table or index is (that is, whether or not you need to rebuild it). The SHOWCONTIG option has the following format:

```
DBCC SHOWCONTIG (table id, [index id])
```

In this syntax, `table id` and `index id` are the IDs of the object found in the `sysobjects` table of the database. For example, the following is the command line and output from a DBCC SHOWCONTIG command performed on the `authors` table in the `pubs` database:

```
DBCC SHOWCONTIG(16003088)
DBCC SHOWCONTIG scanning 'authors' table...
[SHOW_CONTIG - SCAN ANALYSIS]
-----------------------------------------------------------------------
Table: 'authors' (16003088)  Indid: 1  dbid:4
TABLE level scan performed.
```

```
- Pages Scanned................................: 1
- Extent Switches.............................: 0
- Avg. Pages per Extent.......................: 1.0
- Scan Density [Best Count:Actual Count].......: 100.00% [0:1]
- Avg. Bytes free per page....................: 89.0
- Avg. Page density (full)...................: 95.58%
- Overflow Pages.............................: 0
- Disconnected Overflow Pages.................: 0
DBCC execution completed. If DBCC printed error messages, see your System
➥Administrator.
```

Tip

For those of you wondering how to find the table ID using sysobjects, the query used for the authors table is shown here. Remember: To get a table ID for a specific table, you must be in the database when you query sysobjects or make a direct reference to the database such as database..sysobjects. The query (executed from the master database) is as follows:

```
select id from pubs..sysobjects where name = "authors"
```

OTHER SOURCES OF HELP AND INFORMATION

In SQL Server 6.x, Microsoft has done a good job of providing useful and valuable information in Books Online. But as a DBA, it is important for you to know that there are many other good sources of information for Microsoft SQL Server (such as this book). But what happens when the problem is beyond the scope of published resources? The following sections discuss some of the options available to you.

TECHNICAL SUPPORT

When you run across a problem not covered in this book or one of a very critical and urgent nature, it's time to get in touch with your tech support company. If you have purchased SQL Server, you have also (hopefully) purchased a support agreement with Microsoft or with a Microsoft Solution Provider to help you in the event of an emergency. If not, Microsoft can still provide help (you are charged per incident). My experience with Microsoft tech support has been very good. In general, Microsoft's support contracts and agreements are much less expensive than those of some of the other RDBMS companies. A Microsoft Solution Provider is an independent organization that provides consulting and integration services for Microsoft products and also can provide support. Before calling tech support, be sure to have all the information required to start an incident report. You should have the following information:

◆ Hardware platform

◆ Version of Windows NT

◆ Version of SQL Server (you can get this from the error log or by using the @@Version global variable)

◆ Complete error message (number, level, state, and description)

◆ Type of environment (production/development)

◆ Urgency of problem resolution

◆ Description and scenario of the problem and the cause

Tip

> If the problem is one that can be reproduced using SQL commands or a sequence of events, have this information written down so that the tech support person can duplicate the results.

MICROSOFT TECHNET

Before there was SQL Server 6.x Books Online, there was Microsoft TechNet. Microsoft TechNet is a monthly CD subscription that provides a wealth of information about Microsoft products. TechNet provides product white papers, release notes, current patches and drivers, and a knowledge base of product information and problem resolution. TechNet is fairly inexpensive for a yearly subscription of 12 monthly CDs packed with information. (I won't quote a price because it's subject to change!) To find out more about TechNet, call 1-800-344-2121.

Tip

> TechNet is my second line of defense. If I can't resolve the problem based on my knowledge and Books Online, I check TechNet for a information on the problem. Do yourself a favor and subscribe!

The advantage of TechNet is that it is a monthly CD, so problem resolution not available when SQL Server 6.x shipped can be placed in the TechNet knowledge base for your immediate use. TechNet's search facility is similar to the Books Online search facility (or vice-versa, since TechNet was here first), as shown in Figure 17.11. As you can with Books Online, you can perform searches on error numbers or keywords and get a list of articles that contain the keyword or error number.

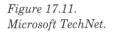

Figure 17.11.
Microsoft TechNet.

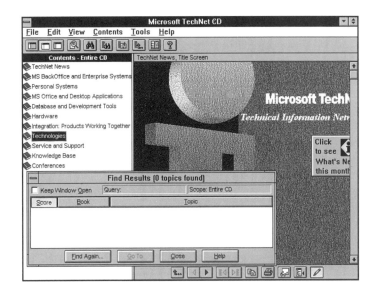

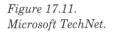
17

TROUBLESHOOTING SQL SERVER

ONLINE SERVICES

To obtain interactive support without using tech support, try one of the interactive Microsoft SQL Server forums. Currently, forums exist on CompuServe (GO MSSQL) and on the new Microsoft Network. Using the online services, you can search for existing messages that deal with problems you are experiencing. You can also post messages asking for help from your peers. I find the online services to be very useful and well worth the small monthly fee. Many individuals have their problems resolved on the online services, but most of these problems are of a noncritical nature because turnaround time for a posted question is an unknown.

USER GROUPS

SQL Server user groups can provide a forum in which you can discuss problems or issues with your local peers. They also tend to enlighten you on current products and future releases.

BETWEEN THE LINES

Following are some of the important points to review when you troubleshoot SQL Server:

◆ SQL Server displays error messages in the following format: Msg #, Level #, State #, Description.

◆ If an error occurs, write down the entire message, not just a part of it.

◆ Use Books Online and the Microsoft TechNet search facilities to help resolve problems.

◆ Make it a point to understand the SQL Server error log.

◆ Check the Windows NT event log for errors by using the Event Viewer search facility.

◆ Stop runaway user processes with the KILL command.

◆ Stay informed by taking advantage of user groups and online services.

SUMMARY

You should now know where to search for SQL Server error messages; you should also understand the format and meaning of SQL Server error messages. This chapter provided the foundation for your understanding of how to interpret and research the error messages you may receive during routine maintenance. Another important point in this chapter is that you have to be a good DBA and get involved in your local SQL Server user group or spend a few hours a week in a online service, interacting with your peers and learning more about SQL Server. In Chapter 25, "Developing a SQL Server Maintenance Plan," and Chapter 26, "Automating Database Administration Tasks," you learn how to perform preventive maintenance on your SQL Server to limit the amount of time you spend troubleshooting.

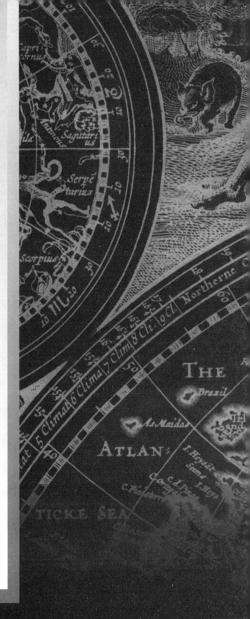

P A R T V

Performance and Tuning

CHAPTER 18 *by Orryn Sledge*

Monitoring SQL Server

SQL Server provides several utilities that allow you to easily monitor SQL Server and its interaction with the operating system. These utilities can help a DBA quickly isolate bottlenecks and determine hardware deficiencies.

UNDERSTANDING THE PERFORMANCE MONITOR

The *Performance Monitor* is an excellent tool for monitoring SQL Server and the Windows NT operating system. The advantage of the Performance Monitor is that it is tightly integrated with the operating system. This enables you to track real-time statistics about SQL Server and Windows NT. You can use these statistics to isolate bottlenecks and track performance.

Note

The Performance Monitor may slightly degrade system performance. The overhead incurred by the Performance Monitor has been found to be 5 percent or less on single processor machines and insignificant on multiple processor machines.

USING THE PERFORMANCE MONITOR

The following step explains how to use the Performance Monitor:

1. Double-click the SQL Performance Monitor icon in the Microsoft SQL Server 6.5 program group. The Performance Monitor dialog box appears (see Figure 18.1).

By default, the Performance Monitor for SQL Server tracks the following five predefined counters:

◆ Cache Hit Ratio

◆ I/O - Transactions/sec

◆ I/O - Page Reads/sec

◆ I/O - Single Page Writes/sec

◆ User Connections

Figure 18.1.
The Performance
Monitor dialog box.

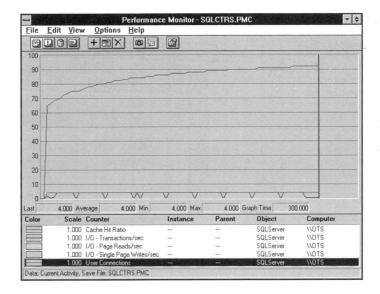

Note

The five default counters are useful but do not give a complete picture of SQL Server or Windows NT. Therefore, you will likely want to add additional counters to get a clearer understanding of system performance.

ADDING COUNTERS

Follow these steps to add counters to the Performance Monitor:

1. From the Performance Monitor dialog box, select Add To Chart from the Edit menu.
2. Select the object type and counter type. Click the Add button to add the counter to the chart (see Figure 18.2).

Note

Chart settings are valid only for the life of the chart. You must manually save the chart if you want to save your chart settings. From the File menu, select Save or Save As to save the current chart to disk.

Figure 18.2.
Adding counters
to a chart.

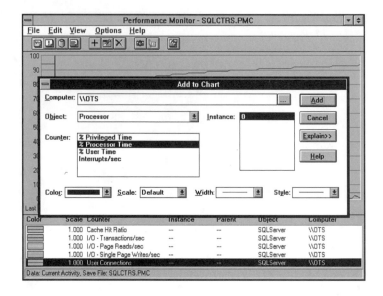

MONITORING KEY AREAS

The Performance Monitor can be overwhelming because it provides so much information. You can track over 70 different counters for SQL Server and hundreds of different counters for Windows NT. Trying to track this much information can drive you crazy!

Instead of trying to track everything at once, you should monitor the following five key areas (see Figure 18.3):

◆ Memory

◆ Processor

◆ Disk I/O

◆ User connections

◆ Locks

These five indicators will quickly clue you in to performance bottlenecks. After you determine the general bottleneck source, you should look into the other types of counters not mentioned in this chapter (use the *Windows NT Resource Guide*, published by Microsoft Press, for additional information).

Figure 18.3.
Some recommended
counters to watch.

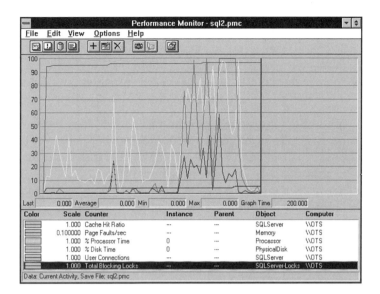

Note

When using the Performance Monitor, it is important to monitor key counters over time and establish patterns before making rash decisions. Be sure that you understand the types of operations being performed by SQL Server before adding a new processor or additional memory. A hardware improvement based on incomplete data may not yield the desired improvement in performance.

MEMORY

SQL Server likes memory. It uses memory to hold data and frequently accessed objects. An increase in memory may enable SQL Server to place more data into the memory cache, which may result in better performance.

When diagnosing memory bottlenecks, the following counters are useful to monitor (see "Adding Counters," earlier in this chapter for information on adding counters):

◆ SQLServer: cache hit ratio

◆ Memory: page faults/sec

◆ Paging file: % Usage

◆ SQLServer: I/O - lazy writes

THE SQLServer: Cache Hit Ratio COUNTER

The SQLServer: cache hit ratio counter monitors the hit rate at which data was found in the data cache. If the data is not in the data cache, the server has to read the data from disk. This counter generally provides an accurate indication of memory allocation that can be used to determine whether you have sufficient memory.

A number consistently less than 85 percent may indicate that you have insufficient memory. Performance may suffer because SQL Server has to read the data from the physical disk. Reading data from the physical disk is an expensive operation. When evaluating this counter, it is important to consider the type of operation being performed on the machine and when the operation occurs. In a transaction processing environment, you can probably improve the cache-hit ratio by adding more memory. In a batch environment that uses very large databases, the cache-hit ratio may never go above 85 percent. Under this scenario, additional memory may not substantially improve performance.

THE Memory: Page Faults/Sec COUNTER

The Memory: Page Faults/sec counter monitors the number of times an operating system virtual page was not found in memory. When a page is not found in memory, the operating system must retrieve the page from disk. The time it takes to retrieve a page from disk is always longer than the time required to retrieve the page from memory.

After SQL Server has stabilized, this number should remain at or near zero. If the number is consistently greater than zero, this indicates that too much memory is allocated to SQL Server and not enough memory is allocated to Windows NT. Therefore, you should reduce the amount of memory allocated to SQL Server.

THE Paging File: % Usage COUNTER

The Paging File: % Usage counter monitors the percent of NT's paging file currently in use. If you find that a large percentage of the page file is in use, you may want to increase the size of the paging file to prevent an out-of-virtual-memory error. An alternative to increasing the page file is to add more memory to your server. Doing so will probably reduce page file utilization. With additional memory, you can improve performance because it is always faster to read data from memory than from the paging file.

Another point to consider when analyzing the paging file counter is a growing page file. A growing page file occurs when you specify an initial page file size smaller than the specified maximum size. From the NT operating system perspective, a growing page file is considered an expensive operation. It is better to set your initial page file size the same as your maximum page file size, which eliminates the need for the operating system to grow the page file.

THE `SQLServer: I/O - Lazy Writes` COUNTER

The `SQLServer: I/O - Lazy Writes` counter monitors the number of flushed pages per second by the Lazy Writer.

A number consistently greater than zero indicates that the Lazy Writer is constantly working to flush buffers to disk. This means that the data cache is too small, which indicates that you have insufficient memory.

PROCESSOR

SQL Server is CPU intensive. Continuously high utilization rates may indicate that your CPU is the bottleneck. The best way to determine if your CPU is the bottleneck is to use the `% Processor Time` counter.

THE `Processor: % Processor Time` COUNTER

The `Processor: % Processor Time` counter monitors the amount of time the CPU spends processing a thread.

A steady-state value above 80 to 90 percent may indicate that a CPU upgrade or additional processors may improve performance.

Note

Scalability (the capability to gain performance through additional processors) has been greatly improved with SQL Server version 6.x. Previous versions of SQL Server did not scale well when multiple processors were added to the computer. Benchmark tests have shown that in an online transaction processing (OLTP) environment, SQL Server 6.x scales in a relatively linear fashion for up to four processors with an out-of-the-box NT Server configuration. SQL Server can scale beyond four processors through vendor-specific extensions to the NT Server operating system.

DISK I/O

You always want to minimize disk I/O when working with SQL Server. However, when SQL Server does read and write to the hard disk, you want to ensure adequate disk performance. If you are not achieving adequate disk I/O, transaction throughput will suffer.

To help detect disk I/O bottlenecks, you should monitor the following two counters:

◆ `PhysicalDisk: % Disk Time`

◆ `PhysicalDisk: Disk Queue Length.`

Note

You must run the `diskperf` command before you can monitor disk performance statistics. To enable `diskperf`, go to the command prompt and type the following:

`diskperf -y,`

You can also control `diskperf` through Control Panel: Devices.

Then shut down and restart the computer.

Caution

Disk I/O values vary from one type of disk system to another. You should contact your disk manufacturer to determine acceptable counter values.

THE `PhysicalDisk: % Disk Time` COUNTER

The `PhysicalDisk: % Disk Time` counter monitors the percentage of elapsed time that the disk is busy with read/write activity.

A consistently high value (one above 2) may indicate that your disk system is a bottleneck.

THE `PhysicalDisk: Disk Queue Length` COUNTER

The `PhysicalDisk: Disk Queue Length` counter monitors the number of outstanding requests on disk.

Sustained queue lengths greater than 3 may indicate a disk-related bottleneck. Also, a consistently high value for one physical disk combined with a consistently low value for your other physical disks indicates that redistributing your data may improve performance. Examine your device and segment configuration.

USER CONNECTIONS

How many times have you been hit with the following problem? System performance crawls during peak business hours. These are the hours when everyone in the company is banging away on the system. Transactions are being processed at a snail's pace and your phone is ringing off the hook with irate users.

I think every DBA, at one time or another, has experienced this problem. It is no secret that as the number of active users increases, the likelihood of performance degradation also increases.

To help track why and when user connection bottlenecks occur, I suggest using the following counters:

◆ `SQLServer: User connections`

◆ `SQLServer: Net - Network Reads/sec.`

THE `SQLServer: User Connections` COUNTER

The `SQLServer: User connections` counter monitors the number of active user connections.

Use this counter to help determine when the number of active users exceeds the capabilities of your system. You may find that performance is exceptional with 50 users, adequate with 75 users, and horrendous with more than 100 users.

Tip

> The `SQLServer: User connections` counter can also be used to help determine the appropriate configuration value for user connections. If the number of active user connections is significantly below the number of available user connections, you are probably wasting memory. Each connection uses 37K of memory, regardless of connection status.

THE `SQLServer: Net - Network Reads/Sec` COUNTER

The `SQLServer: Net - Network Reads/sec` counter monitors the number of data packets read from the network.

If you are currently not using stored procedures and you find that this counter is high and your transaction rate is low, you may be able to improve performance by implementing stored procedures. Stored procedures can help reduce the amount of network traffic. If this counter is extremely high for an extended period of time, you may be able to improve performance by using faster network interface cards (NICs).

LOCKS

SQL Server uses locks to ensure data consistency in a multi-user environment. You will often see various degrees of locking activity during normal processing.

Be on the lookout for blocking locks. A *blocking lock* is a lock that forces another process to wait until the current process is complete. When monitoring blocking, use the SQLServer-Locks: Total Blocking Locks counter.

THE SQLServer-Locks: Total Blocking Locks COUNTER

The SQLServer-Locks: Total Blocking Locks counter monitors the number of all locks that are blocking other processes.

An occasional block or two is usually unavoidable. Be on the lookout for blocking levels consistently greater than zero. This usually indicates serious transaction problems. Blocking can be caused by a variety of factors. Some of the basic causes of blocking are inefficient query design, poor table design, lack of useful indexes, and slow throughput caused by inadequate hardware.

MONITORING USERS

In addition to monitoring SQL Server activity, it may be useful to monitor individual user activity. By using the User Activity Monitor in the Enterprise Manager, you can view user connections, locks, process numbers, and user commands. With SQL Trace, you can monitor and record Transact SQL activity and other statistics.

THE USER ACTIVITY MONITOR

One of the best features of the User Activity Monitor is its capability to view more information about a process. This is a major plus for DBAs: It gives you all the information you need to know about a process. You can use this information to help kill a process or to pinpoint a query that is a burden to the system.

Follow these steps to use the User Activity Monitor:

1. Click the Current Activity toolbar button from the Enterprise Manager window. The Current Activity dialog box appears (see Figure 18.4).

2. From the Current Activity dialog box, you can view three types of information: User Activity, Detail Activity, and Objects Locks. Click the corresponding tab in the Current Activity dialog box to view each type of information (see Figures 18.4, 18.5, and 18.6).

Figure 18.4.
The Current Activity
dialog box, showing the
User Activity page.

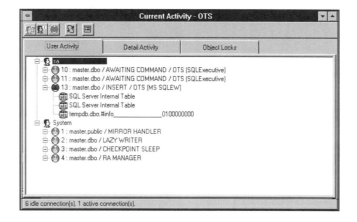

Note

The information displayed in the Current Activity dialog box must be manually refreshed. To perform a refresh, click the Refresh toolbar button in the Current Activity dialog box. When you kill a process, you will want to verify that the process was terminated by clicking the Refresh toolbar button and then reviewing the process information.

Figure 18.5.
The Current Activity
dialog box, showing the
Detail Activity page.

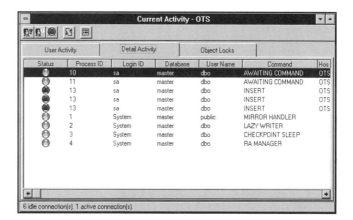

Tip

Click the Display Legend toolbar button to display a legend for activity information (see Figure 18.7).

Figure 18.6.
The Current Activity
dialog box, showing the
Object Locks page.

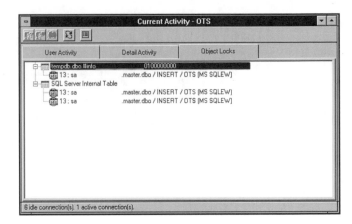

Figure 18.7.
The Activity
Legend menu.

Tip

Be on the lookout for blocking when users are complaining that their transactions are hung. Select the Detail Activity tab in the Current Activity dialog box to view blocked processes.

3. From the Current Activity dialog box, double-click a process to view more information about the process. The Process Details dialog box appears (see Figure 18.8). From this dialog box, you can view the last statement issued by the user, kill a process, and send a message to the user.

Note

The send message feature is available only for Microsoft networks.

Tip

The Transact SQL commands sp_who, sp_lock, KILL, DBCC INPUTBUFFER, and OUTPUTBUFFER can be used to perform functions similar to the functions found in the User Activity Monitor.

Figure 18.8.
The Process Details
dialog box.

Using SQL Trace

SQL Trace is a utility included with SQL Server version 6.5 that allows you to monitor Transact SQL activity for a particular server. Using this utility, you can investigate user activity and generate audit trails. This utility is also useful for observing SQL statements generated by applications and end users. In turn, this information can be used to pinpoint poorly constructed queries or security problems. Another feature of SQL Trace is its capability to save the trace information to a file. This feature allows an administrator or developer to replay the queries from the trace session by cutting and pasting the information into separate query sessions. As you can see, this information can be beneficial when trying to tune queries and stored procedures.

Follow these steps to use SQL Trace:

1. Double-click the SQL Trace icon in the Microsoft SQL Server 6.5 (Common) program group. This starts the SQL Trace utility. The Connect Server dialog box appears (see Figure 18.9).

Figure 18.9.
The Connect Server
dialog box.

2. In the Connect Server dialog box, enter the server name and login information. Click the Connect button to initiate a trace session.

3. If this is the first time you have used SQL Trace, you are prompted to create a new filter. Click the Yes button when prompted. This opens the New Filter dialog box (see Figure 18.10).

4. From the New Filter dialog box, you can create a filter to trace SQL statements. When you create a filter, you can specify the types of information to

trace such as Login Name, Host Name, and so on. After entering the filter information in the New Filter dialog box, click the Add button to save the filter. Clicking the Add button also activates the filter you just created (see Figure 18.11).

Figure 18.10.
The New Filter
dialog box.

Figure 18.11.
An active filter
example.

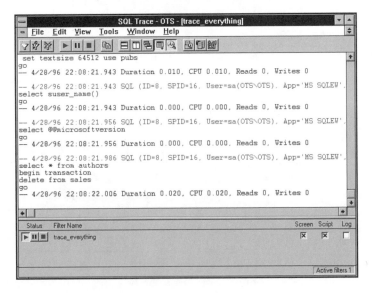

5. When the filter is active, it displays the SQL statements that match your trace criteria. As you can see, the ability to trace SQL statements provides a wealth of information that can be used to analyze SQL activity.

Note

The best method I've found for tracing activity is to create a filter that tightly defines the type of information you are looking for. This eliminates a lot of extraneous information that may not be of interest to you. For example, if you are only interested in tracing the activity for a particular user, create a filter that monitors activity for only that particular user.

When you create a filter, you can specify that the trace information be saved to a log file or to a SQL script. The difference between a log file and a SQL script is the following:

◆ A *log file* is an ASCII text file in a tab-delimited format. This type of file is useful when you want to record trace information and then load the file into a product for further analysis (for example, a SQL Server table, Excel spreadsheet, and so on).

◆ A *SQL script file* is a regular ASCII text file without delimiters. This type of file is useful when you want to copy the trace information into a SQL Server query session or you want to search for certain information through a text editor.

BETWEEN THE LINES

Following are some important notes to remember when monitoring SQL Server:

◆ The Performance Monitor is an excellent tool for monitoring SQL Server and the Windows NT operating system.

◆ On a single-processor machine, the Performance Monitor may slightly degrade system performance.

◆ Don't let the Performance Monitor drive you crazy! Rather than trying to track a multitude of counters, track five to eight key performance indicators. Anything over eight or ten different counters makes it difficult to determine what is going on.

◆ Following are some useful counters to track:

   ◆ `SQLServer: Cache Hit Ratio`

   ◆ `Processor: % Processor Time`

   ◆ `PhysicalDisk: % Disk Time`

   ◆ `SQLServer: User connections`

   ◆ `SQLServer: Net - Network Reads/sec`

   ◆ `SQLServer-Locks: Total Blocking Locks`

◆ You must run `diskperf` before you can monitor disk performance statistics.

◆ Use the User Activity Monitor to track user connections, locks, and process numbers. The User Activity Monitor can also be used to view the SQL commands issued from each user.

◆ Use the SQL Trace utility to trace SQL activity. This tool can monitor SQL activity and save the information to a log file.

SUMMARY

The Performance Monitor and User Activity Monitor are two valuable tools for tracking server utilization and pinpointing bottlenecks. All DBAs should keep an eye on their system by tracking a few key counters. The next chapter discusses server configuration and tuning.

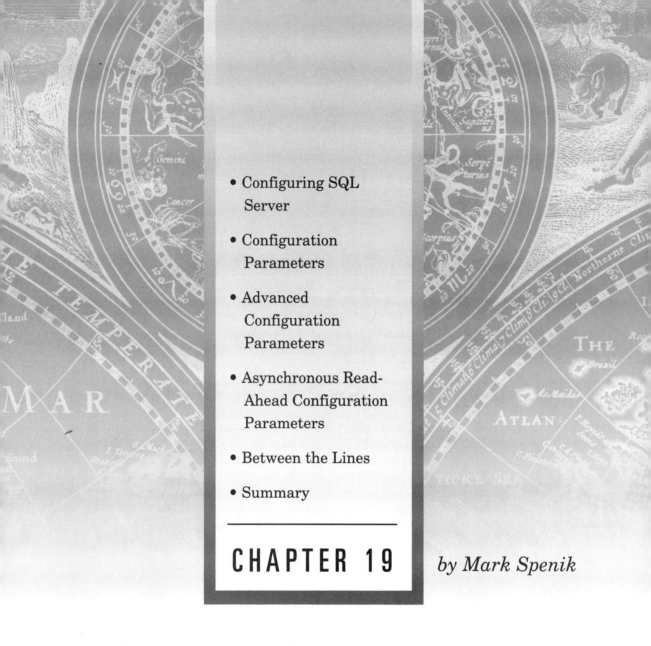

CHAPTER 19

by Mark Spenik

Which Knobs Do I Turn?

You now have SQL Server installed and running. Maybe you are about to roll out your first production database and your boss is breathing down your neck asking, "Mister (or Madam) DBA, have you tuned and optimized the server?" You tell your boss, no, but tuning and optimizing SQL Server was next on your list. You bring up the SQL Enterprise Manager. You begin to stare at the Enterprise Manager configuration screen and ask yourself, "So, which knobs do I turn?"

In this chapter, you learn how to modify SQL Server's configuration parameters. Each configuration parameter, its function, and its effect on SQL Server performance and tuning is examined. When SQL Server is installed, the configuration parameters are given an initial default value. Microsoft has done a good job of selecting default values for the configuration parameters. In many cases, the default values provide the optimum performance for your database server. SQL Server enables you to set close to 50 parameters. We use tips to highlight the most commonly tuned parameters. This is not to say that you do not want to touch the other parameters, but in general, the default settings for the others is sufficient.

To Tune Or Not To Tune?

As you start to tune SQL Server, keep in mind that you are tuning the database server. Other factors, such as the hardware configuration chosen for the database, the network the database clients and SQL Server belong to, and the overall size and structure of your databases also affect the performance of the database server.

I have a friend who used to work for a Fortune 500 company that was bringing several SQL Servers online. He had spent some time tuning SQL Server and everything was up and running quite smoothly. As the days went on, the organization started to experience problems with a particular application running progressively slower. Upper management thought the problem must be a SQL Server configuration problem. My friend tried to explain to them that the problem was not a SQL Server tuning issue but an application issue. He explained how they had done everything right: researched and purchased a very fast RAID 5 machine, tuned Windows NT Server, and then used SQL Server tools to properly configure SQL Server.

Management didn't buy it, so they brought in another consulting firm with a highly certified and expensive specialist. The specialist examined the SQL Server and did not change any configurations parameters because they were all reasonably set. So the hired guns left without fixing anything and people in upper management were left scratching their heads. I stopped by to see if I could help them out, and as it turned out, their problem was a failure to issue a simple command that needed to be executed on three of their tables. (UPDATE STATISTICS, what else?)

The moral of the story is that many things affect the overall performance of SQL Server. Performance issues start from square 1 when you research and purchase the machine and set up Windows NT Server. Too often, the real problems are not understood, so people think tuning SQL Server is the answer. Tuning SQL Server enables the server to use the available resources on the machine optimally but does not prevent problems resulting from poor database and application design or failure to perform periodic maintenance. It is important to understand the value and limitations of tuning SQL Server. Oh yeah, when queries are running slow and the table has the correct indexes—remember the UPDATE STATISTICS command. In many cases, it can fix the problem!

CONFIGURING SQL SERVER

Before discussing the many different configuration parameters, you must learn how to modify SQL Server parameters using the Enterprise Manager. Start up the Enterprise Manager, select a SQL Server, and perform the following steps:

1. From the Enterprise Manager, select SQL Server from the Server menu. From the popout menu, select Configure; the Server Configuration/Options dialog appears (see Figure 19.1).

2. Click the Configuration tab in Server Configuration/Options dialog box (see Figure 19.2).

   The Configuration page displays the SQL Server configuration parameters. The Configuration column displays the SQL Server configuration parameter itself. The Minimum and Maximum columns display the minimum acceptable value for the configuration parameter and the maximum acceptable value for the configuration parameter. The value currently in use by SQL Server is displayed in the Running column. The Current column contains the current value of the SQL Server configuration parameter.

Figure 19.1.
The Server Con-
figuration/Options
dialog box.

Figure 19.2.
The Configuration
tab in the Server
Configuration/Options
dialog box.

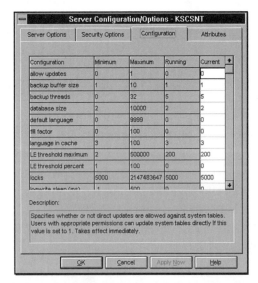

Note

What is the difference between the Running column and the Current column? Most of the time, the two values are the same. As you start to change and modify SQL Server configurations, however, the Current column reflects the changes you have made. These changes do not become the running value until you choose the OK button on the Server Configuration/Options dialog box. For some configuration variables, you have to shut down and restart the server before the parameter changes take effect.

3. To edit a configuration parameter, enter the new value in the Current column of the configuration value you want to modify. Make sure that the value you enter is within ranges displayed in the Maximum and Minimum columns.

Tip

Take advantage of the description that appears in the description box when you select a configuration parameter. The description text gives a summary of the configuration value and when the changed value will take effect (immediately or after stopping and restarting SQL Server).

Special thanks to the Microsoft development team that put this screen together! It makes configuring SQL Server so much easier. (Anyone who has had to use sp_configure and look up minimum and maximum values knows what I mean!)

4. To change the configuration value immediately and stay in the Server Configuration/Options dialog box, click the Apply Now button.

To change the modified variables and exit the Server Configuration/Options dialog box, click the OK button.

To cancel any modifications you have made, click the Cancel button.

Caution

If you modify configuration parameters and then click the Apply Now button, the changes are made to SQL Server. If you then click the Cancel button, the changes are *not* rolled back.

When you click the Apply Now or OK button, the current value of the modified configuration parameters is changed. The running value changes if the value can be modified without stopping and restarting SQL Server.

STRANGER THAN FICTION!

While I was modifying a configuration value that could be updated immediately, I noticed that the value displayed in the Running column of the Server Configuration/Options dialog box did not change to the Current column value when I clicked the Apply Now button. I thought this was pretty strange because *apply now* means just that—

change the configuration and running value now if the value can be changed without restarting SQL Server.

So I pressed F1 to display the help screen, which states:

> Apply Now - Applies the information you have specified. For values that take effect immediately, you must close the Server Configuration/Options dialog box for the value to take effect.

After reading the help, I was even more confused: now I can't determine the difference between the OK button and the Apply Now button. Do they both take effect when you close the Server Configurations/Options dialog box? Well, I brought up a second instance of the Enterprise Manager and did some testing using the Server Configuration/Options dialog box on one instance to change values and using sp_configure on the second instance to check values.

Guess what I found? The configuration values *do* take effect when you click the Apply Now button; however, the Server Configurations/Options dialog box is not refreshed! The configuration value takes effect when you click the Apply Now button, not when you close the window. Closing the window forces you to redisplay the Server Configuration/Options dialog box (that is, it refreshes the display) to see the changed values. Hmmm, because it's in the help file, it must be a *feature* not a bug, right?

To change system configuration parameters the way those poor folks stuck in the dark ages of ISQL (Sybase) do, use the system stored procedure sp_configure, which has the following syntax:

```
sp_configure [configuration_name [, configuration_value]]
```

In this syntax, configuration_name is the configuration parameter name you want to change and configuration_value is the new value for the configuration parameter.

Note

Using sp_configure with no parameters displays the current SQL Server configuration.

SQL Server configuration values are stored in the system table sysconfigures. If you use sp_configure to modify an option, you must use the RECONFIGURE command to make the change take effect. RECONFIGURE has the following syntax:

```
RECONFIGURE [WITH OVERRIDE]
```

The WITH OVERIDE parameter is required only when you set the allow updates configuration parameter to 1. This provides an added security check to make sure that you really want to modify allow updates.

We have mentioned several times configuration parameters that can take effect without restarting SQL Server. These configuration parameters are referred to as *dynamic configuration variables* and are as follows:

◆ allow updates
◆ backup buffer size
◆ cursor threshold
◆ free buffers
◆ LE threshold Maximum
◆ LE threshold Minimum
◆ LE threshold Percent
◆ logwrite sleep
◆ max lazywrite IO
◆ max text repl size
◆ max worker threads
◆ network packet size
◆ RA cache hit limit
◆ RA cache miss limit
◆ RA delay
◆ RA pre-fetches
◆ RA slots per thread
◆ recovery interval
◆ remote conn timeout
◆ remote login timeout
◆ remote proc trans
◆ remote query timeout
◆ resource timeout
◆ show advanced options
◆ sort pages
◆ spin counter
◆ user_option

CONFIGURATION PARAMETERS

The following sections examine each of the SQL Server configuration parameters. The configuration parameters are in alphabetical order, except in special cases when parameters are grouped together (memory configuration parameters, for example). Also, the advanced options are reviewed separately from the standard options. Start with the most important tunable configuration parameters—memory.

Version 6.5

Note

The following configuration parameters are new for SQL Server 6.5:

◆ affinity mask

◆ max text repl size

◆ remote conn timeout

◆ remote proc trans

◆ user_option

MEMORY PARAMETERS

By this time, you have already made several decisions that affect the performance of your SQL Server, such as the type of computer and disk system you have chosen. Now comes the question, "Which knobs do I turn?" or "Which parameters do I change?" As a Microsoft SQL Server DBA, the most important parameters for you to configure are the memory parameters. In general, SQL Server loves memory; that is, the performance of your SQL Server system can be enhanced by adding more memory. SQL Server is not a memory hog and is very smart with memory usage, particularly data caching. So how does SQL Server use memory? Look at Figure 19.3 to understand how memory is allocated.

Figure 19.3.
Windows NT and SQL Server memory usage.

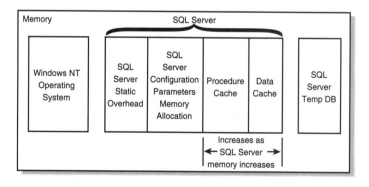

Before you can give memory to SQL Server, you must allocate enough memory for Windows NT Server to run sufficiently. The minimum memory requirement for Windows NT Server is 12M but the amount of memory required by Windows NT varies, depending on the overall use of the NT Server. In the case of a dedicated SQL Server machine, I like to start with 16M of memory for the NT Server and work my way up, if necessary. When the operating system requirements are met, you then can allocate memory for SQL Server. SQL Server requests the memory configuration parameter amount of memory from the Windows NT operating system and then uses the allocated memory to set up shop. SQL Server uses the memory as follows.

First, a certain amount of memory is allocated for SQL Server overhead, which includes the size of the SQL Server executable. The amount of SQL Server static overhead is roughly 2M and is not affected in any way by configuration parameters.

SQL Server then allocates memory for various configuration options, such as user connections and open databases (for example, each user connection configured in SQL Server requires 37K of memory up front). The remaining amount of memory is then used for the procedure cache (which stores the most recently used stored procedures and query trees) and the data cache (which stores the most recently used data and index pages). As you increase the amount of SQL Server memory, the sizes of the procedure cache and disk cache increase, boosting performance because SQL Server can retrieve more information from memory without performing disk I/O to retrieve the information. If the temporary database (`tempdb`) has been placed in RAM, SQL Server requests the memory to create the database from the Windows NT operating system during startup.

Caution

An important point to remember: If the temporary database, `tempdb`, is placed in RAM, the memory allocated to the temporary database is *not part of the memory configured* for SQL Server. I have seen many SQL Server systems fail to start because someone switched the temporary database to RAM and allocated all the remaining memory to SQL Server, assuming that `tempdb` in RAM was taken from SQL Server's memory allocation.

If you find yourself in this situation, you can restart SQL Server using the default settings by adding the startup parameter –f to the SQL Server startup parameter list. You can find the startup parameter list under the option Set Server Options in the SQL setup program.

MONITORING MEMORY

This section offers some tips to help you determine the correct amount of memory for your SQL Server. The primary tools are the SQL Performance Monitor and the DBCC MEMUSAGE command. To determine whether you have enough memory or too much memory, use the Performance Monitor and watch the counters listed in Table 19.1.

TABLE 19.1. PERFORMANCE MONITOR COUNTER FOR TUNING SQL SERVER MEMORY.

Performance Monitor Object	Counter
Memory	Page Faults/sec
SQLServer	Cache Hit Ratio
SQLServer	I/O Page Reads/sec

The first step—and one of the most important steps when trying to tune SQL Server for memory—is to make sure that you are running your typical processes and work loads on SQL Server while you are using the Performance Monitor. The idea behind tuning SQL Server for memory is to keep a high cache-hit ratio (that is, data being retrieved is in the cache), low physical I/O (disk I/O is low because data pages are in memory), and no page faults (a page fault occurs when not enough memory has been allocated to Windows NT, causing Windows NT to rely heavily on virtual memory). If your cache-hit ratio is below 85 to 90 percent, your SQL Server may benefit from increased memory. If the number of I/O page reads per second remains high during your tuning sessions, you may have an insufficient amount of memory allocated to SQL Server (or a substandard disk drive system). An I/O page reads per second counter value of zero means that the data being retrieved is in memory. If you are continuously experiencing page faults, you may have allocated too much memory to SQL Server and not enough to Windows NT. The problem may be corrected by reducing the amount of memory allocated to SQL Server or by adding more physical memory to be used by Windows NT. Before tuning for memory, configure your procedure cache and data cache first and then use the Performance Monitor to determine the correct amount of memory.

Note

When tuning SQL Server memory as just described, many of the counter scenarios used the word *may* instead of *will* to describe whether or not adding more memory could benefit your SQL Server. Why so vague? In many cases, adding additional memory to SQL Server can increase the performance of your system by keeping more information in the cache. However, other factors come into play that cannot be accounted for in a generalized sense. You need to be aware of the type of actions taking place on SQL Server while you are watching the Performance Monitor and tuning SQL Server. For example, if the work load executing on SQL Server is accessing the same values in a table over and over, you should see a high cache-hit ratio, indicating that you have sufficient memory allocated to SQL Server. But if, in your actual production environment, many different tables and databases are being accessed instead of one table, your tuning session did not reflect your production environment and your assumption of sufficient memory may be wrong.

This can also work in reverse. Your tuning session may access many different tables and databases simultaneously, indicating insufficient memory allocation. However, in your actual production environment, the typical situation may be that the same data is being retrieved over and over (that is, enhancing the chance of being in the cache), which would change your assumption of your required memory allocation. Make sure that you tune to your production environment and carefully evaluate your results.

To determine the actual memory pages used by the procedure cache and the data cache, subtract the total SQL Server static overhead and the overhead from SQL Server configuration values from the total amount of memory allocated to SQL Server.

Tip

A new Performance Monitor counter object called `SQLServer-Procedure Cache Object` has been added in SQL Server 6.5. One of the object's counter values is `Procedure Cache Size`, which gives you the size of the procedure cache in 2K pages. The new counter object is discussed later in this chapter in more detail in the section, "`procedure cache`."

Version 6.5

To get the size of the procedure cache, multiply the total cache page value by the default percentage value of the procedure cache. For the data cache, subtract the procedure cache from the total cache value. For example, a SQL Server system has a configuration value of 16M of memory. Assume the static and configuration values overhead are 3M. The amount of memory available for the caches is 16M – 3 M = 13M.

Note

> To determine the amount of memory consumed by configuration
> variables, multiply the configured values for each of the following
> configuration parameters by the approximate amount of memory
> consumed by the object and add the totals:
>
> | | |
> |---|---|
> | Locks | 32 bytes |
> | User Connections | 37 kilobytes |
> | Open Databases | 1 kilobyte |
> | Open Objects | 40 bytes |
> | Devices | 17.9 kilobytes (Total for 255 configured devices in SQL Server 6.x minus 70 bytes for each device) |

To determine the size of the procedure cache using the default value of 30: $13M \times 30\%$
(.30) = 3.9M for the procedure cache. The data cache is 13M – 3.9M (the size of
procedure cache) = 9.1M data cache.

Tip

> The DBA Assistant utility on the CD that accompanies this book
> provides a graphical representation of SQL Server memory allocation
> using the formulas discussed above.

To double-check your memory computations, use the DBCC MEMUSAGE command to get
the exact sizes of SQL Server and configuration overhead, as well as the size of the
procedure and data cache. The partial listing in Listing 19.1 is actual output from
a DBCC MEMUSAGE command.

LISTING 19.1. PARTIAL DBCC MEMUSAGE OUTPUT.

```
Memory Usage:

                          Meg.      2K Blks     Bytes

     Configured Memory:   8.0000      4096      8388608
            Code Size:    1.7166       871       800000
      Static Structures:  0.2385       123       250048
                Locks:    0.2480       127       260000
          Open Objects:   0.1068        55       112000
        Open Databases:   0.0031         2         3220
     User Context Areas:  0.8248       423       864824
            Page Cache:   3.3020      1691      3462416
          Proc Headers:   0.0795        41        83326
       Proc Cache Bufs:   1.3359       684      1400832
```

Using the terminology established earlier to compute the SQL Server memory breakdown, the DBCC MEMUSAGE output translates as follows:

```
Configured Memory = Total Amount of Memory Allocated to SQL Server
Code Size + Static Structures = SQL Server Overhead
Locks + Open Objects + Open Databases + User Context Areas = Configuration Overhead
Page Cache = Data Cache
Proc Headers + Proc Buffers = Procedure Cache
```

The DBCC MEMUSAGE command also prints out the 20 buffered tables and indexes in the cache, as well as the top 20 items in the procedure cache. Listing 19.2 shows a partial listing of the top 20 procedures from a DBCC MEMUSAGE command output.

LISTING 19.2. DBCC MEMUSAGE PARTIAL LISTING: ITEMS IN PROCEDURE CACHE.

```
Procedure Cache, Top 20:

Procedure Name: sp_MSdbuserprofile
Database Id: 1
Object Id: 233051866
Version: 1
Uid: 1
Type: stored procedure
Number of trees: 0
Size of trees: 0.000000 Mb, 0.000000 bytes, 0 pages
Number of plans: 2
Size of plans: 0.144749 Mb, 151780.000000 bytes, 76 pages

Procedure Name: sp_help
Database Id: 1
Object Id: 1888009757
Version: 1
Uid: 1
Type: stored procedure
Number of trees: 0
Size of trees: 0.000000 Mb, 0.000000 bytes, 0 pages
Number of plans: 1
Size of plans: 0.051249 Mb, 53738.000000 bytes, 27 pages
```

19

Note

For each SQL Server 6.5 configuration parameter, the Minimum, Maximum, and Default values are listed in table format; so is the parameter's dynamic variable status.

Version 6.5

memory

The memory configuration parameter sets the amount of memory allocated to SQL Server from the operating system. The values are represented in 2K (2048 byte) units. For example, 16M would be 16M/2K = 8192 pages. In general, adding memory to SQL Server increases the performance of your system.

Tip

If you make calls to many different extended stored procedures, you can use the DBCC command option dllname(FREE) to unload the DLL from SQL Server memory, freeing up the memory to be used by other processes. Otherwise, the DLL remains in memory until SQL Server is shut down.

Use the Performance Monitor and the DBCC command MEMUSAGE to help properly configure your SQL Server with the appropriate amount of memory.

Tip

Is it possible to have too much memory? The answer is *yes*! If you allocate too much memory to SQL Server and not enough to Windows NT, the performance of your SQL Server can decrease because of excessive paging. To determine whether you have allocated too much memory to SQL Server and not enough to Windows NT, use the Performance Monitor and watch the Page Faults/sec counter. If page faults are being continuously generated (after system and SQL Server startup), you are running SQL Server with too much memory. Reduce the configuration amount and check again.

Microsoft prints out a table of suggested memory allocation for SQL Server, based on the amount of memory on the computer, which can be found in Books Online. Remember that the table is just a suggested starting point; you should always determine the correct amount of memory by monitoring your SQL Server.

Minimum: 1000 (2M)
Maximum: 1048576 (2G)
Default: Depends on setup, 8M for computers with <= 32M, 16M for computers with > 32M
Dynamic Variable: No

Caution

Be careful about allocating more memory to SQL Server and Windows NT than is physically available (that is, relying on virtual memory). Configuring SQL Server so that it uses virtual memory exceeding a ratio of 1:1 can hurt SQL Server performance and shows up as excessive paging in the Performance Monitor.

THE `tempdb` DATABASE IN RAM

The temporary database, `tempdb`, is used by SQL Server, applications, and developers as a temporary work area for creating temporary tables or storing temporary information. For example, a developer may create a temporary work table in a stored procedure or SQL Server may create a temporary work table as a result of a query with a `group by` or `order by` clause. The temporary database resides on disk as part of the `master` device and has a default size of 4M. Like a regular database, the size of `tempdb` can be increased using the ALTER database command. In SQL Server 4.21 for Windows NT, Microsoft included the option to allow the temporary database to reside in memory.

Following are the minimum, maximum, and default values for the `config` parameter:

Minimum: 0
Maximum: 2044 (***Note:*** Depends on the size of your temporary database.)
Default: 0
Dynamic Variable: No

DEVELOPERS FEEL THE NEED FOR `tempdb` IN RAM

When the `tempdb` in RAM feature first came out, I was working with a group of developers who had `sa` privileges on one of the development servers. They could not wait to put the temporary database in RAM to help speed up their stored procedures, which made heavy use of temporary tables. The problem was that the development machine had only a modest 32M of memory. SQL Server had been configured with 16M of memory and `tempdb` had the default size of 4M. At the time, the developers thought that the memory from `tempdb` was part of the 16M configured with SQL Server, because the documentation for version 4.21 was not clear about exactly where the memory for `tempdb` in RAM was coming from.

These guys placed `tempdb` in RAM, stopped and restarted the system, and were as happy as could be thinking that they had just gotten a huge performance boost. Later on, they had to shut down SQL Server; when they tried to restart SQL Server, it would not start. This is

continues

> where I came in. Turns out they had several other applications running on the NT Server that grabbed the memory needed to create the `tempdb` in RAM.
>
> When SQL Server failed while creating the `tempdb`, the server halted. I was able to shut down the other processes, restart the server, and place `tempdb` back on disk. The moral of the story is, "Watch out for the developers; they will do everything they can to convince you they need `tempdb` in RAM!"

Microsoft recommends that you not place `tempdb` in RAM unless your NT Server has at least 64M to 128M of memory. I make the same recommendation because it has been my experience that, in systems with less memory, the available memory is better used as part of the data or procedure cache. If you have enough memory to place `tempdb` in memory, run a series of benchmark tests with your queries or stored procedures that use the temporary database. Make sure that placing the temporary database in memory gives you the benefits you want. If you find substantial performance gains, leave `tempdb` in RAM; otherwise, place `tempdb` back on disk and use the memory for larger procedure and data caches.

procedure cache

Version
6.5

The `procedure cache` configuration parameter is often tuned to enhance SQL Server performance. SQL Server 6.5 has added a new Performance Monitor counter object called `SQLServer-Procedure Cache` that can be used to help determine the correct procedure cache value.

Refer back to Figure 19.3 and notice that SQL Server maintains two cache areas that increase as the amount of memory is increased: the procedure cache and the data cache. The procedure cache stores the most recently used stored procedures and also is used for compiling SQL for ad-hoc queries. The data cache is used to store the most recently used data or index pages. Both caches use an LRU/MRU (least recently used/most recently used) management scheme to determine what stays in the cache and what is overwritten.

So how do you know whether you have the correct values for your procedure cache? First, you must understand that stored procedures are not reentrant; that is, if the same stored procedure is executed simultaneously by two users, SQL Server has separate copies of the compiled stored procedure in the procedure cache—one for each user (that is, the two users cannot share the same stored procedure). If 50 users run the same or different stored procedures simultaneously, you have 50 copies of the stored procedures in the procedure cache.

Note

> In the SQL Server Books Online section, "Estimating SQL Server Overhead," the default size of the procedure cache is incorrectly listed as 20 rather than the correct default value of 30. Other parts of the documentation have the correct default value for the procedure cache.

Minimum: 1
Maximum: 99
Default: 30
Dynamic Variable: No

Tip

> Because the procedure cache is of a limited size, it is possible to run out of available memory in the procedure cache, causing error 701 to occur. For example, if your procedure cache is large enough to run 200 stored procedures, and 200 stored procedures are being executed, the next stored procedure or query tree that attempts to load in the cache will be rejected for lack of space. If this occurs frequently, increase the size of your procedure cache.

Now that you understand how users affect the number of stored procedures or query trees in the procedure cache, what about the size of a stored procedure? The minimum size of a stored procedure is 2K. To determine the correct size of a stored procedure, use the DBCC MEMUSAGE command. The following formula, found in the *Microsoft SQL Server Administrator's Companion* in Books Online, can be used to estimate the size of the procedure cache:

```
Procedure Cache = (Max. Number of Concurrent Users) x
                  (Size of Largest Plan) x 1.25
```

To come up with the configuration value, use the following:

```
Procedure Cache Config. Value =
(Procedure Cache/(SQL Server Memory - (Static Overhead + Configuration Overhead) ) )
x 100%
```

A better method of getting a starting value for procedure cache is to determine the most widely used stored procedures and use an average size of the procedures in the preceding formula rather than the size of the largest procedure. If your SQL Server has a large amount of memory available for the cache (greater than 64M), you may want to consider lowering the procedure cache value. For example, if you have 100M available and use the default setting, your procedure cache would be 30M. If the maximum number of concurrent users is 175 with an average plan size of 55K, the following would be true:

```
Procedure Cache = 175 users x (55k plan size) x 1.25 = 12 MB
Procedure Cache Config Value = (12 MB/100 MB) x 100% = 12
```

By using the formulas, you find that you could probably get by with a `procedure cache` configuration value of 12 percent instead of 30 percent, freeing up an additional 18M of memory for the disk cache!

Tip

You have spent some time determining the correct size of the data cache. Now it's time to tune the procedure cache; however, here's the catch: If you modify the procedure cache configuration value, you change the data cache! If you add more memory to SQL Server, you change the size of the data cache and the procedure cache. To size either the procedure cache or data cache without changing the other cache value requires setting both the memory configuration value and the procedure cache value simultaneously, adjusting the two values so that the other cache remains the same. Use this technique when fine-tuning the correct cache values.

Once you have determined a configuration value for the procedure cache, use the Performance Monitor and the new SQL Server 6.5 object `SQLServer-Procedure Cache` to further fine-tune the procedure cache value. Using the `SQLServer-Procedure Cache` object takes the guess work out of selecting a correct value for the procedure cache. Monitor the following counter values during normal and peak periods for your SQL Server:

◆   `Max Procedure Cache Used`

◆   `Procedure Cache Used`

If the `Max Procedure Cache Used` counter value exceeds 95 percent while you are monitoring it, consider increasing the size of the procedure cache (you are very close to running out of memory for the procedure cache). *Note:* If your procedure cache is running out of memory, *definitely* increase the size of `procedure cache`. If, during maximum load periods, the `Max Procedure Cache Used` value does not exceed 70 percent, consider decreasing the amount of memory allocated to the procedure cache.

A DBCC command you can use to help establish the correct cache size is the DBCC `SQLPERF(LRUSTATS)` command. Execute the command after your SQL Server has been running for a few days. Examine the `Cache Flushes` and `Free Page Scan (Avg)` values. The `Free Page Scan (Avg)` value should be less than 10 and the value for `Cache Flushes` should be less than 100. If your values are higher, your current SQL Server cache is not large enough and you can improve your SQL Server performance by increasing the cache size (that is, by adding memory).

Determining the correct size of the procedure cache involves trying different values and monitoring the SQL Server-Procedure Cache object. Getting the correct size for your procedure cache enhances the performance of your system.

allow updates

If the value of allow updates is set to 1, the SQL Server system tables can be modified. But ***do not set this configuration value to 1*** unless told to do so by Microsoft Technical Support.

Caution

Directly updating system tables is risky business and could prevent your SQL Server from running.

If you need to update system tables, use the system stored procedures. If you need to turn on this option, start SQL Server in single-user mode (command-line option −m) to prevent any other users from accidentally modifying the system tables.

Minimum: 0
Maximum: 1
Default: 0
Dynamic Variable: Yes

Note

Stored procedures created to modify system tables while the allow updates option is on can always modify the system tables, even after the allow updates option is turned off.

backup buffer size

A SQL Server 6.x option, backup buffer size, enables you to set the size of the buffer used to load/dump a database to increase the performance of backup/load operations. The value is in 32-page increments.

Minimum: 1
Maximum: 10
Default: 1
Dynamic Variable: Yes

backup threads

The backup threads option is another SQL Server 6.x feature added to speed up dump/load processing. The backup threads configuration value reserves a number of threads to be used for parallel striped backups and recoveries.

Minimum: 0
Maximum: 32
Default: 5
Dynamic Variable: No

database size

The database size option determines the default size allocated to each new database created without specifying the database size. The configuration values are in megabytes.

Minimum: 1
Maximum: 10000
Default: 2
Dynamic Variable: No

default language

The default language option determines the number of the language used to display system messages.

Minimum: 0
Maximum: 9999
Default: Varies (US_English = 0)
Dynamic Variable: No

fill factor

The fill factor option specifies how densely packed you want your index and data pages while creating an index. The default is 0, which leaves room on the nonleaf pages but makes the leaf pages 100 percent full. Use a low fill factor value to spread data over more pages. For more information on using fill factor, see Chapter 21, "Understanding Indexes."

Minimum: 0
Maximum: 100
Default: 0
Dynamic Variable: No

> **Note**
>
> The `fill factor` option is not maintained by SQL Server after index creation and is maintained only when the index is built.

language in cache

The `language in cache` option determines the number of languages that can be held simultaneously in the language cache.

> **Minimum:** 3
> **Maximum:** 100
> **Default:** 3
> **Dynamic Variable:** No

LE threshold maximum

The `LE threshold maximum` is a new configuration parameter that can help ease potential locking problems in environments with extremely large tables.

LE threshold maximum stands for *Lock Escalation threshold maximum* and is a SQL Server 6.x configuration parameter. In previous versions of SQL Server, when many page lock requests began to pile up on a table, SQL Server escalated the lock request to a table lock, preventing other users from accessing the table. The magical number—regardless of the size of the table—was 200 and could not be tuned. Developers working in environments with large amounts of data were penalized because the majority of their transactions could affect over 200 pages. Now you can tune the level of the number of page locks that SQL Server will hold before a table lock is placed on the table.

> **Minimum:** 2
> **Maximum:** 500000
> **Default:** 200
> **Dynamic Variable:** Yes

Note

The use of configurable locking parameters is just one of many ways SQL Server 6.x has improved SQL Server locking capabilities and available options for the developer and DBA. I take my hat off to the folks in Redmond, WA!

LE threshold percent

The LE threshold percent option (a SQL Server 6.x option) enables you to control locking escalation as a percentage rather than a fixed number. A zero value causes a table lock to occur when the LE threshold minimum is reached.

> **Minimum:** 1
> **Maximum:** 100
> **Default:** 0
> **Dynamic Variable:** Yes

locks

The locks configuration variable sets the number of available locks. If you are getting error messages that the SQL Server is out of locks, increase the number.

Tip

The locks configuration parameter is an often-tuned parameter.

> **Minimum:** 5000
> **Maximum:** 214748364
> **Default:** 5000
> **Dynamic Variable:** No

logwrite sleep (ms)

The logwrite sleep (ms) option specifies the number of milliseconds to delay before writing to disk a buffer that is not full. This is done in the hope that other users will fill up the buffer before it is written to disk.

> **Minimum:** –1
> **Maximum:** 500
> **Default:** 0
> **Dynamic Variable:** No

max async IO

The max async IO option is the number of outstanding asynchronous I/Os that can be issued. Modify this option only if you have databases that span multiple physical drives or if you are using disk striping and your database server has separate disk controllers or a smart disk controller (like a Compaq smart array) that supports asynchronous I/O. If you meet these requirements, you may be able to increase your system throughput by modifying the max async IO parameter. Using the Performance Monitor, monitor the SQL Server object counter I/O Batch Writes/sec and the Transactions/sec counter before and after you modify the parameter. You should notice an increase in both values; if you do not, reset the value back to the default. Be careful when increasing this parameter. A value that is too high can cause performance degradation by causing excessive overhead.

> **Minimum:** 1
> **Maximum:** 255
> **Default:** 8
> **Dynamic Variable:** No

max text repl size

The max text repl size option is a new SQL Server 6.5 feature that controls the maximum number of bytes that can be added to a text or image data column during replication in a single data modification statement (INSERT, UPDATE, or DELETE).

> **Minimum:** 0
> **Maximum:** 2147483647
> **Default:** 65536
> **Dynamic Variable:** Yes

max worker threads

Worker threads are used by SQL Server for things such as checkpoints, users, and network support. The max worker threads configuration parameter sets the maximum number of worker threads SQL Server can use. If the configured value is greater than the number of concurrent user connections, each user connection has its own thread; otherwise, the user shares a pool of worker threads.

> **Minimum:** 10
> **Maximum:** 1024
> **Default:** 255
> **Dynamic Variable:** Yes

media retention

The `media retention` option sets the number of days you want to retain backup media before overwriting it with a new dump. If you attempt to overwrite the media before the number of retention days has expired, you get a warning message.

Minimum: 0
Maximum: 365
Default: 0
Dynamic Variable: No

nested triggers

When the `nested triggers` option is set to 1, a trigger can call another trigger (that is, triggers can be nested). When this option is set to 0, calling a trigger from another trigger is prohibited.

Minimum: 0
Maximum: 1
Default: 1
Dynamic Variable: Yes

Note

You can have up to 16 levels of nesting.

network packet size

The `network packet size` option was first introduced in SQL Server 4.21 for Windows NT, but with the major restriction that it could be set only using NETBEUI. With SQL Server 6.x, however, you can now set the packet size for any of the network protocols supported by SQL Server. If you have a network that supports a large packet size, you can increase the network performance with SQL Server by increasing the packet size. The default of 4096 bytes is a welcome change to the anemic 512-byte packet size used in previous versions.

Minimum: 512
Maximum: 32767
Default: 4096
Dynamic Variable: Yes

open databases

The open databases option specifies the maximum number of databases that can be open at one time on SQL Server. If you receive error messages that indicate you have exceeded the number of open databases, increase the number. The overhead is fairly insignificant (about 4K per configured open database).

> **Minimum:** 5
> **Maximum:** 32767
> **Default:** 20
> **Dynamic Variable:** No

Note

> Unlike locks—which are not shared and are per user/per object—the open databases configuration is for the entire server, regardless of the number of users.

open objects

The open objects option specifies the maximum number of database objects that can be open at one time on SQL Server.

> **Minimum:** 100
> **Maximum:** 2147483647
> **Default:** 500
> **Dynamic Variable:** No

recovery flags

Setting recovery flags to 0 displays minimum information during the SQL Server recovery process at startup. When this option is set to 0, a recovery message, along with the database name, is displayed. Setting this option to 1 results in the display of more informational messages (information about individual transactions).

> **Minimum:** 0
> **Maximum:** 1
> **Default:** 0
> **Dynamic Variable:** No

recovery interval

SQL Server uses the `recovery interval` option, the database truncate log on checkpoint setting, and the amount of database activity to determine when a checkpoint should be performed to write the "dirty pages" (modified pages not yet flushed to disk). The `recovery interval` specified is not the amount of time between SQL Server checkpoints; it is the maximum amount of time per database that SQL Server needs to recover the database in the event of a system failure. The checkpoint process checks each database every minute to see whether the database needs to be checkpointed.

The `recovery interval` configuration parameter is an often-tuned parameter.

Minimum: 1
Maximum: 32767
Default: 5
Dynamic Variable: Yes

remote access

The `remote access` option controls the logins from remote SQL Servers. When set to 1, users from remote SQL Servers have access to the server.

Minimum: 0
Maximum: 1
Default: 1
Dynamic Variable: No

remote conn timeout

The `remote conn timeout` option determines the amount of time to wait before timing out inactive connections from a remote server. The timeout value is in minutes. This option has no effect on connections involved in a distributed transaction.

Minimum: –1
Maximum: 32767
Default: 10
Dynamic Variable: No

remote proc trans

When set to 1, the `remote proc trans` option provides a DTC distributed transaction that protects the ACID properties of transactions.

> **Minimum:** 0
> **Maximum:** 1
> **Default:** 0
> **Dynamic Variable:** Yes

show advanced options

The `show advanced options` option displays the advanced configuration options when using the SQL Server Enterprise Manager or the `sp_configure` system stored procedure. Set this value to 1 to display the advanced options.

> **Minimum:** 0
> **Maximum:** 1
> **Default:** 0
> **Dynamic Variable:** Yes

user connections

The `user connections` option specifies the maximum number of simultaneous user connections allowed on SQL Server. If the maximum number is exceeded, you get an error and are unable to establish the new connection until one becomes available. Be careful about setting this parameter too high because each user connection takes up approximately 40K of memory overhead, regardless of whether or not the connection is used.

The `user connections` configuration parameter is an often-tuned parameter.

> **Minimum:** 5
> **Maximum:** 32767
> **Default:** 20
> **Dynamic Variable:** No

PARAMETER OVERKILL

I was once at a site with a well-configured machine (128M of memory for SQL Server); those at the site were wondering whether they had properly configured SQL Server for optimum performance. I issued a DBCC MEMUSAGE command to get an overview of how things looked in memory and I was astounded to see a very large amount of memory being used for user connections (40M)! It turned out that someone had bumped up the number of user connections to 1000, not realizing how SQL Server allocated the memory up front for user connections. The funny thing was they only had 30 users, with at most 60 connections at any one time. We quickly got back an extra 38M of memory for the data and procedure cache.

user_option

The user_option option allows you to set global default options for all users. Using this parameter, you can control implicit transactions, ANSI warnings, ANSI NULLs, ANSI defaults, the distinction between a single quote and a double quote, and several other options. The options set take effect during the user's login session; the user can override them by using the SET statement.

Minimum: 0
Maximum: 4095
Default: 0
Dynamic Variable: Yes

ADVANCED CONFIGURATION PARAMETERS

Caution

The following configuration parameters are considered to be advanced configuration parameters and can be seen only by turning on the show advanced options configuration option. I highly suggest leaving these parameters alone. Microsoft has done a good job setting the default values and you can easily hinder the performance of your SQL Server by incorrectly setting one of the advanced configuration options. If you do modify them, make sure that you fully understand the options and the overall impact of your changes!

affinity mask

The `affinity mask` option allows you to associate a thread to a processor.

Minimum: 0
Maximum: 2147483647
Default: 0
Dynamic Variable: No

cursor threshold

The `cursor threshold` option determines how the keyset for a cursor is generated. If the option is set to -1, all cursor keysets are generated synchronously (which is good for small cursor sets). If the option is set to 0, all cursor keysets are generated asynchronously. Otherwise, the query optimizer compares the number of expected rows in the cursor set; if the number of expected rows exceeds the `cursor threshold` configuration variable, the keyset is built asynchronously.

Minimum: -1
Maximum: 2147483647
Default: -1
Dynamic Variable: Yes

default sortorder id

The `default sortorder id` option shows the current sort order ID installed on SQL Server. Do **not** use `sp_configure` or the SQL Enterprise Manager Configuration dialog box to change the sort order! Changing the sort order is done through the SQL Server setup program and is a major change to your SQL Server.

Minimum: 0
Maximum: 255
Default: Varies
Dynamic Variable: No

free buffers

The `free buffers` option determines the threshold of free buffers available to SQL Server. The values automatically change as the SQL Server memory is changed. The value equals approximately 5 percent of the available memory.

Minimum: 20
Maximum: Varies
Default: Varies
Dynamic Variable: Yes

19

WHICH KNOBS DO I TURN?

hash buckets

You use the hash buckets option to create the number of buckets available for hashing to speed access time when retrieving data from the data cache. The standard default is sufficient for systems with less then 160M of memory.

>**Minimum:** 4999
>**Maximum:** 265003
>**Default:** 7993
>**Dynamic Variable:** No

LE threshold minimum

The LE threshold minimum option sets the minimum number of lock pages required before escalating to a table lock.

>**Minimum:** 2
>**Maximum:** 500000
>**Default:** 20
>**Dynamic Variable:** Yes

max lazywrite IO

Use the max lazywrite IO option to tune the priority of batched asynchronous I/O performed by the Lazy Writer process. Do not modify this option unless told to do so by Microsoft Tech Support.

>**Minimum:** 1
>**Maximum:** 255
>**Default:** 8
>**Dynamic Variable:** Yes

priority boost

If the priority boost configuration value is set to 1, SQL Server runs at a higher priority on the Windows NT server.

>**Minimum:** 0
>**Maximum:** 1
>**Default:** 0
>**Dynamic Variable:** No

Caution

Even if you have a dedicated machine for SQL Server, do not boost the priority of SQL Server. It runs fine as a regular Windows NT service; boosting the priority can cause some unexpected problems when trying to bring down SQL Server or when trying to use other NT tools on the server.

remote login timeout

The `remote login timeout` option specifies the number of seconds to wait before returning from a remote login attempt. The default of 0 specifies an infinite timeout value.

Minimum: 0
Maximum: 2147483647
Default: 0
Dynamic Variable: Yes

remote query timeout

The `remote query timeout` option specifies the number of seconds to wait before timing out as a result of a remote query. The default of 0 specifies an infinite timeout value.

Minimum: 0
Maximum: 2147483647
Default: 0
Dynamic Variable: Yes

resource timeout

The `resource timeout` option specifies the number of seconds to wait for a resource to be released.

Minimum: 5
Maximum: 2147483647
Default: 1
Dynamic Variable: Yes

set working set size

If the value of the set working set size option is set to 1 when SQL Server starts, Windows NT locks all the memory in the memory configuration value and the tempdb value (if it is in RAM), as a working set to increase performance. You can disable the creation of the memory working set by setting the option to 0. When this option is disabled, SQL Server asks the cache manager for memory as needed up to the value in the memory configuration parameter. Memory is still reserved for tempdb (if it is in RAM).

Minimum: 0
Maximum: 1
Default: 0
Dynamic Variable: No

SMP concurrency

The SMP concurrency option determines the number of threads SQL Server releases to Windows NT for execution. The default value for this parameter assumes a dedicated computer for SQL Server, allowing SQL Server to automatically configure itself in an SMP environment or single-processor environment for the best performance.

Minimum: –1
Maximum: 64
Default: –1
Dynamic Variable: No

sort pages

The sort pages option specifies the maximum number of pages allowed to a user performing a sort. This option may require adjusting if SQL Server performs large sorts.

Minimum: 64
Maximum: 511
Default: 64
Dynamic Variable: Yes

spin counter

The `spin counter` option specifies the maximum number of attempts a process will make to obtain a resource.

> **Minimum:** 1
> **Maximum:** 2147483647
> **Default:** 10000
> **Dynamic Variable:** Yes

time slice

The `time slice` option specifies the amount of time a user process can pass a yield point without yielding.

> **Minimum:** 50
> **Maximum:** 1000
> **Default:** 1000
> **Dynamic Variable: No**

ASYNCHRONOUS READ-AHEAD CONFIGURATION PARAMETERS

Version 6.5

19

SQL Server 6.x ships with an exciting new feature called *Parallel Data Scan*, also referred to as *Asynchronous Read Ahead*. The read-ahead technology (RA for short) decreases the time required to perform logical sequential data reads, which translates to improved performance for table scans, index creation, DBCC commands, UPDATE STATISTICS, and covered queries. Microsoft claims that, depending on the hardware platform, databases, and so on, RA technology can boost performance up to a factor of three on some queries over performance in version 4.21. The idea behind the parallel data scan is simple. Using separate threads, SQL Server reads extents (8 data pages or 16K) into memory before the thread running the query needs the extent. When the extent is needed to satisfy the query, the data pages are already in the memory cache thanks to the read-ahead. Figure 19.4 gives you an idea of how RA works.

A user issues a query that performs a table scan on a table called `big_table`. SQL Server gets the query request and begins to process the query. When SQL Server

WHICH KNOBS DO I TURN?

goes to retrieve the first data page, SQL Server first checks to see whether the data page is already in the data cache (memory). If the page is not in memory, SQL Server reads the page from disk and places it in the data cache.

Figure 19.4.
A parallel data scan.

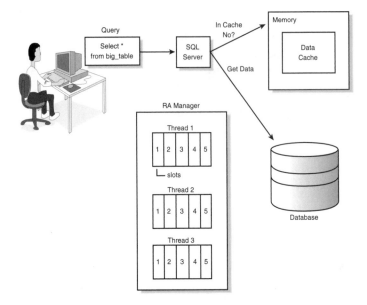

Regardless of whether RA is available, SQL Server always checks the data cache first before reading the data page. So, how does the RA technology fit in? First, a Read-Ahead Manager operates in the background to manage several threads that perform the asynchronous data reads. SQL Server also has several configuration variables that determine how the read ahead will work. For example, there is a parameter that determines the number of read-ahead threads that exist and the number of slots handled per each thread. There also is a parameter that determines how many cache misses can occur in a sequential data operation before the RA Manager assigns a thread to prefetch the data into the data cache.

Look again at Figure 19.4. The query Select * from big_table is being executed by SQL Server. SQL Server checks to see whether the data page is in the data cache. The page is not in the cache, so SQL Server goes out to disk. The RA Manager counts 1 cache miss and compares the number of misses to the SQL Server configuration parameter RA cache miss limit, which defaults to 3 (the value used for this example).

Because the number of cache misses is less than the configuration parameter, nothing happens. The query continues to run and SQL Server checks to see whether the next data page is in the data cache. Again, it's not, so SQL Server reads the page and the RA Manager checks the number of cache misses against the configuration value.

This process continues until the number of cache misses exceeds the configuration value. Then the RA Manager checks thread 1 for an empty slot and assigns the slot to handle read-aheads for the `big_table` query. Thread 1 then begins to prefetch an extent 16K (8 data pages) into the data cache, as shown in Figure 19.5.

Figure 19.5.
The Read-Ahead
Manager using a
thread to prefetch data.

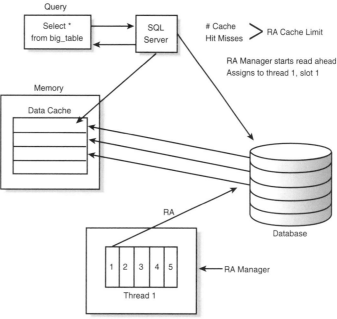

When the query checks to see whether the next page is in the data cache, the answer is *yes*. The thread performing the query does not have to wait for SQL Server to read the data page into memory.

The RA thread prefetches up to a configuration amount of extents into the cache before becoming idle and maintains the number of extents ahead of the operation. If another request comes along and thread 1 has an empty slot, the new request is also assigned to thread 1. Thread 2 does not have any request assigned to it until all the slots in thread 1 are filled. The next sections examine the different configuration parameters for RA technology.

RA cache hit limit

Caution

SQL Server 6.x documentation recommends that you do not modify the `RA cache hit limit` parameter unless instructed to do so by your primary SQL Server support provider.

The `RA cache hit limit` option specifies the number of cache hits that a read-ahead request can have before it is canceled.

> **Minimum:** 1
> **Maximum:** 255
> **Default:** 4
> **Dynamic Variable:** Yes

RA cache miss limit

Caution

> SQL Server 6.x documentation recommends that you do not modify the `RA cache miss limit` parameter unless instructed to do so by your primary SQL Server support provider.

The `RA cache miss limit` option specifies the number of cache misses that can occur before the Read Ahead Manager assigns a thread and slot to begin to prefetch data.

> **Minimum:** 1
> **Maximum:** 255
> **Default:** 3
> **Dynamic Variable:** Yes

RA delay

The `RA delay` option sets the amount of time in milliseconds to wait between the time the read-ahead event is set and when the read-ahead thread is awakened by the operating system. This configuration parameter is required only in non-SMP systems.

> **Minimum:** 0
> **Maximum:** 500
> **Default:** 15
> **Dynamic Variable:** Yes

RA prefetches

The `RA prefetches` configuration parameter specifies the number of data extents the read-ahead thread prefetches in the data cache before becoming idle.

> **Minimum:** 1
> **Maximum:** 1000
> **Default:** 3
> **Dynamic Variable:** Yes

RA slots per thread

The RA slots per thread option specifies the number of slots maintained by each RA thread. A slot corresponds to a read-ahead request and each RA thread simultaneously manages the number of RA slots per thread.

Minimum: 1
Maximum: 255
Default: 5
Dynamic Variable: No

RA worker threads

The RA worker threads option specifies the number of threads available to handle read-ahead requests.

Minimum: 0
Maximum: 255
Default: 3
Dynamic Variable: No

BETWEEN THE LINES

This chapter examined all the SQL Server configuration parameters. Following are some of the more important points to remember about tuning and configuring SQL Server:

◆ Take the time to learn how SQL Server uses memory.

◆ When you tune SQL Server using the Performance Monitor, make sure that the SQL Server is running against the expected real-world work load.

◆ Learn how to start SQL Server with the −f startup option to reset incorrectly configured parameters that may prevent SQL Server from starting.

◆ It is highly recommended that you spend some time tuning the memory parameters such as memory and procedure cache. Verify your settings using the Performance Monitor and DBCC MEMUSAGE.

◆ Understand the impact of changing configuration parameters before you modify them.

SUMMARY

The answer to the question, "Which knobs do I turn?" is "Not many!" The nice thing about SQL Server is that many of the default values provide optimal SQL Server performance for most database installations right out of the box. I have noticed that, with the newer versions of SQL Server, Microsoft has increased the default values for several configuration parameters to meet more real-world needs (and probably to reduce the number of calls to tech support). For example, the default size of the procedure cache is now 30 instead of 20; the configuration value devices has been removed (the old default value was 10), increasing the number of devices to the previous versions' configured maximum of 255. These are just a few of the changes; if you are familiar with previous versions of SQL Server or a Sybase SQL Server, I'm sure that you will also notice the differences. Tune your SQL Server installation for the best possible performance but do not forget that tuning is a many-phase process. It includes the hardware, the installation of the operating system, the installation and tuning of SQL Server, and the overall design of the databases and applications.

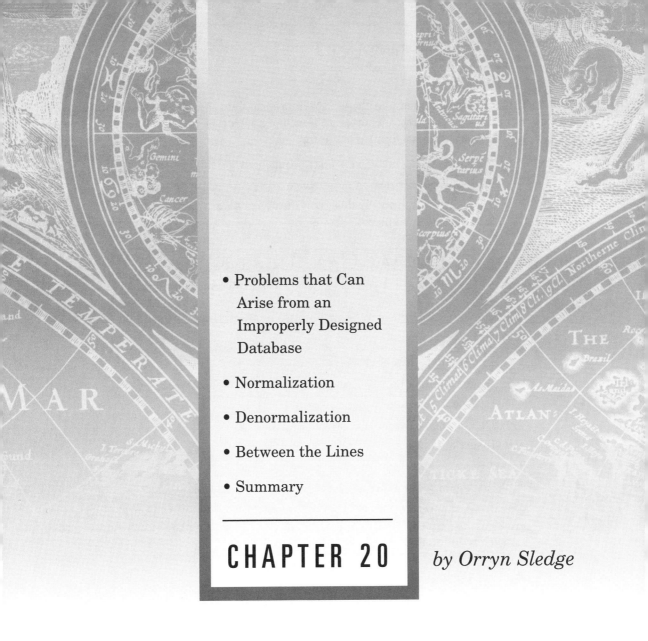

- Problems that Can
  Arise from an
  Improperly Designed
  Database

- Normalization

- Denormalization

- Between the Lines

- Summary

CHAPTER 20   *by Orryn Sledge*

Database Design Issues

A properly designed database can increase data integrity and simplify data maintenance. To help you better understand how to design a database, the following concepts are discussed in this chapter:

◆ Problems that may arise from an improperly designed database

◆ How to correctly design a database

◆ How to take a properly designed database a step backward in order to improve performance

PROBLEMS THAT CAN ARISE FROM AN IMPROPERLY DESIGNED DATABASE

The following problems can occur because of an improperly designed database:

◆ Redundant data

◆ Limited data tracking

◆ Inconsistent data

◆ Update anomalies

◆ Delete anomalies

◆ Insert anomalies

REDUNDANT DATA

As you can see in the sample table in Figure 20.1, several names and descriptions are continuously repeated. This increases the amount of physical storage required to track training data.

Figure 20.1.   Redundant data.

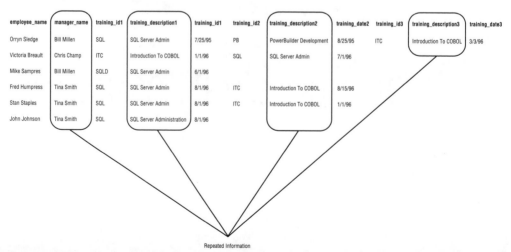

LIMITED DATA TRACKING

The table design in Figure 20.2 is limited to tracking three training courses per employee. Additional columns must be added to the table if you want to track more than three classes.

Figure 20.2.   Limited data tracking.

This table allows a maximum of 3 training courses to be tracked.

employee_name	manager_name	training_id1	training_description1	training_data	training_id21	training_description2	training_date2	training_id3	training_description3	training_date3
Orryn Sledge	Bill Millen	SQL	SQL Server Admin	7/25/95	PB	PowerBuilder Development	8/25/95	ITC	Introduction To COBOL	3/3/96
Victoria Breault	Chris Champ	ITC	Introduction To COBOL	1/1/96	SQL	SQL Server Admin	7/1/96			
Mike Sampres	Bill Millen	SQLD	SQL Server Admin	6/1/96						
Fred Humpress	Tina Smith	SQL	SQL Server Admin	8/1/96	ITC	Introduction To COBOL	8/15/96			
Stan Staples	Tina Smith	SQL	SQL Server Admin	8/1/96	ITC	Introduction To COBOL	1/1/96			
John Johnson	Tina Smith	SQL	SQL Server Administration	8/1/96						

INCONSISTENT DATA

Consider the likelihood of a training class being misspelled when a new record is added to the `employee_training` table (see Figure 20.3). As more records are added to the table, the potential for inconsistent data from typing errors increases.

Figure 20.3.   Inconsistent data.

employee_name	manager_name	training_id1	training_description1	training_date1	training_id2	training_description2	training_date2	training_id3	training_description3	training_date3
Orryn Sledge	Bill Millen	SQL	SQL Server Admin	7/25/95	PB	PowerBuilder Development	8/25/95	ITC	Introduction To COBOL	3/3/96
Victoria Breault	Chris Champ	ITC	Introduction To COBOL	1/1/96	SQL	SQL Server Admin	7/1/96			
Mike Sampres	Bill Millen	SQLD	SQL Server Admin	6/1/96						
Fred Humpress	Tina Smith	SQL	SQL Server Admin	8/1/96	ITC	Introduction To COBOL	8/15/96			
Stan Staples	Tina Smith	SQL	SQL Server Admin	8/1/96	ITC	Introduction To COBOL	1/1/96			
John Johnson	Tina Smith	SQL	SQL Server Administration	8/1/96						

Are these two different training classes or is this a data entry error?

UPDATE ANOMALIES

Suppose that you just realized that the *SQL Server Admin* class should be named *SQL Server Administration* (see Figure 20.4). To change the class name, you must update it in five different places. Wouldn't it be easier if you could change the name in one place and have it automatically reflected throughout the application?

Figure 20.4.   Update anomalies.

employee_name	manager_name	training_id1	training_description1	training_date1	training_id2	training_description2	training_date2	training_id3	training_description3	training_date3
Orryn Sledge	Bill Millen	SQL ①	SQL Server Admin *incorrect*	7/25/95	PB	PowerBuilder Development	8/25/95	ITC	Introduction To COBOL	3/3/96
Victoria Breault	Chris Champ	ITC	Introduction To COBOL	1/1/96	SQL ⑤	SQL Server Admin *incorrect*	7/1/96			
Mike Sampres	Bill Millen	SQLD ②	SQL Server Admin *incorrect*	6/1/96						
Fred Humpress	Tina Smith	SQL ③	SQL Server Admin *incorrect*	8/1/96	ITC	Introduction To COBOL	8/15/96			
Stan Staples	Tina Smith	SQL ④	SQL Server Admin *incorrect*	8/1/96	ITC	Introduction To COBOL	1/1/96			
John Johnson	Tina Smith	SQL	SQL Server Administration *correct*	8/1/96						

You just realized that "SQL Server Admin" should be "SQL Server Administration."
To change the class name you will need to update it in 5 different places.

DELETE ANOMALIES

Suppose that you are no longer interested in tracking the *Introduction to COBOL* training class, so you delete matching records (see Figure 20.5). But wait…you just realized that you deleted other important information. The removal of more than one type of information from a table is considered a *delete anomaly*.

Figure 20.5.   Delete anomalies.

employee_name	manager_name	training_id1	training_description1	training_date1	training_id2	training_description2	training_date2	training_id3	training_description3	training_date3
Orryn Sledge	Bill Millen	SQL	SQL Server Admin	7/25/95	PB	PowerBuilder Development	8/25/95	ITC	Introduction To COBOL	3/3/96
~~Victoria Breault~~	~~Chris Champ~~	~~ITC~~	~~Introduction To COBOL~~	~~1/1/96~~	~~SQL~~	~~SQL Server Admin~~	~~7/1/96~~			
Mike Sampres	Bill Millen	SQLD	SQL Server Admin	6/1/96						
~~Fred Humpress~~	~~Tina Smith~~	~~SQL~~	~~SQL Server Admin~~	~~8/1/96~~	~~ITC~~	~~Introduction To COBOL~~	~~8/15/96~~			
~~Stan Staples~~	~~Tina Smith~~	~~SQL~~	~~SQL Server Admin~~	~~8/1/96~~	~~ITC~~	~~Introduction To COBOL~~	~~1/1/96~~			
John Johnson	Tina Smith	SQL	SQL Server Administration	8/1/96						

You are no longer interested in tracking the "Introduction To COBOL" training class so you delete
matching records. But wait . . . you just realized that you deleted other important information.

INSERT ANOMALIES

Suppose that you want to track a new training course titled *Database Design* and you designate the code DD for training_id1. What values will you use for employee_name and manager_name when you insert the record into the sample table (see Figure 20.6)? Do you leave the values blank? Do you insert a special code such as unknown for employee_name and manager_name?

Figure 20.6.   Insert anomalies.

employee_name	manager_name	training_id1	training_description1	training_date1	training_id2	training_description2	training_date2	training_id3	training_description3	training_date3
Orryn Sledge	Bill Millen	SQL	SQL Server Admin	7/25/95	PB	PowerBuilder Development	8/25/95	ITC	Introduction To COBOL	3/3/96
Victoria Breault	Chris Champ	ITC	Introduction To COBOL	1/1/96	SQL	SQL Server Admin	7/1/96			
Mike Sampres	Bill Millen	SQLD	SQL Server Admin	6/1/96						
Fred Humpress	Tina Smith	SQL	SQL Server Admin	8/1/96	ITC	Introduction To COBOL	8/15/96			
Stan Staples	Tina Smith	SQL	SQL Server Admin	8/1/96	ITC	Introduction To COBOL	1/1/96			
John Johnson	Tina Smith	SQL	SQL Server Administration	8/1/96						
? ?	? ?	DD	Database Design							

You want to track a new training course called "Database Design." Where do you insert the record?

NORMALIZATION

Normalization is a set of standard rules that test the soundness of database design. It can help prevent the problems described in the first part of this chapter. By applying these standard rules, you can pinpoint design flaws that may jeopardize data integrity and complicate data maintenance.

HOW TO NORMALIZE A DATABASE

There are three standard normalization rules. After a design successfully passes a rule, it is said to be in # normal form (where the # represents *1st*, *2nd*, or *3rd*). Rules are cumulative. For example, for a design to be in 3rd normal form, it must satisfy the requirements of the 3rd normal form as well as the requirements for 2nd and 1st normal forms.

Technically speaking, there are other types of normalization rules beyond 3rd normal form. However, for most database designs, the first three normal forms are sufficient. You will seldom need to apply the other types of normalization. Therefore, this section concentrates only on the 1st, 2nd, and 3rd normal forms of database design.

- ◆ **1st normal form**: No repeating groups
- ◆ **2nd normal form**: No nonkey attributes depend on a portion of the primary key
- ◆ **3rd normal form**: No attributes depend on other nonkey attributes

Now that you know the rules regarding normalization, apply them to a sample application.

For this application example, suppose that you are tracking training classes taken by each employee. Figure 20.7 contains a denormalized listing of the data tracked by this application. Each employee may have taken *0* or *N* (zero or many) classes.

Figure 20.7.   A denormalized database design.

employee_id	char(5)
employee_name	char(35)
employee_address	char(35)
employee_city	char(35)
employee_state	char(2)
employee_zip	char(11)
manager_id	char(5)
manager_name	char(35)
training_id1	char(5)
training_description1	char(25)
training_date1	datetime
training_id2	char(5)
training_description2	char(25)
training_date2	datetime
training_id3	char(5)
training_description3	char(25)
training_date3	datetime

1ST NORMAL FORM

Look at the `training_id`, `training_description`, and `training_date` attributes in Figure 20.8. See how they are repeated? This violates the concept of 1st normal form: no repeating groups.

Figure 20.8.   Repeating groups.

employee_table

employee_id	char(5)	
employee_name	char(35)	
employee_address	char(35)	
employee_city	char(35)	
employee_state	char(2)	
employee_zip	char(11)	
manager_id	char(5)	
manager_name	char(35)	
training_id1	char(5)	
training_description1	char(25)	
training_date1	datetime	
training_id2	char(5)	········ Repeating
training_description2	char(25)	Groups
training_date2	datetime	
training_id3	char(5)	
training_description3	char(25)	
training_date3	datetime	

Move the training information into a separate table called `employee_training` and create a relationship between the `employee` table and the `employee_training` table. Now the table design meets the requirements of 1st normal form (see Figure 20.9).

Figure 20.9.   Tables that meet 1st normal form.

employee

employee_id	char(5)
employee_name	char(35)
employee_address	char(35)
employee_city	char(35)
employee_state	char(2)
employee_zip	char(11)
manager_id	char(5)
manager_name	char(35)

employee_training

employee_id	char(5)
training_id	char(5)
training_description	char(25)
training_date	datetime

2ND NORMAL FORM

In Figure 20.10, notice how the `training_description` attribute depends only on the `training_id` attribute and not on the `employee_id` attribute in the `employee_training` table. This violates 2nd normal form: no nonkey attributes depend on a portion of the primary key (the primary key for this table is `employee_id` + `training_id`). This rule is applied only to entities that have compound primary keys (a primary key consisting of more than one attribute).

Figure 20.10.   A nonkey attribute depends on a portion of the primary key.

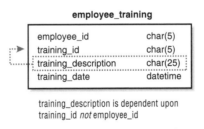

employee_training

employee_id	char(5)
training_id	char(5)
training_description	char(25)
training_date	datetime

training_description is dependent upon
training_id *not* employee_id

Move the `training_description` attribute into a separate table called `training`. Relate the `training` table to the `employee_training` table through the `training_id` attribute. Now the design satisfies 2nd normal form (see Figure 20.11).

Figure 20.11. Tables that meet 2nd normal form.

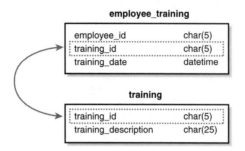

3RD NORMAL FORM

Look at the `manager_name` attribute for the `employee` table in Figure 20.12. The primary key for the `employee` table is the `employee_id` attribute. Does the `manager_name` attribute depend on the `employee_id` attribute? No! This violates 3rd normal form: no attributes can depend on other nonkey attributes.

Figure 20.12. An attribute depends on a nonkey attribute.

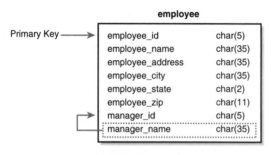

Move the `manager_name` attribute into a separate table called `manager`. The `manager` table can be related to the `employee` table through the `manager_id` attribute. By making this change, the design meets the requirements of 3rd normal form (see Figure 20.13).

Figure 20.13.   Tables that meet 3rd normal form.

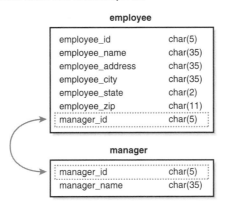

Now you have completed the normalization process (see Figure 20.14). This process helps isolate design flaws that would have led to an awkward and inefficient database design.

Figure 20.14.   A normalized database design.

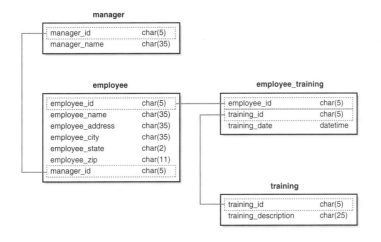

DENORMALIZATION

Denormalization means that you are purposely designing your database so that it is *not* in 3rd normal form. This is done to maximize performance or to simplify end-user reporting. Whenever you denormalize a database, you must be willing to forego the benefits gained from the 3rd normal form.

Note

I recommend that you start your initial database design in 3rd normal form. If you find that performance problems exist, selectively step back to 2nd or 1st normal form. Keep in mind that when you denormalize a database, you do so for a specific set of application requirements. Future requirements may not need or benefit from past denormalization decisions. Only denormalize when you have to.

PERFORMANCE

A database design in 3rd normal form may require more table joins to process a query than a design in 2nd or 1st normal form. These additional table joins can be expensive in terms of CPU and disk I/O.

Suppose that you need a report that lists the training classes taken by each employee (see Figure 20.15).

Figure 20.15.   A sample report.

employee name	manager name	training description	training date
Orryn Sledge	Bill Millen	SQL Server Admin	7/25/95
		PowerBuilder Development	8/25/95
		Introduction To COBOL	3/3/96
Victoria Breault	Chris Champ	Introduction To COBOL	1/1/96
		SQL Server Admin	7/1/96
Mike Sampres	Bill Millen	SQL Server Admin	6/1/96
Fred Humpress	Tina Smith	SQL Server Admin	8/1/96
		Introduction To COBOL	8/15/96
Stan Staples	Tina Smith	SQL Server Admin	8/1/96
		Introduction To COBOL	1/1/96
John Johnson	Tina Smith	SQL Server Admin	8/1/96

Note

The examples used in this section are overly simplistic; however, they *do* explain how multitable joins can complicate data processing.

To retrieve the data from your fully normalized database, you create the following query, which is a sample query for a fully normalized database:

```
SELECT a.employee_name, d.manager_name, c.training_description,b.training_date
FROM employee a, employee_training b, training c, manager d
WHERE a.emp_id = b.emp_id
 AND b.training_id = c. training_id
 AND a.manager_id = d.manager_id
```

As you can see, this simple report requires four tables to be joined. Assume that each table contains one million rows. Can you imagine the work involved to join four tables, each containing one million rows? You can be assured that performance will suffer.

To maximize performance, you sometimes have to step back to 2nd or 1st normal form. If you denormalize your data into a single table, you can use the following query, which is a sample query for a denormalized database:

```
SELECT employee_name, manager_name, training_description, training_date
FROM training_summary
```

AD-HOC REPORTING

Another reason to denormalize a database is to simplify ad-hoc reporting. Ad-hoc reporting is the unstructured reporting and querying performed by end users. End users are often confused when they have to join a significant number of tables. To avoid the confusion, DBAs can create a special set of tables designed for ad-hoc reporting. If the data is used for reporting and not online processing, you can avoid some of the problems associated with a denormalized design.

Tip

> Views can sometimes be used as an alternative to denormalization. Views can present your data in a denormalized manner, which can simplify ad-hoc reporting.

DENORMALIZATION TECHNIQUES

Following is a brief summary of the various techniques you can use to denormalize a database:

◆ **Duplicate data**: Duplicate data can reduce the number of joins required to process a query, thus reducing CPU usage and disk I/O.

◆ **Summary data**: Summary data can provide improved query performance by reducing or eliminating the steps required to summarize your data.

◆ **Horizontal partitioning**: Horizontal partitioning is the splitting of a table into two separate tables at the record level, thus reducing the number of rows per table (see Figure 20.16).

◆ **Vertical partitioning**: Vertical partitioning is the splitting of a table into two separate tables at the column level, thus reducing the number of columns per table (see Figure 20.17).

Figure 20.16.   *Horizontal partitioning.*

id	name	favorite_food	favorite_color	shoe_size
111-11-1111	Orryn Sledge	Pizza	Blue	9.5
222-22-2222	Victoria Breault	Ice Cream	Peach	6.0
333-33-3333	Mike Sampres	Pizza	Silver	9.0
444-44-4444	Fred Humpress	Fish	Red	10.0
555-55-5555	Stan Staples	Meat	Red	8.0
666-66-6666	John Johnson	Poultry	Black	9.0
777-77-7777	Mary Douglous	Pizza	White	6.0
888-88-8888	Jack Johnson	Pizza	Blue	10.0
999-99-9999	Jan Smithe	Pizza	Blue	10.0

With horizontal partitioning, a table is split into two tables at the row level. Usually, the split occurs at a predefined key value.

id	name	favorite_food	favorite_color	shoe_size
111-11-1111	Orryn Sledge	Pizza	Blue	9.5
222-22-2222	Victoria Breault	Ice Cream	Peach	6.0
333-33-3333	Mike Sampres	Pizza	Silver	9.0
444-44-4444	Fred Humpress	Fish	Red	10.0
555-55-5555	Stan Staples	Meat	Red	8.0

id	name	favorite_food	favorite_color	shoe_size
666-66-6666	John Johnson	Poultry	Black	9.0
777-77-7777	Mary Douglous	Pizza	White	6.0
888-88-8888	Jack Johnson	Pizza	Blue	10.0
999-99-9999	Jan Smithe	Pizza	Blue	10.0

Figure 20.17.   Vertical partitioning.

id	name	favorite_food	favorite_color	shoe size
111-11-1111	Orryn Sledge	Pizza	Blue	9.5
222-22-2222	Victoria Breault	Ice Cream	Peach	6.0
333-33-3333	Mike Sampres	Pizza	Silver	9.0
444-44-4444	Fred Humpress	Fish	Red	10.0
555-55-5555	Stan Staples	Meat	Red	8.0
666-66-6666	John Johnson	Poultry	Black	9.0
777-77-7777	Mary Douglous	Pizza	White	6.0
888-88-8888	Jack Johnson	Pizza	Blue	10.0
999-99-9999	Jan Smithe	Pizza	Blue	10.0

With vertical partitioning, a table is split into two separate tables and joined by a common key.

id	name
111-11-1111	Orryn Sledge
222-22-2222	Victoria Breault
333-33-3333	Mike Sampres
444-44-4444	Fred Humpress
555-55-5555	Stan Staples
666-66-6666	John Johnson
777-77-7777	Mary Douglous
888-88-8888	Jack Johnson
999-99-9999	Jan Smithe

id	favorite_food	favorite_color	shoe size
111-11-1111	Pizza	Blue	9.5
222-22-2222	Ice Cream	Peach	6.0
333-33-3333	Pizza	Silver	9.0
444-44-4444	Fish	Red	10.0
555-55-5555	Meat	Red	8.0
666-66-6666	Poultry	Black	9.0
777-77-7777	Pizza	White	6.0
888-88-8888	Pizza	Blue	10.0
999-99-9999	Pizza	Blue	10.0

BETWEEN THE LINES

Following are important notes to remember when designing databases:

◆ Strive for 3rd normal form to maximize data consistency and minimize update anomalies.

◆ When a significant number of tables must be joined to process a query, you may want to selectively denormalize the database to improve performance.

SUMMARY

You can gain tangible benefits by understanding and following the rules of normalization. When a normalized design is not feasible, you should selectively denormalize. Keep in mind the concepts discussed in this chapter when you read the next chapter—your normalization strategy might influence your indexing strategy.

CHAPTER 21

by Mark Spenik

Understanding Indexes

You may be asking yourself, "What in the world is a chapter on indexes and index selection doing in a book about database administration?" My experience as a DBA has shown me that it is important to understand indexes and how SQL Server uses indexes to help developers when they are stuck and come to the DBA looking for some words of wisdom and advice. Not only can you seem like a SQL Server guru by helping a developer quickly tune a query by adding an index, you need to be aware of the disk space requirements of indexes and the performance impact of too many indexes on a single table by an overzealous developer.

This chapter gives you a very basic understanding of an index, the type of structures used by indexes, and how to help developers select the proper indexes for their applications.

To get started, you need to know what an index is. An *index* is a separate physical database structure created on a table that facilitates faster data retrieval when you search on an indexed column. SQL Server also uses indexes to enforce uniqueness on a row or column in a table or to spread out the data on various data pages to help prevent page contention.

GENERAL PRINCIPLE BEHIND INDEXES

Take a high-level look at how indexing can help speed up data retrieval. Figure 21.1 shows a single table called School Employee that lists the name and occupation of each employee in the school.

Figure 21.1.
The School Employee *table.*

School Employee

row	name	occupation
1	John	Janitor
2	David	Principal
3	Adam	Bus Driver
4	Gary	Teacher
5	Lisa	Janitor
6	Chris	Teacher
7	Debbie	Guidance Counselor
8	Denise	Assistant Principal
9	Bryan	Janitor

Using the table shown in Figure 21.1, what would you do if you wanted to select the names of all the people in the School Employee table who were janitors? You would have to read every row in the table and display only the names where the occupation in the row is Janitor. The process of reading every row or record in a table to satisfy a query is called a *table scan*. Now add an index to the Occupation column. Figure 21.2 shows the index on the Occupation column of the School Employee table.

Figure 21.2.
An index on the
Occupation column of
the School Employee
table.

occupation	row pointer
Assistant Principal	8
Bus Driver	3
Guidance Counselor	7
Janitor	1
Janitor	5
Janitor	9
Principal	2
Teacher	4
Teacher	6

The type of index shown in Figure 21.2 contains a pointer to the data. Using the index shown in Figure 21.2, walk through the same query to find the names of all employees who are janitors. Rather than performing a table scan on the School Employee table, you read the first row of the index and check the occupation until you find Janitor. When a row contains Janitor, you use the value in the row pointer column to find the exact row number in the School Employee table of a Janitor. You continue to read the index as long as the occupation is Janitor. When the occupation is no longer Janitor, you stop reading the index. Pretty simple right?

Apply to SQL Server this little bit of knowledge of tables and indexes just described. For starters, SQL Server stores data and index information on a data page (see Figure 21.3).

Figure 21.3.
The SQL Server
data page.

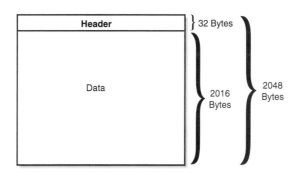

A data page is 2048 bytes in size with a 32-byte header. The remaining 2016 bytes are used for data (that is, table or index information).

Tip

SQL Server allocates space for tables and indexes eight pages at a time, a grouping called an *extent*. When the extent is filled, another extent (8 pages) is allocated. Remember this tip if you take the Microsoft SQL Server certification test. The odds are that you will be asked a question on index and table space allocation.

Suppose that the School Employee table, used earlier, contained other information, such as the employee's home address, phone number, spouse's name, education, and number of years of service. The size of a single row of information for the School Employee table would be around 480 bytes; the maximum size of the Occupation column is 25 bytes. Using these row and column sizes, place the School Employee table (shown in Figure 21.1) and the index (shown in Figure 21.2) on SQL Server data pages (see Figure 21.4).

Note

The layouts of the table information and index information on the data pages shown in Figure 21.4 are not the actual index and table layouts used by SQL Server. They are used here to help you understand the general idea behind data pages, table scans, and indexes.

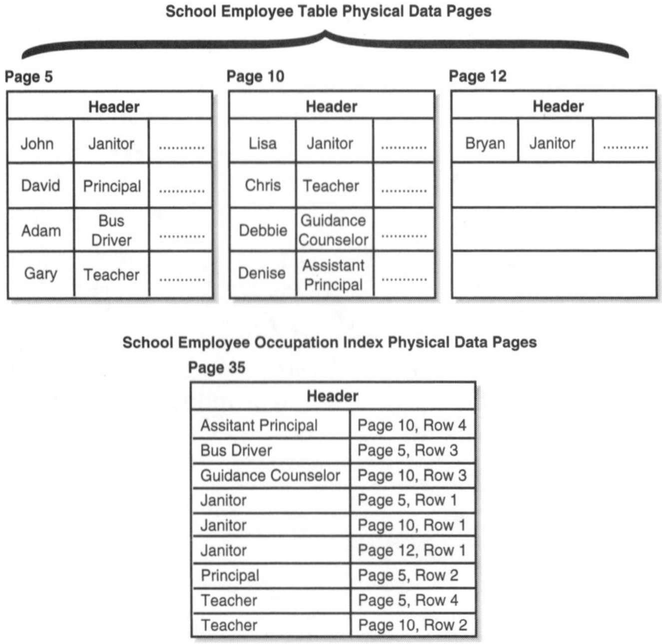

Figure 21.4.
The School Employee
table and index on SQL
Server data pages.

School Employee Table Physical Data Pages

Page 5			Page 10			Page 12		
Header			Header			Header		
John	Janitor	....	Lisa	Janitor	....	Bryan	Janitor	....
David	Principal	....	Chris	Teacher	....			
Adam	Bus Driver	....	Debbie	Guidance Counselor	....			
Gary	Teacher	....	Denise	Assistant Principal	....			

School Employee Occupation Index Physical Data Pages

Page 35

Header	
Assitant Principal	Page 10, Row 4
Bus Driver	Page 5, Row 3
Guidance Counselor	Page 10, Row 3
Janitor	Page 5, Row 1
Janitor	Page 10, Row 1
Janitor	Page 12, Row 1
Principal	Page 5, Row 2
Teacher	Page 5, Row 4
Teacher	Page 10, Row 2

Using the diagram shown in Figure 21.4, how would SQL Server find all the employee names whose occupation is Assistant Principal without the index? First, SQL Server would read data page 5 and search each record for an employee with an occupation equal to Assistant Principal. No records are found on the first page. SQL Server reads the second data page (page 10), searches each record, and displays the fourth record. Because SQL Server has no way of knowing how many records there are with the occupation of Assistant Principal, SQL Server reads and searches the third and final page, page 12.

What happened? SQL Server performed a table scan, reading all the data pages. In this example, a table scan did not seem all that bad because SQL Server only had to read three data pages. But what if the School Employee table had 1,000 times more records for a total of 9,000 records (a small amount for SQL Server)? SQL Server would have to read 3,000 data pages rather than 3 data pages to find all the Assistant Principals, even if there was only one employee who was an Assistant Principal and that record was located on the first data page.

Walk through the same query using the index. First, SQL Server reads the index page and begins to search for Assistant Principal. The first row read is Assistant Principal. SQL Server then checks the pointer, which tells SQL Server that the record is located on data page 10, row 4. SQL Server reads data page 10, goes to the fourth row, and displays the name.

The next row in the index page is checked; because the occupation is not Assistant Principal, SQL Server stops. The number of pages read using the index is two pages as opposed to the three pages read in the table scan example.

What about the Janitor query used earlier? Performing a table scan requires SQL Server to read all three data pages. Using the index requires SQL Server to read all three data pages plus the index page, for a total of four data pages—one more than a table scan! In some cases, a table scan may be faster than using the index. It's the job of the SQL Server query optimizer to determine which index to select and when to perform a table scan.

Tip

You will read many recommendations in this book about keeping indexes small and the row width of a table small for maximum performance. All too often, the reasoning behind small row and index width is left out. It boils down to data pages and how many data pages SQL Server has to read to fulfill a query.

Suppose that you have a table with 500,000 rows; the size of a row (with overhead bytes) is 250 bytes or (2048 bytes in a data page – 32 bytes of overhead) / 250 bytes = 8) 8 records per data page. The number of data pages required for all 500,000 records is (500,000 / 8 = 62,500) 62,500 data pages.

Suppose that you look at your overall table design and decide that you can shrink the size of the maximum row width just over 10 percent so that 9 rather than 8 records fit on a data page. The number of data pages is reduced by almost 7,000 data pages! An index data page is the same. Indexing a 20-character field (with overhead) and a 6-byte field (with overhead), for example, is the difference between 100 keys per data page and 336 keys per data page.

The larger index requires SQL Server to read three times as many data pages to access the same number of keys. (This does not take into account the added B-Tree levels caused by a larger index key!) Normalize your tables and select smart indexes.

STRUCTURE OF SQL SERVER INDEXES

SQL Server maintains indexes with a B-Tree structure (see Figure 21.5). B-Trees are multilevel self-maintaining structures.

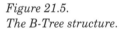

Figure 21.5.
The B-Tree structure.

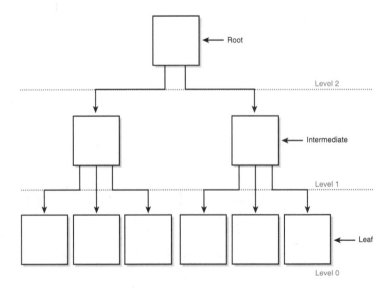

A B-Tree structure consists of a top level, called the *root*; a bottom level, called the *leaf* (always level 0); and zero to many intermediate levels (the B-Tree in Figure 21.5

has one intermediate level). In SQL Server terms, each square shown in Figure 21.5 represents an index page (or data page). The greater the number of levels in your index, the more index pages you must read to retrieve the records you are searching for (that is, performance degrades as the number of levels increases). SQL Server maintains two different types of indexes: a clustered index and a nonclustered index.

CLUSTERED INDEX

A *clustered index* is a B-Tree structure where level 0, the leaf, contains the actual data pages of the table and the data is physically stored in the logical order of the index.

Note

> When a clustered index is created, a lot of disk I/O occurs, the data pages are ordered, the index pages are created, and the nonordered data pages are deleted. Creating a clustered index requires you to have free space in the database that amounts to approximately 1.2 times the amount of data in the table.

Figure 21.6 shows a clustered index on the Name column in the School Employee table. Notice that the data pages are the leaf pages of the clustered index and that the data is stored in logical order on the data pages.

Figure 21.6.
A clustered index on the
Name column of the
School Employee *table.*

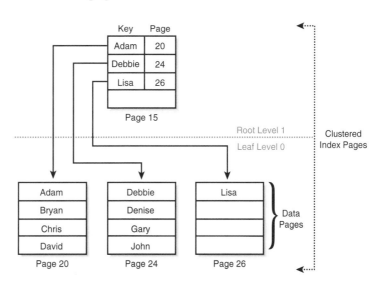

Note

Because data is physically ordered on the data pages, you can have only one clustered index per table. Select the clustered index wisely.

NONCLUSTERED INDEX

With a nonclustered index, the leaf level pages contain pointers to the data pages and rows, not the actual data (as does the clustered index). A nonclustered index does not reorder the physical data pages of the table. Therefore, creating a nonclustered index does not require the large amounts of free disk space associated with creating a clustered index. Figure 21.7 shows a nonclustered index on the School Employee table. Notice that the data in the data pages is in the order in which the data was inserted, not in the order of the index key. Also note that the nonclustered index adds one more level by always arriving at the leaf and then having to read the data page.

Figure 21.7.
A nonclustered index on
the Name column of the
School Employee *table.*

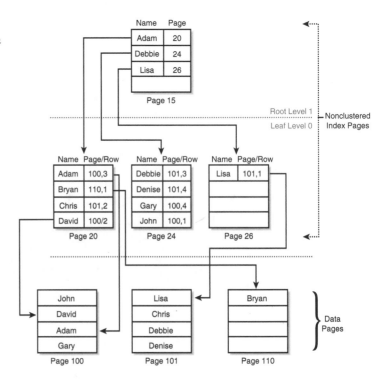

Tip

You can have up to 249 nonclustered indexes on a table, although you would *never* want to create anywhere near 249 indexes on a single table. A large number of indexes on a single table affects the performance of other operations, such as UPDATE, DELETE, and INSERT. In SQL Server 6.5, a single-column index cannot exceed 256 bytes in width; a composite index cannot exceed 900 bytes in width (in SQL Server versions before 6.5, the limit was 256 bytes, regardless of index type). Any index cannot exceed 16 columns. Again, you would *never* want an index that is 900 bytes in width or that contains 16 columns.

Remember to use narrow-width indexes to maximize the number of index keys on a data page. This improves performance by requiring less disk I/O to scan the index. Try not to exceed 4 columns when creating indexes. A table can have both clustered and nonclustered indexes. Because you are allowed to have only a single clustered index on a table, you can meet your other indexing needs with nonclustered indexes. Try not to over-index; in many cases, a clustered index and two to four nonclustered indexes are more than sufficient.

DATA MODIFICATION AND INDEX PERFORMANCE CONSIDERATIONS

It is widely known that an index can help speed data retrievals; from time to time, you may hear someone say that indexes slow down other operations, such as inserts, updates, and deletes—which is true. It has been mentioned that B-Tree data structures are, for the most part, self-maintaining data structures, meaning that as rows are added, deleted, or updated, the indexes also are updated to reflect the changes. All this updating requires extra I/O to update the index pages.

What happens when a new row is added to a table without a clustered index? The data is added at the end of the last data page. What happens when a new row is added to a clustered index? The data is inserted into the correct physical and logical order in the table and other rows may be moved up or down, depending on where the data is placed, causing additional disk I/O to maintain the index.

As the index pages and data pages grow, they may be required to split (a situation beyond the scope of this book), requiring slightly more disk I/O.

In general, you should not worry about the time required to maintain indexes during inserts, deletes, and updates. Be aware that extra time is required to update the indexes during data modification and that performance can become an issue if you over-index a table. On tables that are frequently modified, I try to restrict the tables to a clustered index and no more than three or four nonclustered indexes. Tables involved in heavy transaction processing should be restricted to from zero to two indexes. If you find the need to index beyond these numbers, run some benchmark tests to check for performance degradation.

HOW TO CREATE INDEXES

You can create an index using the Enterprise Manager.

Note

You cannot create an index on the following data types:

```
bit
text
image
```

Indexes cannot be created on a view.

Using the Enterprise Manager, select a database (the following example uses the pubs database). Then follow these steps to create an index:

1. Select Indexes from the Manage menu. The Manage Indexes dialog box appears (see Figure 21.8).

Figure 21.8.
The Manage Indexes
dialog box.

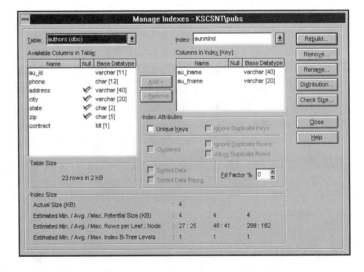

2. From the Index drop-down combo box, select the New Index option. The Index drop-down combo box goes blank. In the now-blank Index drop-down combo box, type the name of the new index.

Tip

Use a meaningful naming convention for indexes and stick with it. I like to prefix my indexes with *cidx* for a clustered index and *idx* for a nonclustered index. If the index is on the primary key table, I add *pk*. If the index is a foreign key, I add *fk*. I then use the column names to remind me at a glance which columns make up the index. For a clustered index on the primary key column on the authors table, au_id, in the pubs database, for example, I would name the index cidx_pk_au_id. The maximum number of characters you can use for an index is 30.

3. Select the column you want to add to the index by single-clicking the column in the Available Columns in Table list box. Click the Add button to move the selected column to the Columns in Index list box (see Figure 21.9). You also can move a column from the Available Columns in Table list box to the Columns in Index list box by double-clicking the selected column.

Figure 21.9.
Adding columns to an index with the Manage Indexes dialog box.

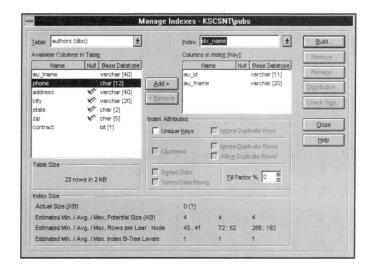

Note

An index that consists of more than one column is called a *composite index*. When creating a composite index, the order of the columns in the index makes a difference. SQL Server keeps density statistics on all columns that make up the index, but only histogram statistics on the first column of the composite index. As a result, if the first column of a composite index has very few unique values, the index may not be used for index selection by the query optimizer. When creating a composite index, select the column with the most unique values for the first column of a composite index. The maximum size of a composite index in SQL Server 6.5 is 900 bytes.

4. To create the index, click the Build button. The Index Build dialog box appears (see Figure 21.10).

The Index Build dialog box enables you to create the index immediately by clicking the Execute Now button; alternatively, you can schedule the index to be built at a later time by clicking the Schedule As Task button. Being able to schedule the index build for a later time is a great new feature of SQL Server 6.x.

Figure 21.10.
The Index Build
dialog box.

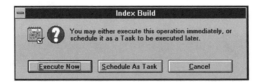

Caution

The table on which the index is being created is locked during index creation. Creating indexes on very large tables or creating clustered indexes (which may reorder the data pages) can take some time to complete. You cannot access the table until the index creation is complete. Try to create clustered indexes and very large nonclustered indexes during non-peak hours.

When an index is created, a row is placed in the sysindexes database system table.

Tip

Always build a clustered index before building a nonclustered index. When a clustered index is built, all nonclustered indexes currently on the table are rebuilt. You also can build an index on a temporary table.

The Transact SQL statement used to create an index is the CREATE INDEX command, which has the following syntax:

```
CREATE [UNIQUE] [CLUSTERED ¦ NONCLUSTERED] INDEX index_name
ON [[database.]owner.]table_name (column_name [, column_name]...)
[WITH [PAD_INDEX,][[,]FILLFACTOR = x][[,] IGNORE_DUP_KEY][[,]
{SORTED_DATA ¦ SORTED_DATA_REORG}] [[,] {IGNORE_DUP_ROW ¦ ALLOW_DUP_ROW}]]
[ON segment_name]
```

Note

Version 6.5

SQL Server 6.x provides another method to create indexes called *constraints*. A constraint is added to a table during the table creation and can be used to maintain referential integrity. The primary key constraint places a unique index, clustered or nonclustered, on the columns defined as the primary key. You cannot drop a constraint index with the Enterprise Manager (using the Manage Index dialog box). To remove a constraint, you must use the ALTER TABLE command. Here's the good news if you use SQL Server 6.5: You can use the DBCC DBREINDEX statement to dynamically rebuild indexes without having to drop and re-create the index or constraint.

The following sections examine in more detail some of the options and information displayed in the Manage Indexes dialog box and the CREATE INDEX command (see Figure 21.11). Start with the Index Attributes frame.

Figure 21.11.
The Manage Index dialog box.

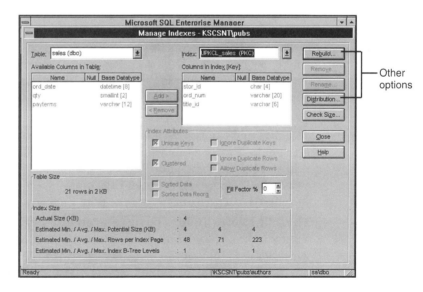

INDEX ATTRIBUTES FRAME

The Index Attributes frame, shown in Figure 21.11, contains checkboxes that enable you to specify the type of index you want to create. These checkboxes relate to many of the options used in the CREATE INDEX command.

◆ **The Unique Keys checkbox.** The Unique option creates a index that enforces uniqueness on the indexed column(s). Use the Unique Keys option when uniqueness is an attribute of the data (for example, the primary key of the table).

Caution

If you try to create a unique index on a column with duplicate data, the index creation will fail. You must remove the duplicate data entries to build the index.

◆ **The Ignore Duplicate Keys checkbox.** The Ignore Duplicate Keys checkbox does not enable you to create a unique index with duplicate values, but if an attempt is made to insert or update a duplicate row, the duplicate row is ignored and an informational message is displayed. If the insert or update is part of a transaction, the transaction continues rather than rolling back on a duplicate key error.

◆ **The Clustered checkbox.** When the Clustered checkbox is selected, a clustered index with the selected columns is created on the table. Remember that you can have only one clustered index per table. When this option is not selected, a nonclustered index is created.

◆ **The Ignore Duplicate Rows and Allow Duplicate Rows checkboxes.** These options are relevant only to clustered indexes. The Ignore Duplicate Rows checkbox prevents duplicate rows from being added by ignoring the duplicate. The Allow Duplicate Rows checkbox enables you to create a nonunique clustered index on a table with duplicate rows and allows duplicate rows to be inserted or updated.

◆ **The Sorted Data and Un-Sorted Data checkboxes.** The Sorted Data checkbox and the Un-Sorted Data checkbox are used for a clustered index. If the data is already in a sorted order, check the Sorted Data checkbox to skip sorting the data while building the index. If a value is found out of order, the index creation halts. Checking the Un-Sorted Data checkbox specifies that you want to sort the data during the index creation process.

◆ **The Fill Factor field.** The Fill Factor specifies how densely packed you want your index and data pages while creating an index. The default is 0, which leaves room on the nonleaf pages with the leaf pages 100 percent full. A high Fill Factor value increases performance for queries because the index pages are packed, reducing the number of index levels. The tradeoff is the increase in time caused by page splitting when performing INSERT and UPDATE statements. Use high Fill Factor values for static tables or tables that are not modified frequently. Specify a low Fill Factor value to spread data over more pages. A low Fill Factor value is good for tables involved with many UPDATE and INSERT transactions because the chance of a page split occurring is reduced by spreading out the data across many pages. The penalty for a low Fill Factor is a decrease in query performance because the number of index levels is increased. *Note:* The default value of 0 is a special case and is not considered a low Fill Factor value because the leaf pages are filled to 100 percent capacity and some space is left on the index pages.

Note

The Fill Factor value is not maintained by SQL Server after index creation; it is maintained only when the index is built.

TABLE SIZE AND INDEX SIZE FRAMES

The Table Size and Index Size frames supply useful information, such as the current size of the table and the amount of disk space used by the index. You can use the information in these two frames to help determine whether to use indexes on a table and if there may be performance problems with the indexes created.

The Table Size frame displays the number of rows and the amount of space occupied by the data. Remember: If the table contains a small number of rows, SQL Server does not use indexes and performs a table scan instead. There is no minimum or maximum number of rows before an index or table scan occurs; you have to test your queries and look at the query plan used by the optimizer.

For an index that already exists, the size of the index in disk space is displayed in the Actual Size field and in the Estimated Min./Avg./Max. Potential Size field.

The Estimated Min./Avg./Max. Rows Per Leaf:Node Page label is displayed for nonclustered indexes; it provides the estimated minimum, average, and maximum number of rows on the leaf pages and the nonleaf pages of the index B-Tree. For a clustered index, the label reads Estimated Min./Avg./Max. Rows Per Index Page. The leaf pages are excluded because they are the actual data pages. Estimated Min./Avg./Max. Index B-Tree Levels displays the number of levels for the expected index B-Tree.

Tip

The levels of the B-Tree can point to possible performance problems or poor index selection. A B-Tree with a large number of levels requires more time to find rows because each level adds more data pages that must be read to get to the leaf pages.

You can reduce the number of B-Tree levels by reducing the width of the indexed columns, which increases the number of index keys per page.

OTHER INDEX OPERATIONS

Let's quickly review other index operations you can perform from the Manage Index dialog box shown in Figure 21.11.

- ◆ **Rebuild button.** Rebuilds the currently selected index.
- ◆ **Remove button.** Removes the selected index, frees the space in the database allocated to the index, and removes the entry for the index from the database system table sysindexes. The Remove button performs the same operation as the Transact SQL command DROP INDEX, which has the following format:

```
DROP INDEX [owner.]table_name.index_name
[, [owner.]table_name.index_name...]
```

- ◆ **Rename button.** Enables you to rename an existing index. The Rename button performs the same operation as the SQL Server system stored procedure sp_rename, which has the following syntax:

```
sp_rename objname, newname [, COLUMN ¦ INDEX ]
```

- ◆ **Distribution button.** Click the Distribution button to display the Index Distribution Statistics dialog box (see Figure 21.12).

  The Index Distribution Statistics dialog box displays the distribution page used by the query optimizer to determine which index (or whether any index) should be used to optimize performance when executing a query. For tables with more than 200 rows, a rating system is displayed to classify the usability of the selected index. The rating system is listed in Table 21.1.

- ◆ **Check Size button.** Use the Check Size button to check and verify the actual size of the index.

Figure 21.12.
The Index Distribution
Statistics dialog box.

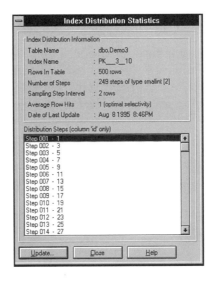

TABLE 21.1. INDEX SUBJECTIVITY RATINGS.

Index Rating	# of Rows Returned	Comment
Optimal	1 row	Good candidate for primary key
Very Good	> 1 row	< 0.5% of rows
Good	> 0.5% of rows	< 1% of rows
Fair	> 1.0% of rows	< 2.5% of rows (Check with query showplan)
Poor	> 2.5% of rows	< 5% of rows (Do not index)
Very Poor	> 5% of rows	No way!

Tip

I'm really impressed with the information provided in the Index Distribution Statistics dialog box. It helps remove some of the guesswork about the data distribution of a table. For developers and DBAs, being able to see the distribution page information and the subjective index rating can help make a sound decision about whether a column is a good index candidate.

Use the information in the Index Distribution Statistics dialog box, along with the Query Analyzer dialog box showplan option (described in the next chapter) to further tune your index selection.

SUGGESTED INDEX STRATEGIES

Index selection is based on the design of the tables and the queries that are executed against the tables. Before you create indexes, make sure that the indexed columns are part of a query or are being placed on the table for other reasons, such as preventing duplicate data. The following sections suggest some indexing strategies.

WHAT TO INDEX

The following list shows criteria you can use to help determine which columns will make good indexes:

◆ Columns used in table joins

◆ Columns used in range queries

◆ Columns used in order by queries

◆ Columns used in group by queries

◆ Columns used in aggregate functions

WHAT NOT TO INDEX

The following list shows cases in which columns or indexes should not be used or should be used sparingly:

◆ Tables with a small number of rows

◆ Columns with poor selectivity (that is, with a wide range of values)

◆ Columns that are very large in width (I try to limit my indexes to columns less than 25 bytes in size)

◆ Tables with heavy transaction loads (lots of inserts and deletes) but very few decision support operations

◆ Columns not used in queries

CLUSTERED OR NONCLUSTERED INDEX

As you know, you can have only one clustered index per table. Following are some situations in which a clustered index works well:

◆ Columns used in range queries

◆ Columns used in order by or group by queries

◆ Columns used in table joins

◆ Queries returning large result sets

Nonclustered indexes work well in the following situations:

- Columns used in aggregate functions
- Foreign keys
- Queries returning small result sets
- When using the DBCC `DBREINDEX` statement to dynamically rebuild indexes (you don't have to drop and re-create the index or constraint)
- Information frequently accessed by a specific column in table joins or `order by` or `group by` queries
- Primary keys that are sequential surrogate keys (identity columns, sequence numbers)

COMPUTING SELECTIVITY

You can determine whether a column is a good candidate for an index by doing some simple math and computing the selectivity of the column. First, you must determine the total number of rows in the table being indexed. You can obtain this information from the Table Size frame of the Manage Indexes dialog box or by using the following SQL command:

```
Select COUNT(*) FROM table_name
```

Then you must determine the number of unique values for the column you want to index. To determine this number, execute the following SQL command:

```
Select COUNT(DISTINCT column1_name) FROM table_name
```

To determine the number of expected rows returned by using the indexed column, calculate the following formula:

```
expected number of rows = (1/number of unique values) * Total number of rows in the
table
```

If the expected number of rows is low compared to the total number of rows in the table, the column is a good candidate for an index. You can further validate this by computing a percentage, as follows:

```
Percentage of rows returned = (expected number of rows/total number of rows in the
table) * 100
```

Compare this value to the values shown in Table 21.1.

COMPOSITE INDEXES

Composite indexes are indexes created with two or more columns (the maximum number of columns for an index is 16 columns). SQL Server 6.x keeps distribution page information on all the columns that make up the composite index, but the histogram of data distribution used by the query optimizer is kept only on the first key, so the order of the keys *does* matter. Use the key with the most unique values as the first key (best selectability). Try not to get carried away by creating composite indexes with a large number of columns. (I try to keep them under four columns.) Too many columns affect performance and make the index key large, increasing the size of the index and requiring you to scan more data pages to read the index keys.

INDEX COVERING

Index covering is a term used to explain a situation in which all the columns returned by a query and all the columns in the WHERE clause are the key columns in a single nonclustered index. SQL Server does not have to read the data pages to satisfy the query; instead, it returns the values on the leaf page of the index. In some cases, a covered nonclustered index can outperform a clustered index.

The downside to index covering is the added overhead to maintain the indexes. Also, it is very difficult to create indexes to cover the many different queries executed by your users. Avoid creating indexes to cover queries. You are better off creating single-column or narrow composite indexes for the query optimizer to use.

"HOW TO START A CONTROVERSY," BY SPENIK AND SLEDGE

I have been to some very good classes covering optimization and tuning using Microsoft SQL Server and Sybase SQL Server. Not to mention a lot of real-world experience in tuning applications. You know the story: optimizing a stored procedure that ran in 16 hours so that it ran in 20 minutes.... In the first edition of this book, I included some brief information about some rare cases in index covering you should experiment with. The tech editors burned me up, complaining that the correct use of covered indexes required much more detail and information than I was providing in my brief description. So I decided to check the Microsoft documentation, which also did not favor the use of index covering. Out voted, two to one, I toned down the recommendation of experimenting with index covering in some critical cases. When the first edition of this book was published, everyone liked the book but pointed out that they do not agree with my stand on covered indexes. I even got e-mail from several respected SQL Server experts who commented on the index covering section.

Okay. In this edition, I'm adding my original recommendation that index covering in many cases can give you better performance than a clustered index when running a query. But in all honesty, do not go crazy and try to cover every query you execute. Trying to cover every query you execute is a ridiculous thought and will end up bringing your system performance to a crawl when performing updates, inserts, and deletes. Keep in mind that the optimizer uses only one index. In general, you should stick with single-column or narrow composite indexes for the query optimizer to use. But if you still need better performance and are not returning a lot of columns or have a large WHERE clause and the query is of a critical nature, experiment with index covering.

I hope this time around I have covered (no pun intended) all the different viewpoints on this topic!

BETWEEN THE LINES

Following are some important points to remember about SQL Server indexes:

◆ SQL Server maintains indexes with a B-Tree structure.

◆ In a clustered index, the leaf contains the actual data pages of the table and the data is physically stored in the logical order of the index.

◆ The SQL Server query optimizer selects at most one index to resolve a query.

◆ Composite indexes are indexes created with two or more columns.

◆ Select indexes carefully.

SUMMARY

It is important that you understand the basic ideas behind SQL Server indexes. In the next chapter, you build on the basic concepts of this chapter and learn about the query optimizer. If you understand indexes and the query optimizer, you will be able to provide valuable support to developers.

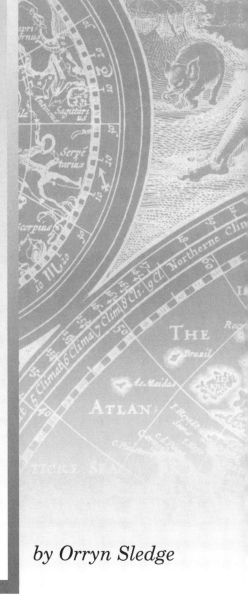

CHAPTER 22

by Orryn Sledge

Understanding the Query Optimizer

The key to extracting maximum query performance is to understand SQL Server's optimizer. If you understand the optimizer, you can write queries that run faster, build better indexes, and resolve performance problems.

Note

SQL Server uses an *intelligent* cost-based optimizer. Don't be misled by the word *intelligent*. I have yet to meet a query optimizer that is more intelligent than a good DBA! Although SQL Server has an excellent query optimizer, there is no way it can ever understand all the nuances and intricacies of your data. Therefore, do not put blind faith in the query optimizer. Instead, try to understand how the optimizer works and how you can finesse it into delivering better performance.

SQL Server's optimizer has been significantly improved in version 6.x. Following is a summary of notable enhancements:

◆ **Enhanced index usage.** SQL Server version 6.x has an improved optimizer that takes better advantage of useful indexes. This can reduce the amount of tuning effort required to achieve maximum performance. The optimizer can also use an index to process a DISTINCT statement (previous versions could not use an index).

◆ **Reverse traversal of indexes.** When you perform a sort in descending order (ORDER BY...DESCENDING), the optimizer looks for useful indexes. Previous versions of SQL Server processed the query by using a worktable and a table scan.

◆ **Improved subquery optimization.** Subqueries are now optimized in regards to the tables in the main query.

◆ **Optimizer hints**: The optimizer can be forced into using an index specified in the FROM clause.

Why SQL Server Uses a Query Optimizer

SQL Server uses a cost-based query optimizer to generate the optimal execution path for an INSERT, UPDATE, DELETE, or SELECT SQL statement. The "optimal" execution path is the path that offers the best performance. Before the query is run, the optimizer assigns a cost based on CPU and disk I/O usage for different execution paths. The optimizer then uses the least expensive execution path to process the query. See Figure 22.1 for examples of execution paths.

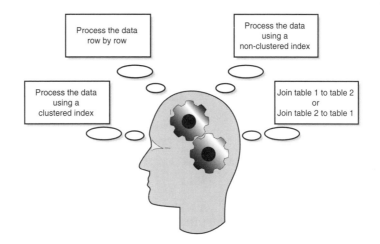

Figure 22.1.
Examples of execution
paths.

The advantage of the query optimizer is that it relieves users from the tedious process of having to decide how their SQL statements should be constructed to use indexes and in what order the data should be accessed. The query optimizer allows users to build SQL statements that *automatically* take advantage of indexes and *automatically* determine the optimal order to process table joins.

UPDATE STATISTICS

Whenever you create an index, SQL Server creates a set of statistics about the data contained within the index. The query optimizer uses these statistics to determine whether it should use the index to help process the query. Over time, you will find that your statistics will become less representative of your data in tables that are frequently modified. In turn, this will cause the optimizer to ignore useful indexes.

To keep statistics up to date, run the UPDATE STATISTICS command whenever a large percentage of the table's index keys have changed. Operations such as BCP and batch inserts, deletes, and updates can cause an index's statistics to become outdated.

```
UPDATE STATISTICS [[database.]owner.]table_name [index_name]
```

If you do not include the [index_name] parameter, all indexes attached to the table are automatically updated.

Tip

In a transaction-oriented environment, it can be advantageous to automate UPDATE STATISTICS (see Chapter 26, "Automating Database Administration Tasks," for more information on automating UPDATE STATISTICS). Doing so can help keep your index statistics current.

Use the Task Scheduler, included with the Enterprise Manager, to schedule UPDATE STATISTICS.

To determine when an index's statistics were last updated, use STATS_DATE() or DBCC SHOW_STATISTICS, as in the following example:

```
STATS_DATE (table_id, index_id)
        DBCC SHOW_STATISTICS (table_name, index_name)
```

BASIC QUERY OPTIMIZATION SUGGESTIONS

The following list of suggestions concentrates on the basics of query optimization. I always recommend starting with the basics when trying to improve query performance. Quite often, a minor modification to a query yields a substantial gain in performance.

◆ **Target queries that run slowly and that run frequently.** By simply adding an index or updating statistics, you can often see a dramatic improvement in query performance.

◆ **Understand your data.** To use optimization tricks, you must understand your query and how it relates to your data. Otherwise, your lack of knowledge may hamper your ability to effectively rewrite a query.

◆ **Record statistics about the existing query.** Before you begin to optimize a query, record a showplan (see "The Showplan Tool," later in this chapter, for more information) and I/O statistics. Doing so provides you with a benchmark against which you can measure the success of your revisions.

◆ **Start with the basics.** Look for the obvious when you start to optimize a query. Do useful indexes exist? Have the statistics been updated recently? Are triggers being executed when the query is run? Does the query reference a view? Does the query use nonsearch arguments?

◆ **Understand the output from a showplan.** It is important to understand what is relevant and what is not when evaluating a showplan. (Use Table 22.1, later in this chapter, to help determine relevant showplan output.)

◆ **Throw conventional wisdom out the window.** Sometimes, you have to break the rules to optimize a query. Your ability to extract maximum query performance is a mix between art and science. What works on one query may not work on another query. Therefore, you occasionally have to go against conventional wisdom to maximize performance.

TOOLS TO HELP OPTIMIZE A QUERY

The following optimizer tools can be used to help optimize a query:

- ◆ Showplan
- ◆ Statistics I/O
- ◆ No Execute
- ◆ Stats Time

THE SHOWPLAN TOOL

A *showplan* provides insight about how SQL Server is going to process a SQL statement. The showplan can be one of the most confusing aspects of SQL Server. Its output is cryptic and based on technical jargon. Yet, if you know how to interpret its cryptic output, it can be useful for tuning queries.

To generate a showplan, click the Query Options button within the Query dialog box from the Enterprise Manager. Select the Show Query Plan option from the Query Flags page of the Query Options dialog box (see Figure 22.2).

Figure 22.2.
Setting the Show Query Plan option.

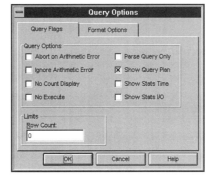

After you execute your query, the output from the showplan appears in the Results window (see Figure 22.3).

Note

Gone, but not forgotten... For some strange reason, Microsoft removed the graphical showplan tool from SQL Server 6.5. I always thought the tool was pretty useful, but I guess the folks at Microsoft didn't think anyone was using it!

Version
6.5

Figure 22.3.
A showplan.

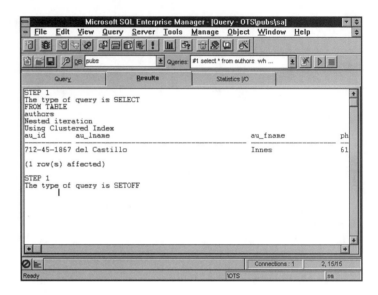

THE STATISTICS I/O TOOL

Statistics I/O is useful in determining the amount of I/O that will occur to process a query. The less I/O you have, the faster your query will run. When tuning queries, try to minimize the amount of I/O used by the query. SQL Server uses I/O statistics to help determine the optimal query execution path.

When you generate statistics I/O, you see three types of I/O measurements: *scan count*, *logical reads*, and *physical reads*. The following list explains the three types of I/O measurements:

◆ *scan count* is the number of table scans required to process the query.

◆ *logical reads* is the number of pages accessed to process the query.

◆ *physical reads* is the number of times the disk was accessed to process the query.

Note

Each time a query is run, the data used to process the query may become loaded into the data cache. This can reduce the number of *physical reads* required to process the query when it is run again. You can detect whether the data is loaded into the data cache by monitoring the *logical reads* and *physical reads* for a query. If *physical reads* is less than *logical reads*, some or all of the data was in the data cache.

SQL Server provides two facilities to generate I/O statistics: graphical and text-based.

To generate graphical statistics I/O, click the Display Statistics I/O button in the Enterprise Manager Query dialog box (see Figure 22.4).

Figure 22.4.
Generating graphical
statistics I/O.

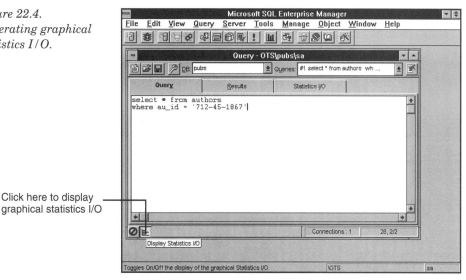

Click here to display
graphical statistics I/O

After you execute your query, click the Statistics I/O tab to view I/O statistics output (see Figure 22.5).

Figure 22.5.
Graphical
statistics I/O.

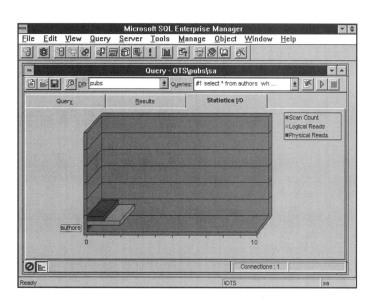

To generate text-based statistics I/O, click the Query Options button in the Enterprise Manager Query dialog box. Select the Show Stats I/O option from the Query Flags page of the Query Options dialog box (see Figure 22.6).

After you execute your query, the output from the statistics I/O appears in the results window (see Figure 22.7).

Figure 22.6.
Setting the Show Stats
I/O query option.

Figure 22.7.
Text-based
statistics I/O.

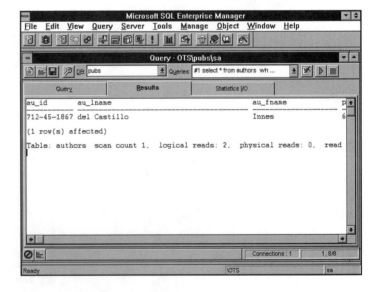

THE NO EXECUTE TOOL

No Execute is an excellent tool for optimizing long-running queries. By using this option, you can determine the showplan for a query without having to actually run the query. When you use this option, the syntax of the query is validated, a showplan can be generated, and any error messages are returned.

To use the No Execute option, click the Query Options button in the Enterprise Manager Query dialog box. Select the No Execute option from the Query Flags page of the Query Option dialog box (see Figure 22.8).

Figure 22.8.
Setting the No Execute
query option.

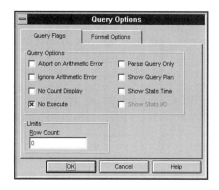

THE STATS TIME TOOL

The Stats Time tool displays the time required by SQL Server to parse, compile, and execute a query.

To use the Stats Time option, click the Query Options button in the Enterprise Manager Query dialog box. Select the Show Stats Time option from the Query Flags page of the Query Option dialog box (see Figure 22.9).

Figure 22.9.
Setting the Show Stats
Time query option.

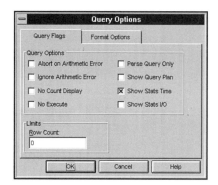

READING THE SHOWPLAN

The showplan provides insight about how SQL Server is going to process a SQL statement. If you know what to look for in a showplan, the information it provides can be useful for tuning queries.

Note

> Those new to SQL Server should not be dismayed by the jargon used in the showplan. For example, the showplan uses words such as SCALAR AGGREGATE. This is just a fancy way of saying that the query contains an aggregate function, such as AVG(), COUNT(), MAX(), MIN(), or SUM(). After you get past the lingo used by the showplan, you will find it a useful tool for optimizing queries.

A large amount of irrelevant information can be generated by a showplan. When you read a showplan, it is important to know what to look for. Use Table 22.1 to help weed out the irrelevant information.

Items in Table 22.1 that are considered irrelevant are those you cannot control. For example, if you use an aggregate function, such as COUNT(), the words SCALAR AGGREGATE or VECTOR AGGREGATE *always* appear in the showplan. Therefore, I consider SCALAR AGGREGATE and VECTOR AGGREGATE to be irrelevant to query tuning because no matter how you modify your indexes or revamp your query, the showplan includes these words.

TABLE 22.1. RELEVANT SHOWPLAN OUTPUT.

Text-Based Showplan Output	Relevant?	New to 6.5?
CONSTRAINT: nested iteration	Yes	Yes
EXISTS TABLE : nested iteration	No	
FROM TABLE	Yes	
FULL OUTER JOIN: nested iteration	No	
GROUP BY WITH CUBE	No	Yes
GROUP BY WITH ROLLUP	No	Yes
GROUP BY	No	
Index : <index name>	Yes	
LEFT OUTER JOIN: nested iteration	No	Yes
Nested iteration	No	
SCALAR AGGREGATE	No	
STEP n	Yes	
Table Scan	Yes	
The type of query is DELETE	No	
The type of query is INSERT	No	
The type of query is SELECT (into a worktable)	Yes	
The type of query is SELECT	No	

Text-Based Showplan Output	Relevant?	New to 6.5?
The type of query is UPDATE	No	
The update mode is deferred	Yes	
The update mode is direct	Yes	
This step involves sorting	Yes	
TO TABLE	No	
UNION ALL	No	Yes
Using Clustered Index	Yes	
Using Dynamic Index	Yes	
Using GETSORTED	Yes	
VECTOR AGGREGATE	No	
Worktable	No	
Worktable created for DISTINCT	No	
Worktable created for ORDER BY	Yes	
Worktable created for REFORMATTING	Yes	
Worktable created for SELECT_INTO	No	

The following sections explain showplan output.

CONSTRAINT: nested iteration

What it means: The query modified data in a table that contains a constraint.

Tip: Use this output to view constraints that are being executed behind the scenes. For example, if you use constraints to enforce declarative referential integrity (DRI), you will see this output when you use INSERT to insert a new record into a table that contains a constraint. If your query is slow to execute and you see this output, you may want to review the indexes used to support the DRI.

Relevant: Yes

EXISTS TABLE : nested iteration

What it means: The query contains an EXISTS, IN, or ANY clause.

Tip: Ignore this output.

Relevant: No

FROM TABLE

What it means: The source of the data for the query.

Tips: Use this output to determine the order in which the optimizer is joining the tables. On complex table joins (usually more than four tables), you can sometimes improve performance by rearranging the order of the tables in the FROM clause and the WHERE clause. To force the optimizer to follow the table order in the FROM clause, you must use the SET FORCEPLAN command.

Relevant: Yes

FULL OUTER JOIN: nested iteration

What it means: The query contains a FULL JOIN clause.

Tip: Ignore this output.

Relevant: No

GROUP BY WITH CUBE

What it means: The query contains a GROUP BY and a WITH CUBE clause.

Tip: Ignore this output.

Relevant: No

GROUP BY WITH ROLLUP

What it means: The query contains a GROUP BY and a ROLLUP clause.

Tip: Ignore this output.

Relevant: No

GROUP BY

What it means: The query contains a GROUP BY clause.

Tip: Ignore this output.

Relevant: No

Index: *<index name>*

What it means: The optimizer found a useful nonclustered index to retrieve the rows.

Tips: Generally speaking, a query that uses an index runs faster than a query that does not use an index. An exception to this rule is a table with a small number of rows. In this scenario, performing a table scan may be faster than using an index; however, the optimal access plan always depends on the number of rows and columns in the table being accessed.

Relevant: Yes

A DISCUSSION ABOUT COMPOUND INDEXES

A *compound index* is an index made up of more than one column. The rules regarding compound index optimization sometimes cause confusion. The source of the confusion stems from when SQL Server takes advantage of the index and when it cannot use the index.

Following is the structure of a table that will be used for this discussion:

```
Table:
CREATE TABLE table1
        (col1 int not null,
        col2 int not null,
        col3 int not null,
        description char(50) null)
Primary Key:
col1 + col2 + col3
Index:
CREATE UNIQUE CLUSTERED INDEX table1_idx ON table1(col1,col2,col3)
Number of rows:
1000
```

When working with a large table, the optimizer takes advantage of the compound index when one of the following is true:

- ◆ All columns in the index are referenced in the WHERE clause and contain useful search arguments.
- ◆ The first column in the index is referenced in the WHERE clause with a useful search argument.

For example, the following queries can take advantage of the compound index:

```
SELECT *
        FROM table1
        WHERE col1 = 100
        and col2 = 250
        and col3 = 179
```

```
SELECT *
        FROM table1
        WHERE col1 = 100
        and col2 = 250

SELECT *
        FROM table1
        WHERE col1 = 100

SELECT *
        FROM table1
        WHERE col1 = 100
        and col3 = 250
```

The following queries *cannot* take advantage of the compound index:

```
SELECT *
        FROM table1
        WHERE col2 = 100
        and col3 = 250

SELECT *
        FROM table1
        WHERE col2 = 100

SELECT *
        FROM table1
        WHERE col3 = 100
```

LEFT OUTER JOIN: nested iteration

What it means: The query contains a LEFT JOIN clause.

Tip: Ignore this output.

Relevant: No

Nested Iteration

What it means: The default approach for queries with WHERE criteria or table joins.

Tip: Ignore this output.

Relevant: No

SCALAR AGGREGATE

What it means: The query contains an aggregate function—AVG(), COUNT(), MAX(), MIN(), or SUM()—and does not contain a GROUP BY clause.

Tip: Ignore this output.

Relevant: No

STEP *n*

What it means: Specifies the number of steps required to process the query. Every query has at least one step.

Tips: Fewer steps means better performance. The GROUP BY clause always requires at least two steps.

Relevant: Yes

Table Scan

What it means: Each row in the table is processed.

Tips: Look out for this plan on large tables. It may slow down your query because each row in the table is processed, which can lead to a lot of I/O. To avoid a table scan, try to build a useful index that matches the WHERE clause.

On small tables, the optimizer may choose to ignore an index and perform a table scan. For small tables, a table scan may process faster than using an index to retrieve the data. On very large tables, you want to avoid table scans.

Relevant: Yes

A DISCUSSION ABOUT TABLE SCAN

The table scan is dreaded when you are working with large tables in an OLTP (online transaction processing) environment. It can lead to poor performance and result in table blocking.

The following example shows the difference in showplans for a retrieval based on a table scan and a retrieval that can use an index. The first listing shows the showplan for a table without an index:

```
Table:
CREATE TABLE sales
          (sales_id int not null,
           descr char(50) null)
Primary Key: sales_id
Indexes: None
Row Count: 1,000,000
Query:
SELECT * FROM sales
          WHERE sales_id = 450
Showplan:
STEP 1
The type of query is SELECT
FROM TABLE
sales
Nested iteration
Table Scan
```

Figure 22.10.
A table scan on a
1,000,000-row table.

Query: SELECT * FROM sales

            WHERE sales_id = 450

SQL Server:
Look at row #1 for sales_id = 450
Look at row #2 for sales_id = 450
....
Look at row #999,999 for sales_id = 450
Look at row #1,000,000 for sales_id = 450

} This occurs
  one million times!

Now consider the inefficiencies involved with a table scan. The user wants only one row returned from the table, but the server had to process *every row* in the table (see Figure 22.10).

To prevent the table scan in this example, create a clustered index on the column `sales_id`. By creating the index, the optimizer can generate a showplan that directly accesses the data without having to look at each row of data (see Figure 22.11). This will significantly improve performance.

```
Index:
CREATE UNIQUE CLUSTERED INDEX sales_idx ON sales(sales_id)
Showplan:
The type of query is SELECT
FROM TABLE
sales
Nested iteration
Using Clustered Index
```

Figure 22.11.
Using a clustered index
to find data on a
1,000,000-row table.

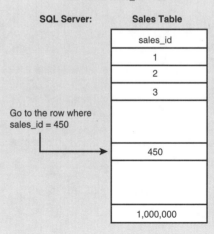

Query: SELECT * FROM sales

            WHERE sales_id = 450

SQL Server: **Sales Table**

sales_id
1
2
3
450
1,000,000

Go to the row where
sales_id = 450

The type of query is SELECT

What it means: The query contains a SELECT clause.

Tip: Ignore this output.

Relevant: No

The type of query is INSERT

What it means: The query contains an INSERT clause; alternatively, a worktable must be used to process the query.

Tip: Ignore this output.

Relevant: No

The type of query is UPDATE

What it means: The query contains an UPDATE clause; alternatively, a worktable must be used to process the query.

Tip: Ignore this output.

Relevant: No

The type of query is DELETE

What it means: The query contains a DELETE clause; alternatively, a worktable must be used to process the query.

Tip: Ignore this output.

Relevant: No

The type of query is SELECT (into a worktable)

What it means: The optimizer decided that a temporary worktable should be built to efficiently process the query. A worktable is always created when a GROUP BY clause is used; a worktable is sometimes generated when an ORDER BY clause is used.

Tips: A *worktable* is an actual table created in the tempdb database. Worktables can degrade performance because they involve additional disk I/O. When the process is complete, the worktable is automatically deleted. A worktable is unavoidable when using a GROUP BY clause.

Relevant: Yes

The update mode is deferred

What it means: Two passes are required to update the data. The first pass generates a log of the changes and the second pass applies the changes. UPDATE, DELETE, and INSERT statements can generate this plan.

Tip: Update deferred is slower than update direct (see the following sidebar for more information).

Relevant: Yes

Update mode is deferred VERSUS Update mode is direct

The update mode is often overlooked when people try to tune queries. By tweaking your table definition, indexes, and SQL statements, you can improve the performance of your UPDATE, INSERT, and DELETE statements.

It is important to determine the type of update mode being used because a deferred update is always slower than a direct update. When a deferred update is used, SQL Server takes two passes to update the data. The first pass generates a log of the changes and the second pass applies the changes. A direct update does not generate a log; instead, it directly applies the changes.

Following is a list of requirements for SQL Server to run a direct update:

◆ The column containing the clustered index cannot be updated.

◆ The table being updated cannot contain an UPDATE trigger.

◆ The table being updated cannot be marked for replication.

The following rules apply to single-row updates:

◆ If the column being modified is variable length, the new row must fit on the same page as the old row.

◆ When updating a column that is part of a nonunique, nonclustered index, the column must be a fixed-length column. If the column being updated is part of a unique nonclustered index, the column must be fixed length and have an exact match in the WHERE clause.

◆ The modified row size must not differ from the original row size by more than 50 percent.

> The following rules apply to multiple-row updates:
> - The column being modified must be fixed length.
> - The column being modified must not be part of a unique nonclustered index.
> - If the column is part of a nonunique clustered index, it must be fixed length; otherwise, the update is deferred.
> - The table must not contain a `timestamp` datatype.

The update mode is direct

What it means: The data can be directly updated. UPDATE, DELETE, INSERT, and SELECT INTO statements can generate this plan.

Tip: Update direct is always faster than update deferred (see the preceding sidebar, "Update mode is deferred versus Update mode is direct," for more information).

Relevant: Yes

This step involves sorting

What it means: The query contains a DISTINCT or ORDER BY clause. To process the query, a worktable is created to sort the data.

Tips: This step is unavoidable if the query contains the DISTINCT clause. If the query contains the ORDER BY clause, you may be able to eliminate this step by creating a useful index.

Relevant: Yes

TO TABLE

What it means: The target table for data modifications. UPDATE, DELETE, INSERT, and SELECT INTO statements can generate this plan.

Tip: Ignore this output.

Relevant: No

UNION ALL

What it means: The query references a view that contains a UNION ALL clause.

Tips: Ignore this output.

Relevant: No

Using Clustered Index

What it means: The optimizer decided to use a clustered index to retrieve the record.

Tips: When working with a large table and retrieving a single record, the use of a clustered index is usually the fastest and easiest strategy to implement for data retrieval.

Relevant: Yes

Using Dynamic Index

What it means: The optimizer decided to build a temporary index to help process the query. This strategy is chosen when the query contains an OR clause or an IN clause.

Tips: A dynamic index is usually faster than a table scan on a large table, but slower than using an existing index. You may be able to avoid this step by creating a permanent index. Use the OR and IN clauses judiciously on large tables—more I/O is required to process the query.

Relevant: Yes

Using GETSORTED

What it means: The query contains a DISTINCT or ORDER BY clause. To handle the sort, a worktable will be created.

Tips: This step is unavoidable if the query contains the DISTINCT clause. If the query contains the ORDER BY clause, you may be able to eliminate this step by creating a useful index.

Relevant: Yes

VECTOR AGGREGATE

What it means: The query contains an aggregate function and a GROUP BY clause. Aggregate functions are AVG(), COUNT(), MAX(), MIN(), and SUM().

Tip: Ignore this output.

Relevant: No

Worktable

What it means: The optimizer decided that a worktable must be created to process the query.

Tips: The use of a worktable requires additional overhead, which can decrease performance. A GROUP BY clause always generates a worktable, so don't spend any time trying to get rid of the worktable if your query has a GROUP BY clause.

Relevant: Yes

Worktable created for DISTINCT

What it means: The query contains the DISTINCT clause. A worktable is always used when the query contains the DISTINCT clause.

Tip: Ignore this output.

Relevant: No

Worktable created for ORDER BY

What it means: The query contains an ORDER BY clause. The optimizer could not find a suitable index to handle the sort.

Tip: Evaluate your indexing strategy. An index may help eliminate this step.

Relevant: Yes

A DISCUSSION ABOUT Worktable Created for ORDER BY

If the ORDER BY clause is generating a worktable, you can use the following strategies to help eliminate the need for a worktable:

- ◆ Sort on the column(s) that contain the clustered index. Doing so always eliminates the need for a worktable. With a clustered index, the data is physically stored in sorted order; therefore, a worktable isn't required to handle the sort.
- ◆ Sort on a column that contains a nonclustered index. This may or may not eliminate the worktable. The optimizer looks at the cost of performing a table scan versus the cost of using the nonclustered index; the optimizer chooses the nonclustered index if the cost is less than the cost of a table scan.

Worktable created for REFORMATTING

What it means: This strategy is used when large tables are joined on columns that do not have useful indexes. The table with the fewest number of rows is inserted into a worktable. Then the worktable is used to join back to the other tables in the query. This reduces the amount of I/O required to process the query.

Tips: This is an easy one to fix! Whenever the optimizer chooses this strategy, look at your indexes. Chances are good that indexes do not exist or that the statistics are out of date. Add indexes to the columns you are joining on or issue an UPDATE STATISTICS command. The optimizer uses this strategy only as a last resort. Try to avoid this strategy.

Relevant: Yes

Worktable created for SELECT_INTO

What it means: The query contains the SELECT..INTO clause. A worktable is always created when SELECT..INTO is used.

Tip: Ignore this output.

Relevant: No

OVERRIDING THE OPTIMIZER

Use the following features to override the optimizer:

◆ Index hints
◆ The SET FORCEPLAN ON command

INDEX HINTS

New to SQL Server 6.x is the capability to override the optimizer. Now you can force the optimizer into using an index or force it to not choose an index.

You usually want to let the optimizer determine how to process the query. However, you may find it beneficial to override the optimizer if you find that it is not taking advantage of useful indexes. Following is the syntax used to override the optimizer:

```
SELECT ...
FROM [table_name] (optimizer_hint)
```

In this syntax, *optimizer_hint* has the following format:

```
INDEX={index_name | index_id}
```

In this format, *index_name* is any valid name of an existing index on the table. *index_id* is 0 or 1; 0 forces the optimizer to perform a table scan and 1 forces the optimizer to use a clustered index.

To force the optimizer to use a clustered index, use the following command:

```
select *
from authors (1)
where au_id = '213-46-8915'
```

To force the optimizer to perform a table scan, use the following command:

```
select *
from authors (0)
where au_id = '213-46-8915'
```

To force the optimizer to use the au_fname_idx nonclustered index, use the following command:

```
select *
from authors (INDEX = au_fname_idx)
where au_fname = 'Marjorie'
```

Tip

> Use the capability to override the optimizer with prudence. Only in cases where SQL Server is choosing a less-than-optimal execution plan should the optimizer be overridden.

THE SET FORCEPLAN ON COMMAND

The SET FORCEPLAN ON command forces the optimizer to join tables based on the order specified in the FROM clause. Normally, you want to let the optimizer determine the order in which to join tables; however, if you think that the optimizer is selecting an inefficient join order, you can use SET FORCEPLAN ON to force the join order.

When forcing SQL Server to use a predefined join order, you usually want the table with the fewest number of qualifying rows to come first in the FROM clause (or the table with the least amount of I/O, if you are dealing with a very wide or a very narrow table). The table with the second lowest number of qualifying rows should be next in the FROM clause, and so on.

The following example shows how SET FORCEPLAN ON can impact query optimization:

```
SET FORCEPLAN ON
select *
from  titleauthor , authors
where titleauthor.au_id = authors.au_id
SET FORCEPLAN OFF
```

22

UNDERSTANDING THE QUERY OPTIMIZER

The following is showplan output with SET FORCEPLAN ON:

```
STEP 1
The type of query is SELECT
FROM TABLE
titleauthor
Nested iteration
Table Scan
FROM TABLE
authors
JOINS WITH
titleauthor
Nested iteration
Table Scan
```

Notice that, with SET FORCEPLAN ON, the optimizer processes the titleauthor table before processing the authors table.

Following is the query:

```
select *
from  titleauthor , authors
where titleauthor.au_id = authors.au_id
```

Here is the showplan output:

```
STEP 1
The type of query is SELECT
FROM TABLE
authors
Nested iteration
Table Scan
FROM TABLE
titleauthor
JOINS WITH
authors
Nested iteration
Table Scan
```

Notice that, without using SET FORCEPLAN ON, the optimizer processes the authors table before processing the titleauthor table.

Tip

Whenever you use SET FORCEPLAN ON, be sure that you turn it off by issuing SET FORCEPLAN OFF. The feature remains in effect for your current connection until the connection is broken or until it is explicitly turned off.

Caution

Use the SET FORCEPLAN ON option as a last resort. You usually want to let the optimizer determine the order in which to process tables.

OTHER TUNING TRICKS

Whenever you try to optimize a query, you should be on the lookout for obstructions that can lead to poor performance. The following sections discuss common causes of poor query performance.

ARE YOU TRYING TO TUNE AN UPDATE, DELETE, OR INSERT QUERY?

If you are trying to tune an UPDATE, DELETE, or INSERT query, does the table have a trigger? The query may be okay, but the trigger may need improvement. An easy way to determine whether the trigger is the bottleneck is to drop the trigger and rerun the query. If query performance improves, you should tune the trigger.

DOES THE QUERY REFERENCE A VIEW?

If the query references a view, you should test the view to determine whether it is optimized. An easy way to test whether the view is optimized is to run a showplan on the view.

ARE THE DATATYPES MISMATCHED?

If you are joining on columns of different datatypes, the optimizer may not be able to use useful indexes. Instead, it may have to choose a table scan to process the query, as in the following example:

```
Table:
CREATE TABLE table1
(col1 char(10) not null)
Index: CREATE INDEX col1_idx ON table1(col1)
Row Count: 1000
Table:
CREATE TABLE table2
(col1 integer not null)
Index: CREATE INDEX col1_idx ON table2(col1)
Row Count: 1000
Query:
SELECT *
FROM table1, table2
WHERE table1.col1 = convert(char(10),table2.col1)
and table1.col1 = '100'
```

This query results in a table scan on table2 because you are joining a char(10) column to an integer column with the convert() function. Internally, SQL Server must convert these values to process the query, which results in a table scan. To avoid this problem, maintain consistency within your database design.

Mismatched datatypes can also cause an UPDATE to be deferred instead of being direct.

22

UNDERSTANDING THE QUERY OPTIMIZER

DOES THE QUERY USE A NONSEARCH ARGUMENT?

Nonsearch arguments force the optimizer to process the query with a table scan. This is because the search value is unknown until runtime.

Following are some common examples of queries that use nonsearch arguments and how to convert them to search arguments that can take advantage of an index:

```
Table:
CREATE TABLE table1
(col1 int not null)
Index: CREATE UNIQUE CLUSTERED INDEX col1_idx ON table1(col1)
Row Count: 1000 rows
```

Following is a nonsearch argument query:

```
select *
from table1
where col1 * 10 = 100
```

Following is a search argument query:

```
select *
from table1
where col1 = 100/10
```

Following is a nonsearch argument query:

```
select *
from table1
where convert(char(8),col1) =  '10'
```

Following is a search argument query:

```
select *
from table1
where col1 =  convert(int,'10')
```

Tip

One way to help reduce the use of a nonsearch argument is to keep the table column on the left side of the equation and to keep the search criteria on the right side of the equation.

DOES THE QUERY USE MORE THAN ONE AGGREGATE FUNCTION?

If your query has more than one aggregate function in the SELECT clause, it may be forced to perform a table scan *regardless* of available indexes. The following query uses the two aggregate functions, MIN() and MAX():

```
Table:
CREATE TABLE table1
(id int not null)
Index: CREATE UNIQUE CLUSTERED INDEX id_idx ON table1(id)
Query:
SELECT MIN(id),MAX(id)
FROM table1
```

If you find that a table scan is being performed, you can rewrite the query by using a subquery in the SELECT statement, as in the next example. This query avoids a table scan by searching the index for both the MIN and MAX aggregate requests:

```
SELECT MIN(ID), (SELECT MAX(ID) FROM TABLE1) FROM TABLE1
```

ARE YOU TRYING TO OPTIMIZE A STORED PROCEDURE?

If you are trying to optimize a stored procedure, you *must* keep in mind the following rules:

◆ A stored procedure's query plan is stored in memory when the stored procedure is first executed. If you add an index after the query plan has been generated, it may not be used by the stored procedure. Whenever you make changes to the tables used by a stored procedure, and the stored procedure does not contain the WITH RECOMPILE statement, *always* use sp_recompile or drop and re-create the stored procedure. Doing so is the only way to ensure that the optimizer has reevaluated the query plan.

Note

> A stored procedure automatically recompiles its query plan whenever you drop an index used by a table within a stored procedure.

◆ Parameters used in the WHERE clause of a stored procedure may produce inconsistent query plans. As mentioned in the preceding rule, a stored procedure saves its query plan in memory. If the first execution of the procedure uses an atypical parameter, the optimizer may place in memory a query plan that is not advantageous for your typical parameter. This may degrade performance when you execute the stored procedure with a typical parameter. Look at the following example:

```
CREATE PROCEDURE usp_example @search_name char(50) AS
SELECT au_lname
FROM authors
WHERE au_lname like @search_name + '%'
Index: CREATE INDEX au_lname_idx ON authors(au_lname)
```

Consider what happens when a user executes the query with 'B' as a parameter:

```
EXEC usp_example 'B'
```

If the table contains numerous records that have a last name beginning with the letter *B*, the optimizer is likely to perform a table scan.

Now consider what happens when a user executes the query with 'BREAULT' as a parameter:

```
EXEC usp_example 'BREAULT'
```

If the table contains only a few records that have a last name equal to *BREAULT*, the optimizer is likely to use an index.

As you can see, the optimizer chooses different query plans based on the value of the parameter passed into the stored procedure. The problem arises when the first query plan is stored in memory. By default, different users receive the same query plan based on the first execution of the stored procedure. If the first user of the stored procedure passed 'B' as a parameter, the query plan would be very inefficient for other users who specify 'BREAULT' as a parameter.

To avoid this problem, use the WITH RECOMPILE option when you execute the procedure. This forces the procedure to regenerate its query plan, as in the following:

```
EXEC ... WITH RECOMPILE
```

The revised query plan is available only for the current execution of the procedure. Subsequent executions of the procedure without the recompile option revert back to the old query plan.

Additionally, you can use the WITH RECOMPILE option when you create the procedure, as in the following:

```
CREATE PROCEDURE ... WITH RECOMPILE
```

This option forces the optimizer to recompile the query plan each time the stored procedure is executed.

BETWEEN THE LINES

Following are some important notes to remember when working with the query optimizer:

◆ You must understand SQL Server's optimizer to get maximum query performance.

◆ Don't forget to use UPDATE STATISTICS.

◆ Keep in mind the following questions when you are trying to tune a query. Any questions you answer with *no* should be used as a starting point for tuning your query:

  ◆ Have useful indexes been created?

  ◆ Have the statistics been updated recently?

  ◆ Does the query use search arguments?

  ◆ Does the query join columns of the same datatype?

◆ Query optimization is part science, part luck. What works on one query may not work on another query. Try different techniques until you get the performance you expect.

◆ Use the showplan, Statistics I/O, No Execute, and Stats Time tools to help tune a query.

◆ The top three items to look for in a showplan are `Table Scan`, `Using Clustered Index`, and `Index: <index name>`.

◆ If you demand OLTP performance, do everything you can to prevent a table scan on a large table.

◆ Use index hints to force the optimizer to use or not use an index.

◆ Stored procedures that do not contain the `WITH RECOMPILE` statement should be recompiled after you make an index change to a table used by the stored procedure.

SUMMARY

A good DBA knows how the SQL Server optimizer works. This knowledge enables the DBA to turn an agonizingly slow query into a fast query. Consequently, knowledge of the optimizer can keep the DBA from creating needless indexes that are never used by the system. The next chapter discusses multi-user considerations.

CHAPTER 23

by Orryn Sledge

Multi-User
Considerations

How many times have you seen an application that works with a single user but when multiple users access the application, all sorts of performance and data problems occur? When these types of problems arise, it usually is up to the DBA to fix them. You have probably heard that SQL Server is a high-performance database capable of handling 100 or more users. That is a true statement. But to extract maximum performance and data consistency in a multi-user environment, you must understand how SQL Server manages transactions. Otherwise, performance and data consistency will suffer. To help you avoid these problems, the topics discussed in this chapter explain how to design multi-user databases that maximize transaction throughput while maintaining data consistency.

LOCKS

SQL Server uses *locks* to maintain data consistency in a multi-user environment. Locking behavior is automatically handled by SQL Server; SQL version 6.x enables the DBA to control additional aspects of locking.

To help understand why locks are important, look at the banking example shown in Figure 23.1. Suppose that you decide to transfer $100 from checking to savings. Your bank decides to run a report that shows your combined balance for checking and savings. What happens if the report is run while the transfer is in progress? Would the report show a balance of $200 or $100?

The answer resides in how SQL Server uses locks to maintain data consistency. When transaction 1 is initiated, SQL Server places a lock on the checking account information and on the savings account information. These locks force other users to wait until the locks are released before they can access the data. This prevents users from reading incomplete or pending changes. Therefore, when the transaction is complete, the report is allowed to access the account data, thus reporting the correct balance of $200.

Note

When pending changes can be read by a transaction, it is known as a *dirty read*. By default, SQL Server prevents dirty reads.

Without locks, the report might have showed a balance of $100, which is incorrect. For example, if the report read the data after the $100 was subtracted from checking but before it was added to savings, the report would show a combined balance of $100.

Figure 23.1.
How locks maintain
data consistency.

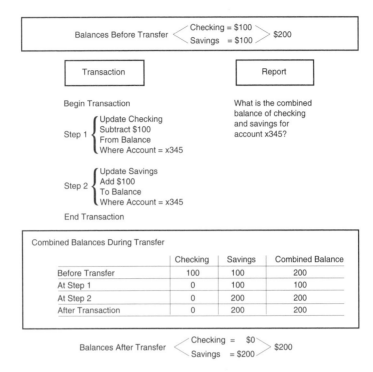

UNDERSTANDING SQL SERVER'S LOCKING BEHAVIOR

If locks are automatically handled by SQL Server you may wonder, "Why are we having this discussion?" The answer is *blocking* and *deadlocks*. Whenever multiple users try to access or modify the same data, the potential for blocking and deadlocks increases.

By understanding SQL Server's locking behavior, you can decrease the likelihood of blocking and deadlocks.

Following are some of the variables that can impact the frequency of blocking and deadlocks:

◆ Transaction management
◆ Query implementation
◆ Indexing scheme
◆ Table design
◆ Hardware configuration

BLOCKING

Blocking occurs when a process must wait for another process to complete. The process must wait because the resources it needs are exclusively used by another process. A blocked process resumes operation after the resources are released by the other process.

For this example, assume that the bank decides to eliminate the monthly service charge for all existing customers (see Figure 23.2). Therefore, the DBA sets the service_charge to $0.00 for all accounts. Not being a good DBA, he runs this transaction during prime hours. This forces transactions 2, 3, and 4 to wait until transaction 1 is complete. The waiting transactions are considered to be *blocked* by transaction 1.

Figure 23.2.
A blocking example.

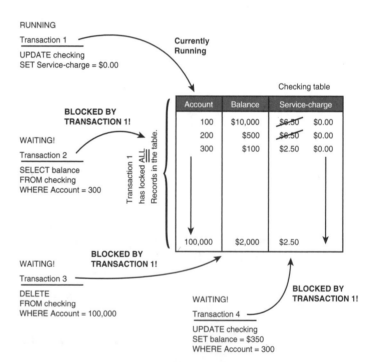

When blocking occurs, it looks like your machine is hung. What has happened is that SQL Server has put your process in a holding queue. The process remains in the queue until it can acquire the resources it needs to complete its tasks.

BLOCKING PROBLEMS

I once was thrown into a project that involved converting a mainframe application to SQL Server. Management was eager to convert the application quickly. They did not want any time spent on table design or index strategy. I tried to explain to them that their existing database design could lead to blocking.

The day the application went into production was a prime example of how blocking can impact a system. Whenever certain components of the application were run, the transaction processing component of the application would halt because of blocking.

The reason the blocking was so severe was because of poor table design and index strategy. The main table used by the application was not properly normalized, thus making it very wide. Very wide tables can substantially slow processing throughput. Additionally, the table lacked any useful indexes. The combination of these factors is a sure-fire way to generate massive blocking.

After management realized what had happened, they were willing to allocate the resources to go back and redesign the table schema and reevaluate the index strategy. After the redesign, the blocking problem went away and the application could be used without impacting the transaction processing aspect of the application.

DEADLOCK

Deadlock occurs when two users have locks on separate objects and each user is trying to lock the other user's objects. SQL Server automatically detects and breaks the deadlock. It terminates the process that has used the least amount of CPU time. This enables the other user's transaction to continue processing. The terminated transaction is automatically rolled back and an error code 1205 is issued.

Figure 23.3 shows an example of a deadlock. Assume that transaction 1 and transaction 2 begin at the exact same time. By default, SQL Server automatically places exclusive locks on data that is being updated. This causes transaction 1 to wait for transaction 2 to complete—but transaction 2 has to wait for transaction 1 to complete. This is classic deadlock. To resolve the deadlock, SQL Server automatically terminates one of the transactions.

Figure 23.3.
An example of
deadlock.

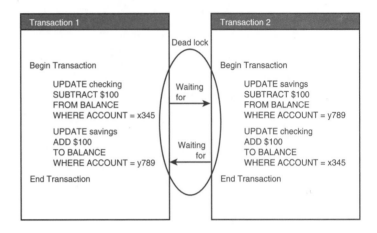

VIEWING LOCKS AND BLOCKING

The following utilities are provided by SQL Server to view locks:

Current Activity dialog box The Current Activity dialog box in the
Enterprise Manager provides graphical
lock and blocking information (see Figure 23.4).

Figure 23.4.
Viewing locks from the
Current Activity dialog
box in the Enterprise
Manager.

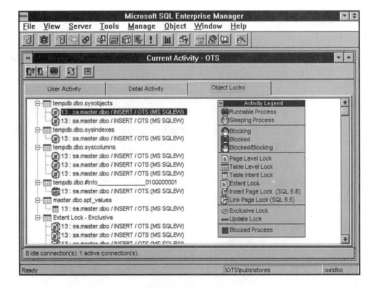

sp_lock

The system procedure `sp_lock` provides text-based lock information (see Figure 23.5).

Figure 23.5.
Sample output from
sp_lock.

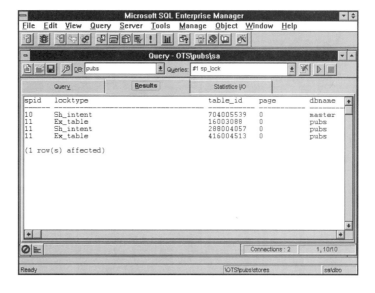

Performance Monitor

The Performance Monitor allows you to graphically track lock information (see Figure 23.6).

Figure 23.6.
Tracking locks with the
Performance Monitor.

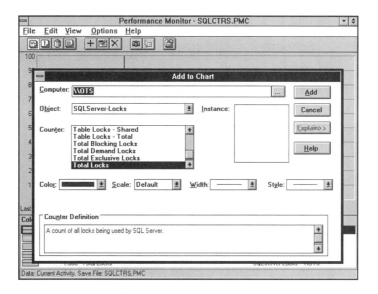

sp_who   The system procedure sp_who provides information about
blocked processes (see Figure 23.7).

Figure 23.7.
Sample output
from sp_who.

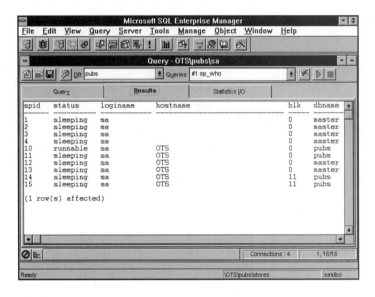

Trace flags   The trace flags shown in Table 23.1 provide extended insight
into locking behavior.

TABLE 23.1. USEFUL TRACE FLAGS.

Trace Flag	Output
1200	Displays process ID and types of locks being requested
1204	Displays locks in use with a deadlock and the command involved in the deadlock
1205	Displays information about the commands used during a deadlock

Tip

The trace flag 1200 can be useful for tracking locking behavior. The
easiest way to use the trace flag is to use the DBCC traceon() function.
You also must turn on trace flag 3604 to echo trace information to the
client workstation, as in the following example:

```
DBCC traceon(3604)
 DBCC traceon(1200)
 UPDATE t_1
 SET c_1 = 0
```

> The following is sample output from DBCC trace flag 1200:
>
> ```
> Process 11 requesting page lock of type SH_PAGE on 7 25
> Process 11 releasing page lock of type SH_PAGE on 7 25
> Process 11 releasing page lock of type SH_PAGE on 7 26
> Process 11 requesting table lock of type EX_TAB on 7 80003316
> Process 11 clearing all pss locks
> ```

ROW-LEVEL LOCKING

For years, users have complained about SQL Server's lack of row-level locking capabilities. Until version 6.5, all locking was done at the page level (a 2K unit of data). The problem with a page-level locking mechanism surfaces when multiple records exist on the same page and multiple processes must access information on the same page. If the page is locked by a process, other processes must wait to access the data.

Version 6.5

To help resolve the issues associated with page-level locking, SQL Server 6.5 *kinda* has row-level locking. The reason I say it *kinda* has row-level locking is because row-level locking is possible only for INSERT operations *and* it must be enabled on a table-by-table basis. In SQL Server 6.5, row-level locking is off by default.

Therefore, you can gain a limited amount of functionality (reduced blocking and the potential for improved INSERT performance) by using row-level locking. Because row-level locking works only with the INSERT statement, it is best suited for tables that meet the following criteria:

◆ A table that contains a unique clustered index based on a counter-type key (for example, an identity column or a column that contains a counter)

◆ A table that does not contain any indexes or a table that contains only nonclustered indexes

To implement row-level locking, use the sp_tableoption system procedure. Following is the syntax for sp_tableoption:

```
sp_tableoption @TableNamePattern  [, '@OptionName'] [, '@OptionValue']
```

For example, to enable row-level locking for all tables in the pubs database, use the following syntax:

```
use pubs
go
EXECUTE sp_tableoption '%.%', 'insert row lock', 'true'
```

23

MULTI-USER CONSIDERATIONS

Note

When you enable row-level locking for all tables in a database, you enable row-level locking for only the currently defined tables in the database. If you add another table to your database and you want to enable row-level locking for that table, you must explicitly configure the table to use row-level locking by using the `sp_tableoption` system procedure.

To enable row-level locking for the `authors` table, use the following syntax:

```
use pubs
go
EXECUTE sp_tableoption 'authors', 'insert row lock', 'true'
```

To disable row-level locking for the `authors` table, use the following syntax:

```
use pubs
go
EXECUTE sp_tableoption 'authors', 'insert row lock', 'false'
```

To view the row-level lock status for all the tables in a database, use the following syntax:

```
EXECUTE sp_tableoption '%.%', 'insert row lock'
```

Caution

Row-level locking can lead to deadlocks if you enable row-level locking on a table and then perform a large number of concurrent INSERT statements followed by an UPDATE statement within a transaction. The deadlock results from contention for the data within the transaction. The following example may lead to deadlock:

```
begin transaction

    /* insert a record */
    INSERT INTO stores (stor_id, stor_name, stor_address, city, state, zip)
    VALUES ('234','some_store_name','some_store_addr','some_city',
    'VA','11111')

    /* update the record we just inserted */
    UPDATE stores
    SET stor_name = 'new_store_name'
    WHERE stor_id = '234'

commit transaction
```

To minimize the risk of deadlock, either disable row-level locking for the table being modified or revise your code to eliminate the update to the record that was just inserted within a transaction.

LOCKING DETAILS

Now that you know why it is important to understand SQL Server's locking behavior and how you can view active locks, you need to get into the nuts and bolts of locking.

Any transaction that reads or modifies data (SELECT, INSERT, DELETE, UPDATE, CREATE INDEX, and so on) generates some type of lock. The degree of locking is determined by the following two questions:

- ◆ Is the data being modified or read?
- ◆ How many rows are being accessed or modified?

To answer these questions, you must look at the two levels of physical locks: page locks and table locks.

PAGE LOCKS

A *page lock* is a lock on a 2K data page. Whenever possible, SQL Server attempts to use a page lock rather than a table lock. Page locks are preferred over table locks because they are less likely to block other processes. There are three main types of page locks:

- ◆ **Shared.** A *shared* page lock is used for read transactions (typically SELECT statements). If a page is marked as shared, other transactions can still read the page. A shared lock must be released before an exclusive page lock can be acquired. Shared locks are released after the page has been read, except when HOLDLOCK is specified. HOLDLOCK forces the page to remain locked until the transaction is complete.
- ◆ **Exclusive.** An *exclusive* lock is used for write transactions (typically INSERT, UPDATE, or DELETE statements). Other transactions must wait for the exclusive page lock to be released before they can read or write to the page.
- ◆ **Update.** When an UPDATE or DELETE statement is initially processed, SQL Server places update locks on the pages being read. It then escalates the update locks to exclusive locks before it modifies the data.

Tip

Typically, read statements acquire shared locks and data modification statements acquire exclusive locks.

TABLE LOCKS

A *table lock* occurs when the entire table (data and indexes) is locked. When this happens, SQL Server has detected that it is faster to process the transaction by locking the table rather than incurring the overhead of locking numerous pages.

SQL Server usually begins the transaction by placing page locks on the data being accessed. By default, if more than 200 pages are acquired within a transaction, SQL Server automatically escalates the page locks into a table lock.

Note

The 200-page limit can be overridden with SQL Server 6.x. See the topic "Lock Escalation" in the "Multi-User Configuration Options" section of this chapter for more information.

The drawback of table locking is that it increases the likelihood of blocking. When other transactions try to access or modify information in a locked table, they must wait for the table lock to be released before proceeding. There are three main types of table locks:

◆ **Shared.** A *shared* table lock differs from a shared page lock in that the lock is at the table level and not at the page level.

◆ **Exclusive.** An *exclusive* table lock differs from an exclusive page lock in that the lock is at the table level and not at the page level. ***Tip:*** In a multi-user environment, you should avoid exclusive table locks during normal processing hours. An exclusive table lock on a commonly used table usually leads to blocking.

◆ **Intent.** An *intent* table lock occurs when SQL Server has the intention of acquiring an exclusive or shared table lock. SQL Server uses intent locks to keep other transactions from placing exclusive table locks on the table in which it is currently processing.

Table 23.2 summarizes the different types of locks that can be placed on an object.

TABLE 23.2. OBJECT LOCK SUMMARY.

Object	Lock Type
Page	Shared
	Exclusive
	Update
Table	Shared
	Exclusive
	Intent

PAGE AND TABLE LOCK SUMMARY

Table 23.3 summarizes the different types of page and table locks used by SQL Server. When viewing Table 23.3, look at the different locking strategies when indexes are used. When a useful index is present, SQL Server is less likely to choose a locking strategy that can lead to blocking.

TABLE 23.3. PAGE AND TABLE LOCK SUMMARY.

Using Index?	Syntax	Table Level Locks	Page Level Locks
N/A	INSERT	Exclusive intent	Exclusive page
Yes	SELECT	Shared intent	Shared page
Yes	SELECT with HOLDLOCK	Shared intent	Shared page
Yes	UPDATE	Exclusive intent	Update and exclusive
Yes	DELETE	Exclusive intent	Exclusive page
No	SELECT	Shared intent	Shared page
No	SELECT with HOLDLOCK	Shared table	None
No	UPDATE	Exclusive table	None
No	DELETE	Exclusive table	None
N/A	Create clustered index	Exclusive table	None
N/A	Create nonclustered index	Shared table	None

23

> *Note*
>
> Before version 6.x, you could run out of exclusive locks when building clustered indexes on large tables. This problem has been resolved with SQL Server 6.x.

TEN TIPS TO HELP MINIMIZE LOCKING AND PREVENT DEADLOCKS

Try using the tips in the following sections to resolve locking problems. These tips can help minimize locking problems and prevent deadlocks.

TIP 1: USE AN INDEX WITH UPDATE/DELETE STATEMENTS

Whenever you issue an UPDATE or DELETE statement that does *not* use an index, an exclusive table lock is used to process the transaction. The exclusive table lock may block other transactions.

To reduce the chance of an exclusive table lock, specify a WHERE clause that takes advantage of an existing index. This may enable SQL Server to use page level locks instead of an exclusive table lock.

TIP 2: CONVERT A LARGE INSERT STATEMENT INTO A SINGLE INSERT STATEMENT WITHIN A LOOP

Inserting a large number of rows into a table may result in an exclusive table lock (for example, INSERT INTO table2 SELECT * FROM table1). To avoid this problem, convert the INSERT statement into an INSERT statement within a loop. For example, the following code opens a cursor and then initiates a loop that fetches the data from table1 into a variable and then inserts the contents of the variable into table2. This approach decreases the likelihood of blocking because it generates exclusive page locks rather than an exclusive table lock. The drawback of this approach is that it runs slower than a batch INSERT.

```
declare @col1 varchar(11)
declare sample_cursor cursor
 for select col1 from table1
open sample_cursor
fetch next from sample_cursor into @col1
while @@fetch_status = 0
 begin
 insert into table2 values (@col1)
 fetch next from sample_cursor into @col1
 end
deallocate sample_cursor
```

TIP 3: AVOID USING HOLDLOCK

HOLDLOCK is one of the keywords that almost every developer new to SQL Server has tried to use. Quite often, the developer uses HOLDLOCK without fully understanding the ramifications behind it.

When HOLDLOCK is used with a SELECT statement, all shared locks (remember that shared locks are acquired whenever a SELECT is issued) remain in effect until the transaction is *complete*. This means additional locking overhead, which degrades performance and increases the likelihood of blocking or deadlocks. When the HOLDLOCK command is not used, SQL Server releases the shared locks as soon as possible rather than waiting for the transaction to complete.

What usually happens is that developers use the HOLDLOCK command, thinking that they can temporarily prevent other users from reading the same data. What they do not realize is that HOLDLOCK only generates shared locks, not exclusive locks. Because the locks are shared, other users can still read the same data values.

TIP 4: PLACE CLUSTERED INDEXES ON TABLES THAT HAVE A HIGH FREQUENCY OF INSERTS

Whenever you insert data into a table without a clustered index, you increase the risk of contention for the last data page. In a high-transaction environment with multiple users, this can lead to blocking.

Add a clustered index to your table to prevent this problem. By adding a clustered index, the inserted rows are distributed across multiple pages, reducing the likelihood of contention for the same page.

TIP 5: KEEP TRANSACTIONS SHORT

Long running transactions—especially data modification transactions—increase the likelihood of blocking and deadlocks. Whenever possible, try to keep the length of a transaction to a minimum. Following are suggestions to help decrease the length of a transaction:

- **Break long running transactions into multiple shorter running transactions.** Whenever you can reduce the duration of a lock, you can reduce the possibility of blocking. For this example, assume that table t_2 has 100 records with a sequential ID going from 1 to 100. The following is a long-running transaction:

```
INSERT INTO t_1
SELECT * FROM t_2
```

You can rewrite this long running transaction into two shorter transactions, reducing the duration of locks in use:

```
INSERT INTO t_1
SELECT * FROM t_2
WHERE t_2.id <= 50
INSERT INTO t_1
SELECT * FROM t_2
WHERE t_2.id > 50
```

- **Minimize nonclustered indexes.** Avoid unnecessary nonclustered indexes. Each index adds additional overhead that must be maintained whenever a record is inserted or deleted or whenever an indexed column is modified. This can decrease throughput.

- **Reduce the number of columns per table.** An INSERT processes faster on a narrow table (a table with few columns) than it can on a wide table (a

23

MULTI-USER CONSIDERATIONS

table with many columns). The reduction of the overall width of a table enables more rows to exist on a page. This means that fewer pages must be accessed to process the transaction, thus shortening transaction times.

TIP 6: UNDERSTAND TRANSACTIONS

Two common misunderstandings in using transactions are nested transactions and user interaction within a transaction.

NESTED TRANSACTIONS

Look at the approach taken in Figure 23.8. Do you see any problems with the code?

Figure 23.8.
A nested transaction:
the common (incorrect)
approach.

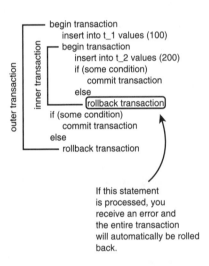

```
        begin transaction
            insert into t_1 values (100)
        begin transaction
            insert into t_2 values (200)
            if (some condition)
                commit transaction
            else
                rollback transaction
        if (some condition)
            commit transaction
        else
            rollback transaction
```

If this statement is processed, you receive an error and the entire transaction will automatically be rolled back.

The problem is with the rollback statement for the inner transaction. If the inner transaction is rolled back, you receive an error message and both INSERT transactions are automatically rolled back by SQL Server, with the following error message:

```
The commit transaction request has no corresponding BEGIN TRANSACTION.
```

To avoid the error message, use the SAVE TRANSACTION statement (see Figure 23.9).

Note

The COMMIT TRANSACTION statement must be issued after the ROLLBACK TRANSACTION INNER_TRANS statement.

Figure 23.9.
A nested transaction:
the correct approach.

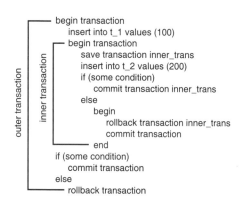

Now look at Figure 23.10. If the outer transaction is rolled back, do you think the inner transaction will also be rolled back? The answer is *yes*. SQL Server always rolls back the inner transaction when the outer transaction is rolled back, even though the inner transaction has been committed. This is how SQL Server handles nested transactions!

Figure 23.10.
The way in which SQL
Server handles nested
transactions.

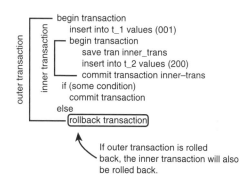

Note

In my experience as a DBA, the way SQL Server handles nested transactions is often contrary to what developers expect. Developers usually expect the inner transaction to *not* be rolled back because it has been committed. Make sure that your developers understand how SQL Server handles nested transactions.

Whenever you nest a transaction, all locks are held for the duration of the transaction (see Figure 23.11). This means that when the inner transaction is committed, its locks are not released until the outer transaction is committed. Be on the lookout for nested transactions; they increase the likelihood of blocking or deadlocks.

Figure 23.11.
The way locks are held
within a nested
transaction.

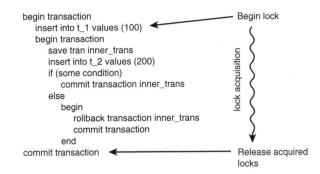

USER INTERACTION WITHIN A TRANSACTION

Keeping a watchful eye on transaction implementation can help ward off blocking. Consider the example in Figure 23.12. This situation virtually guarantees blocking in a multi-user environment. Always avoid user interaction within a transaction.

Figure 23.12.
User interaction within
a transaction.

You should rewrite the transaction to prompt the user first; based on the user's response, you can then perform the DELETE (see Figure 23.13). Transactions should always be managed in a single batch.

Figure 23.13.
The transaction
rewritten to avoid user
interaction.

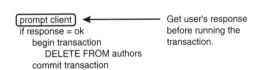

TIP 7: RUN TRANSACTIONS THAT MODIFY LARGE AMOUNTS OF DATA DURING OFF HOURS

You should process CREATE CLUSTERED INDEX and mass UPDATE/DELETE/INSERT statements during off hours. These types of transactions require exclusive table locks and can be resource intensive.

TIP 8: ADD MORE MEMORY TO YOUR SERVER

By adding more memory to your server, you increase the amount of data that can remain in cache. This improves transaction performance, which reduces resource contention.

TIP 9: KNOW HOW TO SAFELY INCREMENT AN ID

Most applications require some type of auto-incrementing ID to be used as a key field. Before a new record is inserted into the table, the application must get the next available ID.

The easiest way to create an auto-incrementing ID is to use the `identity` property. (The `identity` datatype is new with SQL Server 6.x.) This datatype has been optimized for performance and eliminates the need to have a separate table to track the next available ID.

If you cannot use the `identity` property (for example, when you need complete control over the counter values), you can use the following stored procedure to return the next ID. Because the `update` statement is within a transaction, the risk of two users receiving the same ID is eliminated. The following stored procedure returns the next ID:

```
CREATE PROCEDURE usp_next_id AS
declare @next_id integer
begin transaction
 update t_1
 set id = id + 1
 select @next_id = id from t_1
commit transaction
RETURN @next_id
```

The following is an example of how to use the `usp_next_id` stored procedure:

```
declare @next_id integer
exec @next_id = usp_next_id
select @next_id
```

TIP 10: TUNE THE LOCK ESCALATION THRESHOLD

The standard 200-page lock threshold limit can be unnecessarily low for very large tables. By tuning the lock escalation threshold level, you may be able to decrease the frequency of table locks. See the topic "Lock Escalation" in the "Multi-User Configuration Options" section of this chapter for more information.

MULTI-USER CONFIGURATION OPTIONS

SQL Server has several configuration options that allow you to tailor locking and other multi-user considerations. These options provide maximum control for multi-user access.

SERVER LEVEL

At the server level, you can configure the maximum number of locks, the maximum number of open objects, and the point at which lock escalation occurs.

23

MULTI-USER CONSIDERATIONS

All server-level configuration options can be changed by using the Enterprise Manager or the `sp_configure` system procedure. The following steps explain how to change a server configuration option with the Enterprise Manager:

1. Select a server and right-click the server icon.

2. From the shortcut menu that appears, select Configure. The Server Configuration/Options dialog box appears.

3. Select the Configuration tab in the Server Configuration/Options dialog box (see Figure 23.14).

4. Select the appropriate configuration option and enter the corresponding value.

Figure 23.14.
How to configure server
options using the
Enterprise Manager.

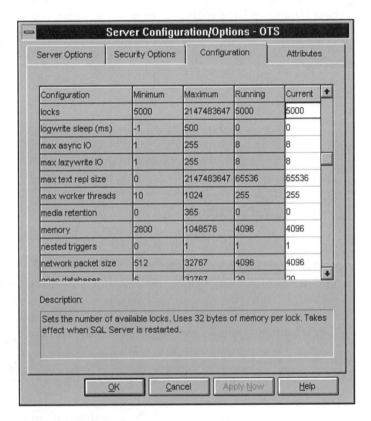

MAXIMUM NUMBER OF LOCKS

To configure the maximum number of locks, modify the `locks` setting in the Server Configuration/Options dialog box. The default installation value is 5000. When setting this value, keep in mind that each lock uses 32 bytes of memory.

The following is the syntax for the sp_configure system procedure:

```
sp_configure 'locks', [value]
```

Note

If you see the following error message, you must increase the maximum number of locks:

```
Error 1204, SQL Server has run out of LOCKS. Re-run your command when
there are fewer active users, or ask your System Administrator to
reconfigure SQL Server with more LOCKS.
```

Typically, the default installation value of 5000 locks is insufficient for most systems.

Tip

Use the Performance Monitor to track lock usage. You can use this value to help determine whether your lock configuration value is reasonable.

MAXIMUM NUMBER OF OPEN OBJECTS

To configure the maximum number of open objects, modify the open objects setting in the Server Configuration/Options dialog box. This setting controls the maximum number of open objects for a server. The default installation value for this option is 500. Each open object uses 70 bytes of memory. The following is the syntax to configure the number of open objects:

```
sp_configure 'open objects', [value]
```

LOCK ESCALATION

Lock escalation occurs when multiple page locks are converted into a single table lock. At this point, SQL Server determines that it is more efficient to process the transaction with a table lock rather than numerous page locks.

Note

The capability to configure lock escalation is new with SQL Server 6.x. Previous versions of SQL Server automatically escalated page locks to a table lock when 200 or more page locks had been acquired.

The default installation value for lock escalation is 200 pages. With a very large table, the default value may not be an optimal setting. For example, a modification to 1 percent of the data in a 200M table automatically produces a table lock. This results in unnecessary table locking, which can lead to increased blocking.

By tuning the lock escalation point, you avoid unnecessary table locking. You can use the configuration settings shown in Table 23.4 to control lock escalation.

TABLE 23.4. LOCK ESCALATION.

Threshold Name	Threshold Type	Default Setting	Minimum Setting	Maximum Setting
LE threshold maximum	Maximum threshold value	200	2	500000
LE threshold minimum	Minimum threshold value	20	2	500000
LE threshold percent	Threshold value based on percentage of table size	0	1	100

Note

LE threshold minimum is an advanced option. To view and set advanced options, you must use the SHOW ADVANCED OPTION syntax with sp_configure. Following is the syntax to show advanced options:

```
sp_configure 'show advanced option',1
```

TRANSACTION ISOLATION LEVEL

With SQL Server, you can configure the transaction isolation level for a connection. A transaction isolation level remains in effect for the life of the connection unless the value is modified or the connection is broken.

Note

The capability to configure the transaction isolation level is new with SQL Server 6.x.

To set the transaction isolation level, use the SET TRANSACTION ISOLATION LEVEL command, as in the following syntax. For an explanation of the differences among transaction isolation levels, see Table 23.5.

```
SET TRANSACTION ISOLATION LEVEL {READ COMMITTED ¦ READ UNCOMMITTED ¦
REPEATABLE READ ¦ SERIALIZABLE}
```

TABLE 23.5. TRANSACTION ISOLATION LEVELS.

Setting	Purpose
READ COMMITTED	SQL Server's default transaction isolation level. Prevents dirty reads; nonrepeatable reads may occur with this setting.
READ UNCOMMITTED	Minimizes locking by issuing locks only for UPDATE commands. Using this setting may result in dirty reads, phantom values, and nonrepeatable reads.
REPEATABLE READ	*See* SERIALIZABLE.
SERIALIZABLE	Prevents dirty reads, phantom values, and nonrepeatable reads. In terms of performance, this setting is the least efficient option.

EXPLICIT LOCKING

With the SELECT statement, you can specify and sometimes override SQL Server's default locking behavior. To specify the locking behavior, use the keyword HOLDLOCK, UPDLOCK, NOLOCK, PAGLOCK, TABLOCK, or TABLOCKX. *Note:* With the exception of HOLDLOCK, the capability to explicitly control locking is new with SQL Server 6.x.

The following is the syntax to control explicit locking. See Table 23.6 for an explanation of the differences among explicit locking levels.

```
SELECT select_list
FROM table list [HOLDLOCK ¦ UPDLOCK ¦ NOLOCK ¦ PAGLOCK ¦ TABLOCK ¦ TABLOCKX]
```

TABLE 23.6. EXPLICIT LOCK SUMMARY.

Lock	Purpose
HOLDLOCK	Forces all locks to be held for the duration of the transaction.
NOLOCK	Turns off locking. Permits dirty reads.
PAGLOCK	Forces page locking rather than table locking.
TABLOCK	Forces table locking rather than page locking and uses a shared lock.
TABLOCKX	Forces table locking rather than page locking and uses an exclusive lock.
UPDLOCK	Forces an update lock to be issued rather than a shared lock. This type of lock ensures consistency when you intend to read data and then perform an update based on the values you just read.

BETWEEN THE LINES

Following are important notes to remember when addressing multi-user issues in SQL Server:

◆ Locks are used to maintain data consistency in a multi-user environment.

◆ Excessive locking can lead to blocking and deadlocks.

◆ Blocking occurs when a process must wait for another process to complete.

◆ Deadlock occurs when two users have locks on separate objects and each user is trying to lock the other user's objects.

◆ Use the Enterprise Manager, Performance Monitor, sp_lock, sp_who, and trace flags to help determine locking behavior.

◆ Almost every SQL operation against a table results in some sort of lock.

◆ Page locks are preferred to table locks because they are less likely to cause blocking.

◆ Read statements acquire shared locks; data modification statements acquire exclusive locks.

◆ Page locks can escalate to table locks. When this occurs, it is more efficient for SQL Server to process the transaction with a table lock rather than a page lock.

◆ A clustered index may reduce contention during an insert.

◆ Always avoid user interaction within a transaction.

SUMMARY

As a DBA, you are guaranteed to run into blocking, deadlocks, and data consistency problems. The more users you have, the more likely you are to experience these problems. Hopefully, the topics discussed in this chapter will help you ward off these problems before they impact your production environment.

Speaking of your production environment, the following chapter can help keep your databases up and running 24×7 (24 hours a day, 7 days a week).

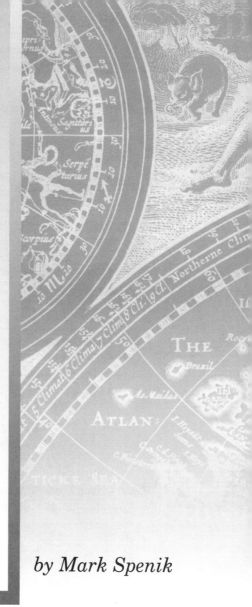

CHAPTER 24   *by Mark Spenik*

Using Stored Procedures and Cursors

Does the topic of stored procedures fall into the realm of developers or DBAs? In the first edition of the *SQL Server DBA Survival Guide*, after much thought and consideration, we decided that the topic belonged to developers. After a few appreciated e-mail messages from readers of the first edition, we realized that we had to include stored procedures in the second edition. Knowledge of stored procedures is required for DBAs and developers alike. As a DBA, you use stored procedures quite frequently. Microsoft supplies many stored procedures you will use to perform database and system maintenance. (*Note:* A list of the system stored procedures is in Appendix C.) You will find that you are frequently required to write your own stored procedures to perform specific DBA tasks for your organization or to help a group of developers solve a complex business problem.

WHAT IS A STORED PROCEDURE?

A *stored procedure* is a series of precompiled SQL statements and control-of-flow language statements. Stored procedures can enhance standard SQL by allowing you to use parameters, make decisions, declare variables, and return information. You can think of a stored procedure as a program or function that is stored as a database object on SQL Server. When a stored procedure is executed, the stored procedure runs on SQL Server—not on the client issuing the request. A stored procedure can be a simple SQL statement such as this one:

```
Select * from authors
```

A stored procedure can also be a series of complex SQL statements and control-of-flow language statements that apply a complex business rule or task to a series of tables in the database.

Tip

A *trigger* is a special type of stored procedure that automatically executes when certain table data modifications are made (for example, inserts, updates, or deletes). Triggers are used to cascade changes to related tables or to perform complex restrictions that cannot be done with constraints.

STORED PROCEDURE PROS AND CONS

Before further defining a stored procedure, here are some of the pros and cons of using stored procedures:

Stored Procedure Pros:

◆ Stored procedures allow you to perform complex operations that cannot be performed with straight SQL.

◆ Stored procedures offer a substantial performance gain over standard SQL statements because the SQL statements in a stored procedure are precompiled. An execution plan is prepared after the stored procedure executes the first time. Once the execution plan is created and stored in the procedure cache, subsequent execution of the stored procedure is much faster than equivalent SQL statements.

◆ Stored procedures can be used as a security mechanism. For example, if you have many tables or views you do not want users to access directly, you can revoke all access to the underlying tables and create a stored procedure granting the users EXECUTE privileges on the stored procedure. The users can then access the tables by executing the stored procedure.

Tip

> Using stored procedures as a security mechanism is one way you can prevent users from accidentally modifying a table with an ad-hoc query tool such as MS-Query or Microsoft Access. Grant the users read-only access to the table and then create stored procedures to perform data modifications like UPDATE or DELETE.

Stored Procedure Cons:

◆ Stored procedures can be difficult to debug. You can write some very complex stored procedures with many different logic points and variables. SQL Server does not provide a debugger (other then a Print statement) to step through the procedures or to display variable values (however, several third-party tools provide full-featured debuggers). In addition, the error messages returned when a syntax error occurs can be difficult to decipher.

◆ Stored procedures can be difficult to manage. When dealing with development projects or special administrative needs, the number of stored procedures can increase dramatically. Trying to remember what each stored procedure does and which other procedures use the stored procedure can become a problem. SQL Server does not provide any administrative capabilities to ease this task; managing stored procedures requires additional work from you.

Tip

One successful method I have used to keep track of stored procedures is to produce a catalog of stored procedures using a Windows help file. Find a utility that allows you to easily create Windows help files. Create a help file to catalog all your stored procedures. Include the name of the procedure, a description of the procedure, a list and description of procedures, tables, or views that procedure accesses, and other procedures called. As you add, modify, and delete stored procedures, keep the help file up to date. The help files are easy to distribute and have very good search utilities. However, this approach requires the cooperation of anyone who creates or modifies stored procedures on your system to keep the help file up to date.

WHAT DOES IT MEAN TO BE COMPILED?

In the preceding definition of a stored procedure, we stated that a stored procedure consists of precompiled SQL statements—but what exactly does it mean when we say *precompiled* or *compiled*? Use Figure 24.1 and walk through the steps SQL Server performs when a stored procedure is created and compiled.

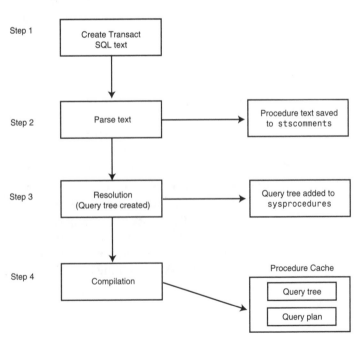

*Figure 24.1.
The SQL Server steps
used to create and
compile a stored
procedure.*

STEP 1: CREATING THE PROCEDURE WITH TRANSACT SQL

The first step in creating a stored procedure is to add the valid Transact SQL statements and valid control-of-flow language statements that make up the stored procedure.

STEP 2: PARSE TEXT

Once a stored procedure is written and sent to SQL Server to be saved, SQL Server parses the text, looking for invalid Transact SQL statements or invalid objects. If a problem is found, the client connection attempting to save the stored procedure is alerted of the problem and the process ends. You must correct all syntax and invalid object errors before SQL Server can save the stored procedure.

Note

> The exception to the invalid object rule is when you call other stored procedures. If a stored procedure called by your new stored procedure does not exist at the time you create the new stored procedure, you are given a warning message and the parsing process continues.

Once SQL Server has validated the Transact SQL statements and the objects used, the ASCII text used to create the stored procedure is saved in the database system table syscomments.

STEP 3: RESOLUTION (QUERY TREE CREATED)

When the text of the stored procedure is saved in syscomments, *resolution* occurs. Resolution is the creation of the normalized form of the procedure (called a *query tree*) that is stored in the database system table sysprocedures. During resolution, external objects such as table names are translated to their internal representation (table names are translated to object IDs from sysobjects) and the SQL statements are converted to a more efficient form. Figure 24.2 shows an example of a query tree used by a stored procedure that performs the following SQL statement:

```
Select * from pubs..authors
```

Figure 24.2.
A sample query tree
from sysprocedures.

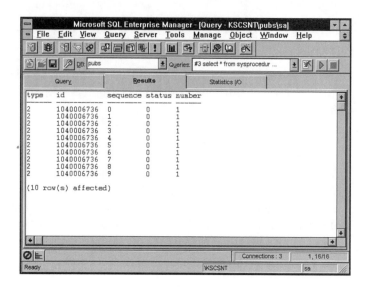

STEP 4: COMPILATION

Compilation is the process of creating the query (access) plan and loading the query plan used by the stored procedure in the procedure cache. Compilation does not occur until the stored procedure is executed for the first time. When the procedure is first executed, the query tree of the procedure is read from the sysprocedures table into the procedure cache. The SQL Server query optimizer then creates the query plan for the stored procedure. The following factors determine the query plan created for a stored procedure:

- ◆ The SQL statements in the query tree.
- ◆ The values of parameters passed to the stored procedure when the query plan is created.
- ◆ The statistics for each table and index used by the procedure.

Tip

Because the query plans are held in memory (procedure cache), the access plans for stored procedures are lost when SQL Server shuts down. The query plan is re-created when SQL Server is restarted and the procedure is executed for the first time.

Once a stored procedure query plan is placed into the procedure cache, the plan stays in the procedure cache as long as there is space in the cache. Subsequent calls to the stored procedure are much faster because the query plan already exists and does not have to be re-created. So what does it mean to be compiled? It means that an access plan (query plan) for the stored procedure exists in the procedure cache.

Tip

Triggers are compiled only once, when the trigger is first created or modified.

REUSABLE BUT NOT REENTRANT

An important fact to remember about stored procedures is that they are *reusable*: once a user executes a stored procedure and the procedure completes, another user can execute the same copy of the stored procedure in the procedure cache. However, stored procedures are not reentrant. To understand what it means when we say a stored procedure is not reentrant, walk through the example shown in Figure 24.3.

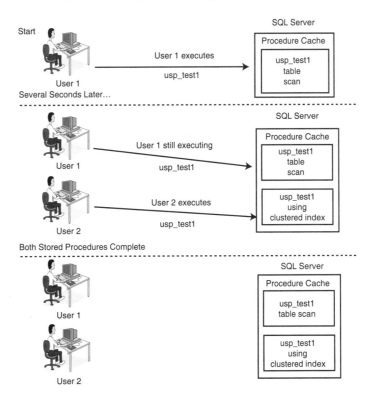

Figure 24.3. Stored procedures are reusable but not reentrant.

User1 begins to execute a stored procedure, `usp_test1`, that is already in the procedure cache. Before `usp_test1` can complete execution, User2 begins to execute the same procedure. Stored procedures are not reentrant, meaning that User2 can't execute the same copy of usp_test1 while User1 is executing it. Instead, SQL Server creates another query plan for usp_test1 and loads it in the procedure cache for User2 to execute. Now two copies of usp_test1 exist in the procedure cache. An interesting point to make (and one that is discussed in detail later) is that not only do two copies of usp_test1 exist in the procedure cache, but in this example each copy of the stored procedure has a different query plan. Remember that several factors determine the type of access plan created by the query optimizer. In this example, User1 passed in a different parameter than User2. The access plan of User1's copy of usp_test1 performs a table scan but the access plan of User2's copy of usp_test1 uses a clustered index. After both users' stored procedures complete, two very different query plans for usp_test1 exist in the procedure cache. If User1 executes the procedure again, there is no way to determine which copy of the stored procedure he or she will get. This uncertainty can cause a performance problem if User1 passes a parameter that would execute faster using a clustered index but uses the stored procedure that performs a table scan instead. This problem is addressed in the following section when discussing the RECOMPILE option.

HOW TO CREATE A STORED PROCEDURE

Version
6.5

To create a stored procedure using SQL Server 6.5, use the Create Procedure statement, which has the following syntax:

```
Create PROCEDURE
[owner.]procedure_name[;number][(parameter1[,parameter2]...[parameter255])]
➥[{FOR REPLICATION} ¦ {WITH RECOMPILE} [{[WITH]¦[,]}ENCRYPTION]] As SQL Statements
```

Note

When you use the Create Procedure statement, you can type the statement Create Procedure as in the following example:

```
Create Procedure usp_test
```

Alternatively, you can use the shortcut statement Create Proc as in the following example:

```
Create Proc usp_test
```

In this syntax, procedure_name is the name of the stored procedure. Stored procedure names conform to the standard SQL Server naming conventions. The maximum size of a procedure name is 30 characters. With SQL Server 6.5, you can create a local temporary stored procedure by adding # to the beginning of the procedure name. A local temporary stored procedure can be used only by the connection that created the stored procedure; it is dropped when the connection ends. You can create a global temporary stored procedure by adding ## to the beginning of the stored procedure name. A global temporary stored procedure can be used by all user connections and is dropped at the end of the last session using the procedure. Suggested stored procedure naming conventions are found in Appendix A.

> ### STRANGER THAN FICTION!
>
> The Microsoft Transact SQL Reference, with Books Online, incorrectly states the maximum size of a stored procedure name to be 20 characters.

Also in this syntax, *number* is an optional integer that can be used to group stored procedures with the same name so that they can be dropped with a single drop statement. *parameter* allows parameters to be passed into the stored procedure. Parameters are optional; a stored procedure can have up to 255 parameters. The text For Replication marks a stored procedure for use only by the replication process.

When the WITH RECOMPILE option is used, the query plan of the stored procedure is not kept in the procedure cache. A new query plan is generated every time the procedure is executed. You cannot use the FOR REPLICATION and WITH RECOMPILE options together.

> ### SOLVING THE WITH RECOMPILE MYTH
>
> The WITH RECOMPILE option is a highly misunderstood option. I have heard things like, "Why would you ever use that? When you use the WITH RECOMPILE option with a stored procedure, you lose the advantage of a compiled query plan. You might as well use straight SQL!" Did you ever think that ignorance is bliss and no wonder your system is slow?
>
> When using the WITH RECOMPILE statement, you do lose the benefit of a compiled query plan, but the stored procedure is still faster than straight SQL because the SQL text has already been parsed and a query tree has been constructed. Even more important, in cases when you use the WITH RECOMPILE option, you lose the small amount of time it takes to create the query plan as opposed to using an incorrect query plan that may cost minutes or hours.
>
> When do you use the WITH RECOMPILE option? When you are passing into a stored procedure parameters that differ greatly in data distribution; these different parameters would cause the query optimizer to create different query plans (refer back to the example in the section,

24

USING STORED PROCEDURES AND CURSORS

"Reusable but Not Reentrant," and refer to Figure 24.3). Also consider using the WITH RECOMPILE option if you pass parameters into a stored procedure and the time to execute the stored procedure is inconsistent. You can force a stored procedure to recompile the next time it is executed by executing the system stored procedure sp_recompile on a table or view referenced in the stored procedure.

The WITH ENCRYPTION option encrypts the text of the stored procedure in the syscomments table so that users cannot query the text of the procedure. Use this option only when necessary.

SQL Statements are the SQL statements or control-of-flow language statements that make up the stored procedure.

Now look at some simple examples of creating stored procedures in the pubs database. The following example creates a stored procedure called usp_show_authors that selects all the columns and rows from the authors table:

```
Create Procedure usp_show_authors
as
Select * from authors
```

The next example creates a stored procedure called usp_Texas_Publisher that selects all the publisher's names from the publishers table using the WITH ENCRYPTION option:

```
Create Proc usp_Texas_Publisher WITH ENCYPTION
as
Select pub_name
From publishers
Where state = 'TX'
```

Tip

Stored procedures are created in the database from which the Create Procedure command is executed; the exception is temporary stored procedures, which are created in the tempdb database.

Use the SQL Query tool (refer back to Figure 24.2) to enter the procedure name and click the green arrow to execute the stored procedure. If the stored procedure is not the first statement, use the EXECUTE statement as follows:

```
execute procedure_name
```

Here is a shortcut and commonly used format:

```
exec procedure_name
```

CONTROL-OF-FLOW LANGUAGE

Before getting into some of the finer points of stored procedures (like using parameters or returning values), it is important to cover a very important topic: control-of-flow language. Control-of-flow language gives your stored procedures added capabilities not found in standard Transact SQL. Using control-of-flow language, you can make use of standard programming techniques such as performing loops or conditional processing on variables.

Tip

> Want to learn how to write good stored procedures? The first requirement is to learn SQL and the many additional Transact SQL features. The next step is to make yourself familiar with the different control-of-flow statements and their uses. Learn these fundamentals, and you are on your way to writing good stored procedures.

The following control-of-flow language statements are quickly reviewed in the following sections:

◆ GOTO label
◆ BEGIN...END
◆ IF...ELSE
◆ WAITFOR
◆ return
◆ while
◆ break
◆ continue

Additionally, the following Transact SQL extensions are reviewed in the following sections:

◆ Declare statement
◆ Print statement
◆ RAISERROR

THE Declare STATEMENT

Using the Declare statement, you can create variables using standard SQL Server datatypes. Variables defined with the Declare statement **must** begin with the

@ symbol. You can declare more than one variable in a Declare statement by using commas to separate the variables. The syntax for Declare is as follows:

```
Declare @parm1 datatype [,@parm2 datatype ...]
```

The following example creates three parameters of different datatypes:

```
Declare @count int, @current_date datetime
Declare @My_Message varchar(255)
```

Note

To initialize or set the value of a variable you create with the Declare statement, use the keyword SELECT. For example, the following statement sets the value of the variable @count to 100:

```
Select @count = 100
```

The following example sets the variable @count to the total number of rows in the authors table located in the pubs database:

```
Select @count = count(*)
from pubs..authors
```

THE GOTO STATEMENT

The GOTO statement performs the same function it performs in many different programming languages like C and Visual Basic. GOTO jumps the execution of the stored procedure to the associated label. The syntax for GOTO is as follows:

```
GOTO label
```

In the following example, the GOTO statement jumps over (skips) the SELECT statement and executes the UPDATE statement:

```
GOTO do_update
SELECT * from authors

do_update:

UPDATE authors
set au_lname = "Spenik"
Where state = 'VA'
```

Note

When defining a label, the label name must end in a colon. When using the GOTO statement, refer to the label name but do not include the colon.

THE BEGIN...END STATEMENT

BEGIN and END statements are considered block statements because they group a series of SQL statements and control-of-flow language into a single entity. BEGIN and END are often used with IF...ELSE blocks. The syntax for BEGIN and END is as follows:

```
BEGIN
    {SQL Statements ¦ statement block}
END
```

THE IF...ELSE STATEMENT

The IF and ELSE statements allow you to check for conditions and execute SQL statements based on the condition. The IF statement checks expressions that return a TRUE or FALSE value (that is, it checks Boolean expressions). If the value returned is TRUE, the block of statements or the single statement that follows the IF statement is executed. If the value returned is FALSE, the optional ELSE statement is executed. The syntax for the IF...ELSE statement is as follows:

```
IF Boolean Expression
  {SQL statement ¦ Statement Block}
[ELSE [Boolean Expression]
  {SQL statement ¦ Statement Block}]
```

Following is an example of IF and IF...ELSE using a single SQL statement and a statement block:

```
If @count = 0
   Select * from authors
else
   Select * from titles

if @Total != 0
begin
   Select count(*) from authors
   Select count(*) from titles
end
else
begin
   Select * from authors
   Select * from titles
end
```

THE WAITFOR STATEMENT

The WAITFOR statement is a delay that allows your stored procedure to wait for a specified time period or until a specific time before execution continues. The syntax for the WAITFOR statement is as follows:

```
WAITFOR {DELAY 'time' ¦ TIME 'time'}
```

24

USING STORED PROCEDURES AND CURSORS

A WAITFOR statement can delay for up to 24 hours. The TIME and DELAY options use the format 'hh:mm:ss'. The following example causes a delay of 10 seconds:

```
WAITFOR DELAY '00:00:10'
```

The following example waits until 11 A.M.:

```
WAITFOR TIME '11:00:00'
```

The RETURN Statement

The RETURN statement causes a stored procedure to exit and return to the calling procedure or application. The syntax for RETURN is as follows:

```
RETURN [Integer Value]
```

You can return an integer value to the calling routine or application using the following syntax:

```
exec @status = procedure_name
```

The following example consists of two parts. The first part is a stored procedure, called usp_return, that returns an integer to the calling procedure or application. The second part is a stored procedure, called usp_call, that calls the stored procedure usp_return and checks the returned value:

```
Create Procedure usp_return
as
Declare @ret_val int

Select @ret_val = 0
Return @ret_val

Create Procedure usp_call
as
Declare @status int
exec @status = usp_return
if(@status = 0)
   Print "Value returned is zero"
```

When executing stored procedures, SQL Server uses the value 0 to indicate success. Negative values indicate that an error has occurred. The return values –1 to –99 are reserved for SQL Server. When you use the RETURN statement, you can return only integer values; if you want to return other datatypes, you must use an output parameter, as described later in this chapter.

The WHILE, BREAK, and CONTINUE Statements

The WHILE statement allows you to perform repeating conditional loops for the execution of a SQL statement or a statement block. The BREAK statement causes an exit from the WHILE loop; CONTINUE causes the WHILE loop to restart, skipping any statements that follow the CONTINUE statement. These statements have the following format:

```
WHILE Boolean Expressions
{SQL statement ¦ statement block}
[BREAK ¦ CONTINUE]
```

Examples of these statements can be found in the sample stored procedures shown at the end of this chapter.

THE Print STATEMENT

The Print statement allows you to return a message to the client's message handler. The message can have up to 255 characters (the maximum size of a varchar datatype). The Print statement has the following syntax:

```
Print {' Any text message' ¦ @local variable ¦ @@global variable}
```

If you print a local or global variable, the variable must be a char or varchar datatype; otherwise, you have to convert the datatype to a char or varchar before printing. Following are some examples using the Print statement:

```
Declare @msg varchar(255), @count int
Select @count = 0
Print "Starting the procedure"
While @count < 5
Begin
    Select @count = @count + 1
    Select @msg = "The Value of @count is " + str(@count)
    Print @msg
end
Select @msg = "This about wraps this procedure up."
Select @msg = @msg + " The value of @count is " + str(@count)
Print @msg
```

Listing 24.1 shows the output generated from the preceding Print statements, executed from the SQL Query tool.

LISTING 24.1. PRINT STATEMENT OUTPUT.

```
(1 row(s) affected)

Starting the procedure

(1 row(s) affected)


(1 row(s) affected)

The Value of @count is           1
```

continues

LISTING 24.1. CONTINUED

```
(1 row(s) affected)


(1 row(s) affected)

The Value of @count is          2

(1 row(s) affected)


(1 row(s) affected)

The Value of @count is          3

(1 row(s) affected)


(1 row(s) affected)

The Value of @count is          4

(1 row(s) affected)


(1 row(s) affected)

The Value of @count is          5

(1 row(s) affected)


(1 row(s) affected)

This about wraps this procedure up. The value of @count is          5
```

Tip

Use Print statements in your stored procedures during testing to help debug the stored procedure. Use the Print statement like a trace statement to print out particular locations or values in the procedure.

THE RAISERROR STATEMENT

The RAISERROR statement sets a SQL Server system flag to signify that an error has occurred and sends back an error message to the client connection. The syntax for RAISERROR is as follows:

```
RAISERROR ({message_id ¦ message_str}, severity, state [,arg1[,arg2]]) [WITH LOG]
```

Use the WITH LOG option to write the error message to the SQL Server error log and the Windows NT event log.

COMMENTS

Comments in a stored procedure follow the C programming language standard. Comments begin with a /* and end with a */. Everything between the /* and the */ is considered part of the comment. Use a lot of comments to make your stored procedures easy to read and maintain. Following are some examples of comments:

```
/* This is a one line comment */
/* This
   Comment
   Spans
   Several lines */
/*
** This is a comment - I think the added ** makes it easier to read.
*/
```

PARAMETERS USED WITH STORED PROCEDURES

Parameters allow you to write flexible stored procedures by executing the SQL statements with values that are determined at run time (not at compile time) and that can be changed at every execution. Parameters follow the same naming conventions as standard stored procedure variables (they must begin with @). Parameters can be input parameters or output parameters.

INPUT PARAMETERS

Input parameters are used to pass values into a stored procedure. Input parameters have the following syntax:

```
Create proc Procedure_name @parm1 datatype, @param2 datatype
```

The following example defines three input parameters of different datatypes:

```
Create procedure usp_input @temp_name varchar(30), @total int, @current_date
➥datetime
```

You can pass the values into a stored procedure in several ways. The standard way to pass the values is as follows:

```
exec usp_input 'Spenik & Sledge', 1000, '03/25/96'
```

When you use the preceding calling form, you must pass the values in the same order as they are declared in the stored procedure. Instead of passing in values, you can also pass in other variables (of the same datatype) as follows:

```
exec usp_input @authors_name, @new_total, @my_date
```

Another way to pass parameters is by using the parameter name. When using the parameter name, you can pass the parameters in any order—but if you use the name for one parameter, you must use the parameter name for all parameters that follow. The following is a valid example of using parameter names:

```
exec usp_input @total = 1000, @temp_name = 'Spenik & Sledge', @current_date =
➥'03/25/96'
```

The following example is **not** valid because, once you start using a parameter name, all the parameters that follow must also include the name:

```
exec usp_input 'Spenik & Sledge', @total = 1000, '03/25/96'
```

Input parameters can also have default values. To assign a default value to an input parameter, use the following syntax:

```
@parameter_name datatype = default_value
```

For example:

```
create proc usp_param @p1 int, @p2 int = 3, @p3 int
```

If the procedure is called without a parameter (as in the following example), the default value is used:

```
exec usp_param @p1=5, @p3=100
```

To use an input parameter in a stored procedure, reference the variable name (just like any other variable). The following example checks the value of the parameter; if the parameter is less than 0, a message is printed:

```
create procedure usp_test @p1 int
as
   if @p1 < 0
      print "The value is less than zero"
```

OUTPUT PARAMETERS

Output parameters are used to return values in a variable to a calling stored procedure or application. The syntax to declare an output parameter is as follows:

```
Create procedure proecdure_name @parameter_name datatype OUTput
```

The following example declares an output parameter called @p1:

```
create procedure usp_test @p1 int OUT
```

To call a procedure with an output parameter, you must declare a variable to hold the returned value (the variable does not have to have the same name as the output parameter used in the create procedure statement). Then use the keyword out (output) as follows:

```
exec usp_test @v1 out
```

After the procedure executes, you can then use the value in the output parameter (in this example, @v1) for further processing. You can also use the parameter name with output parameters, as follows:

```
exec usp_test @p1 = @v1 out
```

The following example multiplies an input parameter by 2 and returns the string version of the result in an output parameter:

```
Create Procedure usp_Double_Value @old_value int, @new_value varchar(20) OUT
as
Declare @temp_value int
Select @temp_value = @old_value * 2
Select @new_value = convert(varchar(20), @temp_value)
```

The following example uses the procedure usp_Double_Value and prints out the results:

```
Declare @start_value int, @computed_value varchar(20)
Declare @msg varchar(50)

Select @start_value = 20
exec usp_Double_Value @start_value, @computed_value OUT
Select @msg = "The computed value is " + @computed_value
Print @msg
```

Listing 24.2 shows the output generated from the preceding routine when executed from the SQL Query tool.

LISTING 24.2. Print STATEMENT OUTPUT.

```
(1 row(s) affected)

(1 row(s) affected)

The computed value is 40
```

COMMONLY USED GLOBAL VARIABLES

SQL Server provides several global variables you can use when writing stored procedures. A *global variable* is distinguished from a standard variable by the @@

that precedes the name. Following is a list of some of the commonly used global variables:

◆ @@Error is probably the most commonly used global variable. @@Error is used to check the error status of a statement executed by SQL Server. @@Error contains a 0 if the statement executed correctly. (***Note:*** @@Error is kept by connection; the value of @@Error for your connection is not changed by other users' statements.)

◆ @@FETCH_STATUS is used to check the status of a cursor's fetch command and is discussed in detail in the section, "What Is a Cursor?," later in this chapter (@@FETCH_STATUS is also kept per connection).

◆ @@IDENTITY holds the value of the last successful identity value inserted (@@IDENTITY is kept per connection).

◆ @@ROWCOUNT holds the value for the number of rows affected by the last SQL statement (@@ROWCOUNT is kept per connection).

◆ @@SERVERNAME specifies the name of the local SQL Server.

◆ @@TRANCOUNT is the number of current active transactions for the current user.

QUICK FACTS ABOUT STORED PROCEDURES

Following is a list of some quick facts, tips, helpful hints, and restrictions that apply to stored procedures:

◆ Stored procedures support up to 16 levels of procedure nesting, meaning that a stored procedure can call another stored procedure, which in turn can call another, until the maximum nesting level of 16 is reached. To determine the current level of nesting, use the global variable @@nestlevel.

◆ You cannot create an object in a stored procedure, drop it, and then try to create another object with the same name.

◆ You cannot perform the following SQL statements within a stored procedure: CREATE VIEW, CREATE DEFAULT, CREATE RULE, CREATE TRIGGER, and CREATE PROCEDURE.

◆ If you create objects in a stored procedure and call another stored procedure, the procedure called can use the objects created by the calling procedure.

◆ You can create temporary tables and indexes on the temporary tables using a stored procedure. All temporary tables are created in the temporary database, regardless of where the stored procedure executes. Any local temporary table created in a stored procedure is removed when the procedure exits.

◆ To remove a stored procedure, use the DROP Procedure command.

◆ To rename a stored procedure, use the system stored procedure sp_rename.

◆ Stored procedures are recompiled when a table is dropped and re-created, when all query plans in the cache are in use, when the procedure is executed with the WITH RECOMPILE option, when an index is dropped, when the procedure is no longer in the procedure cache, or when the procedure is dropped and re-created.

◆ To decrease the overhead of data conversion when using input parameters within a stored procedure on a WHERE clause, make sure that the datatype of the input parameter matches the column datatype. The exception to this rule is a char datatype column with N characters that allows NULL values. SQL Server treats this as a VARCHAR.

◆ A remote stored procedure is a stored procedure that is executed on another SQL Server from your local SQL Server.

◆ A user can execute a stored procedure that accesses tables, views, or other stored procedures to which the user does not have access. The owner of the stored procedure needs the proper access rights to objects used in the procedure. The stored procedure owner then grants to other users the only command permission a stored procedure has: EXECUTE.

LET'S SEE YOU DO THIS WITH SYBASE

SQL Server 6.x has greatly enhanced the EXECUTE command that also exists in Microsoft SQL Server 4.2x and current Sybase systems. For starters, you can use the EXECUTE statement to generate dynamic SQL statements and execute them all at run time. Several of the examples at the end of this chapter use dynamic SQL to perform tasks that are not possible in older versions of Transact SQL. When creating dynamic SQL, remember that you must have the proper access to all the objects you plan to use in the dynamic SQL statement; you are limited to generating dynamic SQL statements that do not exceed the maximum size of a char or varchar datatype (255 characters).

On the performance side, keep in mind that dynamic SQL is parsed and compiled at the time the EXECUTE statement is issued. Here's a hot new feature added to SQL Server 6.5: you can now use the INSERT INTO command and the EXECUTE statement to populate a local database table with information from a remote server using a remote stored procedure. This is a really hot feature, asked for by many of my clients.

Version
6.5

24

USING STORED PROCEDURES AND CURSORS

TIPS FOR USING STORED PROCEDURES

Following are some useful tips and tricks we have learned over the years to help keep track of stored procedures. There are also some tips for testing the stored procedures.

ADD A HEADER TO YOUR STORED PROCEDURES

To make your stored procedures easier to read and maintain, add a header to the start of your stored procedure. Following are two examples of headers you can use in your stored procedures.

Example header style 1:

```
Create Procedure usp_proc_name as
/*****************************************************************************
** Name:
**
** Description:
**
** Parameters:
**
** Returns: 0 - Success
**         -1 - Error
**
** Other Outputs: Populates the table xxxx for Access reports.
**
** History:
**    Mark A. Spenik KSCS, 10/17/95    Initial Release.
**
*****************************************************************************/
```

Example header style 2:

```
Create Procedure usp_proc_name as
/*------------------------------------------------------------

Procedure Name

------------------------------------------------------------
Description:

Called By:

Parameters:

Status Returns:

Other Outputs:

Example: <show an example of calling the stored procedure>
------------------------------------------------------------
History:
------------------------------------------------------------*/
```

TIME HOW LONG A STORED PROCEDURE TAKES TO EXECUTE

When testing stored procedures from the SQL Query tool, you may want to know exactly how long a stored procedure takes to execute. To time the stored procedure and display the start and end times in hh:mm:ss:ms format, use the functions getdate() and convert as follows:

```
select convert(varchar(20), getdate(), 14) 'Start Time'
exec Procedure_name
select convert(varchar(20), getdate(), 14) 'End Time'
```

For a stored procedure that returns several rows of data, you can use the following timing routine, which displays both the start and end times at the end of the stored procedure:

```
declare @startmsg varchar(40)
declare @endmsg varchar(40)

select @startmsg = 'Start Time: ' + convert(varchar(20), getdate(), 14)
/* Execute stored procedure */
exec Procedure_name
select @endmsg = 'End Time:   ' + convert(varchar(20), getdate(), 14)


print @startmsg
print @endmsg
```

VALIDATE STORED PROCEDURES AND COMPLEX SQL STATEMENTS

How do you test a large, complex stored procedure in SQL Server when Microsoft does not provide a debugger? One way to test a large, complex stored procedure is to start a session using the SQL Query tool or ISQL/w. Break the stored procedure into parts, testing each part of the stored procedure and validating the results of each part.

I meet many individuals who have trouble returning the correct number of rows when performing complex joins or using subqueries. One way to determine whether your WHERE clause is correct is to change the SQL statement into SELECT count(*). You can quickly run the complex SQL statement and determine by the row count whether the WHERE clause is correct. The following example shows how to replace an UPDATE statement with SELECT count(*) to validate the WHERE clause. Here's the original code fragment:

```
UPDATE table_a
Set my_name = table_b.old_name
FROM table_a, table_b
```

```
WHERE table_a.id = table_b.id
AND table_a.birth_date IN (Select *
                           From table_c)
```

To test the WHERE clause, change the UPDATE statement to SELECT count(*) as follows:

```
Select count(*)
FROM table_a, table_b
WHERE table_a.id = table_b.id
AND table_a.birth_date IN (Select *
                           From table_c)
```

HOW TO SUBTRACT A DATE

You would be surprised how many times someone asks me, "How do you subtract a date with Microsoft SQL Server? I saw the dateadd() function, but I did not see a datesubtract() function, so what's the deal?" The deal is simple: to subtract a date, use the dateadd() function with a negative number. The following example subtracts 10 days from the current day's date:

```
select dateadd(day,-10,getdate())
```

HOW TO SIZE A STORED PROCEDURE

Stored procedures are limited to 65,025 characters of text. The limitation is a result of storing the text of a stored procedure in the syscomments table, where each procedure can have up to 255 rows of 255 bytes each (that is, 255 rows × 255 bytes = 65,025 bytes). To determine the size of a stored procedure, you can use DBCC MEMUSAGE, which displays the size of the 12 largest objects in the procedure cache. You can determine how many rows the procedure is currently using in syscomments and how many rows are left by issuing the following statement:

```
Select count(*) "Number of rows used", 255 - count(*) "Number of rows remaining"
From syscomments where id = object_id("your procedure name")
```

DISPLAY THE ERROR MESSAGES ASSOCIATED WITH AN ERROR NUMBER

Have you ever received a call from a developer who was running an application that just received an error number (for this example, assume the error number 7935), and the developer wanted to know what the error number meant? The following stored procedure takes an error number as an input parameter and returns the severity and the description of the error number from the sysmessages table (blanks are returned for error numbers that do not exist in sysmessages).

```
create procedure usp_Show_Error_Message @error_number int
as
Select severity "Error Severity", description "Error Message"
from master..sysmessages
where error = @error_number
```

REDUCE THE NETWORK TRAFFIC

You can reduce the amount of extraneous information sent back by a stored procedure (for example, the message N rows affected) by placing the following statement at the top of your stored procedure:

```
SET NO COUNT ON
```

When you use the Set NOCOUNT ON statement, you limit the amount of extraneous information sent back to the calling process, thus reducing network traffic and increasing performance. The following example, created in the pubs database, shows how to use the statement in a stored procedure:

```
Create procedure usp_nocount
as
SET NOCOUNT ON
Select * from authors
```

WHAT IS A CURSOR?

A *cursor* is a SQL result set that allows you to perform row-oriented operations on the result set (this differs from standard SQL result sets, which return all the rows in the result set). Cursors make it possible to process data row by row. With SQL Server's cursors, you can navigate forward and backward through the result set. You can really exploit the power of cursors when you combine them with the EXEC command and a string variable substitution.

Note

ANSI standard cursors are new with SQL Server 6.0. Earlier versions of SQL Server required cursors to be processed at the client through DB-Library function calls or through ODBC.

Cursors can be used in the following locations:

◆ In a control-of-flow batch

◆ Within a stored procedure

◆ Within a trigger

CREATING A CURSOR

Every cursor must have at least four components. The four key components *must* follow this order:

1. DECLARE the cursor.
2. OPEN the cursor.
3. FETCH from the cursor.
4. CLOSE or DEALLOCATE the cursor.

STEP 1: DECLARE THE CURSOR

The DECLARE statement contains the user-defined name used to reference the result set, as well as the SQL SELECT statement that generates the result set. Think of the DECLARE statement as a temporary table that contains a pointer to your actual data source.

SYNTAX

```
DECLARE cursor_name [INSENSITIVE] [SCROLL] CURSOR
FOR select_statement
[FOR {READ ONLY ¦ UPDATE [OF column_list]}]
```

cursor_name	The cursor name.
INSENSITIVE	Specifies that changes in your data source will not be reflected in the cursor. Updates are not allowed to a cursor when this option is specified.
SCROLL	Allows the following FETCH commands to be used: PRIOR, FIRST, LAST, ABSOLUTE n, and RELATIVE n.
select_statement	A SQL SELECT statement. The following SQL commands force a cursor to be declared as INSENSITIVE: DISTINCT, UNION, GROUP BY, and/or HAVING.
READ ONLY	Prohibits updates from occurring against the cursor.
UPDATE [OF column_list]	Allows updates to be performed against the cursor. The optional clause [OF column_list] specifies which columns in the cursor can be updated.

EXAMPLE 1: STANDARD CURSOR

```
declare pub_crsr cursor
for
select pub_id,pub_name
from publishers
```

EXAMPLE 2: READ-ONLY CURSOR

```
declare pub_crsr cursor
for
select pub_id,pub_name
from publishers
FOR READ ONLY
```

EXAMPLE 3: CURSOR THAT ALLOWS UPDATES

```
declare pub_crsr cursor
for
select pub_id,pub_name
from publishers
FOR UPDATE
```

STEP 2: OPEN THE CURSOR

Once you declare a cursor, you must open it. The OPEN statement should immediately follow the DECLARE statement.

SYNTAX

```
OPEN cursor_name
```

cursor_name   The name of the cursor to open.

EXAMPLE

```
OPEN pub_crsr
```

STEP 3: FETCH FROM THE CURSOR

After the cursor has been opened, you can retrieve information from the result set on a row-by-row basis. SQL Server 6.x is one of the few RDBMS products that provides forward-scrolling cursors *and* backward-scrolling cursors.

SYNTAX

```
FETCH [[NEXT | PRIOR | FIRST | LAST | ABSOLUTE n | RELATIVE n] FROM] cursor_name
[INTO @variable_name1, @variable_name2, ...]
```

NEXT	Retrieves the next row.
PRIOR	Retrieves the preceding row.
FIRST	Retrieves the first row.
LAST	Retrieves the last row.

ABSOLUTE *n*   Retrieves a row based on the absolute position within the result set.

RELATIVE *n*   Retrieves a row based on the relative position within the result set.

Tip

Use negative numbers to move backward within a result set when using the ABSOLUTE and RELATIVE arguments. When you use ABSOLUTE, the rows are counted backward from the last row in the recordset. When you use RELATIVE, the rows are counted backward from the current position in the recordset.

cursor_name   The name of the cursor.

INTO @*variable_name1*, @*variable_name2*, and so on   Copies the contents of a column into a variable.

EXAMPLE 1: RETURN THE NEXT ROW IN THE RESULT SET

```
fetch next from pub_crsr
```

EXAMPLE 2: RETURN THE 5TH ROW IN THE RESULT SET

```
fetch absolute 5 from pub_crsr
```

EXAMPLE 3: COPY THE CONTENTS OF THE NEXT ROW INTO HOST VARIABLES

```
fetch next from pub_crsr into @pub_id,@pub_name
```

STEP 4: CLOSE OR DEALLOCATE THE CURSOR

After you finish processing the cursor, you must CLOSE or DEALLOCATE the cursor. The CLOSE statement closes the cursor but does not release the data structures used by the cursor. Use this statement if you plan to reopen the cursor for subsequent use. The DEALLOCATE statement closes the cursor and releases the data structures used by the cursor.

Tip

Always CLOSE or DEALLOCATE a cursor as soon as processing is complete. Cursors consume resources, such as locks, memory, and so on. If these resources are not released, performance and multi-user problems may arise.

SYNTAX

```
CLOSE cursor_name

DEALLOCATE cursor_name
```

> cursor_name   The cursor name.

EXAMPLE 1: CLOSE A CURSOR

```
CLOSE pub_crsr
```

EXAMPLE 2: DEALLOCATE A CURSOR

```
DEALLOCATE pub_crsr
```

POSITIONAL UPDATE AND DELETE

In addition to being able to retrieve data from a cursor, you can perform positional updates and deletes against the data contained in the cursor. When a modification is made to a cursor, that modification automatically cascades to the cursor's data source.

SYNTAX

```
UPDATE table_name
SET column_name1 = {expression1 ¦ NULL ¦ (select_statement)}
[, column_name2 = {expression2 ¦ NULL ¦ (select_statement)}...]
WHERE CURRENT OF cursor_name

DELETE FROM table_name
WHERE CURRENT OF cursor_name
```

> table_name   The name of the table to UPDATE or DELETE.
>
> column_name   The name of the column to UPDATE.
>
> cursor_name   The cursor name.

EXAMPLE 1: UPDATE THE pub_name COLUMN IN THE publishers TABLE

This update is based on the current row position in the cursor:

```
UPDATE publishers
SET pub_name = 'XYZ publisher'
WHERE CURRENT OF pub_crsr
```

EXAMPLE 2: DELETE A ROW IN THE publishers TABLE

This delete is based on the current row position in the cursor:

```
DELETE FROM publishers
WHERE CURRENT OF pub_crsr
```

GLOBAL VARIABLES

The following two global variables can be used to monitor the status of a cursor: `@@fetch_status` and `@@cursor_rows`.

The `@@fetch_status` variable displays the status of a last FETCH command. Following are the possible values for `@@fetch_status`:

0	Successful fetch
-1	The fetch failed or the fetch caused the cursor to go beyond the result set.
-2	The fetch row is missing from the data set.

The following is an example of `@@fetch_status`:

```
while @@fetch_status = 0
    ...do some processing
```

The `@@cursor_rows` variable displays the number of rows in the cursor set. Use this variable *after* the cursor has been opened. Following are the possible values for `@@cursor_rows`:

-n	Cursor is currently being loaded with data. The number returned indicates the number of rows currently in the key result set; however, the number continues to increase as SQL Server processes the SELECT statement (this is known as *asynchronous processing*).
n	Number of rows in the result set.
0	No matching rows in the result set.

PUTTING IT ALL TOGETHER

Now that you know something about cursor statements, positional updates, and global variables, the following cursor examples show you how all these components fit together.

EXAMPLE 1: LOOP THROUGH A TABLE

This example shows how the different components of a cursor (DECLARE, OPEN, FETCH, and DEALLOCATE) are used to loop through the publishers table. The `@@fetch_status` global variable is referenced each time a FETCH is performed. Once the record pointer reaches the end of the result set, the @@fetch_status variable are equal to -1. This arrangement prevents the code inside the while @@fetch_status = 0 section from being executed.

```
/* suppress counts from being displayed */
SET NOCOUNT ON

/* declare a cursor that will contain the pub_id, pub_name columns */
/* from the publishers table */
declare pub_crsr cursor
for
select pub_id,pub_name
from publishers
/* open the cursor *
open  pub_crs

/* get the first row from the cursor *
fetch next from pub_crs

/* loop through the rows in the cursor *
while @@fetch_status =
begi

  /* get next row *
  fetch next from pub_crs
 e n

/* close the cursor *
deallocate pub_crs
```

Output

```
pub_id  pub_name

0736    New Moon Books
0877    Binnet & Hardley
1389    Algodata Infosystems
1622    Five Lakes Publishing
1756    Ramona Publishers
9901    GGG&G
9952    Scootney Books
9999    Lucerne Publishing
```

Example 2: Display Object Names and Object Types

This example displays object names and types for all user-defined objects in the pubs database. It uses two variables (@name and @type) and conditional logic to determine the object type.

```
/* suppress counts from being displayed */
SET NOCOUNT ON

/* declare variables */
declare @name varchar(30)
declare @type char(2)

/* declare a cursor that will contain a list of object */
/* names and object types */
declare object_list cursor
for
select name, type
from sysobjects
where type <> 'S'
order by type

/* open the cursor */
open object_list

/* get the first row from the cursor */
fetch next from object_list into @name,@type

/* loop through the rows in the cursor */
while @@fetch_status = 0
begin
  /* determine object type */
  if @type = 'C'
    select '(CHECK constraint) ' + @name
  if @type = 'D'
    select '(Default or DEFAULT constraint) ' + @name
  if @type = 'F'
    select '(FOREIGN KEY constraint) ' + @name
  if @type = 'K'
    select '(PRIMARY KEY or UNIQUE constraint) ' + @name
  if @type = 'L'
    select '(Log) ' + @name
  if @type = 'P'
    select '(Stored procedure) ' + @name
  if @type = 'R'
    select '(Rule) ' + @name
  if @type = 'RF'
    select '(Stored procedure for replication) ' + @name
  if @type = 'TR'
    select '(Trigger) ' + @name
  if @type = 'U'
    select '(User table) ' + @name
  if @type = 'V'
    select '(View) ' + @name
  if @type = 'X'
    select '(Extended stored procedure) ' + @name

  /* get next table name */
  fetch next from object_list into @name,@type
end

/* close the cursor */
deallocate object_list
```

OUTPUT

```
name                 type

(CHECK constraint) CK__authors__au_id__02DC7882
(CHECK constraint) CK__authors__zip__04C4C0F4
(CHECK constraint) CK__jobs__max_lvl__2719D8F8
(CHECK constraint) CK__jobs__min_lvl__2625B4BF
(CHECK constraint) CK__publisher__pub_i__089551D8
(CHECK constraint) CK_emp_id
(Default or DEFAULT constraint) DF__authors__phone__03D09CBB
(Default or DEFAULT constraint) DF__employee__hire_d__30A34332
(Default or DEFAULT constraint) DF__employee__job_id__2BDE8E15
(Default or DEFAULT constraint) DF__employee__job_lv__2DC6D687
(Default or DEFAULT constraint) DF__employee__pub_id__2EBAFAC0
(Default or DEFAULT constraint) DF__jobs__job_desc__25319086
(Default or DEFAULT constraint) DF__publisher__count__09897611
(Default or DEFAULT constraint) DF__titles__pubdate__0F424F67
(Default or DEFAULT constraint) DF__titles__type__0D5A06F5
(FOREIGN KEY constraint) FK__discounts__stor___2160FFA2
(FOREIGN KEY constraint) FK__employee__job_id__2CD2B24E
(FOREIGN KEY constraint) FK__employee__pub_id__2FAF1EF9
(FOREIGN KEY constraint) FK__pub_info__pub_id__3567F84F
(FOREIGN KEY constraint) FK__roysched__title__1E8492F7
(FOREIGN KEY constraint) FK__sales__stor_id__1AB40213
(FOREIGN KEY constraint) FK__sales__title_id__1BA8264C
(FOREIGN KEY constraint) FK__titleauth__au_id__1312E04B
(FOREIGN KEY constraint) FK__titleauth__title__14070484
(FOREIGN KEY constraint) FK__titles__pub_id__0E4E2B2E
(PRIMARY KEY or UNIQUE constraint) PK__jobs__job_id__243D6C4D
(PRIMARY KEY or UNIQUE constraint) PK_emp_id
(PRIMARY KEY or UNIQUE constraint) UPK_storeid
(PRIMARY KEY or UNIQUE constraint) UPKCL_auidind
(PRIMARY KEY or UNIQUE constraint) UPKCL_pubind
(PRIMARY KEY or UNIQUE constraint) UPKCL_pubinfo
(PRIMARY KEY or UNIQUE constraint) UPKCL_sales
(PRIMARY KEY or UNIQUE constraint) UPKCL_taind
(PRIMARY KEY or UNIQUE constraint) UPKCL_titleidind
(Stored procedure) byroyalty
(Stored procedure) reptq1
(Stored procedure) reptq2
(Stored procedure) reptq3
(Trigger) employee_insupd
(User table) authors
(User table) discounts
(User table) employee
(User table) jobs
(User table) pub_info
(User table) publishers
(User table) roysched
(User table) sales
(User table) stores
(User table) titleauthor
(User table) titles
(View) titleview
```

EXAMPLE 3: UPDATE STATISTICS FOR ALL TABLES IN A DATABASE

This example combines the EXEC command with a cursor to automatically update the statistics for all tables within a database.

```
/* declare variables */
declare @table_name varchar(30)

/* declare a cursor that will contain a list of table */
/* names to be updated */
declare idx_cursor cursor
for select distinct a.name
from sysobjects a,sysindexes b
where a.type = 'U'
and a.id = b.id
and b.indid > 0

/* open the cursor */
open idx_cursor

/* get the first row from the cursor */
fetch next from idx_cursor into @table_name

/* loop through the rows in the cursor */
while @@fetch_status = 0
  begin
    /* issue UPDATE STATISTICS */
    EXEC ("UPDATE STATISTICS " + @table_name)

    /* get next table name */
    fetch next from idx_cursor into @table_name
  end

/* close the cursor */
deallocate idx_cursor
```

STRANGER THAN FICTION!

The SQL Server 6.x documentation incorrectly shows how to use the EXEC statement to execute a command at run time. In the example in the documentation, the concatenation symbol (+) was not included between the command and the variable.

Incorrect Syntax:

```
EXEC ("DROP TABLE "  @tablename)
```

Correct Syntax:

```
EXEC ("DROP TABLE "  + @tablename)
```

EXAMPLE 4: POSITIONAL UPDATE

This example looks at each row in the publishers table. If the pub_id column is equal to '1389', the pub_name column is updated to 'XYZ publisher'.

```
/* suppress counts from being displayed */
SET NOCOUNT ON

/* declare variables */
declare @pub_id char(4),@pub_name varchar(40)

/* declare a cursor that will contain the pub_id, pub_name columns */
/* from the publishers table */
/* NOTE: for UPDATE clause allows position updates */
declare pub_crsr cursor
for
select pub_id,pub_name
from publishers
for UPDATE OF pub_id,pub_name

/* open the cursor */
open pub_crsr

/* get the first row from the cursor */
fetch next from pub_crsr into @pub_id, @pub_name

/* loop through the rows in the cursor */
while @@fetch_status = 0
begin
  if @pub_id = '1389'
    update publishers
    set pub_name = 'XYZ publisher'
    where current of pub_crsr

  /* get next row */
  fetch next from pub_crsr into @pub_id, @pub_name
end

/* close the cursor */
deallocate pub_crsr
```

EXAMPLE 5: BATCH RUN

The following stored procedure and cursor example allows you to schedule a single stored procedure with the SQL Server scheduler that in turn executes any stored procedures in a table of batch procedures. The following example was used for an organization that performed many different types of batch processing using nightly stored procedures. The stored procedures were required to run in a certain order, and the addition of new procedures was a common occurrence. Instead of constantly scheduling the procedures, this example creates a single table, Batch_Procedures, that holds the names of the stored procedures to execute during the nightly batch run. It then creates a stored procedure called usp_Batch_Run that executes each procedure in the Batch_Procedures table.

Note

The current limitations to this stored procedure (which you can easily modify) are as follows:

◆ usp_Batch_Run can execute only stored procedures in the same database as usp_Batch_Run. This limitation exists because the system table sysobjects is checked, as a security measure, to validate that the name in the Batch_Procedures table is an existing stored procedure.

◆ usp_Batch_Run does not support stored procedures with parameters.

The batch processing consists of one support table, one report table, and a stored procedure. The table schema for Batch_Procedures is as follows:

```
CREATE TABLE Batch_Procedures (
   priority int,
   procedure_name varchar (20),
   description varchar (255)
)
CREATE  UNIQUE  CLUSTERED  INDEX cidx_priority ON Batch_Procedures
   ( priority )
```

For example, if you have a stored procedure named usp_rollups that is the first procedure to execute in the batch, you would add the procedure to the table Batch_Procedures as follows:

```
INSERT Batch_Procedures
Values(0,"usp_rollups","First procedure of the batch")
```

The stored procedure usp_Batch_Run opens a cursor on the Batch_Procedures table and executes each procedure in the Batch_Procedures table. The syntax for the Batch_Run procedure is as follows:

```
CREATE PROCEDURE usp_Batch_Run AS
/*-----------------------------------------------------------

usp_Batch_Run

-----------------------------------------------------------
Description: Executes all the stored procedures that are
             stored in the table Batch_Procedures. Results
             from the batch run are stored in the table
             Batch_Results.  This procedure is schedule to run
             via the task scheduler.

Parameters: None.

Status Returns: None.
```

```
Example: usp_Batch_Run
-----------------------------------------------------------------
History:
Mark Spenik, SAMS - DBA Survival Guide - 2nd Edition
March 28, 1996
Initial Release.
-----------------------------------------------------------*/
Declare @status int, @procedure_name varchar(20)
Declare @priority int, @description varchar(255), @id int
Declare @IsProc int

/*
** Declare a cursor to retrieve each stored procedure listed
** in the Batch_Procedures table.
*/
declare  batch_run_crsr  curso
For  Select  procedure_name,priority,descriptio
from  Batch_Procedure
Order  By  priorit

/*
** Clear out the results table from the previous night's run.
*/
truncate table Batch_Results

/*
** Open the cursor to begin running the batch stored procedures.
*/
Open batch_run_crsr
if @@error != 0
   goto Batch_Error

/*
** Get the first Row
*/
fetch next from batch_run_crsr
into @procedure_name, @priority, @description

While (@@fetch_status = 0) And (@@error = 0)
begin

    /*
    ** Make sure it's a stored procedure
    */
    select @IsProc = count(*)
    from sysobjects
    where id = object_id(@procedure_name)
    and type = 'P'

    if @IsProc > 0
    begin
        /*
        ** First log the starting time in the batch results table.
        */
        Insert Batch_Results
        Values(getdate(), NULL, @procedure_name, @description, NULL)
```

```
        /*
        ** Save identity value for the update.
        */
        Select @id = @@identity

        /*
        ** Execute the Stored Procedure
        */
        Execute @status = @procedure_name

        /*
        ** Update the results table.
        */
        UPDATE Batch_Results
            set end_time = getdate(),
            status = @status
        Where id = @id
    END /* If IsProc > 0 */
    /*
    ** Get the next procedure.
    */
    fetch next from batch_run_crsr
    into @procedure_name, @priority, @description

end /* While */

close batch_run_crsr
deallocate batch_run_crsr
return 0

/*
** Simple Error Exit
*/
Batch_Error:
RAISERROR ('Error executing stored procedure usp_Batch_Run',16,-1) return -100
```

The table Batch_Results is truncated every time the stored procedure usp_Batch_Run is executed. The Batch_Results table is used to log the status of the procedures that are executed during the stored procedure usp_Batch_Run. You can enhance the procedure by selecting all the rows from the Batch_Results table and use e-mail to notify users of the status of the batch run. The table schema for the Batch_Results table is as follows:

```
CREATE TABLE Batch_Results (
    id int IDENTITY,
    start_time datetime,
    end_time datetime NULL,
    proc_name varchar (20)  NULL,
    msg varchar (  255 )  NULL,
    status int NULL
  )
CREATE  UNIQUE  CLUSTERED  INDEX cidx_Id ON Batch_Results
    ( id )
```

BETWEEN THE LINES

Following are some important points to remember about SQL Server stored procedures:

◆ A stored procedure is a series of precompiled SQL statements and control-of-flow language statements.

◆ Stored procedures are stored on SQL Server and execute on SQL Server.

◆ Stored procedures are reusable but are not reentrant.

◆ A remote stored procedure is a stored procedure that is executed on another SQL Server from your local SQL Server.

◆ Stored procedures can have input and output parameters.

◆ The only user command permission that can be granted or revoked for a stored procedure is the EXECUTE permission.

◆ When creating stored procedures, use lots of comments and headers to simplify future maintenance.

Following are some important points to remember about cursors:

◆ Use a cursor to perform row-oriented operations on a set of data.

◆ SQL Server's cursors allow you to navigate forward and backward through a result set.

◆ Use the EXEC command inside a cursor to construct SQL statements at run time.

SUMMARY

As a DBA, it is important that you understand how you can use stored procedures and cursors to simplify your daily and weekly routines. If you understand what you can and cannot do with stored procedures and cursors, you can be of great benefit to your organization. You must also understand the concepts of *compiled* and *reusable but not reentrant* if you want to help developers who are trying to improve the performance of their applications.

24

USING STORED PROCEDURES AND CURSORS

- Developing a SQL
  Server Maintenance
  Plan

- Automating Database
  Administration Tasks

- SQL OLE Integration

- New SQL Server
  Utilities

PART VI

Maintaining the Shop

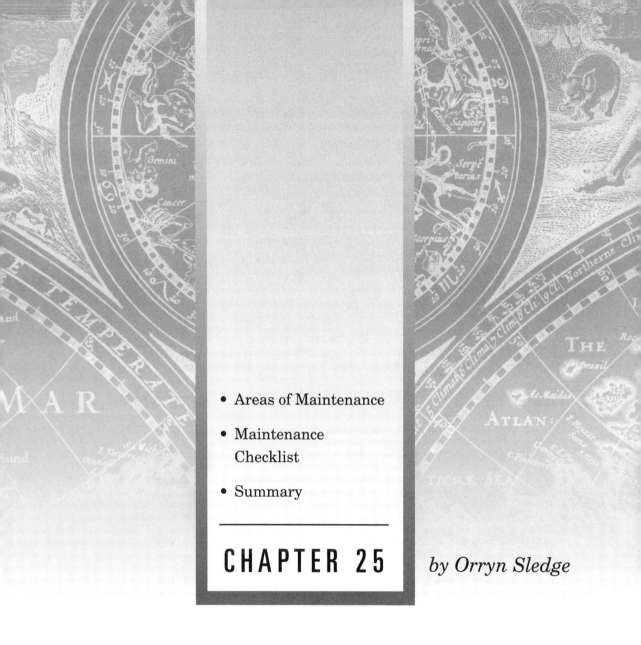

- Areas of Maintenance

- Maintenance
  Checklist

- Summary

CHAPTER 25

by Orryn Sledge

Developing a SQL Server
Maintenance Plan

Developing a SQL Server maintenance plan is a proactive approach that can help minimize system downtime. In terms of maintenance, SQL Server is no different than your car. Both require preventive maintenance and periodic tune ups. To help you keep SQL Server motoring along, this chapter discusses the types of maintenance that should be performed by a DBA.

AREAS OF MAINTENANCE

As a DBA, you should be concerned with four broad areas of maintenance:

◆ SQL Server maintenance
◆ Database maintenance
◆ Table/object maintenance
◆ Windows NT maintenance

SQL SERVER MAINTENANCE

The following list summarizes the types of maintenance that should be performed at the SQL Server database engine level:

◆ Monitor error logs
◆ Record configuration information
◆ Review the number of concurrent users
◆ Manage logins

MONITOR ERROR LOGS

A DBA should frequently review SQL Server's error log. When you review the error log, you should look for messages that do not appear under normal circumstances. Unfortunately, the error log contains more than just error messages. It also contains statements about the status of events, copyright information, and so on. This means that you have to know what to look for when you scan the error log. A good starting point is to look for the following keywords:

◆ `error :`
◆ `table corrupt`
◆ `level 16`
◆ `level 17`
◆ `level 21`
◆ `Severity: 16`
◆ `Severity: 17`
◆ `Severity: 21`

Note

You can view the error log from the Enterprise Manager or from a text editor.

To view the error log from the Enterprise Manager, select Error Log from the Server menu.

To view the current error log with a text editor, open the file c:\mssql\log\errorlog. You also can view the last six versions of the error log by opening the corresponding file (errorlog.1, errorlog.2, and so on).

The following listing shows a sample error log. Items in bold indicate errors a DBA may want to investigate:

```
96/04/29 01:35:59.03 kernel   Microsoft SQL Server  6.50 - 6.50.201 (Intel X86)
     Apr  3 1996 02:55:53
     Copyright (c) 1988-1996 Microsoft Corporation

96/04/29 01:35:59.03 kernel   Copyright (C) 1988-1994 Microsoft Corporation.
96/04/29 01:35:59.04 kernel   All rights reserved.
96/04/29 01:35:59.04 kernel   Logging SQL Server messages in file
'C:\MSSQL\LOG\ERRORLOG'
96/04/29 01:35:59.06 kernel   initconfig: number of user connections limited to 15
96/04/29 01:35:59.06 kernel   SQL Server is starting at priority class 'normal'
with dataserver serialization turned on (1 CPU detected).
96/04/29 01:35:59.15 kernel   Attempting to initialize Distributed Transaction
Coordinator
96/04/29 01:35:59.60 server   Failed to obtain TransactionDispenserInterface:
XACT_E_TMNOTAVAILABLE
96/04/29 01:35:59.62 kernel   initializing virtual device 0,
C:\MSSQL\DATA\MASTER.DAT
96/04/29 01:35:59.62 kernel   Opening Master Database ...
96/04/29 01:35:59.85 spid1    Loading SQL Server's  default sort order and charac-
ter set
96/04/29 01:35:59.97 spid1    Recovering Database 'master'
96/04/29 01:36:00.04 spid1    Recovery dbid 1 ckpt (7958,25) oldest tran=(7958,24)
96/04/29 01:36:00.11 spid1    1 transactions rolled forward
96/04/29 01:36:00.22 spid1    Activating disk 'dev1'
96/04/29 01:36:00.26 kernel   udopen: operating system error 2(The system cannot
find the file specified.) during the creation/opening of physical device
C:\MSSQL\DATA\dev1.DAT
96/04/29 01:36:00.27 kernel   udactivate (primary): failed to open device
C:\MSSQL\DATA\dev1.DAT for vdn 4
96/04/29 01:36:00.27 spid1    Activating disk 'MSDBData'
96/04/29 01:36:00.28 kernel   initializing virtual device 127,
C:\MSSQL\DATA\MSDB.DAT
96/04/29 01:36:00.28 spid1    Activating disk 'MSDBLog'
96/04/29 01:36:00.28 kernel   initializing virtual device 126,
C:\MSSQL\DATA\MSDBLOG.DAT
96/04/29 01:36:00.29 spid1    Activating disk 'salesdat'
96/04/29 01:36:00.29 kernel   udopen: operating system error 2(The system cannot
find the file specified.) during the creation/opening of physical device
C:\MSSQL\DATA\salesdat.DAT
```

```
96/04/29 01:36:00.30 kernel   udactivate (primary): failed to open device
C:\MSSQL\DATA\salesdat.DAT for vdn 1
96/04/29 01:36:00.33 spid1    Activating disk 'salesdat2'
96/04/29 01:36:00.33 kernel   udopen: operating system error 2(The system cannot
find the file specified.) during the creation/opening of physical device
C:\MSSQL\DATA\salesdat2.DAT
96/04/29 01:36:00.34 kernel   udactivate (primary): failed to open device
C:\MSSQL\DATA\salesdat2.DAT for vdn 3
96/04/29 01:36:00.34 spid1    Activating disk 'saleslog'
96/04/29 01:36:00.35 kernel   udopen: operating system error 2(The system cannot
find the file specified.) during the creation/opening of physical device
C:\MSSQL\DATA\saleslog.DAT
96/04/29 01:36:00.36 kernel   udactivate (primary): failed to open device
C:\MSSQL\DATA\saleslog.DAT for vdn 2
96/04/29 01:36:00.39 spid1    server name is 'OTS'
96/04/29 01:36:00.44 spid1    Recovering database 'model'
96/04/29 01:36:00.46 spid1    Recovery dbid 3 ckpt (338,0) oldest tran=(339,0)
96/04/29 01:36:00.54 spid1    Clearing temp db
96/04/29 01:36:03.24 kernel   Read Ahead Manager started.
96/04/29 01:36:03.29 kernel   Using 'SQLEVN60.DLL' version '6.00.000'.
96/04/29 01:36:03.38 kernel   Using 'OPENDS60.DLL' version '6.00.01.02'.
96/04/29 01:36:03.39 kernel   Using 'NTWDBLIB.DLL' version '6.50.201'.
96/04/29 01:36:03.48 ods      Starting SQL Mail session...
96/04/29 01:36:05.34 kernel   udread: Operating system error 6(The handle is
invalid.) on device 'C:\MSSQL\DATA\salesdat.DAT' (virtpage 0x01000018).
96/04/29 01:36:05.54 ods      Using 'SSNMPN60.DLL' version '6.5.0.0' to listen on
'\\.\pipe\sql\query'.
96/04/29 01:36:05.60 spid12   Error : 840, Severity: 17, State: 2
96/04/29 01:36:05.60 spid12   Device 'salesdat' (with physical name
'C:\MSSQL\DATA\salesdat.DAT', and virtual device number 1) is not available.
Please contact System Administrator for assistance.
96/04/29 01:36:05.60 spid12   Buffer 8a24e0 from database 'sales' has page number 0
in the page header and page number 24 in the buffer header
96/04/29 01:36:05.73 spid12   Unable to proceed with the recovery of dbid <6>
because of previous errors.  Continuing with the next database.
96/04/29 01:36:05.73 kernel   udread: Operating system error 6(The handle is
invalid.) on device 'C:\MSSQL\DATA\dev1.DAT' (virtpage 0x04000018).
96/04/29 01:36:05.74 spid12   Error : 840, Severity: 17, State: 2
96/04/29 01:36:05.74 spid12   Device 'dev1' (with physical name
'C:\MSSQL\DATA\dev1.DAT', and virtual device number 4) is not available.  Please
contact System Administrator for assistance.
96/04/29 01:36:05.75 spid12   Buffer 8a24e0 from database 'dev1' has page number 0
in the page header and page number 24 in the buffer header
96/04/29 01:36:05.76 spid12   Unable to proceed with the recovery of dbid <7>
because of previous errors.  Continuing with the next database.
96/04/29 01:36:05.80 spid11   Recovering database 'msdb'
96/04/29 01:36:05.83 spid10   Recovering database 'pubs'
96/04/29 01:36:05.89 spid11   Recovery dbid 5 ckpt (3587,11) oldest tran=(3587,10)
96/04/29 01:36:05.95 spid10   Recovery dbid 4 ckpt (778,31) oldest tran=(778,30)
96/04/29 01:36:06.02 spid11   1 transactions rolled forward in dbid 5.
96/04/29 01:36:06.11 spid10   1 transactions rolled forward in dbid 4.
96/04/29 01:36:06.57 spid1    Recovery complete.
96/04/29 01:36:06.75 spid1    SQL Server's default sort order is:
96/04/29 01:36:06.75 spid1           'nocase' (ID = 52)
96/04/29 01:36:06.76 spid1    on top of default character set:
96/04/29 01:36:06.76 spid1           'iso_1' (ID = 1)
96/04/29 01:36:07.11 spid1    Launched startup procedure 'sp_sqlregister'
```

```
96/04/29 01:36:07.42 ods      Error : 17903, Severity: 18, State: 1
96/04/29 01:36:07.42 ods      MAPI login failure.
96/04/29 01:36:07.44 ods      Error : 17951, Severity: 18, State: 1
96/04/29 01:36:07.44 ods      Failed to start SQL Mail session.
```

Tip

Use the Windows NT FINDSTR.EXE utility to search for text patterns in the error logs. (For the UNIX folks, FINDSTR.EXE is NT's equivalent of GREP.) This utility can help automate the process of scanning the log for errors. The following example shows how to scan the error log for the keyword error :

```
C:\mssql\log>findstr /i /n /c:"error :" errorlog
```

Following is some sample output:

```
C:\mssql\log>findstr /i /n /c:"error :" errorlog
34:95/09/16 11:24:20.42 ods        Error : 17903, Severity: 18, State: 1
36:95/09/16 11:24:20.43 ods        Error : 17951, Severity: 18, State: 1
53:95/09/16 11:24:35.53 ods        Error : 17903, Severity: 18, State: 1
55:95/09/16 11:24:35.54 ods        Error : 17951, Severity: 18, State: 1
```

RECORD CONFIGURATION INFORMATION

Two types of configuration information should be frequently generated and saved: Device Allocation Information and SQL Server Configuration.

DEVICE ALLOCATION INFORMATION

If you have to create a lost or damaged device to restore a database from a backup, you must know the size and type of device used by the database. (For example, was the log on the same device as the database or was it on a different device?) If this information is used to re-create a lost device, it is important to remember that device fragments must be re-created in the same order as they were originally created. Use the following query to generate device allocation information:

```
select b.name 'db_name',a.segmap 'fragment type', a.size 'fragment size'
from master..sysusages a, master..sysdatabases b
where a.dbid = b.dbid
```

Following is sample output:

```
db_name                          fragment type fragment size
-------------------------------- ------------- -------------
master                           7             1536
master                           7             7168
model                            7             512
msdb                             3             1024
msdb                             4             1024
pubs                             7             512
pubs                             7             1024
```

```
sales                3                10240
sales                4                2560
sales                4                2048
tempdb               7                1024
```

Following is an explanation for `fragment type`:

3 Data device

4 Log device

7 Log and data are on the same device

Any other values are user-defined segments.

`Fragment size` is displayed in 2K blocks (512 = 1M).

Tip

Use ISQL to generate device allocation information to a text file and then save the file as part of your nightly backup routine. The following example uses an input file named `device.sql` that contains the SQL statement to generate device information. The information is saved in the file `device_configure.txt`.

Following is the `device.sql` statement:

```
select b.name 'db_name',a.segmap 'fragment type', a.size 'fragment size'
from master..sysusages a, master..sysdatabases b
where a.dbid = b.dbid
go
```

Following is the ISQL statement:

```
isql -U sa -P -i device.sql -o device_configuration.txt
```

SQL Server Configuration

When you are unable to start SQL Server, server configuration information may help Microsoft's technical support group get you back up and running.

Use the system procedure `sp_configure` to generate a list of configuration information, as in the following example:

```
exec sp_configure
```

Following is the output:

```
name                minimum      maximum      config_value run_value
------------------- ------------ ------------ ------------ -----------
allow updates       0            1            0            0
backup buffer size  1            10           1            1
backup threads      0            32           5            5
cursor threshold    -1           2147483647   -1           -1
```

```
database size           1       10000       2       2
default language        0       9999        0       0
default sortorder id    0       255         52      52
fill factor             0       100         0       0
free buffers            20      524288      204     204
hash buckets            4999    265003      7993    7993
language in cache       3       100         3       3
LE threshold maximum    2       500000      200     200
LE threshold minimum    2       500000      20      20
LE threshold percent    1       100         0       0
locks                   5000    2147483647  5000    5000
logwrite sleep (ms)     -1      500         0       0
max async IO            1       255         8       8
max lazywrite IO        1       255         8       8
max worker threads      10      1024        255     255
media retention         0       365         0       0
memory                  1000    1048576     4096    8300
nested triggers         0       1           1       1
network packet size     512     32767       4096    4096
open databases          5       32767       20      20
open objects            100     2147483647  500     500
priority boost          0       1           0       0
procedure cache         1       99          30      30
RA cache hit limit      1       255         4       4
RA cache miss limit     1       255         3       3
RA delay                0       500         15      15
RA pre-fetches          1       1000        3       3
RA slots per thread     1       255         5       5
RA worker threads       0       255         3       3
recovery flags          0       1           0       0
recovery interval       1       32767       5       5
remote access           0       1           1       1
remote login timeout    0       2147483647  5       5
remote query timeout    0       2147483647  0       0
resource timeout        5       2147483647  10      10
set working set size    0       1           0       0
show advanced option    0       1           1       1
SMP concurrency         -1      64          0       1
sort pages              64      511         64      64
spin counter            1       2147483647  10000   0
tempdb in ram (MB)      0       2044        0       0
user connections        5       32767       20      20
```

Tip

Use ISQL and `sp_configure` to save configuration information to a text file and then save the file as part of your nightly backup routine. The following example creates a file named `sp_configure.txt` that contains configuration information:

```
isql -U sa -P -Q"sp_configure" -o sp_configure.txt
```

REVIEW THE NUMBER OF CONCURRENT USERS

It is a good idea to periodically monitor the number of concurrent user connections. Doing so can prevent a surprise phone call from a user complaining that he or she cannot log in to the system because the maximum number of user connections has been exceeded. I recommend using the threshold feature of the Performance Monitor to track the number of active connections. If the threshold is exceeded, you can have an e-mail notification sent to the DBA.

MANAGE LOGINS

As a DBA, you should periodically review who has access to SQL Server. In large organizations, people frequently change jobs. This means that you may have several SQL Server accounts that are not actively being used. You should inactivate these accounts to prevent unauthorized access to SQL Server.

DATABASE MAINTENANCE

The following list summarizes the types of maintenance that should be performed at the database level:

- ◆ Back up database and transaction log
- ◆ Test your backup strategy
- ◆ Run essential DBCC commands
- ◆ Audit database access

Note

Version
6.5

Several of the tasks discussed in this chapter can be automated through the Database Maintenance Wizard included with SQL Server 6.5. For more information about the Database Maintenance Wizard, see Chapter 26, "Automating Database Administration Tasks."

BACK UP DATABASE AND TRANSACTION LOG

To ensure database recovery, it is essential to frequently back up the database and transaction log. Devise a backup strategy that meets your needs and then periodically review this strategy to ensure that it satisfies your backup requirements (see Chapter 14, "Backups," for more information).

Test Your Backup/Recovery Strategy

Many DBAs back up SQL Server on a frequent basis, but only the good DBAs actually test their backup strategy by simulating database recovery. You should frequently test the integrity of your backups by actually performing a database recovery (see Chapter 15, "Recovery," for more information). Try to cover all the scenarios: dead server, lost drives, corrupt database, and so on. Do not put yourself in the position of having to be the one to tell the CEO that your backup strategy didn't work.

Run Essential DBCC Commands

It is important to frequently run key DBCC commands—and, if possible, to run the DBCC commands before you run your backup. These essential DBCC commands alert you to logical and/or physical errors. The reason you want to run these commands before you back up your database is that you may be unable to restore a database if it is corrupt, thus making your backup useless.

Tip

Do not forget to include the master database in your list of databases inspected by DBCC.

Note

Several of the preventive maintenance DBCC commands can be automatically scheduled through the Database Administration Wizard (see Chapter 26, "Automating Database Administration Tasks," for more information about this wizard).

Following is a list of DBCC commands that should be run on a frequent basis. (Refer to Appendix E for a complete explanation of these commands.)

- ◆ DBCC CHECKDB checks all tables and indexes in a database for pointer and data page errors.
- ◆ DBCC NEWALLOC checks data and index pages for extent structure errors.
- ◆ DBCC CHECKCATALOG ensures consistency among system tables in a database.

Tip

Use the `@@error` global variable to help automate nightly DBCC routines. Following is an example:

```
dbcc checkdb(pubs)
if @@error <> o
    run some error reporting routine (such as e-mail notification)
```

AUDIT DATABASE ACCESS

You should periodically perform a review of who has access to your production databases and what type of rights they possess. Doing so can prevent unauthorized access to production data.

TABLE/OBJECT MAINTENANCE

The following list summarizes the types of maintenance that should be performed at the table/object level:

◆ Use UPDATE STATISTICS

◆ Monitor the record count

◆ Audit object permissions

USE UPDATE STATISTICS

Keeping the statistics of an index up to date is crucial for maintaining performance. Frequently issue the UPDATE STATISTICS command for tables that contain indexes subject to frequent data modifications.

Tip

Automate UPDATE STATISTICS by using SQL Server's scheduling feature or by using the Database Maintenance Wizard. See Chapter 26, "Automating Database Administration Tasks," for more information.

MONITOR RECORD COUNT

In a transaction-oriented environment, it may be necessary to establish a limit on the number of records that should exist in your tables. Once the limit is exceeded, the records should be archived from the table. Doing so can ensure a consistent performance level.

AUDIT OBJECT PERMISSIONS

Periodically review the types of permissions (SELECT, INSERT, UPDATE, DELETE, and EXECUTE) that each user has to your production data. Doing so can help prevent security violations.

WINDOWS NT MAINTENANCE

The following list summarizes the types of maintenance that should be performed at the Windows NT level:

- ◆ Monitor the Windows NT event log
- ◆ Back up the registry
- ◆ Keep the emergency repair disk current
- ◆ Run disk defragmentation utilities
- ◆ Monitor available disk space
- ◆ Monitor CPU and memory usage

MONITOR THE WINDOWS NT EVENT LOG

When it comes to monitoring the event log, you should look for two types of errors: system errors and application errors.

System errors are hardware and operating-system specific. Examples include network errors, hardware problems, and driver errors.

Application errors are those errors associated with the application as well as certain types of SQL Server errors. Examples include connection errors, abnormal termination errors, and database failure errors.

BACK UP THE REGISTRY

The registry is vital to the Windows NT operating system. It stores operating system details, hardware information, software information, and user account information. If the registry is damaged, you may be able to restore it from a backup.

To back up the registry, use the tape backup software provided with Windows NT or use REGBACK.EXE (REGBACK.EXE is part of the Windows NT resource kit).

KEEP THE EMERGENCY REPAIR DISK CURRENT

Whenever hardware and software configurations change, you should update the emergency repair disk. Use RDISK.EXE to keep your emergency repair disk current.

RUN DISK DEFRAGMENTATION UTILITIES

You should periodically run disk defragmentation utilities on your server's hard disks. A high degree of hard disk fragmentation can lead to decreased hard disk performance. An NTFS drive must be checked with a third-party product. A FAT drive can be checked with SCANDISK.EXE.

MONITOR AVAILABLE DISK SPACE

It's a good idea to have at least 25 percent of the server's hard disk space not in use. This leaves enough free space for temporary files such as database dumps, BCP imports/exports, script generation, and so on.

MONITOR CPU AND MEMORY USAGE

The easiest way to monitor CPU and memory usage is to use the Performance Monitor (for more information on using the Performance Monitor, refer to Chapter 18, "Monitoring SQL Server"). If you see sustained spikes in CPU usage, it may be time to upgrade your CPU or redistribute the workload. Also keep an eye on memory usage and the number of free bytes. Insufficient memory leads to a high number of page faults, which degrades performance.

MAINTENANCE CHECKLIST

Here's a checklist of items for maintenance.

CHECKLIST

Frequency of Execution	Task
Daily	
	☐ Monitor error logs
	☐ Back up database and transaction log
	☐ Run essential DBCC commands
	☐ Use UPDATE STATISTICS
	☐ Monitor the Windows NT event log
	☐ Monitor CPU and memory usage
Weekly	
	☐ Monitor available disk space
Monthly	
	☐ Test your backup strategy
	☐ Monitor record count
	☐ Review the number of concurrent users
	☐ Manage logins
	☐ Audit database access
	☐ Audit object permissions
As Needed	
	☐ Record configuration information (*SQL Server configuration and **device allocation)
	☐ Back up the registry
	☐ Keep the emergency repair disk current
	☐ Run disk defragmentation utilities

*Information should be recorded whenever SQL Server configuration information is changed.

**Information should be recorded whenever a database is modified or created.

SUMMARY

Several types of tasks are required to maintain SQL Server. Many of these tasks can be automated through SQL Server's scheduler and Alert Manager. The next chapter, "Automating Database Administration Tasks," discusses how to automate common DBA tasks.

CHAPTER 26　　*by Orryn Sledge*

Automating Database Administration Tasks

Virtually every organization can reduce administration effort by automating common DBA tasks. SQL Server 6.x provides two tools that can help automate common tasks: Task Scheduler and Alert Manager; SQL Server 6.5 provides the additional tool Database Maintenance Wizard.

TASK SCHEDULER

The *Task Scheduler* is an easy-to-use and robust scheduler. In addition to being a scheduler, it includes other useful features, such as a history log and the capability to e-mail or page an operator when an event occurs.

Following are just a few of the types of tasks that can be automated with the Task Scheduler:

- ◆ **Automate backups:** Automatic database backups should be an integral part of everyone's production systems. The scheduler can be used to automatically back up a database at a preset interval. See Chapter 14, "Backups," for more information on automatically backing up the database.

- ◆ **Automate UPDATE STATISTICS:** It is important to keep index distribution statistics up to date. Otherwise, the optimizer may ignore existing indexes. To automatically keep statistics fresh, use the scheduler to call a stored procedure that issues the UPDATE STATISTICS command.

- ◆ **Schedule DBCC commands:** DBCC commands should be run frequently to check for corrupt databases and tables. Depending on the size of your databases, try to schedule the DBCC commands before you back up your database. It is important to do this because if you back up a corrupt database, you may be unable to restore it.

- ◆ **Automate data imports and exports:** Many companies that use SQL Server also must import and export data to other non-SQL Server systems within the organization. An easy way to facilitate the transfer of information is to schedule a task that directly calls BCP or to create a stored procedure that in turn calls BCP. The advantage of using a stored procedure to call BCP is that you can chain additional tasks to the procedure, such as validating data, summarizing data, and so on.

Tip

To call BCP from a stored procedure, use the extended stored procedure xp_cmdshell.

USING THE TASK SCHEDULER

Now that you know the types of tasks that can be automated, let's go through a simple example of actually scheduling a task. For this example, assume that you want to schedule a stored procedure that removes any sales data more than seven days old. Also assume that you want the procedure to run on a nightly basis at 3:00 A.M. and that you want to be notified by e-mail that the procedure successfully ran.

The following is a sample procedure:

```
CREATE PROCEDURE usp_remove_old_data AS
/* remove transactions that are 7 or more days old */
DELETE
FROM sales
WHERE DATEDIFF(dd,sales_date,getdate()) > = 7
```

Note

The SQLExecutive service must be running for the Task Scheduler to work. To determine whether SQLExecutive is running, check the SQL Executive status indicator from the Enterprise Manager. The SQL Service Manager can also be used to check the status of the SQLExecutive. To open the SQL Service Manager, go to Program Manager and click the SQL Service Manager icon in the Microsoft SQL Server 6.5 (Common) group. The color of the traffic light indicates the status of the service.

To schedule the `usp_remove_old_data` stored procedure, follow these steps:

1. Click the Managed Scheduled Tasks toolbar button in the Enterprise Manager. The Manage Scheduled Tasks dialog box appears (see Figure 26.1).

2. Click the New Task toolbar button to add a task. The New Task dialog box appears.

3. Enter the following task information: task name, task type, database, and command to execute (see Figure 26.2). From the New Task dialog box, you can execute the following types of commands:

TSQL	Executes Transact SQL statements. Examples include TRUNCATE TABLE authors, UPDATE authors SET au_id = 100, EXEC usp_my_proc, and so on.
CmdExec	Execute a BAT, EXE, or CMD file. Examples include BCP.EXE, ISQL.EXE, CUSTOM.BAT files, and so on.

Distribution   Used in conjunction with replication. Enables you to define replication distribution commands.

LogReader   Used in conjunction with replication. Enables you to define replication log reader commands.

Sync   Used in conjunction with replication. Enables you to define replication synchronization commands.

Figure 26.1.
The Manage Scheduled
Tasks dialog box.

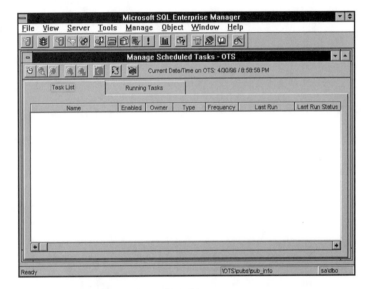

Figure 26.2.
The New Task
dialog box.

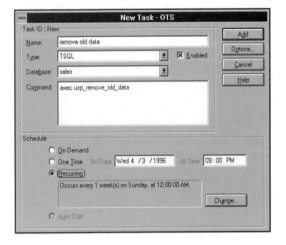

Note

Be sure that you select the appropriate database when running TSQL commands; otherwise, the command may fail.

4. For this example, you want the stored procedure to run every night at 3:00 A.M. To do this, click the Change button. The Task Schedule dialog box appears.

5. From the Task Schedule dialog box, enter the corresponding scheduling information and click the OK button (see Figure 26.3).

Figure 26.3.
The Task Schedule
dialog box.

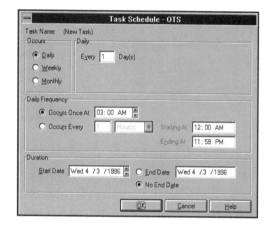

6. Because you want to be notified by e-mail when the task is successfully executed, add the notification by clicking the Options button in the New Task dialog box. The Task Options dialog box appears.

7. For this example, specify an e-mail operator (at this point, you can define a new e-mail operator by selecting the <New Operator> option from the E-mail Operator list box). Select the On Success Write To Windows NT Event Log checkbox (see Figure 26.4). Click OK to save the notification information.

Note

To notify an operator by e-mail, SQL Mail must be running and connected to your e-mail service. Use the SQL Mail status indicator in the Enterprise Manager to validate that SQL Mail is successfully connected.

Tip

Use the extended stored procedure `xp_sendmail` to test whether your e-mail service is properly configured, as in the following example:

```
xp_sendmail 'recipient_name', 'this is a test'
```

Figure 26.4.
The Task Options
dialog box.

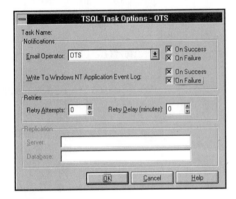

8. To save the task, click the Add button in New Task dialog box.

After a task has been created, it is a good idea to test it by manually executing the task. Follow these steps to manually execute a task:

1. From the Manage Scheduled Tasks dialog box, click the Run Task toolbar button. This action executes the task immediately.

2. To update the task information, click the Refresh toolbar button. This action should always be done *before* clicking the Task History toolbar button. SQL Server's task dialog boxes are *not* automatically refreshed!

3. To determine whether the task ran successfully, click the Task History toolbar button. The Task History dialog box appears (see Figure 26.5). From this dialog box, you can see that the task was successfully executed.

You also can see that this task was successfully executed by looking at your e-mail and NT's event log (see Figures 26.6 and 26.7).

Figure 26.5.
The Task History
dialog box.

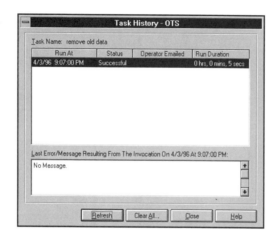

Figure 26.6.
E-mail notification.

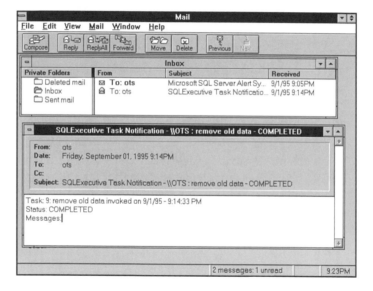

Figure 26.7.
Event log notification.

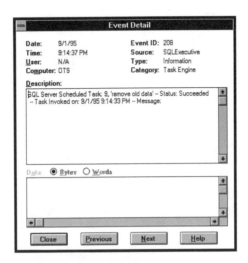

EXTENDING THE TASK SCHEDULER

In the preceding section, you learned how to schedule a task and how to e-mail an operator when the task is complete. This section builds on what you learned in the previous section. For this example, assume that you want to schedule the same task, but you want the e-mail message to contain the number of rows deleted by the stored procedure.

No problem! However, you *do* have to shift the e-mail notification logic to the stored procedure rather than leave it with the Task Scheduler. The Task Scheduler can only send a success or failure e-mail message; it cannot return the number of rows deleted, updated, and so on.

To send an e-mail message that contains the number of rows deleted, you must make a few modifications to the usp_remove_old_data stored procedure. The biggest modification is the additional call to the xp_sendmail extended stored procedure. The xp_sendmail command enables you to e-mail a message that contains the number of rows deleted.

The following stored procedure contains the necessary modifications:

```
CREATE PROCEDURE usp_remove_old_data AS
declare @rows_deleted int
declare @e_mail_message varchar(255)

/* remove transactions that are 7 or more days old */
DELETE
FROM transaction_control
WHERE DATEDIFF(dd,transaction_date,getdate()) > = 7
```

```
/* store number of rows deleted to a variable */
SELECT @rows_deleted = @@rowcount

/* build message */
SELECT @e_mail_message = 'Numbers of rows removed by usp_remove_old_data = ' +
  CONVERT(varchar(20),@rows_deleted)

/* e-mail the results back to the operator */
EXEC master..xp_sendmail 'OTS', @e_mail_message
```

Note

Whenever you call an extended stored procedure, you should include the `master` database in the statement (as in `master..xp_sendmail`). Otherwise, you must be in the `master` database to run an extended stored procedure.

Now when the Task Scheduler executes the `usp_remove_old_data` stored procedure, the number of rows deleted are included in the e-mail message to the operator (see Figure 26.8).

Figure 26.8.
An e-mail message stating the number of rows deleted.

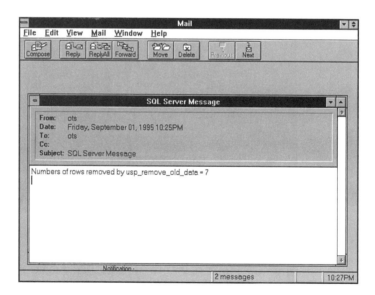

Tip

SQL Server 6.x enables Transact SQL commands to be resolved at run time through the use of the EXEC command. This capability opens up an entire list of DBA functions that can be automated through the use of

stored procedures. For example, the following stored procedure uses
UPDATE STATISTICS for all tables that contain indexes:

```
CREATE PROCEDURE usp_update_statistics AS
         /* declare variables */
         declare @table_name varchar(30)

         /* declare a cursor that will contain a list of table */
         /* names to be updated */
         declare idx_cursor cursor
          for select distinct a.name
            from sysobjects a,sysindexes b
            where a.type = 'U'
            and a.id = b.id
            and b.indid > 0

         /* open the cursor */
         open idx_cursor

         /* get the first row from the cursor */
         fetch next from idx_cursor into @table_name

         /* loop through the rows in the cursor */
         while @@fetch_status = 0
           begin
             /* issue UPDATE STATISTICS */
             EXEC ("UPDATE STATISTICS " + @table_name)

             /* get next table name */
             fetch next from idx_cursor into @table_name
           end

         /* close the cursor */
         deallocate idx_cursor
```

After you create this stored procedure, you can schedule it to execute
automatically on a recurring basis. This helps to ensure that your
index statistics are up to date.

STRANGER THAN FICTION!

The SQL Server 6.x documentation incorrectly shows how to use the
EXEC statement to execute a command at run time. The documentation
example does not include the concatenation symbol (+) between the
command and the variable.

Following is the **incorrect** syntax:

```
EXEC ("DROP TABLE "  @tablename)
```

Following is the **correct** syntax:

```
EXEC ("DROP TABLE "  + @tablename)
```

ALERT MANAGER

The *Alert Manager* enables you to define alerts that are executed automatically on the occurrence of an event. When the alert is executed, an operator can be notified by e-mail or pager. An alert also can execute additional tasks, such as calling another transact SQL command or calling an external program in the form of a BAT, EXE, or CMD file. These features enable a DBA to be more proactive to conditions that require attention.

With the Alert Manager, you can create three types of alerts: standard alerts, Performance Monitor alerts, and business alerts.

Following are examples of standard alerts:

◆ Database out of space

◆ SQL Server was abnormally terminated

◆ Database is corrupt

◆ Table is corrupt

Following are examples of Performance Monitor alerts:

◆ High CPU Utilization

◆ Transaction log almost full

◆ Blocking

Following are examples of business alerts:

◆ Low inventory

◆ Aborted download

STANDARD ALERTS

Now that you have an understanding of the different types of alerts that can be managed, this section runs through a simple example of how to configure the Alert Manager for a standard alert. For this example, assume that you want to define an alert that notifies an operator by e-mail when the pubs database is out of space.

Note

> SQLExecutive must be running for the Alert Manager to work.

To create a sample alert that notifies an operator through e-mail, follow these steps:

1. From the Enterprise Manager, click the Manage Alerts and Operators toolbar button. The Manage Alerts and Operators dialog box appears (see

26

AUTOMATING ADMINISTRATION TASKS

Figure 26.9). From the Manage Alerts and Operators dialog box, you can add, delete, and edit alerts and manage operators.

Figure 26.9.
The Manage Alerts and Operators dialog box.

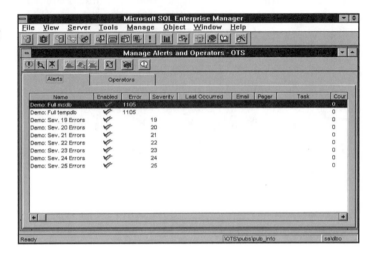

2. From the Operators tab in the Manage Alerts and Operators dialog box, click the New Operator toolbar button. The New Operator dialog box appears.

3. In the New Operator dialog box, type the ID and e-mail name of the person you want to notify of an alert condition (see Figure 26.10). You also can enter pager information. Click OK to save the operator information.

Figure 26.10.
The New Operator dialog box.

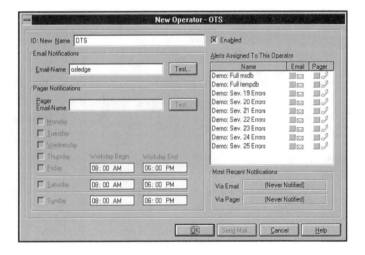

4. Now that you have defined an operator to handle the alert, you must define the alert. Click the Alerts tab in the Manage Alerts and Operators dialog box to make that page active; click the New Alert toolbar button. The New Alert dialog box appears (see Figure 26.11).

Figure 26.11.
The New Alert
dialog box.

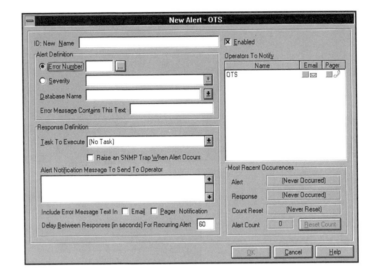

5. For this example, assume that you don't remember which error number is generated when the database is out of space. Click the Manage Error Messages button next to the Error Number field near the top of the New Alert dialog box. The Manage SQL Server Messages dialog box appears.

6. With the Manage SQL Server Messages dialog box, you can find, add, delete, and edit error messages. To help you find the corresponding error message, enter the following message text:

   `out of space`

   Click the Find button to list all matching error messages (see Figure 26.12).

7. You want to base your alert on error number 1105. Highlight the row that contains error number 1105 and click the Select button. The New Alert dialog box reappears, showing the selected error number.

8. After you select an error number, enter the remaining alert information: alert name, alert definition, response definition, and operators to notify (see Figure 26.13).

Figure 26.12.
Finding an error
message.

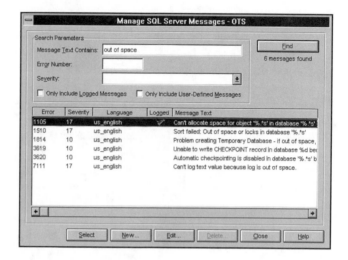

Figure 26.13.
Entering alert
information.

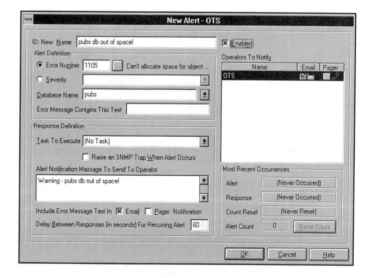

9. Click the OK button to save the new alert.

Congratulations! You just created an alert that will notify an operator when the pubs database is out of space. Figure 26.14 shows the e-mail message the operator receives when the pubs database is out of space.

Figure 26.14.
E-mail notification sent
to the operator when
the pubs *database is out*
of space.

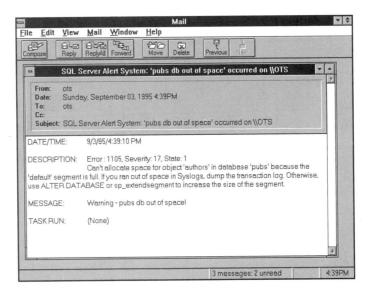

26

PERFORMANCE MONITOR ALERTS

Some types of alerts such as high CPU utilization, transaction log almost full, and blocking require the use of the Performance Monitor, SQLALRTR.EXE, and the Alert Manager. Any type of alert that can be created in the Performance Monitor can be passed to the SQL Server Alert Manager. In turn, the Alert Manager can e-mail or page an operator.

To explain how the Performance Monitor interacts with the Alert Manager, the following steps build an alert that notifies an operator when one or more users are blocked.

1. From the Alert Manager dialog box, click the New Alert toolbar button. The New Alert dialog box appears (see Figure 26.15). For this example, you need to create a custom error. This error will be used by SQLALRTR.EXE.

2. To create a custom alert, click the Manage Error Messages button. The Manage SQL Server Messages dialog box appears.

3. From the Manage SQL Server Messages dialog box, click the New button. The New Message dialog box appears.

4. In the New Message dialog box, enter the error number, severity level, and message text. For this example, use error number 50001 (see Figure 26.16). Be sure to select the Always Write To Windows NT Eventlog option; otherwise, the event is not recognized by the Alert Manager. Click the OK button to save the alert.

Figure 26.15.
The New Alert dialog
box.

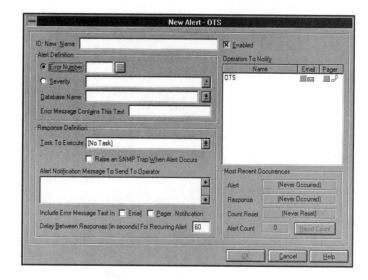

Note

User-defined error messages must use an error number greater than 50000.

Figure 26.16.
Creating a new error
number message.

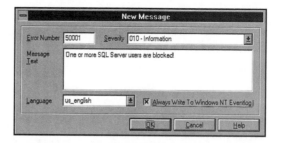

5. Now that you have created a new error number and message, go back to the New Alert dialog box and fill in the remainder of the alert notification (see Figure 26.17). Click the OK button to save the alert.

6. To define the alert in the Performance Monitor, click the SQL Performance Monitor icon in the Microsoft SQL Server 6.5 (Common) group. The Performance Monitor dialog box appears.

7. From the Performance Monitor dialog box, click the View Alerts toolbar button. The View Alerts dialog box appears.

8. From the View Alerts dialog box, click the Add an Alert Entry toolbar button. The Add To Alert dialog box appears.

Figure 26.17.
The alert for blocked
users.

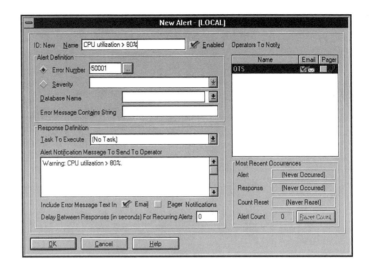

9. For this example, select the SQLServer-Locks object and the Users Blocked counter.

10. In the Alert If box, click the Over button and enter 1 for the alert threshold level. This means that when a user is blocked, an alert will be issued.

11. From the Run Program on Alert box, enter the SQLALRTR.EXE command. For this example, you want to trigger error number 50001.

To trigger error 50001, use the following syntax in SQL Server 6.5:

```
c:\mssql\binn\sqlalrtr /E50001
```

```
sqlalrtr -?  ¦  -E error number
              [-M parameters for error number]
              [-S server name to fire alert on]
              [-T (use trusted SA connection) ¦ -P SA password]
              [-D database name to fire alert from]
              [-V severity of error (1 to 25)]
```

Use the following syntax in SQL Server 6.0:

```
sqlalrtr -E error number [-M parameters for error number] [-S server_name]
         [-T (use trusted SA connection) ¦ -P SA password]
         [-D database name to fire alert from] [-V severity of error
         ➥(1 to 25)]
```

Note

The -P and -T parameters of SQLALRTR.EXE are mutually exclusive—using them together will cause an error.

12. Click the Add button to save the alert (see Figure 26.18).

26

AUTOMATING ADMINISTRATION TASKS

Version
6.5

Figure 26.18.
The finished Perfor-
mance Monitor alert.

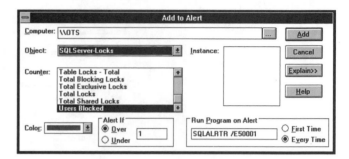

Note

Current alert settings are discarded when the Performance Monitor is closed unless the settings are manually saved (choose Save Workspace from the File menu).

Tip

The Performance Monitor must be running for the Alert Manager to detect that a threshold has been exceeded. The proper way to automatically load the Performance Monitor during the startup of Windows NT is to run the Performance Monitor as a Windows NT Service (see the Windows NT 3.51 Resource Kit for more information).

This completes the Performance Monitor alert example. Figure 26.19 shows the e-mail message an operator would receive when this alert is triggered. Figure 26.20 shows the alert generated by the Performance Monitor.

BUSINESS ALERTS

In addition to handling SQL Server errors and thresholds, the Alert Manager can be used to alert operators to business conditions. Suppose that you own a used car dealership and you want to be alerted by e-mail whenever the number of cars on the lot is below 20.

Assume that the number of cars on your lot can be determined by counting the number of records in a table named cars. Also assume that each time a car is sold, it is deleted from the cars table.

Figure 26.19.
The e-mail message
sent when the blocked
user alert is triggered.

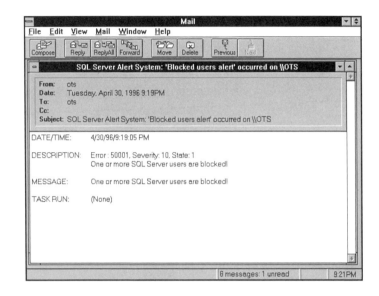

Figure 26.20.
The blocked user alert
in the Performance
Monitor.

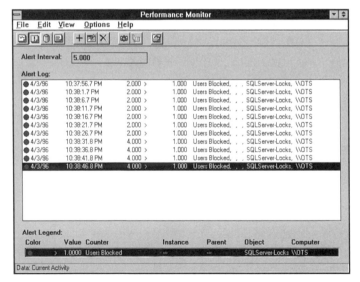

The creation of this type of alert consists of three different steps:

1. Defining the error number and message that corresponds to the alert.

2. Setting the trigger on the event that executes the error that corresponds to the alert.

3. Alert notification.

26

AUTOMATING ADMINISTRATION TASKS

STEP 1: DEFINE THE ERROR NUMBER AND MESSAGE

Follow these steps to define the error number and message that corresponds to the alert:

1. To define a custom error number, click the Manage Messages toolbar button in the Manage Alerts and Operators dialog box. The Manage SQL Server Messages dialog box appears.

2. From the Manage SQL Server Messages dialog box, click the New button. The New Message dialog box appears.

3. In the New Message dialog box, enter the error number, severity, and message text you want to associate with the low inventory message (see Figure 26.21). For this example, use error number 50002.

Figure 26.21.
Adding a new error
message.

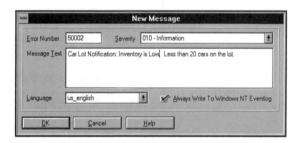

4. To save the error message, click the OK button in the New Message dialog box and click the Close button in the Manage SQL Server Messages dialog box.

STEP 2: SET UP THE EVENT THAT EXECUTES THE ERROR

Every time a car is sold, it is deleted from the cars table. This arrangement enables you to use a trigger that checks to see whether the number of cars on hand is below 20. (Remember that triggers are automatically executed when a DELETE, UPDATE, or INSERT event occurs.)

The following code shows how to create a trigger that automatically issues error number 50002 when fewer than 20 cars are on the lot. In turn, the Alert Manager detects error 50002 and automatically sends an e-mail message to the operator.

```
/* DELETE Trigger Example */
CREATE TRIGGER trg_delete_cars ON dbo.cars
FOR DELETE
AS
/* declare variables */
declare @car_count int
```

```
/* count the number of cars on hand */
SELECT @car_count = COUNT(*)
FROM cars

/* If quantity is less than < 20 */
/* issue error 50002 (user defined error message).  This will */
/* fire an alert which will notify an operator */
IF @car_count < 20
  BEGIN
    /* RAISERROR parameter explanation: */
    /* 50002 = low inventory message */
    /* 16 = severity level (miscellaneous user error) */
    /* -1 = error state */
    RAISERROR(50002,16,-1)
  END
```

STEP 3: BUILD THE ALERT NOTIFICATION

Now that you have defined your error number and trigger, you must build the actual alert notification.

1. In the Manage Alerts and Operators dialog box, click the New Alert toolbar button. The New Alert dialog box appears.

2. In the New Alert dialog box, enter the alert configuration information. Be sure to use the correct error number (in this example, 50002) for the Alert definition. Also enter the notification message and the operator you want to be notified when this condition arises (see Figure 26.22). Click the OK button to save the alert.

Now the low inventory alert is automatically executed whenever the number of cars on hand falls below 20. Figure 26.23 shows the e-mail message that an operator will receive when this alert is triggered.

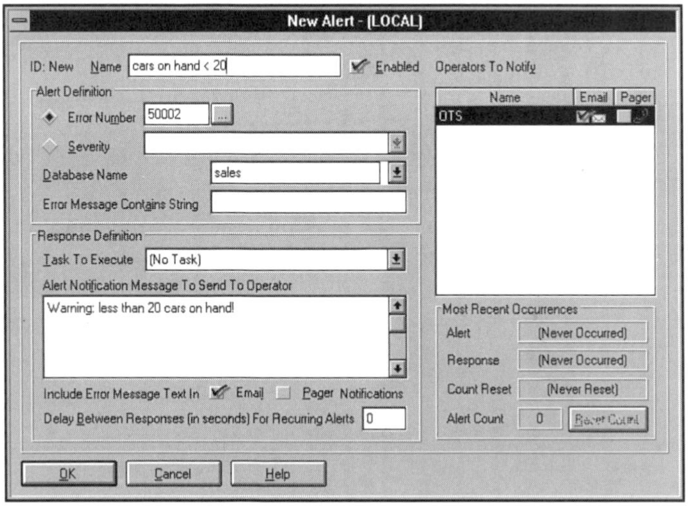

Figure 26.22.
The low inventory alert.

Figure 26.23.
The low inventory
e-mail message.

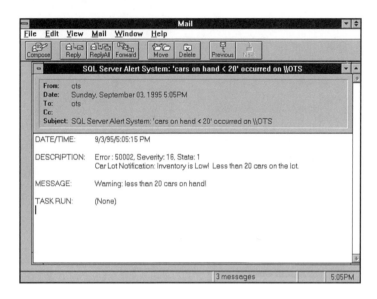

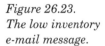 DATABASE MAINTENANCE WIZARD

The Database Maintenance Wizard can automate many of the common tasks a DBA normally performs. Before this wizard was developed, many DBA tasks were script based. With this wizard, however, you can now graphically automate DBCC commands, UPDATE STATISTICS, and other administrative functions. A nice feature of the wizard is its ability to e-mail results to an operator.

The following steps explain how to use the Database Maintenance Wizard:

1. From the Enterprise Manager, click the Database Maintenance Wizard toolbar button. The Database Maintenance Plan Wizard dialog box appears (see Figure 26.24).

Note

Do not forget to include the following system databases when using the Database Maintenance Wizard to automate backups and DBCC tasks: master, model, msdb, tempdb (do not include tempdb in your backup plan). These system databases are actual databases, just as the pubs database or any other database used to store information is a database. It is just as important to back up and run DBCC commands for these databases as it is for any other database.

Figure 26.24.
The Database Mainte-
nance Plan Wizard
dialog box.

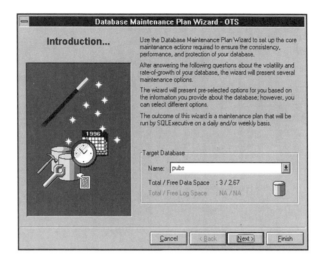

2. From the Database Maintenance Plan Wizard dialog box, select the Target Database and click the Next button to continue. The About the Data In Your Database dialog box appears (see Figure 26.25).

Figure 26.25.
The About the Data In
Your Database dialog
box.

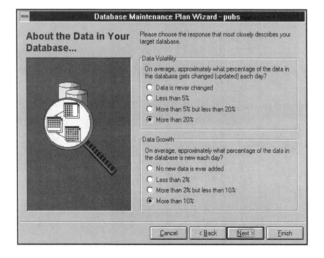

3. From the About the Data In Your Database dialog box, select the appropriate responses for Data Volatility and Data Growth. These responses help the wizard develop a strategy that best suits your needs. Click the Next button to continue. The Data Verification dialog box appears (see Figure 26.26).

Figure 26.26.
The Data Verification
dialog box.

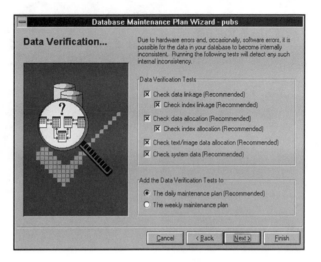

4. From the Data Verification dialog box, select the appropriate Data Verification Tests and when you want to schedule the verification tests. Following are explanations of the Data Verification tests:

- ◆ **Check data linkage:** Selecting this option is the equivalent of using DBCC CHECKDB with the NOINDEX option. This option checks all data pages and tables in the database for pointer and data page errors (see Appendix E for more information on DBCC CHECKDB).

- ◆ **Check index linkage:** Selecting this option is the equivalent of using the DBCC CHECKDB command. This option differs from the DBCC CHECKDB with the NOINDEX option in that the CHECKDB command also verifies index pages (see Appendix E for more information on DBCC CHECKDB).

Note

If possible, you should execute the Check Data Linkage or the Check Index Linkage option only when the database is free from user activity. Ideally, the database should be in single-user mode before you run these options to ensure that the information reported by these commands is accurate. Also, the number of locks generated by these commands can lead to severe blocking and contention for resources if other users are in the database.

- ◆ **Check data allocation:** Selecting this option is the equivalent of using the DBCC NEWALLOC command with the NOINDEX option. This option verifies that each data page is properly tracked within SQL Server (see Appendix E for more information on DBCC NEWALLOC).

◆ **Check index allocation:** Selecting this option is the equivalent of using the DBCC NEWALLOC command. This option differs from the DBCC NEWALLOC command with the NOINDEX option in that the DBCC NEWALLOC command also verifies index pages for allocation errors (see Appendix E for more information on DBCC NEWALLOC).

Note

If possible, you should execute Check Data Allocation or the Check Index Allocation option only when the database is free from user activity. Ideally, the database should be set in single-user mode before you run these options to ensure that the information reported by these commands is accurate.

◆ **Check text/image data allocation:** Selecting this option is the equivalent of using the DBCC TEXTALL command with the FAST option. This option verifies allocation and linkage information for tables that contain text or image data (see Appendix E for more information on DBCC TEXTALL).

◆ **Check system data:** Selecting this option is the equivalent of using the DBCC CHECKCATALOG command. This option checks the system tables for orphaned records and data consistency (see Appendix E for more information on DBCC CHECKCATALOG).

After selecting the appropriate Data Verification tests and adding the verification to the maintenance plan, click the Next button to continue. The Data Optimization dialog box appears (see Figure 26.27).

Figure 26.27.
The Data Optimization
dialog box.

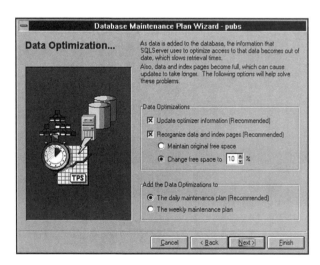

26

5. From the Data Optimization dialog box, select the appropriate Data Optimizations and when you want to schedule the optimization. Following are explanations of the Data Optimization options:

  ◆ **Update Optimizer Information:** Selecting this option is the equivalent of using the UPDATE STATISTICS command (see Chapters 21 and 22 for more information). Select this option when your database has tables that contain indexes and these tables are subject to frequent data modifications. This option regenerates the statistics for each index. If you do not select this option, you may find that the query optimizer ignores useful indexes because the index's statistics do not accurately reflect the data.

  ◆ **Reorganize data and index pages:** Selecting this option is the equivalent of using the DBCC DBREINDEX command (see Appendix E for more information on DBCC DBREINDEX). This option rebuilds all indexes associated with all tables in the selected database (see Chapters 21 and 22 for more information). Using this option may reduce page splitting and improve data modification performance. Additionally, the Maintain Original Free Space and Change Free Space To radio buttons control the fill-factor level.

After selecting the appropriate Data Optimizations and adding the verification to the maintenance plan, click the Next button to continue. The Data Protection dialog box appears (see Figure 26.28).

Figure 26.28.
The Data Protection
dialog box.

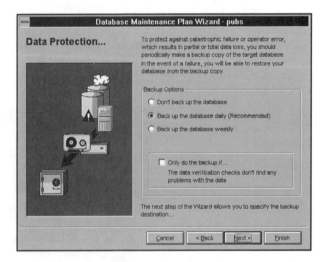

6. From the Data Protection dialog box, select the appropriate Backup Options (see Chapter 14, "Backups," for more information on backing up the database). Select the Only Do the Backup If option if you want the database to be backed up only if it is free from any errors. Click the Next button to continue. The Data Backup Destination dialog box appears (see Figure 26.29).

Note

The Database Administration Wizard does not provide a facility to back up the database log. Log backups must be manually scheduled or scheduled through the backup utility in the Enterprise Manager.

Tip

When working with a database that requires 24-hour access, you may not be able to perform an entire set of DBCC commands before you back up the database. An alternative to running DBCC commands before backing up is to dump the database, load the dump onto another server, and then run the DBCC commands.

Figure 26.29.
The Backup Destination dialog box.

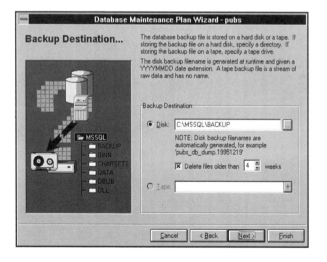

7. From the Backup Destination dialog box, select the appropriate Backup Destination. From this dialog box, you can specify whether you want to store the backup on disk or on tape. Click the Next button to continue. The When To Run, Who To Notify dialog box appears (see Figure 26.30).

Tip

An alternative to backing up directly to tape is to generate the backup to the hard drive and then use NT's backup software (or some third-party software) to back up the entire hard drive. This way, you have your most recent database dump in two places—on disk and on tape.

Figure 26.30.
The When To Run, Who
To Notify dialog box.

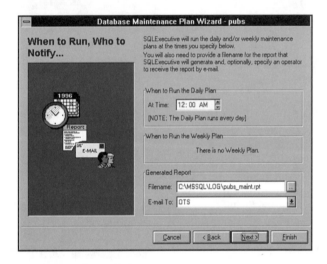

8. From the When To Run, Who To Notify dialog box, select the appropriate When To Run the Daily Plan, When To Run the Weekly Plan, and Generated Report options. Click the Next button to continue. The Wizard Complete! dialog box appears (see Figure 26.31).

Figure 26.31.
The Wizard Complete!
dialog box.

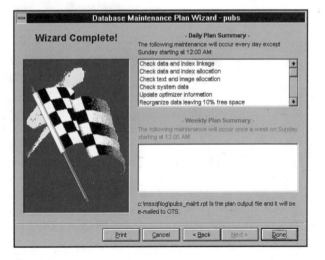

9. From the Wizard Complete! dialog box, review the plan summary information. If the summary information meets your needs, click the Done button to complete the task. The wizard then asks whether you want to run the plan(s) you have created. If possible, I recommend testing the plan at this point. Doing so helps verify that your backup strategy, e-mail notification, and so on are properly configured.

Congratulations! You have completed the Database Administration Wizard task. If you need to modify or review the status of the task, you can go to the Manage Scheduled Tasks dialog box in the Enterprise Manager. From this dialog box, you can add, delete, modify, and enable/disable a task (see Figures 26.32 and 26.33).

Figure 26.32.
The Managed Scheduled Tasks dialog box.

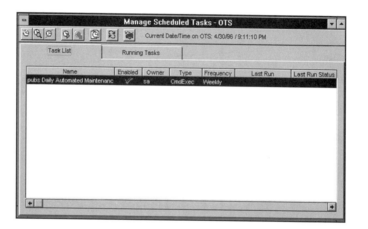

Figure 26.33.
The Edit Task dialog box.

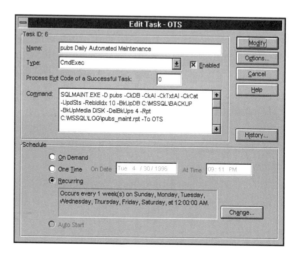

Note

The Database Administrator Wizard uses `sqlmaint.exe` to execute common tasks such as backups, DBCC commands, and so on. The utility can also be run from the command line by typing the following:

```
c:\mssql\binn\sqlmaint.exe
```

Here is a listing of the command-line parameters available with `sqlmaint.exe`:

```
SQLMAINT.EXE /?
 [{-D database_name -Rpt report_file}
 [-S server]
 [-U login_ID]
 [-P password]
 [-To operator_name]
 [-CkAI | -CkDBNoIdx]
 [-CkTxtAI]
 [-CkTxtAi]
 [-CkCat]
 [-UpdSts]
 [-RebldIdx free_space]
 [-BkUpDb backup_path | -BkUpLog backup_path]
 [-BkUpType {TAPE | DISK}]
 [-BkUpOnlyIfClean]
 [-DelBkUps number_of_weeks]]}
```

Between the Lines

Following are some important notes to remember when automating database administration tasks:

◆ Use the Task Scheduler to automate common DBA tasks such as backing up a database, updating statistics, and running DBCC commands.

◆ Use the Alert Manager to automatically notify an operator of problems, such as a database out of space error, high CPU utilization, or low inventory situations.

◆ Use the Database Maintenance Wizard to automate the scheduling of common DBA tasks such as backing up the database, running DBCC, and UPDATE STATISTICS.

◆ The Task Scheduler, Alert Manager, and Database Maintenance Wizard can notify an operator through e-mail or a pager.

SUMMARY

The Task Scheduler, Alert Manager, and Database Maintenance Wizard are three applications that use the SQLExecutive service. In Chapter 27, "SQL OLE Integration," you see how the SQLExecutive and OLE technology can further extend the automation of common DBA tasks.

- SQL Server's Object Model

- Why Use SQL-DMO?

- Creating Applications with SQL-DMO

- Enhancing the SQL Server DBA Assistant

- Summary

CHAPTER 27

by Mark Spenik

SQL OLE Integration

Have you ever felt that Microsoft left out a utility or window of information you thought would really make your life easier? With SQL Server 6.x, you may be able to write that utility yourself! "How?" you ask. The answer is an exciting new feature added to SQL Server 6.0 and extended with SQL Server 6.5—OLE!

OLE stands for Object Linking and Embedding, but in the past few years, it has come to stand for so much more. A few years ago, Microsoft and several integrated system vendors created an open specification for application intercommunication called OLE. The OLE specifications defined more than applications communicating with one another; it also specified how applications can expose parts of their functionality as objects to be used by other applications.

Application developers could then create applications that used parts of other applications to further enhance their own applications. For example, you could create an application that used the charting capabilities of another application or included a spell checker into a text editor application.

What does OLE have to do with SQL Server? In SQL Server 6.x, SQL Server is an OLE object application (also called an *OLE server*). That is, SQL Server exposes several objects, methods, and properties that can be easily controlled programmatically to perform database administrative tasks. Microsoft calls the objects SQL-DMO (SQL Distributed Management Objects). Using SQL-DMO, you can easily create applications that perform many DBA tasks for you!

Note

This chapter almost seems out of place in a book on DBA survival. However, it introduces a technology that truly empowers the DBA, enabling the DBA to create his or her own powerful database utilities. Even if you think this chapter seems too much like a programming chapter, hang in there! The explanations in this chapter are geared toward DBAs, not programmers. Even if you don't know how to program, you will at least understand what *can* be done and you may be able to have someone program your utility for you!

Before going into more detail, here is a quick review of some OLE terminology:

◆ **Container/controller/client application**: An application that can create and manage OLE objects. Visual Basic is an example of a container application.

◆ **Server/object application**: An application that creates OLE objects. SQL Server is an object application.

◆ **OLE automation**: OLE automation is a standard that enables applications to expose their objects and methods so that other applications can use them.

◆ **Object**: Defining an object is a bit difficult. If the OLE definition of an object is used, the discussion gets into many other aspects of OLE, that are covered in detail in other Sams books, but that confuse the topic of this book. This chapter uses a simpler definition: *an object represents some sort of data with properties and methods*. In SQL Server terms, for example, a database is an object and a stored procedure is an object. Figure 27.1 shows the case of a database object.

The object has attributes (in OLE terminology, they are called *properties*). In Figure 27.1, some of the properties of a database object are listed: Name, CreateDate, Size, and Status are all examples of properties of the database object.

The Name property for the database shown in Figure 27.1 is Pubs. A property tells you something about the object. You can read properties, and in some cases, you can also set properties.

Objects also have methods. A *method* is an action the object takes on the data it represents. Examples of the database objects methods are shown in Figure 27.1. The dump method, for example, can be used on the database object. If you invoked the dump method of the database object named pubs, what do you think would happen? If you said, "a database backup," you are correct.

Figure 27.1.
An example of a
database object.

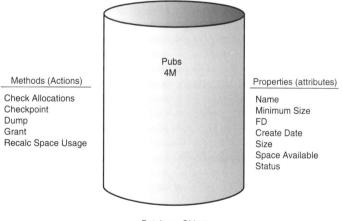

Methods (Actions)

Check Allocations
Checkpoint
Dump
Grant
Recalc Space Usage

Pubs
4M

Properties (attributes)

Name
Minimum Size
FD
Create Date
Size
Space Available
Status

Database Object

27

SQL OLE INTEGRATION

◆ **Collections**: A *collection* is an object that consists of items that can be referred to as a group (see Figure 27.2).

In Figure 27.2, there are several standard SQL Server databases: master, pubs, model, and tempdb. If you group all the databases shown into one large group called databases, you have a collection.

Collections enable you to easily perform tasks on each item in the collection. To perform a DBCC CHECKDB command on every database on your SQL Server, for example, you can use the collection object to get each database on the server and invoke a method that performs that DBA task.

Figure 27.2.
An example of a
collection object.

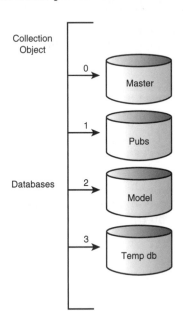

SQL Server's Object Model

To use SQL-DMO, you must understand the SQL Server object model. The *object model* is the hierarchy of exposed SQL Server objects you can use programmatically. SQL Server's object model, taken from the Distributed Management help file, is shown in Figure 27.3.

Follow the object model just like you would a file directory tree. The top level of the object model, for example, is the Application object.

Figure 27.3.
SQL Server distributed
management object
model.

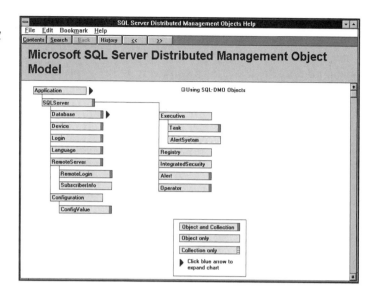

Note

It is standard practice when creating OLE object models from a stand-alone application to include an `Application` object.

Follow the tree to the next level to find the primary object you will use: the `SQL Server` object. If you look at Figure 27.3, you will see that the `Database`, `Device`, `Login`, `Language`, `RemoteServer`, and `Configuration` objects are all below the `SQL Server` object. These objects are said to be *dependent on* the `SQL Server` object; that is, you must have a `SQL Server` object before you can "get to" (that is, *use*) any of the dependent objects.

WHY USE SQL-DMO?

What benefits can you get from learning to use SQL-DMO? The real gain is that you can easily create custom solutions for your database administration environment, allowing you more free time to perform other tasks. For example, you can create a user wizard that performs a series of tasks, such as adding the user to every database based on the user's group.

Using SQL-DMO, you can create applications that you normally have to perform manually. Currently, you can automate many tasks you perform regularly by using stored procedures. The advantage SQL-DMO has over stored procedures for performing administrative tasks is simplicity. By using collection objects, you can easily perform DBCC commands on every database on the server, using only a few lines of code. Many Transact SQL commands have been simplified. The DBCC command and the many different DBCC options become methods of different objects.

Another advantage SQL-DMO has over stored procedures is that you can take advantage of true programming languages that have more powerful programming features than Transact SQL. Not to mention that you can easily integrate your applications into other desktop applications (such as word processors or spreadsheets) to enhance your customized database administration applications. Following is brief list of some of the many administrative tasks you can perform (this is a brief list; SQL-DMO enables you to perform almost any system administrative task):

◆ Back up/restore a database
◆ Generate scripts for stored procedures
◆ Perform the UPDATE STATISTICS command
◆ Perform DBCC commands such as CheckTable, CheckCatalog, and so on
◆ Grant and revoke privileges
◆ Add alerts
◆ Perform BCP
◆ Transfer data from one server to another
◆ Manage users

CREATING APPLICATIONS WITH SQL-DMO

Using SQL-DMO requires a 32-bit programming language that can create OLE controller applications. Such tools as Microsoft Visual C++, Borland Delphi, or Microsoft Excel for Windows NT with 32-bit VBA (Visual Basic for Applications) can easily be used. The examples and code samples shown in this chapter are based on Microsoft Visual Basic 4.0. The choice of Visual Basic is easy because it is the most popular and rapid application development tool available. The core language of Visual Basic 4.0 is VBA (Visual Basic for Applications) and can be found in the Windows 95 releases of Access, Project, and Excel.

The remainder of the chapter focuses on using SQL-DMO objects to perform a variety of database administration tasks using Visual Basic.

USING VISUAL BASIC

Tip

> If you are not familiar with Visual Basic, pick up a beginner's book and learn the Visual Basic basics. Once you know the basics, you can use the suggestions and examples in this chapter effectively to create your own applications. The following discussion of Visual Basic is brief and is given primarily for those who are not familiar with Visual Basic so that they can understand SQL-DMO.

Following is a very brief introduction to Visual Basic to help you understand the terminology used when creating an application that takes advantage of SQL-DMO. The main screen of Visual Basic 4.0 is shown in Figure 27.4.

Figure 27.4.
Visual Basic 4.0.

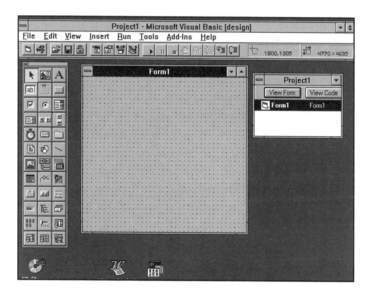

Creating Visual Basic applications consists of creating forms, adding controls to the forms using the toolbar, and adding code to modules and forms that make up the application. The forms and code modules that make up a Visual Basic application are called a *project* and can be found in the project window shown in Figure 27.4. The next sections step you through some Visual Basic basics you will need to create your own SQL-DMO applications or to enhance the application provided with this book (the DBA Assistant).

ADDING A CONTROL TO A FORM AND SETTING PROPERTIES

A Visual Basic *control* is similar to a SQL-DMO object in that they both have properties and methods. Understanding the properties and methods used with a Visual Basic control can help you better understand the concepts of SQL-DMO objects and properties. To add a control to a form, perform the following steps:

1. Click once on the icon on the toolbar of the control you want to add to the form. Common controls used on the toolbar are shown in Figure 27.5.

Figure 27.5.
The Visual Basic
toolbar.

2. Place the mouse cursor on the form; while holding the left mouse button, drag the mouse down. Visual Basic begins to draw a control on the form.

3. Release the left mouse button. You now have added a control to the form.

4. To set properties (such as color, name, height, width, and so on) for the control or the form, click the form or control to make it the active object and press F4. The Properties window for the object appears (see Figure 27.6).

Figure 27.6.
The Visual Basic form
Properties window.

5. To change a property, select the property field and enter a new value. For example, if you want to change the name of the control, edit the Name property.

DECLARING A SQL-DMO OBJECT IN VISUAL BASIC

To use a SQL-DMO object, you must first declare the object in your code. With Visual Basic, you can use the generic object type, which can hold any type of OLE object, or you can declare an object of a specific SQL-DMO object type by using the type library. To create a variable using a generic object, use the following syntax:

```
Dim Variable_Name As Object
```

To create a specific SQL-DMO, use the following syntax:

```
Dim Variable_Name As SQLOLE.SQL_DMO_OBJECT
```

In this syntax, SQL_DMO_OBJECT is the specific SQL-DMO object (such as SQL Server, Database, Table, and so on). For example, to define a SQL-DMO SQL Server object using the type library, enter the following:

```
Dim MySqlServer As SQLOLE.SQLServer
```

Tip

Declare SQL-DMO variables by using the type library and declaring specific SQL Server objects rather than using the generic object. Using specific objects is faster and enables Visual Basic to perform "early binding" (checking that you are using proper objects and methods) during compilation rather than at run time.

CREATING A SQL-DMO OBJECT WITH VISUAL BASIC

After you declare a variable to be a SQL-DMO object, you must create the object before you can use the methods and properties of the object.

Note

Creating an object is also referred to as *getting an instance* of the object.

You can create the object with either the keyword New or the function CreateObject. Following is an example that uses the New keyword when declaring a variable:

```
Dim MySqlServer As New SQLOLE.SQLServer
```

You also can use the New keyword in code, as follows:

```
Set MySqlServer = New SQLOLE.SQLServer
```

The CreateObject function has the following syntax:

```
CreateObject("application_name.object_type")
```

The following code creates a new SQL Server SQL-DMO object with CreateObject:

```
Set MySqlServer = CreateObject("SQLOLE.SQLServer")
```

After you create an object, you can use the objects, properties, and methods to perform DBA tasks.

RELEASING OBJECTS

Just as important as creating an object is releasing the object when you are finished with it. Objects in Visual Basic are released when they go out of scope. If the object is declared in a procedure, the object is released when the procedure completes. If the object is declared in a form, the object is released when the form unloads. Global objects are not released until the application closes.

It is always good Visual Basic coding practice to release your objects in code when you are finished with them by using the keyword Nothing. The following code, for example, releases a SQL-DMO table object called MyTable:

```
Set MyTable = Nothing
```

REQUIRED SQL-DMO FILES

To create SQL-DMO objects using Visual Basic, you must have the following files, which are included with the 32-bit versions of SQL Server client utilities for Windows NT and Windows 95. You can find the following files in the SQL Server 6.5 home directory (C:\MSSQL) in the directory \BINN:

SQLOLE.HLP	SQL-DMO help files, including object hierarchy
SQLOLE65.DLL	In-process SQL-DMO server (in SQL Server 6.0, the filename is SQLOLE32.DLL)
SQLOLE65.TLB	Type library for OLE Automation Controllers (in SQL Server 6.0 the filename is SQLOLE32.DLL)

Note

SQL-DMO is available only in 32-bit Windows environments (Windows NT and Windows 95).

SQL-DMO CHECKLIST

You can use the following checklist when creating SQL-DMO applications. Use this first checklist to ensure that you have the proper files and utilities required to use SQL-DMO:

- ☐ Have Windows NT or Windows 95.

- ☐ Have installed a 32-bit OLE automation controller (Visual Basic).

- ☐ Install the proper SQL-DMO files from the 32-bit SQL Server Client utilities.

The following checklist includes the steps required to create SQL-DMO objects from Visual Basic:

- ☐ 1. Include the SQL-DMO type library in the Visual Basic environment by adding "Microsoft SQLOLE Object Library" to the Visual Basic references.

- ☐ 2. Declare a SQL-DMO SQLServer object.

- ☐ 3. Create the SQLServer object.

- ☐ 4. Connect the SQLServer object to SQL Server.

- ☐ 5. Use the SQL Server objects, properties, and methods, and declare and create any other required SQL-DMO objects to accomplish your required DBA task.

- ☐ 6. Release SQL-DMO objects using the keyword Nothing when you are done using them.

- ☐ 7. Disconnect the SQLServer object.

- ☐ 8. Release the SQLServer object.

ENHANCING THE SQL SERVER DBA ASSISTANT

Now comes the real value-added part of the chapter. As you probably know by now, examples that use SQL-DMO are hard to find. SQL Server ships with a few SQL-DMO samples that are not well documented; the overall SQL-DMO documentation contains very few descriptive examples, concentrating instead on describing the objects and methods.

On the CD-ROM included with this book is a Visual Basic project titled samsdb.vbp. The project contains all the source code for the application and is called the SQL Server DBA Assistant. The source code is included as a foundation that you can modify and enhance to meet your own needs. The following sections discuss the most important parts of the SQL Server DBA Assistant.

Note

The source code for the application is included on the CD-ROM that accompanies this book. The following sections concentrate on the code that uses SQL-DMO, not the Visual Basic code that does not deal with SQL-DMO. The Visual Basic code is well documented so that you can use the code and form to easily add your own functionality to the project.

WHAT'S IN THE SQL SERVER DBA ASSISTANT?

Before getting started on developing the SQL Server DBA application, you must decide what type of functionality you are going to put in the application. First, because the purpose of the utility is for actual DBA work and learning, you should create an application that uses several different SQL-DMO objects.

What do I think is missing from Microsoft SQL Server 6.5? Memory configuration for SQL Server is very important and yet there is no screen that graphically shows how much memory is currently allocated to SQL Server, the procedure cache, data cache, or SQL Server overhead. Although you can always use the DBCC MEMUSAGE command to get this information, the report is not very graphical.

To fix this oversight, the first task your SQL Server DBA Assistant will accomplish is to perform SQL Server memory estimates and breakouts using the formulas published in Chapter 19, "Which Knobs Do I Turn?," and in the SQL Server documentation.

To perform this task, you must use the SQL Server object and the configuration object. You concentrate on setting up a program that enables you to perform table maintenance on several different databases. To perform these tasks, you must use the SQL-DMO database object and the table object. Following is a list of the functionalities of the SQL Server DBA Assistant:

◆ Estimate and graph SQL Server memory breakout
◆ List all the databases in a combo box for selection
◆ Perform table maintenance on selected tables
◆ Perform BCP export on selected tables

CONNECTING TO SQL SERVER

Note

This chapter skips a few steps here that are Visual Basic related, such as creating a new project called samsdba and adding controls to the logon form.

Assuming that you have all the proper files and have added the Microsoft SQLOLE Object Library references to Visual Basic, it is now time to declare a SQL Server object and connect to SQL Server. For logon purposes, use the form shown in Figure 27.7 (frmLogon).

Figure 27.7.
The SQL Server DBA
Assistant Logon form.

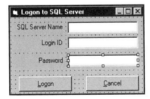

Using your checklist for creating a SQL-DMO application, perform step 2: declare a SQL-DMO object, as follows in the Visual Basic module globals.bas:

```
Public MySqlServer As SQLOLE.SQLServer 'Global SQL Server Object
```

The next step is to create a SQL Server object. The code to create a SQL Server object is located in the Visual Basic module sqlserv.bas in the procedure main. The code for the main procedure is shown in Listing 27.1.

LISTING 27.1. PROCEDURE main: CREATING A SQL SERVER OBJECT.

```
Public Sub main()
'SAMS -MicroSoft SQL Server DBA Survival Guide
'
'Main - The procedure main creates an OLE SQL Server Object
'        and then prompts the user to enter the correct SQL Server
'        name.  If the user properly connects to the SQL Server
'        the main form of the application is shown.
'
'Set up Error handling

On Error GoTo Err_Main

    '
'Check if the application is already running
    '
If App.PrevInstance > 0 Then
    MsgBox "SQL Server DBA Assistant already running on this machine.", _
            vbCritical, "Already Running"
    End
End If

    '
'Create a New SQL Server OLE Object
    '
Set MySqlServer = CreateObject("SQLOLE.SQLServer")

Connected = False 'Set Global to Not Connected
    '
'Set SQL Server Connection Timeout Value
    '
MySqlServer.LoginTimeout = 15 'Set for 15 seconds
    '
'Display the Logon Screen
    '
frmLogon.Show 1
Set frmLogon = Nothing   'Reclaim Object Memory

'If We established a Connection Display the Main form
' Otherwise exit the application
If Connected = True Then
    frmSplash.Show    'Display Splash Screen
    DoEvents          'Allow time to Paint the Splash Screen
    Load frmMain      'Load the Main Form
    frmMain.Show      'Make it Appear
    Unload frmSplash 'Make it disappear
    Set frmSplash = Nothing 'Reclaim Memory
    Exit Sub
End If
    '
'Exit - If not Connected
Quit_App:

    If Not (MySqlServer Is Nothing) Then
        'Release SQL Server Object
        Set MySqlServer = Nothing
    End If
```

```
      End 'End the program
'
'Error Handler
'
Err_Main:
      '
      'Display Error Message
      MsgBox Err.Description, vbCritical, "Connection Error"
      Resume Next

End Sub
```

The following line creates a SQL-DMO SQL Server object using the function CreateObject (as specified in step 3 of the SQL-DMO checklist):

```
Set MySqlServer = CreateObject("SQLOLE.SQLServer")
```

When this line of code executes, the variable MySqlServer contains a SQL Server object.

Before you try to connect to a SQL Server by logging on, you set the login timeout value by setting the SQL Server object property LoginTimeout, as follows:

```
MySqlServer.LoginTimeout = 15 'Set for 15 seconds
```

You now are ready to perform step 4 of the checklist: establish a connection to SQL Server. The logon form appears (refer to Figure 27.7). A user enters the SQL Server, user name, and password and clicks the Logon button on the form. The code shown in Listing 27.2 executes to establish a connection to the SQL Server.

LISTING 27.2. SQL SERVER CONNECTION.

```
Private Sub cmdLogon_Click()

      'Set up the Error Handler
      '
      On Error GoTo Err_Logon
      '
      'Connect to the SQL Server
      '
      If txtServer <> "" Then
          Me.MousePointer = vbHourglass 'Turn Cursor to HourGlass
          '
          'Invoke Connect Method of the SQL Server Object
          '
          MySqlServer.Connect ServerName:=txtServer.TEXT, _
                            Login:=txtLogon.TEXT, _
                            Password:=txtPassword.TEXT
          '
          'Sql Server Connected Correctly - Unload the form
          '
          Connected = True              'Set Global Connection Variable
```

continues

LISTING 27.2. CONTINUED

```
        Me.MousePointer = vbDefault 'Turn Mousepointer back to default
        Unload Me                   'Unload the Logon form
    Else
        MsgBox "You must enter a SQL Server Name to Connect", _
            vbCritical, "Invalid Entry"
    End If
    '
    'Exit the routine - If Not Logged In Try Again
    '
Exit_Logon:

    Exit Sub
'
' Error handler
'
Err_Logon:
    Me.MousePointer = vbDefault
    MsgBox "Error Connection to Server. Error: " & Err.Description, _
        vbCritical, "Error Connection"
    Resume Exit_Logon
End Sub
```

The following lines of code establish a connection with SQL Server using the Connection method of the SQL Server object:

```
    '
    'Invoke Connect Method of the SQL Server Object
    '
    MySqlServer.Connect ServerName:=txtServer.TEXT, _
                Login:=txtLogon.TEXT, _
                Password:=txtPassword.TEXT
```

After you establish a successful connection to SQL Server, you are ready to perform steps 5 and 6 of the SQL-DMO application checklist: perform various tasks by creating objects, invoking methods, and setting properties.

ESTIMATING MEMORY

To configure the memory breakout for SQL Server, you must read the memory configuration parameter to get the total amount of memory. You also must get the configuration value for the procedure cache and subtract that value from 100 to get the percentage of memory used for the data cache. Before the procedure and data cache values can be computed, you must compute the SQL Server overhead.

To compute SQL Server overhead, you must read configuration values, compute the total amount of memory used by each configuration object, and add the value to SQL

Server static memory requirements. Refer back to the SQL-DMO object model shown in Figure 27.3 to see the SQL Server configuration object. Using the configuration object, you can easily obtain the configuration values. To create the configuration object, first declare the configuration object, as follows:

```
Dim MyConfig As SQLOLE.Configuration, ConfigV As SQLOLE.ConfigValue
```

To create the configuration object, use your SQL Server object by executing the following code (the configuration object depends on the SQL Server object):

```
'Get a configuration object
Set MyConfig = MySqlServer.Configuration
```

The variable MyConfig now contains a SQL-DMO configuration object. Using the ConfigValues collection of the configuration object, the configuration values can easily be obtained. To get the running configuration value for the memory configuration parameter, for example, execute the following code:

```
TotalMemory = CInt((DATA_PAGE * MyConfig.ConfigValues("memory").RunningValue) /
MEGA_BYTE)
```

The memory configuration value is in 2K data pages. For the memory estimation graph, all the values are converted to megabytes. Instead of using the ConfigValues collection, you can create an instance of a specific ConfigValue object and then retrieve the values. The following example creates a ConfigValue object for locks and then retrieves the value:

```
'Locks
    Set ConfigV = MyConfig.ConfigValues("locks")
    TempValue = ConfigV.RunningValue * MEM_LOCKS
```

Note

To compute the memory requirements for configuration objects to estimate SQL Server overhead, constants were used; if Microsoft publishes more accurate object memory requirements, you can easily modify the constants located in the global.bas module.

To estimate the SQL Server memory breakdown, the various configuration values are read using the configuration object and ConfigValues collection. The SQL Server overhead, procedure, and data cache are then computed and graphed. The breakout of SQL Server memory is computed during the loading process of the main form (frmMain) of the SQL Server DBA Assistant. The Memory Estimation page of the SQL Server DBA Assistant dialog box is shown in Figure 27.8.

27

SQL OLE INTEGRATION

Figure 27.8.
The Memory Estima-
tion page of the SQL
Server DBA Assistant
dialog box.

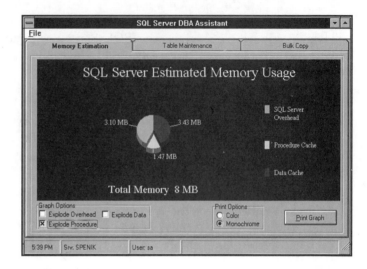

The code to perform the memory estimate and build the graph shown in Figure 27.8 is shown in Listing 27.3.

LISTING 27.3. MEMORY ESTIMATE CODE.

```
Public Sub EstimateMemory()
'
'Define Values to Compute Memory Allocation
'
Dim MyConfig As SQLOLE.Configuration, ConfigV As SQLOLE.ConfigValue
Dim MemoryOverhead As Single, DataCache As Single, ProcCache As Single
Dim TempValue As Single, TotalMemory As Integer

    On Error GoTo Memory_Estimate_Error
    '
    'Use the standard formula to compute Memory usage estimates
    Set MyConfig = MySqlServer.Configuration
    '
    'Get Memory
    '
    '    Note: We will use two different methods to get at the configuration
    '          values (for learning purposes).
    '                    Method 1 uses the Configuration Configvalues collection
    '                    Method 2 creates a ConfigValue Object
    ' Method 1
    TotalMemory = CInt((DATA_PAGE * MyConfig.ConfigValues("memory").RunningValue) /
MEGA_BYTE)
    '
    'Get Procedure Cache and Data Cache Values
    '
    ProcCache = MyConfig.ConfigValues("procedure cache").RunningValue
    DataCache = 100 - ProcCache
    '
    'Do SQL Server Overhead
    '
```

```
MemoryOverhead = MEM_DEVICES + MEM_STATIC_OVERHEAD
'
'Method 2
'
'Locks
Set ConfigV = MyConfig.ConfigValues("locks")
TempValue = ConfigV.RunningValue * MEM_LOCKS
MemoryOverhead = MemoryOverhead + TempValue
'
'Users
Set ConfigV = MyConfig.ConfigValues("user connections")
TempValue = ConfigV.RunningValue * MEM_USER
MemoryOverhead = MemoryOverhead + TempValue
'
'Databases
Set ConfigV = MyConfig.ConfigValues("open databases")
TempValue = ConfigV.RunningValue * MEM_DATABASE
MemoryOverhead = MemoryOverhead + TempValue
'
'Objects
'
Set ConfigV = MyConfig.ConfigValues("open objects")
TempValue = ConfigV.RunningValue * MEM_OBJECTS
MemoryOverhead = (MemoryOverhead + TempValue) / (MEGA_BYTE)
'
'Compute Values
'
TempValue = TotalMemory - MemoryOverhead
ProcCache = TempValue * (ProcCache / 100)
DataCache = TempValue * (DataCache / 100)

'
'Release the Objects
'
Set ConfigV = Nothing
Set MyConfig = Nothing

'
'Setup the Graph With Information
'   Setup Data Points
With grphMemory
    .AutoInc = 1    'Turn Auto Increment On
    .DrawMode = 0   'Disable drawing until the end
    .NumPoints = 3 'Set total number of points
    .ThisPoint = 1 'Start with Point 1
    'OverHead
    .GraphData = CInt(MemoryOverhead) 'Set graph point - Using Integer
    'Procedure Cache
    .GraphData = CInt(ProcCache)
    'Data Cache
    .GraphData = CInt(DataCache)
End With

' Setup Colors for the Graph
With grphMemory
    .ColorData = 7     'Red
    .ColorData = 14
```

continues

Listing 27.3. continued

```
            .ColorData = 12
     End With

     'Setup labels for each graph
     With grphMemory
         .LabelText = Format(MemoryOverhead, "######.00 MB")
         .LabelText = Format(ProcCache, "######.00 MB")
         .LabelText = Format(DataCache, "######.00 MB")
     End With

     'Setup The legend and the title on the bottom
      With grphMemory
         .BottomTitle = "Total Memory " & Str$(TotalMemory) & " MB"
         .LegendText = "SQL Server Overhead"
         .LegendText = "Procedure Cache"
         .LegendText = "Data Cache"
         .DrawMode = 2    'Draw the graph
     End With
'
Memory_Estimate_Exit:
     Exit Sub
'
' Error handler
'
Memory_Estimate_Error:
     Me.MousePointer = vbDefault
     MsgBox "Error estimatin memory configuration." _
         & "Error: " & Err.Description, _
         vbCritical, "Memory Configuration Error"
     Resume Memory_Estimate_Exit
End Sub
```

Filling a Combo Box with Databases

To make the SQL Server DBA Assistant a useful tool during database table maintenance, you will add the capability to select a database from a combo box and then read all the nonsystem tables associated with the database into a Visual Basic list box control.

To read all the databases on the selected server into a combo box, you use the SQL Server SQL-DMO object and the databases collection. The code shown in Listing 27.4 populates a Visual Basic combo box with all the database names in your SQL Server object collection.

Listing 27.4. Populating a combo box with database names.

```
Dim Db As SQLOLE.DATABASE

    CenterForm frmMain
    '
```

```
'Fill the Combo Box on the form with the
'available databases by using the SQL Server databases collection
'
For Each Db In MySqlServer.Databases
    '  Make sure the database is not currently being loaded
    '
    If Db.Status <> SQLOLEDBStat_Inaccessible Then
        cmbDatabase.AddItem Db.Name
    Else
        MsgBox "Database: """ + Db.Name _
            + " "" can not be accessed at this time.", _
            vbCritical, "Database Loading"
    End If
Next
Set Db = Nothing
```

To populate a list box with the tables in the database, you read the tables collection of the selected database. The code to populate the list box using the selected database is shown in Listing 27.5.

LISTING 27.5. POPULATING A LIST BOX WITH TABLE NAMES USING A DATABASE OBJECT AND THE TABLES COLLECTION.

```
Private Sub cmbDatabase_Click()
Dim WorkTable As SQLOLE.TABLE 'SQL-DMO Table Object

    On Error GoTo Get_Tables_Error
    '
    'Database changed - Modify Database Object
    '
    Set WorkDb = Nothing    'Clear the Work Database object
    lstTables.Clear         'Clear tables list box
    lstOperateTables.Clear 'Clear the operate tables list box

    'Get the currently selected database object
    '
    Set WorkDb = MySqlServer.Databases(cmbDatabase.TEXT)


    'Fill the list box with the table names using the database
    'tables collection exclude any system tables.
    '
    For Each WorkTable In WorkDb.Tables 'Do For Each table in the database
        If Not (WorkTable.SystemObject) Then
            lstTables.AddItem WorkTable.Name 'Add to the list Box
        End If
    Next WorkTable

Exit_Get_Tables:
    Set WorkTable = Nothing
    Exit Sub  'Leave the Procedure


' Error handler
'
```

27

SQL OLE INTEGRATION

continues

LISTING 27.5. CONTINUED

```
Get_Tables_Error:
    Me.MousePointer = vbDefault
    MsgBox "Error reading tables collection " & Err.Description, _
        vbCritical, "Filling Combo Box Error"
    Resume Exit_Get_Tables

End Sub
```

Tip

You can begin to see that using SQL-DMO is quite simple once you become familiar with the SQL-DMO object model. Study the model and become familiar with the collections, objects, and the hierarchy.

Getting a list of objects is simple using the Visual Basic FOR EACH - NEXT statement. FOR EACH - NEXT is used to read through all items of an array or collection. Examples of the FOR EACH - NEXT statement can be found in Listings 27.4 and 27.5.

PERFORMING TABLE MAINTENANCE

Once a database has been selected, a database object can easily be created using the selected database name and the SQL Server object, as follows:

```
'Get the currently selected database object
'
    Set WorkDb = MySqlServer.Databases(cmbDatabase.TEXT)
```

Once the line of code executes, you have a SQL-DMO database object for the selected database. If you remember the object model for SQL-DMO, you can easily create a table object using the database object. Once the table object has been created, you then can perform a variety of table maintenance tasks using the different table methods. Following are some examples of the table object methods and the tasks they perform:

CheckTable	Performs the DBCC CheckTable command.
Grant	Grants table privileges to a list of SQL Server users or groups.
RecalcSpaceUsage	Recalculates the space information for the table.
Script	Generates the Transact SQL statements to create the table.
UpdateStatistics	Updates the data distribution pages used by the Query Optimizer to make proper index selection.

For the SQL Server DBA Assistant, you can select the tables on which you want to perform a table maintenance operation and then click a button to perform the appropriate action. The code that scans through the list of selected tables and invokes the method is as follows:

```
'Execute Update Statistics command on selected tables
    '
    For X = 0 To lstOperateTables.ListCount - 1
        ProgressBar1.VALUE = X
        Set WorkTable = WorkDb.Tables(lstOperateTables.List(X))
        '
        'Update Statistics on the Table - using the UpdateStatistics Method
        '
        WorkTable.UpdateStatistics
        'Release the Work Table object
        Set WorkTable = Nothing
    Next X
```

The Table Maintenance page of the SQL Server DBA Assistant dialog box is shown in Figure 27.9.

Figure 27.9.
The Table Maintenance
page of the SQL Server
DBA Assistant dialog
box.

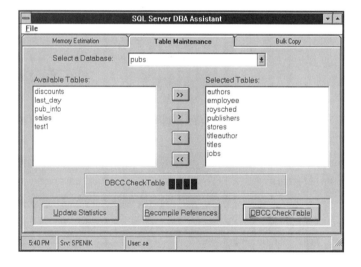

Listing 27.6 shows the code used behind the Update Statistics button (shown in Figure 27.9).

LISTING 27.6. PERFORMING UPDATE STATISTICS ON SELECTED TABLES.

```
Private Sub cmdUpdate_Click()
Dim WorkTable As SQLOLE.TABLE 'SQL-DMO Table Object
Dim X As Integer

    On Error GoTo Up_Stats_Error
```

continues

LISTING 27.6. CONTINUED

```
    SSPanel1.Enabled = False
    frmMain.MousePointer = vbHourglass
    '
    'Setup The Progress Bar
    ProgressBar1.MAX = lstOperateTables.ListCount - 1
    ProgressBar1.VALUE = 0
    lblStatus.Caption = "Updating Statistics"
    frmStatus.Visible = True   'Turn On Progress Bar
    DoEvents 'Allow Screen to repaint
    '
    StatusBar1.Panels("status").TEXT = "Updating Statistics - Please Wait..."

    'Execute Update Statistics command on selected tables
    '
    For X = 0 To lstOperateTables.ListCount - 1
        ProgressBar1.VALUE = X
        Set WorkTable = WorkDb.Tables(lstOperateTables.List(X))
        '
        'Update Statistics on the Table - using the UpdateStatistics Method
        '
        WorkTable.UpdateStatistics
        'Release the Work Table object
        Set WorkTable = Nothing
    Next X
    'Cleanup and Exit
Up_Stats_Exit:
    '
    frmStatus.Visible = False
    StatusBar1.Panels("status").TEXT = ""
    SSPanel1.Enabled = True
    frmMain.MousePointer = vbDefault
    Exit Sub
'
' Error handler
'
Up_Stats_Error:
    Me.MousePointer = vbDefault
    MsgBox "Error Updating statistics on table " & lstOperateTables.List(X) _
        & "Error: " & Err.Description, _
        vbCritical, "Update Statistics Error"
    Resume Up_Stats_Exit
End Sub
```

Tip

We have provided you with the following three table maintenance functions already programmed and ready to use. Look on the CD-ROM that accompanies this book; they're with the SQL Server DBA Assistant.

◆ Update Statistics

◆ Recompile References

◆ DBCC CheckTable

As stated earlier, the purpose of the SQL Server DBA Assistant is to provide you with a foundation from which you can create your own application. If you look behind each of the buttons, you will notice that the code is almost identical except for the methods added. You can easily add more functionality by cutting and pasting the code into new buttons and adding new methods. You also can optimize the application by reducing the code behind the buttons by using a shared function or procedure. The list is endless—what are you waiting for?

PERFORMING TABLE EXPORTS USING BULKCOPY

Version 6.5

One of the new objects added to SQL Server 6.5 is the BulkCopy object (BCP for short). Because the DBA Assistant is all about tools left out of the Enterprise Manager, the ability to perform graphical BCP is very important—especially if you are in environments I find myself in quite often: where the data fed into SQL Server is from mainframe flat files (or vice versa). To take advantage of graphical BCP, you must use the 4.2x Object Manager or create your own graphical BCP tool. For the SQL Server DBA Assistant, we start you down the road of creating your own graphical BCP tool by adding the ability to export data using the BulkCopy object in the following formats:

◆ Tab delimited (default)

◆ Comma delimited

◆ Native format

The BulkCopy object differs from the objects used so far in these example applications because the BulkCopy object does not depend on other objects. To use a BulkCopy object, you create the BulkCopy object, set the various parameters of the BulkCopy object, and then pass the BulkCopy object as a parameter to a table or view object's ImportData or ExportData method. The BulkCopy object has a single method, Abort, to abort a running BCP; this method must be executed from another thread.

For the SQL Server DBA Assistant, the BulkCopy object is created when the object parameter oBcp is declared using the keyword New as follows:

```
Dim oBCP As New SQLOLE.BulkCopy 'Note BCP object is created here using New Keyword
```

Once the BulkCopy object has been created, the next step is to set the desired properties (such as the import batch size or the number of errors to ignore before halting the bulk copy). Here is an example of setting the BulkCopy object's MaximumErrorsBeforeAbort property:

```
'Max Number of errors before BCP quits
    If IsNumeric(txtMaxErrors.Text) Then
        oBCP.MaximumErrorsBeforeAbort = CInt(txtMaxErrors.Text)
    Else
        'Use Default
        oBCP.MaximumErrorsBeforeAbort = 1
    End If
```

When you set the properties of the BulkCopy object to import or export data, you pass the BulkCopy object as a parameter to a table or view object's ImportData or ExportData method. The following example shows the ExportData method being used:

```
iNumRows = BCPTable.ExportData(oBCP)
```

The Bulk Copy page of the SQL Server DBA Assistant dialog box is shown in Figure 27.10.

Figure 27.10.
The Bulk Copy page of
the SQL Server DBA
Assistant dialog box.

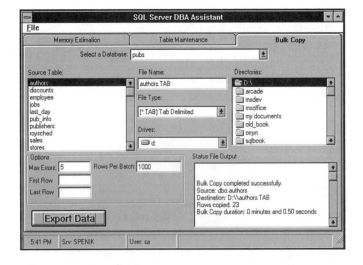

Listing 27.7 shows the code used behind the Export Data button (shown in Figure 27.10).

LISTING 27.7. PERFORMING A BCP EXPORT ON SELECTED TABLES.

```
Private Sub cmdExportData_Click()
Dim BCPTable As SQLOLE.Table      'SQL-DMO Table Object
Dim oBCP As New SQLOLE.BulkCopy   'Note BCP object is created here using New Keyword
Dim iNumRows As Long              'Stores number of rows returned from BCP
Dim oOutputFile As CFile          'Used for file I/O
```

```
Dim sTempBuf As String, sTemp As String 'Temp variables

    'Set up a simple error handler
    On Error GoTo Export_Error

    'Setup display
    SSPanel1.Enabled = False
    frmMain.MousePointer = vbHourglass
    '
    StatusBar1.Panels("status").Text = "Exporting Data - Please Wait..."

    'Step 1 - Get an instance of the table object to perform the BCP
    '
    'Get the table object - to perform the export
    '
    Set BCPTable = WorkDb.Tables(lstBCPTables.Text)

    'Step 2 - Set up the BCP objects properties
    '
    '       (Note: An instance of the BCP object was created above in DIM statement
    '               using the keyword New)
    '
    'Set the BulkCopy input/output file parameter
    oBCP.DataFilePath = Dir1.Path & "\" & txtFile

    'Set the error log and log file parameters
    oBCP.LogFilePath = App.Path & "\sams_bcp.log"
    oBCP.ErrorFilePath = App.Path & "sams_err.log"

    '
    'Do some validation checking and set optional paramters
    '
    ' Batch Size (Not used for exporting - only used in imports
    '               added here for your convenience - should you modify
    '               the program to do imports).
    '
    If IsNumeric(txtBatchSize.Text) Then
        oBCP.ImportRowsPerBatch = CInt(txtBatchSize.Text)
    Else
        'Use Default
        oBCP.ImportRowsPerBatch = 1000
    End If

    'Max Number of errors before BCP quits
    If IsNumeric(txtMaxErrors.Text) Then
        oBCP.MaximumErrorsBeforeAbort = CInt(txtMaxErrors.Text)
    Else
        'Use Default
        oBCP.MaximumErrorsBeforeAbort = 1
    End If

    'First Row to start BCP
    If txtFirstRow <> "" Then
        If IsNumeric(txtFirstRow.Text) Then
            oBCP.FirstRow = CInt(txtFirstRow.Text)
        End If
    End If
```

27

SQL OLE Integration

continues

LISTING 27.7. CONTINUED

```
'Last Row to end BCP
If txtLastRow <> "" Then
    If IsNumeric(txtLastRow.Text) Then
        oBCP.LastRow = CInt(txtLastRow.Text)
    End If
End If

'Set the output type for the BCP- based on combo box
sTemp = cmbType.Text

Select Case sTemp
    Case "(*.CSV) Comma Delimited"
        oBCP.DataFileType = SQLOLEDataFile_CommaDelimitedChar

    Case "(*.TAB) Tab Delimited"
        oBCP.DataFileType = SQLOLEDataFile_TabDelimitedChar

    Case "(*.DAT) Native"
        oBCP.DataFileType = SQLOLEDataFile_NativeFormat

End Select

'Step 3 - Export the Data
'
'Here is the part you have been waiting for -
'Pass the BCP object to the table ExportData method and
'away it goes!
'
iNumRows = BCPTable.ExportData(oBCP)

'The output results are written to a file.
'Create a file object to read the contents
'of the file and display the output file results in the status text box.
'
Set oOutputFile = New CFile
oOutputFile.FileName = oBCP.LogFilePath
oOutputFile.IOMode = "INPUT"
oOutputFile.IOType = "SEQUENTIAL"
oOutputFile.OpenFile
If oOutputFile.Status = 1 Then
    oOutputFile.ReadAll sTempBuf
    txtStatus = sTempBuf
Else
    txtStatus = "Error reading BCP output file."
End If
oOutputFile.CloseFile

'Report the number of rows exported
MsgBox Str(iNumRows) & " rows exported.", vbInformation, "Bulk Copy"

'Cleanup and Exit
Export_Exit:
    '
    Set oBCP = Nothing
    Set BCPTable = Nothing
    Set oOutputFile = Nothing
```

```
    frmStatus.Visible = False
    StatusBar1.Panels("status").Text = ""
    SSPanel1.Enabled = True
    frmMain.MousePointer = vbDefault
    Exit Sub

Export_Error:
    MsgBox Err.Description
    Resume Export_Exit

End Sub
```

Note

The BCP code provided does not import data, but you can modify the code to add this feature. The value of the BulkCopy object property `ImportRowsPerBatch` is set and is included in the export data code—even though it is not used during BCP export—in case you want to modify the code to import data. The log and error files created when performing BCP default to the DBA Assistant application directory (that is, the directory where the DBA Assistant is executing) with the filenames `sams_bcp.log` and `sams_bcp.err`.

SUMMARY

For the non-Visual Basic DBAs in the crowd, I hope the explanations and code examples in this chapter were easy for you to follow and that they motivated you to learn Visual Basic.

If you use SQL-DMO, you can easily create powerful DBA tools that can even be integrated in applications such as Microsoft Word and Excel. Study the various Visual Basic examples that ship with SQL Server and review the code on the CD-ROM that accompanies this book; soon, you will have the power and ability to write your own tools to simplify your job!

27

SQL OLE INTEGRATION

Version
6.5

- SQL Server
  Web Assistant

- MS-Query

- Summary

CHAPTER 28   *by Orryn Sledge*

New SQL Server Utilities

SQL Server 6.5 includes two new graphical utilities that help simplify and automate SQL Server tasks:

◆ SQL Server Web Assistant

◆ MS-Query

SQL SERVER WEB ASSISTANT

The SQL Server Web Assistant automates the generation of HyperText Markup Language (HTML) Web pages. You can use this wizard to publish data that resides in SQL Server on the Internet or Intranet. As you can imagine, this link between SQL Server and the Internet/Intranet creates several new and exciting possibilities for the distribution of information. Following is a list of some of the uses for distributing SQL Server information in the HTML format:

◆ **Customer management.** Use SQL Server to store information about your customers and then use the SQL Server Web Assistant to generate Web pages pertaining to your customers. Summary data, customer trends, credit data, and other types of customer information are just a few examples of the types of information that can be published on the Internet/Intranet.

◆ **Proposal tracking.** Use SQL Server to store hot links to proposals and related documents and then use the SQL Server Web Assistant to generate Web pages that contain the links to your information. This type of application is great for a distributed sales force that has to gather information for past proposals.

◆ **Inventory management.** Use SQL Server to track and manage your inventory and then use the Web Assistant to publish your inventory. Customers, suppliers, managers, and salespeople can all benefit from easy access to inventory information.

USING THE SQL SERVER WEB ASSISTANT

Follow these steps to use the SQL Server Web Assistant:

1. Double-click the SQL Server Web Assistant icon in the Microsoft SQL Server 6.5 (Common) program group. The SQL Server Web Assistant Login dialog box appears (see Figure 28.1).

2. From the SQL Server Web Assistant Login dialog box, enter the server name, login ID, and password. If you are using integrated security, select the Use Windows NT Security option (or you can select a Password option). You do not have to provide a login ID or password if you use integrated security. Click the Next button. The SQL Server Web Assistant Query dialog box appears (see Figure 28.2).

Figure 28.1.
The SQL Server
Web Assistant
Login dialog box.

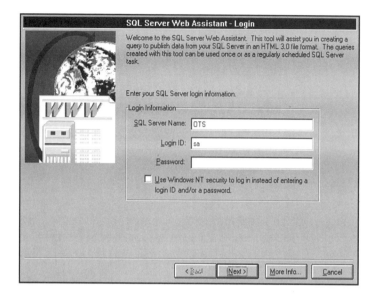

Figure 28.2.
The SQL Server
Web Assistant
Query dialog box.

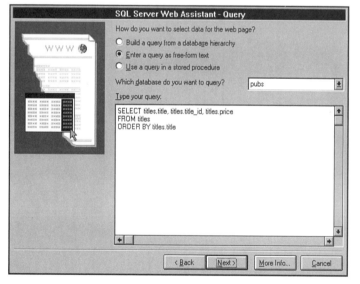

3. From the SQL Server Web Assistant Query dialog box, select your data source. This example uses a free-form text query as the data source (refer to Figure 28.2). The following list explains the data source options:

   ◆ **Build a query from a database hierarchy:** This option allows you to display tables and columns in HTML format. With this option, you can work with multiple tables or views. This option also provides a text box for WHERE, ORDER BY, and GROUP BY clauses.

28

◆ **Enter a query as free-form text:** This option allows you to manually enter SQL syntax as the data source for your Web page. Any valid SELECT statement can be used with the following clauses: FROM, WHERE, GROUP BY, HAVING, and ORDER BY.

◆ **Use a query in a stored procedure:** This option allows you to publish data based on the information returned from a stored procedure.

Click the Next button. The SQL Server Web Assistant Scheduling dialog box appears (see Figure 28.3).

Tip

Use MS-Query to automate the generation of the SQL syntax for a Web page. Build your query in MS-Query. Copy the SQL statement to the Clipboard and then paste it into the SQL Server Web Assistant.

You can use stored procedures to generate Web pages when you need maximum flexibility and management of published data. Stored procedures provide flexibility through the use of temporary tables, multiple queries, cursors, and other types of Transact SQL commands that can gather and present your data (see Chapter 24, "Using Stored Procedures and Cursors," for more information on stored procedures).

Figure 28.3.
The SQL Server Web
Assistant Scheduling
dialog box.

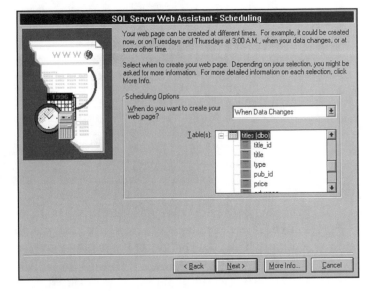

4. From the SQL Server Web Assistant Scheduling dialog box, select the scheduling options. The example in Figure 28.3 regenerates the Web page whenever the data in the `titles` table has changed. When you select the option to regenerate the Web page (when data changes, the following three types of triggers are generated for the `titles` table: `INSERT`, `UPDATE`, and `DELETE`). When the data is modified, the trigger executes a system procedure that regenerates the Web page.

   Click the Next button. The SQL Server Web Assistant File Options dialog box appears (see Figure 28.4).

5. In the SQL Server Web Assistant File Options dialog box, enter a filename, display information, and URL link information. Click the Next button. The SQL Server Web Assistant Formatting dialog box appears (see Figure 28.5).

Figure 28.4.
The SQL Server Web
Assistant File Options
dialog box.

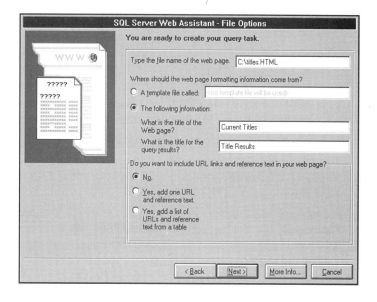

Tip

To display multiple URLs in your Web page, create a table in SQL Server that contains the Internet address and then use the Yes, Add a List of ... Text from a Table option in the SQL Server Web Assistant File Options dialog box. These steps allow you to maintain a list of Internet links in a SQL Server table and then use a query to build a Web page that displays the links.

Figure 28.5.
The SQL Server Web
Assistant Formatting
dialog box.

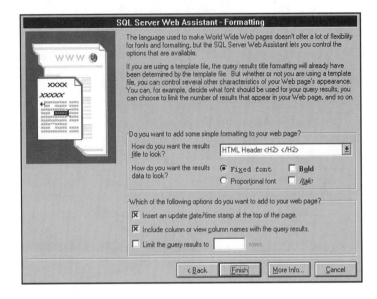

6. From the SQL Server Web Assistant Formatting dialog box, select a formatting style and other Web page options. Click the Finish button to generate the HTML file and any scheduling or trigger options.

Congratulations! You have just designed a Web page that will be generated automatically the next time your data changes. Use a Web browser such as Microsoft's Internet Explorer (shown in Figure 28.6) or the Netscape browser to view the contents of the Web page.

Figure 28.6.
Browsing a Web page
created by the SQL
Server Web Assistant.

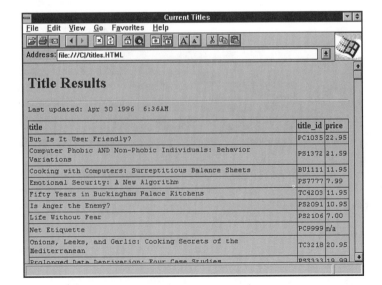

A Behind-the-Scenes Look at the SQL Server Web Assistant

The SQL Server Web Assistant provides a tremendous amount of automation through a simple-to-use graphical interface. However, to fully implement a Web-based solution, you must understand how the wizard performs Web page automation. Understanding the wizard's functionality is useful when you need to modify an existing Web page or correct an error in a Web page. Here is a list of the components used by the wizard; the following sections detail these components:

♦ `sp_makewebtask`, `sp_dropwebtask`, and `sp_runwebtask` system procedures
♦ HTML file
♦ Triggers
♦ Stored procedures
♦ SQL Server's Task Scheduler

The `sp_makewebtask`, `sp_dropwebtask`, and `sp_runwebtask` System Procedures

The following system procedures are used by the SQL Server Web Assistant to generate Web pages: `sp_makewebtask`, `sp_dropwebtask`, and `sp_runwebtask` (refer to Appendix C for more information on these system stored procedures). You can use these system procedures to further extend the functionality of the SQL Server Web Assistant.

HTML File

The output from the SQL Server Web Assistant is an HTML Web page file. This file is a static file that does not contain any live links to SQL Server data. Therefore, if you have to modify an existing HTML file, you can regenerate the entire file or manually modify the file. Manually modifying a file is an easy way to make a quick fix to an existing Web page. Because an HTML file is an ASCII text file, you can use any ASCII text editor (Microsoft Word, Write, Notepad, and so on) to modify an existing HTML file (see Figure 28.7).

Triggers

If you want your Web page to be a current reflection of your data, you will have to regenerate the Web page whenever your data changes. (Remember that the data in an HTML file is static; to reflect updates, the file must be regenerated.) To automate the generation of the HTML file, the SQL Server Web Assistant can create a set of INSERT, UPDATE, and DELETE triggers (see Figure 28.8) that schedule program calls to regenerate the Web page.

Figure 28.7.
Modifying an HTML
file with an ASCII
editor.

Figure 28.8.
A trigger used to
regenerate a Web page.

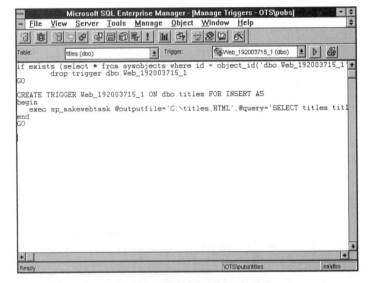

Caution

BCP bypasses a table's triggers. If you are using triggers to regenerate
a Web page, you must manually regenerate the Web page to reflect
the data changes made with BCP.

SQL Server's Task Scheduler

SQL Server's Task Scheduler is another component of the SQL Server Web Assistant. For example, if you want the wizard to regenerate the Web page on an hourly basis, the wizard will schedule a task that, in turn, calls sp_runwebtask (see Figure 28.9). The Web page is rebuilt when this system procedure is executed (see Figure 28.10).

Figure 28.9.
Task Scheduler and
Web page integration.

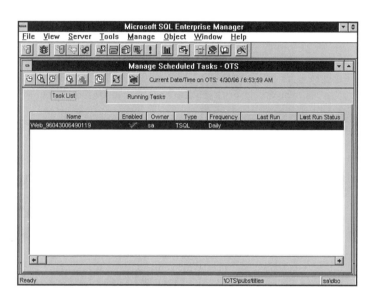

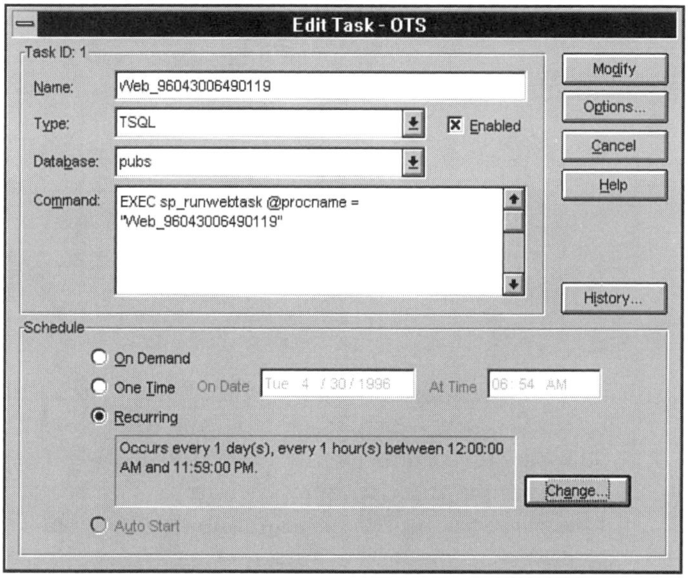

Figure 28.10.
The call to sp_runwebtask
from the Task
Scheduler.

STORED PROCEDURES

When the sp_runwebtask system procedure is executed from the Task Scheduler, it calls a stored procedure generated by the SQL Server Web Assistant. This stored procedure contains the information input by the user when the original Web page was created. To determine the name of the stored procedure being called, look at EXEC sp_runwebtask @procname = *syntax* (refer to Figure 28.10).

MS-QUERY

MS-Query is a graphical query tool that can be used to browse and modify data. Other features of MS-Query include the capability to execute stored procedures, the capability to edit and create table definitions, and extensive sort and filter capabilities.

Follow these steps to use MS-Query:

1. Double-click the MS-Query icon in the Microsoft SQL Server 6.5 (Common) program group. The Microsoft Query window appears (see Figure 28.11).

Figure 28.11.
The Microsoft Query
window.

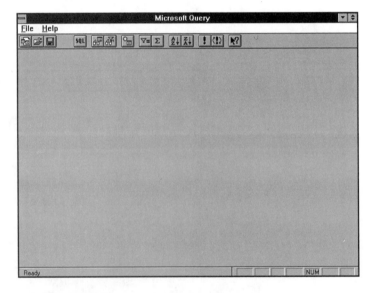

2. To establish a connection to SQL Server from the Microsoft Query window, click the New Query toolbar button. The Select Data Source dialog box appears (see Figure 28.12). From this dialog box, select the appropriate data source and click the Use button. You are prompted for a login and password. Enter this information and click the OK button to continue. The Add Tables dialog box appears (see Figure 28.13).

Figure 28.12.
The Select Data Source
dialog box.

Figure 28.13.
The Add Tables
dialog box.

3. From the Add Tables dialog box, select the tables you want to work with. To add a table, select the table name and click the Add button. If you select multiple tables, MS-Query automatically tries to create a WHERE clause to join the tables. After adding the appropriate tables, click the Close button. The Query1 dialog box appears (see Figure 28.14).

Figure 28.14.
The Query1 dialog box.

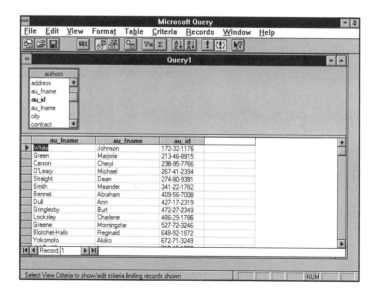

4. From the Query1 dialog box, you can select the data you want to display by dragging and dropping the information from the top half of the window to the bottom half of the window.

Note

If you directly modify data in MS-Query, the data in SQL Server will be updated automatically for you. To enable editing, select the Allow Editing option from the Records menu.

SUMMARY

The SQL Server Web Assistant and MS-Query are two graphical tools that reduce the need to manually generate Transact SQL statements. These two powerful tools often meet the needs of an administrator or developer. When a task exceeds the capabilities of these products, you can still use these tools to generate scripts that can be manually modified.

- Naming Conventions

- Using Extended
  Stored Procedures

- System Procedures

- Function Reference

- DBCC Commands

- System Tables

- Object Manager

- SQL Administrator

- What's on the
  CD-ROM

PART VII

Appendixes

APPENDIX A

Naming Conventions

The following are recommended naming conventions for SQL Server.

Suggested Naming Conventions

Object	Naming Convention	Example
database	*(business name)*	sales
device		
data device	*(business name) + _data*	sales_data
log device	*(business name) + _log*	sales_log
dump device	*(business name) + _dump*	sales_dump
table constraint	*(business name)*	customer
foreign key constraint	*(table name) + _fk*	customer_fk
primary key constraint	*(table name) + _pk*	customer_pk
unique key constraint	*(table name) + _uniq*	customer_uniq
or		
foreign key constraint	*fk_ + (table name)*	fk_customer
primary key constraint	*pk_ + (table name)*	pk_customer
unique key constraint	*uniq_ + (table name)*	uniq_customer
index		
clustered	*(column_name) + _cdx*	customer_id_cdx
nonclustered	*(column name) + _idx*	customer_id_idx
trigger		
delete	*(table name) + _dtr*	customer_dtr
insert	*(table name) + _itr*	customer_itr
update	*(table name) + _utr*	customer_utr
insert and update	*(table name) + _iutr*	customer_iutr
or		
delete	*dtr_ + (table name)*	dtr_customer
insert	*itr_ + (table name)*	itr_customer
update	*utr_ + (table name)*	utr_customer
insert and update	*iutr_ + (table name)*	iutr_customer
stored procedure *(style A)*	*usp_ + (business name)*	usp_customer_inquiry
	(usp stands for *user-defined stored procedure*)	

stored procedure (*style B*)	This style combines the action being performed in the stored procedure with a business name. For example, a stored procedure that deletes the customer profile has the name `del_customer`. If the stored procedure performs multiple business functions, use `oth_` + *(business name)*.		
DELETE	`del_` + *(business name)*	`del_customer`	
INSERT	`ins_` + *(business name)*	`ins_customer`	
SELECT	`sel_` + *(business name)*	`sel_customer`	
UPDATE	`upd_` + *(business name)*	`upd_customer`	
Other types of actions	`oth_` + *(business name)*	`oth_customer`	
view	*(business name)* + `_view`	`customer_view`	

A

NAMING CONVENTIONS

Note

SQL Server is case sensitive. I generally make everything lowercase to avoid confusion.

Using Extended Stored
Procedures

Extended stored procedures were first introduced with Microsoft SQL Server 4.21 for Windows NT. An extended stored procedure is not really a stored procedure; it is a function in a dynamic link library (DLL) that can be executed like a stored procedure from SQL Server; the extended stored procedure can return status codes to the calling process like normal stored procedures. Extended stored procedures can be created by developers and then called from SQL Server; however, only the sa can add an extended stored procedure to the system. This appendix is a reference to the extended stored procedures that come with SQL Server and the stored procedures used to manage extended stored procedures.

Tip

The names of the Microsoft extended stored procedures begin with the characters xp_, unlike the names of the standard system stored procedures, which begin with the characters sp_.

sp_addextendedproc

sp_addextendedproc is a SQL Server stored procedure used to register an extended stored procedure with SQL Server. The command must be executed by the sa in the master database. The syntax for the command is as follows:

```
sp_addextendedproc function, dll
```

In this syntax, function is the extended stored procedure function name and dll is the name of the DLL containing the function.

sp_dropextendedproc

sp_dropextendedproc is a SQL Server stored procedure used to remove (drop) an extended stored procedure from SQL Server. The syntax for the command is as follows:

```
sp_dropextendedproc function
```

In this syntax, function is the name of the extended stored procedure to remove.

sp_helpextendedproc

sp_helpextendedproc displays the extended stored procedures on a SQL Server. The syntax is as follows:

```
sp_helpextendedproc
```

Figure B.1 shows the output from sp_helpextendedproc. Note that the function and DLL name are displayed.

Figure B.1.
Sample output from
sp_helpextendedproc.

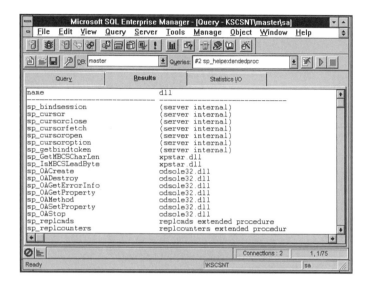

xp_cmdshell

The xp_cmdshell extended stored procedure executes a command string as a system command shell and returns any output.

Tip

> xp_cmdshell is extremely useful for executing commands from stored procedures or triggers. If you need to execute several commands or a single command with a long command string, place the commands in a batch file (with the extension BAT) and execute the batch file.

The syntax for xp_cmdshell is as follows:

```
xp_cmdshell command[, no_output]
```

In this syntax, command is the command to execute and no_output is an optional parameter that tells the server to execute the command but not to return any output.

Note

If you use `xp_cmdshell` to start an application or batch file that does not return immediately, the connection issuing the extended stored procedure will block and wait until the application exits or the batch file completes (even if you use the *no_output* flag).

Caution

`xp_cmdshell` can execute any Windows NT command that SQL Server has permission to execute. If users are given permission to use `xp_cmdshell`, they can execute any commands that SQL Server has permission to execute.

xp_logevent

`xp_logevent` logs user messages to the Windows NT event log and/or the SQL Server error log. The syntax is as follows:

```
xp_logevent error_number, User_Message, [Event_Log_Severity]
```

In this syntax, *error_number* is a number between 50,001 and 2,147,483,647. *User_Message* is a user-defined message up to 255 characters. *Event_Log_Severity* is an optional parameter that can have the value `informational`, `warning`, or `error` (the default is `informational`).

Tip

`xp_logevent` can be used in triggers to audit table changes. Use `xp_logevent` for error reporting in stored procedures.

xp_msver

Added in SQL Server 6.0, `xp_msver` returns information about SQL Server. The syntax for `xp_msver` is as follows:

```
xp_msver [option]
```

In this syntax, *option* can be any of the parameters listed in the `Name` column shown in Figure B.2.

Figure B.2.
Sample output of the
xp_msver command.

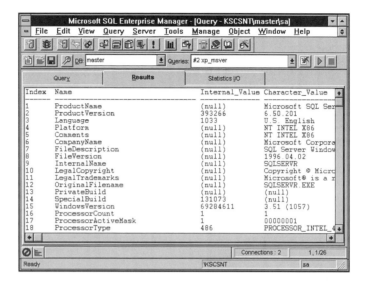

xp_sendmail

xp_sendmail can be used to send a mail message or query from SQL Server to several users using e-mail. xp_sendmail has the following syntax:

```
xp_sendmail recipient, [...recipientn,]]
{@message ¦ @query ¦ @attachments}
[, copy_recipients] [, blind_copy_recipients] [, subject] [, type]
[, attach_results] [, no_output] [, no_header] [, width]
[, separator] [, echo_error] [, set_user]
```

In this syntax, recipient is the user or list of users to which you want to send the mail. @message or @query or @attachment is the body of the mail message. If a query is specified, the results of the query are sent. copy_receipients and blind_copy_recipients are other users to include on the mail list to receive the message. subject is the subject of the message. type is used to send a custom message.

attach_results specifies that the results of the query should be included as an attached file instead of appended to the end of the mail message. no_output specifies not to return results to the mail client. no_header specifies not to include the column header information for a query. width sets the line width for the message.

Tip

Use the extended stored procedure mail functions for error reporting and to send the results of nightly batch runs.

Version 6.5 xp_snmp_getstate

xp_snmp_getstate is new with SQL Server 6.5; it returns the state of the SQL Server SNMP (Simple Network Management Protocol) agent. The syntax is as follows:

```
xp_snmp_getstate [return_status OUTPUT]
```

In this syntax, return_status OUTPUT is a datatype int that holds the return status from the SNMP agent. When the extended stored procedure is executed without any parameters, the status and the definition of the state is returned in the result set.

Version 6.5 xp_snmp_raisetrap

xp_snmp_raisetrap is new with SQL Server 6.5; it allows a client to define and send an SNMP (Simple Network Management Protocol) alert (trap) to an SNMP client. The syntax is as follows:

```
xp_snmp_raisetrap server,database,error_message,
message_id,severity,user,comment,date_and_time,return_status OUTPUT
```

In this syntax, server is the name of the server on which the trap originated. database is the name of the database where the trap originated. error_message is the message for the trap (up to 255 characters). message_id is the message number associated with the error message. severity is the integer value of the SNMP trap.

user is the name of the user raising the SNMP alert (trap). comment is an additional message associated with the trap (up to 255 characters). date_and_time is the date and time at which the trap occurred. return_status OUTPUT is of datatype int and returns the completion status of the extended stored procedure.

xp_sprintf

xp_sprintf was added in SQL Server 6.0; it is similar to the C function sprintf. Use xp_sprintf to build an output string from a format list and a list of strings. The syntax is as follows:

```
xp_sprintf Build_String output, Build_String_Format [, string arguments]…
```

In this syntax, Build_String is the output string for the formatted string. Build_String_Format currently can be only %s (strings), and string_arguments is the list of arguments used to build the output string based on the format string.

xp_sqlinventory

xp sqlinventory is new with SQL Server 6.5; it collects domain information for SQL Server 6.5. The syntax is as follows:

```
xp_sqlinventory @DbName,@TableName,@Interval¦stop
```

In this syntax, @DbName is the name of the database used to store broadcast information. @TableName is the table used to store the server information. @Interval is the amount of time in seconds used to check for broadcast messages. The stop parameter is used to stop all inventory actions in progress.

xp_startmail

xp_startmail starts a SQL Server mail client session. xp_startmail has the following syntax:

```
xp_startmail ['mail_user_name'] [, 'password']
```

In this syntax, mail_user_name is a valid mail user name and password is the password for the user.

xp_stopmail

xp_stopmail halts a SQL Server mail session. xp_stopmail has the following format:

```
xp_stopmail
```

SQL INTEGRATED SECURITY EXTENDED STORED PROCEDURES

The following extended stored procedures are used to set up integrated or mixed security. It is recommended that you use the SQL Security Manager instead of the extended stored procedures to configure security options.

xp_grantlogin

xp_grantlogin adds a Windows NT user group or user to SQL Server. The syntax is as follows:

```
xp_grantlogin 'NT_Account_Name' [, {'admin' ¦ 'repl' ¦ 'user'}]
```

In this syntax, NT_Account_Name is a Windows NT group or user. This optional parameter determines the type of SQL Server privileges assigned to the login: admin = SA, repl=repl_publisher, and user.

xp_revokelogin

xp_revokelogin drops the user account or group from the SQL Server. The syntax is as follows:

```
xp_revokelogin 'NT_Account_Name'
```

In this syntax, *NT_Account_Name* is a Windows NT group or user.

xp_logininfo

xp_logininfo provides SQL Server account access information. The syntax is as follows:

```
xp_logininfo ['NT_Account_Name'] [, 'all' | 'members'] [, variable_name]
```

In this syntax, *NT_Account_Name* is a Windows NT group or user. *'all'* reports all permission paths for the account, *'members'* reports information on all members of the group. *variable_name* is an optional output parameter that returns the permission level of the account (such as admin, repl, user).

xp_loginconfig

xp_loginconfig reports SQL Server login security information. The syntax is as follows:

```
xp_loginconfig ['Config_Name_Parm']
```

In this syntax, *Config_Name_Parm* can be any of the parameters listed in the name column shown in Figure B.3.

Figure B.3.
Sample output from
the xp_loginconfig
command.

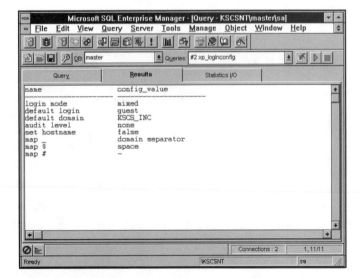

System Stored Procedures

SQL Server comes with many stored procedures that enable you to view and modify the system tables; these procedures are called *system procedures*. This appendix lists the different system stored procedures that ship with Microsoft SQL Server.

sp_addalias

Creates an alias for one user to another in a database.

sp_addalias *login_id, user_name*

login_id	Login ID of user to assign alias
user_name	Database user to alias the login ID

sp_addextendedproc

Registers the new extended stored procedure name with SQL Server.

sp_addextendedproc *function, dll*

function	Function name
dll	Name of the DLL containing the function

sp_addgroup

Creates a group in the database from which the command is executed.

sp_addgroup *group_name*

group_name	Name of the group to add to the database

sp_addlogin

Adds a new login ID to SQL Server and modifies the system syslogins table.

sp_addlogin *login_id* [, *password* [, *default_db* [, *default_language*] [,*login_suid*]]]

login_id	User login ID to add
password	Password for the new login ID
default_db	Default database for the *login_id*
default_language	Default language for the *login_id*
login_suid	Forces SQL Server to set *syslogins.suid* to the value specified in *login_suid*; use this parameter when a user's login in the sysusers table is orphaned and you need to resyncronize the suid with a login

sp_addmessage

Enables you to add custom information or an error message to the sysmessages system table.

```
sp_addmessage message id, severity, 'message text'
        [, language [, {true ¦ false} [, REPLACE]]]
```

message id	Integer message number must be greater than 50001
severity	Severity level of the message (valid levels 1 to 25)
message text	Message description
language	Language of message; US English is the default
{true ¦ false}	If TRUE, message is automatically written to NT event log
REPLACE	Used to overwrite an existing message

sp_addremotelogin

Adds a login ID for a remote user.

```
sp_addremotelogin remote_server [, login_ID [, remote_name]]
```

remote_server	Remote server for which the login_id applies
login_id	Login ID of user on the local server
remote_name	Login ID used by the remote server when logging on to the local server

sp_addsegment

Creates a segment on a device in the current database.

```
sp_addsegment seg_name, logicalname
```

seg_name	Name of the new segment
logicalname	Database device in which the segment will be located

sp_addserver

Adds a remote SQL Server.

```
sp_addserver servername [, LOCAL]
```

servername	Name of the remote server to add
[, LOCAL]	Identifies the server being added as a local server

sp_addtype

Adds a new user-defined datatype.

```
sp_addtype type_name, physical_type [, null_type]
```

type_name	Name of the datatype
physical_type	SQL Server-supplied datatype on which the new type is based
null_type	Defines how the user datatype treats NULLs

sp_addumpdevice

Adds a new dump device to SQL Server.

```
sp_addumpdevice {'disk' | 'diskette' | 'tape'}, 'logical_name', 'physical_name'
[, {{cntrltype [, noskip | skip [, media_capacity]]} | {@devstatus = {noskip |
skip}}}]
```

disk,diskette,tape	Valid types of dump devices
logicalname	Name of the dump device
physicalname	Physical location of the dump device
cntrltype	Not used with version 6.x; SQL Server ignores this setting
media_capacity	Not used with version 6.x; SQL Server ignores this setting
noskip,skip	Reads or skips ANSI labels
@devstatus ={noskip	skip}	Determines whether ANSI tapes are read or ignored; this variable is used when the *ctrltype* or *media_capacity* parameters are not specified

sp_adduser

Adds a new user to the current database.

```
sp_adduser login_id [, user_name [, group_name]]
```

login_id	Login ID of the new user
user_name	User name in the database
group_name	User group name

sp_altermessage

Changes the state of a system error message located in sysmessages.

```
sp_altermessage messageid, WITH_LOG, {true | false}
```

messageid	ID of the message to alter
WITH_LOG	If set to TRUE, the message is written to the Windows NT event log.

sp_bindefault

Binds a default to a table column or user-defined object.

```
sp_bindefault default_name, object_name [, future_only]
```

default_name	Name of the default
object_name	Name of the object having the default bound
future_only	Used for user-defined data types only; prevents existing data from inheriting the new default

sp_bindrule

Binds a rule to a table column or user-defined object.

```
sp_bindrule rule_name, object_name [, future_only]
```

rule_name	Name of the new rule
object_name	Name of the object having the rule bound
future_only	Used for user-defined data types only; prevents existing data from inheriting the new rule

sp_bindsession

Used to attach or remove a session from the Distributed Transaction Coordinator (DTC).

```
sp_bindsession {'bind_token' ¦ 'NULL'}
```

bind_token	Name of the transaction space token
NULL	Used to unbind the session

sp_certify_removable

Verifies that a database is properly configured for removable media distribution and generates a text file containing information about the database.

```
sp_certify_removable database_name[, AUTO]
```

database_name	Name of the database
AUTO	Gives ownership of the databases and objects to the sa and removes user-created database users and nondefault permissions

sp_changedbowner

Changes the database owner.

```
sp_changedbowner login_id [, true]
```

login_id	Login ID of the new database owner
true	Transfers to the new owner aliases and permissions

sp_changegroup

Changes the group of a user.

```
sp_changegroup group_name, user_name
```

group_name	Group name
user_name	User name to add to the group

sp_change_users_login

Used to synchronize login IDs in the sysusers and syslogins tables. Use this procedure when a login ID is orphaned (restoring a database to another server may cause orphaned login IDs).

```
sp_change_users_login {'Auto_Fix' ¦ 'Report' ¦ 'Update_One'} [, UserNameOrPattern
[, LoginName]]
```

Auto_Fix	Automatically synchronizes all orphaned users
Report	Displays orphaned user names
Update_One	Synchronizes a specific user name
UserNameOrPattern	User name or pattern
LoginName	Login name

sp_coalesce_fragments

Consolidates device usage fragment records in the sysusages table for a particular database.

```
sp_coalesce_fragments [DBNamePattern]
```

DBNamePattern	Database name pattern

sp_configure

Sets or displays SQL Server configuration parameters.

```
sp_configure [configuration_name [, configuration_value]]
```

configuration_name	Name of the parameter to modify
configuration_value	New value

sp_dboption

Turns on or off a specified database option. If called with no parameters, displays the current option settings of the default database.

```
sp_dboption [database_name, option_name, {true ¦ false}]
```

database_name	Name of the database to set the option
option_name	Option name
{true ¦ false}	Value of option; true = on, false = off

sp_dbremove

Used to drop a database and, optionally, any device(s) of which the database has exclusive ownership.

```
sp_dbremove database[, drop_device]
```

database	Database to remove
drop_device	Device(s) to remove

sp_defaultdb

Sets the default database for the user identified by login_id.

```
sp_defaultdb login_id, default_database
```

login_id	Login ID of the user
default_database	Default database name

sp_defaultlanguage

Changes the default language of a user.

```
sp_defaultlanguage login_id [, language]
```

login_id	Login ID of the user
language	New default language

sp_depends

Displays object dependencies.

```
sp_depends object_name
```

object_name	Database object for which you want to view dependencies (view, table, trigger, or stored procedure)

sp_devoption

Displays or sets the status of a device.

```
sp_devoption [device_name [, option_name {, true ¦ false} [, override]]]
```

device_name	Name of the device to display or set
option_name	Name of the option (true = on, false = off)
override	Only for read-only option; allows you to set a read/write database to read-only

sp_diskdefault

Determines whether the device can be used as part of the default device pool used for CREATE DATABASE statements without specifying a device.

```
sp_diskdefault database_device, {defaulton ¦ defaultoff}
```

database_device	Device name
{defaulton ¦ defaultoff}	Adds or removes the device from the default pool

sp_dropalias

Drops the alias login_id.

```
sp_dropalias login_id
```

login_id	Login ID of user with alias to drop

sp_dropdevice

Drops a device.

```
sp_dropdevice logical_name [, DELFILE]
```

logical_name	Logical name of the device to drop
DELFILE	Deletes physical file after the device is dropped

sp_dropextendedproc

Removes an extended stored procedure from SQL Server.

```
sp_dropextendedproc function_name
```

function_name	Name of extended stored procedure to remove

sp_dropgroup

Drops a group from a database.

```
sp_dropgroup group_name
```

group_name	Name of the group to remove

sp_droplanguage

Removes an alternate language from SQL Server.

```
sp_droplanguage language [, drop_messages]
```

language	Language to drop
drop_messages	Drops all associated system messages

sp_droplogin

Removes the *login_id* from SQL Server.

```
sp_droplogin login_id
```

login_id	Login ID to remove

sp_dropmessage

Removes a message from the sysmessages table.

```
sp_dropmessage [msgid [, language ¦ 'all']]
```

msgid	Message ID of the message to drop
language	Language of the message to drop
all	Drops message from all languages

sp_dropremotelogin

Drops a remote login ID from the SQL Server.

```
sp_dropremotelogin remote_server [, login_name [, remote_name]]
```

`remote_server`	Server with remote login to drop
`login_name`	Local server's login name to drop
`remote_name`	Remote user name mapped to the local login name

sp_dropsegment

Drops a segment from a database.

`sp_dropsegment segment_name [, logical_name]`

`segment_name`	Segment name to drop
`logical_name`	Database device you no longer want the segment to use

sp_dropserver

Drops a server from SQL Server's list of known servers.

`sp_dropserver server_name [, drop_logins]`

`server_name`	Server name to drop
`drop_logins`	Indicates any remote logins to remove

sp_droptype

Removes a user-defined datatype.

`sp_droptype type_name`

`type_name`	Name of the datatype to remove

sp_dropwebtask

Removes a Web task.

`sp_dropwebtask {@procname = procname ¦ @outputfile = outputfile ¦`
`@procname = procname, @outputfile = outputfile}`

`procname`	Name of the Web procedure to drop
`outputfile`	Name of the Web task to drop

sp_dropuser

Removes a user from the current database.

`sp_dropuser user_name`

`user_name`	User name to remove

sp_dsninfo

Displays ODBC data source name (DSN) information for an installed replication server.

```
sp_dsninfo dsn [, {infotype | NULL}[, login [, password]]]
```

dsn	ODBC data source name
{infotype	NULL}	Type of information to return
login	DSN login ID
password	DSN password

sp_enumdsn

Displays ODBC data source information for the server.

```
sp_enumdsn
```

sp_extendsegment

Expands a segment to another database device.

```
sp_extendsegment segment_name, logical_name
```

segment_name	Segment name to expand
logical_name	Database device to add

sp_fallback_activate_svr_db

Activates a fallback server for specified databases.

```
sp_fallback_activate_svr_db [PrimarySvrName] [, DBNamePattern]
```

PrimarySvrName	Primary fallback server name
DBNamePattern	Database pattern to activate fallback support

sp_fallback_deactivate_svr_db

Deactivates a fallback server for specified databases.

```
sp_fallback_deactivate_svr_db [PrimarySvrName] [, DBNamePattern]
```

PrimarySvrName	Primary fallback server name to deactivate
DBNamePattern	Database pattern to deactivate fallback support

C

SYSTEM STORED PROCEDURES

sp_fallback_enroll_svr_db

Stages a fallback server for activation.

```
sp_fallback_enroll_svr_db {PrimarySvrName, DBName}
```

PrimarySvrName	Primary fallback server to stage
DBName	Database name to stage for fallback

sp_fallback_help

Reports fallback information for a specified server.

```
sp_fallback_help [PrimarySvrNamePattern]
```

PrimarySvrNamePattern	Server name pattern

sp_fallback_permanent_svr

Configures the fallback server as the permanent owner of database(s) specified by the primary server name.

```
sp_fallback_permanent_svr {'PrimarySvrName,' 1}
```

PrimarySvrNamePattern	Server name pattern
1	Specifies override to prohibit this procedure from being inadvertently executed

sp_fallback_upd_dev_drive

Resolves device drive letter differences between a primary and a fallback server.

```
sp_fallback_upd_dev_drive {'PrimarySvrName', 'PrimaryDrive', 'FallbackDrive'}
```

PrimarySvrName	Primary server name
PrimaryDrive	Primary drive letter
FallbackDrive	Fallback drive letter

sp_fallback_withdraw_svr_db

Removes the fallback participation of inactive databases from the fallback server.

```
sp_fallback_withdraw_svr_db {'PrimarySvrName' [, DBNamePattern]}
```

PrimarySvrName	Primary server name
DBNamePattern	Database name pattern

sp_getbindtoken

Generates a distributed transaction session and returns a corresponding bind token ID.

```
sp_getbindtoken return_value OUTPUT [, @for_xp_flag]
```

return_value	Token to use for a shared transaction session
@for_xp_flag	If equal to 1, the token can be passed to an extended stored procedure

sp_help

Displays information on a specific database object; if no parameter is given, displays the objects in the current database.

```
sp_help [object_name]
```

object_name	Name of the object for which you want to display information

sp_helpconstraint

Displays information on the constraints associated with the table.

```
sp_helpconstraint table_name
```

table_name	Table name for which you want constraint information

sp_helpdb

Displays information on the specified database. If no database is specified, displays help on all the databases.

```
sp_helpdb [database_name]
```

database_name	Database name for which to display information

sp_helpdevice

Displays information on a specified device; when called without a parameter, displays information for all system devices.

```
sp_helpdevice [logical_name]
```

logical_name	Device name

sp_helpextendedproc

Displays information for a specified extended stored procedure; when called without a parameter, displays information for all extended stored procedures.

```
sp_helpextendedproc [function_name]
```

    function_name   Name of extended stored procedure

sp_helpgroup

Displays information about the group in the current database; when called without a parameter, displays information for all the groups in the current database.

```
sp_helpgroup [group_name]
```

    group_name   Group name to display information

sp_helpindex

Displays index information on the specified table.

```
sp_helpindex table_name
```

    table_name   Name of the table for which you want to obtain index information

sp_helplanguage

Displays information on the specified language; when called without a parameter, displays information for all the languages.

```
sp_helplanguage [language]
```

    language   Language for which you want to obtain information

sp_helplog

Displays information on the device that contains the first page of the log in the current database. There are no parameters for this procedure.

```
sp_helplog
```

sp_helplogins

Displays login information.

```
sp_helplogins [LoginNamePattern]
```

LoginNamePattern   Login name pattern

sp_helpremotelogin

Displays information on a remote server's specified login; when called without a parameter, displays information for all remote logins.

```
sp_helpremotelogin [remote_server [, remote_name]]
```

remote_server   Server for which you want to obtain login infor-
                          mation
remote_name   Remote user name about which you want to obtain
                          information

sp_help_revdatabase

Produces a script that can be used to create a database; also displays database configuration settings.

```
sp_help_revdatabase [DBNamePattern]
```

DBNamePattern   Database name pattern

sp_helprotect

Displays permissions for a database object and, optionally, a specific user of the object.

```
sp_helprotect object [,granteename] [,grantorname] [,category]
```

object   Database object to display permissions
granteename   Grantee of the database object
grantorname   Grantor of the database object
category   Permission category

sp_helpsegment

Displays information on the specified segment; when called without a parameter, displays information for all segments in the current database.

```
sp_helpsegment [segment_name]
```

    segment_name   Name of the segment for which you want to obtain information

sp_helpserver

Displays information on a specified remote server or replication server; when called without a parameter, displays information for all servers.

```
sp_helpserver [server_name]
```

    server_name   Name of server to display specific information

sp_helpsort

Displays the default sort order and character set. There are no parameters for this procedure.

```
sp_helpsort
```

sp_helpsql

Displays the syntax for Transact SQL statements.

```
sp_helpsql ['topic']
```

    topic   Topic or statement for which you want to display help

sp_helpstartup

Displays the stored procedures that are executed automatically when SQL Server starts. There are no parameters for this procedure.

```
sp_helpstartup
```

sp_helptext

Displays the text for the following objects: stored procedures, views, triggers, or defaults.

```
sp_helptext object_name
```

object_name	Name of object

sp_helpuser

Displays information about a specific user in a database; when called without a parameter, displays information for all users.

```
sp_helpuser [user_name]
```

user_name	User name

sp_lock

Displays information about current locks on SQL Server for a specific system process ID(s) (spid); when called without a parameter, displays information for all the locks.

```
sp_lock [spid1 [, spid2]]
```

spid1	System process ID for which you want to obtain lock information
spid2	System process ID for which you want to obtain lock information

sp_logdevice

Places the syslogs table (that is, the transaction log) on a separate device.

```
sp_logdevice database_name, database_device
```

database_name	Database with the transaction log to move
database_device	Name of the database device to which you want to move syslogs

sp_makestartup

Makes the stored procedure an auto procedure that runs when the system is restarted.

```
sp_makestartup procedure_name
```

procedure_name	Name of the procedure to execute at startup

sp_makewebtask

Creates an HTML script (Web page) that contains data.

```
sp_makewebpage [@outputfile =] filename, [@query1=] query,[[@query2=] query,
[@query3=] query, [@query4=] query,
[@fixedfont=] [0 | 1], [@bold=] [0 | 1], [@italic=] [0 | 1], [@colheaders=] [0 |
1], [@lastupdated=] [0 | 1], [@HTMLheader=] header, [@username_=] username,
[@dbname=] dbname, [@templatefile=] file, [@webpagetitle=] title, [@resultstitle=]
title, [@URL=] url, [@reftext=] reftext, [@table_urls=]url,
[@url_query=]query, [@whentype=] whentype,[@targetdate=] date, [@targettime=] time,
[@dayflags=] flags,
[@numunits=] units, [@unittype=] type,[@procname=] procname, [@maketask=] task],
[@rowcnt = rowcnt,]
[@tabborder = tabborder,] [@singlerow = singlerow,] [@blobfmt = blobfmt]]
```

@outputfile	Filename and location for HTML output
@query1...@query4	SQL query statement
@fixedfont	[0	1] Fixed font option
@bold	[0	1] Bold font option
@italic	[0	1] Italic font option
@colheaders	[0	1] Column header option
@lastupdated	[0	1] Timestamp option
@HTMLheader	HTML formatting code
@username	User name for query permissions
@dbname	Database name
@templatefile	Template filename
@webpagetitle	Web page title
@resultstitle	Result set title
@URL	URL link to another Web page
@reftext	Hyperlink help text
@table_urls	[0	1] Generates links based on data in a SQL Server table
@url_query	SQL SELECT query for URL definitions and text for hyperlinks
@whentype	Schedules a time to update or rebuild the Web page
@targetdate	Date on which the Web page should be rebuilt
@targettime	Time at which the Web page should be rebuilt
@dayflags	Day interval at which to update the Web page
@numunits	Numeric unit that determines when the Web page should be updated
@unittype	Numeric unit time type
@procname	Procedure name

@maketask	Make task option
@rowcnt	Number of rows to return
@tabborder	[0 | 1] Draws border around the output table
@singlerow	[0 | 1] Specifies one row per HTML page
@blobfmt	Specifies text or image datatypes for use in the HTML file

sp_monitor

Displays statistical information on SQL Server. There are no parameters for this procedure.

```
sp_monitor
```

sp_runwebtask

Executes a defined Web task.

```
sp_runwebtask {@procname = procname ¦ @outputfile = outputfile ¦
@procname = procname, @outputfile = outputfile}
```

@procname	Name of the Web procedure to run
@outputfile	Name of the Web task to run

sp_password

Changes the login_id password.

```
sp_password old_password, new_password [, login_id]
```

old_password	Old login ID password
new_password	New login ID password
login_id	Login ID to modify

sp_placeobject

Places future allocation for a table or index on the specified segment.

```
sp_placeobject segment_name, object_name
```

segment_name	Name of the segment for future allocation
object_name	Table or index name to place on segment

sp_processmail

Uses extended stored procedures to process an incoming mail message.

```
sp_processmail [@subject = subject] [[,] @file_type = file_type]
[[,] @separator = separator] [[,] @set_user = user] [[,] @dbuse = database_name]
```

subject	Subject line of the mail message
file_type	File extension to use to send back query results
separator	Column separator
user	Security context in which command is run
database_name	Database context in which command is run

sp_recompile

Recompiles all stored procedures and triggers that use the specified table name.

```
sp_recompile table_name
```

table_name	Table name

sp_remoteoption

Changes or displays the remote login option.

```
sp_remoteoption [remote_server, login_name, remote_name, option_name, {true ¦
false}]
```

remote_server	Remote server name
login_name	Login name
remote_name	Remote user name
option_name	Option name (true = on, false = off)

sp_rename

Renames a database object.

```
sp_rename object_name, new_name [, COLUMN ¦ INDEX  ¦ OBJECT¦ USERDATATYPE]
```

object_name	Old object name
new_name	New object name
COLUMN	Specifies that the object being renamed is a column
INDEX	Specifies that the object being renamed is an index
OBJECT	Specifies the object being renamed
USERDATATYPE	Specifies that the object being renamed is a user-defined datatype

sp_renamedb

Renames a database.

```
sp_renamedb old_db_name, new_db_name
```

old_db_name	Name of the old database
new_db_name	Name of the new database

sp_serveroption

Sets the specified server option.

```
sp_serveroption [server_name, option_name, {true | false}]
```

server_name	Name of the server for which you want to set an option
option_name	Name of the option to set (true = on, false = off)

sp_setlangalias

Sets an alias or changes an alias for an alternate language.

```
sp_setlangalias language, alias
```

language	Language to alias
alias	Alias name

sp_setnetname

Sets a network computer name for a remote computer.

```
sp_setnetname srvname, srvnetname
```

srvname	Server name for RPC syntax
srvnetname	Windows NT server name

sp_spaceused

Displays the number of rows and the overall space usage of the specified object or database.

```
sp_spaceused [object_name] [[,] @updateusage = {true | false}]
```

object_name	Name of the object for which you want to display information
@updateusage	When set to true, issues a DBCC UPDATEUSAGE command before displaying information

C

SYSTEM STORED PROCEDURES

sp_unbindefault

Removes a default from the specified object.

```
sp_unbindefault object_name [, future_only]
```

object_name	Name of the object to unbind the default
future_only	Used only for user-defined datatypes; leaves the default value with the existing data

sp_unbindrule

Removes the rule from the specified object.

```
sp_unbindrule object_name [, future_only]
```

object_name	Object from which to remove the rule
future_only	Used only for user-defined datatypes; leaves the rule with the existing data

sp_unmakestartup

Stops the procedure previously marked as autostart from executing when SQL Server is first started.

```
sp_unmakestartup procedure_name
```

procedure_name	Name of stored procedure

sp_who

Displays information for a specified login_id or a specified process; when called with no parameters, displays information for all users and processes.

```
sp_who [login_id | 'spid' | active]
```

login_id	Login ID for which you want to display information
spid	System process ID for which you want to display information
active	Returns only active processes, ignores idle processes

sp_xpoption

Sets extended stored procedure options.

```
sp_xpoption XPName, OptionName [, OptionValue]
```

XPName	Extended stored procedure name
OptionName	Option name
OptionValue	Option value

APPENDIX D

Function Reference

SQL Server contains several built-in functions that can be used with the Transact SQL language. This appendix categorizes the built-in functions.

AGGREGATE FUNCTIONS

The following sections cover aggregate functions.

> ## PARAMETER EXPLANATION
>
> The ALL parameter applies the aggregate function to all values. ALL is the default.
>
> The DISTINCT parameter applies the aggregate function to only distinct values.
>
> The *expression* parameter is a column name.

AVG([ALL ¦ DISTINCT] *expression*)

Sum of values in a column. NULLs are ignored.

COUNT([ALL ¦ DISTINCT] *expression*)

Count number of non-NULL values in a column. NULLs are ignored.

COUNT(*)

Count number of rows. NULLs are counted.

MAX(*expression*)

Maximum value for a column. NULLs are ignored.

MIN(*expression*)

Minimum value for a column. NULLs are ignored.

SUM([ALL ¦ DISTINCT] *expression*)

Sum of values for a column. NULLs are ignored.

DATE FUNCTIONS

The following sections cover date functions.

> **PARAMETER EXPLANATION**
>
> The *date* parameter is a valid date.
>
> The *datepart* parameter is a date part or abbreviation. (See Table D.1 for valid date part abbreviations.)
>
> The *number* parameter is a valid number.

TABLE D.1. VALID DATE PART ABBREVIATIONS.

Date Part	Abbreviation	Values
year	yy	1753-9999
quarter	qq	1-4
month	mm	1-12
day of year	dy	1-366
day	dd	1-31
week	wk	1-53
weekday	dw	1-7 (Sun.-Sat.)
hour	hh	0-23
minute	mi	0-59
second	ss	0-59
millisecond	ms	0-999

DATEADD(*datepart*,*number*,*date*)

Returns a date incremented by the specified value.

DATEDIFF(*datepart*,*number*,*date*)

Returns the date part difference between a number and a date.

DATENAME(*datepart*,*date*)

Returns the date part of a specified date as a string.

D

DATEPART(*datepart,date*)

Returns the date part of a specified date as an integer.

GETDATE()

Returns the current date and time.

ISDATE(*test_expr*)

Returns 1 if test_expr is a valid date; returns 0 if the expression is not a valid date.

MATHEMATICAL FUNCTIONS

The following sections cover mathematical functions.

ABS(*numeric_expr*)

Returns the absolute value of a specified expression.

ACOS(*float_expr*)

Returns the angle in radians of a cosine expression.

ASIN(*float_expr*)

Returns the angle in radians of a sine expression.

ATAN(*float_expr*)

Returns the angle in radians of a tangent expression.

ATN2(*float_expr1,float_expr2*)

Returns the angle in radians of a tangent expression.

CEILING(*numeric_expr*)

Returns a rounded-up integer based on the specified expression.

COS(*float_expr*)

Returns the cosine of a specified expression.

COT(*float_expr*)

Returns the cotangent of a specified expression.

DEGREES(*numeric_expr*)

Returns the degrees of a specified expression.

EXP(*float_expr*)

Returns the exponential value of a specified expression.

FLOOR(*numeric_expr*)

Returns a rounded-down integer based on the specified expression.

ISNUMERIC(*numeric_expr*)

Returns 1 if *numeric_expr* is a valid numeric expression; returns 0 if the expression is not a valid numeric expression.

LOG(*float_expr*)

Returns the natural logarithm of a specified expression.

LOG10(*float_expr*)

Returns the base-10 logarithm of a specified expression.

PI()

Returns pi.

POWER(*numeric_expr,y*)

Returns the value of *numeric_expr* to the power of *y*.

RADIANS(*numeric_expr*)

Returns the radians of a specified expression.

RAND([*integer_expr*])

Returns a random float number between 0 and 1. Use the optional *integer_expr* as the seed value.

ROUND(*numeric_expr,integer_expr*)

Returns a number rounded to the precision specified by *integer_expr*.

SIGN(*numeric_expr*)

Returns +1, 0, or –1 based on the sign of the expression.

SIN(*float_expr*)

Returns the sine of an angle specified in radians.

SQRT(*float_expr*)

Returns the square root of a specified expression.

TAN(*float_expr*)

Returns the tangent of an angle specified in radians.

NILADIC FUNCTIONS

Niladic functions are new to SQL Server 6.x. These functions allow default values to be inserted into a table. Before version 6.x, you had to use triggers to insert these types of default values. For more information about these functions, see the CREATE TABLE statement in SQL Server's Books Online.

CURRENT_TIMESTAMP

Returns the current date and time.

CURRENT_USER

Returns the name of the person doing the insert.

SESSION_USER

Returns the name of the person doing the insert.

SYSTEM_USER

Returns the login ID of the person doing the insert (same as SESSION_USER).

USER

Returns the name of the person doing the insert (same as SESSION_USER and SYSTEM_USER).

STRING FUNCTIONS

The following sections cover string functions.

+

Concatenates two or more nonnumeric expressions.

ASCII(*char_expr*)

Returns the corresponding ASCII code value of a specified expression.

CHAR(*integer_expr*)

Returns the corresponding character from the specified ASCII code value. The code must be between 0 and 255.

CHARINDEX('*pattern*', *expression*)

Returns the first position of a pattern within an expression.

DIFFERENCE(*char_expr1, char_expr2*)

Determines the similarities between two strings and returns a value rating the similarities on a scale of 0 to 4, with 4 being the best match.

LOWER(*char_expr*)

Converts an expression to lowercase.

LTRIM(*char_expr*)

Removes leading spaces.

PATINDEX('*%pattern%*', *expression*)

Returns the first position of a pattern in the specified expression.

REPLICATE(*char_expr, integer_expr*)

Replicates a character expression *integer_expr* number of times.

REVERSE(*char_expr*)

Returns a reversed expression.

RIGHT(*char_expr, integer_expr*)

Returns *integer_expr* number of characters from a character expression starting at the right side of *char_expr*.

RTRIM(*char_expr*)

Removes trailing spaces.

SOUNDEX(*char_expr*)

Returns a four-digit SOUNDEX code.

SPACE(*integer_expr*)

Returns *integer_expr* number of spaces.

STR(*float_expr [, length [, decimal]]*)

Returns a character string converted from numeric data.

STUFF(*char_expr1, start, length, char_expr2*)

Stuffs *char_expr1* into *char_expr2*.

SUBSTRING(*expression, start, length*)

Returns a portion of a string expression defined by the *start* value and the *length* value.

UPPER(*char_expr*)

Converts an expression to uppercase.

SYSTEM FUNCTIONS

The following sections cover system functions.

APP_NAME()

Returns the application name for the current connection.

COALESCE(*expression1, expression2, ... expressionN*)

Returns the first non-NULL expression in a list of expressions.

COL_LENGTH('*table_name*', '*column_name*')

Returns the length of a column in a table.

COL_NAME(*table_id, column_id*)

Returns the name of a column based on ID.

DATALENGTH('*expression*')

Returns the length of a specified expression.

DB_ID(['*database_name*'])

Returns the database identification number of a specified database name.

DB_NAME([*database_id*])

Returns the database name for a specified database ID.

GETANSINULL(['*database_name*'])

Returns the nullability setting for a database.

HOST_ID()

Returns the workstation identification number.

HOST_NAME()

Returns the workstation name.

IDENT_INCR('*table_name*')

Returns the increment value used for the creation of an identity column.

IDENT_SEED('*table_name*')

Returns the seed value used for the creation of an identity column.

INDEX_COL('*table_name*', *index_id, key_id*)

Returns the index name for an indexed column.

ISNULL(*expression, value*)

Replaces a NULL expression with a specified value.

NULLIF(*expression1, expression2*)

Returns NULL when *expression1* equals *expression2*.

OBJECT_ID('*object_name*')

Returns the ID for a specified object name.

OBJECT_NAME(*object_id*)

Returns the name for a specified object ID.

STATS_DATE(*table_id, index_id*)

Returns a date indicating when an index's statistics were last updated.

SUSER_ID(['*login_name*'])

Returns the login ID for a specified login name.

SUSER_NAME([*server_user_id*])

Returns the login name for a specified login ID.

USER([*user_id*])

Returns the user's database name for a specified user ID (same as USER_NAME()).

USER_ID(['*user_name*'])

Returns the user's database ID for a specified user name.

USER_NAME([*user_id*])

Returns the user's database name for a specified user ID.

TEXT/IMAGE FUNCTIONS

The following sections cover text and image functions.

DATALENGTH('*expression*')

Returns the length of a specified expression.

PATINDEX('*%pattern%*', *expression*)

Returns the first position of a pattern in the specified expression.

TEXTPTR(*column_name*)

Returns the text-pointer value.

TEXTVALID('*table_name.column_name*', *text_ptr*)

Returns 1 if the text pointer is valid and 0 if the pointer is invalid.

TYPE-CONVERSION FUNCTION

The following section covers the CONVERT function.

CONVERT(*datatype*[(*length*)], *expression* [, *style*])

> ### PARAMETER EXPLANATION
>
> The `datatype` parameter is any valid SQL Server datatype.
>
> The `length` parameter is used with `char`, `varchar`, `binary`, and `varbinary` datatypes.
>
> The `expression` parameter is the value to convert.
>
> The `style` parameter is the date format to use with `datetime` or `smalldatetime` data conversion. (See Table D.2 for valid styles.)

TABLE D.2. VALID STYLES.

Without Century (yy)	With Century (yyyy)	Standard	Output
—	0 or 100	Default	`mon dd yyyy` `hh:miAM` (or PM)
1	101	USA	`mm/dd/yy`
2	102	ANSI	`yy.mm.dd`
3	103	British/French	`dd/mm/yy`
4	104	German	`dd.mm.yy`
5	105	Italian	`dd-mm-yy`
6	106	—	`dd mon yy`
7	107	—	`mon dd, yy`
8	108	—	`hh:mm:ss`
—	9 or 109	Default + milliseconds	`mon dd yyyy` `(hh:mi:ss:mmmAM` `(or PM))`
10	110	USA	`mm-dd-yy`
11	111	JAPAN	`yy/mm/dd`
12	112	ISO	`yymmdd`
—	13 or 113	European default + milliseconds	`dd mon yyyy` `hh:mi:ss:mmm(24h)`
14	114	—	`hh:mi:ss:mmm(24h)`

APPENDIX E

DBCC Commands

DBCC stands for *Database Consistency Checker*. Version 6.x of SQL Server extended the scope of DBCC by introducing several new commands that can help a DBA probe into the inner workings of SQL Server. This appendix discusses the traditional DBCC commands along with the enhancements included in version 6.x.

DBCC commands are commonly used to perform the following tasks:

◆ **Routine maintenance**: It is good idea to periodically run the essential DBCC commands listed in Table E.2, later in this appendix. These commands can help detect database and table problems before they manifest themselves into larger issues.

◆ **Investigate errors**: Use DBCC to pinpoint the source of errors such as `Table Corrupt` or `Extent not with segment`.

◆ **Perform before a backup**: Run the essential DBCC commands before backing up the database to ensure that the backup data does not contain errors. Backups that contain errors may be unrestorable.

Note

The majority of the commands discussed in this appendix do not *resolve* errors—they only *report* that the error exists.

QUICK REFERENCE

Table E.1 provides a quick syntax reference for DBCC commands.

TABLE E.1. DBCC QUICK REFERENCE.

Command	Notes
DBCC CHECKALLOC [(*database_name* [, NOINDEX])]	Use NEWALLOC instead (5)
DBCC CHECKCATALOG [(*database_name*)]	
DBCC CHECKTABLE (*table_name* [, NOINDEX ¦ *index_id*]	Performance improved with version 6.x (4)
DBCC CHECKDB [(*database_name* [, NOINDEX])]	Performance improved with version 6.x (4)
DBCC CHECKIDENT [(*table_name*)]	(3)

Command	Notes
DBCC DBREINDEX ([['*db_name.username.table_name*' [, *ind_name*[, *fillfactor* [, SORTED_DATA ¦ SORTED_DATA_REORG]))	(1)
DBCC DBREPAIR (*database_name*, DROPDB [, NOINIT])	
DBCC dllname (FREE)	
DBCC INPUTBUFFER (*spid*)	(3)
DBCC MEMUSAGE	
DBCC NEWALLOC [(*database_name* [, NOINDEX])]	Replaces CHECKALLOC (3)
DBCC OPENTRAN ({*database_name*} ¦ {*database_id*}) [WITH TABLERESULTS]	(3)
DBCC OUTPUTBUFFER (*spid*)	(3)
DBCC PERFMON	(3)
DBCC PINTABLE (database_id, table_id)	(3)
DBCC ROWLOCK (*dbid*, *tableid*, *set*)	(1)
DBCC SHOW_STATISTICS (*table_name*, *index_name*)	(3)
DBCC SHOWCONTIG (*table_id*, [*index_id*])	(3)
DBCC SHRINKDB (*database_name* [, *new_size* [, 'MASTEROVERRIDE']])	(3)
DBCC SQLPERF ({IOSTATS ¦ LRUSTATS ¦ NETSTATS ¦ RASTATS [, CLEAR]} {THREADS} ¦ {LOGSPACE})	New counters with version 6.x (4)
DBCC TEXTALL [({*database_name* ¦ *database_id*} [, FULL ¦ FAST])]	
DBCC TEXTALLOC [({*table_name* ¦ *table_id*} [, FULL ¦ FAST])]	

continues

E

DBCC COMMANDS

TABLE E.1. CONTINUED

Command	Notes
DBCC TRACEOFF (*trace#*)	(3)
DBCC TRACEON (*trace#*)	(3)
DBCC TRACESTATUS (*trace#* [, *trace#*...])	(3)
DBCC UNPINTABLE (*database_id*, *table_id*)	(3)
DBCC UPDATEUSAGE ({0 ¦ *database_name*} [, *table_name* [, *index_id*]]) ¦ USEROPTIONS}[WITH COUNT_ROWS]	Version 6.5 syntax (2)
DBCC UPDATEUSAGE ({0 ¦ *database_name*} [, *table_name* [, *index_id*]])	Version 6.0 syntax (3)
DBCC USEROPTIONS	(3)

The following abbreviations are used in Table E.1:

1 = New in version 6.5

2 = Improved in version 6.5

3 = Introduced in version 6.0

4 = Improved in version 6.0

5 = Use for backward compatibility (to versions before version 6.0)

Tip

When DBCC performance is a primary concern (especially when you are working with very large databases), use the NOINDEX argument with the following commands: CHECKALLOC, CHECKTABLE, CHECKDB, and NEWALLOC. When the NOINDEX argument is specified, only clustered indexes are inspected for errors. All nonclustered indexes are ignored. This option is generally safe to use because damaged indexes can be dropped and re-created without affecting the data within a table.

READING THE OUTPUT FROM DBCC COMMANDS

DBCC commands often generate a great amount of output. The problem is determining what is relevant within the output. Use the following list as a guide to what to look for in the DBCC output:

◆ Any message that contains the string *corrupt* (for example, `Table Corrupt`).

◆ Error messages that range from 2500 to 2599 or 7900 to 7999. DBCC error messages usually contain these error numbers.

◆ Messages that contain the string `error :`.

Tip

To help automate the process of detecting error messages in DBCC output, redirect the DBCC output to an ASCII text file and use the `FINDSTR.EXE` utility provided with Windows NT. Set up `FINDSTR.EXE` to look for keywords such as `corrupt`, `error :`, and so on.

RESOLVING ERRORS REPORTED BY DBCC

When an error is reported by DBCC, you should immediately investigate it. Unresolved errors can propagate throughout a database, increasing the likelihood of permanent data corruption.

The following items provide a general guideline for investigating and resolving errors reported by DBCC:

◆ Save and print DBCC output. On large databases, DBCC commands can sometimes take hours to run. Do not take a chance on forgetting an error message and having to rerun the DBCC command!

◆ With `CHECKDB`, `NEWALLOC`, and `CHECKALLOC`, you may receive erroneous messages if the database is not in single-user mode. If the command was run when the database was not in single-user mode, set the database to single-user mode and rerun the command. This may resolve the problem.

◆ Look up the specific error code in the "Handling Error Messages" chapter in the *Microsoft SQL Server Administrator's Companion* book. That chapter provides error-specific solutions.

◆ Shut down and restart SQL Server. This action flushes out the data cache and may resolve the problem.

◆ Contact Microsoft Support for additional assistance.

ESSENTIAL DBCC COMMANDS

You should run the commands listed in Table E.2 frequently. These commands can detect database and table corruption, along with structure inconsistencies.

TABLE E.2. ESSENTIAL DBCC COMMANDS.

Command
DBCC CHECKDB
DBCC CHECKTABLE
DBCC NEWALLOC
DBCC CHECKCATALOG

COMPARISON OF ESSENTIAL DBCC COMMANDS

Table E.3 details the scope of several DBCC commands, along with their performance and effectiveness.

DBCC COMMANDS FOR TABLES AND DATABASES

The following DBCC commands are used for tables and databases:

CHECKALLOC

CHECKCATALOG

CHECKTABLE

CHECKDB

CHECKIDENT

DBREINDEX

NEWALLOC

TEXTALL

TEXTALLOC

SHOWCONTIG

UPDATEUSAGE

TABLE E.3. COMPARISON OF ESSENTIAL DBCC COMMANDS.

Command	Coverage	Locks Generated	Performance	Effectiveness
CHECKTABLE CHECKDB	page chains, sort order, data rows for *all* indexes	generates shared table lock that is released when table has been checked	slow	high
CHECKTABLE CHECKDB with NOINDEX	page chains, sort order, data row for *clustered indexes*	generates shared table lock that is released when table has been checked	significantly faster than equivalent command without NOINDEX option	medium/high
NEWALLOC CHECKALLOC	page chains	none	slow	high
NEWALLOC CHECKALLOC with NOINDEX	page chains	none	significantly faster than equivalent command without NOINDEX option	high
CHECKCATALOG	system table rows	shared page locks	fast	high

CHECKALLOC

Syntax:

```
DBCC CHECKALLOC [(database_name [, NOINDEX])]
```

CHECKALLOC is designed to be compatible with previous versions of SQL Server. In SQL Server 6.x, use NEWALLOC instead of CHECKALLOC. NEWALLOC provides greater detail and continues to process the remainder of the database after an error has been detected.

CHECKALLOC scans the database to ensure that page allocation is correct.

CHECKCATALOG

Syntax:

```
DBCC CHECKCATALOG [(database_name)]
```

CHECKCATALOG checks the system tables for consistency by ensuring that each datatype in the syscolumns table has a matching entry in the systypes table, that each table and view in the sysobjects table has one or more matching records in the syscolumns table, and that the last checkpoint in the syslogs table is correct. Segment information is also displayed.

Use this command before dumping the database or when you suspect corruption within the system tables.

Example:

```
DBCC CHECKCATALOG (pubs)
```

Sample Output:

```
The following segments have been defined for database 4 (database name pubs).
virtual start addr      size      segments
--------------------    ------    -------------------------
              2052      512
                                          0
                                          1
                                          2
             10756      1024
                                          0
                                          1
                                          2
```

CHECKTABLE

Syntax:

```
DBCC CHECKTABLE (table_name [, NOINDEX ¦ index_id]
```

CHECKTABLE ensures that all pointers are consistent, that data and index pages are properly linked, that indexes match the proper sort order, and that page offsets and page information are correct. Run this command when you suspect that a table is corrupt or as part of your periodic maintenance plan.

Note

When CHECKTABLE is run against the syslogs table, the amount of free space and remaining log space are also reported.

Example:

```
DBCC CHECKTABLE(titles)
```

Sample Output:

```
The total number of data pages in this table is 3.
Table has 18 data rows.
```

Example:

```
DBCC CHECKTABLE(syslogs)
```

Sample Output:

```
The total number of data pages in this table is 4389.
The number of rows in Sysindexes for this table was 198216. It has been corrected
to 198217.
*** NOTICE: Space used on the log segment is 8.78 Mbytes, 95.25.
*** NOTICE: Space free on the log segment is 0.44 Mbytes, 4.75.
Table has 198217 data rows.
```

CHECKDB

Syntax:

```
DBCC CHECKDB [(database_name [, NOINDEX])]
```

CHECKDB checks all tables and indexes in a database for pointer and data page errors. This command may generate the following message:

```
The number of data pages in Sysindexes for this table was 9. It has been corrected
to 1.
The number of rows in Sysindexes for this table was 273. It has been corrected
to 16.
```

Do not be alarmed when you see this message. It means that SQL Server is performing some internal housekeeping to keep row counts accurate for the sp_spaceused command.

In terms of error checking, CHECKDB is the same as CHECKTABLE, except that CHECKDB inspects every table in the database as opposed to checking only a single table in the database.

Caution

Do *not* run DBCC CHECKDB while other users are in the database! This command should be run when the database is in single-user mode. Doing so ensures that the information reported by CHECKDB is accurate. Also, the number of locks generated by CHECKDB could lead to severe blocking and contention for resources if other users are in the database.

Example:

```
/* set database to single user */
sp_dboption pubs,'single user',TRUE
go

DBCC CHECKDB(pubs)
go

/* reset database option */
sp_dboption pubs,'single user',FALSE
go
```

Sample Output:

```
Checking 1
The total number of data pages in this table is 4.
Table has 69 data rows.
Checking 2
The total number of data pages in this table is 4.
Table has 49 data rows.
Checking 3
The total number of data pages in this table is 1.
The number of data pages in Sysindexes for this table was 9. It has been corrected
to 1.
The number of rows in Sysindexes for this table was 273. It has been corrected
to 16.
```

CHECKIDENT

Syntax:

```
DBCC CHECKIDENT [(table_name)]
```

The CHECKIDENT command checks the IDENTITY datatype in a table. It returns the current identity value and the maximum identity value.

Example:

```
DBCC CHECKIDENT(jobs)
```

Sample Output:

```
Checking identity information: current identity value '14', maximum column value
'14'.
```

DBREINDEX

Syntax:

```
DBCC DBREINDEX ([['db_name.username.table_name'[, ind_name
[, fillfactor[, SORTED_DATA ¦ SORTED_DATA_REORG]]]]]) [WITH NOINFOMSGS]
```

The DBREINDEX command rebuilds a table's indexes. When using PRIMARY KEY or UNIQUE constraints, the indexes used to support these constraints can be rebuilt without have to drop and re-create the constraints.

Example (rebuilds all indexes):

```
DBCC DBREINDEX (titleauthor,"")
```

Example (rebuilds a particular index):

```
DBCC DBREINDEX (titleauthor,"auidind")
```

NEWALLOC

Syntax:

```
DBCC NEWALLOC [(database_name [, NOINDEX])]
```

Introduced in SQL Server 6.0, NEWALLOC is the improved version of the CHECKALLOC command. NEWALLOC provides greater detail than CHECKALLOC and continues to process the remainder of the database after an error has been detected (unlike CHECKALLOC, which stops processing when an error has been detected).

NEWALLOC scans the data and index pages for extent structure errors. It ensures that page allocation is correct and that all allocated pages are in use.

Caution

Do *not* run DBCC NEWALLOC while other users are in the database! This command should be run when the database is in single-user mode to ensure that the information reported by NEWALLOC is accurate.

Example:

```
/* set database to single user */
sp_dboption pubs,'single user',TRUE
go

DBCC NEWALLOC(pubs)
go

/* reset database option */
sp_dboption pubs,'single user',FALSE
go
```

Sample Output:

```
Checking pubs
*******************************************************************
TABLE: sysobjects         OBJID = 1
INDID=1     FIRST=1       ROOT=8       DPAGES=4     SORT=0
    Data level: 1.  4 Data  Pages in 1 extents.
    Indid     : 1.  1 Index Pages in 1 extents.
INDID=2   FIRST=40      ROOT=41      DPAGES=1     SORT=1
    Indid     : 2.  3 Index Pages in 1 extents.
TOTAL # of extents = 3
*******************************************************************
TABLE: sysindexes         OBJID = 2
INDID=1     FIRST=24      ROOT=32      DPAGES=4     SORT=0
    Data level: 1.  4 Data  Pages in 1 extents.
    Indid     : 1.  1 Index Pages in 1 extents.
TOTAL # of extents = 2
*******************************************************************
TABLE: jobs       OBJID = 592005140
INDID=1     FIRST=496     ROOT=520     DPAGES=1     SORT=0
    Data level: 1.  1 Data  Pages in 1 extents.
    Indid     : 1.  2 Index Pages in 1 extents.
TOTAL # of extents = 2
*******************************************************************
TABLE: employee       OBJID = 688005482
INDID=1     FIRST=648     ROOT=656     DPAGES=2     SORT=1
    Data level: 1.  2 Data  Pages in 1 extents.
    Indid     : 1.  2 Index Pages in 1 extents.
INDID=2   FIRST=664     ROOT=664     DPAGES=1     SORT=1
    Indid     : 2.  2 Index Pages in 1 extents.
TOTAL # of extents = 3
*******************************************************************
TABLE: pub_info       OBJID = 864006109
INDID=1     FIRST=568     ROOT=584     DPAGES=1     SORT=0
    Data level: 1.  1 Data  Pages in 1 extents.
    Indid     : 1.  2 Index Pages in 1 extents.
INDID=255   FIRST=560     ROOT=608     DPAGES=0     SORT=0
TOTAL # of extents = 2
*******************************************************************
Processed 49 entries in the Sysindexes for dbid 4.
Alloc page 0 (# of extent=32 used pages=57 ref pages=57)
Alloc page 256 (# of extent=26 used pages=35 ref pages=35)
Alloc page 512 (# of extent=15 used pages=38 ref pages=38)
Alloc page 768 (# of extent=1 used pages=1 ref pages=1)
Alloc page 1024 (# of extent=2 used pages=9 ref pages=2)
Alloc page 1280 (# of extent=1 used pages=1 ref pages=1)
Total (# of extent=77 used pages=141 ref pages=134) in this database
DBCC execution completed. If DBCC printed error messages, see your System
Administrator.
```

TEXTALL

Syntax:

```
DBCC TEXTALL [({database_name ¦ database_id}[, FULL ¦ FAST])]
```

TEXTALL checks the allocation of TEXT and IMAGE columns for all tables in a database that contain TEXT or IMAGE columns. The FULL option generates a complete allocation report; the FAST option does not generate an allocation report. FULL is the default report option.

Example:

```
DBCC TEXTALL (pubs, FULL)
```

Sample Output:

```
*****************************************************************
TABLE: sysarticles      OBJID = 16
INDID=255    FIRST=328    ROOT=328    DPAGES=0    SORT=0
   Data level: 1.  1 Data  Pages in 0 extents.
   Indid      : 255.  0 Index Pages in 0 extents.
*****************************************************************
TABLE: pub_info      OBJID = 864006109
INDID=255    FIRST=560    ROOT=608    DPAGES=0    SORT=0
   Data level: 1.  1 Data  Pages in 0 extents.
   Indid      : 255.  73 Index Pages in 0 extents.
```

TEXTALLOC

Syntax:

```
DBCC TEXTALLOC [({table_name | table_id}[, FULL | FAST])]
```

TEXTALLOC checks a specified table for TEXT or IMAGE allocation errors. The FULL option generates a complete allocation report; the FAST option does not generate an allocation report. FULL is the default report option.

Example:

```
DBCC TEXTALLOC (pub_info, FULL)
```

Sample Output:

```
*****************************************************************
TABLE: pub_info      OBJID = 864006109
INDID=255    FIRST=560    ROOT=608    DPAGES=0    SORT=0
   Data level: 1.  1 Data  Pages in 0 extents.
   Indid      : 255.  73 Index Pages in 0 extents.
```

SHOWCONTIG

Syntax:

```
DBCC SHOWCONTIG (table_id, [index_id])
```

SHOWCONTIG determines the amount of table fragmentation. A high degree of fragmentation can lead to poor query performance because more data pages must read by SQL Server to process a query.

Fragmentation occurs when modification statements (DELETE, INSERT, and UPDATE) are performed on a table. A table subject to a lot of modification statements is more likely to become fragmented than a table that is seldom modified.

To determine the degree of fragmentation, inspect the Scan Density, Avg. Page density, and Avg. Overflow Page density values generated by the SHOWCONTIG command. A Scan Density value less than 100% indicates that some fragmentation exists.

To defragment a table, drop and re-create the table's clustered index *or* use DBCC DBREINDEX with the SORTED_DATA_REORG option *or* use BCP to copy out the data, drop the table, re-create the table, and use BCP again to copy in the data.

Tip

Use the object_id() function to determine a table's ID.

Example:

```
/* get table id */
SELECT object_id('sample_table')
-----------
96003373
/* run DBCC command */
DBCC SHOWCONTIG(96003373)
```

Sample Output:

```
TablJ 'sample_table' (96003373)  Indid: 0  dbid:6
TABLE level scan performed.
- Pages Scanned................................: 4096
- Extent Switches.............................: 514
- Avg. Pages per Extent.......................: 8.0
- Scan Density [Best Count:Actual Count]......: 99.42% [512:515]
- Avg. Bytes free per page....................: 89.0
- Avg. Page density (full)....................: 95.58%
- Overflow Pages..............................: 4095
- Avg. Bytes free per Overflow page...........: 89.0
- Avg. Overflow Page density..................: 95.6%
- Disconnected Overflow Pages.................: 0
```

UPDATEUSAGE

Version 6.5

Version 6.5 Syntax:

```
DBCC UPDATEUSAGE ({0 ¦ database_name} [, table_name [, index_id]])
{USEROPTIONS}[WITH COUNT_ROWS]
```

Version 6.0 Syntax:

```
DBCC UPDATEUSAGE ({0 ¦ database_name} [, table_name [, index_id]])
```

Whenever an index is dropped from a table, sp_spaceused inaccurately reports space utilization. Use the UPDATEUSAGE command to correct the inaccuracy.

Caution

The output from the system procedure sp_spaceused should be used only as estimate for space utilization. When an index is dropped, the information returned from sp_spaceused is inaccurate until the UDPATEUSAGE command is executed or until the table is dropped and re-created.

Example:

```
DBCC UPDATEUSAGE('sales','sample_table')
```

Sample Output:

```
DBCC UPDATEUSAGE: Sysindexes row for Table 'sample_table' (IndexId=0) updated:
RSVD Pages: Changed from (4103) to (4120) pages
```

DBCC COMMAND TO DROP A DAMAGED DATABASE

The DBREPAIR command is used to drop a damaged database.

Syntax:

```
DBCC DBREPAIR (database_name, DROPDB [, NOINIT])
```

Caution

DBREPAIR *does not repair* a corrupt database! Instead, it drops a corrupt database.

In SQL Server 6.x, you can drop a corrupt database with the DROP DATABASE command. In previous versions of SQL Server, you must use the DBREPAIR command to drop a damaged database. If you are unable to drop a database with the DROP DATABASE command, use the system procedure sp_dbremove to drop a damaged database.

DBCC COMMANDS TO RETURN PROCESS INFORMATION

The following two DBCC commands return process information.

Syntax:

```
DBCC INPUTBUFFER (spid)
```

```
DBCC OUTPUTBUFFER (spid)
```

The INPUTBUFFER and OUTPUTBUFFER commands allow a DBA to monitor process activity. The INPUTBUFFER command displays the command last executed by a process; the OUTPUTBUFFER command displays the corresponding result. Unfortunately, the information returned from the OUTPUTBUFFER command can be difficult to understand because it is displayed in hexadecimal and ASCII text.

Tip

Use the system procedure sp_who to determine the spid of a process.

Use the INPUTBUFFER command to diagnose blocking and resource utilization problems. When performance begins to suffer, look for data modification queries that do not contain WHERE clauses or SELECT queries that perform table scans on large tables.

Example:

```
DBCC INPUTBUFFER(11)
```

Sample Output:

```
Input Buffer
------------
select *
from authors
```

DBCC COMMANDS TO RETURN PERFORMANCE MONITOR STATISTICS

The following two DBCC commands return Performance Monitor statistics.

Syntax:

```
DBCC PERFMON

DBCC SQLPERF ({IOSTATS ¦ LRUSTATS ¦ NETSTATS ¦ RASTATS [, CLEAR]}
      {THREADS} ¦ {LOGSPACE})
```

The PERFMON command combines the different components of the SQLPERF command (IOSTATS, LRUSTATS, and NETSTATS) into a single DBCC statement.

Example:

```
DBCC PERFMON
```

Sample Output:

```
Statistic                          Value
---------------------------------- -----------------------
Log Flush Requests                 110.0
Log Logical Page IO                112.0
```

```
Log Physical IO              94.0
Log Flush Average            1.17021
Log Logical IO Average       1.19149
Batch Writes                 68.0
Batch Average Size           2.72
Batch Max Size               8.0
Page Reads                   643.0
Single Page Writes           132.0
Reads Outstanding            0.0
Writes Outstanding           0.0
Transactions                 92.0
Transactions/Log Write       0.978723
```

TRACE FLAG COMMANDS

The following commands are used to turn on and off trace flags and to check the status of a trace flag.

Syntax:

```
DBCC TRACEOFF (trace#)

DBCC TRACEON (trace#)

DBCC TRACESTATUS (trace# [, trace#...])
```

Tip

The trace flag 1200 can be useful for tracking locking behavior. You must also turn on trace flag 3604 to echo trace information to the client workstation (see SQL Server's Books Online for a complete list of trace flags).

Example:

```
DBCC traceon(3604)
DBCC traceon(1200)
UPDATE t_1
SET c_1 = 0
```

Sample Output from DBCC Trace Flag 1200:

```
Process 11 requesting page lock of type SH_PAGE on 7 25
Process 11 releasing page lock of type SH_PAGE on 7 25
...
Process 11 releasing page lock of type SH_PAGE on 7 26
Process 11 requesting table lock of type EX_TAB on 7 80003316
...
Process 11 clearing all pss locks
```

Memory and Data Cache Commands

The following sections describe the DBCC commands you can use for tracking memory and data cache information.

MEMUSAGE

Syntax:

DBCC MEMUSAGE

The MEMUSAGE command displays memory usage, buffer cache, and procedure cache information.

Example:

DBCC MEMUSAGE

Sample Output:

Memory Usage:

	Meg.	2K Blks	Bytes
Configured Memory:	8.0000	4096	8388608
Code size:	1.7166	879	1800000
Static Structures:	0.2385	123	250064
Locks:	0.2861	147	300000
Open Objects:	0.1144	59	120000
Open Databases:	0.0031	2	3220
User Context Areas:	0.7505	385	787002
Page Cache:	3.3269	1704	3488480
Proc Headers:	0.0800	41	83936
Proc Cache Bufs:	1.3457	689	1411072

Buffer Cache, Top 20:

DB Id	Object Id	Index Id	2K Buffers
1	5	0	96
1	3	0	41
1	1	0	21
1	1	2	8
1	99	0	8
2	3	0	8
1	2	0	6
1	5	1	6
1	6	0	4
1	36	0	4
1	6	1	3
2	2	0	3

1	45	255	2
1	704005539	1	2
2	99	0	2
3	2	0	2
3	8	0	2
4	1	2	2
4	2	0	2
5	1	2	2

Procedure Cache, Top 9:

Procedure Name: sp_MSdbuserprofile
Database Id: 1
Object Id: 1449056198
Version: 1
Uid: 1
Type: stored procedure
Number of trees: 0
Size of trees: 0.000000 Mb, 0.000000 bytes, 0 pages
Number of plans: 2
Size of plans: 0.171600 Mb, 179936.000000 bytes, 90 pages

Procedure Name: sp_helpdistributor
Database Id: 1
Object Id: 1372531923
Version: 1
Uid: 1
Type: stored procedure
Number of trees: 0
Size of trees: 0.000000 Mb, 0.000000 bytes, 0 pages
Number of plans: 2
Size of plans: 0.042969 Mb, 45056.000000 bytes, 24 pages

Procedure Name: sp_server_info
Database Id: 1
Object Id: 361052322
Version: 1
Uid: 1
Type: stored procedure
Number of trees: 0
Size of trees: 0.000000 Mb, 0.000000 bytes, 0 pages
Number of plans: 2
Size of plans: 0.006332 Mb, 6640.000000 bytes, 4 pages

Procedure Name: sp_MSSQLOLE65_version
Database Id: 1
Object Id: 1481056312
Version: 1
Uid: 1
Type: stored procedure
Number of trees: 0

```
Size of trees: 0.000000 Mb, 0.000000 bytes, 0 pages
Number of plans: 1
Size of plans: 0.001543 Mb, 1618.000000 bytes, 1 pages


Procedure Name: sp_sqlregister
Database Id: 1
Object Id: 985054545
Version: 1
Uid: 1
Type: stored procedure
Number of trees: 0
Size of trees: 0.000000 Mb, 0.000000 bytes, 0 pages
Number of plans: 1
Size of plans: 0.000822 Mb, 862.000000 bytes, 1 pages


Procedure Name: xp_msver
Database Id: 1
Object Id: 1036530726
Version: 1
Uid: 1
Type: stored procedure
Number of trees: 0
Size of trees: 0.000000 Mb, 0.000000 bytes, 0 pages
Number of plans: 1
Size of plans: 0.000578 Mb, 606.000000 bytes, 1 pages


Procedure Name: xp_sqlregister
Database Id: 1
Object Id: 953054431
Version: 1
Uid: 1
Type: stored procedure
Number of trees: 0
Size of trees: 0.000000 Mb, 0.000000 bytes, 0 pages
Number of plans: 1
Size of plans: 0.000578 Mb, 606.000000 bytes, 1 pages


Procedure Name: xp_snmp_getstate
Database Id: 1
Object Id: 921054317
Version: 1
Uid: 1
Type: stored procedure
Number of trees: 0
Size of trees: 0.000000 Mb, 0.000000 bytes, 0 pages
Number of plans: 1
Size of plans: 0.000578 Mb, 606.000000 bytes, 1 pages


Procedure Name: xp_regread
Database Id: 1
Object Id: 585053120
Version: 1
Uid: 1
```

```
Type: stored procedure
Number of trees: 0
Size of trees: 0.000000 Mb, 0.000000 bytes, 0 pages
Number of plans: 1
Size of plans: 0.000578 Mb, 606.000000 bytes, 1 pages


DBCC execution completed. If DBCC printed error messages, see your System
Administrator.
```

PINTABLE AND UNPINTABLE

Syntax:

```
DBCC PINTABLE (database_id, table_id)

DBCC UNPINTABLE (database_id, table_id)
```

The PINTABLE command forces a table to remain in cache until it is removed from the cache with the UNPINTABLE command. You should be careful when pinning a table in the cache. By keeping a table constantly in the cache, you can improve data access performance. However, a large table can dominate the data cache. This could reduce the amount of data held in cache for other tables, thus hindering performance.

Example:

```
declare @id integer
select @id = object_id('authors')
/* 4 = pubs database */
DBCC PINTABLE (4,@id)
```

Sample Output:

```
WARNING: Pinning tables should be carefully considered. If a pinned table is larger
or grows larger than the available data cache, the server may need to be restarted
and the table unpinned.

DBCC execution completed. If DBCC printed error messages, see your System
Administrator.
```

TRANSACTION COMMANDS

Use the OPENTRAN command for information about transactions.

Syntax:

```
DBCC OPENTRAN ({database_name} ¦ {database_id}) [WITH TABLERESULTS]
```

The OPENTRAN command reports the oldest open transaction. An open transaction can stem from an aborted transaction, a runaway transaction, or poor transaction management. If necessary, you can terminate the offending transaction by issuing the KILL command with the process ID returned from the DBCC OPENTRAN command.

Tip

Long-running transactions can lead to contention for resources, which can lead to blocking. Use DBCC OPENTRAN to detect open transactions. If necessary, use the KILL command to cancel the transaction.

Example:

```
DBCC OPENTRAN(pubs)
```

Sample Output:

```
Transaction Information for database: pubs
Oldest active transaction:
        SPID            : 12
        UID             : 1
        SUID            : 1
        Name            : del
        RID             : (14653 , 30)
        Time Stamp      : 0001 0003CB68
        Start Time      : Sep 20 1995  9:30:41:690PM
```

OTHER DBCC COMMANDS

The following sections cover some of the other types of DBCC commands.

ROWLOCK

Syntax:

```
DBCC ROWLOCK (dbid, tableid, set)
```

ROWLOCK allows you to dynamically manage insert row-level locking for a specific table.

Example:

```
declare @id int
select @id = object_id('authors')
/* 4 = pubs database */
DBCC ROWLOCK (4, @id, 1)
```

Sample Output:

```
(1 row(s) affected)
DBCC execution completed. If DBCC printed error messages, see your System
Administrator.
```

SHOW_STATISTICS

Syntax:

```
DBCC SHOW_STATISTICS (table_name, index_name)
```

SHOW_STATISTICS displays index distribution information.

Example:

```
DBCC SHOW_STATISTICS ('authors','aunmind')
```

Sample Output:

```
Updated              Rows         Steps        Density
-------------------- ------------ ------------ --------------------------
Apr  3 1996  3:46AM  23           22           0.0396975

(1 row(s) affected)

All density               Columns
------------------------- ------------------------------
0.047259                  au_lname
0.0434783                 au_lname, au_fname
```

SHRINKDB

Syntax:

```
DBCC SHRINKDB (database_name [, new_size [, 'MASTEROVERRIDE']])
```

Note

The size is specified in 2K pages.

SHRINKDB has two purposes:

- ◆ When a size is not specified, the command returns the minimum size to which a database can be shrunk.
- ◆ When size is specified, the command shrinks the database to the specified size. The MASTEROVERRIDE command is required when the master database is shrunk.

Example:

```
DBCC SHRINKDB (sales , 5376)
```

Sample Output:

```
DBCC execution completed. If DBCC printed error messages, see your System
Administrator.
```

USEROPTIONS

Syntax:

```
DBCC USEROPTIONS
```

The USEROPTIONS command displays the status of SET commands for the current session.

Example:

```
DBCC USEROPTIONS
```

Sample Output:

```
Set Option                    Value
---------------------------   -----------------------------------------------
textsize                      64512
language                      us_english
dateformat                    mdy
datefirst                     7
```

DBCC *dllname* (FREE)

Syntax:

```
DBCC dllname (FREE)
```

This command removes a DLL (dynamic link library) from memory.

APPENDIX F

System Tables

System tables are the tables installed with SQL Server that are used by SQL Server to manage the users, devices, and all the other SQL Server objects. System tables are found in every database. The following sections give brief descriptions of the system tables and their physical layouts. This appendix is divided into two parts: system tables found only in the master database and system tables found in all databases.

SYSTEM TABLES IN THE master DATABASE

The following system tables (in alphabetical order) are found in the master database and are used by SQL Server to manage and maintain the server.

syscharsets

The syscharsets table contains a single row for each valid character set and sort order available.

TABLE STRUCTURE

Column	Datatype
type	smallint
id	tinyint
csid	tinyint
status	smallint
name	varchar(30)
description	varchar(255)
definition	image

INDEX

Unique clustered index on id. Unique nonclustered index on name.

sysconfigures

The `sysconfigures` table contains one row for each user-configurable configuration parameter.

TABLE STRUCTURE

Column	Datatype
config	smallint
value	int
comment	varchar(255)
status	smallint

INDEX

Unique clustered index on `config`.

syscurconfigs

The `syscurconfigs` table contains the current system configuration values: one for each user-configurable parameter and an additional four entries that describe the configuration structure. The `syscurconfigs` table is built dynamically when queried by a user.

TABLE STRUCTURE

Column	Datatype
config	smallint
value	int
comment	varchar(255)
status	smallint

INDEX

Unique clustered index on `config`.

sysdatabases

The sysdatabases table contains an entry for each database on SQL Server.

TABLE STRUCTURE

Column	Datatype
name	varchar(30)
dbid	smallint
suid	smallint
mode	smallint
status	smallint
version	smallint
logptr	int
crdate	datetime
dumptrdate	datetime
category	int

Note

The column category is new for SQL Server version 6.x and is used for publication and constraints.

INDEX

Unique clustered index on name. Unique nonclustered index on dbid.

sysdevices

The sysdevices table contains a row for every device on the SQL Server.

TABLE STRUCTURE

Column	Datatype
low	int
high	int
status	smallint
cntrltype	smallint
name	varchar(30)
phyname	varchar(127)
mirrorname	varchar(127)
stripeset	varchar(30)

INDEX

Unique clustered index on name.

syslanguages

The syslanguages table contains a single row for each language installed on the SQL Server.

> ## *Note*
>
> U.S. English is not in syslanguages but is always available to SQL Server.

TABLE STRUCTURE

Column	Datatype
angid	smallint
dateformat	char(3)
datefirst	tinyint
upgrade	int
namevar	char(30)
aliasvar	char(30)
monthsvar	char(251
shortmonths	varchar(119)
daysvar	char(216)

INDEX

Unique clustered index on langid. Unique nonclustered index on name. Unique nonclustered index on alias.

syslocks

The `syslocks` table is dynamically built when queried by a user; it contains information about active locks.

TABLE STRUCTURE

Column	Datatype
id	int
dbid	smallint
page	int
type	smallint
spid	smallint

INDEX

None

syslogins

The `syslogins` table contains a single row for each valid SQL Server login account.

TABLE STRUCTURE

Column	Datatype
suid	smallint
status	smallint
accdate	datetime
totcpu	int
totio	int
spacelimit	int
timelimit	int
resultlimit	int
dbnamevar	char(30)
namevar	char(30)
password	varchar(30)
language	varchar(30)

INDEX

Unique clustered index on `suid`. Unique nonclustered index on `name`.

sysmessages

The sysmessages table contains the system errors and warning messages returned by SQL Server.

TABLE STRUCTURE

Column	Datatype
error	int
severity	smallint
dlevel	smallint
description	varchar(255)
langid	smallint

INDEX

Clustered index on error, dlevel. Unique nonclustered index on error, dlevel, langid.

sysprocesses

The sysprocesses table is built dynamically when queried by a user; it contains information about SQL Server processes.

TABLE STRUCTURE

Column	Datatype
pid	smallint
kpid	smallint
status	char(10)
suid	smallint
hostname	char(10)
program_name	char(16)
hostprocess	char(8)
cmd	char(16)
cpu	int
physical_io	int
memusage	int
blocked	smallint
waittype	binary
dbid	smallint
uid	smallint

continues

Column	Datatype
gid	smallint
last_batch	char(8)
login_time	char(8)
net_address	char(12)
nt_domain	char(30)
nt_username	char(30)
net_library	char(12)

Note

Version
6.5

The columns last_batch, login_time, net_address, nt_domain, nt_username, and net_library are new for SQL Server 6.5.

INDEX

None.

sysremotelogins

The sysremotelogins table contains a single row for each remote user who is allowed to execute remote procedure calls.

TABLE STRUCTURE

Column	Datatype
remoteserverid	smallint
remoteusername	varchar(30)
suidsmall	int
status	smallint

INDEX

Unique clustered index on remoteserverid, remoteusername.

sysservers

The sysservers table contains a single row for each remote SQL Server. These SQL Servers can execute remote procedures.

TABLE STRUCTURE

Column	Datatype
srvid	smallint
srvstatus	smallint
srvname	varchar(30)
srvnetname	varchar(32)
topologyx	int
topologyy	int

INDEX

Unique clustered index on srvid. Unique nonclustered index on srvname.

sysusages

The sysusages table contains a single row for each disk allocation piece assigned to a database.

TABLE STRUCTURE

Column	Datatype
dbid	smallint
segmap	int
lstart	int
size	int
vstart	int

INDEX

Unique clustered index on dbid, lstart. Unique nonclustered index on vstart.

DATABASE SYSTEM TABLES

The following tables are the system tables found in each database, including the master database, on SQL Server.

sysalternates

The sysalternates table contains a single row for each aliased user in the database.

TABLE STRUCTURE

Column	Datatype
suid	smallint
altsuid	smallint

INDEX

Unique clustered index on suid.

sysarticles

The sysarticles table contains a single row for each article posted by the publishing server. The sysarticles table is new for SQL Server 6.0.

TABLE STRUCTURE

Column	Datatype
artid	int
columns	varbinary(32)
creation_script	varchar(127)
del_cmd	varchar(255)
description	varchar(255)
dest_table	varchar(30)
filter	int
filter_clause	text
ins_cmd	varchar(255)
name	varchar(30)
objid	int
pubid	int
pre_creation_cmd	tinyint
status	tinyint
sync_objid	int
type	tinyint
upd_cmd	varchar(255)

INDEX

Unique nonclustered index on artid, pubid.

syscolumns

The syscolumns table contains a single row for each parameter in a stored procedure and each column in a table and view.

TABLE STRUCTURE

Column	Datatype
id	int
number	smallint
colid	tinyint
status	tinyint
type	tinyint
length	tinyint
offset	smallint
usertype	smallint
cdefault	int
domain	int
name	varchar(30)
printfmt	varchar(255)
prec	tinyint
scale	tinyint

INDEX

Unique clustered index on id, number, colid.

syscomments

The syscomments table contains entries for database objects such as views, rules, defaults, triggers, and procedures.

TABLE STRUCTURE

Column	Datatype
id	int
number	smallint
colid	tinyint
language	smallint
text	varchar(255)

INDEX

Unique clustered index on id, number, colid, texttype.

sysconstraints

The `sysconstraints` table contains constraint mappings to owned objects. The `sysconstraints` table is new for SQL Server 6.0.

TABLE STRUCTURE

Column	Datatype
constid	int
id	int
colid	tinyint
spare1	tinyint
status	int
actions	int
error	int

INDEX

Clustered index on `id`, `colid`. Unique nonclustered index on `constid`.

sysdepends

The `sysdepends` table contains rows for object dependencies.

TABLE STRUCTURE

Column	Datatype
id	int
number	smallint
depid	int
depnumber	smallint
depdbid	smallint
depsiteid	smallint
status	smallint
selall	bit
resultobj	bit
readobj	bit

INDEX

Unique clustered index (ignore duplicate key) on `id`, `number`, `depid`, `depnumber`, `depdbid`, `depsiteid`.

sysindexes

The `sysindexes` table contains a single row for each of the following:

- ◆ Clustered index
- ◆ Nonclustered index
- ◆ Tables with no clustered indexes
- ◆ Tables with text or image columns

TABLE STRUCTURE

Column	Datatype
name	varchar(30)
id	int
indid	smallint
dpages	int
reserved	int
used	int
rows	int
first	int
root	int
distribution	int
OrigFillFactor	tinyint
segment	smallint
status	smallint
rowpage	smallint
minlen	smallint
maxlen	smallint
maxirow	smallint
keycnt	smallint
keys1	varbinary(255)
keys2	varbinary(255)
soid	tinyint
csid	tinyint
UpdateStamp	varbinary

Note

The column `UpdateStamp` is new for SQL Server 6.5.

Version
6.5

INDEX

Unique clustered index on `id`, `indid`.

syslogs

The `syslogs` table is used for the transaction log and is used by SQL Server for roll forward and recovery.

Caution

Do not try to modify the `syslogs` table. Doing so results in an infinite loop until the database fills up.

TABLE STRUCTURE

Column	Datatype
xactid	binary(6)
op	tinyint

INDEX

None.

sysobjects

The `sysobjects` table contains a single entry for each database object, such as tables, views, stored procedures, constraints, rules, and so on.

TABLE STRUCTURE

Column	Datatype
name	varchar(30)
id	int
uid	smallint
type	char(2)
userstat	smallint
sysstat	smallint
indexdel	smallint
schema	smallint
refdate	datetime
crdate	datetime
version	datetime

continues

Column	Datatype
deltrig	int
instrig	int
updtrig	int
seltrig	int
category	int
cache	smallint

INDEX

Unique clustered index on `id`. Unique nonclustered index on `name`, `uid`.

Note

Following are the valid values for the `type` column; they can be used to query for specific database objects (these values sometimes appear on the certification test):

- c Check constraint
- D Default
- F Foreign key reference constraint
- K Primary or unique constraint
- L Log
- P Stored procedure
- R Rule
- S System table
- TR Trigger
- U User table
- V View
- X Extended stored procedure

sysprocedures

The sysprocedures table contains entries for defaults, rules, view, triggers, and stored procedures.

TABLE STRUCTURE

Column	Datatype
type	smallint
id	int
sequence	smallint
status	smallint
number	smallint

INDEX

Unique clustered index on id, number, type, and sequence.

sysprotects

The sysprotects table contains user GRANT and REVOKE permission information.

TABLE STRUCTURE

Column	Datatype
id	int
uid	smallint
action	tinyint
protecttype	tinyint
columns	varbinary(32)
grantor	smallint

INDEX

Clustered index on id, uid, and action.

syspublications

The `syspublications` table contains a single entry for each publication posted by the publishing server. The `syspublications` table is new for SQL Server 6.0.

TABLE STRUCTURE

Column	Datatype
description	varchar(255)
name	varchar(30)
repl_freq	tinyint
restricted	bit
status	tinyint
sync_method	tinyint
taskid	int

INDEX

Unique nonclustered index on `pubid`. Unique nonclustered index on `name`.

sysreferences

The `sysreferences` table contains foreign key table mappings from each foreign key to its respective reference tables. The `sysreferences` table is new for SQL Server 6.0.

TABLE STRUCTURE

Column	Datatype
constid	int
fkeydbid	smallint
rkeyid	int
rkeydbid	smallint
rkeyindid	smallint
keycnt	smallint
fkey1	tinyint
fkey2	tinyint
fkey3	tinyint
fkey4	tinyint
fkey5	tinyint
fkey6	tinyint
fkey7	tinyint
fkey8	tinyint
fkey9	tinyint
fkey10	tinyint
fkey11	tinyint
fkey12	tinyint
fkey13	tinyint
fkey14	tinyint
fkey15	tinyint
fkey16	tinyint
rkey1	tinyint
rkey2	tinyint
rkey3	tinyint
rkey4	tinyint
rkey5	tinyint
rkey6	tinyint
rkey7	tinyint
rkey8	tinyint
rkey9	tinyint
rkey10	tinyint
rkey11	tinyint
rkey12	tinyint
rkey13	tinyint
rkey14	tinyint
rkey15	tinyint
rkey16	tinyint

INDEX

Unique clustered index on `constid`. Nonclustered index on `fkeyid`. Nonclustered index on `rkeyid`.

syssegments

The `syssegments` table contains a single entry for each defined segment.

TABLE STRUCTURE

Column	Datatype
segment	smallint
name	varchar(30)
status	smallint

INDEX

None.

syssubscriptions

The `syssubscriptions` table is used to associate published articles with receiving subscription servers. The `syssubscriptions` table is new for SQL Server 6.0.

TABLE STRUCTURE

Column	Datatype
artid	int
srvid	smallint
dest_db	varchar(30)
status	tinyint
sync_type	tinyint
timestamp	timestamp

INDEX

Unique nonclustered index on `artid` and `srvid`.

F

SYSTEM TABLES

systypes

The systypes table contains a single entry for all user-defined and system datatypes.

TABLE STRUCTURE

Column	Datatype
uid	smallint
usertype	smallint
variable	bit
allownulls	bit
type	tinyint
length	tinyint
tdefault	int
domain	int
name	varchar(30)
printfmt	varchar(255)
prec	tinyint
scale	tinyint

Note

The columns prec and scale are new in SQL Sever 6.0.

INDEX

Unique clustered index on name. Unique nonclustered index on usertype.

sysusers

The sysusers table contains a single row for each user and group allowed to use the database.

TABLE STRUCTURE

Column	Datatype
suid	smallint
uid	smallint
gid	smallint
name	varchar(30)
environ	varchar(255)

INDEX

Unique clustered index on suid. Unique nonclustered index on name. Unique nonclustered index on uid.

Object Manager

The Object Manager is a graphical object administration tool provided with SQL Server 4.x. This tool allows you to manage tables, indexes, stored procedures, and other SQL Server objects.

Note

This appendix is intended to be a reference for users running a version of SQL Server before version 6.x. The Object Manager is *not* included with SQL Server 6.x. Use the Enterprise Manager included with SQL Server 6.x to perform the functions discussed in this appendix.

However, sites that run SQL Server 4.x *and* SQL Server 6.x can use the Object Manager to administer a SQL Server 6.x database. To administer SQL Server 6.x with the Object Manager, you must run one of the following scripts.

If you are using SQL Server 6.5:

`\MSSQL\INSTALL\OBJECT60.SQL`

If you are using SQL Server 6.0:

`\SQL60\INSTALL\OBJECT60.SQL`

STARTING OBJECT MANAGER

To start Object Manager, double-click the SQL Object Manager icon in the SQL Server for Windows NT (Common) group (see Figure G.1).

Figure G.1.
The SQL Object
Manager icon.

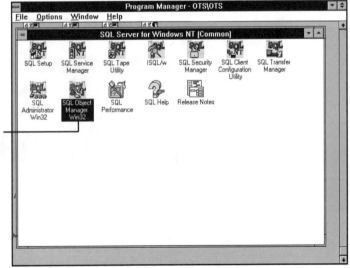

Click here to start
Object Manager

CONNECTING TO THE SERVER

Perform the following steps to connect to the server:

1. Double-click the SQL Object Manager icon in the SQL Server for Windows NT (Common) group. The Microsoft SQL Object Manager and the Connect Server dialog box appear (see Figure G.2).

Figure G.2.
Connecting to SQL
Server.

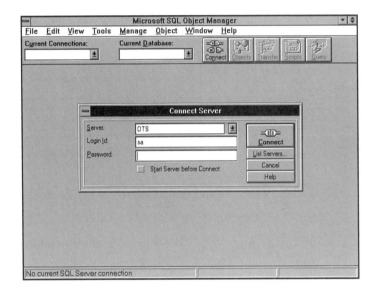

2. To connect to SQL Server, you must enter the server name, login ID, and password.
3. Click the Connect button to connect to the server. The Microsoft SQL Object Manager window appears (see Figure G.3).

Figure G.3.
The Microsoft SQL
Object Manager
window.

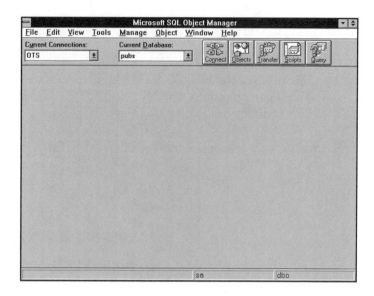

DISCONNECTING FROM SQL SERVER

Perform the following steps to disconnect from SQL Server:

1. From the Microsoft SQL Object Manager window, click the Connect toolbar button. The Connect Server dialog box appears.

2. From the Server drop-down list box, select the name of the server from which you want to disconnect (see Figure G.4).

3. Click the Disconnect button.

Figure G.4.
Disconnecting from
SQL Server

BROWSING DATABASE OBJECTS

From the Microsoft SQL Object Manager window, click the Objects toolbar button. The Database Objects dialog box appears. From here, you can browse all objects contained in a database. From this dialog box, you can directly edit an object by double-clicking the object (see Figure G.5).

Figure G.5.
Browsing database
objects.

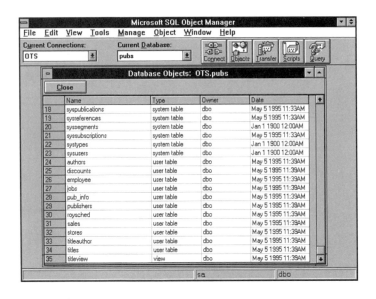

MANAGING TABLES

Starting with the Microsoft SQL Object Manager window, choose Tables from the
Manage menu. The Manage Tables dialog box appears (see Figure G.6). From this
dialog box, you can create, alter, rename, and drop a table.

Figure G.6.
Managing tables.

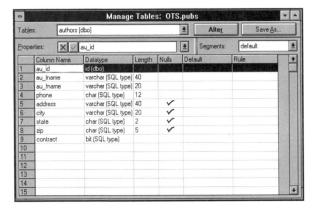

MANAGING INDEXES

Starting with the Microsoft SQL Object Manager window, choose Indexes from the
Manage menu. The Manage Indexes dialog box appears (see Figure G.7). From this
dialog box, you can create, modify, rename, and drop an index.

G

OBJECT MANAGER

Figure G.7.
Managing indexes.

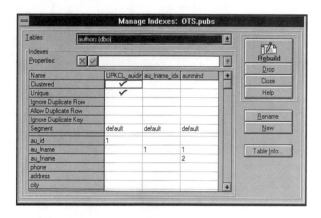

MANAGING STORED PROCEDURES

Starting with the Microsoft SQL Object Manager window, choose Stored Procedures from the Manage menu. The Manage Stored Procedures dialog box appears (see Figure G.8). From this dialog box, you can create and edit stored procedures.

Figure G.8.
Managing stored
procedures.

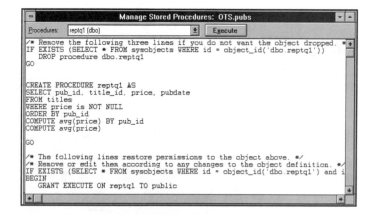

MANAGING OBJECT PERMISSIONS

Starting with the Microsoft SQL Object Manager window, choose Object Permissions from the Object menu. The Object Permissions dialog box appears (see Figure G.9). From this dialog box, you can grant and revoke object permissions.

Figure G.9.
Managing object
permissions.

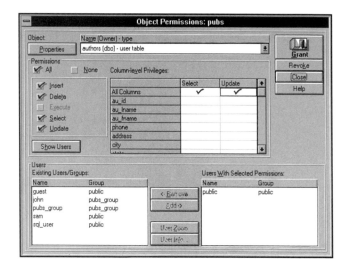

TRANSFERRING DATA

Starting with the Microsoft SQL Object Manager window, click the Transfer toolbar
button. The Transfer Data dialog box appears (see Figure G.10). From this dialog
box, you can graphically import and export data.

Figure G.10.
Transferring data.

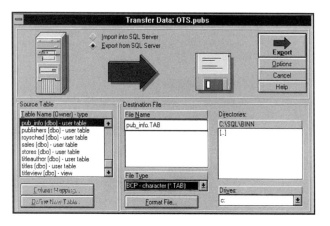

GENERATING SQL SCRIPTS

Starting with the Microsoft SQL Object Manager window, click the Scripts toolbar
button. The Generate SQL Scripts dialog box appears (see Figure G.11). From this
dialog box, you can export SQL object definitions.

Figure G.11.
The Generate SQL
Scripts dialog box.

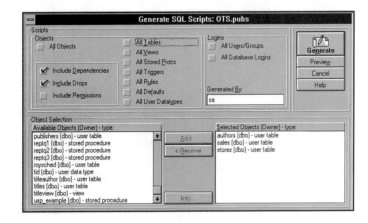

RUNNING QUERIES

From the Microsoft SQL Object Manager window, click the Query toolbar button. The Query window appears (see Figure G.12). From this window, you can build and execute SQL queries.

Figure G.12.
The Query window.

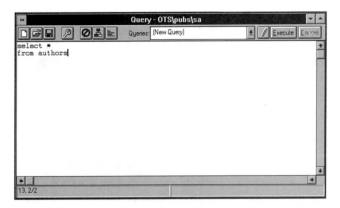

SQL Administrator

The SQL Administrator is a graphical object administration tool provided with SQL Server 4.x. This tool allows you to manage devices, databases, logins, remote servers, and server configuration.

Note

This appendix is intended as a reference for users running a version of SQL Server before version 6.x. The SQL Administrator is *not* included with SQL Server 6.x. Use the Enterprise Manager included with SQL Server 6.x to perform the functions discussed in this appendix.

Those sites that run SQL Server 4.x *and* SQL Server 6.x can use the SQL Administrator to administer a SQL Server 6.x database. To administer SQL Server 6.x from the SQL Administrator, you must run one of the following scripts.

If you are using SQL Server 6.5:

```
\MSSQL\INSTALL\ADMIN60.SQL
```

If you are using SQL Server 6.0:

```
\SQL60\INSTALL\ADMIN60.SQL
```

STARTING SQL ADMINISTRATOR

Perform the following steps to start SQL Administrator:

1. Double-click the SQL Administrator icon in the SQL Server for Windows NT (Common) group (see Figure H.1). The Connect Server dialog box appears. In the Connect Server dialog box, you must enter the server name, login ID, and password.
2. Click the Connect button to connect to the server (see Figure H.2). The Microsoft SQL Administrator dialog box appears (see Figure H.3).

Figure H.1.
The SQL Administrator
icon.

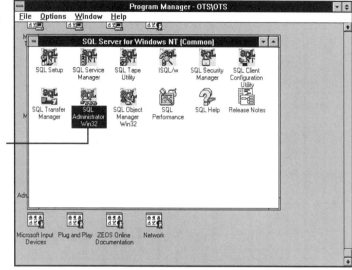

Click here to start
SQL Administrator

Figure H.2.
Connecting to
SQL Server.

Figure H.3.
The Microsoft SQL
Administrator window.

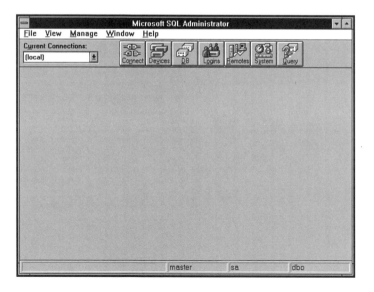

DISCONNECTING FROM SQL SERVER

Perform the following steps to disconnect from SQL Server:

1. From the Microsoft SQL Administrator window, click the Connect toolbar button. The Connect Server dialog box appears.

2. From the Server drop-down list box, select the name of the server from which you want to disconnect.

3. Click the Disconnect button (see Figure H.4).

Figure H.4.
Disconnecting from
SQL Server.

MANAGING DEVICES

From the Microsoft SQL Administrator window, click the Devices toolbar button. The Device Management dialog box appears (see Figure H.5). Using the Manage menu option, you can create, drop, and edit devices. Double-clicking an existing device displays the properties of the selected device.

Figure H.5.
Managing devices.

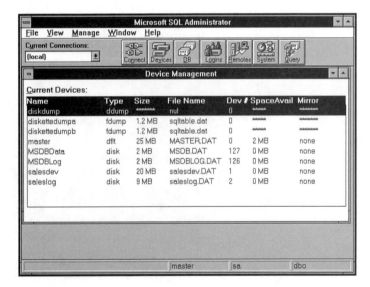

MANAGING DATABASES

From the Microsoft SQL Administrator window, click the DB toolbar button. The Database Management dialog box appears (see Figure H.6). Using the Manage menu option, you can create, alter, drop, and edit a database.

Figure H.6.
Managing databases.

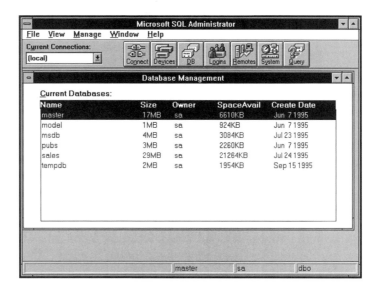

MANAGING LOGINS

From the Microsoft SQL Administrator window, click the Logins toolbar button. The System Logins Management dialog box appears (see Figure H.7). Using the Manage menu option, you can create, edit, and drop a system login.

Figure H.7.
Managing logins.

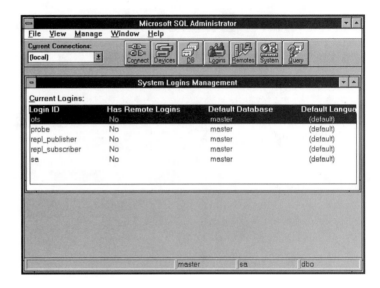

MANAGING REMOTE SERVERS

From the Microsoft SQL Administrator window, click the Remotes toolbar button. The Remote Server Management dialog box appears (see Figure H.8). Using the Manage menu option, you can create, edit, and drop remote server information.

Figure H.8.
Managing remote servers.

MANAGING SQL SERVER

From the Microsoft SQL Administrator window, click the System toolbar button. The Sys Options/Active Resources dialog box appears (see Figure H.9). From this dialog box, you can view system processes. The information in this dialog box can also be obtained by using the sp_who system procedure. Using the Manage menu option, you can configure SQL Server and issue DBCC commands.

Figure H.9.
Managing SQL Server.

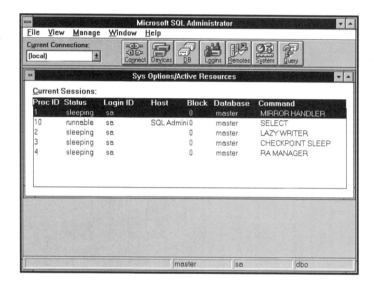

RUNNING QUERIES

From the Microsoft SQL Administrator window, click the Query toolbar button. The Query window appears (see Figure H.10). From this window, you can create and execute SQL queries.

Figure H.10.
Query window.

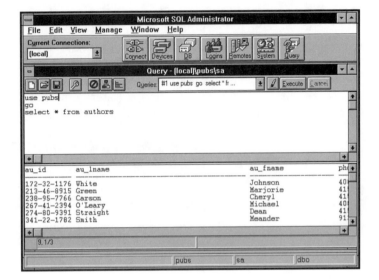

What's on the CD-ROM

The following applications have been included on the CD-ROM that accompanies this book to help you with your database administration tasks:

◆ The SQL Server DBA Assistant

◆ The Database Estimator

THE SQL SERVER DBA ASSISTANT

The SQL Server DBA Assistant is an application written in 32-bit Visual Basic 4.0. Using the SQL Server Assistant, you can perform the following tasks:

◆ Estimate the size of memory

◆ Populate a combo box with database names

◆ Allow exporting of data using graphical BCP

◆ Perform table maintenance functions, including recompiling references, updating statistics, and using the DBCC CheckTable command

The SQL Server DBA Assistant source code is included on the CD-ROM so that you can make your own modifications and enhancements to the application.

Note

The code in the application is discussed in detail in Chapter 27, "SQL OLE Integration."

Following are the prerequisites for using the SQL Server DBA Assistant:

◆ You must be running Windows NT 3.51 or Windows 95

◆ You must have the following files (included with the SQL Server Client Utilities Installation):

SQLOLE.HLP   SQL-DMO help files, including object hierarchy

SQLOLE65.DLL   In-process SQL-DMO server

SQLOLE65.TLB   Type library for OLE automation controllers

INSTALLING SQL SERVER DBA ASSISTANT

To install the SQL Server DBA Assistant, run the executable SETUP.EXE file included on the CD-ROM.

USING SQL SERVER DBA ASSISTANT

Follow these steps to use the SQL Server DBA Assistant:

1. To start the SQL Server DBA Assistant, click the icon installed during setup or run the executable (SAMSDBA.EXE). The Logon Assistant dialog box appears (see Figure I.1).

Figure I.1.
The SQL Server
DBA Assistant
Logon dialog box.

2. Enter the name of the SQL Server to which you want to log on.

3. Enter the login ID and the password and then click the Logon button. An attempt is made to connect to the specified SQL Server. If the logon is successful, a splash screen appears, followed by the SQL Server DBA Assistant dialog box (see Figure I.2).

   The Memory Estimation page displays the estimated memory amounts for the following: SQL Server overhead, procedure cache, and data cache. The values graphed are only estimates based on memory calculation formulas found in Chapter 19, "Which Knobs Do I Turn?" Use the Graph Options at the bottom of the dialog box to explode any of the specified memory break-outs from the pie chart. The Print Options determine how the graph will be printed when you click the Print Graph button.

Figure I.2.
The Memory Estima-
tion page in the SQL
Server DBA Assistant
dialog box.

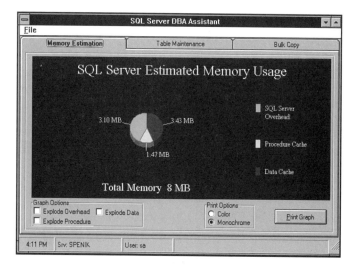

4. To perform table maintenance, click the Table Maintenance tab (see Figure I.3).

Figure I.3.
The Table Maintenance
page in the SQL Server
DBA Assistant dialog
box.

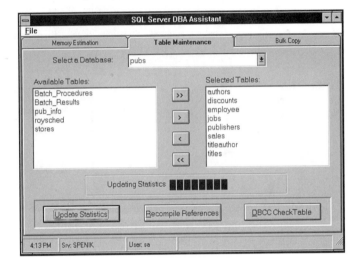

5. Select a database from the combo box. To select a table, click the table name in the left list box. To move a table from the Available Tables list box to the Selected Tables list box, click the > button. Click the < button to move the selected table from the Selected Tables list box to the Available Tables list box. Click the >> or << button to move all the tables.

6. To perform table maintenance, click the appropriate command button. The selected function is performed on all the selected tables. Any error messages or results returned from SQL Server are displayed.

7. To export data, click the Bulk Copy tab (see Figure I.4).

8. Select a database from the Select a Database combo box.

9. Select the table from which you want to export data from the Source Table list box.

10. Select the file export file format from the File Type drop-down list box and specify the name of the file to which you want to export the data (use the Directories pane to specify the path as necessary).

11. Click the Export Data button to export the data to the specified file.

Figure I.4.
The Bulk Copy page in
the SQL Server DBA
Assistant dialog box.

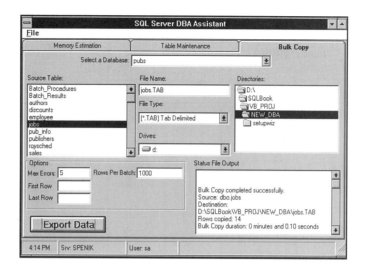

THE DATABASE ESTIMATOR

by Paul Galaspie

Note

The Database Estimator requires you to have the ODBC DLLs installed on your PC. The Database Estimator also comes with a detailed help file that covers all its functionality.

Tired of manually calculating space requirements (see Figure I.5)? Let the Estimator automatically calculate database space requirements! The following sections discuss some of the features of the Estimator product.

Figure I.5.
Calculating database
space requirements
manually.

```
.          Calculate the data row size:
4          (Overhead)
+100       Sum of bytes in all fixed-length columns
+50        Sum of bytes in all variable-length columns
___
154        Subtotal
154        Subtotal
+1         (Subtotal / 256) 1 (Overhead)
+3         Number of variable-length columns 1
+2         (Overhead)
___
160        Data row size
2.         Calculate the number of data pages:
2016 / 160 = 12 Data rows per page
9,00,000 / 12 = 750,000 Data pages
3.         Calculate the size of clustered index rows:
5          Overhead
+4         Sum of bytes in the fixed-length index keys
___
9          Clustered index row size
4.         Calculate the number of clustered index pages:
(2016 / 9) - 2 = 222 Clustered index rows per page
750,000 / 222 = 3378 Index pages (Level 0)
3378 / 222 = 15 Index pages (level 1)
15 / 222 = 1 Index page (Level 2)
5.         Calculate the total number of pages:
Totals:  Pages      Rows
Level 2  (root)     1            15
Level 1  15         3,378
Level 0  3,378      750,000
Data     750,000    9,000,000
3/4----
Total number of 2K pages 753,394
```

INSTALLING THE DATABASE ESTIMATOR

Follow these steps to install the Database Estimator:

1. Create the directory \ESTIMATOR on your destination drive.

Note

This example assumes that you are installing the Estimator on drive C and that the CD-ROM containing the Estimator files is located in drive D.

2. Switch to drive C.

3. Type `cd\` and press Enter.

4. Type `md c:\estimator` and press Enter.

5. Type `copy  d:\estimator.* c:\estimator` and press Enter.

6. Start your version of Windows and create a new program icon with the following properties:

Description: `Estimator`
Command Line: `c:\estimator\estimator.exe`
Working Directory: `c:\estimator`

AUTOMATIC SPACE CALCULATION

Are you creating a new database and do you have to determine how much space is needed to store the data? Do you have an existing database and do you have to predict future space requirements?

The Estimator is designed to help a DBA determine the amount of storage space required for a new or existing table (and associated indexes). The Estimator lets you perform this type of analysis without resorting to complicated formulas (see Figure I.6).

Figure I.6.
Automatic space
calculation.

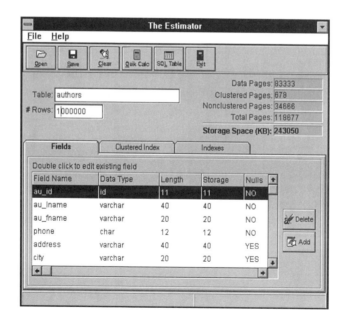

To use the Estimator, you must enter the expected row size and the estimated number of rows. The Estimator can estimate row sizes using three different methods:

◆ Using the table name and column sizes you enter

◆ Using ODBC to read an existing table definition

◆ Using a quick calculation method using only estimated row size

To have the Estimator estimate row sizes based on the table name and column sizes you enter, perform the following steps:

1. Start the Estimator by running `estimate.exe`.

2. Enter the name of your table in the Table text box of the Estimator window.

3. Select the Fields tab; the Fields page opens.

4. Click the Add button to display the Field Definition dialog box. Add the name of the field and the datatype of the field. Click the OK button to add the column.

5. Once you have added all the required table columns, enter the number of rows expected in the table. The Estimator calculates the total storage space required based on your table size and the number of rows expected.

USING ODBC TO READ AN EXISTING TABLE DEFINITION

Have you already created a table and do you have to determine future table size? The Estimator can connect to SQL Server (through ODBC) and load table definitions into the Estimator. To use ODBC, perform the following steps:

1. From the File menu in the main Estimator window, select the Load option. The ODBC data source dialog box appears.

2. Select the ODBC data source on which the table resides. Log on to the SQL Server data source. The Select a Table dialog box appears (see Figure I.7).

3. Select the table on which you want to perform size estimates and click the OK button.

4. The Estimator reads the table and index definitions for the selected table and automatically fills in the information for the table size.

5. In the main Estimator window, enter the number of rows in the # Rows field. The estimated size of the table is computed.

Figure I.7.
Selecting a table in
SQL Server from the
Estimator Select a
Table dialog box.

Loading existing table definitions is useful for determining the impact on storage requirements before you make modifications (such as adding new fields or indexes).

QUICK CALCULATOR

Use the Quick Calculator to get a rough estimate of your storage space requirements without having to resort to field-level definitions (see Figure I.8). Just enter the overall column size, overall index size, and number of rows. Click the Calculate button, and you will have your answer!

Figure I.8.
The Quick Calculator.

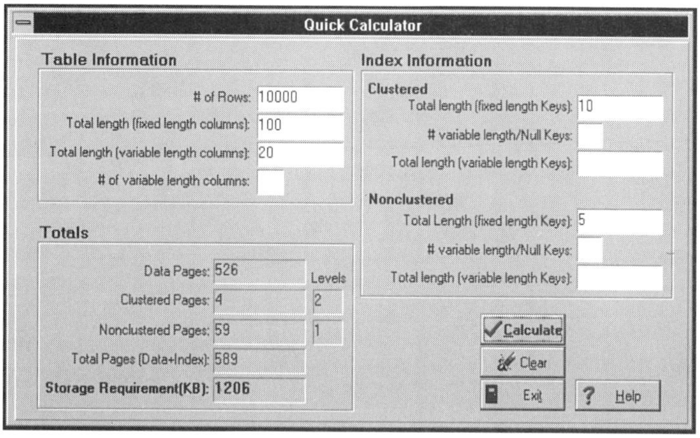

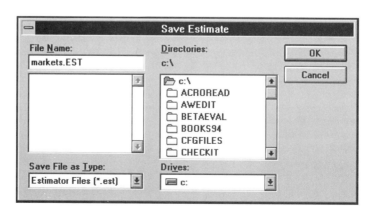

SAVE ESTIMATES

Do you want to save an estimate for future use? No problem! Just click the Save button in the main Estimator window. The Save Estimate dialog box appears (see Figure I.9). Enter the filename and select the directory for the saved estimates. Click the OK button to save the estimate.

Figure I.9.
Saving an estimate.

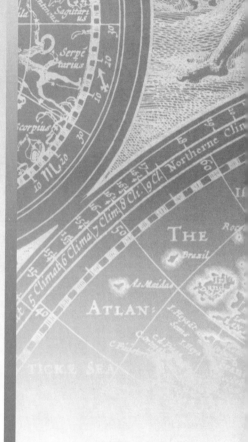

SYMBOLS

Index

G

Add to Your Sams Library Today with the Best Books for Programming, Operating Systems, and New Technologies

The easiest way to order is to pick up the phone and call

1-800-428-5331

between 9:00 a.m. and 5:00 p.m. EST.
For faster service please have your credit card available.

ISBN	Quantity	Description of Item	Unit Cost	Total Cost
0-672-30860-6		Windows NT Server Survival Guide (Book/CD-ROM)	$49.99	
0-672-30849-5		Microsoft BackOffice Administrator's Survival Guide (Book/CD-ROM)	$59.99	
0-672-30902-5		Windows NT 3.51 Unleashed, 3E (Book/CD-ROM)	$49.99	
0-672-30903-3		Microsoft SQL Server 6 Unleashed (Book/CD-ROM)	$59.99	
0-672-30840-1		Understanding Local Area Networks, 5E	$29.99	
1-57521-071-1		Building an Intranet (Book/CD-ROM)	$55.00	
1-57521-018-5		Web Site Administrator's Survival Guide (Book/CD-ROM)	$49.99	
1-57521-047-9		Web Site Construction Kit for Windows NT (Book/CD-ROM)	$49.99	
0-672-30819-3		Microsoft Office Unleashed (Book/CD-ROM)	$45.00	
0-672-30837-1		Visual Basic 4 Unleashed (Book/CD-ROM)	$45.00	
0-672-30745-6		HTML & CGI Unleashed (Book/CD-ROM)	$49.99	
1-57521-040-1		The World Wide Web Unleashed 1996 (Book/CD-ROM)	$49.99	
❏ 3 ½" Disk		Shipping and Handling: See information below.		
❏ 5 ¼" Disk		TOTAL		

Shipping and Handling: $4.00 for the first book, and $1.75 for each additional book. Floppy disk: add $1.75 for shipping and handling. If you need to have it NOW, we can ship product to you in 24 hours for an additional charge of approximately $18.00, and you will receive your item overnight or in two days. Overseas shipping and handling adds $2.00 per book and $8.00 for up to three disks. Prices subject to change. Call for availability and pricing information on latest editions.

201 W. 103rd Street, Indianapolis, Indiana 46290

1-800-428-5331 — Orders   1-800-835-3202 — FAX   1-800-858-7674 — Customer Service

Book ISBN 0-672-30959-9

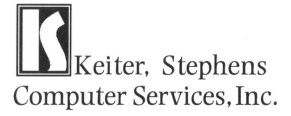